STALIN'S VENGEANCE
The Final Truth about the Forced Return of Cossacks after
World War II

by
NIKOLAI TOLSTOY

STALIN'S VENGEANCE
The Final Truth about the Forced Return of Cossacks after
World War II

by
NIKOLAI TOLSTOY

Academica Press
Washinton~London

Library of Congress Cataloging-in-Publication Data

Names: Tolstoy, Nikolai (author)
Title: Stalin's vengeance : the final truth about the forced return of cossacks
after world war ii | Tolstoy, Nikolai
Description: Washington : Academica Press, 2021. | Includes references.
Identifiers: LCCN 2021945866 | ISBN 9781680538809 (hardcover) |
9781680538816 (paperback) | 9781680538823 (e-book)

CONTENTS

ACKNOWLEDGMENTS

I would like to express my profound gratitude to all those who, in different ways, provided me with information and support of various kinds throughout long and at times difficult years of struggle, in order to bring suppressed evidence to light and (so far as it be retrospectively possible) to right a terrible wrong. They include:

President Boris Nikolaevich Yeltsin of Russia; Major Charles Barrington; Lord Braine of Wheatley; Mr. W. Denis Conolly; Dr. Ludmilla Foster; Major Anthony Gell; Mr. Vladimir Grekoff, director of the Paris Imperial Cossack Museum; Mr. Peter Gwyn; Mr. Martin Gwynne; Mr. Peter J. Huxley-Blythe; Mr. Alun Jones QC; Mr. Sergei Kachkin; Professor Stefan Karner; Sir Ludovic Kennedy; the Rev. Father Georg Kobro, custodian of the Lienz Cossack Museum; Mr. Peter Koltypin; General Alexei Kondaurov; Mr. Sergei Litvinov; Prince Nikita Lobanov-Rostovsky; Mr. Vsevolod Lohmus von Bellingshausen; Professor Sean McMeekin; Mr. Keith Miles; Mr. Max Morgan-Witts; Mr. Nigel Nicolson; Mr. John Odling-Smee; Mr. Sieghard von Pannwitz; Mrs. Zoe Polanska-Palmer; Mrs Evgenia Polskaya; the Earl of Portsmouth; the Rev. Father Michael Protopopov; Mr. Lawrence Rees; Mr. Philipp Schoeller; Dr. Anatol Shmelev; Mr. Alexander Solzhenitsyn; Mr. Mark Stephenson; Mr. Taki Theodoracopulos; Mr. Mark Thomson of Schilling & Lom; Count Andrei Tolstoy-Miloslavsky; General Dmitri Volkogonov; Mr. Auberon Waugh; Brigadier Ian Weston-Smith; and Colonel Rupert Wieloch.

Above all, I must extend especial thanks to that peerless queen of proofreaders, my dear wife Georgina. Her eagle eye can detect the smallest solecism at a bowshot's range. More than this, throughout fifty years of marriage she has lent me such courage and aid, that books such as this which cover dangerous topics might never have been written without her unstinting support. Nor was she in the least alarmed by the hostility of the British government and courts, which she regarded throughout with robust contempt.

Finally, I commend Paul du Quenoy and his Academica Press for taking the project on board. When some publishers at home feared to publish this book, my friend Dr. Anatol Shmelev at Stanford University recommended me to approach Professor du Quenoy at Academica. So far as I am concerned, America remains the Land of the Free!

LIST OF PHOTOGRAPHS

PREFACE

For 75 years, the British betrayal of Cossacks in Austria has remained almost as much a mystery as it was a tragedy. Shrouded in intrigue and secrecy at the time, largely successful measures were subsequently adopted by the British establishment to suppress the truth and protect the reputations of the perpetrators. Thirty years ago, my last book on the subject, *The Minister and the Massacres*, was removed from public and university libraries throughout Britain in response to a forged legal document threatening dire consequences in the event of failure to cooperate in its suppression. The last such occasion of covert official suppression of a book in Britain occurred exactly two centuries earlier. It is ironic that the book in question was Thomas Paine's *The Rights of Man*.[*] Nevertheless, in the words of my famous relative, 'I cannot be silent'.

L. N. Tolstoy, *I cannot be silent* **(1908)**

---

[*] 'The government of George III tried to limit the potential damage [posed by *The Rights of Man*] by commissioning a hostile biography ... It extended to Paine the honor of being the first major publicist in modern times to be savaged by a government muckraking campaign waged publicly through the press' (John Keane, *Tom Paine: A Political Life* (Boston, MA, 1995), p. 320).

In my book *Victims of Yalta*,[*] I acknowledged that 'one half of the source material needed for the story unfolded in this book is inaccessible to scholars', given that 'research in Soviet ... archives is not permitted'. Since then, however, I have been granted access to extensive secret material held in the Russian archives, together with a plethora of other evidence never before made public, which at last enables me to tell the story in detail, with barely any need for recourse to speculative reconstruction.

The focal figure in the story is that of the Cossack General Peter Nikolaevich Krasnov, who led an extraordinarily dramatic life as soldier, statesman, and internationally-renowned author. He served with distinction in the Great War, played a key role in major episodes of the Russian Revolution and Civil War, headed a formidable resistance movement from abroad (generally overlooked by western historians) after the Bolshevik victory in the Civil War, played a controversial part in the German-sponsored anti-Soviet Russian resistance during the Second World War, and was eventually the focal figure at the heart of what is arguably the murkiest and most controversial event in British history.

At the same time, I would emphasise that Krasnov is not the hero of this book, but rather the protagonist. He underwent strikingly dramatic experiences illuminating major historical events, extending from the Russo-Japanese War to the tragedy of the Cossacks betrayed to Stalin forty years later.

General Krasnov lived through exceptionally turbulent times, when on occasion selection of the apparent lesser of two evils effectively provided the only choice available. What some might claim as his two major misjudgements were his turning twice in succession to Germany for military assistance in the struggle against Bolshevik terror. The first occasion was in 1918, when under his leadership the Don Cossacks allied themselves with Imperial Germany, whose armies throughout much of that year occupied the adjacent Ukraine. As there was then nowhere else he could look for effective aid against the Bolsheviks, his choice is comprehensible. While similar considerations obtained after Hitler's invasion of Russia in 1941, his relations with Nazi Germany during the ensuing three years plainly cannot arouse the same sympathy. However, his activities during that time were at most marginal. All in all, pragmatic decisions were made in exceptionally difficult circumstances, which can only be understood by banishing hindsight, refraining from facile judgments, and above all examining the evidence in full.

---

[*] Published in the United States as *The Secret Betrayal*.

I have explored some of the events described in the present work in previous books and articles. Eventually the controversial forced repatriation of 1945 came under intense forensic examination at the famous (or infamous) Lord Aldington show trial in 1989. One unanticipated consequence of that event was that I was eventually enabled to gain access to a previously unknown body of remarkable evidence, which finally makes it possible to reconstruct in revealing detail previously obscured major dramatic events of the turbulent, and in many ways disastrous, twentieth century. The fresh material made available to me when preparing this book is far too extensive to be summarized in a brief preface. Among the most remarkable is undoubtedly the extensive array of hitherto secret documents from the Russian archives, which thanks to President Yeltsin's personal intervention are here deployed for the first time. It is rare indeed even in modern historiography to find hidden troves which to so dramatic an extent illuminate previously obscured major historical events. Their recovery incidentally demonstrates the absurdity of assigning evaluation of major historical events to a court of law.

Key British documents secretly withdrawn by the Foreign Office and Ministry of Defence throughout the Aldington trial and its aftermath were identified by an indignant whistleblower. Once they were belatedly made available to me, their content led to fresh discoveries in British and United States archives. As the reader will discover, it is revealing to learn just what it was that the British government and courts were so concerned to suppress.

Nikolai Tolstoy-Miloslavsky, 2021

CHAPTER I
THE MURDER OF COMMISSAR LINDE

All these precautions having been taken, and it being now quite dark, those in command awaited the result in some anxiety: and not without a hope that such vigilant demonstrations might of themselves dishearten the populace, and prevent any new outrages.

But in this reckoning they were cruelly mistaken, for in half an hour, or less, as though the setting in of night had been their preconcerted signal, the rioters having previously, in small parties, prevented the lighting of the street lamps, rose like a great sea; and that in so many places at once, and with such inconceivable fury, that those who had the direction of the troops knew not, at first, where to turn or what to do.

Charles Dickens, *Barnaby Rudge*

On the night of 24 August 1917, Major-General Peter Nikolaevich Krasnov was summoned to his field telephone, where he received orders to repair with the 2nd Umansky Cossack Regiment to the village of Dukhche, situated some eighteen versts (a dozen miles) from his headquarters at Lutsk, behind the Russian front line. On behalf of the Corps Commander, General Volkovoi, his Chief of Staff Colonel Bogaevsky explained over the field telephone that soldiers of the nearby 444th Infantry Regiment, acting under the influence of seditious agitators, had refused to obey orders, and were effectively in a state of mutiny. Volkovoi considered that deployment of a well-disciplined force of five hundred Cossacks, together with a machine-gun company, should suffice to overawe the rebels and remove the active conspirators.

Krasnov, who shared this opinion, paraded his troops at dawn. To them he explained that the rebels should not be regarded as enemies, but as former comrades who had been misled. Given the generally poor morale of the Russian Army in this revolutionary year, Krasnov was troubled by his Cossacks' dour expressions. Nevertheless, they reacted favourably to his explanatory talk, and rode off to fulfil their mission. Three hours later they arrived in exemplary order at Dukhche, with their band playing and choir singing. On their arrival, Krasnov and General Hirschfelt, commander on the spot, awaited the imminent appearance of Commissar (*i.e.* political officer) Feodor Linde, who had been dispatched by the Provisional Government to appeal to the mutineers to return to their duty.

Commissar Linde addressing troops

At about 11 o'clock Linde arrived in a staff car. As his record testified and events were now to confirm, he decidedly did not lack courage. A diehard supporter of the achievements of the February Revolution, he proved to be a young man of Baltic origin, who retained the slight German accent of his region. His eager, youthful, and somewhat dandified appearance reminded Krasnov of students he had encountered in the Yurievsky University at Dorpat. Linde declared confidently to General Hirschfelt that his parade of armed strength was superfluous: all that was needed was an appeal to the mutineers' patriotic honour and their duty to the revolutionary government. Like Prime Minister Alexander Kerensky, Linde passionately believed that words – especially high-flown revolutionary words – could move mountains. He courageously declined an officer's offer of a pistol. As he earnestly explained to the General, when addressing a crowd one must employ an emotive psychological approach. His confidence in the power of oratory was understandable, given that his eloquence had indeed worked wonders on comparable occasions.

Together Krasnov, Commissar Linde, and General Hirschfeldt drove off to fulfil their mission. Arrived at the forest glade where the soldiers were assembled, they found that the Cossacks had already established themselves before the mutineers' camp, and set up a machine-gun post. Linde walked fearlessly ahead, his expression pale but eager. Climbing onto a pile of logs and glaring angrily around, he upbraided his audience:

> When your homeland is exhausted in its superhuman efforts to defeat the enemy, you allowed yourselves to be lazy and did not fulfil the just demands of your superiors. You are not soldiers, but swine, who should be wiped out. I, the Commissar of the South-Western front, I, who brought the soldiers out to overthrow the tsarist government, in order to give you freedom, freedom which is equalled by no other people in the world, demand that you now deliver up to me those who have been telling you not to obey the orders of the commanders.

Krasnov's Cossacks remained markedly unimpressed by this harangue. As his orderly declared to him afterwards, this sort of talk was considered not very democratic: 'when *you* speak to us you never talk like this, and never swear at us'. Meanwhile, Linde strode along the front rank, while General Hirschfeldt identified twenty-two Bolshevik ringleaders by name. To General Krasnov, they appeared inadequate youthful types, characteristic of urban life. When one of them attempted to blurt out an explanation, Linde yelled at him 'Shut up! Bastard! Scoundrel!' Angry responses from the crowd were swiftly silenced by a menacing movement on the part of the Cossacks. The agitators were taken away under guard.

Both Commissar Linde and General Hirschfeldt were delighted by this apparent submission on the part of the mutineers. Krasnov, however, sensed grave underlying danger, and advised Linde to be content with what he had achieved. 'No, General', responded the Commissar. 'You don't understand anything. The first impression is made. We must take advantage of the psychological moment. I want to talk to the soldiers and explain to them the error of their ways'. Krasnov, with decades behind him of dealing with soldiers of every class and multitudinous races, recognised the peril that faced them. Before him and his five hundred Cossacks were assembled some four thousand soldiers of the 444th Regiment, whose number was being constantly increased by an influx of further men from the 443rd and other neighbouring regiments.

Initially, Linde's procedure appeared promising. In Krasnov's words:

> Linde approached the first battalion. He introduced himself - who he was, and began to utter quite a long speech. As for content, it was a beautiful speech, deeply patriotic, full of passion and suffering for the Motherland. Such words would have been endorsed with pleasure by any of us old officers. Linde demanded unquestioning execution of superior orders, strictest discipline, fulfilment of all duties. He spoke pleadingly,

passionately, strongly, in places beautifully, figuratively – but his accent spoiled everything. Every soldier believed that he was speaking not Russian, but German.

Successive Cossack officers approached Krasnov, warning him urgently:

> Take him away. It will end badly. The soldiers are plotting to kill him. They say he is not a Commissar at all, but a German spy. We cannot cope. They are influencing the Cossacks. See what's going on all around!

Linde's well-intentioned but rash approach swiftly proved disastrous. He passed along the ranks, continuing his scathing harangue. As he moved from the 1st Battalion to the 2nd, mutinous soldiers began to close around him. However Linde had worked himself up into such a fervour of eloquence that he continued blind to what was taking place before his eyes. 'You're frightened' he sneered at Krasnov, when he vainly urged caution. 'Yes', replied the General, 'I am frightened - but I'm frightened for you'.

The situation grew ever more menacing, as soldiers from the 443rd Regiment joined the crowds, arms at the ready. Cries arose from among the rebels, accusing General Hirschfeldt of having betrayed the regiment's position to the Germans, in exchange for a bribe of 40,000 roubles.[1] The situation worsened dramatically as a Cossack officer reported to Krasnov that their machine-gun company was refusing to open fire on the increasingly frantic mob. Blindly confident in the emotional power of his rhetoric, Linde declined every urging by Krasnov to withdraw while opportunity remained. Next moment, shots could be heard from somewhere within the surrounding forest. An agitated Cossack officer rode up to report that he had ordered their machine-gunners to respond, but they had refused. A wild cry of 'to arms!' arose from the ever-increasing mob of soldiers, which the experienced General Krasnov now estimated at some six thousand. The mutineers dashed to their trenches, from which they emerged armed with rifles.

Hopelessly outnumbered, the General's Cossacks galloped off, leaving the Commissar, together with Krasnov, Hirschfeldt, and a couple of officers, to his fate. Linde and Hirschfeldt sprang into the car and attempted to escape likewise. Krasnov and his two companions cantered beside them on horseback. At first it appeared that the mutineers were deliberately shooting high, but before long bullets began striking the vehicle. Seeing that they had become a target, the driver and two passengers swiftly halted and sprang out. Hirschfeldt ran off among the trees, while Linde leaped into a neighbouring trench.

One of the pursuing soldiers came up and struck him on the forehead with his rifle-butt. Linde turned deathly pale, but remained standing. Clearly the blow had not been strong. Then another mutineer shot him in the neck. Linde fell, bleeding profusely. At this, the gathering crowd rushed howling upon the dying man, and stabbed him to death where he lay. Particularly vicious in the assault on the helpless victim was a Bolshevik soldier named Ivan Buschakov, whom an eyewitness, Lieutenant Safronov, saw stabbing the helpless commissar with his bayonet thirty times. The murderer was executed shortly afterwards by a firing squad at Lutsk.

Meanwhile, Krasnov had ridden ahead and reassembled such of his fleeing Cossacks as he could find. After ordering them to return to Dukhche, he rode ahead to the village and from there to the headquarters of the 4th Cavalry Corps. There he received melancholy news. The Corps Commander, General Volkovoi, had ordered General Hirschfeldt to return to his regiment and restore discipline. The latter promptly rode back without an escort. In a forest clearing he found himself suddenly surrounded by a crowd of infuriated mutineers, who raucously demanded the release of their comrades who had been arrested. They then seized the General, stripped him and tied him to a tree, where they tortured and abused him, until they finally put him to death. The atrocity was the more repellent, in that the victim had lost both his arms, amputated in consequence of war wounds.[2]

Similarly horrific crimes were being perpetrated at this time among frontline units everywhere. The Russian army was nearing a state of collapse. In the following month the Germans captured Riga, where they paused within striking distance of the capital, Petrograd. The mighty Russian Empire was disintegrating, with Finland and Ukraine declaring their independence, ever-increasing anarchical violence dominating the streets of cities, and lawless expropriation of property by rebellious peasants becoming endemic throughout the countryside. The unfortunate Linde's murder exemplified the abysmal failure of Prime Minister Kerensky's unworldly confidence that infusing the Army with revolutionary enthusiasm would suffice to defeat the combined might of the German, Austrian, and Ottoman armies.[3]

---

[1] The extent to which revolutionary Russia had become suffused with fantastic conspiracy theories is all but impossible to exaggerate. There can be little distinction between left-wing beliefs that everyone of a different political persuasion was in the pay of capitalists and landowners, or the Germans, and

those on the extreme right who supposed that the Revolution was the satanic offspring of a Judaeo-Masonic conspiracy. While some blame undoubtedly rests with the secretive nature of aspects of pre-revolutionary autocratic rule, greatly increased by requirements of wartime censorship, the Provisional Government's liberal credentials were comparably marred by large-scale corruption of the judicial process in support of delusory spy mania. Cf. William C. Fuller, Jr., *The Foe Within: Fantasies of Treason and the End of Imperial Russia* (New York, 2006), pp. 215-56.

[2] P.N. Krasnov, 'На внутреннемъ фронтѣ', in I.V. Gessen (ed.), *Архивъ Русской Революціи* (Berlin, 1921), i, pp. 105-12; Boris Sokoloff, *The White Nights: Pages from a Russian Doctor's Notebook* (New York, 1956), pp. 15-40; George Katkov, *The Kornilov Affair: Kerensky and the break-up of the Russian army* (London, 1980), p. 65.

[3] Orlando Figes, *A People's Tragedy: The Russian Revolution 1891-1924* (London, 1996), pp. 440-41.

CHAPTER II
A PERILOUS MISSION

Kerensky has again failed us, as he did at the time of the July uprising and of the Kornilov affair. His only chance of success was to make a dash for Petrograd with such troops as he could get hold of; but he wasted time in parleying, issued orders and counter-orders which indisposed the troops and only moved when it was too late. The Bolsheviks have reoccupied Tsarskoe and are now confident of victory.

Sir George Buchanan, British Ambassador to Russia

Peter Nikolaevich Krasnov was born in St. Petersburg in 1869, heir to a celebrated line of Cossack generals, who had distinguished themselves in particular under General Suvorov fighting the Turks in the eighteenth century, and with Ataman Matvei Platov against the French during Napoleon's invasion in 1812. His father was a celebrated historian of the Cossacks – an enthusiasm shared by Peter Nikolaevich throughout his life. After graduating at the Pavlovsky Military Academy in 1888, he was commissioned into the elite Ataman Life Guards Regiment. From an early age he manifested considerable literary talent, much of it reflecting the colourful history of his beloved Cossacks.

Peter Krasnov as a child

Thereafter he pursued a colourfully adventurous career. His writings on military theory continued to attract the attention of his superiors. In September 1897 he was appointed *sotnik* (lieutenant) of the Tsarevich's Ataman Guard Regiment, commanding a Cossack military squadron escorting Russia's first diplomatic mission to the Emperor Menelik of Abyssinia. The mission had a strategic purpose: that of strengthening the Abyssinian Empire as a bulwark against further British expansion in the region. Abyssinian Christianity was regarded by both Russians and Abyssinians as close to Russian Orthodoxy, and it was widely felt that the two empires should become natural allies.

Upon his return to Russia, Krasnov published a detailed account of his adventurous journey, based on the diary he kept at the time, which continues of value to anthropologists and historians.[1] He was further dispatched on a secret mission to Djibouti, in the Horn of Africa. His services attracted widespread recognition, including awards of the Russian order of St. Stanislav, the Star of Abyssinia, and the French Legion of Honor. In 1901 he served during the Boxer Rebellion in China as correspondent for leading Russian military journals.

During the opening years of the twentieth century, Krasnov's adventurous spirit and specialist military duties took him as far afield as Manchuria, Japan, China, and India. Again, he published a substantial work recounting his colourful experiences with infectious enthusiasm and eye for picturesque detail.[2] His travels also provided him with much dramatic material for novels he wrote in subsequent years.

In 1904 this literary skill led to his employment as correspondent for the military journal *Russkii Invalid* throughout the Russo-Japanese War. It was there that he first encountered his future fellow White Army commanders Baron Peter Wrangel and Anton Denikin. Krasnov's lively reporting was conducted from the front line, where the dangers he encountered led to his being decorated for bravery with the Orders of St. Anne and St. Vladimir.

Upon his return from the front he was interviewed by the Emperor Nicholas II, who noted in his diary:

> I received Ataman Krasnov, who has arrived from Manchuria; he recounted much interesting information about the war. He writes articles about it in *Russkii Invalid*.[3]

The Emperor's charm on this and other occasions captured the undying romantic loyalty of the Cossack general. At the same time, Krasnov was not blind to his sovereign's fatal weakness of character, which indeed he regretted as a prime factor in the outbreak of revolution.

In 1909, aged 40, he graduated at the Officers' Cavalry School, and in the following year was promoted to colonel, commanding the 1st Siberian Cavalry Regiment in the Pamir mountains watching over the still uneasy frontier with British India. In October 1913 he commanded the 10th Don Cavalry Regiment, in which he served during the first years of the Great War. Within three months of the outbreak he gained the prestigious St. George's Cross for bravery during fighting on the Austrian front, and was promoted to Major-General commanding the 1st Brigade of the 1st Don Cossack Division.[4]

Командир 1-го Сибирского казачьего Ермака Тимофеева полка полковник П. Н. Краснов. Фото 1912 – 1913 гг. (из архива К. Н. Хохульникова)

Colonel of the 1ˢᵗ Siberian Cossack Regiment

In 1917 the February Revolution broke out, when Emperor Nicholas II abdicated the throne, as did his brother Michael a day later. The

Provisional Government succeeded to power under the leadership of the loquacious lawyer Alexander Kerensky (it was termed 'Provisional', being intended to remain in power only until national elections brought into being a Constituent Assembly at the end of the year). Since there existed at this stage no claimant to the throne,[*] even those, like General Krasnov, who were monarchist by tradition and instinct were prepared to support the new Government. Many loyal military and naval officers were swayed in favour of the new regime by its commitment to continuing the war alongside Russia's Entente allies Britain and France.

Real challenges to the authority of the liberal Provisional Government came from the rival left-wing Petrograd Soviet occupying the Tauride Palace, and the Bolsheviks, who sequestrated the palace of the ballerina Kshesinskaya (formerly mistress of the Emperor Nicholas II) until their expulsion in July.

It was not long before high hopes even among officers that the war would be prosecuted more efficiently by the new Provisional Government, apparently resting on a more popular basis than that of its imperial predecessor, became increasingly dissipated. On 1 March, in a gush of liberal enthusiasm, the government issued its notorious Order No. 1. Originally directed to the garrison of Petrograd alone, its intent was to 'democratize' the armed forces. While some of its provisions were relatively innocuous, or even desirable, both it and subsequent confirmatory orders freed troops to join political associations. The death sentence was rescinded, which together with other concessions fatally undermined the discipline of the Russian Army. Despite its originally restricted application, the order was swiftly circulated throughout the Army, with predictably disastrous effect.[5]

Political agitators, principally though not exclusively Bolshevik, seized upon the proclamation to undermine discipline to a disastrous extent from which the Army would never recover. Commissars were appointed by the government to ensure political control of the armies. Yet more pernicious was the establishment of private soldiers' committees, resulting in widespread refusal to obey orders. Extensive desertions, mutinies, and murders of officers recurred with alarming frequency. Promulgation of the ill-conceived Order No. 1 predictably proved disastrous from the outset of the new campaigning season.[6] Nor was it the sole factor. Widespread hostility to the war had come to permeate much

---

[*] The dynastic heir to Nicholas II and Michael was their first cousin the Grand Duke Kirill Vladimirovich, who had temporarily renounced his claim when registering acceptance of the Provisional Government in the Duma.

of the Army. Not only did it appear far too costly in terms of the terrible casualty rate, but in the vastness of the Russian Empire its aims appeared increasingly remote from the concerns of much of the population.

Peter Krasnov observed with horror the imminent disintegration of a proud military tradition, to which he had devoted his services for nearly forty years. Even among his own troops, he heard on all sides wild cries that the war was now over.[7] Unfortunately for well-meaning liberals in government, the German Army seized opportunity to continue its advance, while Russia's British and French allies received the news with dismay.[8]

Alexander Kerensky, would-be world statesman

As time swiftly showed, the newly-formed Provisional Government was to prove much less capable of administering the military and civil affairs of the country than had been its imperial predecessor.[9] Alexander Kerensky, at first Minister of Justice and then from 3 July Prime Minister, was regarded by many as an impressive orator, adept at uttering rousing liberal platitudes which during the early months of the revolutionary year evoked enthusiastic support from civilians and troops alike. Unfortunately, he was politically naïf, vain, posturing, self-deluding, and ineffectually arrogant. He was not the only leading figure of that turbulent era to be viewed as a new Napoleon, but certainly the least apt for the role. His vanity led him to install himself in the former Emperor's suite in the Winter Palace and the state apartments of the Moscow Kremlin, while he was accustomed to be driven around the streets of Petrograd and Moscow in the Tsar's Rolls-Royce cars. Like Stalin and Mao in their turn, despite possessing no military experience he adopted a spurious semi-military uniform. In later years he complacently described this as 'the one to which the people and the troops had grown so accustomed', and recalled with fond pride how he used to 'salute, as I always did, slightly casually and with a slight smile'.[10]

On 10 April a patriotic emissary of the Provisional Government arriving at Krasnov's headquarters in the field was assured of Cossack loyalty to the Allied cause, which the new regime was committed to maintaining. Quartered as it was at the front opposite occupied Pinsk in Belorussia, the Don Brigade was almost entirely isolated from news of events in the capital Petrograd, accepted the patriotic aims of the Provisional Government, and continued for some months confident of an eventual resolution of problems by the forthcoming Constituent Assembly. However, when news gradually percolated through to the ranks of the chaotic state of affairs in Petrograd, even Cossack discipline was eroded, resulting in increasing defiance of officers and outrages against local civilians.

In June Krasnov was transferred to the 1st Kuban Cossack Division in the vicinity of Moscow, where he found discipline and morale as poor as it had lately become under his previous command. However, he swiftly restored order, instituting improvement of conditions: in particular recreation, morale, and firm reimposition of discipline. For the present these measures appeared satisfactory, but increased tensions on the political front in Petrograd soon began eroding such success as had been attained.

In August, Kerensky sought to counter another feared Bolshevik *coup* in Petrograd, inviting the newly-appointed commander-in-chief, General Lavr Kornilov, to dispatch troops to impose martial law on the city. The Bolshevik cause had for the present suffered a major propaganda setback, following public revelations of the extent to which their activities were being financed by immense sums covertly transmitted by the German Government.[11] However, the vacillating Prime Minister swiftly lost his nerve, duplicitously asserting that Kornilov had instituted his intervention with the unauthorized aim of overthrowing the Revolution, and ordering his arrest for treason. The consequence was that Kornilov's move became overnight discredited, enabling Bolshevik agitators to undermine his troops' discipline. On 1 September the commander-in-chief was placed under arrest.[12]

Shortly before this, on 26 August, Krasnov received a telegram from the General, informing him that he was to be transferred to command of the 3rd Cavalry Corps, after reporting to Kornilov's Headquarters at

Mogilev. At his arrival the Supreme Commander explained that critical difficulties had opened up a rift between him and Kerensky. The Prime Minister was playing fast and loose with him, and he had reluctantly come to the decision to dispatch trustworthy units to restore order in the capital by imposition of martial law. Overall command of the force deployed to occupy Petrograd was now placed in the hands of General Alexander Krymov, whose 3rd Corps was to be reassigned to Krasnov.

> "Are you with us, General, or against us?" - asked Kornilov quickly and firmly.

> "I am an old soldier, your Excellency," I replied, "and I will execute all your orders precisely and without contradiction".

General Lavr Kornilov (center)

From senior officers at the Cossack command, Krasnov learned afterwards that the endlessly vacillating Kerensky was effectively in thrall to the Executive Committee of the Council of Soldiers and Workers Deputies, the council that had issued the fatal Order N°. 1. All that could save Russia now, both from her internal and external foes (the Germans and Bolsheviks, as was now notorious, being close-knit allies) would - so Krasnov felt - be a military government headed by General Kornilov. The son of a peasant Cossack, who had personally arrested the Empress Alexandra,[13] he could scarcely be described as a covert monarchist, seeking to restore the rejected old order.[14] In ironic contrast the principal leaders of the Left – Kerensky, Lenin, and Trotsky – were of comfortable middle-class origin.

Although Krasnov strongly supported any decisive move to restore discipline to the army and crush the anarchic state of affairs in Petrograd, which was not only menaced by a Bolshevik coup d'état, but thanks to the hapless Provisional Government engulfed by an uncontrollably horrific tide of crime and disorder,[15] he felt little confidence in the strategy of the proposed operation. In the first place, why did Kornilov himself not take personal command of the forces being gathered to seize control of the capital?[*] Moreover, both Krymov and Krasnov were new to their designated commands. Kornilov's confidence and that of his staff appeared grievously misplaced in Krasnov's opinion. While he in principle approved Kornilov's twin goals of restoring order at home and gaining victory over the German invader, he considered it tactless in the extreme to proclaim as much. The masses, whether peasants or Cossacks, were as he knew from daily experience desirous only of achieving peace and land. Kerensky, in contrast, cleverly concealed his own desire to continue the war on to victory, laying emphasis instead on Kornilov's hostility to the professed gains of the Revolution. Moreover, like many politicians then and now, Kerensky was susceptible to drawing simplistic historical parallels: in this case, apprehension of a Russian Bonaparte on the Right.[†] This led him into exaggerated fear of the charismatic and intrepid Kornilov, coupled with a gullible underestimate of the potent threat increasingly posed by the German-backed Bolsheviks.[16]

Pressing further, Krasnov found that his superiors were uncertain even of the whereabouts of the force of which he had now been appointed commander. The Army Chief of Staff could not tell whether the 3rd Corps

---

[*] Krasnov remained unaware, when compiling his memoir of these events three years later, that Kornilov had been misled into believing that restoration of order in the Russian capitals was authorized by Kerensky, and it was only when he discovered that he had been betrayed by the shiftless Premier that he briefly contemplated replacing the Government (cf. George Katkov, *The Kornilov Affair: Kerensky and the break-up of the Russian army* (London, 1980). When Kerensky ordered his arrest, he meekly succumbed. An assertion that Krasnov was 'profoundly implicated in the Kornilov conspiracy' (Peter Kenez, *Civil War in South Russia, 1918* (Berkeley, 1971), p. 46) is manifestly untrue. Krasnov's estimate of Kornilov's activity at this time was not high, and throughout all that followed he remained an exceptionally dutiful (if privately critical) servant of the Provisional Government.

[†] Ironically, it was Kerensky himself who self-consciously adopted the pose of a would-be Napoleon!

was still at the headquarters of the Northern Front in Pskov or had already arrived in Petrograd, while the Caucasian Native Division was strung out in trains, denying them communication with Supreme Army Headquarters at Mogilev.

Unaware of increasingly confused relations between Kornilov and Kerensky, Krasnov guardedly trusted that his veteran frontline troops would prove a match for the disorderly mutineers of the Petrograd garrison, despite its juncture with the more formidable support of Red sailors arriving from the nearby naval base at Kronstadt. In any case, he felt obliged to fulfil orders emanating from his superiors. On his journey he was joined by Prince Bagration, commander of the Caucasian Division, who showed him detailed orders from General Krymov providing for the military occupation of Petrograd.

By this time, however, Kerensky's panic-stricken *volte-face*, which led him publicly to denounce Kornilov as a traitor for seeking to implement the instructions he had received from the Prime Minister, began to exercise a pernicious effect on the whole operation. Vladimir Nabokov (father of the writer), who was then secretary to the Provisional Government, recalled that by this stage Kerensky was incapable of decisive action, leaving a void in the leadership which allowed the Bolsheviks to advance their power on a daily basis.[17] Railway workers, who had until now been hostile to the Bolsheviks, turned to obstructing the further advance of troop trains. Within the expeditionary force itself disputes arose among soldiers as to the legitimacy of the operation, when Kerensky and Kornilov were engaged in denouncing each other as traitors. The advance was further hampered by lack of communication between the 3rd Cavalry Corps and the Caucasian Native Division. Krasnov decided that the only practical course was for him to travel immediately to Pskov, where he could obtain an authoritative order at Headquarters from the commander of the Northern Front, General Klembovsky.

At each station along the way, Krasnov descended to stretch his legs by walking up and down the platform. Trains awaiting their departure were packed with troops from a cavalry unit. The General observed ominously what were clearly agents of Kerensky or possibly the Bolsheviks whispering "news" to the troops in the semi-darkness.

'Comrades! Kerensky is for freedom and the happiness of the people, and General Kornilov for discipline and the death penalty. Can you really be with Kornilov'?

'Comrades! Kornilov is a traitor to Russia and is going to lead you into battle to protect foreign capital. He has a lot of money he has received, and Kerensky wants peace'!

Although Krasnov was angered by these disloyal sentiments, privately he acknowledged that they reflected views increasingly espoused by the soldiers. Kerensky himself continued to retain much of his popularity at this time among the troops, largely because it was wrongly assumed that he was as anxious as they to bring an end to the war. Only among the ranks of the Cossacks did Krasnov encounter the old martial spirit, although even among them there existed extensive advocacy of peace and a return to the land. Still, by and large discipline remained instilled among them, and it was for this reason that they and the Caucasian Highlanders had been selected by Kornilov for the occupation and restoration of order in Petrograd.

Meanwhile, Kerensky dispatched a couple of Cossack officers to order General Krymov to confer with him in Petrograd. Whether from weakness or genuine confusion over the political situation, Krymov obeyed. This left the troops of his 3rd Cavalry Corps stranded in railway carriages, often far apart, without any means of knowing what was happening. Throughout this time, the loyalty and discipline of the troops, undermined by lack of any understanding of what was demanded of them, continued to be eroded by subversive elements.

Krasnov arrived at Pskov station at midnight on 30 August. On telephoning headquarters, he was informed that both his immediate superior General Krymov and the Northern Front commander had departed for Petrograd to meet Kerensky. Meanwhile, the latter had issued an order declaring General Kornilov a traitor. It was claimed that the Northern Front Headquarters at Pskov was largely in favour of Kerensky.

Given the situation, Krasnov was regarded with deep suspicion. Despite the chaotic situation in which it found itself, his Corps represented the most formidable fighting force within reach of Petrograd, whose loyalty to Kerensky under these constantly shifting authorities might well be questioned. He was escorted to the premises of the Commissariat, where he was interrogated by Lieutenant Stankevich, Commissar of the Northern Front, who was regarded as Kerensky's right-hand man. With him was his assistant Commissar Voitinsky, a convinced Bolshevik, who nevertheless bore the reputation of being sincerely concerned for the discipline and effectiveness of the Russian Army.

Stankevich evinced suspicion of Krasnov's intention in bringing his corps to Pskov. The General patiently explained that its command had been intended for him well before the revolutionary crisis had arisen.

Indeed, it was purely by chance that he had been given the 3rd Cavalry Corps, rather than the 4th.

> "Did they give it to you for political convictions?" Voitinsky insinuatingly asked me.

> "I am a soldier", I said proudly, "and I stand outside politics. The best proof for you is that I stayed until the last minute when Commissar Linde was killed before my eyes and I tried to save him".

This being the first the commissars had heard of the tragic incident, they requested Krasnov to relate the details. Clearly impressed by his account, they treated him more favourably. Next Voitinsky provided Krasnov with equally unexpected news. On Kerensky's orders, Kornilov had been arrested by his own troops, while Kerensky had appointed himself Supreme Commander.

By this time, it had become apparent to Krasnov that there were no longer any valid orders for him to obey. On the other hand, the two commissars appeared honourable men, who shared his overriding desire to restore the discipline and morale of the army. For the present, the 3rd Cavalry Corps was to remain where it was in the environs of Pskov, where Krasnov himself possessed a flat which he occupied for the duration of his stay.

Next day, he reported to the headquarters of the newly-appointed commander of the Northern Front, General Bonch-Bruevich. The latter dismissed Krasnov's complaint about his arbitrary detention on the previous day, wearily declaring that discipline had all but collapsed in the city. To this he added the startling news that General Krymov had committed suicide on the same day after conferring with Kerensky in Petrograd. Krasnov was now appointed in his place as commander of the 3rd Cavalry Corps. The Corps itself remained concentrated in the region of Pskov.

The task now assigned Krasnov was daunting. Together with a solitary staff officer, he was assigned operational quarters in the former lodgings of the keeper of Pskov gaol. Betrayed by Kerensky, Kornilov was dismissed as commander-in-chief; Krymov was dead; and senior officers of the Northern Front were throwing up their hands in despair at the ever-increasing breakdown in military discipline. Ever a realist, Krasnov understood that order could only be restored by collaboration with the military commissars and their committees, despite the fact that their abolition had been a principal goal of the corps's march on Petrograd. Fortunately for him, he had already established good relations with the two principal commissars, Stankevich and Voitinsky, and despite the waste of time engendered by interminable discussions with their committees, military readiness was greatly improved.

Meanwhile, the collapse of Krymov's advance on the capital exacerbated the situation there. The Bolsheviks had now greatly strengthened their position, to an extent where even the besotted Kerensky was obliged to recognise that the real threat to liberty and order in Russia now lay on the Left. Accordingly, the Prime Minister found himself in a bizarre predicament where he had to appeal for aid to that very 3rd Cavalry Corps whose advance he had on 28 August ordered to be rescinded. On 2 September Krasnov received a telegram from Kerensky, who had now appointed himself Supreme Commander. On the pretext of preventing German troops from crossing over to Russian Finland, the 3rd Cavalry Corps was ordered to concentrate the 1st Don Cossack Division in the Pavlovsk-Tsarskoe Selo area, with its headquarters at Tsarskoe Selo, and the Ussuri Division at Gatchina-Peterhof, headquartered at Peterhof. This placed them within striking distance of the capital.

Krasnov and his colleagues in Pskov recognised immediately that allusion to a possible German attack on the capital via Finland represented a mere fig leaf, disguising the fact that the most dangerous enemy the Government faced was the Bolsheviks, whose propaganda among the already disaffected Petrograd garrison was proving all too effective. Kerensky himself was now bearing the brunt of his misguided and deceptive policy of portraying Kornilov's attempt to restore order in the capital as a reactionary scheme for destroying the gains of the Revolution. The Reds, who in their propaganda had taken advantage of this specious *volte-face*, now posed as guardians of that Revolution which it was in reality their secret aim to divert to their own ends.[*]

Assisted by the two patriotic commissars, Krasnov managed to deploy the Corps as required, and within five days it was concentrated at the designated locations. Krasnov himself repaired to Tsarskoe Selo, fifteen miles outside Petrograd, where stood the great imperial palace of Catherine the Great, whose park had formerly provided the splendid setting for military parades attended by the Emperor every August. Now, however, Krasnov was distressed to find the place almost unrecognisable. Earlier in life he had served there for 26 years in the Guards, on the staff of Grand Duke Vladimir Alexandrovich. Then, discipline had been exemplary, with soldiers of all ranks dressed in splendid uniforms with

---

[*] The accuracy of Krasnov's account of what follows is borne out at critical junctures by copies of signals passing between him and Kerensky. These are now held in the State Archive of the Russian Federation in Moscow.

glittering decorations. Now the General encountered slipshod, ruffianly figures shambling about in dirty, sloppy clothing. The staircase and reception rooms, their magnificent military portraits gazing sternly down upon this motley crew, were now soiled with spittle and expectorated sunflower seeds. The most significant figures were not the humiliated officers, but the all-important commissars.

Despite the intense depression which this spectacle impressed upon him, Krasnov intended to perform his duty to whatever legitimate form of government prevailed in Russia. For the present this meant Kerensky. It was a measure of the latter's ineffectual nature that, despite his entire dependence on the 3rd Cavalry Corps for political survival, he did not pay it or its commander a single visit until it was manifestly too late. Meanwhile, General Krasnov set about restoring order within the regiments. Handicapped by the predictable ill-effects of interfering new commissars (Voitinsky and Stankevich had not accompanied him from Pskov) and Bolshevik agitators, he met with only partial success. Three Cossack regiments were found to be so imbued with revolutionary sentiments that they were dispatched home to the Don.

In order to counteract the pernicious effect of Bolshevik propaganda, coupled with the activities of political commissars and other left-wing agitators, Krasnov instituted practical measures for the restoration of military morale. Frequent maneuvers were followed by discussion of their implementation, regular talks with officers, and establishment of regimental training teams. Lectures and discussions were organised, and troops encouraged to engage in the study of Russian geography and history, political economy, and military science.

The government responded by issuing orders to disperse the regiments, while its commissars hampered Krasnov's restorative measures at every stage. When he objected, he was warned that the new commander of the Northern Front was a strong sympathizer with the Bolsheviks. By the latter half of October, a once formidable force of 50 companies had been reduced to eighteen collected from different regiments. Moreover, under Bolshevik pressure Krasnov was ordered to withdraw his remaining units from Tsarskoe Selo. All these gratuitously destructive measures had been conducted with at least tacit approval by Kerensky, the self-appointed military genius. Within a few days he found himself faced by a Bolshevik uprising, whose only means of resisting lay in that 3rd Cavalry Corps whose strength had been so drastically reduced by the deluded Napoleon of the Revolution.

On 25 October Krasnov received a telegram from Kerensky ordering him to advance the depleted Don Cavalry Division into Petrograd for the purpose of suppressing riots instigated by the Bolsheviks. 'Clever', reflected Krasnov: 'but how in the present utter chaos am I going to move the 1st Don Division immediately to Petrograd?' Fortunately, few Cossacks at this period nurtured warm feelings towards Lenin, recently publicly exposed as a paid agent of the Germans, with whom the Cossack Division had so recently been engaged in combat.[18] Reporting to headquarters in Pskov, Krasnov found the High Command in a state of extreme alarm. News had arrived from Petrograd that the Provisional Government had been overthrown, its supporters having either fled or under siege in the Winter Palace, whose few defenders were even now being overwhelmed by Red Guards. All power in the capital lay now in the hands of the Soviets, headed by Lenin and Trotsky.

From Pskov, Krasnov travelled to Ostrov, the headquarters of the 1st Don Division. So swiftly had events moved that its commanding officer had been caught unawares on leave in Petrograd. It was a still, autumnal night, and the tracks of the railway station were filled with wagons filling up with Cossacks and their horses. Spirits were high, as the Cossacks were aware that they were looked upon unfavourably by the Bolsheviks. Nevertheless, even here Krasnov detected the presence of Red agitators, although fortunately the Cossacks appeared deaf to their insinuations. On the other hand, Kerensky behaved with his usual indecision, authorising a fresh order for the troops to remain in Ostrov.

Krasnov sped back in his car to Pskov, where with difficulty he managed to rouse the new Northern Front commander, General Cheremisov. 'The Provisional Government is in danger', declared Krasnov, 'and we took an oath to the Provisional Government, and our duty'. Cheremisov stared back with a lackluster gaze. 'There is no Provisional Government', he declared wearily. To Krasnov's indignant protest he responded: 'I order you to unload your trains and stay in Ostrov. That is enough for you. Anyway, you cannot do anything'.

Clearly, Cheremisov was incapable of providing a decisive answer, and, at the suggestion of his own chief of staff, Colonel Popov, Krasnov decided to request assistance from the local Commissar, Voitinsky, who as has been seen bore the reputation of an honest man. Upon arrival at his office, they found him absent, and it was not until four o'clock in the morning that he returned. Leading them through a succession of ill-lit empty rooms, after finally reaching his office he carefully locked the doors behind them, and approaching close to Krasnov whispered mysteriously: 'you know, he is here'! 'Who is *he*'? inquired the General curiously. 'Kerensky'! came the startling answer. 'Nobody knows – he has only just arrived secretly from Petrograd – he escaped by car – the Winter Palace is under siege – but he will save us – now that he is with the troops, he will save us. Let's go to him. Or it is better that I tell you his address. It is inconvenient for us to walk together. Go ... go to him. Now'!

Krasnov and Popov set off through the streets on foot, so as not to draw attention by using their car. The moon shone bright, and as they strode through the old city the general humorously envisaged the pair of them as conspirators from a novel by Dumas. As they walked, he reflected on his attitude towards Kerensky, whom as yet he had never met. As Russia descended into chaos during the summer months, he had come to regard the scheming politician with increasing revulsion. So long as Kerensky remained Minister of Justice, he was content to regard him with equanimity. But when overweening conceit led him to appoint himself Supreme Commander, Krasnov was outraged. With absolutely no experience of military life, this vainglorious dilettante was actually destroying the glorious Russian Army.

It seemed chaos had descended upon the counsels of the Provisional Government, and despite pressing enquiries Krasnov was unable to ascertain even Kerensky's whereabouts. His estimate of the Prime Minister was now one of unreserved contempt. As he wrote a few years later,

> I never, not for one minute, was an admirer of Kerensky. I had never seen him, had read very little of his speeches, but everything within me was hostile to him with loathing and contempt.

That Russia, after all her mighty leaders in the past, should have come to be ruled by such a nonentity was entirely repugnant to the general. Nevertheless, he was Russia's appointed leader for the present, and Krasnov felt honor-bound to serve him.

Confiding his contempt for the pompous lawyer, he declared to Popov that he was nevertheless prepared to collaborate with him for the sake of Russia:

> Yes, I'm going. Because I am not going to Kerensky, but to my Motherland, to great Russia, which I cannot renounce. And if Russia is with Kerensky, I will go with him. I will hate and curse him, but I will serve and die for Russia. She elected him, she followed him, she failed to find a more capable leader, I will go to help him if he is for Russia ...

After a lengthy search, the two officers discovered by its illuminated windows the second-floor flat where Kerensky was staying. On entering, they encountered a scene of panic and distress, with sleepless, agitated people bustling about hopelessly. Among them, one hastened to greet Krasnov and his companion. 'General, where is your Corps?,' he exclaimed. 'Is it coming here? Is it already nearby? I was hoping to meet it below Luga'. Russia's would-be saviour presented a sorry figure. Later, Krasnov recalled this first dramatic encounter with Kerensky.

> A face with traces of heavy sleepless nights. Pale, unhealthy, with sore skin and swollen red eyes. Trimmed moustache and trimmed beard, like an actor. The head was too big on its body. A service jacket, riding breeches, boots with leggings - all this made him look like a civilian, dressed up for a Sunday ride on horseback. He looks shrewdly, directly in the eyes, as though looking for an answer in the depths of a man's soul, and not in words; phrases - brief, imperative. He does not doubt that what is said will be fulfilled. But one senses some kind of nervous strain, abnormality. Despite the imperative tone and deliberate harshness of manners, in spite of that "General", which is dropped at the end of every question, there is nothing splendid. Rather, sick and miserable...

> I immediately recognized Kerensky from the many portraits I had seen, from photographs which were then printed in all the illustrated magazines. Not Napoleon, but definitely posing as Napoleon. He listens inattentively. He does not believe what he is told. His whole face says: "I know you; you always have excuses, but you have to do it, and you will do it".

> I reported that not only there was no Corps, but there was no Division either, that the units were scattered throughout north-west Russia, and needed to be assembled first. Moving in small units would be insane.

> "Nonsense! The whole army is behind me against these rascals. I will lead her to you, and everyone will follow me. There, no one sympathizes with them. Tell me what you want? Write down anything the General wants", he said to Baranovsky.[*]

> I began to dictate to Baranovsky, where and what units I had, and how to assemble them. He wrote, but wrote inattentively. We were playing a game. I told him something, and he pretended to write.

> "You will get all your units," said Baranovsky. "Not only the Don [Cossacks], but also the Ussuri Division. In addition, you will be given the 37th Infantry Division, the 1st Cavalry Division, and the entire XVII Army Corps - it seems everything, except for various small units".

> "Now, General. Satisfied?" said Kerensky.

> "Yes," I said, "if all this works out, and if the infantry goes with us, Petrograd will be occupied and freed from the Bolsheviks".

> Hearing about such significant forces, I had no doubt of success. The

---

[*] The Colonel in whose flat this exchange took place.

actuality was otherwise. It was possible to disembark the Cossacks in Gatchina and form a reconnaissance detachment, under cover of which to assemble units of XVII Corps and the 37th Division on the Tosno-Gatchina front, and move quickly, covering Petrograd and cutting it off from Kronstadt and the Morskoi Canal. My task was reduced to simpler actions. It became easier on the soul ... But if that were so, how was it that Cheremisov now sat with the Soviet? ... No, there was something wrong. Doubt crept into my soul, and I stated this to Kerensky.

It seemed to me that he was not only unsure whether the identified units would move according to his order, but he was also uncertain even that Army Headquarters, that is, General Dukhonin [who had replaced Kornilov], had transmitted the order. It seemed that he was afraid of Pskov too. He suddenly collapsed, wilted, his eyes became dull, his movements lethargic.

He needed to rest, I thought, and began to say goodbye.

"Where are you going, General?"

"To Ostrov, to move what I have to secure Gatchina by myself".

"Excellent. I will go with you".

He gave orders to bring his car.

"When will we be there?" he asked.

"If it's good going, in an hour and a quarter we will be in Ostrov".

"Collect divisional and other committees by eleven o'clock, I want to talk to them".

"Oh, what's this for!" I thought, but I agreed. Who knows, maybe he has a special gift, the ability to influence the crowd. What if after all, for some reason, Russia takes it? Would there be ovations, enthusiastic meetings, and love, and worship? Let the Cossacks see him and know that Kerensky himself is with them.

About ten minutes later the cars were ready, I found my own and we drove off. I – on Kerensky's orders – in front, Kerensky with an adjutant behind. The city was still sound asleep, and the noise of two cars did not awake it. We met no one and emerged safely onto the Ostrov highway.

A measure of the confusion attending on the forthcoming operation was provided by an incident as they approached Ostrov. Within five miles of the town they encountered companies of the 9th Don Cossack Regiment dispersing to their quarters in neighbouring villages. When challenged by Krasnov, he was told that they had just received an order from him to leave their trains and return to base. The General responded that he had issued no such order, and that on the contrary Kerensky had arrived, with whom they were about to advance on Petrograd.

In Pskov, the troops still under Krasnov's command were paraded amid great excitement at the news that Kerensky himself had arrived in the town. When all was prepared, Krasnov repaired to his leader's quarters. He found Kerensky sitting asleep at a table. He awoke, and despite evident signs of extreme fatigue set off at once to address the soldiers. Krasnov had received many accounts of Kerensky's brilliance as an orator, and was curious to see how it would go. Making every allowance for the man's state of exhaustion, Krasnov was disappointed. The speech comprised in large part mere hackneyed slogans, with little logical connection between them: "The Russian people are the freest people in the world" – "the Revolution was accomplished without blood" – "the besotted Bolsheviks want to drench it in blood" – "betrayal of the Allies", etc., etc.

His auditors' applause was not only sparse and perfunctory, but interrupted by an angry protest from a Bolshevik sergeant, who accused Kerensky of being another Kornilov. A crowd assembled outside his quarters on his return proved equally equivocal in its reaction. None of this boded well for the success of the forthcoming operation. Again, as the troops prepared to embark in their carriages, the train was obstructed by mutinous soldiers, and their engine-driver declined to cooperate. Ever resourceful, Krasnov overcame the difficulty when he discovered among his Cossacks a young officer who had once served as an assistant driver, and proved competent to take them forward.

At one stop on their journey they encountered officers newly arrived from Petrograd. Among them a Lieutenant Kartashov described the troubled situation in the capital, where the junkers[*] were reportedly still defending the Winter Palace, while the mood of the Petrograd garrison was hesitant and indecisive. At this point Kerensky entered the carriage, where he sought to shake hands with the lieutenant. The latter declined apologetically, declaring himself a firm supporter of Kornilov. Kerensky was visibly shaken by the exchange, which illustrated how far his authority was now threatened by both Right and Left.

The train thundered on through the darkness of a chill October night. After passing through Luga without stopping, they approached their destination. This was Gatchina, the great imperial palace complex 28 miles

---

[*] Cadets were younger pupils of military schools (cadet corps) up to the age of 16 or 17. If they wished to pursue a military career, they entered military colleges (*iunkerskie uchilishcha*) as junkers. After graduation they received their military commissions.

south of Petrograd, which was now the designated base for the forthcoming occupation of the capital. Kerensky appeared in Krasnov's carriage, where he solemnly congratulated the latter on being appointed commander of the advancing army. The general reflected ruefully that the "army" under his command comprised ten companies totaling 700 men – less than a normal regiment. As though this were not daunting enough, should they be obliged to dismount in action – as was likely enough – one-third of the complement would have to be detailed to hold the horses, leaving 466 men to occupy the city and overawe a garrison of some 200,000 men manifesting dubious loyalty! It says much for General Krasnov's sense of loyalty to the civil power – a civil power he thoroughly despised – that his principal reaction was one of amusement at the civilian's gullible delight in playing at soldiers.

Furthermore, before the operation could be undertaken, there was the trifling matter of occupying Gatchina, lying between Tsarskoe Selo and Petrograd, which was garrisoned by a further substantial force. At this point, Krasnov was considerably relieved when a train arrived from Novgorod bringing the 10th Don Regiment with two field guns. Dawn had not yet broken, and Krasnov decided to take the sleeping town by surprise. Information was obtained that reinforcements to the garrison and mutinous sailors had just arrived at the Baltic railway station. Hastening there at the head of his force, he found the newly-arrived force paraded on the platform. To the General's practiced eye they provided a perfect target. He ordered one of his field guns to be set up on the track enfilading the massed soldiers and sailors. After a brief exchange, their officers agreed to hand over their arms. The next problem was what to do with the prisoners, who constituted 360 men to Krasnov's 200! All he could do was discharge them. Shortly afterwards a similar problem arose when it was reported to him that the Warsaw Station was occupied by Cossacks, who had taken prisoner a company with fourteen machine guns. They too were disarmed and released.

Nevertheless, it was clear that Gatchina could not be defended against any major assault by the paltry force at Krasnov's disposal. At the same time, he learned that Kerensky had grandiosely ensconced himself in the Gatchina Palace. Having witnessed the confused reaction of the troops captured by Krasnov's Cossacks, the Supreme Commander expressed confidence that all that remained was to advance on Petrograd and enforce a similar surrender! This the general felt obliged to decline, explaining that it was first necessary to discover what was the situation in Petrograd. Furthermore, the moment they abandoned Gatchina, what was to prevent the bodies of troops they had just overcome from reoccupying the town?

Fortunately, Krasnov's devoted wife Lydia Feodorovna, a talented singer and pianist, was living with a mutual friend in Tsarskoe Selo, fifteen miles outside Petrograd. He managed to telephone her and obtain a first-hand report on the position in the capital. The situation, as might have been expected, was far from promising. While the garrison of 16,000 at Tsarskoe Selo remained quiescent, a ferocious power struggle had erupted in Petrograd. The only troops prepared to fight on the government side were the gallant junkers, still holding out in the Winter Palace. In fact, the Provisional Government itself had been arrested. The Bolsheviks were supported by some 5,000 sailors from the naval base at Kronstadt, who had in turn been joined by the cruiser *Aurora* and other warships, together with an untold number of Red Guards – armed workers, reputedly amounting to more than a hundred thousand men.[19] Overall, the situation appeared to be that while the Bolsheviks were energetically adopting every means of gaining the upper hand, garrison troops supposedly loyal to the government had adopted a passive stance, awaiting a decisive outcome.

In every direction the authority of the government was drawing to a standstill. The new Supreme Commander at Mogilev, General Dukhonin, declined to issue orders. The Northern Front commander, General Cheremisov, was believed to favor the Bolsheviks, while all the major reinforcements promised Krasnov failed to stir from their bases. In this confused situation, no one knew where authority lay, and most of those considered likely to favour the government preferred to await an outcome before committing themselves to any irrevocable action.

Assessing the military situation overall, Krasnov had no choice but to accept that the predominance of force lay overwhelmingly with his potential foes. But never one to be daunted by risks, he recognized that civil war in material ways presented significantly distinct problems from those faced in real war. Despite the overwhelming odds against him, he believed it quite feasible that firm and decisive action could persuade the garrison at Tsarskoe Selo to remain as inactive as their fellows had proved at Gatchina, which in turn could lead a demoralised Petrograd garrison similarly to refrain from active resistance within the capital. Finally, there was the moral factor. On this occasion, the approaching commander-in-chief was not General Kornilov, who reputedly intended to overthrow the Revolution, but the socialist leader Kerensky, who had up to now been idolized by the crowd as its great defender.

Kerensky found committees representing the Cossack rank-and-file in full agreement with his assessment. At two o'clock in the morning of 28 October, Krasnov's diminutive force mounted and rode towards Tsarskoe Selo. As Krasnov later vividly recalled, Gatchina 'barely slept on that alarming night, when horse hooves briskly clattered on stones, thundering heavily as the guns clattered'. Small bodies of infantry attempting tentative efforts to halt their advance were swiftly disarmed and dispersed. As a bright dawn began to break, the Cossacks rode into Tsarskoe Selo. All at once the situation appeared distinctly unpromising, as their advance was challenged by what appeared to be an entire infantry battalion.

Once again, the professionalism and courage of the Cossacks and their commander swiftly carried the day. In response to desultory fire from their ill-organized adversaries, the Cossacks advanced vigorously. Meanwhile, Krasnov directed his artillery to open fire on the Tsarskoe barracks, taking care, however, to aim the guns high. Not the least of his considerations was the fact that his wife's home stood near the barracks. As the Cossacks swept forward into the palace park, they found themselves hugely outnumbered by a great crowd of infantry milling about. Nevertheless, the decisive advantage of discipline and motivation lay with Krasnov. Accompanied by members of the Cossacks' Divisional Committee, he rode up to a figure who appeared to be in command. He was a handsome, middle-aged man, wearing paramilitary dress, who introduced himself as Savinkov. This was the famous revolutionary Boris Savinkov, who was to prove as fearless an adversary of Bolshevik terror as he had been of tsarist autocracy. It is a further measure of Kerensky's erratic rule that he had briefly appointed Savinkov Governor-General of Petrograd, only to relieve him of his duties a few days later.[20] On Savinkov's inquiry about Krasnov's intentions, the latter replied that he intended to advance: 'Either we win, or perish; but if we go back, we will probably die'. Savinkov accepted the situation, praising the loyalty of the Cossacks to their commander. Krasnov was privately astonished by this amicable reception, while relieved to find his position strengthened by the arrival of a small column of cars headed by the Cossacks' own armored car.

Boris Savinkov

Kerensky jumped out of his car, whose fellow-passengers incongruously included some elegantly dressed ladies in a high state of agitation.

"What is happening, General?" he abruptly addressed me. "Why didn't you tell me anything? I was sitting in Gatchina, knowing nothing".

"There's nothing to report," said I. "All is being settled".

And I reported the situation to him.

Kerensky was in a state of acute nervous excitement. His eyes were burning. The ladies in the car, and their holiday appearance recalling picnics, were entirely out of place here, where the guns had just been firing. I begged Kerensky to return to Gatchina.

"Do you think so, General?" says Kerensky, narrowing his eyes. "On the contrary, I will go to them. I will persuade them".

Returning to his car, Kerensky ordered it to be driven forward among the throng of wavering soldiers. From his seat in the open coupe, Krasnov listened again to the familiar hysterical rhetoric. Rather more effective in influencing the crowd was the accompanying advance of their escort of Yenisei Cossacks. The confused mob of revolutionary soldiers surrendered their rifles and returned sheepishly to their barracks. When the Cossacks arrived at the gates of the palace, however, matters proved more daunting. Someone appeared to be in charge of troops stationed there, whose superior numbers enabled them to begin surrounding the Cossack squadron. At the same time, Krasnov received a disturbing report that revolutionary soldiers were preparing to open fire from the direction of Pavlovsk. Observing this, he asked Kerensky to drive back and summon the Don Cossacks' artillery battery, who on their arrival uncoupled their guns and swiftly fired a couple of shells over the heads of the revolutionaries. Shrapnel rattled on the roofs of the barracks. The effect was devastating. The huge crowd fled the scene to the railway station, where they sprang into awaiting railway carriages and yelled frantically to be taken back to Petrograd.

By that evening, Tsarskoe Selo was effectively in the hands of the Cossacks, who occupied the railway station, together with the radio and telephone stations. Although it was no longer necessary for his small force to occupy the entire town, Krasnov felt it obligatory for psychological reasons to garrison the principal palaces. Unless that occurred, neither in Tsarskoe Selo nor Petrograd would it be credited that the forces of the Provisional Government were in control. Equally, the moral advantage precariously enjoyed by their diminutive force could only be sustained by continuing the advance on the capital.

Even the hardy Cossacks had momentarily reached an impasse. Hugely outnumbered at every stage of their advance, they had passed two nights without rest. Worse still, it was clearly impossible to maintain their hitherto successful advance without Kerensky's promised infantry support. Hoping against all odds for the reinforcements, Krasnov ordered the next day to be treated as a day of rest in Tsarskoe Selo.

Meanwhile, his officers, who were all loyal to the core to their commander, expressed indignation at the lack of leadership provided by Kerensky. News of this reached Savinkov, who reappeared to suggest that Krasnov place Kerensky under arrest and assume leadership of the expeditionary force himself. "Do that, and everyone will follow you!" urged the diehard revolutionary. Krasnov, however, felt compelled to decline, feeling it his duty to continue serving as General, while the overthrow and arrest of Kerensky would inevitably make a hero of the Prime Minister, exacerbating an already precarious situation. Above all, the General had become convinced that the only way to restore order in the army and society was to negotiate an immediate armistice with the Germans, which would be a task far beyond his capacity to achieve. Finally, Kerensky had entrusted himself to Krasnov's protection, which it would be dishonorable to renounce.

Although sparse reinforcements trickled in that evening, the military force placed at his disposal to occupy the capital comprised nine companies of Cossacks, eighteen artillery pieces, an armored car, and an armored train. Despite the patent inadequacy of this minuscule force to occupy the sprawling capital city, and faced with mounting discontent manifested by elements of the troops under his command, Krasnov prepared to continue his advance. Once in the city, it would primarily be up to Kerensky and Savinkov to establish order.

Now, however, the committees of the 1st Don and Ussuri Divisions appeared before the general. They insisted that the Cossacks could not continue the advance without the support of an adequate infantry force. Pointing out that they had already seized Gatchina and Tsarskoe Selo with no infantry support, Krasnov nevertheless conceded that their nine companies could not occupy Petrograd unsupported. Instead of ordering a full-scale advance, he now proposed to undertake a reconnaissance mission, testing the water by engaging whatever force was sent against them. Should the odds prove too great, they could withdraw and await reinforcements.

The next morning (30 October) General Krasnov dispatched a characteristically buoyant telegram to headquarters at Pskov, reporting that the desertion of one regiment left him with a force of only three squadrons of Don Cossacks, one of Amur Cossacks and two of artillery. Despite this, morale was improving by the day, with enemy strength believed to be dwindling. All that was required for success was reinforcement by railway of infantry and armored cars (essential for street-fighting).[21]

At this point a daring schoolboy arrived, having managed to slip out of revolutionary Petrograd. He carried a secret message addressed to Krasnov from the Council of the Union of Cossack Troops, which recounted the dire situation in the capital:

> The situation of Petrograd is terrible. The junkers, who are at present the only defenders of the population, are being beaten. Infantry regiments are hesitating and standing still. The Cossacks are waiting for infantry units to arrive. The Council requests your swift advance on Petrograd. Your delay threatens a total extermination of the boy-junkers. Do not forget that your desire to seize power without bloodshed - is a fiction, as there will be a total liquidation of the junkers. You will learn details from the despatches.

Chairman A. Mikheev. Sec. Sokolov.

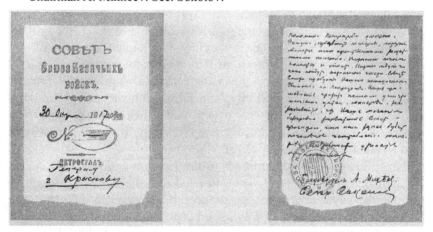

The secret message from Petrograd, later described by Krasnov as 'A melancholy witness to the beginning of a bloodstained nightmare'.

This appeal inspired the chivalrous spirit of the Cossacks, and largely restored order in the ranks.

The next morning, a sunny day which gradually turned to rain, Krasnov led his force in the direction of Pulkovo, fifteen miles on the road towards Petrograd. On its outskirts they arrived at a deep ravine, whose further side was strongly defended by Bolshevik troops. Through his binoculars, Krasnov could see that the slope was competently entrenched, defended by what he estimated at five or six thousand Red Guards.

An incongruous episode provided a farcical prelude to the impending tragedy. As desultory rifle fire broke out, an officer with two young ladies who had bicycled over to watch the spectacle swiftly escorted them from the scene. They left behind them a sizeable body of local men and women contentedly assembled with their children, settling down under the delusion that they were witnessing peaceful military maneuvers, complete with blank cartridges. When Krasnov dispatched officers to warn them off, they indignantly complained that they had never been turned away on previous occasions, when they assembled to enjoy the spectacular parade of the Tsar's troops on summer maneuvers.

Assessing the situation, Krasnov observed that while his Cossacks were greatly outnumbered by the enemy force, their principal advantage lay in his possession of artillery. As far as the enemy was concerned, Red Guards occupied the center and detachments of mutinous sailors from Kronstadt the two flanks. They also possessed three armored cars, whose firepower proved no match for his own field guns, whose shells promptly destroyed one of the armored cars, and continued flinging over enough shrapnel to keep the enemy at a distance. Nevertheless, the strategic situation was unpromising. At about noon, a report arrived of the approach of a large column of some 10,000 troops coming to reinforce the enemy.

The Reds had proved unwilling to advance under the Cossacks' artillery fire, but the disparity of force left Krasnov with little room to maneuver. In the absence of requested reinforcements, he decided that the most he could do was continue to engage the enemy for at least the remainder of the day. It was essential that the wavering Petrograd garrison should be aware of the approach of a relief force. At present the grotesquely outnumbered Cossacks were fighting with great gallantry, but as evening wore on it became plain that their position was untenable. Although the Red Guards eventually withdrew in some panic, the sailors stood firm. A desperate charge by Cossacks of the Orenburg Regiment came to a halt when they unexpectedly found themselves bogged down in a swampy ditch. The cavalrymen had to return on foot, while their stampeding horses were almost all shot and killed by the Reds.

At the same time, Krasnov learned that his men were fast running out of shells and cartridges. When he sent a dispatch rider to the artillery depot at Tsarskoe Selo requesting fresh supply, the depot's heavily armed guards declined to comply. The Cossacks at Pulkovo were becoming increasingly outflanked, and he received a warning that the garrison at Tsarskoe Selo was preparing an attack on his rear. When the Red sailors installed a long-range naval gun on the Pulkovo Heights and opened fire, he reluctantly conceded that the grossly unequal struggle must be abandoned. After giving orders to retreat to the railway line, Krasnov, handicapped by a lame left leg, found himself last to leave the battlefield. Fortunately, he was saved from capture by the onset of a pitch-black night.

On the other side of the nearby railway embankment, he stumbled upon a *dacha* (country house) abandoned by its owners. From their janitor he obtained a smoky kitchen lamp, by the light of which he wrote a dispatch to the 3rd Cavalry Corps, in which he explained that the odds against further advance were overwhelming, in consequence of which he and his men now found themselves obliged to retreat to Gatchina, where they could take up a defensive position while they awaited reinforcement. At the same time, he was perfectly aware that no such promised reinforcement was coming.

In the morning, having rejoined his troops, Krasnov found them in an understandably depressed state. Many of the wounded and dead were discovered to have been hideously mutilated by the Bolsheviks. Fortunately, he managed to find his faithful horse and followed his troops in their withdrawal to Tsarskoe Selo. Finding no one at headquarters, he dispatched his car to bring his wife. Clearly, it was not safe for her to remain in the town.

Krasnov rode on to Gatchina, where he arrived at one in the morning. There he found Kerensky awaiting his arrival. 'What can we do, General'? he enquired apprehensively. 'Will there be reinforcements'?, I asked him. 'Yes, yes, of course. The Poles promised to send their Corps. They probably will'.

This was scarcely encouraging, and Krasnov responded firmly: 'If the infantry arrives, then we will fight and take Petrograd. If no one comes, nothing will come of it. We'll have to leave'.

So desperate was the situation that many of Krasnov's Cossacks were now refusing to continue fighting. Pro-Bolshevik agitators infiltrating their ranks laid emphasis on the hopelessness of their position, and the need to make peace swiftly, both with the Germans and between the rival powers now contesting control of Petrograd. 'It's Kerensky's affair', was a frequent complaint. However, Boris Savinkov, who had accompanied the Cossacks during their advance, urged a continuance to the fighting, and set off to summon the Polish Corps, on whose support Kerensky counted.

Krasnov and his officers played no part in what they regarded as the political dimension of these negotiations, but remained emphatic in asserting that there was no possibility of victory without substantial reinforcements. Their predicament was worsening by the hour. That evening alarming telegrams arrived from Moscow and Smolensk, where serious outbursts of violence had broken out. To Krasnov it was clear that 'not a single soldier stood up for the Provisional Government. We were alone and betrayed by all'. Kerensky was plainly terrified, not without reason. The effectiveness of the small garrison at Tsarskoe Selo was diminishing by the hour. While the Cossacks were for the most part hostile to the Bolsheviks, they did not acknowledge any necessity for risking their lives in fighting them for a cause few now believed in.

On the morning of 1 November, remarkable exchanges occurred which, like so many in Krasnov's experiences during this tragically momentous year, might conceivably have tipped the scales of history. A truce having been negotiated between the Bolsheviks and Krasnov's Cossacks, a representative of the former arrived in Gatchina. This was the famous sailor Dybenko, a charismatic muscular giant with black curly hair, moustache and beard, of cheerful appearance with sparkling white teeth, and a ready humour which delighted not only the Cossacks, but even many of their fiercely anti-Bolshevik officers.

"Give us Kerensky, and we will give you Lenin, we want to exchange ear for ear here!" proposed Dybenko jovially. Whether the offer was sincere or not, it impressed the Cossacks, who reported back to Krasnov, declaring enthusiastically that they would hang Lenin right there at the palace.

> "Let Lenin be brought here, then we will speak," I said to the Cossacks, and drove them from me. But around noon Kerensky sent for me. He had heard about these conversations and was worried. He requested that the Cossack guard at his door be replaced by a guard from the junkers.
>
> "Your Cossacks will betray me," said Kerensky with chagrin.
>
> "Before, they would have betrayed *me*," I said, and ordered the Cossack sentries to be removed from the doors of Kerensky's apartment.
>
> Something vile was going on. It smelled of ugly betrayal.

Not long after a committee of Don Cossacks burst into the General's room. They demanded peremptorily that Kerensky be handed over, and that they would take him under guard to Bolshevik headquarters at the Smolny Institute in Petrograd. Krasnov angrily replied that he would permit nothing of the sort. Cossacks could not be traitors, and if any punishment were to be inflicted on Kerensky it should be at the hands of a court of law. The Cossacks departed, shouting that they would place a guard on Kerensky. With their departure, Krasnov hastened to Kerensky's quarters. He was deathly pale, and listened attentively while Krasnov explained that he could no longer ensure his safety. Pointing out that there were several unguarded exits from the palace, he added that he could only guarantee the leader's safety for the space of half an hour. During that time Krasnov made arrangements to distract the Cossacks, and when they finally arrived to inspect the Prime Minister's premises they found the bird had flown.

He was just in time. Shortly afterwards a dense column of troops could be seen approaching the Gatchina Palace. On their arrival they proved to be the Finnish Lifeguards Regiment, which was effectively in the service of the Bolsheviks. Such was the Bolshevik truce! reflected Krasnov wearily. He descended to the square, where he explained to his Cossacks that Kerensky had indeed fled. However, he went on, this was to their advantage. The overwhelming superiority of the enemy meant that they could no longer honourably fulfil their duty of protecting the Prime Minister. 'We would have given him up', went up a grim cry from the ranks. 'But did you get hold of Lenin? How would you reconcile the betrayal with your honour'? the General enquired sardonically. The Cossacks fell silent at this, and Krasnov hastened to improve the psychological advantage he had gained over them. 'I know what I'm doing. I brought you here and I will bring you out of here. Do you understand this? Trust me, and you will not perish, but be on the Don'. With this, the General calmly passed through their ranks and returned to his rooms.

Meanwhile, chaos had been unleashed on the palace. Sailors, Red Guards, and soldiers staggered about the rooms, carrying carpets, pillows, mattresses. Evening was approaching, when Krasnov received yet another remarkable visitation. Already that turbulent summer he had encountered three of the leading protagonists of the Revolution: Kornilov, Kerensky, and Savinkov, each of whom in different ways sought his assistance. Now, a civilian of markedly Jewish appearance burst angrily into the room. Krasnov demanded to know who he was. 'I am Trotsky'! shouted the newcomer, insisting that he be freed from the Don Cossack sentry who had followed him in. Before the discussion could proceed further, the Bolshevik leader stormed out. Trotsky's appearance made it dramatically clear that the truce was now being openly violated.* The Red Guards were becoming increasingly truculent, although a semblance of order continued to be imposed by the sailor Dybenko.

Before long Krasnov was informed that he must repair to the Smolny Institute in Petrograd for a discussion. 'Am I under arrest'? enquired Krasnov. No, he was assured that he was not a prisoner, but it remained abundantly clear that he was not being given a choice in the matter. The next morning a car arrived to drive the General, who was accompanied by two of his Cossack officers, to the Bolshevik headquarters. The journey was not without its perils. A giant soldier levelled his rifle at the passengers, declaring that all generals should be shot. Driving off at speed, the car was hit by a bullet as it sped past the recent battlefield at Pulkovo.

Finally, they found themselves being driven through the streets of Petrograd until they arrived at Smolny, formerly a school for the daughters of the high aristocracy, now the Bolshevik headquarters. A crowd was gathered before the building, and a movie camera whirred. Clearly, the occasion was being treated as a major Bolshevik victory, under the assumption that the commander of the 3rd Cavalry Corps was arriving to negotiate its surrender, being the last military unit to serve the Provisional Government.

Inside Smolny, chaos reigned. The building swarmed with ragged 'comrades' and attendant young women of patently dubious morality. Krasnov and his escorts ascended to the third story, where they were taken to a room guarded by two armed sailors at its entrance. The crowd within contained a number of people who were clearly prisoners. They included officers loyal to the Kerensky government. When Krasnov enquired whether he and they were being treated as prisoners, he received a grimly affirmative reply.

> "An arrest indeed", they answered me. "But it will be worse. Yesterday they took General Karachan, commander of the Artillery School, out of Smolny and shot him in the alley. How has it not happened to you, General?", said one.

Exhausted by a succession of sleepless nights, Krasnov found temporary refuge in a neighbouring washroom. Rolling up his overcoat to make a pillow, he lay on the asphalt floor considering his perilous

---

* As yet another measure of his spectacular incapacity, Kerensky had recently suppressed a parade of Cossacks loyal to his government, while ordering the release from gaol of Trotsky and his fellow Bolshevik leaders (Dmitri Volkogonov, *Троцкий: Политический Портрет* (Moscow, 1992), i, p. 132). It is not unlikely that Trotsky's bail of 3,000 roubles was advanced at a remove by a grateful German government.

situation. It was obvious that he had been lied to, and that the so-called 'truce' was nothing more than a duplicitous trap. Suddenly he heard an outburst of agitated discussion next door, and rising to see what was happening found a group of armed Cossack officers from the Committee of the 1st Don Division, all bearing sabres, who had come in search of him. They were accompanied by the doughty Red sailor Dybenko, who imparted an impression of order to the otherwise lawless proceedings.

After half an hour Krasnov and the others were taken to another room, where he was given a chair. No indication was provided of what awaited him, but eventually a man entered, dressed in a baggy tunic with ensign's epaulettes. An unimpressive figure, at least in Krasnov's eyes, he was introduced as Ensign Krylenko, the newly-appointed Bolshevik Commissar for War. That the General's predicament was not so dire as it had hitherto appeared became plain when Krylenko opened his address with a prefatory 'Your Excellency'. He explained that a dispute had arisen over the treatment of Krasnov's Cossacks. The Bolsheviks had decided that the safest course was to rid themselves altogether of this dangerous force, and agreed to allow them to return to the Don with their weapons. From these Krylenko excepted their artillery, which he claimed was needed for the Northern Army. However, this proved a sticking point, which the proud Cossacks were not prepared to concede.

> "But, judge for yourself, here the Committee of 5th Army requests these guns", said Krylenko. "Such is our position. We must fulfil the request of the Committee of 5th Army. Comrades, please come here".
>
> The soldiers, standing at the door, entered the room and with them burst in the Committee of the 1st Don Division.
>
> There began a fierce argument, at times approaching abusive, between the Cossacks and the soldiers.
>
> "While we're alive we will not give up our guns!" yelled the Cossacks. "We will not act dishonourably. How will we appear at home without guns! The old folk will not look at us, the women will be laughing".
>
> In the end they convinced them, that the guns would remain with the Cossacks. The Committee, cursing, went off. We remained with Krylenko.

It was plain that the Bolsheviks, whose superior numbers plainly made them capable of overwhelming the Cossacks, would nevertheless be likely to incur severe casualties in the process. Meanwhile,

"Tell me, Your Excellency", said Krylenko to me, "do you not have tidings of Kaledin [Ataman of the Don Cossacks]? Is it true that he's near Moscow?"

"What's this!" I thought. "You are still not strong. Nor are we victorious. The fight continues".

"I don't know", said I with a significant expression. "Kaledin is my good friend... But I doubt he has any motive for hastening here. Especially, if you don't touch him, and he is left with his Cossacks".

I knew that on the Don Kaledin was barely holding out, and was aware from private understanding that it was impossible to raise the Cossacks [to fight the Bolsheviks].

"Bear in mind, Ensign", said I, "that you promised to release me after an hour, but you have kept me for a whole day. This may anger my Cossacks".

"I cannot release you, so far as that goes, but I have nowhere here to hold you. Do you not have here somewhere where you can stay, while your business is being clarified?"

"I have a flat in Officers' Street", said I.

"Good. We will despatch you to your flat, but before that I will speak with our Chief of Staff".

Krylenko went off with Popov [Krasnov's Chief of Staff]. I despatched Chebotarev with the car to Gatchina to enable my wife to travel to Petrograd. Soon Popov returned. He was grinning broadly.

"You know why they called me?" said he.

"Why?" I asked.

"Trotsky asked me, how you would consider it, were the Government - that's to say the Bolsheviks, obviously - to offer you some high position!"

"Well, and what did you reply?"

"I said: go and ask him yourselves, and the General will give you a punch on the snout!"

I warmly shook Popov's hand. This Popov was the best of fellows. In those difficult, hard minutes he not only did not lose his presence of mind, but he did not abandon his native good humour. Throughout our day of confinement in Smolny, he was criticizing and laughing at our regime in the Smolny Institute. He remained throughout true to himself. That we were risking our heads, we did not consider ...

"You know, Your Excellency", said Popov to me gravely, "it seems to me that the matter is not yet fully played out. It seems that when he asked me about Trotsky's offer, that they fear you. They don't believe in victory".

Trotsky's proposed invitation to Krasnov to accept a command in the Red Army, implausible as it might appear, accorded with his pragmatic policy of employing officers of the Imperial Army to lead the inexperienced Red Army.[*]

In fact the General heard no more of this offer, and shortly afterwards he was driven under guard to his old home, where he was soon joined by his wife Lydia. There for a short space they were able to live a quiet normal life. At the same time, he kept in close touch with officers of the 3rd Cavalry Corps, which was now quartered at nearby Velikie Luki. He was able to contact his troops through representatives of the Don Cossack Committee. Finally, on the evening of 6 November, two of their officers brought him a pass permitting him to depart from Petrograd. Next evening a powerful car belonging to his Corps staff arrived. Together with his wife and two officers from the Corps (all three in full-dress uniform, and bearing weapons), they were driven off, waved past by Red Guards, and tore along the highroad to Novgorod, which they reached at ten o'clock. Meanwhile, as Krasnov learned subsequently, a Red Guard had in the interval arrived at their flat with a warrant signed by Trotsky for his arrest. After replenishing their petrol in Novgorod they drove on to Velikie Luki, where he resumed his position as corps commander.

Although his Cossacks continued fully armed and in good military array, there was much confused discussion in the ranks about their future. Now that the advance on Petrograd had been halted, it remained unclear what was their position. It soon became evident that the majority was determined on returning to the Don, not in order to participate in General Kaledin's attempt to raise an anti-Bolshevik army, but to resume their peacetime life back in their homes. Krasnov reported the situation to Kaledin, suggesting that their desire be fulfilled, while contemplating the prospect that vigorous recruitment and training of new recruits could more effectively re-establish the efficacy of the Cossack Host.

In his response, Kaledin expressed pessimistic reserve. Meanwhile, the Cossack regiments were being successively dispatched to their homelands, until all that remained in Velikie Luki were the General and his staff. As a consequence, Bolshevik elements in the infantry garrison

---

[*] Volkogonov, *Троцкий*, i, pp. 217-18. In Krasnov's epic novel *From Double Eagle to Red Flag* (Berlin, 1921), his hero General Sablin similarly declines a Bolshevik offer to change sides in order to become 'the Murat of the Revolution'.

became increasingly threatening. On one occasion Krasnov himself was pursued by soldiers armed with knives, and on another he was fired upon. Clearly, the time had come when escape could not be postponed further. But how was this to be managed? They were now closely watched by suspicious Red spies. Alone, he might have escaped by failing to return from one of his regular horseback rides in the vicinity. But that would have meant abandoning his wife and remaining staff officers, which was inconceivable. Finally, they satisfied their captors by reluctantly handing over the corps's considerable military pay chest, in return for which they were provided with a train to take them south.

Krasnov himself traveled south separately, accompanied by his wife. It swiftly became clear that the communists were determined to lay hands on him. It appeared that he had been sentenced to death, and "wanted" notices were posted at railway stations. Abandoning his uniform, he donned workman's clothing. At one point the carriage was searched by a sailor accompanied by two Red Guards. Taking care to stand in shadow, Krasnov showed his false passport, with which they appeared satisfied. However, it was worrying that passengers' luggage was now being searched. The General's suitcase contained his military uniform with its epaulettes, together with such tell-tale documents as his service record and diaries. In the event, however, the searchers became bored with their task and left without checking his luggage.

Eventually, they crossed the border into the territory of the Don Cossacks. There he was swiftly recognised and welcomed by Cossacks who had served under him in previous campaigns. At last he was safe! But now he received devastating news that Ataman Kaledin had shot himself, to be succeeded as Ataman by Major-General Anatoly Nazarov. What would happen now? That evening Krasnov paced the bank of the swift-flowing Don, on the far side of which he could see the twinkling lights of Novocherkassk, capital of the Don Cossack territory. What was to be done? Where could he find refuge from the vengeful Reds? Russia was falling apart, and the threat of a bloody Bolshevik conquest now loomed. On 1 February he set off for the city to discover whether the situation could be remedied.[22]

NOTE

It is widely claimed in Soviet sources that while he was in the hands of the Bolsheviks, General Krasnov owed his release to his solemn undertaking not to participate in any further military action against the Bolshevik regime – a promise he allegedly broke a few months later, when he succeeded Kaledin as Ataman of the Don Cossacks.[23] This version of events appears to have originated with Trotsky himself at the time of the supposed event and was subsequently espoused by Stalin.[24] The latter declared that all the Soviet leaders (by inference, including Trotsky and Stalin himself) save Lenin had supported this arrangement, and that when Lenin found himself outnumbered he conceded the point.[25] Remarkably, this version of events has been uncritically accepted by Western historians, in one extreme case going so far as to insinuate that it was possible to read Krasnov's mind when perpetrating his treachery:

> ... Krasnov, who promised not to fight the new regime, was therefore allowed to go. Krasnov was soon [*i.e.* seven months later, in unanticipatable circumstances!] to violate his word, and we have no evidence that he did so after much mental anguish.[26]

Perhaps most regrettable of all was the use made of this Soviet propaganda smear by a British apologist for Krasnov's betrayal in 1945, who sought to justify the elderly General's delivery to SMERSH with the unsubstantiated assertion that 'Years before Krasnov had broken his parole to the Soviet authorities'.[27]

Krasnov drew for his account of his activities in 1917 on his diaries and memory, writing his recollection of events less than three years afterwards.[28] Nowhere in his detailed narrative is there mention, or indeed possibility, of his having entered into any such engagement as that ascribed him by his enemies. In his capacity as novelist, journalist, and high-ranking soldier he was possessed of an outstandingly retentive memory, which enabled him to describe his experiences accurately down to the last trifling detail.

It might be urged that Krasnov deliberately omitted recounting an event which, if true, was much to his discredit. This seems unlikely for a variety of reasons. For a start, it would have been necessary for him not merely to have omitted the alleged incident, but to have doctored much else in his detailed narrative of events following the battle at Pulkovo. Nor does it seem that at the time he wrote his memoir Krasnov was aware of Trotsky's accusation. Had he been, he might be expected to have made some attempt to repudiate the charge in his narrative.

Further to this, Trotsky's tale remains intrinsically implausible. It seems unlikely that he would have relied upon a mere verbal undertaking on the General's part not to fight against Bolshevik power. There was in fact at the time little likelihood of Krasnov's ever being in a position to resume the conflict. His Cossacks were in the process of being repatriated and disbanded, and Trotsky was well aware that it was their intention to return to their homeland *stanitsas*, where they declared their concern to abandon any further military activity. Meanwhile, until it was dispersed and safely removed from the scene, the 3rd Cossack Cavalry Corps remained a formidable fighting force. It has been seen how anxious the Bolsheviks were to appropriate the Cossacks' artillery, while their grudging acceptance of a flat refusal reveals the essential weakness of their position. Any attempt on the life or liberty of the popular General could have imperilled the entire Bolshevik movement, whose grip on Petrograd at this juncture hung in the balance.

Again, while Trotsky was a strong proponent of the policy of employing tsarist officers in the Red Army, he profoundly mistrusted their loyalty. Retention and killing of hostages, together with murder of those suspected of betrayal, were among draconian measures he instituted for guarding against their betrayal of a cause they were suspected of secretly detesting.[29] Mere reliance on a senior White general's word of honour in the circumstances in which Krasnov was placed would have been highly uncharacteristic of the relentlessly suspicious Trotsky.

Finally, Krasnov's elevation in May 1918 to the post of Ataman of the Don Cossacks must in this context have appeared a considerable embarrassment to Trotsky. Before Kaledin's unexpected suicide no one could have anticipated that Krasnov would emerge as leader of a vigorously anti-Bolshevik Don Cossack army. The Bolshevik leadership (especially those who, like Stalin, envied and hated Trotsky) might well have asked how Krasnov had been allowed to escape, when he was effectively their prisoner.[30] Trotsky was after all the leader who had treated with the Cossacks after the skirmish at Pulkovo. He could not escape the fact that Krasnov had slipped through his fingers, and the accusation that he had obtained his word of honour not to fight the Bolsheviks might have appeared the best justification of his failure that Trotsky could provide.[*]

Finally, and perhaps most significantly, no mention of Krasnov's alleged violation of his parole was raised during his lengthy trial by the NKVD in 1946. The truth of this matter may never be known for certain, but on balance it seems more likely that Trotsky invented Krasnov's alleged breach of promise, than that any such pledge actually occurred.

---

[*] It may be significant that no Soviet source (so far as I am aware) records to whom it was that Krasnov is supposed to have given his word of honour not to serve further against the Bolsheviks. Nor do the detailed proceedings of Krasnov's secret interrogations in Moscow in 1945-46 contain any reference to the allegation of bad faith in 1917 – which is where one might most expect to find it included. The General's memory was incidentally quite extraordinary. At his interrogation on 20 June 1945, for example, he recalled with minute accuracy the precise dates and locations of events in 1917, despite the fact that he possessed only the scantiest of notes or memoranda.

[1] P.N. Krasnov, *Казаки въ Африкѣ': Дневникъ Начальника Конвоя Россійской Императорской Миссій въ Абиссиніи въ 1897-98 году* (St. Peterburg, 1899).

[2] P.N. Krasnov, *По Азіи: Путевые очерки Манчжуріи Дальная Востока, Китая, Японіи и Индіи* (St. Peterburg, 1903).

[3] K.F. Shatsillo (ed.), *Дневники Императора Николая II* (Moscow, 1991), p. 245. Krasnov's heartfelt patriotism led him at times into underestimating the skill and courage of the Japanese foe.

[4] V.Y. Chernaev, 'Писатель генерал Краснов', in V.G. Bortnevsky (ed.), *Русское Прошлое: Историко-Документальный Альманах* (St. Petersburg, 1993), iv, pp. 352-53; Vasily Matasov, *Белое Движение на Юге России 1917-1920 годы* (Montreal, 1990), p. 206.

[5] Allan K. Wildman, *The End of the Russian Army: The Old Army and the Soldiers' Revolt (March-April 1917)* (Princeton, 1980), pp., 228-34; Sean McMeekin, *The Russian Revolution: A New History* (London, 2017), pp. 113-14, 122-23, 126, 137.

[6] George Katkov, *Russia 1917: The February Revolution* (London, 1967), pp. 367-74; Wildman, *The End of the Russian Army*, pp. 228-34.

[7] P.N. Krasnov, 'На внутреннемъ фронтѣ', in I.V. Gessen (ed.), *Архивъ Русской Революціи* (Berlin, 1922-37), i, pp. 97-100. At the same time, in the south around Kishinev, Krasnov's future Kuban Cossack colleague Andrei Shkuro witnessed comparably horrifying scenes of chaos (V. Tretyakova (ed.), *Тайны Истории в романах повестях и документах* (Moscow, 1996), i, pp. 20-22).

[8] McMeekin, *The Russian Revolution*, p. 126.

[9] *Ibid.*, p. 344.

[10] Laura Engelstein, *Russia in Flames: War, Revolution, Civil War 1914-1921* (New York, 2018), p. 180; Harvey Pitcher, *Witnesses of the Russian Revolution* (London, 1994), p. 163; Orlando Figes and Boris Kolonitskii, *Interpreting the Russian Revolution: The Language and Symbols of 1917* (New Haven and London, 1999), pp. 76-96. A rare and unconvincing defence of Kerensky's conduct in 1917 was propounded by Robert Paul Browder, 'Kerenskij Revisited', in Hugh Maclean, Martin E. Malia, and George Fischer (ed.), *Russian Thought and Politics* (*Harvard Slavic Studies*, iv) (Cambridge, Mass., 1957), pp. 421-34.

[11] The German Foreign Minister reported to the Kaiser on 3 December 1917 that 'It was not until the Bolsheviki had received from us a steady flow of funds through various channels and under varying labels that they were in a position to be able to build up their main organ, *Pravda*, to conduct energetic propaganda and appreciably to extend the original narrow basis of their party' (George Katkov, 'German Foreign Office Documents on Financial Support to the Bolsheviks in 1917', *International Affairs* (London, 1956), xxxii, p.

189). The fullest and most reliable account of German funding of the Bolshevik Party is now provided by McMeekin, *The Russian Revolution*, pp. 127-36. Cf. also Michael Futrell, 'Alexander Keskuela', in David Footman (ed.), *St Antony's Papers, Number 12: Soviet Affairs Number Three* (London, 1962), pp. 23-52. Foreign Minister Pavel Miliukov ascribed the Army's collapse in morale to 'the penetration of agitators, sent by the Soviets' (Thomas Riha, *A Russian European: Paul Miliukov in Russian Politics* (Notre Dame, Ind., 1969), p. 310).

[12] The liberal statesman P.B. Struve condemned Kerensky's short-sighted betrayal of Kornilov and alliance with the extreme Left as 'acts not only of "unparalleled baseness" but of "immense political stupidity" as well' (Richard Pipes, *Struve: Liberal on the Right, 1905-1944* (Cambridge, Mass., 1980), pp. 309-10).

[13] Andrei Malyunas and Sergei Mironenko (ed.), *A Lifelong Passion: Nicholas and Alexandra; Their Own Story* (London, 1996), p. 555.

[14] The cult of Kornilov is described by Figes and Kolonitskii, *Interpreting the Russian Revolution* (New Haven and London, 1999), pp. 96-100. General Krasnov himself took Kornilov for a revolutionary sympathizer (Gessen (cd.), *Архивъ Русской Революцiи*, i, p. 117).

[15] Tsuyoshi Hasegawa, *Crime and Punishment in the Russian Revolution* (Cambridge, Mass., 2017), pp. 64-71.

[16] Cf. George Katkov, *The Kornilov Affair: Kerensky and the break-up of the Russian army* (London, 1980), pp. 442-64; Richard Pipes, 'The Kornilov affair: A tragedy of errors', in Tony Brenton (ed.), *Historically Inevitable?: Turning Points of the Russian Revolution* (London, 2016), pp. 109-22; McMeekin, *The Russian Revolution*, pp. 185-91.

[17] V. Nabokov, 'Временное Правитьелство', in Gessen (ed.), *Архивъ Русской Революцiи*, i, p. 83.

[18] *Ibid.*, pp. 132-36, 172-79.

[19] For the key part played by the Red sailors in halting Krasnov's advance at Pulkovo, cf. Evan Mawdsley, *The Russian Revolution and the Baltic Fleet: War and Politics, February 1917-April 1918* (London, 1978), pp. 99-100, 113-14.

[20] Katkov, *The Kornilov Affair*, pp. 126-27.

[21] Telegram preserved in the Central Archive of the October Revolution, Stock 1052, File 343, p. 7.

[22] Gessen (ed.), *Архивъ Русской Революцiи*, i, pp. 97-190.

[23] Cf. S.S. Khromov (ed.), *Гражданская Война и Военная Интервенция в СССР: Энциклопедия* (Moscow, 1983), p. 300.

[24] Dmitri Volkogonov, *Троцкий: Политический Портрет* (Moscow, 1992), p. 217; Emil Ludwig, *Leaders of Europe* (London, 1934), p. 373.

[25] Volkogonov, *Троцкий*, i, p. 172.

[26] Peter Kenez, *Civil War in South Russia, 1918* (Berkeley, 1971), p. 46. Isaac

Deutscher went so far as to justify the Red Terror as a consequence of Krasnov's alleged bad faith! (*Stalin: A Political Biography* (Oxford, 1949), p. 178).

[27] Carol Mather, *Aftermath of War: Everyone Must Go Home* (London, 1992), p. 238.

[28] Gessen (ed.), *Архивъ Русской Революціи*, i, p. 190.

[29] Volkogonov, *Троцкий*, i, pp. 224-25, 290-92. For one example amongst a plethora testifying to Trotsky's sanguinary treatment of White prisoners, cf. his instruction of 28 August 1920 for the liquidation of White suspects in the recently-occupied Kuban (I.I. Basik, S.N. Ivanov, S.O. Panin and V.S. Khristopherov (ed.), *Русская Военная Эмиграция 20-х-40-х годов: Документы и Материалы* (Moscow, 1998-), i, pt. i, pp. 133-36).

[30] Stalin was particularly concerned to downplay Trotsky's revolutionary role in 1917 (Dmitri Volkogonov, *Сталин: Политический Портрет* (Moscow, 1994), i, p. 82).

CHAPTER III
COSSACK BANNERS ON THE DON

White Guard, your path is set noble and high:
Black muzzles – your breast and temple defy.

Godly and white is the cause you die for:
White is your body – in sands to lie.

That is no flock of swans in the sky there:
Saintly the White Guard host sails by there,
White, as a vision, to fade and die there...

One last glimpse of a world that's gone:
Manliness – Daring – Vendée – Don.
Marina Tsvetaeva, 11 March 1918[*]

No sooner had Peter Krasnov arrived in his home territory of the Don, than he received the shocking news of the suicide of Ataman Kaledin. The Ataman had been an able military commander and staunch conservative, who nevertheless introduced representation of poor peasants (*inogorodnye*) into the Don parliament (*Krug*). However, with the New Year of 1918 the Don territory suffered an invasion by a numerically vastly superior Red Army. General Kornilov, who had made his way south where he raised the anti-Bolshevik Volunteer Army, declared his intention of preserving the Army by withdrawal to the Kuban. Apparently despairing of being able to remedy a fast-deteriorating situation, on 12 February Kaledin shot himself through the heart. His successor, General Nazarov, attempted briefly to continue the armed conflict. After a desultory struggle, it became clear that victory lay for the present with the Reds. The Volunteer Army entered on its immortal Ice March in an attempt to liberate the Kuban from local Bolshevik rule, while the Red Army occupied the Don capital Novocherkassk and overran almost the

---

[*] Robin Kemball (ed.), *Marina Tsvetaeva: The Demesne of the Swans; Лебединый Станъ* (Ann Arbor, 1980), p. 63.

entire region. Nazarov was captured and summarily murdered. The situation remained chaotic.

Now the Cossacks learned what it was to live under Red rule. Although a substantial element of the population had for various reasons supported the invasion, almost all had become alienated by the realities of Bolshevik conquest. Both Lenin and Trotsky were committed to all-pervasive terror as the preferred instrument of imposing their authority.[1] Thus in August Lenin ordered local Communists at Penza to select victims at random from among disaffected peasants: 'Hang (hang without fail, so the people see) no fewer than 100 known kulaks, rich men, bloodsuckers'. In the next month he instructed Party secretary Krestinsky: 'It is necessary secretly – and urgently – to prepare the terror'.[2]

During the few weeks of Bolshevik rule in the Don territory, thousands of people were butchered, few if any of whom had actively opposed the Bolshevik occupation – as often as not, in circumstances of atrocious brutality.[3]

Fortunately for the inhabitants, it was not long before the situation was dramatically altered by larger events. By the opening weeks of 1918 the demoralised Russian Army was incapable of any effective resistance to the remorseless advance of the Germans. As early as 4 December 1917 (old style) an armistice was agreed between the Central Powers and the nascent Soviet Union. Negotiations for a formal treaty opened, with each side duplicitously seeking to undermine the other's position. While Ludendorff was determined to take advantage of Russia's weakness by preserving existing conquests in eastern Russia from the Baltic to the Black Sea, Lenin was left with little hope of countering an imposed annexationist peace, beyond a hope that an outraged European proletariat would in due course rise up and overthrow the Carthaginian peace imposed on their comrades in the East.

Owing to the effectiveness of the Allied naval blockade, the populations of the Central powers had become subjected to ever-increasing malnutrition, with the ultimate prospect of starvation. Germany's overriding strategic aims were retention of conquests in Courland and eastern Poland, and control of the grain-producing Ukraine and oil-rich Caucasus. There existed hopes among many of its population that an independent Ukraine might somehow escape the turmoil and brutality afflicting the broken Empire. Equally, the Bolshevik dictatorship was determined to frustrate any such secession. When the Central Council (*Rada*) of the newly-emergent Ukrainian Republic declared independence, with its capital at Kiev, the Bolsheviks established a rival regime centered on the eastern city of Kharkov. The military resources of the *Rada* proving inadequate, Kiev fell to the Red Army on 8 February. Once again, the familiar pattern of ensuing atrocities succeeded in alienating much of the population from its conquerors.[4]

While the Red Army proved more than a match for Ukrainian levies, it was helpless in face of continuing German advance into the territory. By the end of April German and Austrian forces had occupied Kiev and advanced their front line as far as the Don in the east and Crimea in the south. When the *Rada* failed to ensure provision of the occupying force with the requisite grain, Field Marshal von Eichhorn dissolved the assembly and elevated a former officer of the Russian Imperial Army, General Pavel Skoropadsky, as Hetman of the province. He was an old comrade of Ataman Krasnov, having served with him at the front in the 1st Guards Cavalry Division. A flamboyant figure, he was wholly dependent on the German occupying force for maintenance of his authority, which collapsed when the occupying force came to be withdrawn.[5]

When Trotsky and his fellow-delegates met the Germans to negotiate peace at Brest-Litovsk they were in no position to defend Russian interests, having themselves effectively destroyed the Russian Army. On 3 March 1918 they signed the infamous treaty which capitulated to virtually every German demand. At the same time, neither party regarded it as anything but formalising acceptance of the current military *status quo*, whose ultimate fate depended on the outcome of the Great War itself.[6] Had Germany won the war (as it appeared that summer it might), a vast swathe of Russian territory would have remained in perpetuity a collection of German satrapies.

Meanwhile the situation in Russia became ever more confused and polarised. Throughout 1917, the great majority of the Russian officer class continued content to abide by the outcome of the elections to the Constituent Assembly, being primarily concerned to prosecute the war effectively against the common enemy Germany. Russian national honour demanded continued support of the Allied cause, and ejection of the Central Powers' occupation of Russian soil. However, the Bolsheviks' armed suppression of the Assembly when they found the national vote cast against them, coupled with mounting evidence that they were working hand-in-glove with their German paymasters, and finally their manifest commitment to terror as the prime instrument in their determination to gain power by force, led to an ever-increasing conviction that Red oppression could only be effectively countered by military measures.[*]

The Volunteer Army was assembled in the south, under the leadership of Generals Alexeev, former Chief of Staff of the Imperial Army, and Kornilov. Initially the Whites were isolated, and Kornilov was obliged to evacuate his small but resolute army from the Soviet Don in what became the legendary Ice March. Arrival of the German Army on the west bank of the Don dramatically changed the strategic situation. While the Germans were not prepared to engage in military operations against the Bolshevik regime, their presence guaranteed the left flank of the White Army. On 6 May the Germans occupied Rostov, and the Bolshevik occupiers of the Don territory withdrew to Tsaritsyn on the Volga (afterwards Stalingrad).

General Kornilov was killed during the Ice March at the siege of Ekaterinodar. His successor as commander of the Volunteer Army was General Anton Denikin, a capable and honourable, though less inspiring leader, who in due course became commander of the White Armies in southern Russia.

Meanwhile, in the Don territory the savagery of its Bolshevik occupiers had alienated the greater part of the population. In April a Don Provisional Government was formed under the leadership of a conservative, G. P. Yanov. Amicable relations were established with the Germans, who had seized Taganrog and Rostov, together with the Ukrainian government (also under German control) at Kiev, and elections were called to the Don Cossack assembly, or *Krug* ('Circle'), in the newly-recovered regional capital Novocherkassk.

Since his arrival in the Don at the beginning of the year, General Krasnov had been living in obscurity two hundred miles from the Don river, in Konstantinovska *stanitsa*, to avoid attracting the attention of Bolshevik executioners. Dismayed by the Cossacks' failure to resist the Bolshevik onslaught, he declined an initial invitation to take command of

---

[*] There was of course a White terror, as well as Red. Fundamental distinctions between the two lay in the facts (i) that the Red terror comprised from the outset a (arguably *the*) basic element of Soviet rule; (ii) its use was consistently advocated and enforced by every Bolshevik leader; (iii) its deployment continued unabated for decades after Bolshevik victory in the Civil War (George Leggett, *The Cheka: Lenin's Political Police* (Oxford, 1981), pp. 171-203). Neither Krasnov, Denikin, Kolchak, nor Wrangel regarded terror *per se* as a valid instrument of state power. While a White victory could well have resulted in authoritarian military rule over Russia, comparable to the regimes of Mannerheim in Finland or Piłsudski in Poland (both, incidentally, former officers of the Tsar), it is worth noting that the principal White war aim was that of reconvening the Constituent Assembly.

the Don territory. By the spring, however, the situation began to improve, and at the beginning of May a Cossack army recaptured the capital of Novocherkassk. Now Krasnov decided to attend the meeting of the *Krug*. His distinguished military record and intellectual gifts, together with his considerable talent as an orator, led to his election by an overwhelming majority of the delegates on 16 May as Ataman of the Don Cossacks. His political programme effectively constituted a return to the state of affairs as it stood on the eve of the February Revolution. His profound knowledge of Cossack history assisted reintroduction of many colourful traditions from the heroic Cossack past. All this appealed greatly to Don Cossack pride, and played a major part in reinvigorating a Cossack 'national' spirit.

This assembly became known by the historic title of 'The *Krug* of Salvation of the Don'. It did not concern itself overly with legislative issues, regarding itself as a provisional government whose pressing and immediate task comprised liberation of the entirety of the Don from its Bolshevik oppressors. Once that was achieved, a full *Krug* would be assembled to decide on the region's future. As Krasnov put it: 'In the meantime, the only goal was: save the Don'!

A pressing issue lay in the relationship of the Don with the Germans and Skoropadsky's regime in Kiev. The attitude to be adopted towards the Germans presented a thorny problem. Krasnov and his fellow-soldiers had fought long and hard for the Allied cause. On the other hand, German occupation of the Ukraine had removed the threat of Bolshevism from the region, and by its presence went far to ensure the Cossacks' survival. The Allies were far away, and in any case unprepared to endorse the separatist policy of the Cossacks. On purely pragmatic grounds, Krasnov opted for good relations with the Germans.[7] In addition, he and his Cossacks resented any attempt by Denikin to assume overall command of the anti-Soviet movement.

On the evening of 14 May Krasnov delivered by invitation an eloquent address to the *Krug*. Many in his audience had served under his command during the War and previous campaigns. These veterans held him in high regard for his military talent, and the adroit manner in which he frequently emerged from the most dangerous predicaments led to his being widely regarded with almost superstitious reverence. His love for the Cossacks, their exemplary military record, and colorful history was patent. Now, however, he lamented that the Russian Empire was being destroyed under the tyranny of the Bolsheviks, while the Don had become isolated and largely occupied by the Red enemy. Given this dire situation, until Russia were restored the Don must become an independent state, with its own political and military institutions.

So far as her immediate neighbours were concerned, Krasnov continued, it was necessary to cooperate with the Germans until their army were to withdraw peacefully. Meanwhile the Don should work closely with General Denikin's Volunteer Army and Skoropadsky's regime in the Ukraine. The ultimate aim was for the Don to recover her historical autonomy within a renewed Russian Empire.

Krasnov's speech was received with great acclaim. Two days later he was elected by an overwhelming majority of the *Krug* as Field Ataman of the Don Cossacks. His position gave him supreme command over all military matters, and empowered him to conduct relations with neighbouring states. However, the predicament he faced appeared dire. The Bolsheviks still occupied the greater part of the Don, German cavalry had advanced within striking distance of the capital Novocherkassk, and the shattered land was all but overwhelmed by social chaos, corruption, and near-famine.

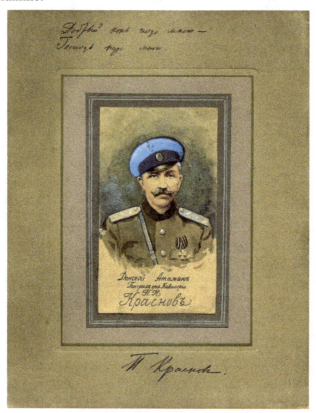

Ataman P. N. Krasnov

Krasnov began immediate measures to recover the military situation. Radical improvements were undertaken under his guidance in discipline, morale, and recruitment. By the next month his inspired leadership resulted in a more than doubling of the Don Cossack Army to 40,000 troops.[8] Emissaries were swiftly dispatched to the German Field Marshal von Eichhorn and Hetman Skoropadsky in the Ukraine. Friendly relations were likewise established with their fellow Cossacks of the Kuban and with the newly-declared Georgian Republic. Meanwhile, Krasnov wrote a personal letter to Kaiser Wilhelm, requesting collaboration with his army in the Ukraine. The German response was swift and positive. The disputed region they had occupied around Donetsk was they accepted based on a misunderstanding that it belonged to Ukraine, and both parties agreed to co-operate constructively with the common aim of expelling the Bolsheviks from the Don.[9]

A pricklier problem arose in regard to relations with General Denikin's Volunteer Army. Denikin sought unity between their forces, urging that the Don Army come under his overall command. While this made sense from a military point of view, other considerations made it unacceptable from the Ataman's viewpoint. Krasnov pointed out that he was no longer a mere subordinate in rank to the General, but now headed a nation of five million people. A still more serious difference lay in the irreconcilability of Krasnov's pragmatic policy of maintaining mutual understanding with Eichhorn's army of occupation in the Ukraine, while Denikin remained uncompromisingly loyal to the alliance with Britain and France.

Nevertheless, the Ataman accepted that a unified command would become necessary in the event that a common front developed. The strategy advocated by Krasnov was to unite their armies in an assault on the city of Tsaritsyn. A peasant uprising against the Bolsheviks in Saratov province proffered opportunity for the advance. As Krasnov explained:

> Tsaritsyn will give General Denikin a purely Russian base, with weapons and munitions factories and large stores of military material – to say nothing of money. The Volunteer Army would cease to depend on the Cossacks. Besides, taking Tsaritsyn would bring the Army closer to, and possibly unite it with, the Czechoslovaks[*] and Dutov[†], and create a single menacing front. With the support of the Don *voisko*, the

---

[*] Liberated Czech prisoners of war had formed a Legion which fought alongside the White Army of Admiral Kolchak in Siberia.
[†] Ataman of the Ural Cossacks.

[Volunteer] Army could begin its march to Samara, Penza, Tula, and
then the Don soldiers would take Voronezh.

Disappointingly, Denikin declined to participate. His preference was
to protect his rear base by joining with the Kuban Cossacks in
overthrowing local Bolsheviks. That achieved, the Volunteer Army would
return to assist in operations against Tsaritsyn. It is hard not to conclude
that Krasnov's forward policy was preferable. Denikin was confident of
an eventual Allied victory on the Western Front, but this was far from
being a certain outcome during the summer of 1918. In any case, while the
Allies could play no part in the current critical situation, the Germans in
the Ukraine were covertly providing the Don Army with a substantial flow
of munitions and economic supplies.[10] When reproached on this count,
Krasnov responded ironically:

> Yes, yes, gentlemen! The Volunteer Army is pure and infallible. But
> after all, it's me, the Don Ataman, I take German shells and cartridges
> with my dirty hands, wash them in the waves of the Quiet Don and give
> them clean to the Volunteer Army! All the shame of this business lies
> with me![11]

The Germans appreciated the need for discretion in their relations with
the Don government and army. Although concerned not to become
embroiled in the Russian civil war, their presence freed the Don from
stationing troops along the 500-verst frontier. Moreover, they initially
provided active military assistance, suffering considerable losses in
repelling a Red Army attempt to seize the city of Taganrog.

On 28 June General Krasnov dispatched, through the medium of a
mutual friend, the Russo-German Duke of Leuchtenberg, a further eight-
page letter to Kaiser Wilhelm, appealing for recognition of the
independence of a neutral Don territory. The result was a material increase
in German aid, and even an offer to assist in the capture of Tsaritsyn. This
however Krasnov declined, trusting that with the eventual support of the
Volunteer Army the city would fall to Russian arms alone.[12]

Under Krasnov's energetic direction, based on extensive training and
greatly improved equipment, the Cossack host swiftly achieved expulsion
of the Red Army from the whole of the Don territory.

On 28 May Krasnov met Denikin, and urged that the latter's Volunteer
Army unite with the Don Cossacks in a bold strike to seize the city of
Tsaritsyn. Strategically located between the rivers Don and Volga, the city
was well placed to impede shipping passing up and downstream. It boasted
a population of 150,000, was an important railway center, and contained
major arms factories. It was also a critical junction for transport of grain

to the south, at a time when workers in Moscow and Petrograd were receiving a bare four ounces of bread every other day. Now that Admiral Kolchak's White Army and its Czechoslovak allies were advancing westwards from Siberia into European Russia, capture of Tsaritsyn could prove decisive in the creation of a common front against the retreating Red Army. Denikin however rejected the proposal, which if pursued with vigour by their combined armies might conceivably have tipped the balance in favour of a White victory in the Civil War.

Although Denikin was an honourable man and able commander, it is hard not to accept the superior efficacy of Krasnov's strategy. As the latter urged:

> If General Denikin considers it possible to leave the Kuban with his volunteer detachments and head for Tsaritsyn, then all the Don troops of the Lower Chirsky and Grand Ducal regions will be automatically subordinated to General Denikin. On the basis of the situation observed in Saratov district, an attack on Tsaritsyn promises full success to the Volunteers. In Saratov district an uprising of the peasants has already begun. [13]

By July, Bolshevik forces had been entirely destroyed or driven out of the southern Don territory, the capital Novocherkassk was liberated, and with discipline restored and morale high, the Don Army prepared to take the fight beyond the Don lands. But here Krasnov came up against an endemic problem. While his Cossacks were fully prepared to fight with determination and skill against the Red occupiers of their land, it was a very different matter to continue the war beyond the Don border. Why shed their blood in a struggle which did not concern them? Many remained deaf to the Ataman's pleas that the Don would never be safe so long as the Bolshevik regime endured. But as Krasnov urged again and again,

> For the best support of our borders, the Don Army must advance beyond the region, occupying the cities of Tsaritsyn, Kamyshin, Balashov, Novokhopersk and Kalach in the areas of Saratov and Voronezh provinces.

While a solid core of Don Cossacks remained true to their oath of obedience, the reluctance of many to participate in a campaign beyond the frontiers placed Krasnov's strategy in peril. He appealed urgently to Denikin to abandon his campaign in the Kuban, and join the common crusade to deal a mortal blow to the Bolshevik enemy of Russia and mankind. Denikin rejected the appeal: as a responsible commander, he felt he could not leave his rear unsecured. Krasnov suspected him of concern at the prospect of his numerically inferior command's being subordinated to that of the Don Ataman.

Ataman P. N. Krasnov,
bearing the ceremonial mace (*bulava*) of the Don Cossacks

On 26 August Ataman Krasnov held a mass parade of his retrained and rearmed Army at a ground outside the Don capital of Novocherkassk. His heart swelled with pride as he rode past the eager faces of his beloved Don Cossacks. As he recalled afterwards,

> In all there were 7 battalions, 33 squadrons of dismounted Cossacks, 6 batteries without harnesses (one crew), 16 mounted Cossack squadrons, one mortar battery and 5 aeroplanes.

At the same time a formidable little navy was established to protect communications along the Don, on occasion conveying landing-parties for expeditions against Bolshevik positions in the vicinity of the river. Training of personnel was conducted at a base established in the town of Taganrog.[14]

As the year drew on, it became clear that the Western Allies, with United States forces arriving in ever-increasing strength at the front line, must before long be victorious, with the Central Powers correspondingly doomed. It would not be long, Denikin believed, before German occupation of the Ukraine melted away and powerful Allied fleets arrived in the Black Sea. Where he was wrong, Krasnov reckoned in turn, was in trusting that they would bring them a military force of sufficient strength to turn the tide against the Bolsheviks. On 20 October he travelled to the Ukraine, where he conferred with a despondent Hetman Skoropadsky. Together they issued a vain appeal to Denikin. But Denikin knew, as they knew, that an imminent Allied victory would cause the German protectorate to melt away like ice in the spring. He rejected any possibility of an alliance. Nor should it be forgotten that he was intensely loyal to Russia. The creation of semi-independent states carved out of southern Russia was as repugnant to him as his loyalty to Russia's wartime allies was firm.[15]

In Moscow the Bolshevik leadership was in a state of panic. In May Lenin had dispatched a former Imperial staff officer, Andrei Snesarev, to assume control of the garrison of Tsaritsyn. This constituted a motley collection of ill-disciplined partisans, and in mid-July the Soviet leader sent one of his favourite colleagues to establish socialist order in the city and restore the vital grain supply. This was Joseph Stalin, who set about his task with relentless vigor.

Stalin's most congenial instrument for imposing Bolshevik discipline was the local Cheka (political police). Its headquarters occupied a two-story building overlooking the Volga, whose ground floor was converted into cells. Many prisoners were crammed into a barge moored below the bloodstained building, where they died of starvation or were summarily murdered. Suspects were subjected to appalling tortures, whose specialities included sawing through prisoners' bones, mutilations repeatedly inflicted before execution, snapping arms backwards, and the like. A chance visitor was horrified to witness the Cheka chairman Cherviakov and his aides examining four prisoners (three men and a woman). Without warning, they began battering their victims with revolver butts, warning that any cry of pain would be met with a bullet. A Cossack officer showed another visitor how his interrogation had been conducted. First he was placed for some time barefoot on a red-hot frying-pan, then he was lashed with a whip equipped with metallic tips until his back was one bleeding mass of mutilated flesh. The next day he was contemptuously shot. A total of some 5,000 people were slaughtered during this extended purge. As was almost always the case on such sanguinary occasions, few if any of the victims were guilty of any crime; the prime purpose of the Red Terror was just that: to terrify the population into submission.[16]

Unsurprisingly, such atrocities provoked White retaliation, and so the grim cycle continued.

In all this Cherviakov was directly answerable to Stalin, who notoriously relished torture, the crueller and more protracted the better. A few years later, on learning that some erstwhile colleagues had refused to confess to imaginary crimes, he snarled: 'Give them the works until they come crawling to you on their bellies with confessions in their teeth!' He personally advised on methods of torture, exclaiming on occasion in his crude Georgian accent: 'beat, beat and, once again, beat'.[17]

Before long, Stalin intrigued with Trotsky to have the garrison commandant of Tsaritsyn dismissed, to be replaced by himself with a couple of subservient colleagues as organisers of the city's defense.

That autumn Tsaritsyn remained under siege by Krasnov's army, which on 15 October gained the city's outskirts. This, however, represented the high tide of Don Cossack success. Within ten days they were driven back across the Don. This close-run Bolshevik victory was largely owing to the garrison's immense superiority in numbers, combined with an unexpected attack on the Cossacks' rear by a Bolshevik division of 15,000 men, which had skilfully outwitted Denikin's army and conducted a forced march northward from the Caucasus front. The Don Army had no choice but to withdraw.[18] Although Stalin played no direct part in the military command, and in fact left the city shortly before the siege was lifted, his ruthless repression of dissent had played a significant part in maintaining Bolshevik control over the city.[19] (How far his murderous activities really contributed to victory is another matter). Given his prominent contribution, he might be expected to have regarded his adversary Ataman Krasnov with grudging respect. This however would be gravely to misread his vengeful attitude towards anyone whom he regarded as having presented a threat to his authority.

As 1918 drew to a close, the state of affairs in Russia appeared deeply threatening to the Don. When on 11 November an exhausted Germany was obliged to accept an armistice with the Allies, the terms included abrogation of the Treaty of Brest-Litovsk, imposing withdrawal of all German forces from occupied territories there and elsewhere.[20] With them departed the unfortunate Hetman Skoropadsky, whose authority was wholly dependent on the arms of his German ally. The briefly independent Ukraine subsided into a chaotic internecine struggle, vividly depicted in Bulgakov's novel *The White Guard*.[21]

There can be little doubt that the narrow survival of the Red Army defenders of Tsaritsyn exercised a profound effect on Stalin's accruing self-assurance. After initial reservation that his henchman's reign of cruelty might have represented a 'mistake' (although needless to say *not* a crime), Lenin swiftly came to relish Stalin's butchery as wholly beneficial.[22] Following the latter's rise to power over the Soviet Union, the city was in 1925 renamed Stalingrad. When in 1942 it again became the focus of the successful defense of Soviet power, his thoughts harked back to his earlier success.[23] The siege of Tsaritsyn in 1918 was the second occasion that he had come up against Peter Krasnov as his most formidable adversary. In the previous year he had played a similar role in the defense of Petrograd against Krasnov's abortive attempt to seize the city, described in the previous chapter.[24]

With the withdrawal of Krasnov's Cossacks to their homeland, the Ataman came under increasing pressure. His policy of *rapprochement* with the Germans reflected no ideological preference, but pure *Realpolitik*. Their occupation of the Ukraine assured the security of his vulnerable left flank, while their massive provision of arms and material played a vital part in the Whites' recovery of the Don territory.[25] Until the close of 1918 the Allies were in no position to afford any aid to the Cossacks, but now the victorious British and French navies arrived in the Black Sea. Denikin and his Volunteer Army had remained loyal to the Entente cause throughout, and were now naturally preferred as trusted allies.

Krasnov, who had earlier fought long and hard for three years in the Allied cause, could not expect to avoid a degree of mistrust for his pragmatic switch to alliance with the enemy.[26] He himself entertained no inhibitions over the enforced choice, and in his novel *From Double Eagle to Red Flag* likened acceptance of German aid to the Kievan state's appeal to the Varangians (Vikings) in early Rus' a thousand years before.

The attitude of the Allies was however initially understanding of the Ataman's predicament vis-à-vis his German neighbours. On 25 November, an Allied mission arrived in Novocherkassk. The party sailed to Mariupol in destroyers, and then travelled by rail to Taganrog, Rostov and Novocherkassk. They were entertained in the Ataman's luxurious railway train, which included a restaurant carriage serving rich food and wines. Arrived in the Don capital Novocherkassk, they were received by an honor guard of the 4th Don Cossack Regiment. The two-mile route

from the station to the cathedral was guarded by Don Cossack infantry,
cavalry and artillery.

Novocherkassk was replete with colourful guests. To impress the
Allies with the military power of the Don, representatives of Denikin's
Volunteer Army, the Kuban Cossacks, and the peoples of the North
Caucasus and Astrakhan had been invited to attend the celebrations.
Prominent among them was a striking figure, who was to play a major part
in the triumph, travails, and ultimate tragedy of the Don Ataman Peter
Krasnov. This was the Kuban Cossack Andrei Grigorievich Shkuro, whom
General Krasnov probably first encountered in February 1918, when
Denikin dispatched his regiment north to participate in the assault on
Tsaritsyn.[27]

A dashing figure even by Cossack standards, he had enjoyed a colorful
career which might have been drawn from the pages of Gogol's heroic tale
Taras Bulba. Despite being only thirty-one at the time of Krasnov's
reception at Novocherkassk, he had been appointed a full colonel in
consequence of daring feats achieved by his partisan force, operating
during the war behind German lines. Agile and tough, Shkuro was utterly
fearless and a centaur among horseman, whose curly hair and merry smile
made him a favourite of the ladies.

By the end of May 1918, he had raised a force of ten daring followers
in the mountains near Vladikavkaz. However, in no time at all his
reputation gained him a greater following, at whose head (dressed in an
elegant Circassian coat) he conducted a series of raids against local
Bolshevik forces. A particularly impressive attack on the city of
Kislovodsk gained him almost legendary status, and before long he headed
a host several thousand strong. At the same time, he was intelligent enough
to realise that he could not liberate the Kuban single-handed: his
cavalrymen could seize a town, but not hold it against Red infantry and
artillery. Accordingly, he placed his force under Denikin's command.
Initially, the regular officers of the Volunteer Army regarded him as little
better than a bandit, but under pressure from the Kuban *Rada*, General
Denikin promoted him to the rank of general a month after his attendance
at Krasnov's reception in Novocherkassk.[28]

Over the year that followed, Shkuro's 'Wolves' wrought havoc among
Red detachments. In correspondence the moderate socialist Don Cossack
Filipp Mironov repeatedly refers to the dreaded 'black banner of General
Shkuro with its wolf's head and slogan "Forward for a great united
Russia"'.[29] Although his Wolves gained a daunting reputation for looting,
there was a chivalrous side to his nature. During his occupation of

Kislovodsk, for example, he rescued from prison a group of girls whom local Bolsheviks planned to 'socialise' into enforced prostitution.[30]

To British officers and men serving with the Military Mission to the Don Cossacks, he was a picturesque hero. Major Williamson of the Royal Artillery described him well:

> Short, weatherbeaten and sporting a long yellow moustache, Skouro [*sic*] was one of the characters of the Civil War. Never without his wolfskin cap and the red, blue and white ribbon of the Volunteer Army on his sleeve, he was a Caucasian from one of the mountain tribes, savage and cruel as the best of them, and his regiment of three to four hundred cavalrymen all wore wolfskin caps instead of astrakhan wool. They had their headquarters in their own special collection of railway trucks, on which were painted a pack of wolves in pursuit of prey, and they were a particularly fierce and relentless collection of mountaineers, carrying the usual armoury of a *kinjal* or dagger at their waist, a sword slung over the shoulder, a revolver whenever possible, and rows of cartridge cases for rifles across each side of their chests. Skouro was undoubtedly a great cavalry leader but, as we'd been told, he was also a bit of a brigand and, on one occasion, accompanied by three or four of his officers, he entered the ballroom of a big hotel in Rostov where dancing was in progress and invited all the guests to contribute in jewellery or cash towards the maintenance of his Wolves. Confronted by glittering eyes beneath the shaggy wolf's hair and remembering the Wolves' reputation for ruthless pillage and lack of mercy, no one argued. He made a very successful haul.[31]

Shkuro's 'Wolves'

In 1919 Major-General Holman, head of the British Military Mission
to General Denikin, formally decorated Shkuro with the Commandership
of the Bath. As Shkuro later recalled,

> ... I arrived at the English military mission and was received there by an
> honour guard. General Holman addressed me with these words:
>
> 'This high order is bestowed on you by His Majesty', he said to me,
> presenting me with the order, 'for your service in the struggle against
> Bolshevism, as a world evil'.
>
> Much moved, I replied with a few words of gratitude that my service was
> appreciated.[32]

Returning to Krasnov, the Don Ataman likewise possessed a genius
for the picturesque and theatrical, and his guests were impressed by the
lavish splendour of their reception. However, the Allied delegates proved
to be of subordinate rank, and had been assigned no authority to negotiate.
The British and French governments were prepared only to recognise a
single Russian national government, and remained committed to support
of General Denikin as its leader.

Allied intervention was swift. The first troops to arrive in South Russia
were French. On 18 December 1918, 1,800 French troops disembarked at
Odessa, to be followed by reinforcements (including Greeks, Romanians,
and Poles) that before long amounted to some 65,000 men. Unfortunately,
their morale was poor, the situation in Ukraine was complicated by its
multi-sided civil war, and five months later what survived of the
expedition was withdrawn. General Franchet d'Espèrey, commander of
French forces in the near East, had advised against the operation from the
beginning.

British support of the loyal General Denikin and his Volunteer Army
was considerably more effective, although much more restricted in
personnel. On 14 November the War Office approved the policy of
intervention, and dispatched Major-General Frederick Poole to visit
General Denikin and assess the strength of the Volunteer Army. On 24
November a Colonel Blackwood with an advance party of British officers
arrived at the port of Novorossiisk, where they conferred with Denikin and
his staff. However, when they sought to approach General Krasnov in the
north, they were told that the Don Cossacks were suspicious of the Allies,
whom they feared might seek to impose a form of government on Russia
unacceptable to the Cossacks. The Volunteers were naturally concerned to
exaggerate forces at their disposal, and Blackwood was persuaded that
they represented the only military force in Russia capable of facing up to
the Bolsheviks.

His mission was succeeded a month later by another headed by Poole himself, who was overall impressed by the Volunteer Army's spirit and fighting record. At the same time, he felt it essential to secure the co-operation of Krasnov's Cossacks. Poole travelled to the Don, where Krasnov entertained him to a lavish banquet, whose highlights the susceptible British general was delighted to discover included a bevy of attractive gypsy girls. But when it came to business, Poole was firm. While Krasnov was naturally to remain Ataman of the Don, he must expect to be subordinated to Denikin, whom the British recognised as Commander-in-Chief of the White Armies in South Russia. This Krasnov agreed to accept – 'rather grudgingly', as Poole reported. At the same time he added that General Krasnov 'stands out both in ability and capacity far above any Russian officer'. On 26 December Krasnov formally acknowledged Denikin's authority.

The British intelligence agent Sidney Reilly, who accompanied General Poole, reported that

> General Krasnov is first and foremost an opportunist [*i.e.* pragmatic] and once he is given to understand in a most decided manner that the way to Allied support in the matter of equipment, arms, goods, etc. lies *via* Denikin he will submit and being a clever man, he will do so with good grace and workable amount of *bona fides* ... The [Don] Cossacks if well supplied in the matter of equipment and armament will follow Krasnov in a campaign against Moscow if the campaign promises to be short, but they will *not* remain in the field for an indefinite time'.

Reilly's assessment was perceptive, as was also his pen-sketch of the character of General Denikin,

> a man of about 50, of fine presence, the dark Russian type with regular features; he has a dignified, very cultured manner, and could be classed as belonging to the "higher staff officer type" rather than to the "fighting type". He gives one the impression of a broad-minded, high-thinking, determined and well-balanced man – but the impression of great power of intellect or of those characteristics which mark a ruler of men is lacking.[33]

By the turn of the year the position of the Whites in southern Russia was deteriorating seriously. While the British proved generous with supplies of arms and munitions to Denikin's Volunteer Army and Krasnov's Don Army, they failed to respond to requests for sufficient British troops to be dispatched in force to protect the rear and supply lines of the White Armies. Although the state of morale among Entente troops was better among British soldiers than French, they were not for the most part intended to participate in frontline fighting. Unfortunately, there existed grave misapprehension among politicians in London with regard to the threat posed by Bolshevism.[34]

The British Prime Minister David Lloyd George was reluctant for Britain to become actively involved in the Russian Civil War, his policy interventions being marred throughout by his extreme ignorance of the situation. On 16 April 1919 in the House of Commons, he endorsed the policy of supplying the Whites with goods but not troops, declaring that

> I do not in the least regard it as a departure from the fundamental policy of Great Britain not to interfere in the internal affairs of any land that we should support General Denikin, Admiral Koltchak and General Kharkoff.[35]

Not only was 'Kharkoff' a blunder for 'Krasnov', but by the time of Lloyd George's speech the former Ataman had departed the Don for good two months earlier.

Unfortunately, although General Poole and other British officers were understanding of Krasnov's pragmatic decision to work with the Germans throughout their occupation of the Ukraine, Lloyd George's policy *inter alia* undermined the Ataman's position *vis-à-vis* Denikin, who remained throughout loyal to the Allied cause. Krasnov now acted swiftly to repair the situation. On 19 November 1918 he sent a deputation to General Franchet d'Espèrey's headquarters at Jassy in Romania, bearing florid assurances of the Don territory's devout wish to work with the Entente. Unfortunately, his dissatisfaction with Denikin's policies led him to urge the latter's replacement as commander-in-chief. Not only was the French commander in no position to enforce such an action, but Krasnov's reservations with regard to Denikin brought him into bad odour with many who might otherwise have supported him. Pressure grew for subordination of the Don Army to Denikin's command. At a meeting on 8 January 1919, Krasnov grudgingly accepted a face-saving agreement, which acknowledged Denikin's supremacy.[36]

Krasnov's predicament was further worsened by renewed Red Army advances into the Don territory. Equally, his acceptance of unification of the Don Army with the Volunteer Army laid the basis for creation of a formidable White Army in the South. Krasnov's concession had in part been motivated by the hope of receiving swift Allied help on the deteriorating front: a hope that failed to materialise in time. This in turn led his adversaries in the Don *Krug* to assert that it was the notoriety of his alliance with the Germans which antagonised the Allies, and now deprived the Don of desperately needed assistance. On 14 February (new style) the

Krug assembled, when a demand was made for resignation of the Ataman's two principal generals. It being now plain that he had lost the confidence of the Assembly, Krasnov resigned his leadership.[37] In the circumstances, his departure, although regretted by many of his faithful Cossacks, represented a cruel necessity. He was succeeded as Ataman by General A. P. Bogaevsky, who had long enjoyed cordial relations with Denikin.[38]

Whatever the political and military situation, the Cossacks gathered in crowds to attest their heartfelt appreciation of all that General Krasnov had accomplished for them. At his departure by train from Rostov, a deputation of the *Krug* of Cherkass region presented the Ataman with a touching address endorsed by sixty-two signatures, and his wife Lydia with a beautiful bouquet of fresh flowers. When other members of the *Krug* learned the contents of the address, they also subscribed to it and collected further signatures.[39]

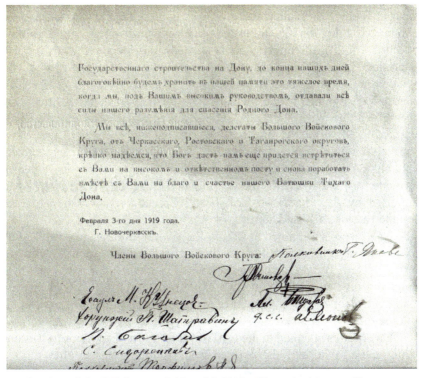

Section of the 3 February (old style) 1919 address to Ataman Krasnov from leading Don Cossacks, thanking him for his services to the Don.

Although Krasnov's term of office concluded in disappointment, his fall from power was probably inevitable, given his compromising rapprochement with the German occupiers of Ukraine, and his consequent poor relationship with Denikin. But he had saved the Don from the Red Terror, and might conceivably have turned the tide of the Civil War had Denikin joined him in force at the siege of Tsaritsyn. Eventually, his services and devotion to his homeland earned him the lasting admiration of the Cossack peoples, continuing to the present day. His uncompromising hostility to Bolshevism further cemented loyalty to their former Ataman once the Don was finally subjugated by the Soviets. On 24 January 1919, a decree from Moscow declared

> that the only correct approach is the merciless fight against all Cossack elites by means of their complete annihilation. No compromises, no halfway measures can be accepted.

The decree was signed by Iakov Sverdlov, organizer of the murder of the Imperial Family at Ekaterinburg. An estimated 10,000 Cossacks were summarily slaughtered, thousands more imprisoned in appalling conditions, and grim oppression laid waste the Don and Kuban for a generation. In particular, anyone associated with General Krasnov was high on the list for execution.[40]

Upon resigning office, Krasnov immediately departed the Don together with his wife Lydia, and settled at the port of Batum on the Black Sea coast of Georgia. While there, he offered his services to the White Army commander General Wrangel.[41] The offer was however declined, probably on account of Krasnov's earlier alliance with the defeated Germans: an embarrassing association now that the White Army was supported by the victorious British and French. Krasnov nevertheless remained a close ally and admirer of Wrangel's leadership.

The Krasnovs remained at Batum for several months, until on 22 July 1919 (new style) Peter Nikolaevich received an invitation to join the North-Western White Army of General Yudenich, which was then advancing on Petrograd. Yudenich explained regretfully that he had no immediate place for a commander of his rank, and assigned Krasnov a post with the reserve.

There he was attached to the staff of General von Glasenapp, a Russian Baltic veteran who had also arrived from Southern Russia after serving heroically with the Volunteer Army. The Krasnovs were quartered first at Yamburg, then at Gatchina, scene of Krasnov's adventures during his 1917 advance on Petrograd. His duties involved assisting refugees from the vicinity of the front. More importantly, he returned to his literary métier, editing a propaganda newspaper *Prinevsky krai* ('Land in the Region of the River Neva'). He wrote articles in many of its fifty issues, principally on Russian history.[42]

This episode in General Krasnov's peripatetic career was not destined to endure long.[43] In November 1919 Yudenich's North-Western Army, destroyed as much by a terrible typhus epidemic as by the Red Army, was compelled to withdraw to Reval (Tallinn), capital of the newly-established independent state of Estonia. Disarmed on crossing the frontier, by early spring the Army was dissolved, many of its personnel departing to enlist in the French Foreign Legion in North Africa and Syria. In March 1920 Peter Krasnov left Estonia to settle in Germany.

---

[1] Orlando Figes, *A People's Tragedy: The Russian Revolution 1891-1924* (London, 1996), pp. 642-49.

[2] Richard Pipes (ed.), *The Unknown Lenin: From the Secret Archive* (New Haven, 1996), pp. 50-51, 56-57. For further evidence of Lenin's deep-rooted belief in terror as the principal instrument of Bolshevik power, cf. *ibid.*, pp. 152-55; Bertram D. Wolfe, *Khrushchev and Stalin's Ghost* (New York, 1957), pp. 293-94; Lennard D. Gerson, *The Secret Police in Lenin's Russia* (Philadelphia, 1976), pp. 130-88; Jonathan R. Adelman, 'Soviet Secret Police', in *idem* (ed.), *Terror and Communist Politics: The Role of the Secret*

Police in Communist States (Boulder, 1984), pp. 79-85; Dmitri Volkogonov, *Сталин: Политический Портрет* (Moscow, 1994), ii, p. 573.

[3] S.P. Melgounov, *La "Terreur Rouge" en Russie (1918-1924)* (Paris, 1927), pp. 107-13; Peter Kenez, *Civil War in South Russia, 1918* (Berkeley, 1971), 118-21; Vasily Matasov, *Белое Движение на Юге России 1917-1920 годы* (Montreal, 1990), pp. 34-35; Laura Engelstein, *Russia in Flames: War, Revolution, Civil War 1914-1921* (New York, 2018), pp. 376-77.

[4] Wolodomyr Kosyk, *La Politique de la France à l'égard de l'Ukraine: Mars 1917 - Février 1918* (Paris, 1981), pp. 258-59.

[5] Skoropadsky has received a bad press from historians (*e.g.* Figes, *A People's Tragedy*, p. 549). However, while scarcely an impressive figure, it is hard to see how he could have achieved more than he did (Andrew Wilson, *The Ukrainians: Unexpected Nation* (New Haven and London, 2000), pp. 126-27).

[6] John H. Wheeler-Bennett, *Brest-Litovsk: The Forgotten Peace March 1918* (London, 1939), pp. 241-308; Gerhard Ritter, *The Sword and the Sceptre: The Problem of Militarism in Germany* (London, 1972-73), iv, pp. 84-117; Alexander Watson, *Ring of Steel: Germany and Austria-Hungary at War, 1914-1918* (London, 2014), pp. 492-98.

[7] P.N. Krasnov, 'Всевеликое Войско Донское', in I.V. Gessen (ed.), *Архивъ Русской Революціи* (Berlin, 1922), v, p. 221.

[8] Kenez, *Civil War in South Russia*, pp. 141-42.

[9] Gessen (ed.), *Архивъ Русской Революціи*, v, pp. 199-200.

[10] *Ibid.*, pp. 200-201.

[11] *Ibid.*, pp. 206-7. 'In the first month and a half, the Germans donated 11,651 rifles, 46 guns, 88 machineguns, 109,104 artillery shells and 11,594,721 rifle cartridges to the Don, Kuban and Volunteer Army' (*ibid.*, p. 209).

[12] *Ibid.*, pp. 210-13. Kenez notes unfortunate indiscretions contained in Krasnov's second letter to the German Emperor (*Civil War in South Russia*, pp. 143-45). Ludendorff's principal strategic aim was to establish a friendly (or at least neutral) force on the Don to counter the pro-Allied Volunteer Army (Michael Kettle, *The Road to Intervention: March-November 1918* (London, 1988), p. 126).

[13] Gessen (ed.), *Архивъ Русской Революціи*, v, p. 201.

[14] *Ibid.*, pp. 228-30.

[15] *Ibid.*, pp. 237-40.

[16] Melgounov, *La "Terreur Rouge" en Russie*, pp. 152, 156, 164; Gerson, *The Secret Police in Lenin's Russia*, pp. 142-43; George Leggett, *The Cheka: Lenin's Political Police* (Oxford, 1981), pp. 198, 464; Stephen Kotkin, *Stalin: Volume I: Paradoxes of Power, 1878-1928* (New York, 2014), pp. 302, 304-5.

[17] Alexander Orlov, *The Secret History of Stalin's Crimes* (London, 1954), pp. 129, 137-38; Bertram D. Wolfe, *Khrushchev and Stalin's Ghost* (New York,

1957), pp. 202-4; Strobe Talbott (ed.), *Khrushchev Remembers* (Boston, 1970), pp. 170, 137-38; Roy A. Medvedev, *Let History Judge: The Origins and Consequences of Stalinism* (London, 1971), pp. 296-98.

[18] Kenez, *Civil War in South Russia*, pp. 173-75; Kotkin, *Stalin*, i, pp. 300-310.

[19] 'There is no question that Stalin contributed to the successful defense of Tsaritsyn from the Ataman Krasnov's Cossack bands in 1918, and thus an extremely important strategic bastion was preserved from the Whites' (Adam B. Ulam, *Stalin: The Man and his Era* (New York, 1973), p. 176).

[20] John W. Thompson, *Russia, Bolshevism, and the Versailles Peace* (Princeton, 1966), p. 310.

[21] The novel was dramatized under the title *The Days of the Turbins*. While the Bolsheviks remain off-scene, the White family of the Turbins appears throughout center-stage, with one character departing to join Krasnov's Cossacks. Despite the portrayal of class enemies as consistently honorable and courageous, Stalin expressed his approval of the play and attended several performances (cf. Volkogonov, *Сталин*, i, p. 233; Stephen Kotkin, *Stalin: Vol. II: Waiting for Hitler, 1928-1941* (London, 2017), 148-49). It is said that he regarded it as a measure of the Bolshevik achievement that it achieved victory over such principled and fearless adversaries.

[22] Kotkin, *Stalin*, i, pp. 320-21.

[23] Volkogonov, *Сталин*, ii, pp. 314, 319.

[24] *Ibid.*, i, pp. 94-95.

[25] Sean McMeekin, *The Russian Revolution: A New History* (London, 2017), pp. 267-69.

[26] Kenez, *Civil War in South Russia*, 1918, pp. 253-55; Frank Grelka, „Zwischen Kollaborationismus, Kriminalisierung und Kanonenfutter", in Harald Stadler, Rolf Steininger, and Karl C. Berger (ed.), *Die Kosaken im Ersten und Zweiten Weltkrieg* (Innsbruck, 2008), pp. 96-97.

[27] Matasov, *Белое Движение на Юге России*, pp. 97, 103.

[28] Kenez, *Civil War in South Russia*, 1918, pp. 181-82.

[29] V. Danilov, T. Shanin, L. Dvoinykh, V. Vinogradov, and O. Naumov (ed.), *Филипп Миронов: Тихий Дон в 1917-1921 гг.* (Moscow, 1997), pp. 507, 543, 641.

[30] Douglas Smith, *Former People: The Last Days of the Russian Aristocracy* (London, 2012), p. 154.

[31] John Harris (ed.), *Farewell to the Don: The Journal of Brigadier H.N.H. Williamson* (London, 1970), pp. 68-69. A White propaganda film showed Shkuro and his wolves riding into captured Kharkov during the advance on Tsaritsyn (*ibid.*, p. 105).

[32] V. Tretyakova (ed.), *Тайны Истории в романах повестях и документах* (Moscow, 1996), i, p. 155.

[33] Michael Kettle, *Churchill and the Archangel Fiasco: November 1918-July 1919* (London, 1992), pp. 40-41.

[34] *Ibid.*, pp. 77-82.

[35] E.L. Woodward and Rohan Butler (ed.), *Documents on British Foreign Policy 1919-1939: First Series* (London, 1949), iii, p. 311.

[36] Richard H. Ullman, *Britain and the Russian Civil War: November 1918-February 1920* (Princeton, NJ, 1968), p. 49.

[37] Kenez, *Civil War in South Russia,* 1918, pp. 260-71.

[38] Matasov, *Белое Движение на Юге России*, pp. 96-97.

[39] Gessen (ed.), *Архивъ Русской Революціи*, v, p. 321. The original of the Cossack testimonial to Krasnov is now held in the Cossack Museum in Paris.

[40] Engelstein, *Russia in Flames*, pp. 475-77.

[41] Nikolai Ross, *Врангель в Крыму* (Frankfurt, 1982), p. 250.

[42] V.Yu. Chernyaev, 'Писатель генерал П.Н. Краснов', in V.G. Bortnevsky (ed.), *Русское Прошлое: Историко-Документальный Альманах* (St. Petersburg, 1993), iv, p. 356.

[43] The background to Yudenich's campaign to seize Petrograd is described by Ullman, *Britain and the Russian Civil War*, pp. 254-93.

CHAPTER IV
RUSSIA ABROAD

Russia Abroad - that great spiritual world, in which Russian philosophy was flourishing, there were Bulgakov, Berdyayev, Lossky, whose Russian art enchanted the world, there were Rachmaninov, Chaliapin, Benois, Diaghilev, Pavlova, the Don Cossack Chorus of Zharov, profound studies of Dostoevsky were being undertaken there (at a time when he was generally reviled by us), that the incredible writer Nabokov-Sirin existed out there, that Bunin himself was still alive and had been writing for these twenty years.

Alexander Solzhenitsyn[*]

The unique character of Russian emigration arising from the Bolshevik seizure of power in 1917 and the ensuing Civil War is not infrequently belittled or ignored by historians. With a diaspora extending from China to Persia and Western Europe to the Americas, numbers are always likely to baffle precise reckoning. Estimates range from one million to three, with a figure of one and a half to two million likely to be nearest the mark. Of these, perhaps three-quarters of a million settled in Western Europe.[1] To them may be added that extensive population of the Russian Empire which found itself living outside the USSR, following post-Civil War treaties with Finland, the Baltic States, Poland, and Romania.[2] All this created the enormous total of between one and two million Russians living beyond the reach of the new masters of the land.[3]

In his magisterial survey of the Russian emigration, Marc Raeff has described the extent to which it was distinguished not only in size, but also in character from other political emigrations of modern times. Although broad ranges of political opinion existed among the exiles, the savagery of the Red Terror had touched too many directly for there to be many desirous of return, so long as the regime endured.[4] On the other hand, the emigrants were broadly unconcerned with integration into their host countries or cultures. In the first place, they were generally sufficient in number to form inclusive communities. Again, Bolshevism was widely regarded among

---

[*] *Архипелаг ГУЛаг: Опыт Художественного Исследования 1918-1956* (Paris, 1973-75), i, p. 268.

émigré Russians as so brutal, inefficient, and unnatural a system of government as to lead many to believe in its imminent collapse, and the exiles' consequent return home. Most White emigrants were devoutly Orthodox and bonded together by their faith, which was undergoing savage persecution in their native land.[5] Other motives for this widespread acceptance of exile lay in the fact that thousands were veteran soldiers, accustomed to acting as a unity and bound by loyalty to a common cause, while international hostility to the threat posed externally to Western European countries by a militaristic and expansionist Soviet Union, and internally by the Communist International, gained the emigrants widespread sympathy in their host nations.[6]

Regardless of their political views, most Russians were deeply concerned to preserve all that was valuable in Russia's political, cultural, and spiritual traditions, safe from the destructive bloodshed and repression they were fortunate to have escaped. In Raeff's words,

> the émigrés were committed to carrying on a meaningful *Russian* life. They were determined to act, work, and create as part and parcel of *Russia*, even in a foreign environment. They needed "producers" and "consumers" of cultural "goods" and values maintained in exile. Russia Abroad was a society by virtue of its firm intention to go on living in "Russia," to be the truest and culturally most creative of the two Russias that political circumstances had brought into being. Though it was a somewhat distorted society in strictly sociological terms ... the émigrés did think of themselves as a "country" or society. They strove to act creatively as if the emigration represented Russia in the fullest cultural and philosophical sense.[7]

On his deathbed in California in 1943, Sergei Rachmaninov was heard to murmur: 'We have not left Russia, we will never leave Russia'.

While the great majority of exiled Russians struggled for economic survival, their scattered population was the reverse of being culturally impoverished. It is remarkable that 'outside the boundaries of the USSR, 108 Russian newspapers and 162 journals were being produced for a readership of more than two million', while publishers like the respected YMCA Press in Paris catered to an intellectual readership.[8] As Solzhenitsyn affirmed, the high culture of the Russian emigration is surely unparalleled in history. The names of some of the more illustrious practitioners of the arts in Russia Abroad (*Русское Зарубежье*) speak for themselves. In music the names of Sergei Rachmaninov, Igor Stravinsky, Vladimir Horowitz, and Feodor Chaliapin resound, while international ballet was dominated by the *Ballets Russes*, with Pavlova, Karsavina, and Nizhinsky drawing rapturous audiences worldwide. Serge Lifar,

Alexandre Benois,[9] and Leon Bakst designed exquisite theatrical sets and costumes, while émigré painters included such figures as Kandinsky, Chagall, and Leonid Pasternak. In the cinema, directors Sacha Guitry in France and Anatole de Grunwald in England were internationally acclaimed. In 1933 Ivan Bunin (who wrote exclusively in Russian, and that in pre-revolutionary orthography) won the Nobel Prize for Literature (to Soviet fury, as Maxim Gorky was their preferred figure), while Vladimir Nabokov created fiction as adroitly in English as in Russian. Russian poets writing abroad included Georgi Ivanov and Marina Tsvetaeva, the latter memorably hymning the tragic courage of the doomed White Armies.[10] Another Nobel Prize was won by the renowned geneticist Feodor Dobzhansky, a devout Russian Orthodox patriot, while the emigration of Igor Sikorsky in 1919 ensured that it was America rather than Russia that benefited from the development of the helicopter. In short, it is difficult to conceive of a sovereign state at the time that could boast a more extraordinary galaxy of talent than the stateless diaspora of Russia Abroad.[11]

With the defeat and exile of the last White commander, General Wrangel, from the Crimea in 1920, it became clear – at least, for the time being - that no foreign government, however hostile its attitude towards to the Soviet Union, contemplated further military intervention on the Whites' behalf. A partial exception was provided by King Peter I of Yugoslavia, who, in gratitude for Russia's alliance with Serbia during the Great War and recognition of their shared Orthodox religion, invited remnants of Wrangel's army to settle in his country. There they retained their military structure, armed and drilling in preparation for an eventual triumphant return to their homeland.[12] A smaller force was welcomed and maintained by the Bulgarian government.[13] In 1923, however, this section of General Wrangel's army was sabotaged by a Comintern-directed campaign of efficiently-directed propaganda and terror.[14]

In a particularly daring exploit, a Cossack unit from Yugoslavia, under the command of General Sergei Ulagai, played a decisive part in 1924 in the coup d'état which resulted in King Zog's accession to the throne of Albania. Following the German occupation of Yugoslavia in 1941, White Russian formations were equipped with German arms and uniforms. The *Russkii Korpus*, as it became known, fought against Tito's Communists, and finally succeeded in battling its way into Austria in 1945, where it surrendered to British forces.[15] In addition, thousands of Russian civilians evacuated by the British and French navies from Black Sea ports accompanied Wrangel's troops to new homes in Yugoslavia and elsewhere.[16]

In other Western European countries during the inter-war period, White Russians were likewise discreetly permitted to conduct paramilitary training. France having been Wrangel's ally during the Civil War, it was appropriate that many White Russian émigrés relocated to Paris.[17] Although for the most part impoverished and obliged to search for whatever livelihood proffered itself,* members of the scattered community maintained Russian-language newspapers, churches, hospitals, old people's homes, schools, Boy Scout and *Vityaz* organizations for the young, as well as the *Sokol* gymnastic movement.[18] Russian volunteers were prominent among all ranks of the Foreign Legion,[19] and yet more alarming to the Soviet leadership was the extent to which the French government accepted the existence of paramilitary cadet schools and training camps across the country.[20]

Ideologically, the Russian Orthodox Church provided the most potent common focus of spiritual union within the emigration, extending from Paris to Manchuria.[21] It is in addition an ironic fact that provinces of the Russian Empire now lying outside the Soviet Union (such as Finland and the Baltic states) provided incomparably closer continuity of traditional Russian life and culture than anything to be found in the atheist and ideologically-structured Bolshevik state.[22]

The new rulers in the Kremlin viewed with dismay the existence of extensive Russian communities beyond their control free to espouse and express what political views they chose. Newspapers and books emanating from émigré publishing houses ensured that they continued well-informed about the state of affairs within their ravaged homeland. Even allowing for inevitable political prejudice, there can be little doubt that the émigrés were generally far better apprised of realities of life within the Soviet Union than were their host populations. From the perspective of the Soviet leadership, they appeared particularly dangerous, being the only Russians free to propagate whatever views they chose *in Russian*, who were at the same time well placed to expound the brutal realities of Soviet life to the world.

The special status of Russian refugees was acknowledged by successive conventions of the League of Nations, several of which specifically prohibited their enforced repatriation to the Soviet Union.[23] In 1922 the League regularized the émigrés' position by granting applicants who had not acquired citizenship from their country of residence the right

---

* Readers of George Orwell's *Down and out in London and Paris* (1933) will recall the Russian restaurant waiters with whom he worked in Paris, who departed each evening to attend military drill.

to bear a 'Nansen passport', named after its initiator the Norwegian explorer and humanitarian Fridtjof Nansen.[24]

Particularly dangerous in Soviet eyes was the astonishing eminence of émigré Russians in the arts and sciences: an achievement bearing worldwide testimony to the fact that so many of Russia's brightest and best rejected the Soviet regime. Few of them could be regarded as overtly political figures, but their fame abroad attested to a proud Russian tradition wholly independent of Marxist dogma and Bolshevik practice. In Solzhenitsyn's words: 'Russia Abroad was a great spiritual world'.[25] Lenin, as self-acclaimed genius and voracious, judgmental, but not very perceptive reader,[26] nurtured jealous resentment towards Russian intellectuals.[27] Large numbers whose views failed to accord with his ideological preconceptions were arbitrarily expelled from the Soviet Union between 1921 and 1923.[28]

At a less exalted but possibly still more influential level, during the interwar years émigré Russian aristocrats were widely portrayed in popular novels, films, and plays as elegant, sophisticated, courageous, and above all romantic, while almost everywhere save in entrenched left-wing circles their Bolshevik adversaries featured as brutally uncouth (preferably bearded and bomb-bearing) spies, kidnappers, and assassins.* It would take an independent study to cover this factor adequately, but it conceivably exerted greater influence over public perceptions in the Western world than any other. Successful films such as *Tovarich* (1937), starring Claudette Colbert and Charles Boyer, and *Ninotchka* (1939), with Melvyn Douglas and Greta Garbo, perpetuated the opposed stereotypes, as also did innumerable works of popular fiction such as the Bulldog Drummond stories of 'Sapper', Dennis Wheatley's (also filmed) *The Forbidden Territory* (1933), or Hergé's comic but starkly accurate portrayal of the contemporary USSR in *Tintin dans le pays des Soviets* (1930).

Aristocratic Russians, however impoverished, found ready acceptance in influential social circles in the West. The Dowager Empress Maria Feodorovna rejoined her Danish royal relatives, while King George V provided Nicholas II's sister the Grand Duchess Xenia with a home at Hampton Court, and entertained her at Balmoral. To the Bolshevik leadership, these and other examples conveyed a disturbing perception of White Russian influence at an eminent political level, despite its being in

---

* As a small boy I delighted in the immensely popular *Daily Mirror* cartoon series 'Pip, Squeak and Wilfred', whose supporting cast included Popski, a bearded Bolshevik customarily bearing behind his back a large black bomb with smoking fuse.

reality of little practical effect. Stalin himself nurtured a degree of awed respect for the resilience of aristocracies generally.[29]

There were however other figures from the recent Russian imperial past, who were with reason regarded as overtly dangerous. Among them was Field Marshal Baron Gustav Mannerheim, who led the Finnish army against the Soviet Union between 1939 and 1944. In an earlier incarnation he had enjoyed a distinguished career as a general in the Russian Imperial Army, when he was closely associated with the Emperor Nicholas II. He also pursued an adventurous career as a Russian intelligence agent, roaming in the wilds of Mongolia and the margins of the Chinese Empire. When Finland gained independence from Russia in 1918, he led White forces to victory over Finnish Bolsheviks. The Estonian Chief of Staff in 1939, General Laidoner, was a former tsarist staff officer,[30] while the future World War II Polish hero General Władysław Anders had served in a crack Lancer regiment of the Russian Imperial Army, before becoming Chief of Staff to Marshal Piłsudski during the Polish-Russian war of 1919-21.*

To the Soviet leadership under Stalin, in greater or lesser degree ignorant of the outside world, and viewing foreign states largely through the distorting prism of Marxist-Leninist dialectic, Russia Abroad appeared a uniquely potent menacing conspiracy against socialist rule in Russia. In the immediate aftermath of the final defeat of the Whites in late 1920, Lenin himself expressed acute apprehension at the threat they posed in emigration. Estimating their total number as between one and a half and two million, he declared that

> They are skilfully taking advantage of every opportunity in order, in one way or another, to attack Soviet Russia and smash her to pieces ... These counter-revolutionary émigrés are very well-informed, excellently organized and good strategists.[31]

This alarmist outlook was if anything espoused to an even greater extent by Lenin's successor, Joseph Stalin. While Lenin's ideological obsessions gained him a reputation among Soviet loyalists as an outstanding intellectual, Stalin had learned little during his boyhood as a seminarian, spoke no foreign language, and possessed a scant and distorted understanding of history and the contemporary outside world. Much of his

---

* On 9 May 1952, General Anders wrote to my great-aunt Maria Pavlovna: 'I can myself confirm the moral and material sufferings which have subjected the Russian people to the Soviet yoke... Understanding of this danger and the solidarity of those who seek to overthrow this scourge form the basis of a victory which should be the common aim of the free world'.

voracious reading constituted ideological literature, which provided him
with a legitimating rationale for his career as criminal tyrant.[32]

Throughout the 1920s and 1930s eager hopes were nurtured within
the Russian emigration of an end to the Soviet dictatorship, whether
arising from internal revolt or foreign intervention – or, more likely, a
combination of both. To this end, White military units were kept in being
by the Russian Military Union based in Paris, initially under the able
leadership of General Wrangel. In the context of the present study,
however, the actual extent of the threat this posed to Soviet power is less
significant than its perception by the Soviet leadership. And there can be
no doubt that the rulers of the Soviet Union and its security services took
the danger very seriously indeed.

Stalin's Civil War experience of the commitment and courage of the
White armies compelled him to regard them as formidable adversaries,
whose services hostile foreign powers might naturally be expected to
recruit in the event of any conflict with the Soviet regime. In 1920 he was
convinced that Marshal Piłsudski's victorious Polish army planned a
White restoration in Russia.[33] In the same year a widespread peasant
uprising against the Bolsheviks was condemned by the latter as the
'Tambov Vendée' – an allusion to the formidable royalist uprising against
Revolutionary France. The communist leadership was persuaded that the
'Greens' (as the peasant resistance termed itself) were subordinated to the
supreme White command in Paris, although in reality their links with the
Whites were minimal.[34]

Similarly, the impeccably revolutionary sailors' uprising at the naval
base of Kronstadt in 1921 was credited with being masterminded by the
exiled White command. Although individual White Russian émigrés
encouraged the Finns to supply aid to the defendants, no such assistance
was in fact provided. At the same time, fortuitous circumstances make it
clear that the claim represented no insincere Bolshevik slur, but was
genuinely credited by the Soviet leadership.[35]

In all that followed in the inter-war period the exiled Russian military
command and its forces continued effectively at war with the Soviets.
Throughout their protracted struggle against Soviet power, they regarded
themselves, not as irregular saboteurs, but as continuing a Civil War that
for them had not ended in 1920. In the following year, Wrangel threatened
to return to Russia at the head of 60,000 men.[36]

Soviet fears of White Russian interventions in the interior of the Soviet
Union were by no means delusory. In March 1924 Grand Duke Nikolai
Nikolaevich, former commander-in-chief of the Russian Imperial Army,
summoned his fellow-émigré General Alexander Kutepov to Paris to

supervise underground operations in the USSR. Kutepov, earlier an able and intrepid commander under Wrangel's command, threw himself into the task with energy and skill.

On 1 September of the same year, a formal organization was established to unite the internationally-distributed elements of the exiled White Army. This was the 'Russian All-Military Union' (*Русскій Обще-Воинскій Союзъ*), generally known by its initials ROVS. Its titular leader was Grand Duke Nikolai Nikolaevich, while Wrangel administered it until his death in 1928. Although active blows against the Soviet Union were instigated by ROVS, its primary purpose was to preserve military discipline, readiness, and cohesion among White Army veterans so that in the event of the communist dictatorship's collapse the emigrants could provide a focus for reestablishment of all that was exemplary in the Russian tradition. The ROVS did not advocate forceful restoration of the monarchy, nor any other form of government 'imposed by bayonets'. Nevertheless, every effort was to be made to topple the godless regime, by violence where possible. Only in the late 1930s did the effective authority of ROVS dwindle, in consequence of the continuing failure of the hoped-for collapse of Stalin's regime, ageing membership, the changed political situation in Europe (above all the rise of Hitler), and effective retaliation by the OGPU (predecessor of the NKVD).[37]

The Soviets were well informed of the danger posed by this threat, and already in 1922 a senior official of the OGPU had publicly warned:

> We are watching this second Russia and we assume that its armed forces will reappear somewhere on our borders and that we will have to resume the struggle.[38]

The fear was realistic enough. During the first decade of its existence and for some time thereafter, the vast frontiers of the Soviet Union remained permeable at points known to secret emissaries and saboteurs as 'windows'.

A particular bugbear of Stalin and his security services was the threat posed by exiles operating among Cossacks and Caucasians in southern Russia. Both groupings had fought with ferocious valor against the Red Army, and after being driven into exile maintained military formations abroad, eager at any time to resume the armed struggle. In the Far East, elements of the Transbaikal Cossack Host, commanded by the ferocious Ataman Grigory Semenov, had been driven into Mongolia and Manchuria at the conclusion of the Civil War. However, for years thereafter they returned to conduct raids across the frontier deep into Soviet territory.

Among other precautions, Stalin implemented ingenious measures to counter threats posed by ROVS and other anti-Soviet elements. From 1922 the Soviet political police OGPU skilfully created a false monarchist underground organization known as 'The Trust', which widely penetrated the White movement abroad and eliminated many of its agents operating within the Soviet Union. Inflicting grave damage on White paramilitary activities, it continued effective until its exposure in 1927.[39]

Also in 1928 Stalin established a 'Jewish Autonomous District' in the frontier region of Birobidzhan. Ostensibly, the purpose was to provide a home for Russian Jews in that remote and inhospitable region. In reality, it was designed to counter White incursions, on the assumption that Jews would be particularly hostile to Cossacks.[40] However, the extent of the Soviet Union's vast and in large part unpopulated frontier regions meant that the threat could never be entirely dissipated. At his show trial in 1937, Bukharin was driven to disclose that his associates in the North Caucasus had conspired with White émigré groups.[41] Whether or not the Soviet leadership actually believed his enforced confession, it confirms the extent to which it regarded the White movement as a credibly dangerous foe.

Such fears might readily be multiplied. It is true that the Whites represented traditional bogeymen, a threat which might be evoked whether or not it existed in reality. On the other hand, the extraordinary nature of Marxist dictatorship resulted in a state of affairs where truth and falsehood became inextricably mixed throughout every level of society. Dismissal of alleged threats was perilous to an extent that resulted in almost any official claim's gaining widespread credence.[42]

Few believed more in the universality and credibility of conspiratorial threats to the regime than Stalin himself.[43] None among the clique of fawning misfits with which he surrounded himself dared question any suspicion that crossed their Leader's mind, ensuring that his naturally morbid disposition encountered apparent confirmation of his alarmist fears at every turn.[44] At the same time, the obsessive fear that he was surrounded by malevolent enemies was far from unrealistic.[45]

The extent to which 'White Guardists' loomed large in Stalin's catalogue of relentless foes was in any case by no means irrational. The Russian emigration provided a unique cloud of witnesses, who were better placed than any to proclaim the realities of Soviet tyranny. First-hand accounts of the horrors of Soviet gaols and slave labour camps appearing both in Russian and foreign-language publications abroad were regularly taken up by influential critics of Communism in host countries.[46] Recognizing the danger this posed him, Stalin took close interest in the emigrant press and literature.[47]

A related consideration loomed large in the Soviet attitude towards the emigration. As General Walter Bedell Smith, US Ambassador to the Soviet Union, explained:

> I wondered, immediately after the war, at the sustained and active campaign to force the return to the Soviet Union of all Soviet nationals who had been displaced, many of whom refused to return and some of whom even killed themselves when they thought they would be forced to do so ... During the Paris Peace Conference [1946] I discussed this with a Communist statesman who occasionally spoke more frankly than his colleagues, and he put the Politburo's position and apprehension regarding Soviet displaced persons with one pithy sentence.

> "That's the way we got our start!" he said, and of course that was true.[48]

Nevertheless, although General Wrangel had nurtured hopes of employing the exiled White Army in a renewed crusade against Bolshevism, it was not long before it became apparent that the prospect of a full-scale invasion remained for the time being impractical. Following the Polish-Soviet Treaty of Riga in 1921, countries bordering on the Soviet Union had little choice but to maintain peaceful relations with their malevolent and unpredictable neighbour. This uneasy situation prevailed until the militantly anti-communist Hitler became Chancellor of Germany in 1933.

---

[1] '... citizens who emigrated abroad... numbered between one and a half and two million. The bulk of the émigrés initially went to Germany and France, each of which is estimated to have absorbed some 400,000. An estimated 100,000 sought refuge in China' (Richard Pipes, *Russia under the Bolshevik Regime 1919-1924* (London, 1994), p. 139). Cf. Catherine Andreyev, *Vlasov and the Russian Liberation Movement: Soviet reality and émigré theories* (Cambridge, 1987), pp. 171, 194; Marc Raeff, *Russia Abroad: A Cultural History of the Russian Emigration, 1919-1939* (New York, 1990), p. 24; Miroslav Iovanovich, 'Россия в изгнании: Границы, масштабы и основые проблемы исследования', in A. Arseniev, O. Kirillova, and M. Sibinovich (ed.), *Русская змиграция в Югославии* (Moscow, 1996), p. 36.

[2] The distinction between 'Russia Abroad' and the parent country was accentuated by the fact that the Soviet republic at an early stage abandoned the very name of Russia, becoming first the RSFSR (Russian Soviet Federative Socialist Republic), and subsequently the USSR.

[3] Arseniev, Kirillova, and Sibinovich (ed.), *Русская змиграция в Югославии*, pp. 35-40.

[4] S.P. Melgounov, *La "Terreur Rouge" en Russie (1918-1924)* (Paris, 1927), pp. 10-12. Of the few who opted for return, most (like the the historian Prince

Dmitri Svyatopolk-Mirsky) came to a grim end. A notorious exception was the unsavoury Soviet writer Alexei Nikolaevich Tolstoy (cf. my *The Tolstoys: Twenty-Four Generations of Russian History 1353-1983* (London, 1983), pp. 281-320).

[5] Vladimir Stepanov, *Свидетельство Обвинения: Церковь и государство в Советском Союзе* (Moscow, 1980), i, pp. 61-201; Dimitry V. Pospielovsky, *A History of Soviet Atheism in Theory and Practice, and the Believer* (Basingstoke, 1987-88), i, pp. 27-68; *idem*, 'The Survival of the Russian Orthodox Church in her Millennial Century: Faith as *Martyria* in an Atheistic State', in Geoffrey A. Hosking (ed.), *Church, Nation and State in Russia and Ukraine* (London, 1991), pp. 273-84; Raeff, *Russia Abroad*, pp. 118-55.

[6] From its inception the Soviet Union made no secret of its intention to set no limits to Red Army occupation of other counties, under pretext of liberating their proletariats from bourgeois oppression (Elliot R. Goodman, *The Soviet Design for a World State* (New York, 1960), pp. 285-308).

[7] Raeff, *Russia Abroad*, p. 5; cf. pp. 3-8, 44-46.

[8] Andreyev, *Vlasov and the Russian Liberation Movement*, p. 12; Raeff, *Russia Abroad*, pp. 78-79, 82-90.

[9] For Benois' career in emigration, cf. Prince Nikita D. Lobanov-Rostovsky's memoir *Эпоха. Судьба. Коллекция* (Moscow, 2010), pp. 127-36.

[10] For the achievements of Tsvetaeva and Remizov, cf. Greta N. Slobin, *Russians Abroad: Literary and Cultural Politics of Diaspora (1919-1939)* (Boston, 2013), pp. 57-73.

[11] Cf. Pipes, *Russia under the Bolshevik Regime*, pp. 139-40.

[12] Paul Robinson, *The White Russian Army in Exile 1920-1941* (Oxford, 2002), pp. 81-85.

[13] A vivid personal vignette of émigré life in Sofia appears in Lobanov-Rostovsky, *Эпоха. Судьба. Коллекция*, pp. 9-13.

[14] Robinson, *The White Russian Army in Exile*, pp. 69-70, 75; W.G. Krivitsky, *I was Stalin's Agent* (London, 1939), p. 66.

[15] D.P. Vertepov (ed.), *Русский Корпус на Балканах во Время II Великой Войны 1941-1945 г.г.* (New York, 1963), pp. 9-34; B. Prianishnikoff, *Новопоколенцы* (Silver Springs, Md., 1986), pp. 109-37; Alexis Wrangel, *General Wrangel: Russia's White Crusader* (New York, 1987), pp. 229-32. Earlier, Russian émigrés in France had raised a contingent to fight Bolshevism in Spain, where they served with Spanish royalist levies (Carlists) of General Franco's army (I.B. Ivanov, *Русский Обще-Воинский Союз* (St. Petersburg, 1994), pp. 8-10; Andrei Korliakov, *Русская Эмиграция в Фотографиях Франция 1917-1947* (Paris, 2001), ii, pp. 218-23).

[16] Alexei Arseniev, 'Русская диаспора в Югославии', in A. Arseniev, O. Kirillova, and M. Sibinovich (ed.), *Русская змиграция в Югославии* (Moscow, 1996), pp. 46-99.

---

[17] Paul Avrich, *Kronstadt 1921* (Princeton, 1970), pp. 103-5. Paris became the effective 'capital' of the early emigration (Prianishnikoff, *Новопоколенцы*, p. 1; Robert H. Johnston, *"New Mecca, New Babylon": Paris and the Russian Exiles, 1920-1945* (Kingston and Montreal, 1988), p. 21).

[18] While the Soviets declined to participate in the international Boy Scout movement, the Russian Scouts in emigration (NORS) continued to be officially recognized from 1928 to 1945 (A.V. Okorokov, *Русская Змиграция: Политические, военно-политические и воинские организации 1920-1990 гг.* (Moscow, 2003), pp. 42-44). The *Vityazi* ('Knights') provided a further White Russian equivalent, whose permanent camp at Laffrey in the French Alps I attended in 1957. Cf. *ibid.*, pp. 36-42; Korliakov, *Русская Эмиграция в Фотографиях Франция*, ii, pp. 142-71. The popular international *Sokol* youth movement is described by Okorokov, *Русская Змиграция*, pp. 65-74.

[19] After reading *Beau Geste* at an impressionable age, my late friend John Yeowell joined the Foreign Legion at Sidi Bel Abbes in the 1930s. There he was gratified to find his battalion CO a Prince Obolensky, complete with silver-topped cane and monocle.

[20] Georges Coudry, *Les camps soviétiques en France: Les «Russes» livrés à Staline en 1945* (Paris, 1997), pp. 164-93. For the cadet schools, cf. *ibid.*, pp. 182-83; Korliakov, *Русская Эмиграция в Фотографиях Франция*, ii, pp. 78-83, 120-29.

[21] Raeff, *Russia Abroad*, p. 43.

[22] George Kennan, who worked from 1931 to 1933 at the American legation in Riga, remarked on 'the atmosphere of the Baltic States, where more of the prerevolutionary Russia was still present than in Russia proper' (*Memoirs 1925-1950* (Boston, 1967), p. 49).

[23] Julius Epstein, *Operation Keelhaul: The Story of Forced Repatriation from 1944 to the Present* (Old Greenwich, Conn., 1973), pp. 13-16.

[24] Elizabeth White, 'The Legal Status of Russian Refugees, 1921-1936', *Zeitschrift Fur Globalgeschichte Und Vergleichende Gesellshaftsforschung* (Leipzig, 2017), xxvii, pp. 18-38. My father bore a Nansen passport until he acquired British citizenship well after World War II. By that time he had been practising for years as a barrister at the English bar, and travelled abroad freely. Only when his movements in England became severely restricted during World War II was he inconvenienced by his alien status.

[25] The poetess Zinaida Hippius likewise proclaimed the view that the emigration constituted another Russia, preserving all that was best in their national tradition (Johnston, *"New Mecca, New Babylon"*, p. 10).

[26] Peter Reddaway, 'Literature, the Arts and the Personality of Lenin', in Leonard Schapiro and Peter Reddaway (ed.), *Lenin: The Man, the Theorist, the Leader; A Reappraisal* (New York, 1967), pp. 37-70.

[27] Dmitri Volkogonov, *Ленин: Политический Портрет* (Moscow, 1994), ii, pp. 174-201.

28 Pipes, *Russia under the Bolshevik Regime*, pp. 334-36; Raeff, *Russia Abroad*, pp. 28, 62, 126; Pipes (ed.), *The Unknown Lenin*, pp. 168-69, 174. Full documentation of this philistine expulsion is to be found in the excellent compendium by V.G. Makarov and V.S. Khristoforov (ed.), *Высылка вместо Расстрела: Депортация Интеллигенции в Документов ВЧК-ГПУ 1921-1923* (Moscow, 2005).

29 '... Stalin ... said to me on one occasion that nations which had been ruled by powerful aristocracies, like the Hungarians and the Poles, were strong nations' (George Urban, 'A Conversation with Milovan Djilas', *Encounter* (December, 1979), p. 21).

30 Dmitri Volkogonov, *Сталин: Политический Портрет* (Moscow, 1994), ii, p. 43.

31 Christopher Andrew and Vasili Mitrokhin, *The Sword and the Shield: The Mitrokhin Archive and the Secret History of the KGB* (New York, 1999), pp. 32-33.

32 Volkogonov, *Сталин*, i, pp. 189, 394-406. Stalin's secretary, who enjoyed opportunity to observe him at close quarters over a period of years, perceived that the dictator's criminal nature derived legitimacy from Marxist doctrine (Boris Bajanov, *Bajanov révèle Staline; Souvenirs d'un ancien secrétaire de Staline* (Paris, 1979), pp. 141-42). Djilas similarly observed that Stalin utilized Leninism as a cloak for reality (Milovan Djilas, *Conversations with Stalin* (London, 1962), p. 166).

33 Piotr S. Wandycz, *Soviet-Polish Relations, 1917-1921* (Cambridge, Mass., 1969), pp. 198, 361; John W. Thompson, *Russia, Bolshevism, and the Versailles Peace* (Princeton, 1966), p. 344.

34 Oliver H. Radkey, *The Unknown War in Soviet Russia: A Study of the Green Movement in the Tambov Region 1920-1921* (Stanford, 1976), pp. 80-94, 386; Viktor Bortnevsky, *Белое Дело: (Люди и события)* (St. Petersburg, 1993), pp. 35-39. Thenceforth it became official Soviet dogma that the Green leader Antonov was surrounded by White officers, and in close league with 'counter-revolutionaries' (S.S. Khromov (ed.), *Гражданская Война и Военная Интервенция в СССР: Энциклопедия* (Moscow, 1983), p. 39).

35 George Katkov, 'The Kronstadt Rising', in David Footman (ed.), *St Antony's Papers · Number 6: Soviet Affairs Number Two* (London, 1959), pp. 43-44, 55-56; Avrich, *Kronstadt 1921*, pp. 95-135; A.V. Smolin, 'Кронштадт в 1921 году: новые документы', in V.G. Bortnevsky (ed.), *Русское Прошлое: Историко-Документальный Альманах* (St. Petersburg, 1991), ii, pp. 348-60.

36 E. Malcolm Carroll, *Soviet Communism and Western Opinion 1919-1921* (Chapel Hill, 1965), p. 233. Hopes continued to run high for some years. My late friend Prince Leonid Lieven recalled, when living as a boy in Belgium in the early 1920s, the sudden arrival of Baron Wrangel, a family friend. The General brought joyful news that the Communist regime would be

overthrown within the year!

[37] Robinson, *The White Russian Army in Exile*, pp. 97-130; Okorokov, *Русская Змиграция*, pp. 112-24.

[38] 'Geoffrey Bailey', *The Conspirators* (London, 1961), p. 11. 'Geoffrey Bailey' was the pseudonym of the late Prince Georgi Vassilchikov (Gordon Brook-Shepherd, *Iron Maze: The Western Secret Services and the Bolsheviks* (London, 1998), pp. 8-9). The murder of the Leningrad Communist Party Secretary, Sergei Kirov, in December 1934 was ascribed to White Guardists (Robert Conquest, *Stalin and the Kirov Murder* (London, 1989), pp. 44-58). In the same month Ivan Maisky, the Soviet Ambassador to Britain, recorded in his diary that 'over the past three or four months the Soviet authorities had established the existence of a large terrorist conspiracy against our Party leaders, beginning with Comrade Stalin. It is being organized and financed by the German 'Nazis'. Its agents are Russian White Guards and all those dissatisfied little groups which exist inside the USSR. The White Guards secretly cross the border in Poland, Latvia and Finland with the assistance of the listed countries and, once in the USSR, enter into contact with conspirators of Soviet citizenship' (Gabriel Gorodetsky (ed.), *The Maisky Diaries: Red Ambassador to the Court of St James's 1932-1943* (New Haven and London, 2015), p. 25).

[39] 'Bailey', *The Conspirators*, pp. 1-86; George Leggett, *The Cheka: Lenin's Political Police* (Oxford, 1981), pp. 297-98

[40] Pavel Sudoplatov, *Спецоперации: Лублянка и Кремль 1930-1950 годы* (Moscow, 1997), p. 462.

[41] Volkogonov, *Сталин*, i, p. 505. In the same year the province of Krasnoyarsk was believed to be infested with enemies of the people, including 'Kolchakites' – surviving elements of the army of the White commander in Siberia, Admiral Kolchak (*ibid.*, p. 514).

[42] Gábor Tamás Rittersporn, 'The omnipresent conspiracy: On Soviet imagery of politics and social relations in the 1930s', in J. Arch Getty and Roberta T. Manning (ed.), *Stalinist Terror: New Perspectives* (Cambridge 1993), pp. 99-115. 'The imagery of omnipresent subversion and conspiracy denoted a dark feeling of suspicion and threat among leaders and the populace. This feeling did not necessarily appear as fear of a specific danger, and the underlying experience of anxiousness varied according to age, personal background, and social status. It nevertheless permeated the relationships of social categories to each other and to the regime. As social groups define themselves in their relations to each other and to the state, the representation of ubiquitous wrecking and plots revealed a strong inclination of officialdom and the masses alike to identify themselves as potential victims of impenetrable machinations' (*ibid.*, pp. 114-15). In the 1930s, even within the security services purported 'enemies of the state' were accepted as authentic conspirators (Sudoplatov, *Спецоперации*, p. 142). All in all, the Soviet

leaders 'lived in a world of Lies, Cynicism, Cruelty' (Volkogonov, *Сталин*, i, p. 279).

[43] Lars T. Lih, Oleg V. Naumov, and Oleg V. Khlevniuk (ed.), *Stalin's Letters to Molotov 1925-1936* (Yale, 1995), pp. 44-49.

[44] A lifetime of ruthless struggle led Stalin to fear and hate imaginary foes as much as real ones (Volkogonov, *Сталин*, ii, p. 438). His daughter noted with increasing revulsion his prevailing characteristics of ambition, secretiveness, cynicism, atheism, revolutionary hatred of society, increasing persecution mania, violent temper, and callous cruelty (Svetlana Alliluyeva, *Only One Year* (London, 1969), pp. 339-52).

[45] Bertram D. Wolfe, *Khrushchev and Stalin's Ghost* (New York, 1957), pp. 158, 204, 240; Robert Conquest, *The Great Terror: Stalin's Purge of the Thirties* (London, 1968), pp. 298, 302, 312, 316; Strobe Talbott (ed.), *Khrushchev Remembers* (Boston, 1970), pp. 257-58, 281, 307, 481; Roy A. Medvedev, *Let History Judge: The Origins and Consequences of Stalinism* (London, 1971), pp. 305-6.

[46] Cf. Libushe Zorin, *Soviet Prisons and Concentration Camps: An Annotated Bibliography 1917-1980* (Newtonville, Mass., 1980), pp. 17-28. Evidence provided by fugitives and other witnesses led to embarrassing investigations by foreign governments and the Anti-Slavery Society (David J. Dallin and Boris I. Nicolaevsky, *Forced Labor in Soviet Russia* (London, 1948), pp. 218-22).

[47] Volkogonov, *Сталин*, i, pp. 398-99.

[48] Walter Bedell Smith, *Moscow Mission 1946-1949* (London, 1950), p. 115.

CHAPTER V
THE BROTHERHOOD
OF RUSSIAN TRUTH

Thou gav'st us courage
For five-score lifetimes!
Though planets gyrate,
We stay – unshifting.
Maria Tsvetaeva[*]

After arriving in Germany in March 1920, General Peter Nikolaevich Krasnov and his wife Lydia stayed in Upper Silesia. On 23 September 1920 they travelled to Bavaria together with the General's friend Count Grabbe, former commander of the Emperor's elite Cossack bodyguard.[1] Upon arrival the little party received an hospitable welcome from their mutual friend the Duke of Leuchtenberg, at his 'castle' of Seeon on an island at Lake Chiemsee in Bavaria (Leuchtenberg was a cousin of the heir to the Bavarian throne).[†] A direct descendant both of Napoleon's stepson Eugène de Beauharnais and Tsar Nicholas I, Leuchtenberg stood distantly in the succession to the Imperial House of Russia.[2] He had been close to his cousin Nicholas II, and in 1918 entered into covert negotiations with Field Marshal von Eichhorn, commander-in-chief of the German army of occupation in Ukraine, for the rescue of the imperial family from their captivity in Ekaterinburg. The project foundered on Kaiser Wilhelm's refusal to authorize the project.[3] A fervent monarchist, Leuchtenberg had been closely associated with General Krasnov, especially once the latter became Ataman of the Don Cossacks in the same year.[4]

Leuchtenberg's wealth enabled him to fund several Russian émigré publishing houses in Berlin, as well as assisting anti-Soviet activities generally.[5] Combined with his influential social position, this naturally led him to be regarded with acute suspicion by the Soviet regime. In 1926 an

---

[*] Robin Kemball (ed.), *Marina Tsvetaeva: The Demesne of the Swans; Лебединый Станъ* (Ann Arbor, 1980), p. 107.
[†] The 'castle' is in fact a former ancient Benedictine monastery bestowed by Napoleon on Prince Eugène Beauharnais, who is buried there.

OGPU report from Paris informed Moscow that the Duke held in a Swiss safe a collection of immensely valuable diamonds, whose sale he was understood to be negotiating – implicitly, in order to subsidize anti-Bolshevik activities. The agent continued by advising his superiors of Leuchtenberg's contacts with influential figures in Conservative Party circles in London, conducted through the Grand Duke Nikolai Nikolaevich's representative in Britain, Prince Beloselsky-Belozersky.[6] In the same year, Leuchtenberg hosted an important émigré conference at his castle, prominent among those present being Generals Krasnov and Wrangel.[7]

Particularly alarming was the Duke's close relationship with General Krasnov, who was regarded by the OGPU as one of the most dangerous leaders of the Russian military emigration.[8] A report of 12 November 1921 describes him as follows:

> General Krasnov – enjoys the respect of the majority [of White émigrés]; much loved by the Don Cossacks; apparently a superb organiser and administrator.[9]

Three months later another Chekist agent submitted one of many similarly agitated reports on the subject:

> Above all it may be concluded that a descent on Odessa and on the Cossack coast is being prepared under the command of General Krasnov, who will soon arrive in Bulgaria and take upon himself command of all campaigning together with Generals Wrangel and Kutepov.[10]

Prominent among émigré newspapers at this time was *Russian Truth* (*Russkaia Pravda*), founded in Berlin in 1921. On 25 January of the same year, it assisted in organizing a major conference in Berlin under the ægis of General Krasnov, at which provisional plans for a White Guard movement continuing the struggle against Soviet power were adopted. From the newspaper evolved an active political organisation bearing the title 'The Brotherhood of Russian Truth' (*Bratstvo Russkoi Pravdy*). As well as the Duke of Leuchtenberg and General Krasnov, it enjoyed the support of the two other leading White Russian generals Wrangel and Kutepov.[*]

At an early stage the BRP was penetrated by the OGPU in the person of a General Monkevits, whose betrayal was not exposed until 1926.

---

[*] This makes it difficult at times to distinguish between activities in the field of 'The Brotherhood of Russian Truth' (BRP) and the better-known 'Russian All-Military Union' (ROVS), with which the Grand Duke Nikolai Nikolaevich and Generals Wrangel and Kutepov were also closely associated.

However, the organisation continued active, in many instances effective, into the next decade, being reinforced by the creation of autonomous subordinate units, which were before long established in most countries of Western Europe and the United States. In 1927 its active fighting membership amounted to some 3,000 committed adherents.[11]

As the Soviet leadership swiftly discovered, this was no café gathering of languid exiles lamenting their unjust fate, but a formidable organization led and manned by soldiers of all ranks, hardened in most cases by years of war, and fearlessly determined to strike by any means possible at 'the Bolshevik beast'. Through the frontier forests of Finland, the Baltic States, Poland, Romania, and the mountains of the Caucasus, small groups infiltrated the forbidden territory, striking swiftly at military installations, Communist assemblages, rail and road communications, and other strategic targets. In 1927 agents planned to blow up the entire Red leadership at the opening of the Lenin Mausoleum in Red Square. In 1934 a well-planned operation to kill Stalin and Voroshilov was barely foiled by the OGPU. Responsibility for these operations largely rested for some years in the capable hands of General Kutepov. Because the Soviet Union was at ideological odds with almost every neighbouring country, including such major military powers as Britain, France, and Japan, Moscow suspected with some justification that the Brotherhood of Russian Truth was on occasion covertly aided by foreign governments.[12]

Politically, the purpose of the movement was focussed on overthrowing the Stalinist dictatorship, leaving the ultimate fate of Russia to be decided by the Russian people following their liberation. Particularly unnerving to the Kremlin was vigorous advocacy in its publications of the assassination of Stalin himself.[13]

Сталину-Джугашвили

Отъ Братства

Русской Правды

новогоднее пожеланіе.

New Year's greeting from the Brotherhood of Russian Truth to Comrade Stalin

The sympathies of the leadership of the BRP lay broadly in the direction of restoration of the monarchy, without commitment to either of the two principal candidates (the Grand Dukes Kirill Vladimirovich and Nikolai Nikolaevich). While the first was the legitimate dynastic heir, the second enjoyed enormous prestige from having been commmander-in-chief of the Russian Imperial Army. At the same time, the movement eschewed advocacy of the restoration of the monarchy at all, should it not accord with the people's wishes.[14]

A principal leader of this formidable organization, with its headquarters in Prague, was General Peter Krasnov;[15] although the commander in the field was the younger and more active General Kutepov. Nevertheless, Krasnov was no idle figurehead. His literary talent had manifested itself during his pre-war career, and he now settled down to write a succession of remarkably successful novels. In 1922 he published his most celebrated work, *From Double Eagle to Red Flag*, which went on to sell more than two million copies internationally.[16] This epic work follows the career of the fictional General Sablin from peacetime Guards officer in St. Petersburg to wartime cavalry commander, and finally as witness to horrific experiences during the Revolution. Although the treatment is strongly antagonistic to the Bolsheviks, the author does not baulk at assigning blame also to endemic failings of the *ancien régime*. All this of course reflected the General's own dramatic experiences in 1917 and before.[17]

The book's stirring pace and epic treatment attracted an extensive international readership, being eventually translated into fifteen languages. One reader is of especial interest here. When an aide showed him a copy of the four-volume novel shortly after its publication in Berlin, Stalin refused even to touch it, exclaiming angrily: 'When did he manage to write it, the swine?' Again, on another occasion his language suggests bitter hatred for the author, rather than contempt: 'The novel, like the General himself, is shit'.[18] This suggests that Stalin did after all read the book. He also resentfully recalled Krasnov's daring escape from Soviet power in 1917, as well as his own part in the narrowly-gained victory over Krasnov's Don Army in 1918 at Tsaritsyn (boastfully renamed Stalingrad).[19]

However, the novel which had reason above all to provoke Stalin's resentment and fear was Krasnov's *The White Coat* (Бѣлая Свитка), which was originally published in Berlin in 1928 and promptly translated into numerous foreign editions. The book is dedicated to 'The Brotherhood of Russian Truth', being (as the author emphasizes in his preface) based largely on fact, save for its imaginative conclusion. Krasnov presents it as a sequel to *From Double Eagle to red flag*, which will at the same time introduce the beginning of a new cycle, the name of which is *From the red flag to the Double Eagle*'.[20]

Briefly summarized, the novel's plot is as follows. The Brotherhood of Russian Truth has succeeded in establishing a military enclave in a remote and inaccessible forest region on the Polish frontier with the Soviet Union.[21] An early section, reflecting Krasnov's participation in the widespread early twentieth-century penchant for mysticism,[22] is devoted to a Russian girl's seduction into worship of the Devil.* Following this bizarre digression, the narrative turns to a strikingly convincing 'alternative history' of the near-destruction of the White outpost by Red artillery, followed in turn by an efficiently-staged military coup headed by officers of the old Imperial Army, whose superior discipline and tactics achieve a victory in which the Bolshevik regime is overthrown and replaced by restoration of 'the Grand Duke'. Throughout these dramatic turns of fortune's wheel, great emphasis is placed on the devastating effect of a combination of the lamentable morale of the Red Army with tacit support of the oppressed and exploited population for its courageous deliverers.

This longed-for liberation is set in what is clearly the imminent future. Allusions to current events in the tale are numerous, Krasnov being particularly well-informed of contemporary political intrigues, and are almost exclusively confined to events directly relevant to the immediate time of writing, which the author explains was 'April 1927-January 1928'.[23] The earliest explicit allusion is to the OGPU's capture and execution of the celebrated British spy Sidney Reilly, and his Russo-Finnish comrade Georgi Elvengrön in 1925.[24] Other references are to events occurring at the time of writing, including recent exposure of 'the repulsive 'Trust'';[25] the murder of the Soviet ambassador in Warsaw Peter Voikov by a sixteen-year-old émigré Boris Koverda in June 1927;[26] Krasnov's intrepid colleague Maria Zakharchenko-Schultz's bombing in the same month of an OGPU building beside its Lubianka headquarters in Moscow, and her subsequent death in a forest shoot-out;[27] in September a

---

* It is possible that General Krasnov underwent some genuinely mystical experience during his service in the Pamirs before the Great War. In his novel *Kostia the Cossack*, which is set in the seventeenth century, the hero becomes immersed in a powerfully-described shamanistic rite in the wastelands of Mongolia. On the other hand, it may be that the episode in *The White Coat* symbolizes Russia's succumbing to her Bolshevik oppressors.

further White agent Iosif Traikovich murdered by OGPU agents inside the Warsaw Soviet Embassy.[28]

In 1946 Krasnov recalled that

> In particular, Kutepov arranged for continuous infiltration of espionage materials into the Soviet Union, to be collected there, and for the perpetration of terrorist and sabotage activities by a group headed by the wife of a White Guardist officer, called Zakharchenko-Schultz. Through her I dispatched to the Soviet Union for distribution there 60 copies of an anti-Soviet book called "United Undivided" [published in Berlin in 1925]. On her return to France, Zakharenko-Schultz told me that my book appeared to enjoy great success among the population.

Peter Nikolaevich Krasnov the author

Copies must inevitably have fallen into the hands of the OGPU, and it may reasonably be assumed that the still more dangerous *White Coat* was in its turn likewise smuggled across the frontier and brought to the attention of the ubiquitous secret police and their apprehensive master in the Kremlin.

Although cast as a novel, much of Krasnov's *White Coat* reads like a blueprint for a forthcoming overthrow of the Soviet regime. Strong emphasis is laid on the necessity of arousing the crushed Russian masses to rise up against their oppressive masters. The function of the well-trained and patriotically committed emigrants in their fortified outpost at Borovoye was to strike a blow across the frontier that would enable the uprising to take place. In the meantime, widespread sabotage and assassinations of key Red figures would shake Communist morale.

Krasnov repeatedly stresses that these operations are directed by the real-life Brotherhood of Russian Truth, of which he himself was a principal leader. In his novel, the charismatic leader of the Whites, an eponymous figure known only as 'the White Coat' explains:

> We have a distant leader, the Supreme Commander-in-Chief [i.e. the Grand Duke Nikolai Nikolaevich].* We listen to his voice, and we cherish his general precepts. And he says, and we know it ourselves, that fundamental questions of the reconstruction of the Russian state can only be decided on Russian soil and in accordance with the wishes of its own people. That is why we go out to work in Russia herself. We do not bring any political programme with us. We are first of all soldiers, everyday workers, our aim is to liberate Russia from the shackles of the Third International. We do not seek to avenge the past. For us there is neither religious, nor tribal intolerance. We believe, that future Russian state power authority will be above classes and parties. It will be a Russian, national power. We do not wish to take the land from the peasants, but to strengthen the legality of their full possession.[29]

All this might appear to reflect wishful fantasies characteristic of emigrant political movements throughout history, whose effect might safely have been dismissed by the Soviet authorities. In reality, the activities of the Brotherhood of Russian Truth and its sister-organization the ROVS were profoundly disturbing to Stalin and the Soviet regime. BRP propaganda activities were particularly successful. Their literature was constantly being smuggled into the Soviet Union through channels ranging from the regular international post to passengers on ships and trains arriving at the frontiers. A particularly ingenious approach was the launch of thousands of party balloons bearing BRP literature on favourable winds from Finland and the Baltic States, delivering the organization's message to great tracts of Belorussia as well as the densely-populated city of Leningrad and its environs.[30]

---

* The Museum of the Emigration in Moscow possesses a copy of *The White Coat* bearing the author's inscription to the Grand Duke Nikolai's wife Anastasia Nikolaevna (Bazanov, *Братство Русской Правды*, p. 92; plate opposite p. 225).

P. N. Krasnov's *The White Coat* **(1928)**

Still more galling to the regime were successful operations involving sabotage of Soviet strategic sites and assassinations of leading Bolshevik figures. Real-life guerrilla operations such as those depicted in Krasnov's novel were frequent in the 1920s and early 1930s, being fully documented in P. N. Bazanov's scholarly history of the movement.[31] In the novel, the White Coat explains to a sceptical colleague how a courageous agent crosses the Soviet frontier without a passport.

> The brave and bold have no need of passports, nor visas. The brave and bold will turn into a wolf and make his way through the woods. I have been all over the world, and I do not know what is such a thing as a passport. Our visas – the misty marshes, our passport – the dark forest, while the consuls are our Russian peasants.[32]

One episode in particular must surely have brought disquiet to its readers in the Kremlin. On 7 June 1927, the same day that Ambassador Voikov was assassinated in Warsaw, Iosif K. Opansky, deputy chief of the OGPU in the military district of Belorus, was killed together with his chauffeur between Zhdanovichi and Minsk. His death was ascribed to sabotage conducted by agents of the Brotherhood of Russian Truth.[33] In *The White Coat*, which Krasnov was writing at that very time, the event is incorporated thinly disguised into his tale, when a brutal Commissar Patz is shot dead by the White Coat himself in a Belorussian railway station.

It is possible that the Soviet leadership found a specific aspect of this dramatic episode of Krasnov's book still more disturbing than the impunity with which White agents could strike deep within the frontiers of the Soviet Union. The White Coat is described as 'a tall, handsome man, in a white coat and a white astrakhan hat'. The climax of the book is provided by his seizure of Leningrad at the head of a well-disciplined force of White cavalry and infantry, to be followed by the restoration of the exiled Tsar (implicitly the Grand Duke Kirill, first cousin to Nicholas II and heir to the Throne). While the physical description of the White Coat is not apt to Krasnov or Kutepov, another figure to whom it might well have been applicable was surely too obvious to escape attention in the Kremlin.

Marshal Tukhachevsky

The Soviet General (in 1935 promoted to Marshal) Mikhail Tukhachevsky was just such a figure. One of the principal architects of victory in the Civil War, he was the ablest of the Red Army high command. In addition, there was much about him that was calculated to confirm Stalin's jealous apprehensions.[34] A member of an old aristocratic family,[35] he had served in the Great War as an officer of the élite Semeonovsky Guards. His personal qualities further suggested the camp of the Whites rather than that of the Reds: his impressive height, splendid physique and dashing good looks, easy self-confidence, elegance, and cultured tastes all smacked of the *ancien régime*.[36] During official visits to London and Paris in 1936, public popularity aroused by his gentlemanly appearance, confident courtesy, and fluent French provoked among others the jaundiced resentment of his incompetent rival Voroshilov.[37]

By the mid-1920s, both Red and White circles identified Tukhachevsky as a potential Bonaparte, who might yet overthrow the continuingly vulnerable Bolshevik regime. His own predilection for Napoleonic history aroused contrasted hope or fear in the opposed camps, while the continuing presence of a strong proportion of former tsarist officers in the Red Army was sufficient to provoke acute alarm in Bolshevik breasts.[38] Reds and Whites alike were prone (from differing perspectives) to dwell on the precedent of General Bonaparte's military *coup* of 18 Brumaire in 1799, when he overthrew the Revolutionary government of France.[39] Stalin entertained oscillating degrees of mistrust of Tukhachevsky's dangerously charismatic, ruthless, and energetic character. In 1925 he expressed suspicion of the General's supposed Bonapartist ambitions, and in 1930 he read an OGPU report of Tukhachevsky's alleged 'monarchist-military plot to seize power'.[40]

It was probably fear as much as doubt that postponed the inevitable dénouement. In 1937 N. I. Yezhov, head of the NKVD, passed Stalin an intercept of a message purportedly emanating from the émigré military organization ROVS in Paris. It reported preparations by a group of senior officers of the Red Army for a coup d'état in the USSR, to be headed by Tukhachevsky.[41] The NKVD having conveniently provided further incriminatory evidence, Tukhachevsky and his fellow 'conspirators' were summarily convicted at a secret trial and executed.

Reverting to Krasnov's novel, it is not unlikely that Stalin was further disturbed by the curious fact that the name of the charismatic and daring White Coat is never revealed, as well as the persistent failure even to affirm explicitly that he is an émigré. One wonders how General Krasnov's vivid portrayal in 1928 of the fictional coup d'état effected by the White Coat served to exacerbate Stalin's suspicions. After all, if anyone was aware of the extent of the Brotherhood of Russian Truth's clandestine activities and intrigues within the Soviet Union, it was its chief General Krasnov. In 1927-8 alarmist reports from OGPU agents abroad stressed extensive White emigrant plans for military intervention within the Soviet Union, Krasnov's BRP being regarded with particular apprehension.[42]

Unsurprisingly, Stalin nurtured a virulent mixture of fear and hatred for the White Russian military leadership, operating as it did with seeming impunity particularly in Poland, relations with which country had gravely deteriorated following the Voikov assassination. In the same year successive OGPU reports recounted detailed accounts of a planned uprising of the ubiquitous Russian monarchists in various cities of the USSR, while the doughty exiled General Wrangel continued to prepare for all-out war.[43] Two years after publication of *The White Coat*, an OGPU report noted:

> Evidence was given that a foreign expeditionary corps, combined with remnants of Wrangel's army and Krasnov's Cossack units, was preparing for military intervention in 1930. These formations were allegedly supposed to strike a combined blow against Moscow and Leningrad.[44]

Interviewed by the German writer Emil Ludwig at the end of the following year, Stalin justified the continuance of extreme oppression in the Soviet Union by comparing it with what he regarded as the Bolsheviks' excessive leniency at the time of the Revolution. As he recalled bitterly,

> When the white-haired General Krasnov marched upon Leningrad and was arrested by us, under the military law he should have been shot or at least imprisoned, but we set him free on his word of honour. Afterwards it became clear that with this policy we were undermining the very system that we were endeavouring to construct.[45]

As a consequence, the General was now free both to write pernicious anti-Soviet literature and encourage and direct terrorist acts within the USSR, operating from 1923 with relative impunity under protection of the French Government. The dictator is known to have made a close study of émigré literature and journals, and it is scarcely open to doubt that *The White Coat* stood high on the list of works dangerous to the Soviet Union generally, and its leader in particular.[46]

Krasnov now became a marked man. Of leading figures in the active White movement abroad, General Wrangel and the Grand Duke Nikolai died in 1928 and 1929, respectively. The principal commanders perpetuating resistance to Soviet power were now General Kutepov, head of the ROVS, and General Krasnov, head of the Brotherhood of Russian Truth. Of the two, Kutepov was the more dynamic and active leader. While Krasnov's age and commitment to his literary career inhibited active participation in political events, his charismatic figure particularly inspired the Cossacks.[47] At the same time, his writing instigated widespread hostility to the Soviet Union and gained him international acclaim.

From 1920 to 1923, the General lived in Germany, where he was supported in his political endeavors by his wealthy friend and colleague the Duke of Leuchtenberg. On 23 November of the latter year, at the invitation of the Grand Duke Nikolai Nikolaevich he moved to France, where he took up residence in a house close to the Grand Duke's residence at the Château de Choigny, an elegant nineteenth-century mansion at Santeny, some twenty miles from the center of Paris. In recognition of the Grand Duke's sterling services to the Allied cause during the Great War, the French Government had in addition provided him with a marshal's pension, together with secret service protection.

Château de Choigny

Here Krasnov enjoyed a peaceful refuge for his writing, while the chateau's spacious reception halls provided an aptly impressive setting for the Grand Duke's headquarters, as well as affording space for major conferences of the principal emigrant military organizations.[48]

At the time Krasnov was writing *The White Coat*, the redoutable General Kutepov, Wrangel's successor as head of the ROVS ('Russian All-Military Union' (*Русский Обще-Воинский Союз*),[49] pursued a relentless campaign of sabotage and armed action inside the frontiers of the USSR.[50] However ultimately ineffectual such a policy might appear with hindsight, there can be no doubt that in the conspiratorial mind of Joseph Stalin it posed an exceptionally dire and persistent threat. The more the regime imposed draconian measures to suppress any expression of opinion not wholly laudatory of the Great Leader, the harder it became to discover what people really thought. There can be no doubt that the *Vozhd* genuinely believed in the potency of the White threat – and was indeed justified in his fear.

Eventually, so alarming did the activities of General Kutepov appear that intructions were transmitted through Yakov Serebriansky, head of the

Spetsburo (the Soviet organization responsible for perpetrating assassinations abroad), to abduct the White general and bring him to the USSR. In 1930 he was kidnapped in the streets of Paris, during the course of which he suffered a heart attack. He was secretly buried in the house of a resident NKVD agent just outside the city.[51]

Three months after the judicial murder of Tukhachevsky in 1937, Stalin struck again. In Paris, General Kutepov had been succeeded as head of the White military organization ROVS by General Evgeny Miller, former commander of the White Russian Army of the North serving alongside British forces in 1918. In contrast to his predecessor's policy of conducting daring forward operations within the Soviet Union, Miller was persuaded that the current political situation was better met by husbanding ROVS resources, until the volatile state of Europe should afford opportunity for resumption of the armed struggle.[52]

Just how menacing Stalin considered the émigré resistance generally and the ROVS in particular is attested by Kutepov's abduction and that of his successor. For on 22 September 1937 General Miller was kidnapped in the heart of Paris by NKVD agents, rushed to a waiting Soviet ship in the Channel, and transported to Moscow. For two years he was held prisoner in the USSR, where he withstood pressures one can only imagine to issue an appeal to the White emigration to abandon the struggle against Soviet power. Eventually, in 1939 he was shot in the Lubianka. In his memoirs, NKVD General Sudoplatov claims that this operation resulted in a total breakdown of the White military organization, together with its plans for collaboration with the Germans in a future war against the Soviet Union.[53]

Although Sudoplatov was well informed concerning the facts of the operation and its aftermath, his explanation of its motive is implausible. Miller was in reality profoundly distrustful of Nazi Germany,[54] while the White cause was if anything strengthened by this brutal confirmation that their sinister foe regarded the ROVS as a force to be reckoned with. A further material consideration was the indignation the outrage aroused with the French Government and public opinion. The likely explanation of the dangerously provocative kidnapping in Paris is that Stalin had genuinely become persuaded that Tukhachevsky was conspiring with the White leadership in Paris.

Despite the success of this operation, on the eve of the outbreak of World War II, Walter Krivitsky, NKVD 'Resident' at The Hague, was assigned the dual task of monitoring 'the Red Army's two chief enemies, Hitler's Gestapo and the remnants of the Czarist White Army in Paris'.[55] In June 1937 (the month of Tukhachevsky's execution) the NKVD in western Siberia uncovered a purported monarchist conspiracy centered on Tomsk, led by princes Volkonsky and Dolgoruky. Some 3,107 of these 'conspirators', many of them nobles, were promptly rounded up and shot.[56] Thereafter, special sections of the NKVD directed from the Lubianka were deployed to conduct operations against the continuing threat posed by dangerous elements of the White Russian emigration.[57]

It can scarcely have been chance that led General Krasnov about this very time to depart France and return to Germany. It had now become abundantly clear that the French police could no longer afford sufficient protection against the abduction or murder of leading White leaders like himself, who were being ferociously targeted by skilled assassins employed by the NKVD (as the OGPU had now become). On the other hand, communist assassins were likely to receive short shrift in what had become Hitler's Germany.[58]

---

[1] I.I. Basik, S.N. Ivanov, S.O. Panin and V.S. Khristopherov (ed.), *Русская Военная Эмиграция 20-40-х годов XX века: Документы и Материалы* (Moscow, 1998-), i, pt. 1, p. 183.

[2] Marquis of Ruvigny, *The Titled Nobility of Europe* (London, 1914), p. 915; S.V. Dumin (ed.), *Дворянские Роды Российской Империи* (St. Petersburg, 1993-98), ii, pp. 13-16.

[3] Helen Rappaport, *The Race to Save the Romanovs* (New York, 2018), p. 235.

[4] Duke G. Leuchtenberg, 'Какъ началась «Южная Армія»' in I.V. Gessen (ed.), *Архивъ Русской Революціи* (Berlin, 1923), viii, pp. 166-82.

[5] P.N. Bazanov, *Братство Русской Правды – самая загадочная организация Русского Зарубежья* (Moscow, 2013), p. 83.

[6] Basik, Ivanov, Panin and Khristopherov (ed.), *Русская Военная Эмиграция*, vi, pp. 398-99. According to Soviet intelligence, Leuchtenberg was a monarchist, while not committed to the claims either of the Grand Duke Kirill Vladimirovich or that of the supporters of Nikolai Nikolaevich (*ibid.*, p. 576).

[7] Bazanov, *Братство Русской Правды*, pp. 83-84. Wrangel set out his views on restoration of the monarchy in Russia on 16 January 1922 in a lengthy letter to Krasnov, a copy of which duly fell into the hands of the OGPU (Basik, Ivanov, Panin and Khristopherov (ed.), *Русская Военная Эмиграция*, i, pt. 2, pp. 160-63.

[8] Cf. *ibid.*, ii, pp. 68, 216.

[9] *Ibid.*, i, pt. 2, p. 109. Cf. pp. 146, 643. Two days earlier (10 November 1921), Krasnov was described in a Cheka report as 'one of several leaders, whose name has brought together the hopes and expectations of all. Colossal popularity among all sections of the Volunteer Army and Cossacks' (*ibid.*, p. 97; cf. p. 643; *ibid.*, v, p. 279).

[10] *Ibid.*, i, pt. 2, p. 585. The former Ataman was also believed to have established

influential American contacts (*ibid.*, pp. 637-38; *ibid.*, v, pp. 603, 608).

[11] Bazanov, *Братство Русской Правды*, pp. 5-12, 33-38.

[12] Details of these relentless assaults on Soviet power are provided in *ibid.*, pp. 115-98.

[13] *Ibid.*, pp. 64-65.

[14] A.V. Okorokov, *Русская Эмиграция: Политические, военно-политические и воинские организации 1920-1990 гг.* (Moscow, 2003), pp. 7-8.

[15] Bazanov, *Братство Русской Правды*, p. 242.

[16] *Ibid.*, p. 89.

[17] The novel still repays reading, although readers may find allusions to the Jewish element in Bolshevism distasteful. Space forbids adequate consideration of this factor here, which can only be properly understood in the context of its time. It was not only reactionary Whites who found Jews disproportionately influential among the Bolshevik leadership. For example, in July 1917 a liberal intellectual in Petrograd recorded his dismay at the predominance of Jewish Bolshevik leaders such as Trotsky, Kamenev, and Steklov, who for what he assumed to be sinister motives operated like criminals under pseudonyms (G.A. Knyazev, 'Из записной книжки русского интеллигента за время войны и революции 1915-1922 г.', in V.G. Bortnevsky (ed.), *Русское Прошлое: Историко-Документальный Альманах* (St. Petersburg, 1991), ii, p. 161). Elements of Russian Jewry at the time perceived Bolshevism as a movement providing liberation from discrimination and persecution endured under the old regime (their aliases in some cases originated in pre-revolutionary clandestine activities), and Jews consequently featured disproportionately in the ranks of the Party and political police during the early decades of the Soviet regime (Leonard Schapiro, *Russian Studies* (London, 1986), pp. 284-87, 388-89; Stephen Kotkin, *Stalin: Volume I: Paradoxes of Power, 1878-1928* (New York, 2014), pp. 340-41). Adverse depiction of Jews in Krasnov's novels is generally confined to those prominent or active in the Bolshevik regime, while non-Bolshevik Jews are widely depicted as ordinary citizens of the multi-national Russian Empire, who on occasion feature as victims of the Red Terror (P.N. Krasnov, *Бѣлая Свитка* (Berlin, 1928), pp. 128, 159). Red pogroms were indeed a frequent occurrence (Dmitri Volkogonov, *Троцкий: Политический Портрет* (Moscow, 1992), ii, p. 290; Richard Pipes (ed.), *The Unknown Lenin: From the Secret Archive* (New Haven, 1996), pp. 77, 116-17, 128-29. The London *Jewish Chronicle* observed on 12 July 1918 that 'Bolshevism, for all its alleged Jewish origin, has been a nightmare and a curse to the Jewish population of Russia. Under its wings anarchy has flourished again and the Jews of Russia are living today under a terror rarely matched in all the dark days of Tsarism' (Sharman Kadish, *Bolsheviks and British Jews: The Anglo-Jewish Community, Britain and the Russian Revolution* (London, 1992), p. 78). A measured survey of the causes and effects of anti-Semitic outrages

perpetrated during the Civil War is to be found in Richard Pipes, *Russia under the Bolshevik Regime 1919-1924* (London, 1994), pp. 99-114.

[18] Dmitri Volkogonov, *Сталин: Политический Портрет* (Moscow, 1994), i, p. 238.

[19] Cf. *ibid.*, ii, pp. 314, 319; Dmitri Volkogonov, *Ленин: Политический Портрет* (Moscow, 1994), i, p. 245.

[20] Krasnov, *Бѣлая Свитка*, p. 3.

[21] *Ibid.*, pp. 182, 218-19, 232-33. In 1931 the emigrant General Sobolevsky urged the creation of just such a White Russian buffer state on Siberian territory in the Far East, operating under Japanese protection and supported by a dissident faction of the Red Army (R.W. Davies, 'Soviet Defence Industries during the First Five-Year Plan', in Linda Edmondson and Peter Waldron (ed.), *Economy and Society in Russia and the Soviet Union, 1860-1930: Essays for Olga Crisp* (Basingstoke, 1992), p. 257).

[22] For the influence of lurid forms of occultism widespread in high society before and during the Revolution, cf. Laura Engelstein, *Russia in Flames: War, Revolution, Civil War 1914-1921* (New York, 2018), p. 97.

[23] Krasnov, *Бѣлая Свитка*, p. 360.

[24] *Ibid.*, pp. 268-71.

[25] *Ibid.*, p. 136. The Trust was a notorious OGPU organization, which for several years penetrated the major White political movements (cf. Gordon Brook-Shepherd, *Iron Maze: The Western Secret Services and the Bolsheviks* (London, 1998), pp. 249-56; Kotkin, *Stalin*, i, p. 841).

[26] *Бѣлая Свитка*, pp. 75, 135. Voikov was not assassinated for his rôle as diplomat, but for the part he played in the murder of the Imperial Family in 1918 (cf. Mark D. Steinberg and Vladimir M. Khrustalëv, *The Fall of the Romanovs: Political Dreams and Personal Struggles in a Time of Revolution* (Yale, 1995), pp. 315, 363, 366, 392). The Soviet Government avenged Voikov's death by authorising random killing of a score of nobles and monarchists living in the USSR.

[27] *Бѣлая Свитка* pp. 135-36. Ambivalent aspects of Maria Schulz's role are discussed by Gordon Brook-Shepherd, *Iron Maze: The Western Secret Services and the Bolsheviks* (London, 1998), pp. 284-95, 318-22, 374.

[28] Krasnov, *Бѣлая Свитка*, pp. 250, 262. Cf. the OGPU report in Basik, Ivanov, Panin and Khristopherov (ed.), *Русская Военная Змиграция*, vi, pp. 338-39.

[29] Krasnov, *Бѣлая Свитка*, pp. 137-38. Hopes of a peasant uprising within the USSR were far from delusory. As a former Soviet journalist and Red Army officer recalled,

'*Émigré* military associations were active in Paris and constituted a serious threat to Bolshevism. In 1929 and 1930 the Ukraine and the lands along the Don, the Kuban, and the Terek were seething with discontent; peasants refused to work the *kolkhoz* fields; they refused to plough, sow, or harvest.

When I was living in Kuban, the Kuban Cossacks believed that outside help was at hand; rumours circulated constantly that White Cossacks had landed near Novorossiysk ... The fact remained that the internal unrest was associated with the presence of Russian *émigrés* in Paris. Small wonder that the N.K.V.D. agents took the trouble to kidnap and destroy General Kutepov and Miller, who stood at the head of the Paris military asociations' (Mikhail Koriakov, *I'll Never Go Back* (London, 1948), pp. 168-69).

[30] Bazanov, *Братство Русской Правды*, pp. 104-14.

[31] *Ibid.*, pp. 114-19.

[32] Krasnov, *Бѣлая Свитка*, p. 138.

[33] Bazanov, *Братство Русской Правды*, p. 163. According to Georgi Wassilchikov, Opansky 'was shot down in the neighbourhood of Minsk' ('Geoffrey Bailey', *The Conspirators* (London, 1961), p. 84).

[34] As early as 1925 Stalin brooded over the possibility that Tukhachevsky and other generals might emerge as leaders of a Soviet 18 Brumaire (Boris Bajanov, *Bajanov révèle Staline; Souvenirs d'un ancien secrétaire de Staline* (Paris, 1979), 127).

[35] Alexander Bobrinskoy, *Дворянскіе Роды внесенные въ Общій Гербовникъ Всероссійской Имперіи* (St. Petersburg, 1890), i, p. 178. The common ancestor of the Tukhachevskys and my own family was a Lithuanian warlord named Indris, who settled with his military retinue in Chernigov in 1353.

[36] Solomon Volkov, *Testimony: The Memoirs of Dmitri Shostakovich* (London, 1979), pp. 72-79). Although the authenticity of the 'testimony' has been challenged, it is clear that its content largely reflects what was being said and observed at the time. A subsidiary accusation levelled against the cultured Tukhachevsky was misuse of military orchestras to entertain parties at his country house (Pavel Sudoplatov, *Спецоперации: Лубянка и Кремль 1930-1950 годы* (Moscow, 1997), p. 135).

[37] Volkogonov, *Троцкий*, ii, pp. 249-50.

[38] Stephen Kotkin, *Stalin: Volume I: Paradoxes of Power, 1878-1928* (New York, 2014), pp. 574-75.

[39] 'Certainly Communist leaders since 1917 displayed a healthy fear of "a man on horseback"' (Adam B. Ulam, *Stalin: The Man and his Era* (London, 1973), p. 448).

[40] Bajanov, *Bajanov révèle Staline*, p. 127; Kotkin, *Stalin: Volume I*, pp. 52, 54, 58.

[41] Volkogonov, *Сталин*, i, pp. 531-32, 538. Although General Volkogonov considered the document a forgery, it may well have been a 'plant', deliberately leaked by the White high command to sow dissension among the Soviet leadership. Cf. Roy A. Medvedev, *Let History Judge: The Origins and Consequences of Stalinism* (London, 1971), p. 300-301.

[42] *e.g.* Basik, Ivanov, Panin and Khristopherov (ed.), *Русская Военная Эмиграция*, vi, pp. 305-7. Particular emphasis was laid on the threat posed

by the Brotherhood of Russian Truth (pp. 339-40). The years 1926-29 were deeply fraught for the Soviet Union, when the regime believed itself threatened by war with Britain and other hostile nations extending from Finland to China (Gabriel Gorodetsky, *The Precarious Truce: Anglo-Soviet Relations 1924-27* (Cambridge, 1977), pp. 231-40; Lars T. Lih, Oleg V. Naumov, and Oleg V. Khlevniuk (ed.), *Stalin's Letters to Molotov 1925-1936* (Yale, 1995), pp. 133-44, 178). A concomitant of war was anticipated as foreign invasion combined with internal uprisings organised by the omnipresent White monarchists (Kotkin, *Stalin: Volume I*, pp. 625, 634-5, 639, 644, 646-47, 668).

[43] Basik, Ivanov, Panin and Khristopherov (ed.), *Русская Военная Змиграция*, vi, pp. 305, 328-29. Detailed plans were believed to be being drawn up for further assassinations of Soviet diplomats (pp. 325, 329-40).

[44] Lih, Naumov, and Khlevniuk (ed.), *Stalin's Letters to Molotov*, p. 194.

[45] *Leaders of Europe* (London, 1934), p. 373.

[46] Stalin's obsessive concern with emigrant publications is described by Volkogonov, *Stalin: Volume I*, pp. 398-9. *The White Coat* was regarded with particular apprehension in the Soviet Union (Bazanov, *Братство Русской Правды*, p. 106). On 15 September 1946 Krasnov told his NKVD interrogators that his books were frequently transmitted to the Soviet Union hidden among imported foreign goods. Stalin would in any case have encountered no difficulty in obtaining a copy from Soviet embassies and other agencies operating abroad. As a young seminarist, he had read Victor Hugo's historical novel *Ninety-three* (*Quatrevingt Treize*) (Robert C. Tucker, *Stalin as Revolutionary 1879-1929* (London, 1974), p. 86). The tale is set at the time of Royalist resistance in Brittany to the Revolutionary government in Paris. A leading protagonist is the Marquis de Lantenac, who is characterised by ruthless courage and relentless hostility to the Republican dictatorship. A further parallel with the current situation lay in the fact that the French counter-revolutionary movement is backed by British military support.

[47] An OGPU report of 5 December 1923 emphasises Krasnov's enormous popularity among the Cossacks (Basik, Ivanov, Panin and Khristopherov (ed.), *Русская Военная Змиграция*, ii, p. 395; cf. v, p. 279).

[48] Cf. *ibid.*, pp. 602-9; vi, pp. 387, 397-98, 403-5.

[49] For the history and organization of ROVS, cf. Okorokov, *Русская Змиграция*, pp. 112-24.

[50] *Ibid.*, pp. 81-82.

[51] Sudoplatov, *Спецоперации*, pp. 94, 138-39. Kutepov's son fell into Soviet hands during the war, when he was sentenced to twenty-five years' slave labour. When the young man protested that he was only an ordinary prisoner-of-war, the prosecutor explained: 'In your case nothing else is needed. You are your father's son' (Unto Parvilahti, *Beria's Gardens: Ten Years'*

Captivity in Russia and Siberia (London, 1959), p. 45).

[52] 'Bailey', *The Conspirators*, pp. 118-20.

[53] Sudoplatov, *Спецоперации*, pp. 63-64.

[54] 'Bailey', *The Conspirators* pp. 132, 260. For General Miller's abduction, cf. further *ibid.*, pp. 229-67; Prianishnikoff, *Новопоколенцы*, pp. 64-73; Vadim J. Birstein, *SMERSH: Stalin's Secret Weapon* (London, 2011), p. 207.

[55] W.G. Krivitsky, *I was Stalin's Agent* (London, 1939), p. 263. In the 1930s, 'The main "enemies of the people" were still considered to be the White Guards' (Christopher Andrew and Vasili Mitrokhin, *The Sword and the Shield: The Mitrokhin Archive and the Secret History of the KGB* (New York, 1999), p. 41). In July 1937 NKVD chief Lev Mekhlis reported to Stalin the arrest of numerous members of a musical ensemble, whose 'anti-Soviet elements' included 'former [*i.e.* White] officers' (Volkogonov, *Сталин*, i, p. 358). It is significant that these and other comparable reports were intended for internal consumption only. As their principal recipient was Stalin himself, whatever the validity of the report Mekhlis must have assumed that the dreaded Boss would credit it.

[56] Douglas Smith, *Former People: The Last Days of the Russian Aristocracy* (London, 2012), pp. 348-49.

[57] Furmanov was 'the chief of the counter-espionage section operating among White Russians abroad' (Krivitsky, *I was Stalin's Agent*, pp. 253-54, 261). In 1937 he was 'Resident of the NKVD in Czechoslovakia' (Alexander Orlov, *The Secret History of Stalin's Crimes* (London, 1954), p. 215). In Vienna, the NKVD representative was Ivan Zaporozhets, whose 'main job consisted in keeping an eye on the remnants of the armies of General Wrangel' (Elisabeth K. Poretsky, *Our Own People: A Memoir of 'Ignace Reiss' and His Friends* (Oxford, 1969), p. 65). For further allusions to Soviet surveillance of the émigrés, cf. Vladimir and Evdokia Petrov, *Empire of Fear* (London, 1956), p. 257; Sudoplatov, *Спецоперации*, pp. 92-93.

[58] Samuel J. Newland, *Cossacks in the German Army 1941-1945* (London, 1991), pp. 95-96, 188 note 25. Krasnov's Berlin publisher suggested the transfer, doubtless having Krasnov's safety in mind. That this was the prime motive for his move appears more likely than a suggestion that he was looking to Germany for aid against the Soviet Union (Bazanov, *Братство Русской Правды*, p. 261).

CHAPTER VI
REFUGE IN THE REICH

Question: You composed an appeal?

Answer: Yes. At the beginning of June 1943 I published an appeal, in which I called upon the Don Cossacks to unite with the Germans and take part in armed conflict against the Soviet Union.

In this appeal I pointed out that the Cossacks had already in 1918 accepted active assistance from the Germans, then occupying the Ukraine, and undertook a relentless fight against the Bolsheviks, and that with their help I succeeded in occupying the whole of the Don territory.

– NKVD interrogation of General Krasnov, 19 September 1946.

On his arrival in Germany in 1937, Peter Krasnov and his wife Lydia settled in the village of Dahlewitz, on the southern outskirts of Berlin. Although he continued to work for the anti-Soviet cause, he does not appear to have maintained any significant contact with the German government.[1] He continued his literary work, writing articles (principally on military topics) for influential emigrant newspapers such as *Sentinel* (*Chasavoi*) and *Russian Invalid* (*Russkii Invalid*). Among the emigration generally and the Cossacks in particular his prestige was immense, while his fame as internationally acclaimed author gained him respect in influential circles in the West. Such work occupied him until the German invasion of its close ally the Soviet Union on 22 June 1941 abruptly changed everything.

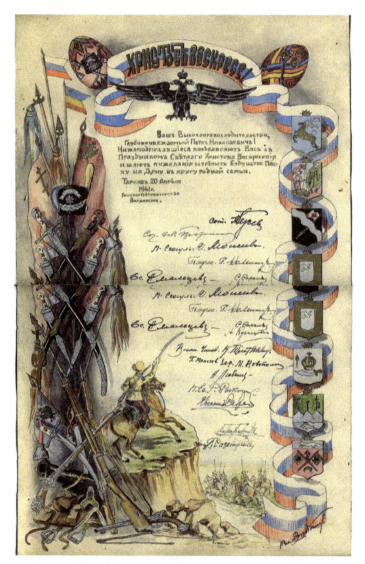

Cossack Easter greetings to Ataman Krasnov, 20 April 1941

As the Wehrmacht eventually encountered increasingly potent Red Army resistance, intelligent elements of the German military began looking to peoples of the Soviet Union hostile to the socialist regime as potential allies. These included Turkomans, other martial ethnicities of Central Asia, and fiercely independent mountaineers from the Caucasus. Above all, the Cossacks' impressive record in combating Soviet power during the Civil War and interwar period commended them as potential co-belligerents in the colossal struggle now unfolding. High regard for their fighting abilities was held in German military circles, and on 15 April 1942 Hitler formally permitted recruitment of Cossacks by the Wehrmacht, both for combating Soviet partisans in rear areas, and at the front. In an attempt to reconcile their status with Nazi racial doctrines, an ingenious theory was advanced asserting that Cossacks were not Slavs as was generally believed, but descendants of Germanic Ostrogoths dwelling north of the Black Sea in the early centuries AD.[2]

Individual Wehrmacht commanders began authorizing recruitment of Cossack units from an early stage of the invasion. Hatred of their Soviet oppressors, combined with their outstanding fighting qualities, swiftly earned them the respect of the German military, who employed them in increasing numbers under the command of Cossack and German officers.[3] Apart from the Cossacks, many Soviet citizens for varying reasons supported the German war effort, and by March 1943 an estimated 430,000 volunteers from occupied regions of the Soviet Union were serving alongside the German Army.[4] As Solzhenitsyn sardonically observed, defection on such a scale remains unparalleled in the history of Russia, or indeed any other country.[5]

L'Oberst (colonel) Ivan Nikitich Kononov, chef du 5e régiment de Cosaques du Don.
Colonel Ivan Nikitich Kononov, commander of the 5th. Don Cossack Regiment.

Ivan Nikitich Kononov

Two months after the German invasion of the USSR, the Red Army's 436rd Infantry Regiment defected to the Germans. Its commander was a Don Cossack, Major Ivan Nikitich Kononov, who had an impressive record of service in the Red Army. However, as frequently occurred, Red brutality had long destroyed any vestige of his loyalty to the regime. The Bolsheviks had murdered three of his brothers, while most of his remaining relatives were either killed or dispatched to slave labor camps.[6] Kononov's services were promptly welcomed by General von Schenkendorff, commanding Army Group Center's rear area, and the Regiment's strength was increased by volunteers from other captured Red Army prisoners. Toward the end of the year Kononov received a congratulatory letter from General Krasnov, who expressed his conviction that recruits would be found across Cossack lands from the Don to the Urals, eager to help in liberating all Cossacks from communist rule.[7]

General Krasnov at home in 1942

In the following year German Army Group A occupied the greater part of the Don and Kuban Cossack territories. Field Marshal Maximilian von Weichs set about reassuring the population of decent treatment, and recruiting Cossacks willing to fight against their Bolshevik oppressors.

Volunteers flocked to the colors, churches were reopened, Cossack cadet schools re-established, and civil liberties restored. Misbehavior on the part of the occupying force was strictly prohibited, and German troops became widely accepted as liberators.[8] German propaganda disseminated behind Red Army lines gained a receptive response.[9]

At the beginning of March 1942, well before German occupation of the Don territory, a secret body of Cossack resistance leaders gathered in the capital Novocherkassk. An envoy from their committee, Captain Alexander Siusiukin, managed to cross over to the Germans, where he arranged for a message to be transmitted to General Krasnov in Berlin. Before long, thousands of copies of Krasnov's appeal to the Cossacks to come over to their liberators were dropped behind Red Army lines.[10]

However, with the crushing defeat of the Germans at Stalingrad and ensuing Red Army reoccupation of the Cossack lands, this brief 'liberation' came to a swift and deadly end. On 19 March 1943 NKVD Deputy People's Commissar Vsevolod Merkulov reported to Stalin that in the Rostov region of the Don alone 2,804 people had been arrested. He noted that

> in the city of Rostov the German command undertook measures for creation of a 'Cossack government of the Don, Kuban and Terek'.

> In this connexion in November 1942 there resided in Germany the White Guardist general KRASNOV who handled matters with especial regard to the Don Cossacks. However this 'government' was not formed by the Germans.[11]

Once again Krasnov was drawn to Stalin's attention as an inveterate foe of Soviet power. And just over two years later Krasnov and Merkulov were to meet face-to-face in unforeseeable circumstances.

Meanwhile, as Samuel Newland observes in his study of the Cossacks in the Second World War,

> In 1942, in addition to the other activities mentioned, Himpel [of the *Ostministerium*] contacted General Krasnov, who was still living in Berlin, and asked him to join the staff of the Cossack central office. At first Krasnov refused, but on January 25, 1943 he joined the central office and began working in cooperation with the German force. Apparently Krasnov found it advantageous to be within the political structure rather than to remain an outsider. In addition, Krasnov thought it wise to be within Berlin's political structure to counter the influence of the [pro-Nazi Cossack] Glaskow and his group who were repeatedly trying to influence German policies through their contacts within the S.S. and the *Gestapo*.[12]

On 21 April 1943 the celebrated 15th Cossack Cavalry Corps, commanded by the talented and charismatic General Helmuth von Pannwitz, was formally brought into existence. The officers were for the most part German and Austrian, and also included a number of native Russian-speakers from the Baltic States. Cossack martial skills were much appreciated by their officers. As the Russian-speaking Colonel Alexander von Bosse explained,

> the Cossacks far surpassed the German personnel in taking advantage of terrain and in the art of camouflage. Thus, for example, after each rush the Cossacks always rolled a few yards to one side in a previously selected position and so escaped enemy observation. It was not necessary to teach them to dig in, as they did so instinctively.

> Each regiment was assigned an Orthodox chaplain, whose ministrations were received by the Cossacks with great reverence.

> Although attendance by Germans was expressly prohibited by the leaders in the Wehrmacht High Command, General Von Pannwitz nevertheless encouraged the presence of German personnel, and I noticed that the Cossacks were always grateful for this sign of recognition.

> A large number of the Cossacks who had grown up in the Soviet Union were not baptized and had been given the queerest kinds of first names, such as: "May," "Tractor," or "Ni[n]el" (reversed spelling of "Lenin"). These men were all baptized and received Christian names of their choice. The old custom by which every Russian Orthodox Christian wears a cross around his neck was re-introduced, and each Cossack given an aluminum cross of this kind and wore it on his chest.

Their instinctive piety was tempered by other traditional Cossack practices.

> Choral singing and Cossack dances, preferably with rather than without vodka, were the favorite evening amusements in camp. On Sundays and holidays the men executed the famous "Dshigitovka" riding feast [feat?] with enthusiastic applause and loud cheering. Parties given by the various units ended in drunken orgies which had to be supervised and kept in check by details appointed for this purpose in advance, especially whenever indiscriminate shooting began, which, although all a part of the game, met with scant sympathy on the part of the German officers and garrison headquarters. However, no accident ever occurred.[13]

The Cossack Division was quartered beside the town of Mielau (Mława), north of Warsaw, where intensive recruiting and training took place.[14] As time passed, many White émigré officers possessed of valuable military experience joined the Division.[15]

Eventually, on 12 September 1943 the *Wehrmacht* chief of staff General Zeitzler telegraphed von Pannwitz at Mielau:

> I can no longer afford to let a complete division remain inactive. Report immediately your readiness to depart by 15 September. Further orders will follow.

Although the Cossack Division had originally been intended for combat on the Russian front, Hitler's fanatical objection to employing Russians in the liberation of their country obstructed the opportunity. While other Russian units in German service were redeployed in Western Europe, it was decided as a palliative that the Cossacks' skill in guerilla warfare made them ideally suited to combat Tito's Communist partisans in the mountains and forests of northern Yugoslavia. In view of the fact that his men were burning to fight the hated Bolshevik armies of Stalin, von Pannwitz arranged to assuage their disappointment with a magnificent parade of the Division, at which General Peter Krasnov was invited as guest of honour.[16] It is a measure of his legendary status among all Cossacks that his name continued a byword among men who had for the most part lived for nearly a quarter of a century within the bounds of the Soviet Union. The parade provided a magnificent spectacle, which impressed itself on the memory of all present.

Generals Krasnov and von Pannwitz at Mielau

Colonel Heinrich-Detloff von Kalben was among the officers present who never forgot the stirring magnificence of that day.

At the gate of the camp, under the banner of the 1. Don Regiment, the Don Cossack guards appeared in their uniform with the Cossack fur cap and sabre. A guard of honour, all mounted on greys, accompanied the car of the principal guest and General v. Pannwitz on their journey through the entire camp at Mielau, past 15,000 Cossacks and their numerous families, who stood beside the camp lanes. An indescribable cheer greeted the revered General. This was followed by visits to the stables and barracks, field service, shooting and riding, and in the evening outdoor celebrations of individual regiments with singing, dancing and various demonstrations. The General Ataman was convinced that the Cossacks were well treated under German leadership, and between them and the German soldiers a sense of brotherhood and camaraderie had developed. In successive speeches to the soldiers of individual regiments he expressed his joy that Cossacks and Germans would fight together for liberation of peoples from Bolshevik rule. At the end of this visiting day, the choir of the Division performed Russian songs in a ceremony in the camp hall of Mielau. The Russian Lord's Prayer was sung movingly. The trumpeter corps of the Division played here for the first time, the parade march of the Cossack division "Prinz Eugen, the noble knight". The event concluded with the "Circassian Tattoo", which concludes with the "God Protect the Tsar" of the Russian Imperial anthem. While the power of the sound of this musical work had a strong effect on the Germans, it brought back their youth to the older Cossacks when they had served in the Tsar's Army in their homeland. They were not ashamed of their tears. Pannwitz had managed to ensure that the 1 Cossack Division was the only formation of the German *Wehrmacht* permitted to play this tattoo on official occasions.[17]

During the summer of 1943, Krasnov was visited at his home in Dahlewitz by a delegation of 38 Cossacks from the Soviet-reoccupied Don, Kuban and Terek regions. They discussed the possibility of a renewed overthrow of Soviet power with German assistance. Not long after this the General was approached by officers of the German secret police (*Sicherheitsdienst*). He agreed to provide the text of an appeal to renew the struggle against Bolshevism. 'From this' he later recalled, 'I understood that the Germans in this struggle were helping the Cossacks, as they helped in 1918'.

Unfortunately, the German government of 1943 was very different from that of 1918. Hitler entertained no intention of permitting the restoration of a free Russia. As he declared to Keitel and Zeitzler at a conference in the Berghof on 8 June 1943, 'A differentiation must be made between the propaganda which I make in Russia and what we ourselves will do in the end'.[18]

Although he took his duty seriously, Krasnov (who was by now 74) was no longer able to lead troops in battle. Equally, he must have been gratified to discover that he was now if anything more popular with Cossacks from the Soviet Union than he had been in the at times divisive days of 1918. Many of the German officers with whom he dealt on behalf of Cossack formations serving in the *Wehrmacht* were sincere supporters of the revival of a free Russia following the overthrow of Bolshevism. They included such significant figures as Count Claus von Stauffenberg, subsequently hero of the plot to kill Hitler, and the celebrated German intelligence chief Reinhard Gehlen.[19] Von Pannwitz himself was no admirer of the Führer as military leader, and declined Himmler's proposal to place the 15th Cossack Cavalry Corps (as it became on 25 February 1945) under Waffen SS command. Instead, a form of words was agreed enabling the Corps to receive advanced weaponry uniquely available to the SS, in exchange for acknowledging a nominal SS connection. Even this face-saving arrangement provoked resentment among the Corps' German and Austrian officers.[20] In reality, however, von Pannwitz had conceded little or nothing to *Reichsführer* Himmler. The 15th Cossack Cavalry Corps continued to operate exclusively within the Wehrmacht chain of command, while its officers retained their Wehrmacht uniforms, ranks, and identification.[21]

General von Pannwitz's attitude towards Nazism generally, and its racial doctrines in particular, is illustrated by a striking episode. *Oberleutnant* Ernst Walter von Mossner had joined the 1st Division of the 15th Cossack Cavalry Corps during its formation at Mielau. On one occasion during subsequent fighting in Croatia, he was attending on General von Pannwitz at a hilltop observation post. All at once, a distant staff car was glimpsed making its way towards them. On arrival, two smartly-uniformed SS officers jumped out and saluted the General. To his enquiry, they explained that the *Reichsführer* wished to speak with von Mossner, who was to accompany them to his headquarters.

It was common knowledge that von Mossner (originally Moses) was of Jewish origin, his grandfather having been decorated by Kaiser Wilhelm II for distinguished military service. Nevertheless, it was not hard to guess the nature of Himmler's interest. Von Pannwitz looked his emissaries up and down, then addressed them sharply. 'You see those gentlemen there?' he snapped. 'If you are not gone from here within two minutes, I'm handing you over to them'. The SS officers took one look at the General's ferocious-looking Cossack bodyguards, and, springing back into their car, tore off the way they had come. Nothing more was heard of the matter.

General von Pannwitz's bodyguard

This episode was recounted to me independently by Ernst von Mossner himself and Captain (*Rittmeister*) Philipp von Schoeller, who witnessed the encounter.

Another old friend of mine, Major George Druzhakin, was a White émigré from Paris who had formerly served in General Krasnov's Don Army in 1918. Recruited to join the staff of Colonel Constantin Wagner's 1st Cossack Cavalry Division, he was astonished by the overt extent of hostility to Nazism and the Führer he encountered in the divisional mess.

General Krasnov, however, did not share this view. He mistakenly took the situation to be not dissimilar from that arising from the pragmatic alliance with the Germans he had engineered in 1918. More realistically, he recognized that the overthrow of Stalin could now only be effected by German military might, and believed that considerations of *Realpolitik* required active collaboration with their German ally.

At the same time, many sympathetic Germans disapproved Krasnov's refusal to enter into any formal co-operation with General Vlasov, commander of the 'Russian Liberation Army' (ROA) recruited by the Germans from their colossal pool of Red Army prisoners-of-war, and condemned his stance as perverse and reactionary.[22] However, since the Vlasov 'army' was not permitted to play an active part in the war until its final days, it does not appear that any real damage resulted from Krasnov's controversial attitude. Nor was his mistrust of the ROA total, as he conferred with Vlasov on a couple of occasions, and maintained association between the latter's command and the *Kazachi Stan* through

Vlasov's liaison officer on his staff, the Cossack Colonel A. M. Bocharov.[23]

Although Krasnov's concern to reestablish an independent or autonomous Cossack state in a restored national Russia was doomed to failure, both on account of Hitler's malign racial policy and larger events beyond the control of either, he played a positive role as prestigious mediator between the German command structure and the Cossacks. While he boosted morale with visits to the Cossack Corps in Yugoslavia, his principal activity lay in support of a major Cossack settlement centered on the town of Novogrudok in Belorussia. The *Wehrmacht* high command had authorized establishment of a self-governing region, to which thousands of Cossacks repaired. The creation of this short-lived 'free Cossackdom' owed much to General Krasnov's influence with the *Ostministerium*.[24] Among other services, he arranged for numerous military White emigrants to join the settlement.

On 31 March 1944, General Köstring, who bore responsibility for the Cossack and other eastern 'legions', established a central administration of the Cossack army, *Hauptverwaltung*. General Krasnov was appointed titular head of the organisation.[25] He approved the succession of Sergei Pavlov to the German Major Müller as Field Ataman of the *Kazachi Stan*, as the settlement now became known. An experienced and respected officer in both the White and Red Armies successively, Pavlov was unfortunately killed in an exchange of fire with Red partisans on 17 June 1944.[26]

As Newland explains,

> In practice, the *Hauptverwaltung* had very little if any power delegated to it since by 1944 National Socialist Germany was fighting for its survival and could not afford to release combat-ready forces under its command to an agency, such as the *Hauptverwaltung*, outside its direct control. Nonetheless, the *Hauptverwaltung* continued to exist and function until the end of the war and served to represent the Cossack interests within the German military and political structure.[27]

On 25 June General Krasnov appointed as Pavlov's successor Timofei Domanov, who had likewise served in the White Army during the Civil War, and afterwards in the Red Army.[28] However the continuing advance of the Red Army required an urgent withdrawal, when Krasnov secured permission to transfer the *Kazachi Stan* to North Italy. On 6 July the Cossacks began their last long trek: a protracted move which was not completed until September.[29]

[1] Throughout the period of the 1939-41 Nazi-Soviet alliance, the German government was concerned to repress anti-Soviet activities within the Reich (Raymond James Sontag and James Stuart Beddie (ed.), *Nazi-Soviet Relations 1931-1941: Documents from the Archives of The German Foreign Office* (Washington, 1948), p. 145).

[2] Petr N. Krikunov, 'Collaborationism: Some Issues in Participation of Cossacks in the Second World War', in Harald Stadler, Rolf Steininger, and Karl C. Berger (ed.), *Die Kosaken im Ersten und Zweiten Weltkrieg* (Innsbruck, 2008), pp. 122-23.

[3] Jürgen Thorwald, *The Illusion: Soviet Soldiers in Hitler's Armies* (New York, 1975), pp. 24-62.

[4] Samuel J. Newland, *Cossacks in the German Army 1941-1945* (London, 1991), pp. 86-92.

[5] A. Solzhenitsyn, *Архипелаг ГУЛаг: Опыт Художественного Исследования 1918-1956* (Paris, 1973-75), i, p. 248.

[6] Konstantin Cherkassov, *Генерал Кононов: (Ответ перед Историей за Одну Попытку)* (Melbourne, 1963-65), i, pp. 22-26; K.M. Alexandrov, *Офицерский Корпус Армии Генерал-Лейтенанта А.А. Власова 1944-1945* (Moscow, 2009), p. 502.

[7] Cherkassov, *Генерал Кононов*, i, pp. 146-47. For Kononov's biography, cf. Alexandrov, *Офицерский Корпус Армии Генерал-Лейтенанта А.А. Власова*, pp. 491-510.

[8] General V. Naumenko (ed.), *Великое Предательство: Выдача Казаков в Лиенце и Других Местах (1945-1947); Сборник материалов и документов* (New York, 1962-70), i, pp. 19-31, 54-64. The account in Naumenko's collection is by the Don Cossack Nikolai Nazarenko, who at the time played a key part in events in his homeland. Cf. also Newland, *Cossacks in the German Army*, pp. 90-92, 129-31; Stadler, Steininger, and Berger (ed.), *Die Kosaken im Ersten und Zweiten Weltkrieg*, pp. 125-27.

[9] Ortwin Buchbender, *Das tönende Erz: Deutsche Propaganda gegen die Rote Armee im Zweiten Weltkrieg* (Stuttgart, 1978), pp. 148-54.

[10] Naumenko (ed.), *Великое Предательство*, i, pp. 25-26.

[11] V.N. Khaustov, V.P. Naumov, and N.S. Plotnikova (ed.), *Лубянка: Сталин и НКВД-НКГБ-ГУКР «Смерш» 1939 – март 1946* (Moscow, 2006), p. 363.

[12] Newland, *Cossacks in the German Army*, p. 139.

[13] Alexander von Bosse, *The Cossack Corps* (Headquarters US Army European Command, 1950), pp. 6-17.

[14] Newland, *Cossacks in the German Army*, pp. 113-25.

[15] Naumenko (ed.), *Великое Предательство*, i, p. 41; A. Petrowsky, *Unvergessener Verrat!: Roosevelt - Stalin - Churchill 1945* (Munich, 1965), p. 159.

[16] Thorwald, *The Illusion*, pp. 166-78.

[17] Heinrich-Detloff v. Kalben and Constantin Wagner, *Die Geschichte des XV.*

Kosaken-Kavallerie-Korps (Münster, 1988), p. 14.

[18] George Fischer, *Soviet Opposition to Stalin: a case study in world war II* (Cambridge, Mass., 1952), p. 177.

[19] Thorwald, *The Illusion*, pp. 31-43; E.H. Cookridge, *Gehlen: Spy of the Century* (London, 1971), pp. 82-84.

[20] Erwein Karl Graf zu Eltz, *Mit den Kosaken: Kriegestagebuch 1943-1945* (Donaueschingen, 1970), pp. 144, 145-46, 207, 209.

[21] Thorwald, *The Illusion*, p. 193; Hans Werner Neulen, *An deutscher Seite: Internationale Freiwillige von Wehrmacht und Waffen-SS* (Munich, 1985), p. 320; Matthias Hoy (Ph.D. thesis), *Der Weg in den Tod: Das Schicksal der Kosaken und des deutschen Rahmpersonals in zweiten Weltkrieg* (Vienna, 1991), pp. 152-55, 473-76; Werner H. Krause, *Kosaken und Wehrmacht: Der Freiheitskampf eines Volkes* (Graz, 2003), pp. 202-6.

[22] Wilfried Strik-Strikfeldt, *Against Stalin and Hitler: Memoir of the Russian Liberation Movement 1941-5* (London, 1970), p. 210. For Krasnov's relationship with Vlasov, cf. Joachim Hoffmann, *Die Geschichte der Wlassow-Armee* (Freiburg, 1984), pp. 82-89, 94; B. Prianishnikoff, *Новопоколенцы* (Silver Springs, Md., 1986), pp. 206-7; Catherine Andreyev, *Vlasov and the Russian Liberation Movement: Soviet reality and émigré theories* (Cambridge, 1987), pp. 64, 132.

[23] Naumenko (ed.), *Великое Предательство*, i, pp. 108, 116. For Bocharov's career, cf. Alexandrov, *Офицерский Корпус Армии Генерал-Лейтенанта А.А. Власова*, pp. 211-14.

[24] Naumenko (ed.), *Великое Предательство*, i, pp. 80-82.

[25] Neulen, *An deutscher Seite*, p. 316.

[26] Newland, *Cossacks in the German Army*, pp. 117, 133-34.

[27] *Ibid.*, p. 141.

[28] Naumenko (ed.), *Великое Предательство*, i, pp. 88, 106-7. A detailed account of Domanov's checkered career is provided by Alexandrov, *Офицерский Корпус Армии Генерал-Лейтенанта А.А. Власова*, pp. 381-91. Domanov had served for a few years in the NKVD in the early 1920s, but nothing suggests that this affected his actions when in British custody during May 1945.

[29] The protracted and frequently arduous itinerary from Poland to Italy is described in detail by a participant, Mikhail Rotov (Naumenko (ed.), *Великое Предательство*, i, pp. 89-100).

CHAPTER VII
ASYLUM IN AUSTRIA

I recall snatches of conversations between old émigrés and the eternally mistrustful, ever 'on the look out' former Soviet citizens. As the first to have fled, we with fervent enthusiasm assured those, who many times had been deceived over their fate, deceived by people, that, before us unquestionably lay a peaceful life as ordinary citizens – yes, we affirmed, as emigrants, but in territory occupied by the army of the great civilized British monarchy, bound by close ties to our former Russian dynasty.[*]

– N. N. Krasnov

In September 1944, the German authorities allocated the *Kazachi Stan* a fresh asylum in Northern Italy, a region chosen because it was far removed from the Soviet line of advance, while being at the same time one of the few non-German territories still lying within the power of the rapidly dwindling Reich. From a military point of view, they could also prove useful in countering an increasingly troublesome threat to German communications posed by Italian partisans.

Across Poland, Germany and Austria moved the little Cossack 'nation', still with its train of wagons, cattle, horses and dromedaries. In Italy they were settled first at Gemona in Friuli, then at Tolmezzo in the Carnia. Before the Cossacks' arrival, land and houses had been temporarily appropriated for their use, which naturally aroused resentment amongst the inhabitants. With the ever-nearing advance of Allied armies up the peninsula, Italian partisans were becoming increasingly active. Once again the Cossacks established a vignette of life in a Don *stanitsa*, continuing primarily as a settlement rather than a military force, although as before their regiments fought when required against Communist partisans. Such was the situation in the spring of 1945, as the war drew to its close.[1]

Throughout the time of the Cossacks' migration to Italy, General Krasnov remained in Berlin, while his nephew Semeon Nikolaevich fulfilled the role of chief of staff at the *Kazachi Stan*. However, by

---

[*] N. N. Krasnov, *Незабываемое 1945-1956* (San Francisco, 1957), pp. 19-20.

February 1945 Berlin itself was threatened by the Red Army, and Peter Krasnov made his way south, joining the *Kazachi Stan* in Italy on the 12th of the month. He explained that he regarded himself as a guest, and would not interfere with measures authorised by the Field Ataman Domanov. Krasnov's role was almost entirely honorary at this time. Among other ceremonial activities he travelled into Croatia to visit the 15th Cossack Cavalry Corps, where he was once again received with acclaim by General von Pannwitz and his Corps.[2]

The old General was as ever accompanied by his wife Lydia. An Italian eyewitness later described the elderly couple, who lived for a while in the little town of Verzegnis near Udine. Observing Peter Krasnov walking in the streets,

> His wife often accompanied him, recalls Zorzut, the princess [in a complimentary sense] Lydia, whom he treated with chivalrous devotion, and who strolled about with a dignified air while acknowledging with kindliness and goodwill those ladies who greeted her in the street, deferential and overawed. 'This pathetic etiquette made one laugh', remarked the old sacristan in one of his letters, 'but the elderly couple possessed a genuine presence which the ironical emphasis of the situation could not efface: the lofty nature of their conjugal love and fidelity, the beauty of a shared life, of a love which revealed itself in their gestures, in their habits, and in the details of their daily life'.[3]

Near the Cossacks at Tolmezzo was a settlement of several thousand Caucasians: Georgians, Armenians, Azerbaidjanis, Ossetians and others. Their history and reasons for being in North Italy were similar in many ways to the circumstances of the Cossacks. They comprised detached units or survivors of national legions formed by the Germans with the ostensible purpose of liberating their homelands. When this became no longer feasible, some of the more martial units were employed on the Western front in France and the Low Countries, whilst many of the Azerbaijanis found themselves serving on the Italian front in the 162nd Turkoman Division, a front-line unit with a reputation for tough fighting. Scattered Caucasians were instructed by the Germans to settle in the Carnia. Their headquarters was at Paluzza, in the mountains some miles north of the Cossack settlement at Tolmezzo. Their discipline and organisation were much inferior to that of the Cossacks, possibly on account of the difficulty of imposing uniform order on a series of tribes speaking (it is said) seventeen separate languages, and ranging in religious belief from the Orthodox Christians of Georgia to the Shiite Moslems of Azerbaidjan. Like the Cossacks, during their peregrinations they had attracted numerous compatriots wandering individually or in groups through the chaos of central Europe. At the time it was believed that the Caucasians were responsible for scattered depredations and violence committed in the region against the inhabitants.[4] Owing to the difficulty of identifying individuals at the time, it is clear that crimes ascribed the Cossacks were more often than not perpetrated by ill-disciplined Caucasians.[5]

Years later, Harold Macmillan and some of his supporters asserted that the forced repatriations were justified as retribution for atrocities perpetrated by the Cossacks during their stay in Northern Italy and exodus into Austria. In order to establish this accusation, all mention of the presence – let alone activities – of the Caucasian levies in Italy is omitted in their accounts.

Sir Carol Mather, a former Conservative MP, devoted an entire chapter of his book to alleged brutalities perpetrated by the *Kazachi Stan* in Italy. Were the issue not so grave, it would be hard not to smile at his catalogue of horrors. Among other dismaying episodes, his readers learn that some Cossacks burned a hole in their living-room floor when cooking *prosciutto*; a Cossack cow was tethered in a garden, rather than housed in a stall; a Cossack unsuccessfully tried to milk a villager's cow; a group sowed potatoes in nearby fields and kept dromedaries, while others taught local girls Cossack songs; a further group perversely reprieved villagers wrongly suspected of having murdered Cossacks. Perhaps most dreadful of all, Cossacks in Montegliano 'did nothing wrong', while a captured partisan was invited to join Cossacks singing songs at a New Year's Eve party ... *und so weiter*.

In a couple of instances, Mather describes what were real crimes: that is, assuming they occurred and were indeed perpetrated by Cossacks, rather than Caucasian or German SS troops active in the region. Thus he was shown a funerary inscription at Imponzo commemorating a man allegedly 'battered to death' by Cossacks[*]. Among thousands of men stationed in a country of whose language they were ignorant, harassed at every stage by rival Italian bands of partisans (whose undoubted atrocities Mather is careful to suppress), it would be well-nigh incredible had no outrages occurred. However, given his overt aim of blackening the reputation of the Cossacks, combined with near total

---

[*] Even so serious a claim must be open to some doubt, in view of Mather's shameless conflation of alleged Cossack misdeeds with entirely distinct operations undertaken by German SS units in the region (cf. his *Aftermath of War*, p. 202).

ignorance of the facts, it is difficult to assign credibility to anything he writes.[*]

The dubious validity of Mather's aged witnesses, none of whom could speak Russian or German, and testifying half a century after the supposed events, is illustrated by an old lady's alarming description of General Krasnov's second-in-command:

> A man with a *barba bianca* [white beard], right down to his waist. So much hair on his face that you could only just see his eyes.

It is a little hard to recognise here the clean-shaven Major-General Semeon Krasnov – but when denigrating the Cossacks it is evidently not requisite to be overly particular.[6]

Yet more whimsical is the claim by Harold Macmillan's commissioned biographer Alastair Horne:

> In Northern Italy and Carinthia, where they were finally rounded up, the Cossacks - employed by the Germans to hunt down partisans in the last stages of the war - left an outrageous trail of murder and rape.[7]

So far as Carinthia is concerned, it is strange that this 'outrageous trail' passed entirely unnoticed at the time by British forces, to whom the Cossacks had surrendered on the first day of their arrival in Austria.

It was shortly after the Cossacks' arrival in Italy in the autumn of 1944 that Allied Force Headquarters at Caserta became alerted to their presence. Operating in Friuli at the time in a roving SOE unit was Patrick Martin-Smith. He was informed by local non-Communist partisans (*Osoppo*) that the Cossacks had established contact with them, with a view to collaboration with the Allies. Martin-Smith at once became excited by the possibility of persuading the Cossacks to cut the Villach-Udine railway line, one of the two main German lines of communication into Italy.[8]

His report reached Harold Macmillan at Allied Force Headquarters in October 1944, providing the Minister's first involvement in the Cossack problem. As he recorded in his diary on 11 October 1944:

> There are said to be 30,000 Russian prisoners of war working for the

---

[*] Mather might with advantage have consulted Pier Arrigo Carnier's *L'armata cosacca in Italia (1944-1945)* (Milan, 1965), and his *Lo Sterminio Mancato: La dominazione nazista nel Veneto orientale 1943-1945* (Milan, 1982), pp. 139-47. In his flowery account of the Cossacks during their sojourn in Italy, Claudio Magris recounts tales of the Cossacks in Italy acquired from local inhabitants, but fails to identify a single Cossack crime. This is noteworthy, because the author is unrelentingly hostile to the Cossacks, and General Krasnov in particular - as well as being an enthusiast for the Bolshevik coup in October 1917 (*Enquête sur un sabre* (Paris, 1987)).

Germans in northern Italy. These men want to desert to us, but want a guarantee that they will *not* be sent back to Russia. This is a delicate point, and we telegraphed to F.O. for their views. I fear that they will object, but it seems a pity not to get them over somehow' .[9]

The last thing the Soviets wanted was to accept the existence of an independent Russian military force fighting in collaboration with the Western Allies. When at about the same time the British government proposed formalizing the position of liberated Russian prisoners held in camps in England under the Allied Forces Act, the Soviets proved suspicious and obstructive in the extreme.[10]

Moving on, by the second week of April 1945 Field Marshal Alexander's armies had surged irresistibly forward, seizing Imola and Bologna. By the end of the month the Allies themselves were in a position to pounce on Tolmezzo.

It was 8th Argyll and Sutherland Highlanders who, on the night of 6 May, received orders to move against the Cossack Division. Advancing from the east along the mountainous valley of the Tagliamento, they left camp at dawn in full fighting order. When it soon became apparent that no resistance was likely to be offered, the Battalion pushed on at greater speed. By noon they were in Tolmezzo to find the birds had flown – 'probably back into Austria'. All they found of the departed legions were a few dispirited Turkomans. British troops were not displeased to find their entry so easy, and just after teatime came 'the best news of the war', as the Brigade War Diarist put it:

> The unconditional surrender of all German forces in the field had been confirmed. Unfortunately the B[attalio]n was not in a suitable position to celebrate but an extra beer issue was authorised. The evening passed very quietly.[11]

Further north, a Georgian unit surrendered, many of whose officers were princes, and whose commanding officer was a beautiful Georgian princess named Mariana. These noble Georgians lived in a romantic dream-world, soon to be destroyed forever. Only ten days before, Prince Irakly Bagration had knocked on the door of the British Embassy in Madrid, offering to arrange the surrender of a hundred thousand Georgians serving in the German army, provided guarantees could be given that they would not be sent to the Soviet Union. The Foreign Office instructed the Embassy not to reply.[12]

Meanwhile, where were the main bodies of Cossacks and Caucasians, who had apparently melted away from Tolmezzo? With the impending collapse of German power, arguments had swayed this way and that as to

the best course to be adopted in the circumstances. *Obergruppenführer*
Odilo Globocnik, the local Nazi commander, ordered them to stay put, but
the Cossacks paid little heed to his impotent threats and the Nazi leader
fled the scene.[13] Next, German officers commanding the Caucasian
Division disappeared one night, leaving a leading émigré, Sultan Kelich
Ghirei, in command. The exiles were free to decide their fate, but their
choice seemed distinctly limited. Eventually it was effectively made for
them.

Now that the final destruction of Nazi power was clearly only a matter
of days away, Italian partisans began operating increasingly openly, in
larger and better-equipped units. A formidable communist band led by a
Catholic priest appeared particularly threatening. One day the Cossack
military hospital in Amara was burned to the ground with many wounded
Cossacks inside.[14] Finally, on 27 April, three Italian officers came to the
Cossack commander General Domanov's headquarters in Tolmezzo,
demanding that the Cossacks surrender all their arms and withdraw from
Italian soil. Little inclined to place himself so totally at the mercy of such
enemies, Domanov agreed to lead his Cossacks from Italy, but declined to
give up their arms. The Italians agreed, and on 28 April virtually the whole
of the Cossack formation and a large detachment of Caucasians struck
camp and began the arduous march northwards.

They set off at midnight, bearing with them everything that could be
borne in wagons or on their backs. The mounted units came first, led by
Domanov's staff: first came the Don Regiment, then the Kuban, and after
them the Terek. Trailing behind these wound a seemingly endless column
of wagons, bearing supplies and personal possessions and as many of the
old, sick or very young horses could draw. Near the head of the column
drove a Fiat car carrying the aged General Peter Krasnov. Domanov
himself waited with his bodyguard regiment for a detached unit from
Udine to catch up with the main column. A rear guard of several hundred
Don and Kuban Cossacks was placed south of Tolmezzo to check the
partisans from launching an attack on the unwieldy column as it set off
northwards.

The withdrawal of the Cossacks into Austria was a journey of
appalling hardship and danger. In the early stages they had to fend off
attacks by the Italian partisans. Then, as they ascended the heights to
where the road winds perilously around the precipitous chasms of the
Plöckenpass, the weather also turned against them. Torrential rain fell
upon the struggling column, to be followed higher up by a prolonged
snowstorm. There were numerous deaths, first from partisan bullets, and
later from cold, or the precipitous, snow-covered trackway where a missed

foothold could be fatal. In the midst of the driving storm the Cossacks crossed the Austrian frontier and descended from the rocky fastnesses of the towering Hohe Warte, round wooded and boulder-strewn crags until they reached the shelter of the Gailtal. Late in the evening of 3 May advance units of Domanov's staff arrived in the first village in Austria, Mauthen-Kötschach. General Krasnov's Fiat had broken down, and was being towed by a transport bus. The trumpets of the bedraggled Don Regiment blared out defiantly from behind as two officers from the staff went forward to see what reception they would receive. After all, the Reich still stood, if shakily, and the Cossacks had been strictly forbidden to leave Italy.

An eighteen-year-old Austrian girl in Kötschach later described to me the arrival of 'a seemingly never ending column of horse drawn waggons laden with all kind of household gear, and accompanied by armed men, their women and children as well as some cows, fowls, pigs, and even camels'.[15]

It was accepted after discussion with the sympathetic local Gauleiter that the Cossacks should move on northwards to the valley of the Drautal. Thus, their destination, soon to be the scene of dramatic and tragic events, was chosen quite by chance.

The Cossacks accepted this arrangement, and for three days and two nights the serpentine column wended its way over the mountain pass and into Austria. In Mauthen, the first village in Austria, the railway hotel was placed at the disposal of the Cossack generals and staff. General Krasnov took up quarters there, and from his window witnessed with melancholy resignation scenes that presaged the end of all his hopes. The Cossacks, destitute of fodder for their beloved horses, were straggling on northwards, camping at night on the roadside wherever they happened to find themselves.

On 4 May, Domanov brought up the Cossack rearguard and joined Krasnov in the Mauthen Hotel Bahnhof. There they conferred on their next move. Meanwhile, the cavalcade of thousands of Cossacks with their baggage-train (it was the movement of a people rather than an army) streamed on northwards to the valley of the Drau. Crossing the Gailbergsattel, they moved slowly up the valley. A few miles upriver the land broadens out beneath the mountains, where the sleepy Carinthian town of Lienz stands among carefully-cultivated fields. Here at least was a place where there was room to erect tents and pasture their thousands of horses.[16] It was Easter, a day of hope, and the priests conducted services in the fields. 'Christ is risen!' cried the Cossacks, kissing each other in the meadows as they met.

The two Cossack leaders, Domanov and Krasnov, discussed long and urgently what should be done next. The choice was small, being virtually limited to the question of whether to surrender to the Americans or the British. Krasnov, who as an émigré had by far the greater knowledge of European affairs, urged that the British would view their case with more sympathy and understanding. It was they, after all, who had been the most ardent supporters of the White cause in the struggle against the Bolsheviks during the Civil War, and it had been Churchill, then Secretary for War, who was the most vociferous supporter of British military intervention on the anti-Communist side. Years had passed and times had changed, but surely English chivalry would come to the aid of a former ally in distress? Krasnov looked, too, to the influence of the Allied Commander-in-Chief in Italy, Field Marshal Alexander. For at the time that Churchill had been dispatching men and munitions to assist Denikin's armies, Alexander had been fighting the Bolsheviks in Courland, where Krasnov served in the White General Yudenich's Reserve. The Field Marshal still bore proudly a Russian Imperial order, bestowed on him by Yudenich, and must surely appreciate the Cossacks' predicament. Among the rank-and-file Cossacks there had even grown up a romantic legend that Alexander had, in his admiration for all things Russian, wooed and won a beautiful Russian bride.

To this Domanov, who had been a simple major in the Red Army, was not in a position to argue, and he acquiesced. It was decided to send the delegation back across the Plöckenpass to parley with the nearest British force. The party was headed by a General Vasiliev, who was accompanied by young lieutenant Nikolai Krasnov, great-nephew of the General, and an English-speaking Cossack lady, Olga Rotova. The latter both left first-hand accounts of these negotiations.

Hastily pinning a piece of white sheeting to their car as a flag of truce, the party set off southwards. As Olga Rotova thought, 'what was awaiting us ahead, God only knew'. But even as they began to leave the village, they were unexpectedly halted by a British armored car. On explaining their mission, they were sent on to Regimental Headquarters at Paluzza. There the Colonel in turn transferred them to Brigade Headquarters in Tolmezzo. It was somewhat disconcerting to find themselves back where they had started the week before, particularly as their uniforms were recognised by Italians who shook their fists and howled 'Cossack barbarians!' The building which had housed General Domanov's headquarters a week before was now that of Major-General Robert Arbuthnott, commanding the 78th Infantry Division.

Escorted inside, General Arbuthnott greeted the envoys politely. General Vasiliev asked whether he could speak privately with him, and Arbuthnott ushered the Russians into his office. He offered them seats, but Vasiliev, a former officer of the Emperor in the Cossacks of the Guard and a man of impressive personality and appearance, insisted on standing whilst he explained his purpose. Although Vasiliev spoke English, he and Arbuthnott were unwittingly speaking at sadly cross purposes.

Vasiliev explained that the Cossacks had no quarrel with the Western Allies, and only wished to continue their struggle against Bolshevism. In order to prosecute this aim, he requested that they be permitted to join General Vlasov. 'Who is this General Vlasov?' asked Arbuthnott. Vasiliev explained about the ROA, its hopes and plans. The Englishman replied: 'You must first hand over all your arms'.

Vasiliev enquired whether that meant they were to become prisoners of war. No, replied Arbuthnott, that term applied only to soldiers captured in battle; the Cossacks would be regarded merely as having voluntarily given themselves up.[*] This enigmatic distinction was mistakenly accepted by the Cossacks as implying a status less subject to arbitrary treatment than that of prisoners of war.

Before the important question of status could be discussed further, Brigadier Geoffrey Musson of 36th Infantry Brigade entered the room. At Arbuthnott's request, Vasiliev again explained the Cossacks' position. Musson waited until the latter had finished, and then repeated that it was essential the Cossacks be disarmed as quickly as possible. Vasiliev explained that he could not answer in this for General Domanov, and so, after a brief consultation, the two British generals declared that on the following morning they would attend at Domanov's headquarters at Kötschach and settle terms.

Knowing that Domanov and Krasnov would be impatiently awaiting their return, Vasiliev and his party were anxious to return across the pass as soon as possible. But Arbuthnott and Musson would hear nothing of this, and insisted that they stay for tea. In this more relaxed atmosphere, Arbuthnott asked young Lieutenant Krasnov some friendly questions

---

[*] The journalist Christopher Booker sought to belittle the reliability of Olga Rotova's description of the conversation with Musson and Arbuthnott by dismissing it as a 'subsequent account' (*A Looking-Glass Tragedy: The Controversy over the repatriations from Austria in 1945* (London, 1997), p. 154). Had he been able to read Russian, he would have learned that her source was her diary, which she kept on a daily basis. (Russian friends in Canada have made vigorous efforts to trace the current location of Olga's diary, so far without success).

about himself. Nikolai explained that he had left Russia as a baby with his parents, and thereafter lived in Yugoslavia. When war broke out he had served in King Peter's army against the Germans. He was taken prisoner, and was later offered and accepted the chance of joining an anti-Soviet Cossack unit. But he had refused to serve in Africa, as that would have involved serving against Russia's allies of the previous war.

Although in thus showing interest in his young guest's history, Arbuthnott's motive was undoubtedly simple curiosity coupled with good manners, it is important to remember that from his very first dealings with the Cossacks it was apparent to many within 5th Corps that the most distinctive element were patently not Soviet citizens.

Before their departure, Musson pressed on Olga Rotova, the interpreter, a large packet of tea, sugar and chocolate. He brushed aside her thanks, and, together with Arbuthnott, came into the street to see the party off. This demonstration of British goodwill greatly impressed the volatile Italian crowd: cries of 'evviva!' rent the air, and a girl, overcome with emotion, thrust a bouquet of lilies into Olga's arms. Escorted by British armored cars, General Vasiliev and his party drove back up the mountain pass to Kötschach, arriving at 9.30 p.m. at Domanov's Headquarters, where they reported to Generals Domanov and Krasnov on their mission. In the Cossack headquarters that night all stayed up late, vainly trying to prise deeper implications from the largely noncommittal replies of Arbuthnott and Musson.[17]

Next morning, half an hour earlier than expected, Brigadier Musson and his staff arrived at the Cossack headquarters. The meeting was held in the dining-room of the hotel occupied by Domanov. After handshakes all round, the discussion proceeded on a cordial note. The Cossacks, eagerly pinning extravagant hopes to any demonstration of British goodwill, noted that they did not appear to be treated as enemies or prisoners, but as colleagues in an administrative operation. Brigadier Musson's opening words appeared encouraging also: he told the Cossacks that they were to keep their arms while en route to their concentration area. A map was then spread out on the table, and he explained that all Russian forces must foregather in the Drau Valley – the Cossacks upriver between Lienz and Oberdrauburg, and the Caucasians downstream between Oberdrauburg and Dellach.

This was all that was discussed concerning conditions of the Cossack surrender. The Cossacks were relieved that the British appeared so understanding, and Brigadier Musson likewise felt that what might have been an awkward business had passed off very smoothly. As 36th Infantry Brigade War Diary explained, the Cossacks 'would have been still a force to be reckoned with if they had refused to capitulate and until that capitulation was complete we could not feel secure'. The serious business over, both sides took breakfast, drinking wine and chatting in friendly fashion.

Later in the day newspaper correspondents from the *Times* and the *Daily Mail* arrived to interview the Cossack leaders. They wanted to know how and why the Cossacks had left Russia and come all these hundreds of miles to Austria. Speaking through the interpreter Olga Rotova, General Domanov explained with the aid of a map how the Bolshevik regime had waged virtual war on the Cossack lands, how they had made the arduous journey from the Kuban and Don to Tolmezzo, not knowing where they were going nor what would happen to them, and determined only on one thing: that they should never again fall into the hands of Stalin. General Vasiliev had been similarly interviewed the day before, presumably by the same reporters. Regrettably neither of these fascinating interviews, nor the photographs taken at the same time, was published.

That evening the first formations of 36th Infantry Brigade descended into Austria. The two foremost battalions, 8th Argyll and Sutherland Highlanders and 5th Buffs, were assigned the tasks of controlling the Cossacks and Caucasians respectively. As the Russians moved into their allotted areas, the British never ceased to be intrigued by their picturesque appearance.

> As an army they presented an amazing sight. Their basic uniform was German, but with their fur Cossack caps, their mournful dundreary whiskers, their knee-high riding boots, and their roughly made horse-drawn carts bearing all their worldly goods and chattels, including wife and family, there could be no mistaking them for anything but Russians. They were a tableau from the Russia of 1812. Cossacks are famed as horsemen and these lived up to their reputation. Squadrons of horses galloped hither and thither on the road impeding our progress as much as the horse-drawn carts. It was useless to give them orders; few spoke German or English and no one who understood seemed inclined to obey. Despite this apparent chaos it was remarkable how swiftly and completely they carried out their orders to concentrate ... by next morning they were all in position – men, women, children, baggage, horses, carts, tyres and – camels![18]

***Kazachi Stan* camels in North Italy**

Initially, the administrative problem facing 36th Infantry Brigade appeared daunting. As General Musson subsequently explained to me:

> Commanders and staffs had a multitude of problems. Conditions were chaotic with the ending of hostilities, after a very rough winter, and the occupation of Austria. The Austrians were 'lost' and did not know where they stood. There were masses of people wandering about, some friendly and some hostile, all homeless and all with their own problems. Distances were great and conditions bad. (We had no helicopters in those days!). Our headquarters were on a wartime basis and we were working in tents or billets.

The numbers alone were formidable. A census was taken in the Cossack camp by the British authorities, and a 78th Division report of 16 May lists the Cossacks at Lienz as:

1533 officers
13847 Cossacks
4193 women
<u>2436 children.</u>

i.e. 22,009 in all.[19]

The Caucasians raised the number by a further 4,800, but for both these figures it was reckoned that a 10 percent deduction could be allowed, although the Cossacks' own estimates were considerably higher. Their reckonings varied from totals of 30,000 to 35,000, but as there had latterly been so many desertions and accessions it is impossible to say exactly how many were present in the Drau Valley in May 1945.[20] However, the figure for the Caucasians would appear to be about right, as one of their officers provides the figure of 5,000 as having been at Tolmezzo shortly before their removal to Austria.[21]

By the second week of May the Cossacks were concentrated in the valley between Lienz and Oberdrauburg. Through the encampments ran the turbulent river Drau, and a main road and railway line. In the central square of Lienz itself General Domanov and Colonel Alec Malcolm of the Argylls set up their respective headquarters in the Hotel Goldener Fisch.

On 2 May General Krasnov and his wife Lydia had been driven in their Fiat staff car to the hamlet of Piana d'Arta on the Italian side of the Carnian mountain range. There they spent a restless night, disturbed by echoing gunfire. Guards were posted against any assault by Italian partisans. Next day they pressed forward up the steeply winding road ascending to the Plöckenpass. It was late that evening that they arrived at the village of Kötschach-Mauthen, where quarters were arranged for the distinguished fugitives at the Van Gogh hotel beside the railway station. Meanwhile, the endless column of Cossacks rode on to the fertile area of the valley of the Drau between Oberdrauburg and Lienz.

Gazing down from his window in Mauthen on 4 May, the General was concerned to witness grave breakdowns of discipline among the retreating Cossacks. In particular, attacks on demoralised accompanying German troops provoked his indignation. Similar outrage was expressed by Colonel Bocharov, General Vlasov's liaison officer with the Cossacks. However, their anger achieved little to prevent such assaults.[22] Relief was aroused by news brought by General Domanov, who had returned under a white flag to confer with British troops of the 8th Argyll and Sutherland Highlanders, who were pressing hard on their heels. No doubt Domanov and his companion General Vasiliev believed the British General Arbuthnott's assurance to the General that there could be no question of the Cossacks' being delivered over to the Soviets. The contrast between the savage wintry weather of the snowbound Plöckenpass and the lovely flower-bespangled green of the Drau valley served also to endorse the harassed Cossacks' revived optimism. That evening Domanov held a champagne reception, which Krasnov however did not attend.

Krasnov was preoccupied at this time with a twenty-page letter he wrote in French to the Supreme Allied Commander, Field Marshal Alexander. In it he renewed the secret proposal received by AFHQ in the previous October, offering to deploy his Cossacks under Allied control. He further recounted at length the situation of the *Kazachi Stan*, and reminded Alexander of their common struggle against the Bolsheviks in Northwest Russia in 1919. Explaining that he no longer exercised any formal command over the Cossacks, he offered to assist in a liaison capacity with the British military. Happening to encounter a German general (according to another version, colonel) who spoke English and asserted that he was on his way to Alexander's headquarters, he entrusted the letter to him.

Amlacher Hof[*]

Although Krasnov wished to remain in his hotel at Kötschach, on 9 May the British transported him and his wife Lydia by staff car to a villa originally intended for Domanov, who was instead installed with his staff in the Hotel *Goldener Fisch* in Lienz.[23] The Krasnovs' dwelling for the rest of May was the Amlacher Hof at Amlach, a village not far from Lienz. The house is a handsome yellow-plastered mansion, which also provided ample room for members of the General's staff. There he settled down in what his wife Lydia described as a small but snug flat, where they talked of his devoting himself in his coming retirement once more to his literary work.[24] In later years a lady, a little girl at the time, recalled a visit Krasnov paid to her school in Peggetz camp. Under direction from their

---

[*] General Krasnov and his wife Lydia occupied the first-floor suite on the right.

young schoolmistress, the little girls excitedly repeated after her: 'Greetings, Mr. General!'[25]

Andrei Grigorievich Shkuro

Meanwhile another celebrated old émigré general had surrendered to the British. This was the colourful Kuban Cossack Ataman Andrei Shkuro, who had cooperated with General Krasnov during the turbulent year of 1918. During the Second World War he fulfilled a largely honorary position among the Cossacks, among whom he enjoyed immense popularity owing to his formidable military reputation gained during the Civil War, and archetypally flamboyant Cossack personality. Although he maintained cordial relations with the *Kazachi Stan* and 15th Cossack Cavalry Corps, he was formally attached to neither.[26] During the dying days of the Third Reich he was principally based in Vienna, having been appointed titular head of a Cossack reserve regiment. On 6 May he arrived at Kötschach, where he was reunited with the Krasnov family and General Domanov, commander of the *Kazachi Stan*.[27]

On 10 May he surrendered to the British 56th Recce Regiment, whose war diary records:

> At Rennweg the surrender of a Cossack Rft. Regt. was accepted, including the personal surrender of an old Cossack Gen. Schkuro, who had fought under Denikin.[28]

This further confirmed that there was widespread recognition within the 5th Corps that many of the most prominent Cossack commanders were White Russians, who were not subject to surrender to the Soviets under the terms of the 8th Army order of 13 March.

Between 16 and 20 May Shkuro's Reserve Regiment was moved from Tamsweg to the village of St. Michael, while he himself joined General Domanov and his staff at their quarters in the Hotel *Goldener Fisch* in Lienz. That these events were notified to 5th Corps headquarters as soon as they occurred, is confirmed by the fact that on 21 May Brigadier Low specifically included Shkuro's formation among those designated for handover to the Soviets: 'Following will be treated as Soviet nationals ... Res[erve] units of Lt-Gen Chkouro'.[29]

Of the White Russian generals whose handover was about to be requested by the Soviets on 11 May, Generals Semeon Krasnov (nephew of Peter) and Shkuro were living in the same building in Lienz under the eye of the local British command, while General Sultan Ghirei was held under guard with his Caucasian Division at neighbouring Oberdrauburg. Only General Peter Krasnov was housed apart from the *Kazachi Stan*, in his private quarters at the village of Amlach.

The Caucasians were moved to Grofelhof further down the valley, while the Buffs' headquarters was situated at nearby Dellach. The Caucasian leader, Sultan Kelich Ghirei, had surrendered on behalf of his motley band of followers at the same time as Domanov. Like Krasnov, Ghirei was an old émigré who had cooperated with the British forces of General Holman in the Civil War, and remained with Baron Wrangel until the failure of the last abortive raid launched from the Crimea in 1920. As heir to the medieval Tartar khans of the Crimea, Ghirei enjoyed great prestige among the peoples of the Caucasus. Soon after he and his followers were installed at Grofelhof, he assembled them, 'and made a speech to the effect that those who were able to try to leave as soon as possible – especially the young – and forget about the dream of freeing the Caucasus and the nations therein. He however was too old to continue and would honour his surrender and wait to see what was to happen'.

A number so exhorted seized opportunity of disappearing, which serves to illustrate the important fact that, although the Cossacks and Caucasians were technically prisoners, the British were unable to prevent large-scale desertions should they occur. The camps were not wired, and largely self-policed. Despite this, however, there were for the moment few absconders from the Cossack camp. The steep snow-topped mountains walling in the valley formed a daunting obstacle, as did the knowledge that they were in an alien country of whose language and people they were ignorant. A far greater consideration than this was that the Cossacks were banded together by a lively hope that they would be allowed to hold together as a community, and be permitted to find asylum somewhere in the free world.

It is important to realise that many intelligent Cossacks genuinely believed Britain and the United States would adopt a realistic attitude towards the Soviet Union once Germany had surrendered and the temporary bond of unity was dissolved. It should also be kept in mind how relatively recent were the events of the Russian Civil War. The vast cataclysm of the Second World War has produced a watershed sharply dividing the worlds before and after. Today the Russian Revolution seems a remote event, but in 1945 it was a story familiar and readily recalled by many.

Although too young to have served in the Great War, at 5th Corps Headquarters Brigadier Edward Tryon recalled only warm admiration for the Cossacks' gallantry during the Great War.[30] While more pressing events had long preoccupied their minds to the exclusion of a cause now dead, there were many in British military circles to whom the history of the Cossacks was far from unfamiliar.

Sophisticated men like General Krasnov did not imagine that the British would authorise an immediate onslaught on Red Army lines in Styria. But he did hope and expect that something might be done, not only to provide the Cossacks with asylum in the West, but also to enable them to keep together and so preserve their unique heritage.

Such was the man to whom the Cossacks looked for advice and inspiration to guide them out of their present troubles. Now, as has been mentioned, their camp had been joined by another figure from the heroic past – one almost equally celebrated, although of a very different character.

Ataman Shkuro left Russia in 1920 to join the emigration. At one time he took to performing daredevil feats on horseback at circuses in France, Germany, and England. He was also a trusted supporter and emissary of the heir to the Russian Throne, Grand Duke Kirill Vladimirovich, being active in the political and military wings of the White Russian emigration. Although he was often to be found deep in play at the roulette table, he was entrusted by leaders of the emigration with disposal and disbursement of substantial sums of money for the cause. Unsurprisingly, his name featured prominently in pre-war secret OGPU and NKVD reports to Moscow.

When Germany attacked the USSR, he came forward to volunteer his services. Lacking the moral and intellectual stature of Krasnov, Shkuro

nevertheless had a name to conjure with. A hundred tales of his bravery
and cunning were circulated wherever Cossacks gathered in their camps
or *stanitsas*, and he maintained what may be described as a roving
commission, visiting Cossack units everywhere. Notionally in charge of
the training regiment for the 15th Cossack Cavalry Corps, he did in fact
much as he pleased. This generally consisted in visiting the camps and
appearing in the center of any company when a vodka bottle was being
opened. His soldier's repertoire of bawdy jokes and songs was apparently
limitless. Colonel Constantin Wagner told me that he would not allow
Shkuro to approach his 1st Cossack Cavalry Division in Croatia, since all
his stories related to 'between here, and here' – indicating the waist and
knees. He felt that such language from a general was unbecoming and bad
for discipline; but to many simple Cossacks the visits of *batka* Shkuro
were a source of delight.

So it was that the Cossacks with heartfelt relief found asylum with the
good-natured British tommies. At last they were free from constant
harassment, and might look forward to settling with their families in some
distant land, safe from persecution by the Soviets or exploitation by the
Nazis.

Colonel Malcolm of the Argylls reported of Peggetz, 'This camp
accomodated about 5000 men, women & children, being the families and
followers of the Domanov Cossack Division'.[31] After all the perils to
which the Cossacks had experienced, culminating in the terrifying
crossing of the Carnian Alps, the camp appeared a veritable paradise. A
British soldier recalled how

> ... I was on one occasion required to attend a refugee camp at Peggetz. It
> was I believe an old German camp and had a fence round it, although it
> was broken in many places. It was located on the North bank of the river
> Drau across which was an old wooden bridge and directly opposite was
> an entrance into the camp. It was generally understood in the barracks
> that most of the refugees were White Russians, some of whom were
> Mongolians, but most of whom were known as Cossacks... I recall that,
> although the camp was very crowded, everyone was extremely well-
> behaved; they were just standing or sitting around. There was certainly
> no chaos. Everything seemed to be well-organised and in good order...
> Also when I went out on my patrols which took me along the banks of
> the river Drau, I remember seeing about a hundred or so Cossacks living
> in among their wagons on the other side of the river. They seem to me to
> be very happy and content and we used to exchange waves and smiles...
> I remember also seeing refugees coming out of the holes in the fence
> which surrounded the camp.[32]

During the three weeks following their arrival, the camp was organized by British soldiers and Cossacks working together. In no time at all the run-down camp had become an astonishing smoothly-run settlement – almost like a little country town. The beauty and spring tranquillity of the green valley of the Drautal, with its dramatic mountain setting, soothed troubled nerves. Combined with British kindliness and assurances of good faith, the sense of relief and happiness was universal. Major Davies, together with his interpreter Captain Butlerov, regularly moved around the camp, the former distributing chocolates to laughing children crowding round.

With characteristic efficiency, the British had in almost no time established all requisite facilities. Following the Cossacks' arrival, Rusty Davies arrived with a party of engineers to arrange stoves, shelter, and lavatories, all spades and other tools being secured nightly within his office in the camp. A football pitch was created in the center of the camp, while schools, theatrical groups, and further sports for young people and children were swiftly established. A hospital was established in a school building at nearby Nusdorf, and religious services were held daily in a hastily constructed church. The *Kazachi Stan* newspaper continued publication with British approval. Olga Polskaya, the editor's wife, noticed with amusement British tommies strolling around singing 'It's a long way to Tipperary' – a chorus taken up by the Cossacks, a Russian version having become popular during the Great War.[33] By 25 May all was in such good order that Davies was able to supervise elaborate preparations for a Cossack concert.[34]

Among survivors, those three weeks remained fixed in memory as a time of unsullied relief and contentment, after years of enduring cruel maltreatment at the hands of Stalin, Hitler, or both – to say nothing of their recent savage harassment at the hands of Italian Communist partisans. Under the genial protection of the British Army, all looked forward to a peaceful existence working in Canada, Argentina, Australia – anywhere lying far from the clutch of their Soviet persecutors.[35]

No one anticipated that, at long last liberated from persecution, the last and cruellest blow would come, with brutal suddenness, out of the blue from their kindly British 'protectors'.

---

[1] General V. Naumenko (ed.), *Великое Предательство: Выдача Казаков в Лиенце и Других Местах (1945-1947); Сборник материалов и документов* (New York, 1962-70), i, pp. 19-110, 256-58; Józef Mackiewicz, *Kontra* (Paris, 1957), pp. 81-91.

[2] A. Petrowsky, *Unvergessener Verrat!: Roosevelt - Stalin - Churchill 1945* (Munich, 1965), p. 223; Erich Kern, *General von Pannwitz und seine Kosaken* (Göttingen, 1964), photograph opposite p. 192.

[3] Claudio Magris, *Enquête sur un sabre* (Paris, 1987), pp. 36-37.

[4] N.N. Krasnov, *Незабываемое 1945-1956* (San Francisco, 1957), pp. 19-20.

[5] An April 1944 SOE report details the German strength in Slovenia as follows: 'According to sources which I think reliable this 20,000 is made up as follows: 10,000 Germans (at the very maximum); 7,000 Foreign legionaries (Mongols, Poles, Czechs, French, etc.); 3,000 Italian Fascists. Though nominally they belong to the 162 Legionary division, these troops for the most part have no real divisional organization and consist of detachments whose task is to garrison towns, communications, and other vulnerable points' (Thomas M. Barker, *Social Revolutionaries and Secret Agents: The Carinthian Slovene Partisans and Britain's Special Operations Executive* (Boulder, 1990), p. 106). The British author of this report went on to declare that 'For sheer opportunism, bestial cruelty, and general unstrustworthiness the Mongol legionary can have few equals'. Despite (or because of?) this, 'the [Communist] Partizans welcomed these proselytes into their ranks with a father's welcome for a a prodigal son' (p. 107).

[6] Carol Mather, *Aftermath of War: Everyone Must Go Home* (London, 1992), pp. 201-12.

[7] Alistair Horne, *Macmillan: 1894-1956* (London, 1988), p. 262. Horne was naturally unable to cite any evidence in support of his bizarre accusation.

[8] Letter of 3 March 1978 from Patrick Martin-Smith to the author.

[9] Harold Macmillan, *War Diaries: Politics and War in the Mediterranean January 1943-May 1945* (London, 1984), p. 550. The Russians in question were clearly the Cossacks of the *Kazachi Stan*, who had arrived in North Italy in the previous month (General V. Naumenko (ed.), *Великое Предательство: Выдача Казаков в Лиенце и Других Местах (1945-1947); Сборник материалов и документов* (New York, 1962-70) , i, p. 257).

[10] Nikolai Tolstoy, *Victims of Yalta* (London, 1977), pp. 100-11. '... the Soviet Union had an almost obsessive fear of its subjects abroad bearing arms' (p. 104).

[11] WO.170/4988. On 2 May General von Vietinghoff surrendered all German forces in Italy, thus ending the official military campaign.

[12] WO.170/4461; WO.170/47955.

[13] Naumenko (ed.), *Великое Предательство*, i, p. 114; ii, pp. 21-22; Pier Arrigo Carnier, *Lo Sterminio Mancato: La dominazione nazista nel Veneto orientale 1943-1945* (Milan, 1982), p. 248.

[14] Mackiewicz, *Kontra*, pp. 121-23; Naumenko (ed.), *Великое Предательство*, i, p. 258. For a further partizan atrocity, cf. Pier Arrigo Carnier, *L'armata cosacca in Italia (1944-1945)* (Milan, 1965), p. 245.

[15] Letter to the author of 25 May 1988 from Mrs Helga Forster.

[16] Naumenko (ed.), *Великое Предательство,* i, p. 135. For accounts of the terrible journey from Tolmezzo to Lienz, *v. ibid.,* pp. 112-19, 132-35, 258; ii, pp. 21-22; Peter J. Huxley-Blythe, *The East Came West* (Caldwell, Idaho, 1964), pp. 117-21; Carnier, *L'armata cosacca in Italia,* pp. 255-65; Mackiewicz, *Kontra,* pp. 125-33; T. Kubansky, *A Memento for the Free World* (Paterson, N.J., 1960), pp. 39-41; Evgenia Polskaya, *Это мы, Господи пред Тобою...* (Nevinnomyssk, 1998), pp. 21-24.

[17] Naumenko (ed.), *Великое Предательство,* i, pp. 20-28; Krasnov, *Незабываемое,* p. 19.

[18] WO.170/4461.

[19] Information kindly provided by Major R.C. Taylor, at the time a staff officer at Divisional Headquarters (letter dated 28 October 1980).

[20] Naumenko (ed.), *Великое Предательство,* i, pp. 139, 142, 170. A roll had been taken in Gemona seven months previously (8 September 1944) (*ibid.,* pp. 95-96).

[21] *Ibid.,* p. 101. On 26 May the Buffs compiled a census of the Caucasians (WO.170/4993).

[22] Naumenko (ed.), *Великое Предательство,* i, pp. 115-16; Polskaya, *Это мы, Господи пред Тобою...,* p. 24.

[23] Naumenko (ed.), *Великое Предательство,* i, pp. 139-40.

[24] *Ibid.,* p. 158.

[25] 'Воспоминания Галины Захарьевны Блашинской' in Elena Shupilina (ed., *Станичный Вестник* (Montreal, 2005), xxxix, p. 37). Galina miraculously escaped, but ten days later her 27-year-old schoolmistress was hurled into a truck and handed over to SMERSH. She was never heard of again.

[26] Naumenko (ed.), *Великое Предательство,* i,, p. 195.

[27] *Ibid.,* p. 95. On 2nd May he was at Völkermarkt (Lt. Gen. Pavlo Shandruk, *Arms of Valor* (New York, 1959), p. 273).

[28] WO.170/4396. Three days later, on 13th May, 8th Argyll and Sutherland Highlanders reported 'General Schkouro Commanding Cossacks at S. Mickael passed a letter by our L.O. to General Dominoff at Lienz giving details' (WO.170/4988).

[29] It is surprising that neither Lord Aldington nor his supporters ever attempted to distance him from responsibility for inclusion of Shkuro among those delivered to the Soviets, on grounds that that it was his formation, rather than he himself, that was ordered to be handed over. It is further telling that throughout a protracted exchange on this topic in court, while Aldington's responses were as evasive as may be, they never extended to distinguishing Shkuro from members of his Reserve Regiment whom he sentenced to be surrendered to the Soviets (Trial Transcript, Day 8). Perhaps he preferred conceding the point to inviting closer examination by seeking to evade it.

[30] 'Well, from the point of view that my own previous knowledge of the Cossacks had been going back to the First World War, and that was that they were a

jolly fine crowd of outfits' (Trial Transcript, Day 11).

[31] WO.170/4461.

[32] Constable Witness Statement, 1989 Aldington trial.

[33] Polskaya, *Это мы, Господи пред Тобою ...*, pp. 19, 25-27.

[34] Naumenko (ed.), *Великое Предательство,* i, p. 122; ii, p. 50.

[35] For a vivid account of life in the camp at Peggetz and its horrific conclusion by a survivor who was a little girl at the time, cf. Shupilina (ed.), *Станичный Вестник*, xxxix, pp. 37-41.

CHAPTER VIII
SOVIET CITIZENS AND OLD EMIGRANTS

Article 1.

All **Soviet citizens** [bold inserted] liberated by the forces operating under British command and all British subjects liberated by the forces operating under Soviet command will, without delay after their operation, be separated from enemy prisoners of war and will be maintained separately from them in camps or points of concentration until they have been handed over to the Soviet or British authorities, as the case may be, at places agreed upon between those authorities

Yalta Agreement, 11 February 1945[*]

What follows in the ensuing chapters was originally intended to be assembled within a single narrative, following chronological order. Eventually I found this course unsatisfactory: first, because the chapter was becoming inordinately long; second, and more importantly, because four interrelated strands of the narrative cover aspects more readily followed if examined independently. They are as follows.

1. General Keightley's secret compliance with the Soviet request for the handover of senior White Russian émigré officers, together with large numbers of refugees who were likewise notoriously not Soviet

---

[*] FO.916/1189. Note that the terms of the agreement do not envisage use of force, and are exclusively concerned with repatriation of Soviet citizens. Furthermore,
'If it were a lawful handing over, the Yalta Agreements were legally superfluous, whatever their diplomatic value in securing an easing of our relations with the USSR. If the handing over was a violation of the laws of war, the Yalta Agreements would not remove the taint of illegality, but only advertise it to the world, once the Agreements were published. For this legal issue, the question of the knowledge of the UK authorities as to the likely fate of the Soviet nationals handed over to the various Soviet commands in occupied Europe was relevant... But the deliberate handing over of persons to another State in the knowledge that most of them would be, if not killed outright, grossly maltreated, is an example of known, but not desired, consequence with which the criminal law of most States in familiar' (Michael A. Meyer and Hilaire McCoubrey (ed.), *Reflections on Law and Armed Conflicts: The Selected Works on the Laws of War by the late Professor Colonel G.I.A.D. Draper, OBE* (The Hague, 1998), p. 259).

citizens: a concession contrary alike to the wording of the Yalta
Agreement, policy directives of the Allied governments, and
consequent orders transmitted to 5th Corps in Austria by Allied
Force Headquarters in Naples.
2. Covert obstruction by 5th Corps Headquarters of the Allied move
to evacuate *all* Cossacks to safety in the American zone of
occupation in Austria.
3. Policy secretly adopted by 5th Corps, contrary to orders from
higher command, to employ brutal force to dispatch thousands of
Cossack men, women, and children into the merciless hands of
SMERSH. As will be shown, this atrocity arose as a direct
consequence of the 5th Corps conspirators' overriding
determination to extract the White officers from their thousands of
followers, in order to ensure the officers' delivery to their vengeful
enemies.
4. The part played by Harold Macmillan in the unfolding tragedy.

It is unavoidable that these four chapters, unravelling as they do in
detail sinister circumstances surrounding the Cossack handovers, break
the narrative flow of General Krasnov's colourful life. Readers who wish
to pursue his career uninterrupted may if they choose pass on to Chapter
Eleven, where the narrative chronicle is resumed. On the other hand, the
unique extent of the conspiracy, combined with its subsequent official
cover-up, is so extraordinary that I imagine most readers will wish to get
to the bottom of it.

These distinct aspects of a conspiracy to perpetrate what is
undoubtedly the greatest war crime in British history are closely
interwoven within the space of three hectic weeks. By their nature,
conspiracies (especially one of this complexity) involve intricate
deception during their perpetration. In the case of the present study,
confusion has been compounded by publication of a succession of official
and semi-official 'reports' and books, whose principal intent has been to
distort the facts and suppress incriminating evidence. Normally, past
disinformation of such a nature may be safely ignored. However, several
of these publications have received official government imprimatur, and
their conclusions remain widely accepted in Britain and elsewhere as
authoritative. At the same time, my previous book on the subject *The
Minister and the Massacres* was removed from most public and university
libraries. In consequence, I have little choice but to examine the evidence
as comprehensively and scrupulously as possible. While I find this
detective work fascinating, readers who prefer to follow the ongoing

narrative without intermission may as I say choose to pass over this and the three ensuing chapters.

A remarkable array of fresh evidence has become available to me since publication of my previous book on this subject over thirty years ago. Among these revelations, the most significant is probably the extensive range of documents from Soviet archives, made available to me through personal intervention of the late President Yeltsin, and for the most part here made public for the first time. Also revealing is the range of testimony provided at the notorious Aldington libel hearing in 1989, and its aftermath. Yet again, the U.S. National Archives, which have not been subjected to extensive 'weeding' comparable to that applied to records held by its British counterpart, have yielded copies of important archival material covertly removed at an early stage from British records.

Readers may incidentally be intrigued to read Lord Aldington's explanation of this disappearance of compromising contemporary signals.

> I can say what I have been told - that when 5th Corps headquarters left Austria, I think to be disbanded, at the end of the year [1945], there was an accident in the night, a wall fell down or something. Many of the trucks in which the documents were, were damaged.[1]

It seems that the wall fell with ingenious selectivity, its bricks destroying signals (such as the 6 March 1945 AFHQ screening order), which were almost exclusively those likely to be harmful to the reputation of 5th Corps command, while others neutral or apparently favourable to forcible repatriation escaped unscathed. It is unfortunate that, beyond Lord Aldington's assertion, there appears to be no evidence of the existence of the collapsing wall and its selective destruction of single sheets from Corps records.

We now return to the situation in Austria in the second week of May 1945. As I say, readers may feel that the narrative is straying from the life-story of General Krasnov. However, it is impossible to account for his terrible end without understanding the murky conspiratorial circumstances which brought it about. In fact, this and the ensuing three chapters might have been reduced to two or three pages had Harold Macmillan not issued his fateful 'verbal directive' to General Keightley, or had the latter obeyed repeated orders from his military superiors to screen Cossacks before their delivery to SMERSH, and abstain from use of violent force to compel their return. Again, had 5th Corps not obstructed arrangements concerted by Eisenhower and Alexander to evacuate the Cossacks to the American zone of Austria on 20-21 May, this story would again have drawn to a summary close on a largely or even wholly happy note.

The fact is that Generals Krasnov, Shkuro, and their fellow émigré officers represent throughout these machinations the largely ignored elephant in the room. Despite their central importance to the events that follow, *their very existence is suppressed in every signal emanating from 5th Corps or Harold Macmillan to their superiors.* Even Lord Brimelow, in 1945 a relentlessly cold-blooded advocate of forced repatriation, in the late 1980s privately posed this disquieting query to his colleagues in the British Government cover-up:

> I have found no trace of or reference to the appeals of the emigre Cossacks to Alexander etc. What happened to them?

The allusion is primarily to two lengthy letters General Krasnov wrote to Field Marshal Alexander on 8 and 24 May. No allusion to them is to be found in the relevant war diaries. In fact, we know on impeccable authority that one or both was passed by 5th Corps command directly into the hands of SMERSH. As will now be shown, the terrible events which occurred during the last days of May and first of June resulted from Keightley's ruthless determination to accede to the Soviet demand of 11 May for Krasnov, Shkuro and a score or so other emigrant generals and officers. The SMERSH list which Brigadier Tryon gave to General Keightley is also absent from British files – although I am now able to cite a SMERSH report reflecting the original, which confirms the accuracy of Brigadier Tryon-Wilson's memory of the exchange.

In the event a horrifying degree of brutality was employed during the first days of June in order to hand over thousands of Cossacks to their Soviet persecutors. As will be shown in Chapter Thirteen, during this operation several hundred casualties were inflicted by British soldiers on their helpless victims, a large proportion of whom were old men, women and children. While it is incontrovertible that these atrocious operations were concealed at the time from higher command, shortly after the event Field Marshal Alexander and General McCreery (commanding the 8th Army) acquired an inkling of outrages against humanity perpetrated under their respective commands. Alexander's Chief of Staff, General Sir William Morgan, told me when we met in September 1974 that reports of atrocities filtering through after the event 'caused Alex to hit the roof'.

Count Ariprand von Thurn-Valsassina, whose castle at Bleiburg was situated within 5th Corps command, acted as interpreter for Brigadier Pat Scott of 38th Infantry Brigade and Field Marshal Alexander on 5 June 1945 during the latter's visit to Austria. Alexander expressed his indignation at the brutal handover of the Cossacks to their Bolshevik foes, and his resentment at the way in which 'politicians' had taken the matter out of his hands to perpetrate a betrayal that should never have occurred. Although Alexander was not specific in his charge, he was in a position to know better than anyone that the sole politician to have played any part in authorizing the tragedy was Harold Macmillan.[2]

Immediately after the brutal Cossack handovers in Austria, Alexander arrived for a tour of inspection of 5th Corps zone. Evidence makes it clear that his primary purpose was to call a halt to the atrocious operation. Eleven years later, young Nikolai Krasnov was informed by his wife and mother that

> Suddenly, on 4 June, a new order arrived: All those who had lived outside the limits of the Soviet Union since before 1939 were not subject to repatriation. Such persons were to be considered DPs.[3]

It was on the same day (4 June) that Field Marshal Alexander did indeed arrive in Austria, where he belatedly called a halt to the operations. That he was author of the intervention was unknown to the Krasnovs, then or later. No record of Alexander's issuance of this order on the day of his arrival is to be found in the relevant war diaries (that collapsing wall again?), but first-hand evidence establishes that it was urgently transmitted by him on the spot in the form of oral commands over field telephones.[4]

Again, the Field Marshal's horrified reaction was confirmed to me by Louise Buchanan, who as a young girl was close to the Field Marshal's family in Northern Ireland. When Alexander returned home on leave in 1945, Mrs. Buchanan was witness to much uninhibited conversation:

> Certainly the return of ... the Cossacks was mentioned and I remember being puzzled by hearing that 'Alex's protests were absolutely ignored and how sick and furious it made him'. Like Wavell & Tedder, he was something of a romantic in his soldiering, you know. And that is hard to explain in 1980. Something stemming from a boyhood ideal of the 'parfit, gentil knight – sans peur et sans reproche!'[5]

Field Marshal Alexander

Alexander toured 5th Corps command on 4 and 5 June, where he received harrowing first-hand accounts of the betrayal from indignant British officers. He shared their outrage, intervening on the spot to forbid further use of force, and ordered rigorous checking of any further claims to non-Soviet citizenship.[6]

While there can be no doubt that the wool was largely pulled over his eyes, the Field Marshal subsequently obtained more than a glimpse of the extent of cruelties nominally perpetrated under his authority. He was *par excellence* a commander, not only of outstanding military talent, but much loved among all ranks of the Allied armies as indeed a *chevalier sans peur et sans reproche*.[7] Winston Churchill regarded him with particular affection and respect. As his physician Lord Moran recalled,

> The P.M. can never say no to Alex, whatever he asks; he keeps a place for him in his heart, apart from the others ... What he loved in Alex was that he had justified his own feelings about war, tried them out in the field and made sense of them. Alex had redeemed what was brutal in war, touching the grim business lightly with his glove. In his hands it was still a game for people of quality. He had shown that war could still be made respectable ... Winston drew a clear line between Alex's gallant bearing and the blind courage of a man like Gort. 'Dainty,' 'jaunty' and 'gay' were the terms he chose for his knight errant as he flitted across the sombre scene. Here Winston's instinct was sound.[8]

With regard to the Cossacks, Alexander's deep-rooted concern to uphold what he termed 'the etiquette of war' was doubtless increased in their case by the fact that 26 years earlier he had been appointed to command the Baltic *Landeswehr*,[9] which in 1918 fought the Bolsheviks in collaboration with the White Russian army of General Yudenich.[10] Throughout his military career he retained strong feelings of loyalty to his former comrades, proudly bearing alongside his British and foreign decorations the Order of St. Anne conferred on him by Yudenich,[11] taught himself Russian and German, and continued wearing his jaunty *Landeswehr* field cap while commanding Allied armies in World War II. Although he possessed no means of knowing, he may well have assumed (correctly) that former comrades were likely to been found among officers of the 15th Cossack Cavalry Corps, now held in Austria.[12]

When later that summer Alexander declared to his friend Field Marshal Alan Brooke that 'So far I have refused to use force to repatriate Soviet citizens',[13] he was as ever being entirely truthful.

All relevant orders emanating from him expressly or implicitly (reflecting previous orders) prohibited use of force to repatriate the Cossacks, and rigorously stipulated retention of non-Soviet citizens.[14] How then did 5th Corps command come to feel entitled to perpetrate what (it must be reiterated) was at once the cruellest, most unnecessary, and least accountable war crime in British military history?[15]

We turn now to a British general of markedly contrasted character to Field Marshal Alexander. Lieutenant-General Charles Keightley is a key figure in the conspiratorial events occurring in British-occupied Austria during the months of May and June 1945. As commander of the British 5th Corps, he had proved a capable officer, valued by his superiors for his decisiveness and dash, but whose character was marred by a streak of coldness and arrogance that could, if occasion arose, descend into callous brutality. Count Thurn-Valsassina, who acted as his interpreter at the time, subsequently described him to me as being 'like the worst type of Prussian officer'.

At the same time, his outwardly forceful character may have concealed an unsettling degree of social unease, illustrated by the following entertaining vignette. On 12 May 1945, shortly after he had led 5th Corps into Austria, Keightley came upon a retreating column of the 6th Terek Cossack Regiment. Their Colonel was the tall and distinguished Prince zu Salm-Horstmar. As they chatted briefly, the Prince was amused to note that the General was surreptitiously shifting his position on the hillside in order to bring himself onto a level with his taller interlocutor.[16]

Lieutenant-General Sir James Wilson, who served in the Rifle Brigade in Carinthia at the time, told me that Keightley was (as I jotted down while he spoke)

> ... not popular. Out for self with superiors, rather than concerned with subordinates. Personally ambitious, and likely to jump at chance to ingratiate himself with influential superior.

This assessment was widespread. Major J. A. Friend informed me that

> My Father was the last pre-war Cavalry Commander in Cairo when we controlled the Middle East. Charles Keightly was his Brigade Major. He had very little behind him other than ambition... Keightly was an able man, but considered that, as long as he carried out orders, his career was safe-guarded.[17]

Lieutenant-General Charles Keightley, 'the Smiling Snake'.

Keightley's reputation as a coldly ambitious commander followed him into the post-war period. In Lord Halifax's diary account of a visit to Germany in 1948, he describes a meeting with the General, mentioning in passing that he was nicknamed 'Killer' Keightley by his officers and men.[*] Such a character could prove useful under battle conditions, but potentially dangerous in other contexts. In 1954 Rear-Admiral P. W. Brock, Flag Officer in the Middle East, worked close to Keightley, who was by then Commander-in-Chief Middle East Land Forces. Brock described him as a 'professional good-fellow; known to his own staff as 'The Smiling Snake''. Ruthless drive in battle, failure to suppress arrogance towards his subordinates,[18] a degree of social unease, a narrow intellect, and a concern to ensure professional advancement by ingratiating himself with accessible politicians – such appear to have been among Keightley's less attractive characteristics. It seems clear that the duplicitous aspect of his nature arose, not from concern with political issues *per se*, but rather to engage the favour of politicians in a position to assist his advancement.

Having set the scene, we now return to the gathering tragedy in Austria.

On 10 May, shortly after the arrival of his Corps in Austria, Keightley and his chief of staff Brigadier Toby Low paid a formal visit to Voitsberg in the newly-occupied Soviet zone, where they conferred with the neighbouring Red Army commander, Lieutenant-General Dreer of the 6th Guards Corps. Boundaries were agreed between their respective areas of occupation,[19] and possibly a request in general terms for handover of the Cossacks was presented to the British commander. As Low later recalled,

---

[*] Reference kindly provided by Andrew Roberts. The epithet was confirmed by Major Patrick Waller, then serving with 12 Lancers in Austria, who informed me that 'the soldiers' nickname was "Killer Keightley". Not a happy nickname for a general!!'

this occurred over a lavish luncheon in an open field, with entertainment provided by a troupe of dancing girls flown in from Moscow.[20]

Dismayed by the quantity of vodka obligatorily consumed at such meetings, on his return Keightley told his second Chief of Staff (A/Q), Brigadier Tryon (in later years Tryon-Wilson): 'I'm not going up there again. You're next!'. Accordingly, at the ensuing appointment next day Tryon travelled with a driver in a jeep to Voitsberg. At a similarly lavish luncheon held again in the open field, Tryon was approached by a Soviet officer, undoubtedly a member of SMERSH, the organization whose principal task at this time was entrapment of the vast number of Russians at large in Western Europe.[21] This officer explained to Tryon that the Soviets were particularly anxious to gain possession of a number of senior Cossack officers understood to be in the British zone of Carinthia, and presented the Brigadier with a typed list of some twenty names. In successive conversations with me (several being tape-recorded), Tryon-Wilson was emphatic that this list of 'wanted' Cossack officers included about half a dozen whose names were picked out in capital letters. He was particularly struck by that of General Shkuro, in view of the fact that he was 'the old boy who had the CB'. In the first official 'Cowgill Inquiry' report published in 1988, of which Tryon-Wilson was co-author, he emphasized that the list handed to him on 12 [recte 11] May 1945[*] 'included several names picked out in capital letters whom Brig. Tryon-Wilson believes included the 'White Russian' heroes of the Civil War, Gens Krasnov, Shkuro and Sultan Kelitsch-Ghirei'.[22]

This detail bears out the remarkable reliability of Tryon-Wilson's memory. In the following month Viktor Abakumov, head of SMERSH, sent a report of the Cossack generals' handover to Beria, in which the list singles out eight leading Cossack generals (including Krasnov, Shkuro and Sultan Kelitsch-Ghirei), whose names are indeed as in the list described by Brigadier Tryon-Wilson distinguished by capital letters.

Abakumov's report confirms Tryon-Wilson's memory in another striking respect. On 20 August 1987 the Brigadier, in response to an enquiry by Lord Aldington, included these details.

> **The list contained some 20 to 25 names** ... What I do remember clearly about the list is that **it contained some 5 names which were in block capitals as against the remainder in normal type** [bold inserted]. I can

---

[*] The date has often been given as the 12th, but Brigadier Tryon-Wilson was consistent in his early conversations with me that his visit to Voitsberg occurred the day following Keightley's journey there on the 10th. For practical purposes the difference is immaterial.

only conjecture that the names in block capitals referred to the White Russian Generals or Emigrés.

That the total number of names of 'wanted' Cossack officers on the SMERSH list comprised 20-25 in Tryon-Wilson's recollection, of whom about five were singled out in capital letters, tallies too closely with corresponding figures in Abakumov's contemporary report to represent mere coincidence. For the latter specified the total number of 'wanted' Cossack leaders as a precisely comparable figure:

> I report that at the end of May on Austrian territory there were handed over to the Soviet command 20 White Guardists who were thereupon arrested and delivered to the Main Command of "SMERSH" ...

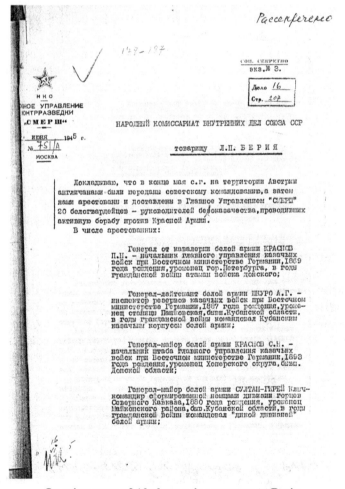

Opening page of Abakumov's messsage to Beria

That Tryon recognized the most prominent names within three days of the Cossack surrender might strike the reader as unlikely. However, this would be to ignore the dramatic effect their colourful prisoners exerted on soldiers of all ranks within 5th Corps. It has been seen that on 8 May General Arbuthnott, commanding 78th Infantry Division, and Brigadier Musson, commanding 36th Infantry Brigade, to whom the main body of Cossacks (*Kazachi Stan*) had surrendered, obtained first-hand accounts of the Cossacks from the White Russian General Vasiliev and the elderly General Krasnov's great-nephew Nikolai. Arbuthnott gained a very favourable impression of the Cossacks, and was shortly afterwards prominent among those senior officers in 5th Corps who raised vigorous objection to their betrayal to the Soviets. It was about the same time that General Krasnov wrote his lengthy appeal to Field Marshal Alexander described earlier.[23] He gave the letter to a German officer who claimed to possess means of passing it to the Field Marshal. The German must however have become a prisoner-of-war within the next twenty-four hours, when the letter would inevitably have passed into the hands of his captors. (The purpose of his mission would have been defeated had he retained it). Given its significance, it is unlikely that any untoward delay was incurred in forwarding it to 5th Corps Headquarters. By 11 May, it is consequently more likely than not that Keightley had seen the letter (which was written in French), and become familiar with the status of Krasnov in particular and the Cossacks generally.

On his return from Voitsberg, Tryon restored his befuddled wits (he had eventually managed after each toast to empty his glass surreptitiously onto the ground) with a plunge into the icy waters of the Wörthersee, before reporting to Keightley, to whom he handed the list. Aware that, with one exception (General Domanov), none of the principals featured on it was a Soviet citizen, and hence not liable to repatriation under the Yalta Agreement, Keightley expressed indignation at what he regarded as Soviet effrontery in submitting the demand, declaring emphatically that it would happen only 'over my dead body!' That the British command in Austria initially objected to handing over the Cossack officers is confirmed not only by the testimony of the SMERSH representative at subsequent negotiations (see Chapter 12 *infra*), but also by General Shtemenko, at the time Chief of the Red Army Main Operations Directorate, who recalled in his memoirs that

> The gang of enemies of our motherland who had finally fallen into the hands of the law was soon swollen by new members. In the foothills of the Alps some ancient enemies of the Soviet regime were discovered: Generals P. N. Krasnov, A. G. Shkuro, K. Sultan-Ghirei, and others...

With great losses they slowly made their way to the British lines and, considering that both the British and Americans would soon be waging war against the Soviet Union, they offered them their services. But they had guessed wrong... The Soviet Government made a firm [*i.e.* official] representation to our allies (*Советское правительство сделало тогда решительное представление*) in the matter of Krasnov, Shkuro, Sultan-Ghirei, and other war criminals. The British delayed a little (*Англичание немного повременели*); but since neither old White Guard generals nor their troops were worth much, they put them into trucks and delivered them to the Soviet authorities.[24]

The 'delay' to which Shtemenko referred can only be that elapsing between Keightley's initial opposition to compliance with the SMERSH demand, and his contrasted agreement nearly a fortnight later. The Soviet General's account also confirms that a direct request was issued and eventually fulfilled for the named émigré generals in particular. As a loyal protégé of Stalin's security chief Lavrenty Beria, Shtemenko was well-placed to be informed of secretive circumstances surrounding the surrender of the White generals – as indeed his account confirms he was.[25]

Keightley's exchange with Tryon raises several telling points. It confirms that the presence of the leading émigré Cossack generals was already known at 5th Corps Headquarters, and that Keightley anticipated a cruel fate for them were he to comply with the SMERSH demand. Equally, he initially envisaged no problem likely to arise from responding with a firm refusal.

Within 48 hours, however, his attitude had diametrically altered, and thenceforward he remorselessly disobeyed successive orders from his superiors in order to pursue a policy designed to ensure, come what may, that the Soviets obtain their prey. This shadowy conspiracy has been shrouded in secrecy and misrepresentation for the past three-quarters of a century, and only now is it possible to reconstruct events with a major degree of certitude. The extent of Keightley's drastic *volte-face* is revealed by the fact that his initial reaction not only reflected military standards of honour and decency (Field Marshal Alexander's 'etiquette of war'), but endorsed the directive issued by 8th Army on 13 March 1945, which laid down that

All persons of undoubted Soviet Citizenship will be repatriated irrespective of their own wishes.

In cases where nationality is in doubt, personnel concerned will be sent to 373 PW Camp [in Italy] for adjudication.[26]

Although the ruling was undoubtedly intended *inter alia* for 5th Corps, no record of its receipt has survived in the Corps war diary.

Since Keightley had recognized some of the names singled out in the Soviet list as those of prominent émigré generals, his instinctive personal reaction was confirmed by the second stipulation.[27] So what unanticipated contingency brought about his abrupt change from humanitarian concern to obsessive determination to comply with the Soviet demand, regardless of Allied policy? That this transformation reflected some higher political consideration rather than military pragmatism is evinced by the startling extent to which he henceforward flouted his orders, in the process deliberately deceiving his superiors at 8th Army and above, in order to dispatch the Cossack officers to death or slavery.

Here it may assist to outline the chain of command. Allied Force Headquarters in the Mediterranean was established in the huge former royal palace of Caserta, situated outside Naples. The Supreme Allied Commander-in-Chief (SACMED) was Field Marshal Sir Harold Alexander, whose command was Allied Force Headquarters, abbreviated as AFHQ. Allied command in north Italy was entrusted to the American General Mark Clark, commanding 15th Army Group, whose headquarters was situated outside Florence. His command included the British 8th Army, controlling the north-east region of Italy and part of southern Austria, commanded by Lieutenant-General Sir Richard (Dick) McCreery. Finally, the 8th Army occupied the southern region of the Austrian province of Carinthia occupied by the British 5th Corps under Lieutenant General Charles Keightley, together with north-eastern Italy facing the Yugoslav frontier, which was held by 13th Corps commanded by Lieutenant-General John Harding. These two corps were divided by the massive range of the Carnian Alps – a striking geographical feature which may in some degree explain how Keightley and his chief of staff were enabled to conduct a policy concealed from higher command in Italy.

Palace of Caserta (Alexander's headquarters at AFHQ)

In accordance with military practice, orders and reports were normally passed up and down from one command to another. Thus, General Keightley received his orders from McCreery at the 8th Army, even though they might merely repeat those which Mark Clark at 15th Army Group had in turn received from AFHQ. An instruction, too, could be copied to a subordinate command, which might be expected to fulfil it. On the other hand, higher command could on occasion bypass this procedure, while keeping the chain of command informed.

Once the crisis with Tito's regime (described in the next chapter) had been resolved, repatriation of Soviet citizens was authorized, with the major proviso that this should only occur where they could be sent home without use of force. Alexander's concern to free 5th Corps of responsibility for the Cossacks was directly related to preparations for conflict with the Yugoslavs. As will also be shown in the next chapter, Alexander and Eisenhower swiftly concerted measures for evacuating *all* Cossacks to safety in the US zone of Germany.

Consequently, late on the evening of 21 May, the 8th Army sent this puzzled query A 4073 to AFHQ.

> Reference your FX-75383 dated 14 stating all Russians to be handed over to Soviet Forces and SHAEF 399 Fwd 21870 stating Cossacks accepted by [US] 12 Army Group.
>
> Request earliest information whether approved policy is to despatch to SHAEF or to endeavour to secure direct return to Russians by Eight Army negotiations.[28]

In response, AFHQ issued this fresh policy order the next day:

> Ref your A 4073 of 21 May asking for policy re Cossacks.
>
> 1. all who are Soviet citizens and who can be handed over to Russians without use of force should be returned direct by Eighth Army.
>
> 2. any others should be evacuated to 12 Army Group.
>
> 3. definition of Soviet citizen is given in AFHQ letter CR/3491/G1-British of 6 May [*recte* March] addressed to 15 Army Group and Main Eighth Army. ref your A 4073 of 21 May asking for policy re Cossacks.[29]

With the immediate Yugoslav crisis over, that evening Alexander sent this modification of the foregoing order to the 8th Army and 5th Corps:

> You have authority to pass Cossacks direct to Russians provided force has not repeat not to be used.[30]

So it was that, by the morning of 23 May, General Keightley was in receipt of *two* AFHQ orders prohibiting use of force to repatriate

Cossacks. The first additionally reminded him in very specific terms of the requirement to screen and retain non-Soviet émigrés in accordance with the March AFHQ ruling. As will be shown below, these humane orders were never rescinded.

These directives were presumably known to Major-General de Fonblanque, when he travelled as 5th Corps representative to meet the Soviet delegates at Wolfsberg on the afternoon of 23 May. Unfortunately, minutes of the meeting are absent from the 5th Corps War Diary, as are those of an earlier one also held by de Fonblanque on the 21st.[31] However, since we know that it was only at a subsequent conference on 24 May that 5th Corps finally ratified a formal agreement to surrender the Cossacks to their enemies, discussions at the two earlier conferences must of necessity have been conducted on a provisional basis.

Responsibility for the delay in finalizing the agreement lay entirely with the Soviets. This might appear odd, given their relentless determination to lay hands on the Cossacks as a whole, and the White émigré generals in particular. However, Soviet evidence shows that the problem arose from administrative, and still more logistical, problems of dealing with so large a body of men desperately hostile to Soviet power. In the event, the Cossacks' reception was handled by 57th Red Army at Judenburg, where they were then handed over to SMERSH, whose responsibility it was (together with the NKVD) to guard and administer them during their long journey across eastern Europe and much of Russia, to the desolate Kemerovo Oblast complex of camps of the GULAG administration.

Organizing transport for so large a body raised major problems. A fair idea of the difficulties involved is provided in a subsequent report by 57th Red Army on 15 June.

> They [the British] have no more Vlasovites [*i.e.* Cossacks], but there are 25000 Soviet citizens and former Red Army PW.
>
> The envoys of our commission are ready to prepare the reception of the stated 25000. However it is impossible to prepare for the reception without precise arrangement and means of transporting these masses.
>
> The fact is that the British are not providing motorized transport, and I am offering to move them by rail transport, on condition that the coal will be ours.
>
> For this transport 300 tons of coal is required. The possibility of requisitioning the required quality of coal in the neighbourhood of the Judenburg region on territory controlled by the Red Army, obviously, will be reported.

I ask for instructions [in response to] the questions: ...

Who and when will be accepted from the 3 Ukrainian Front protected deportation points. Delay on this question will not permit continuance of the reception and the transportation of the repatriates from Allied territory, so that 3 Ukrainian Front removal of repatriates from the advanced protected deportation points was discontinued; the latter are overcrowded, in particular at Melk and Anzendorf, instead of the calculated quotas of 10,000, on 15.6.45 there are over 15,000 people at each point. Derevianko.

Reverting to the position of General Keightley and his senior staff officers when at 10am on 21 May, he presided over the Corps Commander's conference, his orders required him *either* to allow the Americans to remove the Cossacks to safety in their occupation zone, *or* to dispatch them to the Soviets. (This overridingly significant issue is fully explained in the next chapter). The latter choice, as Macmillan had accepted during his conference with Keightley nine days earlier, meant 'condemning them to slavery, torture and probably death'. However, all this was kept secret from 5th Corps divisional commanders, who were never informed of the existence of the alternative humane directive. On the contrary, they were duped throughout by their Corps Commander and his Chief of Staff into believing that forcible return of *all* Cossacks to the Soviets, whether Soviet nationals or White emigrants, represented undeviating AFHQ policy.

Those attending the Corps Commander's conference of 21 May included Keightley himself, his two chiefs of staff, Brigadiers Low and Tryon, Major-General de Fonblanque, and the three divisional commanders or their representatives.[32] Although it would have been normal practice for the Brigadier General Staff (BGS) to be present at such a meeting, Lord Aldington at his libel trial in 1989 swore on oath that he was not.[33] It is clear that this disclaimer arose from legal advice requiring him to distance himself as far as possible from responsibility for the Cossack repatriation.

In fact Aldington had been prepared to acknowledge the fact that he was present at the conference long before any libel action was contemplated. In a letter written on 27 June 1978, Aldington informed General de Fonblanque:

So far as I recollect ... I was there for the conference ... I have a clear recollection that Buthie [Arbuthnott] and, to a lesser extent, the man I called the Pope ! [Major-General Murray?] were objecting to the whole business but eventually saw that we had to carry out the Yalta Agreement ...

So he even recalled details of the session!

In 1981 Aldington confirmed to Brigadier Tryon-Wilson that 'I do remember being involved in the arguments'. While Low had no sympathy for the Cossacks, Tryon admired them as Britain's allies during the Great War. On the other hand, the New Zealander General Weir, commanding the 46th Infantry Division, appears to have accepted the policy of forced repatriation without compunction. Lastly, 5th Corps' two other divisional commanders, Generals Arbuthnott and Murray, were vigorously opposed to it on principle.

General Horatius 'Nap' Murray, commanding the 6th Armoured Division, was throughout an unwavering opponent of a course he regarded as being as needless as it was dishonorable. The policy he pursued, as he recalled to me in after years, was to make plain to Keightley his rooted hostility to the projected operation, while ensuring that the relevant orders received minimal compliance within his divisional area. As he recalled of his relations with his commanding officer, 'he knew that I was unlikely to be a very helpful subordinate in this way'.[34] It is a measure of the precarious path the Corps Commander knew himself to be treading at this time that, instead of issuing the firm order he was entitled to expect his subordinate to obey, he instead adopted the subterfuge of arranging for the majority of the 15th Cossack Cavalry Corps to be transferred from Murray's control to that of the amenable General Weir's 46th Infantry Division.

For it was on 22 May, as the 6th Armoured Division war diary recorded, that 'Bulk of 15 Cossack Corps, comprising 9,500 Cossacks was handed over to 46 Div[ision]'.[35] The 5th Corps's official pretext was that this was arranged in order to ease congestion within the 6th Armoured Division's area,[36] but since it was planned to deliver all Cossacks to the Soviets within the week it is hard to believe that this can have been the true reason.[37] Soldiers implementing the operation at a lower level learned another story. George Rhodes, then serving as a sergeant in the 277th Battery of 70th Field Regiment Royal Artillery within 46th Infantry Division, was seconded with other NCOs of his unit to escort Cossacks being sent to Judenburg. As he recalled:

> With other NCOs I was ordered to report to our colonel. We were told other ranks were not to be used. The young officer who briefed me said that the Cossacks had to go back to Russia and that apparently the British 6th Armoured Division had refused to do the job.[38]

It was the conference of 21 May that provided the first occasion when vigorous objections to Corps policy were voiced by the commander of 78th Infantry Division, Major-General (subsequently Viscount) Robert

Arbuthnott. Lord Aldington recalled Arbuthnott's protesting hotly that 'we should be no party to this affair'. He

> disliked sending any of them back - he thought it just as wrong to send a Soviet Cossack back as to send a non-Soviet Cossack back. Because he said that they had both been fighting for the Germans, and they're just going to be killed... He didn't mind ... which ... White or Red ... that's the one thing I do remember. One had to harden one's heart, and we had been fighting against the Germans for six years, and we weren't awfully sorry for people who'd been fighting for the Germans... I said: 'this is Yalta. Why we have got to do this is Yalta'.[39]

Significantly, Aldington's account intimates that General Arbuthnott understood that his (Low's) 'Definition' required the sending of 'a non-Soviet Cossack back' as definitively as sending 'a Soviet Cossack back'. It also confirms that, contrary to the official claim that 5th Corps command remained up to the last minute ignorant of the presence of White émigrés among the Cossacks, the issue was the subject of heated debate no later than 21 May.

Low's emphasis on Yalta was intended to convey the impression that the policy now being imposed on 5th Corps divisional commands to hand over Soviet and non-Soviet Cossacks emanated from the highest political and military sources. As General Musson, Arbuthnott's subordinate commanding 36th Infantry Brigade, explained to me,

> The overriding impression that I had then, and still have, is that **all the officers had to be sent to the East**. All discussions that I had with superior commanders and their staffs confirmed this and I was told that **the order had come from Field Marshal's headquarters and was H.M. Government policy** [bold inserted in each case]... I must also emphasise how much we all hated the whole business. It was a horrible situation.[40]

Arbuthnott and Musson had of course been deliberately deceived. The Yalta Agreement was concerned exclusively with Soviet citizens, and had nothing to say about use of force. Neither the British Government nor Alexander ever contemplated handing over White émigrés, and every order (save the ignored Robertson order of 14 May) passed down through 8th Army asserted or implied that Soviet citizens alone were liable to return – and then *only* if it could be implemented without use of force. The deception cannot have originated with General Arbuthnott, who as we know was vigorously hostile to handing over anyone by force, let alone individuals who had never been Soviet citizens. Clearly, the lie that Alexander (and beyond him, Churchill) had authorized both use of force and inclusion of White Russian officers originated at Keightley's headquarters.

Aldington's wording confirms both that the question of the handover of non-Soviet Cossack officers was raised by Arbuthnott in Aldington's presence at the 21 May conference, and that the latter instructed him that *all* Cossacks were ordered to be handed over, regardless of their citizenship or wishes. Aldington's reference to Yalta suggests too that the decision had been presented by Macmillan to Keightley as a higher *political* measure, which there was no means of evading. Macmillan himself later falsely asserted that his instructions emanated from the Combined Chiefs of Staff and Winston Churchill himself (see note to Chapter Eleven). No reference was made to alleged considerations of overcrowding of the 5th Corps area, nor a subsequent concocted claim by Macmillan and his defenders that liberated British prisoners were obtained in exchange from the Red Army.[41] In conversations with me, Brigadier Tryon-Wilson was emphatic that Keightley would not of himself have undertaken any political decision.

The only politician involved was Harold Macmillan.

In his book *The Last Secret*, Lord Bethell explains how he was informed by General Keightley that

> The repatriation of the Cossacks was of course an order from Army Group and certainly stemmed from Westminster, probably from Winston [Churchill] himself. Whether we were happy about the operation or not, therefore, did not really come into it.[42]

Since nothing in any signal reaching 5th Corps from higher command alludes to political intervention at this high level, the assertion presumably derived from the only person Keightley encountered at the time who was in a position to know. This was the Minister Resident, Harold Macmillan, who discussed the issue with him on 13 May. In reality, as the record shows, Churchill strongly opposed the handover of Cossacks to the Soviets, and (as will be described in in the next chapter) intervened with Eisenhower to *protect* them from being delivered up to their enemies.

Reverting to events on the ground, General Arbuthnott at the 78th Infantry Division was not only deeply concerned by the inhumanity of the proposed treatment of the Cossacks, but correspondingly exercized about the effect of the forthcoming operation on his own troops. From the moment it became known that transfer of the Cossacks to the Soviet zone was under contemplation, protests arose from all ranks within his 78th Infantry Division. Lieutenant-Colonel A. C. 'Bala' Bredin, who as A/Q to the Division[43] was responsible for assessing the morale of troops, reported widespread revulsion throughout the other ranks. 'This isn't what we fought the war for, sir!' was a recurring protest that arose on all sides.[44] Similarly, in the 6th Armoured Division a subaltern in the Royal Irish Fusiliers explained that

> The whole world now knows of the horror when those Cossack thousands with their women and children were tricked into returning over the Hungarian frontier and there butchered by Russian troops. I am only grateful that my own Regiment was spared the filthy task of handing them over, if only for the fact that we would have faced that dread of all good regiments, *mutiny*.[45]

So it was that the fateful resolution was reached at 5th Corps Headquarters. It was by any standards an extraordinary decision. Arrived at contrary to the wishes of most soldiers of all ranks under Corps command, it contravened policies agreed by the two Supreme Allied Commanders at SHAEF and AFHQ, made known in signals to 5th Corps on the previous day. It was as inimical to the military interests of 5th Corps, as it was inhumane and contrary to the provisions of international law.[46] Finally, and perhaps most incongruent of all, it was totally unnecessary, since (as will be recounted in the next chapter) alternative measures were already in train to transfer the Cossacks to safe asylum with the Americans.

We now return to the situation at 5th Corps Headquarters on 21 May, by which time the secret decision had been taken to implement Macmillan's secretive 'advice' to deliver the Cossacks and White Russians among them to the Soviets. That morning Brigadier Low, Keightley's Chief of Staff, to whom the latter assigned responsibility for the handover operations, presided over a conference at which the decision was formally announced to surrender *all* Cossacks, *regardless of their citizenship*, to the Soviets. By now it will probably come as no surprise to learn that minutes of the conference have not been preserved. After its conclusion, major-generals commanding 5th Corps' three divisions were issued the following directive.

Subject: Definition of Russian Nationals.

Ref conference am 21 May at Main 5 Corps on transfer Soviet Nationals.

1. Various cases have recently been referred to this HQ in which doubt has been raised as to whether certain f[or]m[atio]ns and groups should be treated as Soviet Nationals in so far as their return to the Soviet Union direct from 5 Corps is concerned. Rulings in these cases are given below.

Russian Schützkorps (incl Rumanians in this fmn) will not be treated as

Soviet Nationals until further orders.

Following will be treated as Soviet nationals:-

Ataman Group

15 Cossack Cav Corps (incl Cossacks and Calmucks)

Res units of Lt-Gen Chkouro

Caucasians (incl Mussulmen)

2. Individual cases will NOT be considered unless particularly pressed. In these cases and in the case of appeals by further units or fmns, the following directive will apply:-

(a) Any individual now in our hands who, at the time of joining the German Forces or joining a fmn fighting with the German Forces, was living within the 1938 b[oun]d[ar]y of USSR since 1930, will be treated as a Soviet National for the purposes of transfer.

(b) Any individual although of Russian blood who, prior to joining the German Forces, had not been in USSR since 1930, will NOT until further orders be treated as a Soviet National.

(c) In all cases of doubt, the individual will be treated as a Soviet National.

ARW Low
Brigadier General Staff.[47]

As befits a document drawn up by a devious lawyer,[*] it obfuscates the issue to an extent which in one major respect misled me when preparing my book, *The Minister and the Massacres*. At that time I had not seen a copy of the relevant definition of a Soviet national transmitted earlier by the Foreign Office to AFHQ, and from them to 5th Corps. This was because copies were abstracted from all relevant British files at some point after the war. It was not until shortly after the book's publication in 1986 that I came upon a copy when working on US files held at the National Archives in Washington. This fortuitous survival occurred because 5th Corps came under Anglo-American command (15th Army Group, under U.S. General Mark Clark). As a consequence, many signals were duplicated between the parallel commands, eventually to be preserved in British and American archives. That the British authorities selected this particular signal for destruction confirms its embarrassing nature.

---

[*] Over lunch at the Lansdowne Club in 1985, Aldington's colleague Brigadier Tryon-Wilson impressed on me that 'Low was a lawyer, and saw things differently from regular soldiers'.

In *The Minister and the Massacres* I assumed that Low's 'Definition' was broadly intended to provide an authentic reflexion of the AFHQ ruling on screening. Since it was clear from the consistent testimony of officers involved, as well as the events themselves, that *no* screening was effected and none intended, I suggested that oral instructions were issued by Brigadier Low to the effect that the Corps 'Definition' was designed to be ignored.* My belated discovery of the text of the suppressed AFHQ ruling of 6 March made it plain that, on the contrary, Low's 'Definition' was itself skilfully designed to evade the provisions of this crucial directive.[48]

In the first place, collective classification of entire units comprising thousands of individuals of nationalities other than Soviet as 'Soviet nationals' finds no authority in relevant orders emanating from AFHQ and 8th Army.[49] Low's system of classification was patently designed to *prevent* screening, not least since non-Soviet citizens in formations identified as Soviet were deliberately redefined *ipso facto* as Soviet Nationals.

Low's classification of '15 Cossack Cav[alry] Corps' as 'Soviet nationals' was peculiarly disgraceful, given that the Corps included a substantial number of German and Austrian officers and NCOs, who unmistakably came under protection of the 1929 Geneva Convention on Prisoners-of-War.[50] (Needless to say, no British government has apologized, let alone provided compensation, for this deliberate violation of the laws of war). 'Res[erve] units of Lt-Gen Chkouro' identifies the General who was among those officers whose names headed the list of White Russians handed by the Soviets to Brigadier Tryon at Voitsberg on 11 May. Low knew full well that General Shkuro was one of the leading White Russian generals whose handover had been secretly approved by Macmillan during his visit to Corps Headquarters on 13 May, and was clearly concerned to secure his betrayal.[51]

The provision that 'Individual cases will NOT be considered unless particularly pressed' is not only wholly at variance with AFHQ instructions, but was in this case deliberately designed to prevent individual screening. Since entire formations are classified in Low's 'Definition' as Soviet nationals, no opportunity was afforded anyone to

---

* This was partially correct, in that oral orders within 5th Corps emphatically required that all held in the Cossack camps were, without exception, to be handed over. What my discovery of the US copy of the 6 March 'screening order' showed was that Low's 21st May 'Definition' was *not* worded in order to convey the impression that it protected non-Soviet citizens from handover, but rather to ensure that they *were* included.

raise effective objection while being beaten into cattle-trucks by monolingual British troops armed with pickaxe helves and rifle butts. And how were small children and babies supposed to 'press' their citizenship? The order appears all but designed to mock its victims.

Not only this, but oral orders arising from this 'Definition' were issued by 5th Corps to Divisions that *every* Cossack without exception was to be handed over. When in 1974 I interviewed General Musson, who at the time commanded 36th Infantry Brigade with responsibility for the principal handover, I pressed him on this point. His reply was emphatic.

> Musson. My order was that *all* were to go back.
> Tolstoy. Yes.
> Musson. Particularly the officers.
> Tolstoy. And you had no leeway really, did you?
> Musson. No.

That no screening of Cossacks occurred, nor was intended to occur, is confirmed (along with related atrocious factors) by a report drawn up by British Red Cross supervisor Joan Couper, following a tour of inspection at Lienz a week after the bloodbath at Peggetz camp. During an interview with Captain Martyn, officer in charge of the camp, she

> ... explained that Red Cross workers in the camp were being inundated with appeals for help in tracing persons said to have been forcibly carried away & asked for the facts. The Adjutant gave me the following information:-
>
> a the people in the camp had been fed by the Argylls for some days before evacuation took place. No attempt was made during that time to register the camp inmates or ascertain, if they all were, in fact, Cossacks.
>
> b no official Russian interpreter arrived until the day after the first trainload had been sent off. Until his arrival the only means of communication with the camp inmates was through one or two of their number who could speak a little English.
>
> c the Adjutant said that he knew nothing relating to the categories of person to be classed as Soviet citizens & that their orders were to put the entire camp on to the train.
>
> d the first train-load (about 1200 including women & children) were sent off without any preliminary investigation & no-one, in fact, knew, either the names or the number of persons finally sent off on that train.
>
> e subsequently [*i.e.* after the major handovers were completed], cases were dealt with individually & investigations made...
>
> I understand that there is already clear evidence

a that many people who are not 'Soviet Citizens' as laid down in the circular referred to in 2c above, are being forcibly sent into Russian territory.

b that families are being split & force used on women & children.

c that sick persons, unfit to travel, have been included in the mass repatriation.

Appended to Miss Couper's report are two grim accounts by Miss M. Blair of the Red Cross, concerning two badly injured Russian children who were abducted by the British military from their respective hospitals and their mothers, to be handed over to the Soviets. In the case of one, the doctor responsible 'emphatically said that it was extremely dangerous and that he was surprised that the military had ordered all patients to be removed regardless of their condition'. In the second case, that of a ten-year-old girl:

On the 7 June 1945 I visited the chief Surgeon and he said that the child would certainly die [if moved]. On the 8 June I spoke to Dr Henke Assistant Chief at Villach Krankenhaus [hospital] and he was astonished that the child had been included in the general order to move. He corroborated Dr Fleck's statement that the child had septic fever and that she required absolute quiet. Dr Fleck told me that the journey must have been agonising to her.[52]

Immediately following this, Sir John Selby-Bigge, Assistant Commissioner for Military Government in Austria, took up the issue in person with 8th Army commander Sir Richard McCreery. As Selby-Bigge wrote in his ensuing report,

A serious situation soon arose in the refugee camps controlled by 5th Corps, and to a lesser extent in the M.G. camps. Forcible repatriation was being exercised in a most discreditable manner. White Russian emigres, who had joined the Cossack regiments of the German Army to fight the Bolsheviks, were loaded up by force and driven off to the Soviet boundary - including wives and civilians. These emigres had mostly become citizens of Poland and Jugoslavia, after leaving Russia in 1918... From our point of view, as Red Cross workers, the position was untenable; and I don't think the Army officers or their soldiers were much happier about it.

Selby-Bigge decided that the British Red Cross could not be associated with so shameful a policy, and prepared a report for his Commissioner in Rome, in which he declared that 'the British Zone of Austria was not a suitable field of operations for the B.R.C.'. Before dispatching this, however, he engineered a meeting with General

McCreery himself at his headquarters in Udine. McCreery covered his subordinate, explaining

> the difficulty of the military situation, which had necessitated the clearance of a certain area without delay. Under such circumstances, hasty decisions and injustices were bound to occur. But my main thesis he accepted and regretted. He then gave me his assurance that 'there would be no more forcible repatriation at all without proper screening by qualified M.G. officers'.

More might be written concerning Low's duplicitous 'Definition', but it will suffice here to cite its closing sentence:

> **In all cases of doubt, the individual will be treated as a Soviet National.**

It cannot have escaped the attention of its framer that this protected no one. Since *all* members of the identified formations (save the 'Russian Schützkorps') were classified *ipso facto* as Soviet nationals, the issue of doubt necessarily arose should any one of their number claim another nationality. Besides, since the Cossacks were unaware of the existence of Low's 'Definition', how could they become aware of this course of action? Again, who was empowered to decide 'cases of doubt'? On this point it is needless to say more, since we have the reaction of no less a figure than General McCreery himself. As we further learn from Selby-Bigge's interview with the 8th Army commander,

> Pearson and Miss Couper (B[ritish].R[ed].C[ross].) promptly collected evidence and saw Selby-Bigge. As a result, Selby-Bigge and Pearson went to H.Q. 8th Army where they saw the Head of M[ilitary].G[overnment]. and the Army Chief of Staff. The General [Sir Richard McCreery] was shocked by the evidence and forthwith issued instructions that <u>no</u> sick people were to be moved and no D[isplaced].P[ersons].s were to be repatriated against their will. Further, **he rescinded an outrageous instruction that in cases of doubt refugees were to be classified as Soviet Nationals** [bold inserted]. In parenthesis, a number of refugees had been rescued from evacuation by B.R.C./F.A.U.[*] workers who classified them as "Polish Ukranians" and similar categories.[53]

It is clear that General McCreery's attention was not drawn to Low's 'Definition' until after the repatriation operations had occurred and Low

---

[*] British Red Cross and Friends' [*i.e.* Quaker] Ambulance Unit.

himself was safely back in England.* In fact, anyone conspiring to flout orders in order to send thousands to slavery and death would undoubtedly have taken great care to avoid alerting Lieutenant-General Sir Richard McCreery to the fact. Finally, it is significant that in a subsequent (13 June) signal to Keightley, McCreery made blunt reference to

> the fact that men, women and children have been included in the parties [handed over to the Soviets] who are not Soviet nationals as defined in AFHQ letter CR/3491/G1-Br of 6 March 45, contents of which were notified to you in this HQ letter M 6251 A of 13 Mar 45.

This was the official instruction implementing British Government policy, which required screening and retention of non-Soviet citizens. Moreover, **McCreery's citation shows that it had continued throughout binding on repatriation operations, and confirms that at no time did he receive or issue any order that could be understood to rescind the provisions of the 6 March screening order**. Yet this is the ruling Christopher Booker and his associates in the Government-sponsored Cowgill Inquiry pronounced to have been effectively dead letter so far as 5th Corps was concerned!

McCreery further confirmed that

> On no account is any force to be used in connection with any repatriation scheme.[54]

A brilliant tank commander, and close personal friend of Field Marshal Alexander, McCreery was the last man likely to approve a perfidious scheme devised to send tens of thousands of helpless people needlessly to the cruellest fate imaginable. As Major-General John Strawson, who knew him well, wrote:

> McCreery was deeply religious, and very much a family man...

---

* Both the deceptive title 'Definition of Russian Nationals' and cunning legalistic framing of the text suggest a lawyerly hand. Aldington subsequently claimed that all was above board, since 8th Army officers were present at the preceding conference. During the 1989 libel trial, his counsel (now Judge) Charles Gray QC emphasized in his closing address to the jury: 'May I draw to your attention, in view of some of the charges that are apparently made, to the fact that there was **on the evidence** [bold inserted], at least one officer from 8th Army present at this discussion which took place on 21st May in the morning' (Trial Transcript, Day 36, 55D). Although the Judge allowed this assertion to remain unchallenged, both he and Gray knew full well that no such evidence had been submitted to the Court. As Aldington had himself conceded a month earlier, 'I would have thought there would have been somebody present from 8th Army, but I cannot remember and it is very unfortunate that there is no list available' (Day 8, 51C; cf 70H).

McCreery seemed to be composed of gentler, simpler elements than most men and with a rare clarity of heart and mind: a man of fierce loyalties and without humbug. A legendary horseman, he came to be at once the doyen and the conscience of the British cavalry of his day.[55]

Brigadier Low's 'Definition', which was so patently designed to deceive, does indeed bear a strongly 'lawyerly' look. After all, why did he not reiterate the simple description contained in the authoritative 8th Army ruling of 13 March?

> All persons of undoubted Soviet Citizenship will be repatriated irrespective of their own wishes.
>
> (c) In cases where nationality is in doubt, personnel concerned will be sent to 373 PW Camp [in Italy] for adjudication.

This would automatically have excluded thousands of Cossacks who had never lived in the Soviet Union, and who bore passports of other countries or League of Nations 'Nansen Certificates'. It must have been clear for a start that the numerous babies and small children flung into cattle-trucks at Peggetz on 1st June were patently too young to have been born in the Soviet Union.

On 2 November 1981, Low (by then appointed Lord Aldington by his patron Prime Minister Harold Macmillan) wrote to Serena Booker:

> All I can say now is what I remember distinctly; and what is confirmed by the records; namely, that right up to the time when I left the policy of H.Q. 5th Corps was to follow Yalta strictly and to separate those you call "White Russians" from the Cossacks and to follow very closely the definition in 8th Army Order of March 1945.

This provides interesting matter for reflection on Aldington's conception of honesty, but little for the reality of what occurred in 1945.

To achieve their single-minded pursuit of a goal which almost no one else (the solitary known exception being that of Major-General Weir,[*]

---

[*] As a New Zealander, Weir may have been less informed of European affairs than his colleagues. I have been unable to discover evidence throwing light on his attitude. He was given to understand that 'The German increment of the Cossack Corps will also be handed back, many being wanted [by whom?] for war crimes' (WO.170/4352). Evidently Weir was prepared to ignore the fact that, even were the unsubstantiated charge true (which he possessed no means of confirming), all German military personnel (including Cossacks in German uniform) in his charge remained entitled to protection under the 1929 Geneva Convention on Prisoners of War. The fact that Weir felt impelled to circulate this spurious charge suggests awareness that many if not most troops under his command were likely to regard the forthcoming operation with distaste. Finally, given that the alleged war crimes could only have been perpetrated

commanding 46th Infantry Division) of significance in the chain of command believed necessary or desirable, Keightley and Low were impelled to deceive or browbeat trusted subordinates into submission, while concealing what can only be described as a conspiracy to collaborate in mass murder from their superiors at 8th Army and AFHQ.

It was in the middle of the day on 22 May that AFHQ sent its signal FX 79904 to the 8th Army, authorizing 5th Corps to hand over *willing* Soviet citizens to the Red Army, any *unwilling* to be transferred to American control. A copy was forwarded to Lieutenant-Colonel T. D. Gerrett, the staff officer dispatched by 15th Army Group with authority to monitor the removal of German and Cossack prisoners from 5th Corps area.[56] At 7pm that evening, a further signal F80197 was dispatched by Alexander to McCreery, with a copy forwarded to 5th Corps. It included this instruction:

> You have authority to pass Cossacks direct to Russians **provided force has not repeat not to be used.**[57]

In this way the policy was modified, with a restricted degree of repatriation to the Soviets being now authorized. Brigadier Low's plea on behalf of 5th Corps that the Americans should be prevented from taking over responsibility for the Cossacks had been accepted with the material qualification at AFHQ. In successive editions of the Cowgill Inquiry this minor policy shift is accorded no historical context, making it appear that Alexander was no longer so concerned to protect the Cossacks as hitherto.

Here, however (as is generally the case with historical studies), context is everything. On 22 May, Operation Fairway, involving a massive Allied advance under the command of General Mark Clark into Trieste and adjacent regions occupied or infiltrated by Communist Yugoslav forces, proved gratifyingly successful. Faced by overwhelmingly superior Allied ground, air, and naval reinforcements, Tito hastened to back down. As Geoffrey Cox, intelligence officer to the commander of the New Zealand Division, recalled:

> It was not just a display of force but a display of very real and very ready force. It worked with hardly a hitch. The Allied forces had reached a much more effective defence line. We were still not up to the Morgan line at all points but we had made a significant move towards it.[58]

---

in Yugoslavia or Italy, how could they constitute a concern of the Soviet Union? At his 1989 trial, Aldington was concerned to denigrate the Cossacks as brutish villains unworthy of sympathy, while Macmillan in his 1976 BBC interview with Ludovic Kennedy dismissed them as 'practically savages' (cf. Chapter 11).

In southern Austria the invaders were similarly forced to retreat. As the 6th Armoured Division war diary records, the 'Tits' were compelled to withdraw into Yugoslavia by the evening of 21 May.

> 5 Corps Op Instr No. 24 received detailing action to be taken should it become necessary to eliminate Yugoslavs in 5 Corps area. Fortunately it was never necessary to implement the Corps Instr. At 0001 hrs [20 May] BGS 5 Corps telephoned Main Div the news that Yugoslav forces would withdraw south of the 1939 Yugoslav-Austrian frontier b[orde]r by 211900B apart from small rear parties. The great bluff was over. Orders were issued that the Yugoslav withdrawal would be facilitated in every way possible and GOC held a conference ['0930' hrs] of comds at 61 Inf Bde and explained the new developments ...

> The evac continued throughout 21st and by nightfall the sole Yugoslav forces remaining were a b[attalio]n area Ferlach D 2370 and a b[riga]de area Rosenbach D 0271.[59]

An ancillary effect of this triumph was that there no longer remained any necessity for the Americans to occupy the greater part of the region administered by 5th Corps in Austria, nor for Eisenhower to accept the heavy administrative burden of Cossack prisoners held in the region.

When the successive AFHQ signals received by the 5th Corps on 22 May are compared, it can be seen that the second contains a modification of the first, arising from dissipation of the Yugoslav threat.

> FX 79904

> 1. all who are Soviet citizens and who can be handed over to Russians without use of force should be returned direct by Eighth Army.

> 2. any others should be evacuated to 12 Army Group...

> F80197

> You have authority to pass Cossacks direct to Russians provided force has not repeat not to be used.

With the Yugoslav crisis effectively over, clause 2 of FX 79904 was rescinded in response to Brigadier Low's callous intervention. Instead of being sent to the US zone of Austria or Germany, the Cossacks were after all to be evacuated to the Soviet zone of Austria. However, AFHQ's emphatic prohibition of any resort to force, together with continued insistence on screening, required that only Soviet citizens who volunteered for return would be affected. At Alexander's distant headquarters in the palace of Caserta it might reasonably be expected that the number of genuine volunteers would be sufficient to placate the Soviets. While many doubtless dreaded repatriation, elsewhere in Europe numerous Russians did in fact volunteer for return. This was for a variety of reasons, ranging from overwhelming longing to return to the Motherland, misplaced confidence in Stalin's 'amnesty', and fear of the consequences of refusal. Besides, it was clearly inconceivable that Soviet citizens who wished to return home should be prevented from doing so.

Although F80197 makes no allusion to the requirement that only Soviet citizens should be returned, it clearly could not be interpreted as rescinding the proviso. The fact is that AFHQ at no time contemplated enforced repatriation of non-Soviet citizens, whose identity could only be established by an effective system of individual screening – such as was being practised at this very time in the camp at Mestre in Italy. So far as higher command was concerned, however, Low's spurious 5th Corps 'Definition' of 21 May made it appear that screening *had* been conducted within the 5th Corps area. After all, 5th Corps had consistently concealed the presence of large numbers of old émigrés among the Cossacks – above all those whom Low forty years later still recalled as 'distinguished people who were wanted by the Soviet Russians': *i.e.* Generals Krasnov, Shkuro and other officers on the list handed to Brigadier Tryon at Voitsberg on 11 May. (This incidentally suggests that Low was familiar with the list at the time of its receipt – as is plainly much more likely than not).

As a consequence, the sole controversial consideration aired outside 5th Corps throughout the whole of this time was that of use of force. On 20 August, Alexander explained to his friend Field Marshal Brooke that

So far I have refused to use force to repatriate Soviet citizens, although I suppose I am not strictly entitled to adopt this attitude - nevertheless, I shall continue with this policy unless I am ordered to do otherwise.[60]

All evidence bears out the truth of this assurance.

Continuance of the prohibition on use of force prevented Keightley from repatriating *all* Cossacks, including Krasnov, Shkuro, and other leading former officers of the Russian Imperial Army. Twenty-four hours after receipt of Alexander's renewed prohibition on use of force, at 7.15 on the evening of 23 May Keightley's Chief of Staff (who may by then have been Low's successor Major-General de Fonblanque)[*] dispatched this remarkably revealing message to 8th Army Chief of Staff.

O539. Secret. Personal BGS for C of S [Floyd].

'Ref AFHQ F80197 dated 22 personally for Gen McCreery and copy to

[*] The hour of Low's departure from Austria on 23 May is unrecorded, although there are reasons for supposing it was in the evening.

5 Corps. **As a result of verbal directive from Macmillan to Corps Comd at recent meeting we have undertaken to return all Soviet nationals in Corps area to Soviet forces** [bold inserted]. Macmillan mentioned no proviso about use of force and we have issued instructions that force may be used if absolutely necessary. Consider quite impossible to guarantee to return Cossacks and so honour our verbal agreement with Soviet forces unless we are allowed free hand in this matter. Cossacks will view any move with suspicion as to destination. Consider therefore may be necessary use force to move Cossacks at all from present area. Longer they remain present area more likely force have to be used. Request you confirm our freedom of action in this.[61]

This signal was Keightley's response to General Morgan's signal F80197 prohibiting use of force, a copy of which must have reached 5th Corps no later than that morning.[62] It was probably that afternoon that Brigadier Low departed for leave in England, and the signal's wording suggests that it was he who drafted the appeal.[63]

This signal is of prime importance both as clarifying 5th Corps command's attitude towards the Cossack handover, and establishing the extent of Macmillan's intervention, which has provoked so much controversy. The Cowgill Inquiry was at pains to emphasize that

in military matters Macmillan was in no position to 'direct'. He could only offer advice... In the chain of authorization through military channels there are no missing links.[64]

In reality, all available evidence points to the contrary conclusion. The first factor to note is Keightley's assertion (mentioned earlier) that 'at recent meeting we have undertaken to return all Soviet nationals in Corps area to Soviet forces'. The implication is that the undertaking had been given in good faith before receipt of Alexander's explicit prohibition on use of force. In fact, the insinuation is deceptive. The 'recent meeting' must be that held at Wolfsberg on the previous day (21 May). In reality the discussion had been broadly provisional, as this signal from 5th Corps next day attests.

Representatives of 5 Corps & Russian Force met yesterday [21 May] at Wolfsberg Y6305. **NO final decision was made** [bold inserted] but both agreed 1) that Russians accept COSSACKS & CAUCASIAN surrendered personnel in Corps area with their German Cadre 2) that they be moved by train to JUDENBERG B 2565 & evacuation completed by 11 June 3) that Russians Ex PW be returned on 22 – 24 May & Russian civilians 26 May. Russian representative returns tomorrow after speaking with Russian higher commander.[65]

It was not until two days later (24 May) that a firm commitment was entered into with Soviet representatives at Wolfsberg: *i.e.* comfortably *after* receipt of Alexander's order.[66]

Secondly, the signal throws penetrating light on Macmillan's role. Initially Keightley had reported his decision to hand over the Cossacks as having been undertaken 'on advice Macmillan'. Now, however, we learn that it was a 'verbal directive' that the Minister issued to the 5th Corps commander. The Robertson order of 14 May (which provided for return of 'all Russians') was incidentally ignored as though it had never existed. This implies either that Macmillan's original 'advice' was in reality very much more forceful than had initially been intimated, or that Keightley and Low, disturbed by Alexander's 22 May prohibition on use of force, obtained renewed confirmation of his decision from the influential Minister Resident.* The latter interpretation appears the more plausible, in that Keightley might on the initial occasion be expected to have emphasized the authority of Macmillan's intervention to its maximum extent. Moreover, had there been no subsequent communication between them, Keightley possessed no means of knowing on 23 May whether Macmillan might not have come to concur with Alexander's attitude during the intervening ten hectic days following the Minister's visit to Klagenfurt.

Furthermore, the wording 'at recent meeting we have undertaken to return **all Soviet nationals** [emphasis added]' is unequivocally deceptive. As will be shown in due course, we know that discussions with Soviet representatives, starting with Brigadier Tryon's visit on 11 May, were concerned (in the words of the leading SMERSH negotiator) with 'the handover to the Soviet Army of the remainder of the enemy force, **together with the White Guard generals**'. That this was throughout the focus of negotiations is further confirmed by Macmillan's diary account of his meeting with Keightley on 13 May, together with the war diary of the 57th Red Army at the end of the month:

> On the basis of arrangements with the allied military command [in Austria] the latter finally agreed to hand over in their entirety the 15 Cossack Corps / Vlasovites/ the whole collection of Russian traitors to the Motherland **and the White emigrants**. Point of handover – JUDENBURG.

---

* Macmillan had returned the previous afternoon from his consultation with Churchill, where it seems he suppressed reference to his advice to hand over the Cossacks.

Yet again, it has been seen that Red Army General Shtemenko confirmed that it was above all the White generals whom the Soviets were concerned to secure: a point conceded by 5th Corps after a brief delay.

As 5th Corps command instructed divisional commanders the next day, 'It is of the utmost importance that all the off[ice]rs **and particularly senior com[an]d[er]s** are rounded up and that none are allowed to escape'. What this implied is made explicit in the war diary of the 2nd Battalion of the Lancashire Fusiliers:

> An agreement was reached with the Russians to return them [the Cossacks] all to Russia, a move they would hardly appreciate, having fought on the German side. The Russians were particularly keen on the return of the officers, **many of whom were Tsarist émigrés.**[67]

Similarly, the Inniskilling Fusiliers reported that

> The removal of the Cossack officers was carried out. As **we had been warned that this was the crucial point in the whole operation**, everybody was more than usually vigilant.[68]

Finally, we come to Keightley's concluding request in his signal O539.

> Cossacks will view any move with suspicion as to destination. Consider therefore may be necessary use force to move Cossacks at all from present area. Longer they remain present area more likely force have to be used. Request you confirm our freedom of action in this.

This plea was wholly disingenuous. At 5th Corps headquarters detailed planning was devoted to the duping of Cossacks and Yugoslavs into thinking they were be transported to freedom in the U.S. zone of Austria or Italy. As General K. C. 'Ted' Cooper, commanding 7th Armoured Brigade, explained to me,

> I remember some of those meetings where we thrashed it out. It was very detailed in the end, it had to be, so as the timing was correct.

Keightley and Low proved correctly confident that 'the word of a British officer' would suffice to lure the prospective victims into travelling without resistance to their fate. **Thus it was *not* anticipated that 'Cossacks will view any move with suspicion as to destination'.** There was only one anticipated exception to this rule, which arose from Corps determination to circumvent the screening requirement in the case of the leading émigré officers.

In the event, the Cossack officers at Lienz were as planned duped into travelling to Judenburg without protest, while the unique use of force to compel the other ranks and civilians to follow them three days later inevitably arose from their discovery of the officers' fate. **Had 5 Corps'**

secret agenda not required extraction of the officers from the other ranks and civilians, there appears no reason why deception should not have worked as effectively around Lienz as it did elsewhere in the Corps area. The grim consequences of this implication are described in Chapter Thirteen.

Of key documents relating to the handovers, this urgent appeal is one of the most significant and revealing. First, although the term 'verbal directive' would normally be alien to a military context, it is incontrovertible that Keightley accepted it as an order. For it has hitherto oddly escaped attention (my own, among others) that **Keightley *obeyed* Macmillan's 'verbal directive',** *without any referral to McCreery for authorization*:

> As a result of verbal directive from Macmillan to Corps Comd at recent meeting we have undertaken to return all Soviet nationals in Corps area to Soviet forces.

It is accordingly indisputable that Macmillan's 'verbal directive' corresponded to an order, and was accepted by Keightley as such.

It was Keightley's further request to McCreery in the same signal that raised *the entirely distinct issue* of being permitted to use force when repatriating Cossacks.

In contrast, when on 14 May Keightley reported Macmillan's 'advice' to surrender the Cossacks to the Soviets, although anxious to implement it, he acknowledged that he 'had no power to do this without your [McCreery's] authority'. The distinction between Macmillan's two interventions in Keightley's signal of 23 May is clear beyond contention.[69]

The 'verbal directive' was issued by a Government Minister: one, moreover, who just two days before had returned from consultation with the Prime Minister. On 13 May (the signal was sent in the middle of the night) it must have seemed that 8th Army or AFHQ would accede to a seemingly innocuous appeal for authority to repatriate 'this large number Soviet nationals', in view of the deceptive emphasis on 'Soviet'. Now, however, with AFHQ having unexpectedly declared itself committed to evacuating *all* Cossacks to safety in the American zone, Macmillan's 'advice' has become replaced by his 'verbal directive'.

What could have occurred in the interval to bring about this dramatic shift? On the face of it, Keightley had no reason to seek to frustrate AFHQ policy. If Alexander and McCreery wished to relieve him of responsibility for the Cossacks, instead passing them directly across to SHAEF control, what motive had he for objection? Of the two divergent policies, the new one was infinitely preferable from the point of view of 5th Corps. Instead of a possible bloody confrontation with the Cossacks, to say nothing of perpetrating a major war crime, they were to be peacefully relieved of their charges overnight, who would then become an exclusively American responsibility. Furthermore, the planned transfer to SHAEF overtly precluded any necessity for 5th Corps to undertake the potentially dangerous operation of disarming the Cossacks.

As 5th Corps Chief of Staff, it fell to Brigadier Low to draft both messages, and it was clearly he who attached such weight to the 'advice Macmillan'. On 19 May Macmillan had flown to England to confer with Churchill, but he was back at Caserta on the afternoon of the 22nd. Did Toby Low make use of the direct line between his Headquarters and Caserta to consult the Minister? Or did the Minister himself, disturbed by Churchill's expressed sympathy with the Cossacks, contact 5th Corps Headquarters? Either way, it was now that Macmillan transformed his 'advice' of 13 May into an unequivocal 'verbal directive'.

Low was after all a lawyer, and an intimate friend of no less a figure than the Foreign Secretary, Anthony Eden. It would be remarkable were Keightley not to have been influenced on such a patently political issue by his politically well-connected, unscrupulous, and oleaginous Chief of Staff. Lieutenant-General Sir James Wilson, who was serving in Austria at the time and came to know him well after the war, described Low to me as having 'Too many fingers in too many pies? Influenced by political ambitions, shared with Macmillan'. Everything known about him, both at the time and subsequently, confirms this perceptive judgment.

Keightley's signal makes only secondary allusion to what the official Inquiry terms the the military 'chain of authorization'.[70] *He had obeyed Macmillan's directive without seeking his superiors' authority.* It is further significant that in Keightley's 23 May appeal to be permitted to use force, General Robertson's order of 14 May ordering the Cossacks to be handed over to the Soviets by 5th Corps is ignored as though it had never been issued.

On 12 August 1978, Major-General de Fonblanque (from 23 May 1945 Chief of Staff to 5th Corps) wrote a letter to Lord Aldington, in which he declared:

> What I can say, however, is that increasingly Charles Keightley resisted sending anyone until finally overridden by the F.O.

In reality, nothing suggests that the Foreign Office was ever informed – let alone involved. The Corps commander's assertion presumably reflected what he was assured by Macmillan. We know that Keightley was initially opposed to handing over the Cossacks, which implies that he was subsequently confronted with some overwhelmingly persuasive reason, not only for compliance with the Soviet demand, but still more significantly for his repeated deception and disobedience of his superiors in order to perpetrate an atrocious war crime.

In conclusion, the 'advice' Macmillan gave Keightley on 13 May is so radically distinct from his 'verbal directive' ten days later, that it is impossible to suppose that the latter expression merely echoed the former. The sole inference compatible with the facts, therefore, is that Macmillan issued the 'verbal directive' after his return from England on the morning of 22 May, or the day after. Communication between Macmillan and 5th Corps Headquarters did not cease after the former's visit to Klagenfurt, and nothing prevented the Minister Resident at Naples from making his wishes known to the Corps Commander at Klagenfurt. Direct communication existed between them, 5th Corps being linked by radio transmission to AFHQ.[71] As Brigadier Tryon-Wilson recalled to me,

> I think when the history of that campaign is dealt with you will find that in many cases 5 Corps were in a position sometimes to go to Harold Macmillan, sometimes direct to Alex.

Consider quite impossible to guarantee to return Cossacks and so honour our verbal agreement with Soviet forces ['at recent meeting'] unless we are allowed free hand in this matter.
The 8th Army's fresh order of 22 May, which effectively superseded the Robertson order, placed Keightley (so he now claimed) in a gravely embarrassing position. He expresses a desire to fulfil the original order, in consequence of the need to honour a commitment subsequently entered into in good faith.

The inference is unmistakable. The 5th Corps was pledged to a firm commitment to the Soviets, from which it would be embarrassing or even dangerous to withdraw. But if the suggestion be that this agreement was ratified *before* AFHQ's prohibition on the use of force came to be known at 5th Corps, then the evidence proves it false. The AFHQ signal was received no later than the afternoon of 22 May, at which time negotiations with the Soviets in Austria continued at a provisional stage. Final agreement was not in fact reached until two days later, *after* receipt of AFHQ's fresh policy directive. In any case, whatever the date of the agreement, it could be overruled by AFHQ at any time.

Such was the situation on 23 and 24 May. Remarkably, no reply is recorded from the 8th Army in response to Keightley's 23 May request to be permitted to employ force in repatriating Cossacks. For whatever reason, McCreery failed to endorse Macmillan's verbal directive. On 24 and 25 May he visited 5th Corps, where he called at the 6th Armoured

Division, which held captured Yugoslavs and the greater part of the 15th Cossack Cavalry Corps. The Cowgill Inquiry asserted that the 8th Army's commander was apprised during his visit of 5th Corps' intention to return *all* the Cossack officers. It further claimed that he would *inter alia* have learned of this from Colonel Robin Rose Price, commanding 3rd Welsh Guards, who is on record as being resolutely hostile to the proposed Cossack handover. Surely, it is claimed, Rose Price must have seized opportunity to speak frankly to McCreery.[72]

Like so many of Cowgill's speculations, advanced as though they were fact, it is entirely groundless. Members of the Cowgill Inquiry never met Robin Rose Price. I did on successive occasions, and became friendly with him in consequence of our shared distaste for the betrayal of the Cossacks. At no time during our lengthy discussions (some tape-recorded) did he mention having raised so pertinent an issue with General McCreery, which I am certain he would had he done so. Since Keightley was also present at their meeting, it is further unlikely that Rose Price as a subordinate officer would have raised so controversial a topic with the Army Commander. Indeed, it seems likely that he (Rose Price) did not receive definite instructions for the forthcoming handover until after McCreery's departure.[73] Yet again, McCreery's shocked reaction on belatedly learning of atrocities perpetrated during the handovers makes it inconceivable that it was he who authorized them.

A still greater blow to Cowgill's facile conjectures lies in a signal McCreery sent Keightley on 13 June, in which the 8th Army commander implicitly reproached the latter for his violation of earlier orders requiring rigorous screening of Russians on an individual basis:

> Reports have reached this HQ to the effect that in the course of evacuation to Russia of Soviets and displaced personnel considerable hardship has occurred in a number of cases. This has been due to the fact that men, women and children have been included in the parties [delivered to the Soviets] who are not Soviet nationals as defined in AFHQ letter CR/3491/G1-Br of 6 March 45, contents of which were notified to you in this HQ letter M 6251 A of 13 Mar 45.

It is inconceivable that General McCreery could have issued such an account, had he earlier transmitted an order authorizing abandonment of screening.

Conscious of the weakness of their case, the Cowgill Inquiry members made a further desperate attempt to establish that the brutal atrocities in Austria were fully authorized by higher command. This time it was to invoke the authority of conferences held immediately after McCreery's visit to 5th Corps, on 26 and 27 May at 8th Army Headquarters, proceedings of which were circulated by a Colonel Jackling of AFHQ Military Government.

COSSACKS

(i) Cossacks will be treated as Soviet Nationals* and will be returned to Russian hands.

(ii) Other Soviet Nationals including SS troops and other arrestable categories will be treated in the same way.[74]

The Cowgill Inquiry's interpretation of this section of Jackling's report runs as follows.

> Firstly, this order that all Cossacks were to 'be treated as Soviet Nationals appeared to sanction the sending over of any Germans or emigres among them. Secondly, there are no qualifications at all here about 'the use of force'. The Cossacks are to be handed over, by whatever means are deemed appropriate...

> Now it is clear that an answer was implicitly given to 5 Corps' request, by a conference which included representatives both of Eighth Army and of AFHQ itself. In the full light of 5 Corps' [23rd May] insistence that the Cossacks could not be handed back without the use of force, the conference ruled that nevertheless the Cossacks should be handed back, without qualification. **If force was to be used, it would be with the authorization of the full chain of command up to Allied Forces Headquarters** [bold in original] ...

> Even though we have no record of how this was communicated to 5 Corps, we assume that in view of the urgency of the situation, the decision was passed on from HQ Eighth Army by telephone.

All this represents either ignorant nonsense, or wilful distortion of the evidence. In fact, it is clear that the latter is the case. Hitherto all relevant orders emanating from AFHQ (save General Robertson's order of 14 May, which was initially ignored and superseded a week later) had included the explicit provisos reported by Alexander Kirk to the U.S. State Department on 24 May,

> that Cossacks who are Sov citizens and who can be handed over to Russians without use of force should be sent back direct by Eighth Army. All others should be evacuated to Twelfth Army Group.

---

* At the 1989 libel trial, Aldington acknowledged that 'I imagine the point that might be taken is that the words "other Soviet nationals" must mean that Cossacks were only Soviet nationals there [*i.e.* that all were Soviet nationals]. I don't read it like that' (Trial Transcript, Day 4). He was unable to explain how he arrived at a conclusion so manifestly at variance with the plain meaning of the document's wording.

In other words, the only Cossacks who could be delivered up to the Soviets were those who were (a) Soviet citizens, and (b) volunteers for return.[75]

In reality the decision of the Treviso Military Government conference that 'Cossacks will be treated as Soviet Nationals and will be returned to Russian hands' can have played no part whatever in implementation of operations in Austria. Given that the official Inquiry relies almost exclusively on this report to validate its assertion that '**If force was to be used, it would be with the authorization of the full chain of command up to Allied Forces Headquarters**', readers may consider the following:

1. No evidence exists for Cowgill's imaginary 'telephone call', whether it be to 8th Army (Ops) or 5th Corps.

2. Participants at the conference could not have intended inclusion of 'émigrés' among Cossacks to be handed over, since their presence in Austria had been wilfully concealed by 5th Corps in every report passed to 8th Army and above. In particular, the presence of a substantial number of White émigrés among the Cossacks was suppressed by Toby Low in his notorious 'Definition' of 21 May, a copy of which was passed to 8th Army.

3. How is it that no one involved cited the findings of the Treviso conference as justification for the deliberate inclusion of German personnel and White émigrés in the Cossack handovers? Neither Keightley nor anyone else concerned ever evinced at the time or subsequently awareness of Jackling's report.

4. As will shortly be described, all arrangements for disposal of the Cossacks in Austria were at this time being handled on the spot by Colonel Gerrett, official emissary of Fifteenth Army Group. Had the Treviso conference borne any relevance to treatment of the Cossacks, Gerrett would have been first to be informed. He was not.

5. Throughout their detailed four-page discussion of the conference, Cowgill and his colleagues withheld the fact that (as its heading proclaims) the report of the Treviso conference on 26-27 May was not circulated until 29 May – by which time 5th Corps had not only concluded arrangements for "Operation Cossack" five days earlier, but had on the previous day *already* handed over the émigré officers and German personnel![76] This deliberate omission makes it clear that the authors of the Cowgill Inquiry were aware of the inescapable fact that the circulated report of the conference "arrangements" can have played no part in initiating an operation which had in its most significant respect already occurred.[76]

These considerations must be obvious to anyone familiar with military procedure. It may be wondered, then, why I have troubled to examine them in any detail. The answer is twofold. In the first place, the Cowgill Inquiry advanced their four-page misrepresentation as uniquely decisive evidence proving that it was not Macmillan, Keightley, or Low who were responsible for the treachery and brutality that occurred in May and June 1945. Implicitly, therefore, responsibility for the tragedy was shifted onto the shoulders of Field Marshal Alexander and Lieutenant-General McCreery. This was what Macmillan subsequently affirmed, when interviewed by Ludovic Kennedy.

The falsehood, palpable as it is, has effectively passed into the record as established fact – which is why I am obliged to counter the claim in some detail. So far as I am aware, no academic historian of any stature has ventured to challenge it.[77] No British newspaper was prepared to allow me to counter even so brazen a distortion of evidence, despite its patent implausibility. Meanwhile, my book *The Minister and the Massacres* was secretly removed from almost all British public and university libraries[*] – as often as not to be replaced by the Cowgill Inquiry's mendacious 'Report'.[†]

Moving on from this palpable red herring, further evidence withheld from the Cowgill reports confirms beyond contention that higher command *never* contemplated use of force to repatriate Cossacks. At 12.30 p.m. on 20 May, when Operation Coldstream, which involved the planned evacuation of Cossacks to American control, was already under way, 15th Army Group in Italy (General Mark Clark) sent the following notification to the American 12th Army Group (General Omar Bradley), enabling direct communication between the two armies concerning the transfer of Cossack and German prisoners to American control.

> To facilitate handling and movement personnel to your area sending today from this headquarters Lt Col T D Gerrett to Eighth Army for attachment 5 Corps. This officer will be on the spot representative 15 Army Group and is authorised to deal directly with your Headquarters

---

[*] This ban was imposed in response to circulation of a forged document drawn up by Lord Aldington's lawyers, Messrs. Allen and Overy, which falsely asserted that my book was prohibited by a court injunction.

[†] Dr. Thorpe declared that 'The two vast volumes of the Cowgill report and of the associated documents ... stand as one of the most remarkable and comprehensive historical investigations of recent years. Indeed, these volumes have been held up, especially in American universities, as a model of how such historical investigations should be conducted' (D.R. Thorpe, *Supermac: The Life of Harold Macmillan* (London, 2010), p. 229). Thorpe's own apologia for Macmillan's role in the Cossack and Yugoslav handovers provides an exemplary instance of official propaganda dressed up as history. He visited me to discuss the events, only to ignore the evidence and publish an obsequious apologia in which the pertinent evidence is suppressed

on any matters concerning transfer. He will communicate with your Headquarters on any matters concerning transfer. He will communicate with your Headquarters immediately upon reaching 5 Corps. For Eighth Army. One. Upon arrival Col Gerrett your Headquarters request you despatch him earliest to 5 Corps and advise 5 Corps his mission. Two. Arrange to provide communication for Col Gerrett with 12 Army Group.[78]

The following afternoon (21 May) 8th Army, as yet seemingly unaware of Gerrett's mission, sent this request to AFHQ.

Many urgent questions constantly arising concerning treatment of various nationals both members of armed forces and others. Matters constantly complicated by claims of diplomatic privilege members of armed forces or civilians, etcetera.

Consider it essential proper principles are consolidated so that action can be taken in each case without reference to you.

Will you fly to us tomorrow a representative who can lay down principles and answer specific questions. Will then organize conference at which present problems can be cleared and principles laid down.

If possible, representative should stay at this HQ as advisor on unfor[e]seen problems.[79]

The nature of the problems recapitulated suggest that this was an immediate reaction on the part of 8th Army to receipt of Brigadier Low's 21 May 'Definition' of 'Soviet nationals' liable to repatriation, which was copied to 8th Army at this time.

Colonel Gerrett arrived at 5th Corps Headquarters on 20 or 21 May, where he received a copy of Field Marshal Alexander's FX 79904, ruling (as was seen earlier) that Cossacks 'who are Soviet citizens and who can be handed over to Russians without use of force should be returned direct by Eighth Army. any others should be evacuated to [U.S.] 12 Army Group'.

Next, at 10.20 on the evening of 25 May, Gerrett reported to 15th Army Group from 5th Corps Headquarters that

(B). Approx 90000 [German POW] from Lienz to Bruck E8467 [within the US zome of Austria] commencing approx 30 May at rate NOT yet firm as dependent on Third Army's capacity of acceptance...

Ref Freedom FX79904 of 23. 5 Corps confirm that approx 42000 Cossacks to be handed over to Russians are Soviet citizens within definition of cited AFHQ letter. Any NOT eligible for transfer to Russians will be included in surrendered personnel at first (B) above.[80]

Thus Gerrett was duped by 5th Corps Headquarters into believing that the Cossacks had *already* been screened according to the AFHQ ruling of 6 March, which required establishment of nationality *on an individual basis* – not *en masse* as members of a particular formation. It scarcely needs stressing that Gerrett was deceived, since no such screening was ever ordered – let alone occurred. Gerrett was further informed that an unspecified number was now expected to be screened and retained as non-Soviet citizens for transfer to American custody.

Finally, on 29 May Colonel Gerrett submitted his full report to 15th Army Group. Since this provides the conclusive account of the circumstances of the handovers, which began the same day, it is well to cite the relevant section in full.

NOTES ON VISIT OF AAG* [Gerrett], HQ 15 ARMY GROUP TO EIGHTH ARMY ... 20-28 MAY, 1945

OBJECT

1. To arrange hand over to 12 Army Group of approximately 150,000 surrendered personnel, (GERMANS and COSSACKS) held in 5 Corps area...

COSSACKS

3. By arrangements between 5 Corps and Russian Authorities, approximately 42,000 Cossacks are to be handed over to the Russians commencing 29 May and completing by approximately 10 June.

4. I drew the attention of 5 Corps to instructions contained in AFHQ signal FX 79904 of 23 May which sets out the policy as regards handing over of Soviet citizens to Russians.[†]

5. Any Cossacks not handed over to Russians will be despatched to 12 Army Group as surrendered personnel. It is estimated that these personnel will total approximately 10,000. They will be routed to Bruck (E.8467), after completion of move of German surrendered personnel to that destination...

13. 5 Corps are dealing direct with XV and XX (US) Corps on detail of moves and will obtain from them firm dates on which personnel can be accepted in concentration areas. Pending receipt of this information 5 Corps have issued instructions to 78 Inf Div and 6 Armd Div to prepare surrendered personnel to move in accordance with programme given above.[81]

---

* Assistant Adjutant General.
[†] *i.e.* no use of force, and individual screening.

Thus on 29 May Gerrett was informed by 5th Corps command that 42,000 Cossacks whose Soviet citizenship had been established through individual screening, and who could be returned without use of force, would be delivered to the Soviets forthwith. Another 10,000, excluded on grounds that they were either non-Soviet citizens or required use of force to compel their return, were to be transferred to the Americans. That this 5th Corps smokescreen was designed to deceive Keightley's superiors is incontrovertible.

The 5th Corps response to Colonel Gerrett's enquiries includes a further significant lie:

> ... 5 Corps have issued instructions to 78 Inf Div and 6 Armd Div to prepare surrendered personnel to move in accordance with programme given above.

In fact, no 5th Corps divisional commander was ever informed by Corps headquarters that 10,000 Cossacks opting not to travel to the Soviet Union were to be dispatched to the American zone of Austria.

The impressive figure of 10,000 exempted from compulsory handover was as arbitrary as it was false. The statistic was clearly envisaged by 5th Corps as a number sufficiently substantial to render it credible. On the other hand, the figure of 42,000 effectively opting for return might at first sight appear too large to be realistic, given the appalling fate which it was widely appreciated awaited them in their homeland. However, it clearly *was* considered authentic, being accepted by Colonel Gerrett and implicitly by recipients of his report at 8th Army and 15th Army Group. Nor was it in fact so unreasonable as to arouse suspicion. All over Western Europe substantial numbers of Soviet citizens volunteered for a variety of reasons to return to the Motherland.[82] Neutral Liechtenstein provides the unique instance where Soviet fugitives were granted a genuinely free option whether to stay or return. Significantly, of 494 Russian soldiers some 200 eventually opted for repatriation.[83]

Given the overwhelmingly damaging effect of Gerrett's 29 May report on the apologia for war crimes presented by the Cowgill Inquiry, readers will doubtless be curious to learn how its members explained it away. The answer is that they did not. Readers of all three versions of the Inquiry's report, to say nothing of ancillary ventures by Alistair Horne, Carol Mather, John Keegan, *et al.*, will find *no* citation of Gerrett's signal of 29 May. The preface to the volume of reproduced documents contained in the accompanying volume declares that 'This companion volume ... contains all the key documents of the time ...'[84] By now the reader will not be surprised to learn that Colonel Gerrett's decisive signal is nowhere to be found among those 'Key Documents'.[85]

Further insight into the crucial significance of Gerrett's 29 May report is provided by an event accompanying the second publication issued by the Inquiry. On 18 October 1990 its committee members, Brigadier Cowgill, Lord Brimelow, and Christopher Booker, Esq (a title he insisted upon including on the book's title page in both its first and second editions),[*] held a press conference to launch their *magnum opus*. To their evident dismay, I attended the meeting as representative of the Croatian newspaper *Nove Hrvatska*, where I quoted from Gerrett's report cited above. In his ensuing account of the event, published seven years later, Booker describes the exchange.

> One key document which made complete nonsense of our case was a signal he [Tolstoy] had found from 15th Army Group on 29 May, which stated quite plainly that '10,000 of the Cossacks are not Soviet nationals'. I at once thought 'he has made this up. It is quite inconceivable that such a document exists. We were never to hear of his supposed document again'.[86]

Apparently a fundamental tenet of this novel school of historiography is that any document challenging their preconceptions *ipso facto* cannot exist.[†]

On the other hand, it is gratifying to read Booker's frank acknowledgment that, in the event it *did* exist, this 'key document ... made complete nonsense of our case'.

At the same press conference, Alistair Horne announced that, as a former serving soldier, he found it inconceivable that so deep-rooted and secretive a conspiracy as I had described could possibly have occurred within the framework of the British Army. How far Horne's youthful subaltern service nowhere near Austria qualified him to pronounce on so broad a perspective is a distinct matter. Nevertheless, his point may be considered. Ironically, it is effectively answered by a member of the

---

[*] Could the unusual insistence on 'Esq.' have borne a significance apt to Booker's function in the Cowgill Inquiry? Samuel Kent's *Grammar of Heraldry* (1716) tells us that 'The *Esquire* bears a sidelong Helmet, after this manner; as it were attentively beholding his Master the Knight, to receive his Commands'.

[†] As Booker conducted no researches himself, it is not unlikely that he was misled by his employers Cowgill and Brimelow. I was prevented by a court injunction from publishing anything material on the subject so long as Lord Aldington lived, and even now British publishers continue apprehensive of publishing anything by me on the subject. Only under this system of covert self-censorship have the Government-authorized Cowgill Inquiry's fabrications been enabled to prevail to this day.

Cowgill Inquiry, Lord Brimelow, in correspondence with Brigadier Cowgill himself.

On 24 October 1985 Brimelow sent Cowgill a detailed overview of questions I had raised in my books, which he felt necessary for their Inquiry to consider, and if possible answer.

The following considerations make it difficult to assert with confidence that there was no cover-up...

- I have found no trace of or reference to the appeals of the emigre Cossacks to Alexander etc. What happened to them?

- The first paragraph of Keightley's signal of 00.15 14 May to McCreery contained the sentence (at the top of fo. 41 in the papers I sent you) "Cannot see any point in keeping this large number Soviet nationals who are so clearly great source of contention between Soviets and ourselves." An unbriefed reader would assume from this that the Cossacks were Soviet citizens. Most of them were, but some were not. The impression created by the sentence was misleading.

- if there was nothing to conceal, why were the two repatriation officers from AFHQ who visited Klagenfurt on the 15th of May (fo. 3 of the papers I sent you) told that no approach could be made to the Russians in Graz as negotiations were in progress between V Corps Commander and the Commander of Russian 57 Army, and that permission could not be granted for them to go into the Russian Zone?

- similarly, when Captain R. Thompson visited HQ 5 Corps on 7-8 June why did he find that "there were no details of any incidents during the handover available at Corps. However it is known that incidents did occur, and Corps are obtaining details of these." (fo. 83 in the papers I sent to you)...

- at a later date in 1945, outside the period covered by this letter, HQ 5 Corps asked an UNRRA officer to explain why, without the permission of HQ, he had given an account of the handing over of Yugoslavs to Lt. Col Hammer of CADP, W[ar]O[ffice]. In his reply he said that he had been in London and that Hammer, who was conducting an enquiry, had asked him for information. The implication was that HQ were strictly controlling the passing on of information. I have found nothing in the FO archives about the outcome of Hammer's enquiries.

- Keightley's account to Lady Limerick of the handing-over (Tolstoy p.299) seems to have been somewhat guarded.

- in 1947 I had occasion to make an official request to the WO for information about the handings-over. It took the WO a long time to reply, and when they did reply they said that HQ British Troops Austria had had difficulty, because of the lapse of time, in obtaining the information requested. The information supplied was scanty. Was the lapse of time the sole cause of difficulty?

It is to Lord Brimelow's credit that he posed these pertinent questions so fluently and succinctly. Less so is the fact that the first two Cowgill Inquiry reports, of which he was co-author, either gloss over or wholly suppress the queries he raised in this and other internal correspondence.

That Brimelow was right in suspecting Keightley's command was engaged in a major cover-up is further confirmed by this 5 Corps order transmitted to divisions on 28 May:

> 1. Many offrs and O[ther]R[anks] in the Army are aware that the Allies have made great use of cover and deception plans in s[up]p[ort] of factual ops.
>
> 2. It is of the highest importance that NO unauthorised disclosures of Allied practice on this and kindred subjects should be made in any form whatever, even now that hostilities have ceased. This applies to methods used in specific ops and to gen policy. Any knowledge of the subject will continue to be treated as TOP SECRET.
>
> 3. **It is undesirable that this order should arouse undue comment** [emphasis added] and its distribution will be limited to comds down to B[attalio]n level, Staff offrs, and F[iel]d Co[mpan]y comds.[87]

Thus, a policy devized to preserve secrecy of military operations from the enemy in time of war, was now invoked to withhold from Allied higher command awareness of war crimes perpetrated in peacetime! In the event of their transfer, Article 26 of the Geneva Convention requires prisoners of war to be informed of their new destination. It does not require an expert on international law to infer that this implies being told their *true* destination.[88]

In conclusion, I am conscious that this chapter requires careful and at times complex analysis of the evidence. However, unravelling the skein of an elaborate conspiracy – especially when complicated by a still more complex cover-up long after the event – necessitates scrupulously careful presentation of the facts. Even the smallest omission would be seized upon by surviving influential supporters of forced repatriation. As a concluding reminder of the more striking evidence for the 5th Corps conspiracy, we may note the following:

(i) On no occasion (save the inoperative Robertson order of 14th May) did 5th Corps receive orders to abandon screening or employ force in handing over Cossacks. On the contrary, Keightley was explicitly and repeatedly ordered to enforce both policy directives.

(ii) No credible reason has been advanced by apologists to explain 5th Corps' consistent deception of higher command, nor its inflexible determination to flout successive orders to retain Cossacks who were not Soviet nationals, and its disobedience to explicit prohibitions on the use of force. Why did they not welcome both provisions, on grounds of humanity and that risk to British soldiers' lives which 5th Corps Headquarters itself anticipated?

(iii) Why was 5th Corps so determined on frustrating Alexander's and Eisenhower's planned evacuation of the Cossacks to the American zone of Austria?

(iv) At no time were 5th Corps divisional commanders informed of the official policy of screening and retaining non-Soviet citizens, nor of successive prohibitions on the use of force.

(v) It appears unlikely in the extreme that it was Keightley who undertook on his own account this flagrant disobedience of orders. To what end would he have risked doing so? And what of his initial principled objection to compliance with the Soviet demand of 11th May, which was only reversed following Macmillan's visit two days later?

(vi) The evidence is overwhelming that it was Macmillan who initiated and masterminded the covert policy of deliberately handing over Krasnov, Shkuro, and thousands of other White Russians. Indeed, his intervention provides the sole plausible explanation of Keightley's otherwise inexplicably conspiratorial actions. Removing Macmillan from the picture makes the whole affair appear motiveless and unaccountable.

(vii) Any attempt to adduce pragmatic considerations (the alleged impossibility of maintaining so large a body of prisoners-of-war in occupied Austria, the necessity for placating Stalin, the recovery of our own prisoners-of-war in Soviet hands, etc) must first explain why neither Churchill, Alexander, Eisenhower, Patton, Clark, nor McCreery was for a moment deterred by such hypothetical contingencies when they arranged for the Cossacks to be evacuated to the US zone of Austria. Could it be that they were better placed than former 2nd Lieutenant Alistair Horne to judge of the matter?

NOTE

While General McCreery was visiting 5th Corps, 8th Army received a curious signal from 15th Army Group, copied to 5th Corps. Once again, the Cowgill Inquiry attempted to make capital out of it, but as it represents yet another official red herring a brief discussion is added here in order not to interrupt the narrative. This is the signal:

A 4152 top secret. **ref this HQ A 4149 dated 25** [bold added]. Ruling
now received 15 Army Gp. all SOVIET CITIZENS including arrestable
categories will be treated as surrendered personnel and will therefore be
handed over to RUSSIANS. For 5 Corps. please take action accordingly.
NO further SOVIET CITIZENS to be evacuated [*i.e.* to Italy].[89]

A 4149, to which this A 4152 is the response, was exclusively
concerned with 'arrestable categories' of prisoners who were Soviet
citizens. Here is its text:

Reference your FX-75753 date 15 giving arrestable categories of
surrendered personnel for evacuation to Italy.

Request immediate ruling on treatment Soviet citizens who fall within
these categories. Are they to be treated as liberated Soviet citizens as
defined in CR/3491/2/G1 dated 15 March and handed back to Russians
in accordance with your FX 79904 of 22, or are they to be treated as
PW?[90]

The originating signal A 4152 was in one respect carelessly phrased,
although its recipients at the time cannot have failed to understand its
correct meaning. As can be seen, 8th Army signal A 4152 above represents
the response to 5th Corps enquiry 4149 regarding treatment of Soviet
nationals who were believed to be members of various unsavoury Nazi
organizations, such as SS police units, war criminals, etc.[*] Hitherto these
categories had been evacuated to a camp in North Italy for interrogation
and classification.[91] The question now arose: should this vetting procedure
continue, or should suspected Soviet collaborators with the Nazis be
retained in Austria and treated no differently from other Soviet citizens
being handed over to the Soviets, as laid down in FX 79904 of 22 May?

Thus, these exchanges concerned individual Nazi suspects who were
Soviet citizens, and *not* Cossacks (who were normally described as such).
Indeed, no reference is to be found in the relevant war diaries to dispatch
Cossacks for interrogation in Italy on suspicion of being war criminals.
(This incidentally further refutes the accusation that many Cossacks were
guilty of such crimes, for had they been suspected at the time they should
have been sent to the camp at Mestre for investigation). The number of
Soviet citizens in Austria classified as 'arrestable categories' was
incidentally substantial. Thus, on 17 May 5th Corps recorded that 'Russian
SS in area Y 52 total 1200'.[92]

---

[*] The stipulated categories (including 'war criminals') are listed in AFHQ order
FX-75753. This signal is again among those withheld from the Cowgill Inquiry's 'Key
Papers'.

Thus the two related signals under review were exclusively concerned with treatment of Soviet citizens suspected of having perpetrated war crimes or collaborated with the Nazis in other ways. The instruction 'all Soviet Citizens including arrestable categories will be treated as surrendered personnel and will therefore be handed over to Russians' was carelessly phrased. Being a response to 8th Army's A 4149, which had no concern with Cossacks, A 4152 ruled that henceforth suspected war criminals and the like should be included among Soviet citizens in Austria liable for return to the USSR. That the Cowgill Inquiry suppressed the vital reference to the earlier signal to which A 4152 was the response, suggests that they had drawn the same conclusion: one with which they were naturally unhappy.

It is unquestionable that 8th Army signal A 4152 was *not* understood by its recipients to override Alexander's recent prohibition on use of force when repatriating Cossacks. As described above, Colonel Gerrett, 15th Army Group's emissary, had on 20 May been dispatched to 5th Corps with authority 'to deal directly with ... any matters concerning transfer' of Cossacks and Germans to the US zone. Had signal A 4152 been intended to halt that operation in respect of the Cossacks, Gerrett must certainly have been shown a copy. Immediately ensuing events establish that he was not. Nor was the signal ever cited at the time as having borne the intent claimed by the Cowgill 'Inquiry'.

Accordingly, 15th Army Group's A 4152 cannot be held to have superseded Alexander's repeated prohibitions on use of force, together with his firm requirement to retain non-Soviet citizens. It is essentially irrelevant to the Cossack issue. It is telling that the Cowgill Inquiry deliberately omitted the crucial reference in A 4152 attesting to its being a response to A 4149.[93] By depriving the signal of its context, the false impression was ingeniously conveyed that the query was exclusively concerned with Cossacks. Moreover, even Cowgill was compelled to concede that the 25 May signal 'did not explicitly set aside AFHQ's previous ruling that *'force has not, repeat not, to be used''*.[94]

---

[1] Trial Transcript, Day 10.

[2] Nikolai Tolstoy, *The Minister and the Massacres* (London, 1986), pp. 308-10. As will be seen in due course, Macmillan's express responsibility for the handovers was confirmed by his US counterpart, Alexander Kirk.

[3] N.N. Krasnov, Jr., *The Hidden Russia: My Ten Years as a Slave Laborer* (New York, 1960), p. 332. Nikolai Krasnov learned of the order from his mother and wife, who had escaped the bloody handover at Peggetz camp by fleeing

to the mountains.

4 Tolstoy, *The Minister and the Massacres*, pp. 306, 312-13. As ever, the first-hand testimony of eyewitnesses is ignored by the Cowgill Inquiry.

5 Letter of 2 February 1981. Alexander particularly admired Rommel, against whom he fought in the desert, both as 'a most able battle commander, and a fine tactician' and 'a very chivalrous enemy' (John North (ed.), *The Alexander Memoirs 1940-1945* (London, 1962), p. 13).

6 A full account of Alexander's intervention, based on contemporary records and eyewitness accounts, is to be found in *The Minister and the Massacres*, pp. 305-13. Overall, it appears that the principal purpose of his visit was to investigate and, so far as possible, halt the brutal forced repatriation operations.

7 General Sir William Jackson and Group Captain T.P. Gleave, *The Mediterranean and Middle East* (London, 1988), vi (part iii), pp. 361-63. Eisenhower's admiration was unstinted: 'I regarded Alexander as Britain's outstanding soldier in the field of strategy. He was, moreover, a friendly and agreeable type; Americans always liked him' (Dwight D. Eisenhower, *Crusade in Europe* (New York, 1948), p. 211. 'In the opinion of many of his American associates, Alexander was then the ablest of British generals in the Mediterranean theatre of war. I am still of that opinion' (Robert Murphy, *Diplomat among Warriors* (London, 1964), p. 236). '... we had been, in a sense, close partners for months, and I had come to have great admiration for his qualities of decision and leadership' (Allen Dulles, *The Secret Surrender* (London, 1967), p. 242.

8 Lord Moran, *Winston Churchill: The struggle for survival* 1940-1965 (London, 1966), pp. 172, 173-74. As no scholarly biography of Field Marshal Alexander has yet appeared, probably the best account remains that of Sir David Hunt, in E.T. Williams and C.S. Nicholls (ed.), *The Dictionary of National Biography: 1961-1970* (Oxford, 1981), pp. 18-23.

9 E.L. Woodward and Rohan Butler (ed.), *Documents on British Foreign Policy 1919-1939: First Series* (London, 1949), iii, p. 18.

10 Norman Hillson, *Alexander of Tunis: A Biographical Portrait* (London, 1952), pp. 34-40.

11 When Alexander met Red Army Marshal Tolbukhin in 1945, the latter expressed regret that, although he had received the same decoration during the Great War, he was not now permitted to wear it (North (ed.), *The Alexander Memoirs*, p. 133).

12 General von Pannwitz's Chief of Staff, Colonel von Renteln, had been Alexander's adjutant in 1919, and they subsequently met at the Field Marshal's (Guards) club in London. On surrendering in 1945 he declared that, if only he could speak with Alexander, all would be well with the Cossacks. It is melancholy to think that he was probably right. Cf. General V. Naumenko (ed.), *Великое Предательство: Выдача Казаков в Лиенце*

и Других Местах (1945-1947); Сборник материалов и документов (New York, 1962-70), ii, p. 320; Erich Kern, *General von Pannwitz und seine Kosaken* (Göttingen, 1964), p. 140; Nikolai Tolstoy, *Victims of Yalta* (London, 1977), pp. 228-29; Erwein Karl Graf zu Eltz, *Mit den Kosaken: Kriegestagebuch 1943-1945* (Donaueschingen, 1970), p. 228). Von Renteln was among German officers delivered by Keightley to SMERSH, who ended up in some of the harshest camps in the GULAG, where he died (Father Michael Protopopov, *"Живых Проглотим их...": Пут от Георгиевского Креста к Голгофе* (Melbourne, 2000), pp. 86, 96, 110-16; Karl-Gottfried Vierkorn, *Gefangen in Sibirien: Achteinhalb Jahre hinter Stacheldraht* (Oberaudorf, 1994), p. 261.

[13] WO.214/63A. It comes as no surprise that yet again this signal is among those omitted from Cowgill's 'key documents of the time'.

[14] Two days before his message to Brooke, Alexander had conferred with a Soviet General Basilov, who demanded the repatriation of 10,000 'Soviet nationals' held at Cesenatico in Italy. Alexander coolly explained that he 'was not ... at present empowered to make people return to Russia against their will', and when challenged by Basilov added 'that if ordered to do so, he would use force to effect repatriation'. As he neither sought nor received such an order, the issue never arose during the time that Alexander remained Supreme Allied Commander (Tolstoy, *Victims of Yalta*, pp. 340-41). His son Shane informed me that his father, when Governor-General of Canada 'persuaded the immigration authorities there to grant Canadian citizenship to a number of Latvians, Lithuanians, Ukrainians and other White Russians so that they and their families would be able to settle in Canada' (letter of 19th May 1986).

[15] Cf. my paper, 'The Application of International Law to Forced Repatriation from Austria in 1945', in Stefan Karner, Erich Reiter, and Gerald Schöpfer (ed.), *Kalter Krieg: Beiträge zur Ost-West-Konfrontation 1945 bis 1990* (Graz, 2002), pp. 131-53.

[16] Account related to the author by Prince zu Salm.

[17] Letter of 1 June 1986 to the author.

[18] John Donovan (ed.), *'A Very Fine Commander': The memoirs of General Sir Horatius Murray* (Barnsley, 2010), pp. 181-82.

[19] 'Contact made by 27 L[ancers] with 6 Guards Donaiskaia Inf Corps at Voitsberg. Conference between two Corps Comds produced b[oun]d[ar]y to mutual satisfaction' (WO.170/4241,18).

[20] Trial Transcript, Day 3.

[21] 'A.I. Romanov' [Captain Boris Bakhlanov], *Nights are Longest There: Smersh from the Inside* (London, 1972), pp. 169-71. Cf. P.I. Kuleshov, *Хождение по этапам* (Sydney, 1987), p. 29.

[22] Brigadier Anthony Cowgill, Christopher Booker Esq, Lord Brimelow, and Brigadier Teddy Tryon-Wilson, *Interim Report on an Enquiry into the*

Repatriation of Surrendered Enemy Personnel to the Soviet Union and Yugoslavia from Austria in 1945 and the Alleged 'Klagenfurt Conspiracy' (London, 1988), p. 22. Tryon-Wilson's account of his visit to Voitsberg, published in 1988, vitiates the greater part of everything then and thereafter written by the Cowgill team. They belatedly came to appreciate its acutely embarrassing implications, and by the time of the 1989 libel trial Tryon-Wilson, testifying on Lord Aldington's behalf, succumbed to pressure to abandon his prior repeated assertions of having recognized the names of the émigré officers. In the second Report, published two years later in 1990, all reference to Tryon-Wilson's receipt of the list is omitted. (Both Reports curiously lack an index, which, whether designedly or otherwise, makes it difficult to check references). In what was effectively the third Cowgill Report, Christopher Booker claims to have persuaded Tryon-Wilson, when they first met in the autumn of 1986, that he had not after all recognized the names in the Soviet list (*A Looking-Glass Tragedy: The Controversy over the repatriations from Austria in 1945* (London, 1997), pp. 96-97). Unfortunately for the credibility of this unsubstantiated assertion, it was two years *after* Booker's 1986 brainwashing attempt that Tryon-Wilson repeated his earlier assertions that he *had* recognized the principal names in the Soviet list! Booker either overlooked this, or hoped that it might escape attention, since his strange book omits mention of Tryon-Wilson's 1988 explicit account of what passed at his meeting with the Soviets on 11 May 1945.

[23] Naumenko (ed.), *Великое Предательство*, i, pp. 139-40.

[24] General S.M. Shtemenko, *Генеральный Штаб в Годы Войны* (Moscow, 1973), p. 450.

[25] Amy Knight, *Beria: Stalin's First Lieutenant* (Princeton, 1993), pp. 120-21, 168.

[26] WO.204/10449. The Government Inquiry makes great play of the fact that the 13th March signal to 8th Army 'completely omitted the previous passage from para 2 of 6 March letter, emphasising that 'any person who is NOT a Soviet Citizen under British law will NOT be sent back to the Soviet Union unless he expresses a desire to be so'. **This was the only instruction on repatriation to USSR available at HQ 5 Corps** [bold in original]' (Cowgill, Brimelow, and Booker Esq, *The Repatriations from Austria in 1945: The Report of an Inquiry*, p. 61; cf. Booker, *A Looking-Glass Tragedy*, pp. 219-20). In reality (although the reader is not supposed to notice the fact), the omission in no way qualifies the AFHQ order, which confines involuntary repatriation to 'persons of undoubted Soviet Citizenship', and provides for all others to be sent to Italy for formal screening ('adjudication'): *i.e.* to be retained, if found not to be Soviet citizens. Yet more significant is the fact that AFHQ signal FX 79904 of 22nd May, copied to 5th Corps, included a reminder of the definition of a Soviet citizen contained in the 13th March order.

[27] 'No guidance had been sought about White Russians, and none had been given' (Cowgill, Brimelow, and Booker Esq, *The Repatriations from Austria in 1945: The Report of an Inquiry*, p. 57; cf. p. 59). This is a deliberate misrepresentation: the 13 March order explicitly states that all non-Soviet citizens (of whom the overwhelming majority were White emigrants) were to be dispatched at 373 PW camp (in Italy).

[28] NA.383.7-14,67.

[29] WO.170/4183,487; FO.1020/42,133.

[30] FO.1020/42,135.

[31] In a journal compiled later de Fonblanque recalled: 'The Cossack problem was on us and in connection therewith I had at least two conferences with Russians at Wolfsberg'.

[32] These are listed as invited by 46th Infantry Division war diary on the previous day (WO.170/4352). The BGS is not included in this list, but appears as a recipient of the minutes distributed the next day. Some alteration in plan is possible, since the time of meeting was brought forward at the last minute from 1400 hours to 1130. Generals Weir and Arbuthnott were certainly in attendance (Diary of Captain Norrie, ADC to General Weir; WO.170/4388).

[33] Trial Transcript, Day 4.

[34] Conversation between General Sir Horatius Murray and the author, 12 February 1975. Cf. Donovan (ed.), *'A Very Fine Commander'*, p. 181.

[35] WO.170/4337.

[36] WO.170/4241.

[37] It may be urged that 46th Infantry Divisional area touched on the handover points, initially envisaged as Voitsberg and subsequently Judenburg. But this appears wholly inadequate as a reason for causing thousands of men to break camp and reestablish themselves a few miles nearer their destination for the space of a week. Moreover, if administrative convenience provided the reason, why were the Cossacks within 78th Infantry Division (who were situated furthest of all from the handover points) not likewise shifted in preparation for the handovers?

[38] *Western Morning News*, 7 June 1990.

[39] Conversation with the author on 8 May 1985.

[40] Letter to the author of 1st April 1975.

[41] On the evening of 22nd May, at the height of 5th Corps preparations to hand over the Cossacks, Alexander informed the War Office that 'Agreement with Russians at Graz only applies to handover of Soviet citizens in British Zone Austria. No reciprocal guarantee in respect of British ex PW obtained apart from halfhearted promise which so far has not been honoured. Evacuation [of British PW] to Odessa still continuing from this area' (FO.916/1207).

[42] Nicholas Bethell, *The Last Secret: Forcible Repatriation to Russia 1944-7* (London, 1974), p. 92; cf. p. 206.

[43] Lt-Col Bredin was seconded from command of 2 Irish Rifles to HQ 78th Infantry Division on 24th May (WO.170/4465).

---

[44] Conversation with the author, 17 October 1975.

[45] Colin J. Gunner, *Front of the Line: Adventures with the Irish Brigade* (Belfast, 1991), p. 149.

[46] Cf. Karner, Reiter, and Schöpfer (ed.), *Kalter Krieg*, pp. 131-53, and Appendix A *infra*.

[47] WO.170/4241.

[48] This correction was utilized by Aldington's Counsel and Judge Michael Davies in the 1989 trial to confuse the jury, ascribing to me views they knew I no longer held.

[49] The exceptions were Macmillan's and Robertson's deliberately deceptive introduction of the blanket term 'Russians', uniquely adopted in order covertly to include Soviet and non-Soviet citizens alike.

[50] Records held in the Central State Archive of the Soviet Army record that 139 German officers from the 15th Cossack Cavalry Corps were handed over by the British at Judenburg. In addition 644 German NCOs were delivered up (Vierkorn, *Gefangen in Sibirien*, p. 6). Vierkorn lists 82 Germans known to him who died from murder or maltreatment in GUPVI camps (*ibid.*, pp. 261-63). In fact the original number in British hands was much greater: '1172 troops were German out of a total strength of 18,792. However, as many as 199 out of the 452 officers were German and the officers staff of Corps Headquarters had only one Cossack representative' (WO.170/7211). Many escaped handover, primarily thanks to warnings given by Major-General Murray and Brigadier Usher (General V. Naumenko (ed.), *Великое Предательство: Выдача Казаков в Лиенце и Других Местах (1945-1947); Сборник материалов и документов* (New York, 1962-70), ii, 159, 160, 321). Of the 783 Germans despatched to lethal slavery by the British Army to whom they had surrendered, only 230-240 survived.

[51] Despite characteristic evasiveness, Aldington conceded 45 years later at his trial that he had been aware of Shkuro's identity. Richard Rampton QC asked 'Did you know that General Shkuro was one of the old émigrés - what elsewhere you have described as White Russians with French nationality, or something like that?' Aldington replied: 'I think I must have known that, but it is difficult for me to say yes or no to that. I knew that General Shkuro was there, obviously; how much I knew I am not sure' (Trial Transcript, Day 8).

[52] I am grateful to Mrs Margaret Poulter, Archivist of the British Red Cross, for providing me with a copy of Miss Couper's report.

[53] Report by John Rose and Peter Gibson of the Friends Ambulance Unit of their interview with the Army Commander at the end of June 1945, obtained for me by Denis Connolly, who was in 1945 serving with the Friends Ambulance Unit in Austria. A copy of Low's 'Definition' was passed to 8th Army, which was evidently mistaken for valid guidance on screening, not requiring further consideration. In an interview with Gordon Brook-Shepherd published in the *Sunday Telegraph* on 23 December 1984, Aldington speciously sought to

assign responsibility for failure to screen Cossacks to 78th Division command. 'One of the forward divisions of 5 Corps did not have time to screen properly all the White Russians in its area ...' This is in flat contradiction to his own oral orders to General Arbuthnott that *all* Cossacks were to be indiscriminately handed over.

[54] FO.1020/2838,31A.

[55] Lieutenant-General John Strawson, 'McCreery, Sir Richard Loudon', in E.T. Williams and C.S. Nicholls (ed.), *The Dictionary of National Biography: 1961-1970* (Oxford, 1981), p. 691. Field Marshal Alexander shared Strawson's high estimate of McCreery's character (North (ed.), *The Alexander Memoirs*, p. 17).

[56] WO.170/4146.

[57] FO.1020/42,135.

[58] Geoffrey Cox, *The Race for Trieste* (Letchworth, 1977), pp. 252-54. In a letter to me dated 7th December 1987, Sir Geoffrey volunteered that 'I believe your case against Macmillan to be ... well founded'.

[59] WO.170/4337. A useful account of these events is provided by Felix Schneider, '„Freeborn" und „Coldstream" – Vorboten des Kalten Krieges in Österreich und Venezia Giulia 1945', in Karner, Reiter, and Schöpfer (ed.), *Kalter Krieg*, pp. 115-29. The Cowgill Inquiries ignore the contextual significance of the Yugoslav crisis at this juncture altogether (Cowgill, Brimelow, and Booker Esq, *The Repatriations from Austria in 1945: The Report of an Inquiry*, pp. 101-2; Booker, *A Looking-Glass Tragedy*, pp. 229-30.

[60] WO.214/63A. Booker's interpretation (tucked away in a footnote) of Alexander's avowal is that he 'was referring here to the general repatriations which were still taking place from the Mediterranean area under his command ...' (*A Looking-Glass Tragedy*, p. 430). No such qualification appears in Alexander's letter, and Booker's cavalier distortion provides yet another specimen of his treatment of any evidence inconveniently contradicting his conspiracy theory. It is incontrovertible that from May 1945 onwards Alexander neither received nor issued at any time an order to use force to repatriate Russians.

[61] FO.1020/42.

[62] 5 Corps' (missing) copy of Morgan's signal to McCreery was transmitted directly from AFHQ, obviating any delay in forward transmission by 8 Army.

[63] On day 35 of the Aldington trial in 1989, Richard Rampton QC pointed out the close stylistic resemblance between the text of the 13th May 'on advice Macmillan' signal, and that of the 23rd May 'verbal directive'. Since Aldington accepted that he drafted the first, it is probable that he was likewise responsible for its successor.

[64] Cowgill, Brimelow, and Booker Esq, *The Repatriations from Austria in 1945: The Report of an Inquiry*, p. 112; cf. pp. 222-26.

[65] WO.218/248. It is noteworthy that there is no mention of the return of British

PW in Soviet hands, which was clearly treated as an altogether distinct issue.

[66] On 25 May, 5th Corps Headquarters reported to 46th Infantry Division: 'Conference with 57 Russian Army reps held at Wolfsberg Y60 yesterday. Russians agreed to accept Cossacks from 6 Armd Div & 78 Div areas by train at Judenburg and those from 46 Div by march at Voitsberg' (WO.170/4352).

[67] WO.170/5034.

[68] WO.170/5018.

[69] As Nigel Nicolson pointed out to Christopher Booker in a letter of 15 October 1988, 'Macmillan may not have been in a position to give a 'verbal directive' to 5 Corps, but his eminence, personality and the fact that he went to Klagenfurt as Alex's personal emissary, meant that anything he said on the 13th would have made, and obviously did make, a profound impression on Keightley and his staff. They were still quoting it ten days later, in spite of several intervening orders that contradicted it'. The point had already been emphasized by John Grigg: 'It is quite clear from this that he authorized the transfer, though it did not in fact take place until the end of the month. John Keegan, writing in the *Daily Telegraph*, insists that what Macmillan gave was "political guidance" rather than a "directive", and disputes Tolstoy's thesis on this narrow semantic ground. But surely there is not much distinction in the difference, given that the point at issue was political, and Macmillan, as the British government's senior representative on the spot - a minister of cabinet rank - the most authoritative local figure on all political matters. Guidance from such a source must have been almost tantamount to a directive' (John Grigg, 'Mac and the massacres: good intent but a bad decision', *The Times*, 23 August 1986). Keightley himself had of course described Macmillan's instruction as a 'directive'. The decisive point, however, is that Keightley obeyed Macmillan's verbal directive without consulting McCreery: it was the secondary consideration of use of force for which he requested authorization.

[70] Cowgill, Brimelow, and Booker Esq, *The Repatriations from Austria in 1945: The Report of an Inquiry*, p. 112.

[71] WO.170/4185,639.

[72] Cowgill, Brimelow, and Booker Esq, *The Repatriations from Austria in 1945: The Report of an Inquiry*, pp. 107-8. The Inquiry's account of McCreery's visit to 5th Corps is a classic of the Cowgill approach to historical investigation, with its repeated deployment of 'we think that' and 'we believe that' – all without a scrap of evidence in support.

[73] It was only on 26th May that Rose Price 'spent day discussing and recceing area for OP COSSACK' (WO.170/4982).

[74] NA Kirk Papers.

[75] That AFHQ never envisaged the handover of non-Soviet citizens not covered by the Yalta Agreement was acknowledged by Lord Aldington himself: 'I share the view ascribed to Field Marshal Alexander that the Cossacks to be

returned were being done so under the terms of the Yalta treaty' (letter of 11 February 1981 to Serena Booker).

[76] Cowgill, Brimelow, and Booker Esq, *The Repatriations from Austria in 1945: The Report of an Inquiry*, pp. 108-12. Cf. also Booker, *A Looking-Glass Tragedy*, pp. 240-41. At the 1989 trial Aldington himself relied on the Cowgill interpretation of the 26-27 May conference (Trial Transcript, Day 8). In his third edition of the Cowgill 'Inquiry', Christopher Booker was still more specific in suppressing the fact that Colonel Jackling's report was not circulated until 29 May. Confident that lawyers would prevent my responding, he glibly assured his readers: 'With these rulings from the conferences at Eighth Army headquarters **on 27 May**, Eighth Army was now in a position to give 5 Corps all the authority it required ... to begin the complex operations required to hand the various groups of Cossacks back to the Russians. **Planning for these had now been completed down to divisional and brigade level, and they were due to begin the following day, 28 May** [emphasis added]' (*A Looking-Glass Tragedy*, p. 241).

[77] An exception was Professor Hugh Trevor-Roper, writing in *The Independent Magazine* for 23 December 1989, He claimed that 'The error of Mr Tolstoy is that he ... is a simplifier'. Setting aside his own ability to interpret evidence (he is now perhaps best known for his gullible endorsement of the forged 'Hitler diaries'), the true simplifiers were surely Trevor-Roper himself and members of the 'Cowgill Inquiry', who claimed that no aspect of the forced repatriations was in any way remiss or regrettable. In contrast, by allowing participants of every rank and nationality involved to recount their differing experiences and responsibilities, I was able to show just how varied they were. Furthermore, readers will have noted the extent that I have constantly modified my conclusions in light of accumulated fresh evidence, while the 'Cowgill Inquiry' suppressed or doctored all evidence damaging to their overriding conclusion.

[78] WO.170/4146.

[79] WO.204/2864; FO.1020/42,148.

[80] WO.170/4184.

[81] WO.170/4146.

[82] 'A.I. Romanov', *Nights are Longest There*, p. 169. Soviet reassurances included such affectionate pledges as: 'All those who return home will be treated with maximum of care and attention... Dear Countrymen! who are in Italy, you have the opportunity to come back to your country and your families, do your duty and work for your people and native land' (National Archives 1945: 801.2). In the Far East, many Russian exiles from Shanghai and elsewhere were similarly enticed into voluntary repatriation – needless to say, with appalling consequences (Aino Kuusinen, *Before and After Stalin: A Personal Account of Soviet Russia from the 1920s to the 1960s* (London, 1974), p. 194). A startling proportion of White émigrés in Paris succumbed to the

patriotic glamour of the Red Army's victories, combined with gullible acceptance of Soviet propaganda. An eyewitness account is provided by Mikhail Koriakov, *I'll Never Go Back* (London, 1948), pp. 166-94. The allure of the Soviet appeal and its horrifying consequences were powerfully dramatized in the 1999 French film *Est-Ouest*, starring Catherine Deneuve and Oleg Menshikov.

[83] Tolstoy, *Victims of Yalta*, pp. 391-92.

[84] *Ibid.*, p. vii.

[85] Among reviewers duped by the Cowgill Inquiry's doctored evidence, it is disappointing to find Lieutenant-General Sir James Wilson ('The Repatriations from Austria in 1945: The Cowgill Inquiry – Report and Documentary Evidence', *Army Defence Quarterly Journal* (London, 1991), cxxi, pp. 61-63). A pattern of honour himself, it seems he was unable to detect falsehoods of such staggering extent.

[86] Booker, *A Looking-Glass Tragedy*, p. 416.

[87] WO.170/4352.

[88] Gustav Rasmussen (ed.), *Code des prisonniers de guerre: Commentaire de la convention du 27 juillet 1929 relative au traitement des prisonniers de guerre* (Copenhagen, 1931), p. 116).

[89] WO.170/4183,460; FO.1020/2838.

[90] NA 383.7-14.

[91] FO.1020/42,97; NA 383.7-14.

[92] WO.170/4241.

[93] Cowgill, Booker Esq, Brimelow, and Tryon-Wilson, *Interim Report on an Enquiry into the Repatriation of Surrendered Enemy Personnel to the Soviet Union and Yugoslavia from Austria in 1945 and the Alleged 'Klagenfurt Conspiracy*, p. 45; Cowgill, Brimelow, and Booker Esq, *The Repatriations from Austria in 1945: The Report of an Inquiry*, p. 109; Booker, *A Looking-Glass Tragedy*, p. 239.

[94] Cowgill, Brimelow, and Booker Esq, *The Repatriations from Austria in 1945: The Report of an Inquiry*, p. 109.

CHAPTER IX
'CLEARING THE DECKS'

My administrative problem is a big one, as we have about one million prisoners in Villach - Klagenfurt area to look after, so I am trying to get SHAEF to accept them, but so far without much success. I must clear the decks in this area.

Field Marshal Alexander to Winston Churchill, 16 May 1945.

The 'Klagenfurt Conspiracy', as I have termed it elsewhere,[1] involved both at the time and since much intricate chicanery, which inescapably requires detailed unravelling. Not only did General Keightley conceal his insubordinate actions from his superiors, but his covert violations of their orders had in addition to be withheld from all ranks in his own 5th Corps, save for one or two compliant senior staff officers. As explained at the outset of the previous chapter, clarification of its ramifications is best served by separate examination of parallel strands of what may justly be termed a secret history.

Throughout the week following Macmillan's unexpected intervention in Austria on 13 May, the Western Allies were preoccupied with the threat posed by the self-appointed Marshal Tito's determination to occupy by force the city of Trieste and adjacent Italian territory, together with much of Austria south of the river Drau. President Truman at first declared himself unable to commit American troops to any conflict, unless the Yugoslavs opened fire first. Accordingly, on 8 May the British 8th Army in north Italy and southern Austria was ordered 'Force NOT to be used pending negotiations'.

In Italy Tito had advanced his troops not only into the city of Trieste, but in addition further inside Italian territory up to the Isonzo river, while from 5th Corps General McCreery at 8th Army learned that 'HQ 14 Yugoslav Div is established [at] Klagenfurt and Keightley reports that there is no sign of a stop to the Northernly move of Yugoslav forces into our zone of Austria'.[2]

Apart from Truman's worrying reservation, two other major considerations troubled Field Marshal Alexander. Were use of force to provide the only means of halting and throwing back the Yugoslav

advance, the Supreme Allied Commander frankly warned the Combined
Chiefs of Staff on 11 May:

> The foregoing is based on the assumption that my forces would display
> the same fighting spirit and high endeavour in battle as hitherto. In view
> of the announcement of VE day and the long publicity given to Tito's
> operations in aid of the Allied cause, I am doubtful whether in fact this
> would be the case. In my view, both U.S. and Brit troops would be very
> reluctant to engage at this stage of the war in a fresh conflict against the
> Jugoslavs.
>
> If the Russians decided to support Tito, such support might vary between
> open hostilities and the provision of volunteer formations operating
> under Tito's command. In either case, it is impossible to estimate the
> resources that would be required. They would clearly be beyond
> everything that I have available in this theatre.[3]

However, it was on the same day that Allied policy became
dramatically clarified. Suddenly President Truman assured Churchill of
his wholehearted support for vigorous action to check Tito's apparently
insatiable desire to expand Communist Yugoslavia into neighbouring
states.

> The problem is essentially one of deciding whether our two countries are
> going to permit our Allies to engage in uncontrolled landgrabbing or
> tactics which are all too reminiscent of those of Hitler and Japan.

Stalin was to be informed of this resolute shift in policy.[4] The two
Communist dictators were no longer dealing with the vain and vacillating
Roosevelt, but with a no-nonsense President confident in his country's
strength and probity.

Meanwhile, the brutality and rapacity of Tito's ruffianly army swiftly
antagonized Allied troops as much as they terrified local Italians and
Austrians subjected to their reign of terror. Ironically, this served to
antagonize Allied troops to the extent that any lingering admiration for
their 'gallant ally' was transformed overnight into contemptuous disgust.
In Trieste, Geoffrey Cox, Intelligence Officer to General Freyberg,
observed that New Zealand troops had overnight become ready to fight the
thuggish 'Jugs'.[5] David Bendall, at the time G2-Ops at 5th Corps, recalled
that in Austria too:

> One impression which remains quite indelible is the rapidity with which
> the troops themselves reached the conclusion that the Communist forces
> whether partisan or otherwise were not friendly and gallant allies but a
> nasty, ruthless bunch of thugs.[6]

On 17th May Alexander reported to the Combined Chiefs of Staff:

Jugoslav behaviour both in Austria and Venezia Giulia is making a very unfavourable impression on Allied troops both United States and British. Our men are obliged to look on without power to intervene whilst actions which offend their traditional sense of justice are permitted. Further, our men feel that by taking no action they are condoning such behaviour. As a result feeling against Jugoslavs is now strong and is getting stronger daily.

It is now certain that any solution by which we shared an area with Jugoslav troops or partisans or permitted Jugoslav administration to function would not work.

Despite Truman's altered view, for some days the United States continued cautious with respect to unleashing war against a former ally so soon after the crushing of Nazi Germany – particularly at a time when the President and his military advisers were concerned to focus on defeat of the Japanese. Now, however, General George Marshall, US Army Chief of Staff, shrewdly determined on a show of force so overwhelming that Tito would (with any luck) be left with no choice but to back down. On 16 May he outlined his plan to General Eisenhower at SHAEF Headquarters.

I have just talked to the President who consulted me regarding the increasingly acute situation with Tito and the Yugoslavs. I saw Alexander's message to you requesting that you take over control of certain Austrian provinces that are in his bailiwick.

The President is naturally most anxious to avoid the tragedy of an open fight; at the same time he feels that the actions of the Yugoslav Government and of Tito have become so aggressive and contemptuous of the Allied authority and responsibility in the matter that there is a limit to how far we can go in tolerating further adverse development of the situation. He asked me my views, I have previously urged him against committing himself to action which might, in my opinion, provoke fighting and which was being urged on him. I told him that we might play another card by strongly reinforcing Alexander with armored forces and that, for example, if three or four or even five armored divisions moved into the region and if Patton's name could be connected with them it might solve the problem without an open rupture. He was particularly enthusiastic over the psychological effect of Patton's name and was in accord with my suggestion that I communicate with you on the basis that if you could make such a force available you might informally discuss the matter with Alexander and if you and he were in agreement it could then be confirmed by the Chiefs of Staff.

There would be command complications because Alexander has the V British Corps in control of the situation operating in the Eighth British Army with our 91st Division as part of the Corps and the Eighth Army

under Clark. However these are details, the main issue being the desire
of the President to make this sort of an effort in the hope of reconverting
the Yugoslavs to a more reasonable and tractable course. We do not
know here to what extent you could free armored divisions for this work
and how long it would take them to move, speed of action being very
necessary.[7]

As early as the evening of 14 May Alexander had sent an urgent plea
to SHAEF to free 5th Corps of responsibility for 'about 500,000' refugees
and prisoners of war clogging up the British zone of Austria, 'by accepting
concentration under your control in RADSTADT area or elsewhere more
convenient to you' in the American zone of Austria.[8] The 5th Corps was
informed of Alexander's appeal the next morning,[9] and continued
thereafter fully informed of developments intended *inter alia* to relieve 5th
Corps of all responsibility for the Cossacks.

As Alexander emphasized to Churchill.

My administrative problem is a big one, as we have about one million
prisoners in Villach - Klagenfurt area to look after, so I am trying to get
SHAEF to accept them, but so far without much success. I must clear the
decks in this area.[10]

The Prime Minister was prompt to endorse Alexander's proposal.

I entirely agree with your telegrams (NAF 971 and NAF 972). Except in
the case of some definite emergency, you will no doubt await the reply
of the C.C.S.* Always count on me should trouble come.[11]

Meanwhile on 16 May, Alexander's chief of staff Lieutenant-General
William Morgan had visited 5th Corps, whence he reported back to
AFHQ:

5 Corps situation difficult owing to very widespread commitments and
guards required for prisoners and surrendered personnel.

Prisoners and surrendered personnel total about 220000[†] of whom ...
46000 Cossacks 25000 Croats 25000 Slovenes. consider that SHAEF
should be asked to take over 5 Corps front ...[12]

It is clear that Morgan had throughout his visit to 5th Corps
Headquarters been deliberately kept in ignorance of the fact that it was

---

* Combined Chiefs of Staff.
[†] Wide disparities in estimates of the total figure of prisoners and surrendered
personnel in Austria at this time were largely due to the feared irruption of an
estimated 200,000 Croats seeking refuge within 5th Corps area. However, by the
evening of 16th May they had been persuaded to surrender to Tito's forces, and
withdrew into Yugoslavia.

intended (on the authority of Macmillan's 'advice' and the consequent 'Robertson order' of 14 May) to resolve the problem of the 46,000 Cossacks by their imminent delivery to the Soviets, and presenting the 50,000 Croats and Slovenes to the genocidal dictator Tito. In marked contrast, Morgan proposed that the grave problem of guarding and sustaining 'prisoners and surrendered personnel' in Austria should immediately be transferred to Eisenhower's command at SHAEF (Supreme Headquarters Allied Expeditionary Force).

A further urgent plea (FX 76939) from Alexander urged on Eisenhower:

> Latest report indicates that prisoners and surrendered personnel total about 220,000 of whom ... 46,000 Cossacks ...

> My earnest appeal to you is to come to my assistance as regards surrendered German armed forces including Cossacks. I request urgently your agreement that these surrendered forces ... be transferred to your area soonest at a point agreeable to you in status of surrendered personnel. **The only alternative** [emphasis added] is that as matter of operational and administrative necessity I shall be compelled to disband them, which would produce confusion in contiguous German territory under your command.[13]

It will not have escaped the reader that the one alternative Alexander did *not* contemplate was that of surrendering the Cossacks to the Soviets. Nor did his good friend Eisenhower contemplate any such atrocious action. Yet it is evident from everything that follows that Alexander's Chief of Staff General Morgan was told nothing of the 14 May Robertson order (requiring immediate handover of Cossacks to the Red Army) during his visit to 5th Corps command, and it becomes equally clear that Alexander remained likewise ignorant of its existence.

Initially Eisenhower jibbed at taking on such a massive responsibility at a time when SHAEF was faced with maintaining several million refugees and prisoner of wars. However, faced with a supportive appeal from Winston Churchill, he acknowledged the necessity of coming to Alexander's assistance. On 17 May Alexander received this encouraging message from SHAEF.

> 1. You have seen SCAF 397.* In our opinion paragraphs 3 and 4 substantially meet operational desires of SACMED [Supreme Allied Commander: *i.e.* Alexander]. We urge prompt implementation of

---

* An earlier lengthy signal, in which Eisenhower *inter alia* proposed the dispatch of five U.S. divisions to oppose Tito's aggressive moves in Austria (FO.371/48817).

paragraph 4. Request your comment earliest.

2. We have also put forward suggestion that Cossacks and surrendered German forces other than Austrians, Hungarians and arrestable categories in V Corps area should be instructed by V Corps to move forthwith via LIENZ and INNSBRUCK for disposal by Seventh Army. This is being discussed finally tonight and we hope that SHAEF may be able to help us.[14]

Innsbruck lay to the west, in the American zone of Austria.

A striking consideration featuring in this flurry of exchanges is to be found in Alexander's FX 77292, sent to the Combined Chiefs of Staff in the early evening of 17th May.

To assist us in clearing congestion in Southern Austria we urgently require direction regarding final disposal following three classes:-

(a) Approximately 50,000 Cossacks including 11,000 women, children and old men. These have been part of German armed forces and fighting against Allies.

(b) Chetniks whose numbers are constantly increasing. Present estimate of total 35,000 of which we have already evacuated 11,000 to Italy.

(c) German Croat troops total 25,000.*

In each of above cases to return them to their country of origin immediately might be fatal to their health [emphasis added]. Request decision as early as possible as to final disposal.[15]

While the threat of military aggression by Tito provided the prime reason for 'clearing the decks' in Austria, it is clear that for Alexander the humanitarian consideration also loomed large. Indeed, there was no conflict between the two perspectives. As yet there existed no formal agreement to transfer the Cossacks to the Soviets, largely because the latter had yet to put in place logistical means of transporting them from the demarcation point at Judenburg to the camps of GULAG. Thus, their transfer to SHAEF-controlled territory provided not only the most humane, but also the speediest means of removing them from the potential scene of conflict.

A striking aspect of these exchanges, together with the extensive troop movements which followed, is that from 17 May onwards[16] none of the leading proponents of this forward policy, from Truman, Churchill, and Alexander down to Keightley, expressed any fear or misgiving that Stalin

---

* These were Croats who had managed to infiltrate the British zone while the majority of their compatriots were being denied entry at Bleiburg.

might intervene as Tito's ally. Indeed, events made it clear to observers on the ground as early as 19 May that Stalin was unprepared to assist Tito in his annexationist adventure.[17] Yet Macmillan claimed subsequently it was fear of a Red Army attack on the Western Allies that provided one of his principal motives for advising acceptance of the Soviet demand for the Cossacks and White Russians.

On 18 May, copies of signals relating to the foregoing policy directives were forwarded to 5th Corps:

> Personal for Gen Keightley from Army Comd.
>
> The attached copies of three AFHQ signals are forwarded for your information. FX 77363 FX 76939 FX 77382.[18]

The originals of all three messages had been dispatched on the previous day. FX 77363 contained a copy of Alexander's signal to Eisenhower requesting SHAEF takeover of 'Northern section of V Corps front facing the Russians'. FX 76939 contained Alexander's plea to Eisenhower to accept the Cossacks in the American zone, the *sole* alternative being to disband them in Austria. FX 77382 contained General Morgan's report on his return from 5th Corps on the worsening situation in Venezia Giulia and Austria.

This establishes conclusively that from the morning of 18 May Keightley was fully apprised of his superiors' plans to relieve 5th Corps of responsibility for the Lienz district, and to dispose of the Cossacks by means of alternative measures intended to preserve them from being sent eastwards to the Soviets.

Immediately ensuing events show these humane measures being ignored by the corps commander and his chief of staff, who by the same token withheld their intention of covertly implementing General Robertson's errant order of 14 May, providing for the handover of 'all Russians' in the Corps area to the Soviets. In any case, the proposals contained in the first two signals plainly superseded the Robertson order, which promptly became irrelevant.

So it was that, while Eisenhower's and Alexander's planned transfer of responsibility for the Cossacks to SHAEF continued apace, Keightley continued secretly implementing Macmillan's recommendation for their delivery to their implacable persecutors in the east.

On appreciating the critical situation faced by 5th Corps in Austria, confirmed by receipt of an urgent appeal from Churchill to Eisenhower, urging him to come to Alexander's aid,[19] and yet further strengthened by a visit of two of Alexander's senior staff officers, Eisenhower agreed to accept the surrendered enemy personnel within his command. On 19 May he informed AFHQ:

> As result of meeting with Generals Macleod and Eberle we understand the enemy personnel required to be moved into 12th Army Group area [in the US zone of Germany] consist of a maximum of 150,000 surrendered enemy of which approximately 105,000 are Germans NOT yet totally disarmed and 45,000 are Cossacks still fully armed.
>
> The Cossacks may be expected to move more or less as organized bodies intact ...
>
> In order further to assist any possible operations by A.F.H.Q. forces in Austria against Jugoslavs, we are willing to accept the enemy personnel mentioned above in the status of "disarmed enemy forces".
>
> Request subject personnel be directed to move over routes agreed 15th and 12th Army Groups to assembly area designated by 12th Army Group and that 15th Army Group be authorised to deal direct with 12th Army Group in this connection.
>
> In their area 12th Army Group will be responsible for disarming any of the above personnel, as necessary...
>
> Accompanying the Cossacks are an estimated additional 11,000 camp followers (women, children and old men). Until these persons can be segregated and properly disposed of as displaced persons they should be accorded the same treatment as the forces they accompany...
>
> *Copy sent to 5 Corps by G(Ops).*[20]

Copies were also sent to 15th Army Group and 8th Army.[21]

The next day Winston Churchill sent General Ismay this pressing query:

> Could I have a further report on the 45,000 Cossacks, of whom General Eisenhower speaks in his SCAF.399. How did they come in their present plight? Did they fight against us?

No doubt aware of the Prime Minister's sympathy for the Cossacks, originating in his heartfelt support for the White cause in the Russian Civil War, Ismay hastened to reassure him by referring him to Eisenhower's

> Scaf 399 dated 19.5.45 – urgency of moving into 12th Army Group area 150,000 surrendered enemy, including 45,000 fully armed Cossacks.[22]

Henceforward there developed a sharp divergence between measures adopted by SHAEF and AFHQ as to disposal of the Cossacks on the one hand, and Macmillan's diametrically opposed policy covertly pursued by 5th Corps Headquarters on the other. Thus, on 21 May AFHQ G-5 Section reported that '45,000 Cossacks plus 11,000 camp followers are being disposed of under SHAEF arrangements'.[23] Yet it was on the morning of the same day that 5th Corps Headquarters conferred on the planned delivery of Cossacks to the Soviet Union. No minutes of this decisive conference reached 8th Army, nor are they preserved in 5th Corps war diary. That afternoon the Corps Chief of Staff Brigadier Low drew up his deceptive 'Definition', which effectively ruled that all Cossacks be treated as Soviet nationals, a copy of which was forwarded to 8 Army.

It was now, too, that SHAEF and AFHQ began putting into effect the greatest military operation of the immediate post-war period in Europe. On the same fateful 21 May, General Eisenhower informed General Omar Bradley, commanding 12th Army Group, that 'Codeword our immediately preceding cable is quote COLDSTREAM unquote'.[24] The plan, as has been seen, was to provide such overwhelming American support to 5th Corps in Austria as to render Titoist resistance nugatory.[*]

'Lienz-Spittal', the intended destination of the American relief force, was of course the district where one of the two principal bodies of Cossacks and Caucasians was held (the 15th Cossack Cavalry Corps was interned further to the east). Under the Hague and Geneva Conventions 'camp followers' are required to be treated with the same humanity legally accorded prisoners of war.[25]

Eisenhower reported with satisfaction to Churchill that 'we are already doing everything we can to help out Alexander, including an offer to take over some of the prisoners'.[26] He further informed the Combined Chiefs of Staff 'that I have already agreed to allow 150,000 surrendered enemy to be moved northwards into my area. Steps are being taken to implement this forthwith'.[27] At the same time, no nonsense was anticipated in the event of war with Tito's thuggish army: as Patton's chief of staff General Hobart R. Gay notified his counterpart at 15th Corps, 'If Tito wants to fight do a good job'. Evacuation of the Cossacks and German prisoners of

---

[*] No mention of Operation Coldstream, which is fundamental to understanding of the Cossack tragedy, is to be found in the first two Cowgill Inquiry reports. The crucial bulky file WO.219/290 ('OPERATION COLDSTREAM. PLAN FOR REINFORCEMENT OF 15th ARMY GROUP') is discreetly omitted from the authors' list of 'all the key documents of the time' (*The Repatriations from Austria in 1945: The Documentary Evidence Reproduced in Full: Cowgill Inquiry* (London, 1990), pp. vii, 340). Christopher Booker eventually made extensive allusion to Operation Coldstream in his book *A Looking-Glass Tragedy: The Controversy over the repatriations from Austria in 1945* (London, 1997), pp. 201, 212-13, 230, 276 – while carefully omitting all reference to the proposed evacuation of Cossacks, together with every allusion to the proposed American occupation of the Lienz area.

war was regarded as a vital prerequisite to freeing 5th Corps of responsibility for their custody in the event of military moves to clear the Yugoslavs out of Austria. Speed was of the essence: as Alexander explained to Generals Bradley and McCreery,

> All surrendered enemy personnel should if possible be disarmed before being moved into Twelfth Army Group area. It is however likely that Cossacks may not submit to being disarmed until after they are evacuated in which case Para 5 of SCAF-399 will be effective:[28]

i.e. they were to be disarmed by the Americans on arrival, so relieving 5th Corps of the potentially hazardous and time-consuming responsibility.

On the same afternoon (20 May) the Combined Chiefs of Staff informed Eisenhower and Alexander that they approved the proposals and ordered 'direct action in accordance therewith'.[29] The forthright General Patton instructed his troops:

> If the Jugoslavian Partisans behave and do what they are told, leave them alone. If they do not behave, clean them out.[30]

Under his dynamic command advance US forces covered the ground at unexpected speed. Although obstructed by snow four feet deep on the highways, 3rd Cavalry Corps had traversed fifty miles by the dawn of 21 May, when they reached Mauterndorf on the river Mur. There for the first time they encountered British troops, who reported their arrival to 5th Corps Headquarters at the Villa Angerer on the Wörthersee.

General George S. Patton

Meanwhile, that evening a message from 15th Army Group to 8th Army was copied to 5th Corps, confirming that the advancing American forces would shortly 'in conjunction with 15th Army Group arrange evacuation and disposal of "disarmed enemy forces" as directed in FWD 21870 of 19 May', and 'undertake ground and air recces to make contact with tps of 5 Brit Corps in areas Lienz - Spittal and Tamsweg – Judenburg and take such other measures as will facilitate the rapid deployment of 3rd Army forces into these areas on later orders'.[31]

The natural expectation would be that 5th Corps was overjoyed at the prospect of being overnight relieved of its grave and pressing responsibility for the Cossacks. In reality, the reaction was of one of increasing dismay – much greater, it seems, than had they been required to retain responsibility for custody of 150,000 German and Cossack prisoners while simultaneously waging war on the Yugoslav Army.

Meanwhile, in blithe ignorance of this opening resistance on the part of 5th Corps, General Omar Bradley copied to 15th Army Group his order to the US 3rd and 7th Armies to evacuate the German prisoners and Cossacks northwards to the American zone. The latter in particular presented no problem, since

> It is expected that the Cossacks will continue to move as organised bodies intact whereas the German units may be substantially reduced by individual straggling to the north'.[32]

Apologists for 5th Corps' savage treatment of the Cossacks when delivering them to SMERSH ten days later rely heavily on the claim that they represented an intolerable burden to 5th Corps, which was at the time facing the threat of a purportedly mighty Yugoslav invasion.[33] One of the leading proponents of this view, Sir Carol Mather, was inspired to extravagant heights of metaphorical imagery:

> British troops in Austria really had their hands full, even a gigantic colander could scarcely strain the dregs of war.[34]

It is instructive to compare this lurid description by Mather, who was never anywhere near the scene, with that of Captain Nigel Nicolson (intelligence officer to 1st Guards Brigade), who was at the heart of it:

> To us the German/Austrian soldiers were not the defeated, hated enemy, so much as fellow-travellers of a long ordeal. I hate to say so, since it sounds so trivial, but the atmosphere was that of a match-tea after a hard-fought rugger-match. We exchanged reminiscences, we shared the duty of feeding, housing and even guarding the vast number of people in their open prison- and internment-camps, and because we had to rely so largely on the German officers to handle these masses, a sort of

professional camaderie succeeded our hostility...

Everyone was pretty happy. There was a common sense of relief that the war was over, and the various national groups felt secure under our tutelage. Even Tito's partisans gave us little trouble because they were so poorly equipped and organised.[35]

Besides, as is immediately apparent, no 'gigantic colander' was required, since *fulfilment of the policy concerted by Alexander and Eisenhower, and approved by Churchill and the Combined Chiefs of Staff, would have resolved 5 Corps' pressing problem over a week earlier than actually occurred*. Vociferous spokesmen for the British government's official viewpoint, such as Mather, Cowgill, Booker, Horne, and Keegan,[*] were only able to maintain their position by suppressing or obscuring this fundamental point. At the Aldington trial, one of his witnesses, a retired judge John Taylor who had been on Keightley's staff in 1945, declared on oath:

It looks as though General Eisenhower was ready to accept them, but how on earth you were going to get those Cossacks over those mountains I do not know.[36]

On the ground at the time (as Judge Taylor appears conveniently to have forgotten), the search for a solution was rather different. When at 5.45 on the afternoon of 21 May troops of the US 3rd Cavalry Group encountered the British 78th Infantry Division at Mauterndorf, instead of being welcomed with relief as deliverers, they learned that 'They do not need or want us'.[37]

The first of a gathering chorus of ever shriller protests was passed on to General Mark Clark by 8th Army at 10.45 that morning:

V Corps report 800 vehicles arrived in area A6056 and Mautendorf A5054 and camping there tonight.

Most important main bodies of Third Army do NOT move until final arrangements made. V Corps are NOT handing over until position clarified.[38]

Next day (22 May), General Omar Bradley ordered:

Third [US] Army will concentrate without delay in the LIENZ-SPITTAL area a Corps of 2 Divisions and in the TAMSWEG-JUDENBURG area, a Corps of 3 Divisions including at least 1 Armored Division. V British Corps in these areas will be relieved.[39]

---

[*] On the other hand, it is surely telling that (so far as I recall) no academic historian of any repute supported the sycophantic chorus.

The 5th Corps command was becoming seriously concerned by this dramatically altered turn of events. Keightley and Low were dismayed by the speedy arrival of the American relief force, which posed an unanticipated threat to the enforced handover of 'Cossacks and White Russians' to the Soviets concerted by Macmillan and Keightley during the former's visit to Klagenfurt on 13 May.

Alexander's orders plainly superseded any prior directive issued by AFHQ, and it must have been clear to 5th Corps command that the Supreme Allied Commander continued unaware of the 'Robertson order' of 14 March, with its requirement that 'all Russians' should be handed over to the Soviets. Now that American troops had arrived at the 5th Corps boundary, with the declared purpose of taking over relevant sections of the British zone in order to evacuate all 45,000 Cossacks to American custody, Keightley had no choice but to decide whether he should concur with this development, or continue following Macmillan's 'advice' to deliver them up to the Soviets. Following Macmillan's return from England on 22 May (as will be described in Chapter Eleven), he became determined on fulfilling the latter course, despite the fact that he ought naturally (not to say humanely) to have fulfilled orders from Alexander clearly replacing any prior order.

It was presumably the arrival of the massive convoy of 800 American vehicles that belatedly alerted Keightley to the necessity of discovering whether he should continue to implement Macmillan's 'advice', or accede to Alexander's succeeding orders which unequivocally overrode it. At 11.15 p.m. on 21 May, 8th Army (whose command, like everyone concerned save Keightley, had hitherto ignored the Robertson order) forwarded this enquiry A 4073 (copied to 5th Corps) to AFHQ:

> Reference your FX-75383 [the 'Robertson order'] dated 14 stating all Russians to be handed over to Soviet Forces and SHAEF 399 Fwd 21870 [dated 19 May] stating Cossacks accepted by 12 Army Group.
>
> Request earliest information whether approved policy is to despatch to SHAEF or to endeavour to secure direct return to Russians by Eight Army negotiations.[40]

Next morning, without awaiting a response, a further fateful conference was convened at 5th Corps Headquarters, presided over by Keightley and attended by his Chief of Staff Brigadier Low.

> Notes on the Conference held by the Corps Commander at Main HQ 5 Corps on 22 May at 1130 hrs...
>
> Priority will be given as follows (i) first to **the control, disarmament and evacuation to the Soviet Army of the Cossacks**...

4. B[oun]d[ar]ys

(a) It is not yet certain whether the Northern Corps bdy with SHAEF will be altered. In any case **a request will be made that they do NOT take over Spittal or Lienz, but that the b[oun]d[ar]y be all incl 5 Corps**...

5. Evacuation of Cossacks to the Russians

(a) CCRA* [de Fonblanque] reported on his discussions of 21 May; these will be confirmed or otherwise by Russians at Wolfsburg p.m. 23 May. Q [Tryon] to give orders on t[rans]p[or]t and handover of Cossacks according to programme to be arranged by CCRA on 23 May.

(b) Divs will be prepared to shoot at Cossacks to enforce the evacuation plan.[41]

From this it can be seen that Keightley and Low were stretching every nerve to *retain* the Cossacks for their violent delivery to the Soviets, despite the fact that an agreement to this effect had yet to be ratified. So far from wishing to rid themselves of the problem in the most efficacious, speedy, and humane manner possible, they preferred to kill Cossacks (including women and children, as the event was to show) in order to fulfil their unaccountable but nevertheless demonstrable eagerness to collaborate with the Soviets in dispatching their victims to Macmillan's anticipated 'slavery, torture, and probably death'.

By mid-morning on the same day (22 May), Keightley had read a copy of McCreery's signal A 4073 to AFHQ, which he had received the previous night at 5th Corps Headquarters.

Reference your FX-75383 dated 14 stating all Russians to be handed over to Soviet Forces and SHAEF 399 Fwd 21870 stating Cossacks accepted by 12 Army Group.

Request earliest information whether approved policy is to despatch to SHAEF or to endeavour to secure direct return to Russians by Eight Army negotiations.[42]

FX-75383 was the order extracted by Macmillan from General Robertson (the 'Robertson order') the morning after his return to Naples from Klagenfurt. Keightley was now made unequivocally aware that 8th Army Commander was awaiting a ruling from AFHQ as to whether the

---

* Corps Commander Royal Artillery. That this was still de Fonblanque's function incidentally confirms that he was not yet BGS, and accordingly that Low did not in fact depart on leave on the morning of 22 May, as he asserted on oath in court. This is among a plethora of evidence that Aldington perjured himself over the date of his departure from Austria. It can be seen too that at this stage Keightley expected de Fonblanque to be still CCRA on the following afternoon.

Cossacks should be handed over to the Red Army, or evacuated to safety in the American zone administered by SHAEF. The implication of the signal was clear. McCreery's enquiry whether he should instruct 5th Corps 'to endeavour to secure direct return to Russians by Eighth Army negotiations' reminded 5th Corps that, so far as the Army Commander was aware, *on 22 May there as yet existed no formal agreement with the Soviets to hand over the Cossacks*.

In addition, 5th Corps had that morning[43] received Eisenhower's signal Fwd 399, referred to in McCreery's signal. This was a copy of Eisenhower's message of 19 May to the Combined Chiefs of Staff, in which he stated his willingness to receive and disarm the 45,000 Cossacks, and requesting that

> subject personnel be directed to move over routes agreed 15 and 12 [US] Army Groups to assembly area designated by 12 Army Group and that 15 Army Group be authorised to deal direct with 12 Army Group in this connection.

Implicit in McCreery's signal was requirement for a stay on 5th Corps' engaging in any further action affecting movement of the Cossacks, until the requested ruling was received from AFHQ. Ensuing discussion between 5th Corps and the Red Army relating to any Cossack handover should accordingly have been put on hold forthwith. In addition, since arrangements for the transfer of German and Cossack prisoners-of-war from AFHQ control to SHAEF were well advanced (Eisenhower's message to that effect was already three days old by the time of the 5th Corps conference of 21 May), while McCreery's message made it clear that he did not regard 8th Army as bound by any commitment to the Soviets regarding the Cossacks, it must have appeared to Keightley from an early stage that AFHQ intended to accept Eisenhower's offer to accept control of the Cossacks.

Following lunch after the Corps conference on 22 May, 46th Infantry Division noted receipt of instructions from Corps Headquarters:

> Conference with Russian Gen taking place at Wolfsberg 23/5. Same arrangements as 21/5. Will let us know if any food has to be provided.[44]

Unknown to divisional commanders, it was about the same time as the 22 May Corps conference that Brigadier Low urged his counterpart Brigadier Floyd at 8th Army to call a halt to the arrival of American trucks dispatched to rescue the Cossacks, concluding:

> Do NOT now consider necessary for us to be relieved up to boundary suggested in our O 449 dated 16th as situation in Lienz well in hand and can be organized by one unit.[45]

That the author of this signal was Brigadier Low, rather than de Fonblanque who succeeded him as BGS on 23 May, was confirmed by Brigadier Tryon-Wilson in a recorded interview held at the Imperial War Museum:

> ... Brigadier Low ... at the *moment critique* ... decided that he didn't want that help, because operationally we were in a position to deal with it as we thought right and proper, and - which he did do'.[*]

Low's coldly cursory request effectively represented a death sentence for thousands of Cossack men, women, and children held by the British in Austria. It alone suffices to refute the official Cowgill Inquiry claim that their handover to the Soviets reflected decisions taken 'at a time of grave operational necessity, [which] led the chain of military command to take decisions some of which were not in line with Government policies'.[46] In reality, it was *not* 'the chain of military command' that authorized the surrender of Soviet and non-Soviet citizens alike to the Soviets, but the Minister Resident Harold Macmillan. So far as Churchill, Alexander and Eisenhower were concerned, the 'grave operational necessity' required immediate evacuation of the Cossacks to US custody.

At the 22 May 5th Corps Conference, reference had been made to General de Fonblanque's 'discussions of 21 May; these will be confirmed or otherwise by Russians at Wolfsburg p.m. 23 May'. That nothing had yet been finalized is likewise clear from the reference to Brigadier Tryon's giving 'orders on transport and handover of Cossacks according to programme to be arranged [with the Soviets] by CCRA [de Fonblanque] on 23 May'. The phraseology overall confirms that as yet no irretrievable commitment had been entered into: hence the need for a further meeting with the Soviets. As 5th Corps war diary on 23 May records: 'Negotiations for handover of Cossack tps to Russians opened'.[47]

Accordingly, the next conference with the Soviets was arranged for three o'clock on the afternoon of 23 May.[48] By that morning, however, 5th Corps had received messages whose implications clearly proved disconcerting to the Corps Commander and his immediate entourage. McCreery had sent his enquiry to AFHQ as to which of the two divergent policies should be adopted towards the Cossacks on the evening of 21 May. Were they to be delivered up to the Soviets (providing they were proven Soviet citizens, and no force employed), or transported to safety in the US zone of Austria?

---

[*] Cf. note at the end of this chapter.

The next day (23 May), Field Marshal Alexander himself arrived at Trieste to observe the unfolding of Operation Coldstream. He was joined there by a number of senior commanders, including Generals Mark Clark, McCreery, and Geoffrey Keyes, commanding the U.S. 2nd Corps, which had been brought up from Italy to strengthen 8th Army.[49] Orders were promptly issued in Alexander's name, confirming (with a minor logistical distinction) arrangements already in train for transfer of the Cossacks to the Americans at Innsbruck, and responding directly to McCreery's enquiry as to which policy he should pursue. General Mark Clark, commanding 15th Army Group, was instructed:

> For your information Combined Chiefs of Staff have approved proposals in SCAF 397 and NAF 979. You should therefore take action accordingly dealing direct with [US] 12th Army Group.

The first of these signals referred to Alexander's request of 17 May:

> Immediate operational need is to relieve 5 Corps of their present responsibilities in JUDENBURG and LIENZ areas of AUSTRIA to enable them to concentrate on Austro-Jugoslav frontier in readiness for opns against Jugoslavs should these be necessary. This would be achieved if the forces mentioned in your paragraph 3 could be directed from RADSTADT and BRUCK respectively into the MUR River Valley towards TAMSWEG and JUDENBURG and the MOLL and DRAU River Valleys towards LIENZ and SPITTAL.[50]

The second of these signals, sent at 12.57 on 22 May (*i.e.* the previous day), had been transmitted by AFHQ to General McCreery at 8th Army. Numbered FX 79904, it read as follows:

> Ref your A 4073 of 21 May asking for policy re Cossacks.
>
> 1. all who are **Soviet citizens** and **who can be handed over to Russians without use of force** should [be] returned direct by Eighth Army.
>
> 2. any others should be evacuated to 12 Army Group.
>
> 3. definition of Soviet citizen is given in AFHQ letter CR/3491/G1-British of 6 May [*sic* - read 'March'] addressed to 15 Army Group and Main Eighth Army. ref your A 4073 of 21 May asking for policy re Cossacks.[51]

These signals were issued by two of Alexander's senior staff officers, Generals Eberle and Macleod. It was they who had travelled from AFHQ at Naples to SHAEF Headquarters a few days earlier in order to negotiate Eisenhower's acceptance of Cossacks and Germans held in Carinthia, and whom Alexander described as 'officers fully acquainted with situation in 5 Corps area and [who] are familiar with my plans'.[52] There can thus be no doubt of Alexander's continuing concern for the welfare of the Cossacks, and given the circumstances it is likely that he discussed the matter in person with McCreery and Clark that day.[53]

A copy of the second message (A 4073 of 21 May) was sent to 'Main Five Corps for Gerrett' (the staff officer dispatched by 15th Army Group to supervize arrangements). It must have reached Colonel Gerrett either that evening (22 May), or possibly early on the morning of 23 May. It is uncertain whether Gerrett received the message before his departure from Corps Headquarters, which occurred on the same day. That morning 5 Corps reported to 8th Army:

> Nothing to report. An officer (Lt-Col [*i.e.* Gerrett]) of A Branch 15 Army Gp is flying from 5 Corps to 3 US Army this morning 23 May to arrange hand over of PW.[54]

Gerrett must have shown Keightley this signal. It is a measure of the latter's continuing duplicity that his reaction was to proceed as swiftly as possible with commiting his command to an agreement with the Soviets to hand the Cossacks over.

The 8th Army's earlier A 4073 enquiry whether the Cossacks were to be handed over to the Red Army or transferred to the Americans no doubt reflected a pressing enquiry from Keightley. AFHQ's decision (with its vital qualifications, no use of force, and requirement for individual screening as stipulated in the 6 March order) clearly represented a response to 5th Corps' vigorous objection to the proposed rescue of the Cossacks by Patton's 12th Corps.

Henceforward, so far as 5th Corps was concerned, AFHQ policy remained absolutely clear: Cossacks could be handed over to the Soviets *provided* no force were used to compel them, and *provided* they were Soviet citizens, as stipulated in the AFHQ ruling of 6 March.

The effect of this news on General Keightley is unrecorded, although it is not hard to guess that it must have caused him to reflect hard on what he was doing. Furthermore, the order transmitted to Gerrett was not the only one 5th Corps received on the topic. At seven o'clock the same evening (22 May) a further message was dispatched to 8th Army from AFHQ. Numbered F80197, it read:

> Personal for General McCreery from General Morgan [Alexander's Chief of Staff]. Reference telephone conversation with my M.A. 1800B hrs, this evening.

> One. SHAEF movements into 5 Corps area should be arranged between 15 Army Group and 12 Army Group in accordance with advice 8 Army. Gruenther is arranging.

Two. You have authority to pass Cossacks direct to Russians **provided force has not repeat not to be used** [bold inserted].[55]

A copy was forwarded by 8th Army to 5th Corps - presumably as a matter of urgency, since McCreery's telephone call to General Morgan was made in response to a pressing request from 5th Corps (received only three-quarters of an hour earlier), in which Keightley once again requested authority to block forward movement of units of 12th US Army Group into the Corps area.[56]

A major contention by supporters of forced repatriation to the Soviets is that the Cossacks represented an intolerable burden on the resources of 5th Corps. In fact, Corps command's determination not to allow the Cossacks to be rescued by the Americans *postponed* their departure from the Corps area by over a week!

Meanwhile Keightley had continued throughout the 22nd fully apprised of AFHQ policy intentions. At the time he began his conference that morning, Colonel Gerrett (present at 5th Corps Headquarters as representative of Mark Clark's 15th Army Group) received this message from US 15th Army Group, commanded by the energetic George Patton:

> For Fifth Army. 150,000 surrendered enemy now in British 5 Corps sector are to be moved to United States 3 Army sector. Route designated for movt is Lienz - Vipiteno - Innsbruck. Desire arrangements for mov[emen]t over portion this route in your sector be made directly with Eighth Army. 3 US Army is dealing with rep[resentative] 15 Army Gp now at 5 Corps HQ [*i.e.* Gerrett] on details of movt. For Eight Army. When details of movt worked out deal directly with 5 Army movement over portion route that sector. For Lt Col Gerrett 5 Corps. Keep Eight Army inf[or]m[ed] plans for movement to enable prompt movement arrangements to be made with 5 Army. Incl[ude] in your daily sit[uation]rep[orts] numbers moved.[57]

Gerrett will have drawn this message to the attention of Keightley and his staff on the afternoon or evening following the conference, but was vouchsafed no inkling that 5th Corps had that morning arrived at a decision to hand the Cossacks over to the Soviets, in preference to evacuating them by the designated route to safety under SHAEF control. Nor was he made aware of continuing vigorous resistance by 5th Corps command to the planned American assumption of responsibility for the thousands of Cossacks encamped in the Drau Valley between Lienz and Spittal. That Gerrett was being misinformed by 5th Corps command becomes increasingly clear, culminating in the report he sent 15th Army Group at the end of the month (see the conclusion of Chapter Eight *passim*). That same afternoon 5th Corps sent this urgently-worded objection to U.S. XX Corps:

> Most grateful your prompt action in moving south but in view of improvement in local situation understand that higher authority is proposing to SHAEF NO move your main bodies takes place south of Kleine Tauern until further orders. Suggest therefore you confine movement in our area to reconnaissance parties until then. 78 Div have been informed of this. This not to affect arrangements already made as to hand over of surrendered personnel. Will send liaison officer to clarify situation when further orders received from Eighth Army. Please inform 3 US Army of above.[58]

At the same time Brigadier Low sent an equally emphatic message to his counterpart at 8th Army:

> in the event main bodies US troops being ordered to move consider that in view of present situation b[oun]d[ar]y should be ... to [US] 12 Army Group Mautendorf ... and should not include to 12 Army Group Spittal and beyond as indicated in SHAEF signal. Do NOT now consider necessary for us to be relieved up to boundary suggested in our 0 449 dated 16th as **situation in Lienz well in hand and can be organized by one unit**.[59]

This message throws a flood of light on subsequent claims by apologists for the ensuing atrocities that the Cossacks at Lienz represented an overwhelming administrative burden for 5th Corps.[60] Even had they remained *in situ*, the reality, as Brigadier Tryon-Wilson (who was responsible for their maintenance and transport) explained at the 1989 Aldington trial, was that 'As far as 78th Div was concerned there was no problem with them at all'.[61]

Thus, at the precise moment the Cossack handover to the Soviets was being planned by 5th Corps headquarters, the Americans were assured: 'situation in Lienz well in hand and can be organized by one unit'!* Likewise, should it still be contended that the Cossacks represented the overwhelming burden or embarrassment to 5th Corps that is affirmed by apologists for forced repatriation,[62] it can now be seen how unaccountably resolute was Keightley's determination *not* to rid himself of the problem

---

* It is not hard to see why all reference to this signal is suppressed in officially-authorized apologias for forced repatriation, such as the works by Cowgill, Booker, Mather, and Horne. On 20 July 1986 the same Brigadier Low (by then Lord Aldington) informed the *Sunday Telegraph* that the handover of Cossacks to the Soviets was necessitated by a 'considerable threat of disorder and shortage of food, and the inevitable problems of the aftermath of a long war'!

by the most efficacious path available. Also striking is 5th Corps' suppression in all exchanges with the US command of the fact that measures were afoot to ensure that the Cossacks were to be disposed of by their delivery to the Soviets.

Low's overriding concern on 22 May 1945 to **prevent the Americans from removing the Cossacks that very day**, contrasts revealingly with his justification of his actions to the boys at Winchester College forty years later.

> We were under instructions not to let the Russians to advance further. **We needed therefore to clear the area** so that we could defensively dispose and support our three divisions... That, coupled with the shortage of food, and the tremendous problems of dealing with hundreds of thousands of people, can at least explain why **General Keightley ... was so anxious to clear the 5th Corps area of all prisoners of war... we felt that we simply had to clear the area of prisoners of war as soon as possible.**

Thus it was that by the evening of 22 May, just as the success of Operations Fairway and Coldstream in checking the Yugoslav threat to Venezia Giulia and Carinthia appeared assured, intense pressure from 5th Corps succeeded in halting Patton's vigorous efforts to relieve Keightley of responsibility for the Cossacks quartered in the Drau Valley around Lienz. Returned to 15th Army Group Headquarters at Florence, Mark Clark signalled Omar Bradley at the U.S. 12th Army Group as follows:

> personal to Gen Bradley from Clark.

> I have just returned from visit with McCreery's Eighth Army. He is concerned about the rate of movement of your Third Army to areas south of initial concentration in Enns river valley and feels that these movements unless closely coordinated with General Keightley's 5 Corps may cause congestion in his area.

> I deeply appreciate the speed with which you are assisting us. However as your liaison group has not yet arrived at this HQ I am not in a position to know whether your moves are in fact complicating Keightley's situation. Will you please have someone contact him at Klagenfurt in order that moves may be co-ordinated.[63]

Clearly McCreery's objection to the U.S. 3rd Army's proposed assumption of responsibility for the Cossacks reflected a protest on Keightley's part. On 26 May Eisenhower reported to AFHQ:

> At present only reconnaissance elements of Third [US] Army have reached "COLDSTREAM" objectives. These were informed by 5 Corps units that congestion and shortage of supplies makes further buildup in

subject areas undesirable.[64]

The remarkable extent to which 5th Corps was determined to retain control over the purportedly overwhelmingly intractable problem of maintaining the troublesome Cossacks is illustrated by the fact that a major purpose of the 'Coldstream' operation was to relieve 5th Corps of the major cause of 'congestion and shortage of supplies' arising from the problem of maintaining the German and Cossack prisoners of war. Moreover, if everything was above board, why did 5th Corps not state the true reason for their not needing American assistance in this regard: *viz.*, that agreement was nearing completion with the Soviets for the Cossacks' imminent handover at Judenburg?

Although Patton's proposed occupation of Lienz and Spittal continued to be discussed in signals,[65] the danger (as 5th Corps command clearly regarded it) was now effectively over. Three American officers from Patton's 3rd Army visited Arbuthnott's Headquarters to advise that their forces would not advance further unless required. Meanwhile (as was seen) it was confirmed by 78th Infantry Division that the trucks whose advance had been checked at Mauterndorf had arrived for the express purpose of evacuating Cossack and other prisoners held in the Lienz-Spittal area of the Drautal:

> L[iaison]O[fficer]s from three SHAEF f[or]m[atio]ns visited 78 Div with object of r[oa]d recce in case they should be called on to come south and take over part 78 Div sector. They had no infm that main bodies were to follow. 15 US Corps: 106 Cav G[rou]p thought to be going into Tamsweg - Mautendorf - Murau area. 20 US Corps: 3 Cav[alry] G[rou]p and 20 US Armd Div in Lienz - Spittal area.
>
> **800 veh[icle]s believed from 3 Cav Gp and were believed to be for evac[uation] of PW** [bold inserted].[66]

800 vehicles would have provided sufficient transport to remove *all* estimated 25,000 Cossacks held in the Drautal - had 5th Corps Headquarters been genuinely concerned to see themselves relieved of the responsibility.[67] It is worth noting, too, that the Cossacks would in that case have passed under control of commanders whose attitude towards prisoners-of-war in their custody contrasts strikingly with that of Keightley.

> General George Patton, always closer to insubordination than servility in his relation to authority, did not bother with appearances. He simply released 5,000 Russian POWs in mid-June 1945, orders notwithstanding.
>
> Again,

On 25 August, aiming at a review of standing orders, General Alexander Patch, commander of the U.S. Seventh Army, requested SHAEF to spell out American policy "on the use of troops to turn over unwilling repatriates to the Soviet authorities." In the meantime, he would suspend the use of force.[68]

Thus, 5th Corps' undeviating reaction to the proposed American takeover of the Drau Valley above Spittal, where the majority of Cossacks was encamped, was one of vigorous objection, prevarication, and finally obdurate resistance. At the same time 5th Corps Headquarters provided higher command with no intimation that they were determined on brutally violent entrainment of the Cossacks *eastwards* into the Soviet zone of Austria – still less, that they planned to include some thousands of prisoners whose nationality was other than Soviet.[69] Learning of elaborate practical arrangements concerted by 15th Army Group and the U.S. 12th Army Group for the Cossacks' evacuation to the US zone, 5th Corps strained every sinew to frustrate Generals Omar Bradley and George Patton – in order to oblige Red Army Marshal Tolbukhin and SMERSH.

Meanwhile, in advance of any agreement with the Soviets or authorization from 8th Army, 5th Corps began preparations for handing over *all* Cossacks, regardless of their citizenship, and with use of whatever violence the anticipated brutal operations might require. As ever, Keightley entrusted the planning to his obliging and energetic Chief of Staff, Toby Low.

The most blatant suppression of screening occurred within 36th Infantry Brigade in and around Lienz, where the *Kazachi Stan* was quartered. Yet perhaps the most curious factor in Low's deceptive 21 May 'Definition' is its failure even to mention the *Kazachi Stan*! Although a copy of the document was received at Brigade Headquarters the next day,[70] it was clearly (like that forwarded to 8th Army) designed for 'cover', rather than implementation. As Brigadier Musson repeatedly emphasized to me, 'I don't honestly think that screening, you know, in my area was really ever considered'. The 'overriding thing of getting them all – the officers out of the Valley and to Spittal' required that 'screening didn't really play any (I don't think) significant point in my mind till I'd come to talk with you'.

General Arbuthnott, Musson's divisional commander, twice or thrice raised outraged objection to handing over Cossacks in his custody, and only grudgingly succumbed when given a direct order by Keightley himself. It seems that *any* allusion to the *Kazachi Stan* in Low's 'Definition' risked being seized upon by Arbuthnott or others within 78th Infantry Division to justify implementing some form of screening.

Inclusion of the *Kazachi Stan* among categories to 'be treated as Soviet nationals' would at once beg the question how the substantial number who patently did not belong to that category was to be treated. And who were among the most obvious candidates for retention, but the elderly Generals Krasnov, Shkuro, and Kelich Ghirei, dressed as they were in Russian imperial uniforms?

This reconstruction is not entirely hypothetical. Further east, in 6th Armoured Divison area, last-minute discovery of a copy of the 21 May 'Definition' order enabled sympathetic officers in 1st Kings Royal Rifle Corps to make use of a charitable interpretation of its provisions to reprieve a small party of Cossack officers from being surrendered to the Soviets.[71] There can be little wonder that Keightley and Low were not anxious for 78th Division command to examine the small print of their 'Definition' too attentively.

So it was that 5th Corps command successfully schemed to disobey repeated orders to screen non-Soviet from Soviet prisoners. As was seen at the end of the last chapter, higher command, in the form of Field Marshal Alexander and Generals Mark Clark and Richard McCreery, was deceived into believing that 10,000 Cossacks were being dispatched to the Americans, having either been screened, or whose return would require use of force. I suspect readers will share my view that it is inconceivable Keightley engaged in this protracted deception, both of his superiors and subordinates, out of mindless malice towards his prisoners. Clearly some more potent influence was at work behind the scenes. As will be shown in Chapter Eleven, the evidence is clear that this shadowy figure was Harold Macmillan, who recorded in his diary that

> ... among the surrendered Germans are about 40,000 Cossacks and 'White' Russians, with their wives and children... We have decided to hand them over ...

APPENDIX

In November 1990 Brigadier Tryon-Wilson conducted a recorded interview with Dr. Lyn Smith of the Imperial War Museum, in which he stated:

> ... this is why we had to clear the decks. We knew about it, and the Divisional commanders knew about it, but nobody else did. And if you remember at one stage, I think it was Alex got on to General Eisenhower and said: "Look, can you relieve 5 Corps, and take all the Cossacks and Russians, and take them over. Can you come in and take over that area and that area there, so that we can concentrate on this area of the front instead of the enormous area which we were operating in". And

probably, when you spoke to Brigadier Low, he will have told you that
at the *moment critique* he decided that he didn't want that [American]
help, because operationally we were in a position to deal with it as we
thought right and proper, and - which he did do.

The reference can only be to signal O.527 (which it unmistakably
paraphrases), dispatched at a quarter past five on the afternoon of 22 May
1945 by 5th Corps Chief of Staff (Brigadier Low) to 8 Army Chief of Staff,
in which the former pleaded that

> in the event main bodies US troops being ordered to move consider that
> in view of present situation b[oun]d[ar]y should be (now ?) to [US] 12
> Army Group ... and should NOT include to 12 Army Group Spittal and
> beyond as indicated in SHAEF signal. Do NOT now consider necessary
> for us to be relieved up to boundary suggested in our O 449 dated 16th
> as situation in Lienz well in hand and can be organized by one unit.[72]

Tryon-Wilson's admission was inadvertently doubly damaging to
Aldington's account given on oath at the 1989 trial, for it showed, firstly,
Aldington's claim to have departed 5th Corps on leave on the morning of
22 May to be false; secondly, that it was he personally who intervened to
frustrate the Allied plan for the U.S. 12th Army to advance into the British
zone of Austria and 'clear the decks' (Alexander's expression) by
removing the Cossacks to the U.S. zone.

The signal O.527 accordingly comprized a significant piece of
evidence in an action for perjury brought by my lawyers against Lord
Aldington in October 1994, on grounds that he had throughout the 1989
trial falsified the date of his departure from Austria in 1945. By this time
Tryon-Wilson was 85, and was either unable to attend the hearing in
person, or dissuaded from doing so by Aldington's lawyers who feared his
being exposed to cross-examination. Messrs Allen and Overy accordingly
induced him to subscribe his name to an affidavit,[*] the relevant section of
which is cited here in full:

> I, Charles Edward Tryon-Wilson of Dallam Tower, Milnthorpe, Cumbria
> LA7 70G MAKE OATH and say as follows:- ...
>
> 3. I refer in particular to the passage on pages 5/6 in which I said that "at
> [le] moment critique he [Lord Aldington] decided that he didn't want
> that help, because operationally we were in a position to deal with it as
> we thought right and proper". My recollection of events is as follows: in

---

[*] The deposition is couched in unmistakable legalese, wholly uncharacteristic of
Brigadier Tryon-Wilson's normal manner of writing (we corresponded over a period
of years).

the early part of May 1945, 5 Corps were engaged in planning for
Operation Beehive, which was designed to prepare for the eventuality of
war breaking out with forces commanded by Tito. I do recall that at an
early stage there was a proposal that, for the purposes of Operation
Beehive, US forces should take over a large part of the 5 Corps area. It
was subsequently deemed unnecessary for them to come so far South to
achieve the state of operational readiness required by Operation Beehive.
Signals to that effect were sent by General Morgan on 16th May and by
Lord Aldington on 18th. None of this had anything to do with the
question of whether 5 Corps or US forces should be responsible for the
Cossacks.

4. In his Second Affidavit, Count Tolstoy misunderstands what I told Dr.
Smith at pages 5 and 6 of the transcript. The reference I there make to a
decision by Brigadier Low (Lord Aldington) was to the decision which
he took, in conjunction with others, on about 18th May, that it was not
operationally necessary for the purposes of Operation Beehive that the
Americans should relieve 5 Corps of so much of their territorial
responsibilities.* That took place before the Corps Commander's
Conference. As I said on page 21 of the transcript, the last order which
Lord Aldington made was on 21st May 1945.

This revised explanation is unsustainable. No such decision or signal
as that claimed on Tryon-Wilson's behalf is anywhere to be found in
connexion with Operation Beehive 'on about 18th May', nor was any
reference cited by Aldington's lawyers at the hearing to substantiate their
assertion.[73] On the contrary, detailed instructions for Operation Beehive
issued by 5 Corps to divisions late on the evening of 18 May confirm the
essential role intended for U.S. forces, and conclude with a reference to
'move of 15th US Corps and 20th US Corps to the South'.[74] The parallel
Operation Coldstream, which included provision for US forces'
occupation of Lienz and evacuation of the Cossacks to safety, continued
unabated until halted in consequence of Low's message of 22 May.

On Day 4 of the 1989 trial, Lord Aldington stressed that at the time he
did not feel confident of the Yugoslav withdrawal until it actually occurred
on 22 May:

I suppose one should believe what one is told, but I think we felt that it
would be wise to wait until it had happened before we took too much
comfort.

---

* This is demonstrably untrue. Plans for 'Beehive' were not drawn up and issued to
divisions until late at night on 18 May. They anticipated 'move of 15 US Corps and
20 US Corps to the South' (WO.170/4241).

Again, the wording of 5 Corps' signal O.527 of 22 May clearly implies that this was the *first* occasion on which the 5th Corps Chief of Staff requested a halt to the US advance into the Corps area.

Do NOT **now** consider necessary for us to be relieved up to boundary suggested in our O 449 dated 16th as situation in Lienz well in hand and can be organized by one unit.

The adverb 'now' unmistakably confirms that there had been no prior signal objecting to the proposed move.

There is incidentally no requirement to infer that Brigadier Tryon-Wilson perjured himself in order to assist a former colleague. At his advanced age and inaccessibility in his Lake District home to relevant documents, it is unsurprising that he accepted Aldington's lawyers' ingenious reconstruction.

As the Court evaded providing my lawyers with a transcript of the three days' proceedings at the secret hearing,* while the presiding Judge Andrew Collins ruled any solicitor audacious enough to act for me liable for costs incurred, any opportunity for further raising the issue in a court of law was thenceforth conveniently blocked.

---

[1] Nikolai Tolstoy, 'The Klagenfurt Conspiracy', *Encounter* (London, 1983), lx, pp. 24-37.

[2] FO.1020/42.

[3] FO.371/48814.

[4] Geoffrey Cox, *The Race for Trieste* (Letchworth, 1977), pp. 232-34.

[5] *Ibid.*, pp. 245-46. Cf. C.R.S. Harris, *Allied Military Administration of Italy 1943-1945* (London, 1957), pp. 328-50; Bogdan C. Novak, *Trieste, 1941-1954: The Ethnic, Political, and Ideological Struggle* (Chicago, 1970), pp. 179-87, 192-94.

[6] Letter of 14 August 1978 to Lord Aldington. Another former officer on Keightley's staff, John Crawley, recalled that Bendall also 'said he found it painful to take part in the Russian [Cossack] operation because the Russians felt sure they were going to their death, and he believed them. I even believe he said: "You're lucky not to be involved"' (letter of 11 October 1997 to Nigel Nicolson). Yet Aldington claimed at trial that almost no-one on 5th Corps staff anticipated the outcome.

[7] Eisenhower Library, Kansas.

[8] WO.170/4183. Christopher Booker claimed that Alexander's request was restricted to German PW only (*A Looking-Glass Tragedy: The Controversy*

---

* Court officials explained to my solicitors that the regular tape-recording machines (there were two to guard against any breakdown) had regrettably broken down on each successive day of the hearing.

over the repatriations from Austria in 1945 (London, 1997), p. 202). He was only enabled to advance the claim by ignoring the fact that Alexander's signal urges US acceptance of the 'total' of 500,000 refugees and PW in the 5th Corps zone. That the Cossacks were included in this total is made explicit in ensuing signals.

[9] FO.1020/42.

[10] WO.106/4059,363. The second Cowgill Inquiry report asserts that that this signal really emanated from General Robertson (Brigadier Anthony Cowgill, Lord Brimelow, and Christopher Booker Esq, *The Repatriations from Austria in 1945: The Report of an Inquiry* (London, 1990), p. 74). Their failure to explain how this is to be reconciled with the explicit heading 'Signed : Alexander', and its incompatibility with Robertson's own order of 14 May that 'all Russians should be handed over to Soviet forces', provide sufficient refutation of this characteristic distortion of the evidence. Indeed, that it was forwarded by Robertson's office begs the question why he did not immediately draw Alexander's attention to the incompatibility of the two signals.

[11] WO.106/4059,199.

[12] WO.170/4184,674.

[13] WO.219/290; WO.106/4059,372-73.

[14] WO.219/290; NA.383, 7-14.

[15] WO.106/4059,371.

[16] In his signal FWD 21699 of 17 May, Eisenhower pointed out to General Marshall the potential danger posed by Soviet military intervention in support of Tito (Eisenhower Library, Kansas), but thereafter the likelihood of such a contingency was dismissed without further discussion. Yet Macmillan subsequently cited this imaginary threat as the principal justification for the handovers.

[17] '19 May ... The terrific news is announced this morning that Tito has agreed to withdraw behind his frontier. Just in time, too. Corps had already got to the stage of issuing an Op. Order in the event of hostilities. Two U.S. Corps were moving down here also, & in general it must have become clear to Tito that we both prepared to use force, & able to do so successfully.

'I deduce also that Moscow has denied him support. Three days ago, Herr Hanni, a C.P. member of the Prov. Carinthian Govt., resigned & joined the rival Tito-inspired Slovene Govt. But yesterday he stated he had received orders from the Carinthian C.P. to rejoin the Austrian Govt: so it appears that Moscow does not now support this particular Tito claim' (Crosland Diary).

[18] FO.1020/42,108.

[19] On 19th May Eisenhower reassured Churchill that 'we are already doing everything we can to help out ALEXANDER, including an offer to take over some of the prisoners' (WO.219/290).

[20] FO.1020/42. Cf. WO.219/290.

[21] WO.170/4146.

[22] PREM 3/364/17. In 1919 Ismay had participated in measures concerted to frustrate a Bolshevik threat to India (*The Memoirs of General the Lord Ismay* (London, 1960), pp. 60-62.

[23] WO.204/2664.

[24] WO.219/290.

[25] James Brown Scott (ed.), *Les conventions et déclarations de La Haye de 1899 et 1907* (New York, 1918), p. 112; Gustav Rasmussen (ed.), *Code des prisonniers de guerre: Commentaire de la convention du 27 juillet 1929 relative au traitement des prisonniers de guerre* (Copenhagen, 1931), p. 112. Cf. Christiane Shields Delessert, *Release and Repatriation of Prisoners of War at the End of Active Hostilities: A Study of Article 118, Paragraph 1 of the Third Geneva Convention Relative to the Treatment of Prisoners of War* (Zürich, 1977), pp. 119-122.

[26] Alfred D. Chandler and Louis Galambos (ed.), *The Papers of Dwight David Eisenhower* (Baltimore and London, 1970-2001), vi, p. 67; WO.219/290.

[27] *Ibid.*

[28] WO.219/290.

[29] NA. 383.7-14.

[30] HQ US 3 Cavalry Gp Journal (NA. CAVG-3-0.7).

[31] FO.1020/42,123; WO.219/290.

[32] WO.219/290.

[33] Alistair Horne declared that 'the Yugoslav partisans had suddenly transformed themselves from an essentially guerilla organisation into one of the most powerful, and determined, armies on the European battlefield' (*Macmillan: 1894-1956* (London, 1988), i, p. 245). The claim is of course a fantastic absurdity, illustrating Horne's astonishing ignorance of the state of affairs in Europe in 1945.

[34] Mather, *Aftermath of War*, p. 132.

[35] Letter to Christopher Booker of 15 October 1988 – *not* cited in the Cowgill Inquiry's report.

[36] Trial Transcript, Day 12.

[37] NA. CAVG-3-0.

[38] WO.204/1615.

[39] WO.219/290.

[40] NA.383.7-14,67.

[41] WO.170/4241.

[42] NA.383.7-14,67.

[43] The 8th Army copy of SCAF 399 is stamped '21 May' (FO.1020/42,122), and bears a handwritten note: 'Copy sent to 5 Corps by G(Ops)'. The Cowgill Inquiry omits reference to this significant fact, while Lord Aldington swore in court that he never saw the message (Trial Transcript, Day 9).

[44] WO.170/4352. It is wearisome but necessary to point out that the Cowgill Inquiry here follows its customary practice of omitting all reference to a document when

its content appears dangerous to the Inquiry's commissioned purpose.

[45] WO.170/4184,921.

[46] Cowgill, Brimelow, and Booker Esq, *The Repatriations from Austria in 1945: The Report of an Inquiry*, p. 229.

[47] WO.170/4241.

[48] 'Negotiations for handover of Cossack t[roo]ps to Russians opened' (WO.170/4241). 78th Infantry Division war diary records on 23rd May: 'It was learnt today that the Cossack and Caucasian Divs are to be sent back to Russia in the near future' (WO.170/4388). Once again, the Cowgill Inquiry omits reference to these documents.

[49] Cox, *The Race for Trieste*, pp. 253.

[50] WO.219/290.

[51] WO.170/4183,487; National Archives, 383.6-31 (TS). Cf. 8 Army Adm Instruction No. 41 of 24 May: 'With regard to the Russians [in Austria] all who are Soviet citizens and can be handed back to the Russians without the use of force will be returned direct; any others will be returned through 12 Army Gp (SHAEF)' (FO.1020/2838).

[52] FO.1020/42.

[53] That some such discussion occurred at Trieste seeking protection for the Cossacks is described by Pier Arrigo Carnier, *Lo Sterminio Mancato: La dominazione nazista nel Veneto orientale 1943-1945* (Milan, 1982), p. 319. Although not entirely accurate in its detail, Carnier's account is too specific not to reflect a reasonably well-informed source.

[54] WO.170/4183.

[55] FO.1020/42,135.

[56] WO.170/4184, 921.

[57] FO.1020/42,130. Cf. WO.219/290.

[58] WO.170/4184,914. No copy of this signal is to be found in 5th Corps war diary (WO.170/4241). The Cowgill Inquiry likewise omits reference to the document.

[59] WO.170/4184,921.

[60] *e.g.* Mather, *Aftermath of War*, p. 130.

[61] Trial Transcript, Day 11.

[62] Sir Carol Mather declared that 'it was his [Alexander's] own headquarters which had issued the instructions 'to clear the decks', and for the repatriations to begin' (*Aftermath of War*, p. 170: cf. the chapter-heading on p. 118). In fact Mather was well aware that the 'clear the decks' request referred specifically to Cossacks being *evacuated to safety* under the care of SHAEF. Mather concludes his book with the claim that it was written 'by someone who was involved in the whole affair, and its aftermath' (p. 200). This is scarcely candid. In reality he never ventured anywhere near Austria at the time, and only learned about the forced repatriation from very limited material drawn to his attention half a century later later by members of the 'Cowgill Inquiry'. His book is a strange one. Its first fifty pages and

concluding chapter have nothing to do with events in Austria in 1945, and the muddled account of the repatriations sandwiched between reads almost as though compiled by another writer. This oddity was explained by a lady named Susan Hayworth, next to whom I sat at a friend's dinner on 6 April 1994. It turned out that she knew Mather well, and began singing his praises. When I cautiously inquired whether he would not have done better to have written an entirely autobiographical memoir, she promptly replied: 'That's what he wanted to do, but they insisted on the other book'. I asked who 'they' were, but she looked awkward and avoided answering. Later on, she mentioned that it was not the publisher who wanted the book commissioned, but 'these people'. I further received the impression that the publication had been subsidized. To my wife, next to whom my interlocutor sat afterwards, she confirmed that the book's purpose was to 'counter' what I had written.

[63] FO.1020/42,134; WO.219/290. Yet again, the Cowgill Inquiry omits reference to these documents.

[64] WO.219/290.

[65] At 8.40 on the evening of 22 May, 15th Army Group notified 8th Army that U.S. troops were moving 'to Lienz area to implement decision of Combined Chiefs of Staff that SHAEF forces will enter Southern Austria to assist AFHQ in dealing with operational **and disarmed enemy problems therein**' (WO.170/4141,141 = WO.170/4184,924).

[66] WO.170/4183,182. As ever, the Cowgill Inquiry omits reference to the document.

[67] It was also proposed to transport PW from British-occupied Austria to the US zone by trains operating from Mallnitz in 78th Infantry Division area (WO.170/4388,136).

[68] Mark R. Elliott, *Pawns of Yalta: Soviet Refugees and America's Role in Their Repatriation* (Urbana, 1982), pp. 106, 107.

[69] Although 5th Corps itself sent no report to 8th Army at this time, the Phantom signals unit based at its HQ informed 8th Army: 'Representatives of 5 Corps & Russian Force met yesterday [21 May] at WOLFSBERG Y6305. **NO final decision was made** but both agreed 1) that Russians accept COSSACKS & CAUCASIAN surrendered personnel in Corps area with their German Cadre 2) that they be moved by train to JUDENBERG B 2565 & evacuation completed by 11 June' (WO.218/248). If McCreery was shown this signal, it no doubt further spurred him to despatch his enquiry A 4073 of the next day to AFHQ.

[70] WO.204/10449.

[71] WO.170/5026.

[72] WO.170/4184,921.

[73] No such signal features among the Cowgill Inquiry's 'Key Papers', which were compiled with Lord Aldington's assistance. Nor did Aldington allude to such a signal during the relevant section of his testimony at the 1989 libel action (Trial Transcript, Day 4).

[74] WO.170/4241.

CHAPTER X
BY FRAUD OR FORCE?

O what a tangled web we weave,
When first we practise to deceive!
Sir Walter Scott, *Marmion*

Ensuing events show that Alexander was kept in ignorance of General Robertson's order of 14 May ordering the handover to Stalin of 'all Russians'. A week later Keightley was obliged to request clarification on being informed of the policy concerted by SHAEF and AFHQ for transfer of the Cossacks to American custody. For this confusion Alexander has by some been apportioned a degree of responsibility, arising from his well-known dislike of paper work and tendency to leave detailed application of operational orders to his staff.[1] In addition, throughout much of this critical time the Field Marshal was preoccupied with the major crisis arising in mid-May from Tito's aggression in Italy and Austria. Finally, political factors were implicit in connexion with treatment of the Cossacks, and these Macmillan might reasonably be better expected to understand than the military command at AFHQ.

Robertson's 14 May order was forwarded by 8th Army to 5th Corps at 9.25 a.m. on 15 May.[2] That evening, 5th Corps received a copy of the signal from Alexander's headquarters to Eisenhower, in which he 'earnestly' requested that he assume responsibility for the Cossacks and other prisoners of war in the British zone of Austria.[3] Why then did Keightley not immediately draw his superiors' attention to the irreconcilable contradiction between this and the Robertson order?[*]

That afternoon (15 May) two officers from AFHQ, Colonel Derry and Major May, landed at Klagenfurt aerodrome. At a meeting with Brigadier Tryon's deputy, Major Taylor, they explained that they had been sent to enquire what assistance 5th Corps required in respect of the vast number

---

[*] McCreery would also have seen both signals. Since no one thought to apprise Eisenhower of the Robertson order, it may be surmised that the 8th Army commander assumed it to be 'on hold' now Keightley was aware of the proposed removal of the Cossacks to the US zone. This would explain why from its inception the Robertson order was treated as dead letter, barely to be cited again.

of surrendered enemy personnel (including Cossacks) hindering 5th Corps's operational efficiency in face of the mounting threat from Tito. Their report back to Naples is revealing, and was privately acknowledged by Lord Brimelow as providing a likely instance of conspiratorial activity on the part of 5th Corps headquarters:

> ... It was obvious [ran the report] that some assistance had to be given to V Corps, whose commitments in regard to the various types of Allied prisoners-of-war, Displaced Persons, refugees, Cossacks and other surrendered enemy personnel was proving a hindrance to their operational role. A signal to this effect was sent to AFHQ.

Taylor stressed that no approach could be made to the Russians in Graz as negotiations were in progress between 5th Corps Commander and the Commander of the Russian 57th Army. Permission could not be granted for any member of the [visiting AFHQ] Repatriation detachment to attempt to enter the Russian zone.[4]

Apparently 5th Corps negotiations were so secretive, that even AFHQ must be denied access to the exchanges![5] Speaking as a witness on Lord Aldington's behalf at the 1989 trial, Major (by then Judge) Taylor asserted that the reason for frustrating the visiting officers' mission was that 'General Keightley was dealing with Marshal Tolbukhin, and it was far too hot for a DAAG [i.e. himself] to handle'.[6] In reality it does not appear that any negotiations on the topic were being conducted at the time with the Red Army. On the day of Derry and May's visit Keightley and other senior 5th Corps officers were being entertained by the commander of the Red Army 30th Corps at a luncheon party at Leoben, which the British participants ruefully pronounced to have been little more than a drunken hooley.[7]

On 17 May a Soviet envoy, Major Skvortsoff, arrived at 5th Corps Headquarters from Marshal Tolbukhin's Headquarters to discuss mutual exchange of liberated Allied prisoners-of-war. His British opposite number was again Major Taylor, who recorded that

> The question of the disposal of 75,000 Cossacks was raised [i.e. by Taylor*], but Skvortsoff stated that he was only empowered to deal with these [non-Cossack] ex-PW in the Wolfsberg area, but that he would inform Tolbukhin of this and had no doubt that arrangements would be made for their reception in Russian territory.[8]

---

* So the issue was *not* 'far too hot for a DAAG [i.e. Major Taylor] to handle'! Besides, why should it have been 'hot' at all, if everything were above board?

Thus, agreement had yet to be reached regarding the return of the Cossacks, while the exchange of liberated prisoners of war was being treated on an entirely distinct basis.

On the morning of 22 May Keightley held a conference, at which measures for handing over the Cossacks were laid down.

> Priority will be given ... to the control, disarmament and evacuation to the Soviet Army of the Cossacks.

In this connexion,

> CCRA reported on his discussions of 21 May: these will be confirmed or otherwise by Russians at Wolfsberg p.m. 23 May.

There was still no agreement to hand over the Cossacks!

The CCRA (Corps Commander Royal Artillery) was Major-General Edward ('Dolly') de Fonblanque, who had opened preliminary discussions with Soviet representatives at Wolfsberg for the handover of surrendered Cossacks.[9] Although the Soviets had yet to agree to the proposal, it was now ordered that 'Div[ision]s will be prepared to shoot at Cossacks to enforce the evacuation plan'. As we know, the blanket term 'Cossacks' included an estimated 11,000 old men, women, and children – many of whom were indeed destined to be shot and killed by British troops.

It will be seen in Chapter Thirteen how bloody and brutal the operations proved when put into effect. It is a striking fact that those who planned them at 5th Corps Headquarters anticipated from the outset that they might prove *more* violent even than the horrifying extent that occurred in the event. Large numbers of heavily armed troops and armored vehicles were to be deployed. On 26 May, 46th Infantry Division (Major-General Weir) issued a grim order, which included this revealing passage:

> If it appears that Brit life or property is in danger, or if any Cossack would otherwise escape, tps will have no hesitation in using firearms. Mass shootings will, if possible, be avoided...

The deliberate killing of prisoners of war fleeing violent treatment by their captors represents a gross and obvious violation of the laws of war. The Nazis had defined Russians as subhuman (*Untermenschen*), and now the British were likewise preparing to treat them as lying beyond the pale of civilization. A grave charge against Nazi war criminals tried at Nuremberg in the following year was their application of

> a broad directive concerning the use of arms against Soviet prisoners of war. This says that if a prisoner of war tries to escape he must be shot immediately.[10]

Clearly mass shootings were envisaged as a real possibility, and Cossacks were to be killed merely for attempting to escape from unprovoked brutal maltreatment. No tears need be shed for victims of this policy, since 'A very large number of the Cossacks are wanted for war crimes'.[11] This was a straightforward lie, no investigation of the issue having been conducted at any time by their British captors, nor did the Soviets ever claim or try them on such grounds. Who were they wanted by, and why is there no record of these alleged crimes being pursued by the Yugoslavs or Italians?[12] In any case, the implication that all were tainted by the alleged activities of some smacks once again more of the methods of Nazi Germany than the high ideals for which the Allies professed to be fighting.[13] Finally, how can perpetration of one war crime be used as justification for committing another?

Ilya Pinoci, who had earlier served with the *Russkii Korpus*,[14] together with his parents and little sister, had joined the *Kazachi Stan* during its withdrawal into Austria. General Shkuro having been a family friend from earlier days in Belgrade, Pinoci was well-informed about the general situation. Asked in court at the Aldington trial whether the 11,000 old men, women, and children at Peggetz and its environs were 'families of the serving men', he explained:

> Yes and no. There was a large number of refugees who just joined them.
> I would say that two-thirds were Cossack families who had somebody in
> the armed forces and the rest were political refugees, I think.

Many of these refugees were scattered individuals who, as the War drew to a close, sought refuge in Vienna. There General Shkuro directed measures for gathering them together.[15]

Dr. Pinoci further informed me:

> I left Belgrade at the end of September 1944 and saw Shkuro again only
> in February 1945 in Vienna ... Vienna was teeming with civilian Russian
> refugees from the Balkans at that time. What to do with them? Where to
> send them to? How to feed them all? At that time there was only one
> place in the world where Russians had a place to gather together and to
> remain under a half-way autonomous Russian administration: the
> Cossack camp in Tolmezzo, Italy. Shkuro organized a collection point
> for Russian refugees in Vienna at Radetzky Platz. This was a rallying
> point for Russian civilians of all ages and sexes and their families. From
> there they were transferred by military lorries and rail to Domanoff's
> camp. This camp was, although labelled as a military camp, filled with
> Russian émigrés and refugees, most of them civilians who never were
> Soviet citizens.[16]

Had *German* officers justified sending women and children to die in slave-labour camps on grounds that *some* men with whom they had come in contact *might* have been war criminals, one may conjecture the likely reaction of the Nuremberg War Crimes Tribunal.

Following this digression, the question may again be posed: why, on receiving from Alexander his twin AFHQ policy directives FX 79904 and F 80197 of 22nd May, both expressly prohibiting use of force, did 5 Corps Chief of Staff feel impelled to urge his pressing plea for permission to use that same force, while secretly issuing orders to put it into effect without awaiting that permission? Why did he and Keightley not prefer the course of obedience to orders, to say nothing of natural humanity?

It is further significant that in only one major instance did 5th Corps adopt brutal force on a massive scale to repatriate Cossacks. This was when thousands of Cossack and Caucasian other ranks and civilian refugees held by 78th Infantry Division in the Drau Valley were clubbed, bayonetted and shot during the first days of June, in order to transport them into the hands of SMERSH units awaiting them in Judenburg. In other divisional commands Cossack prisoners were successfully duped into being transported to SMERSH, generally on receipt of solemn assurances that they were being assigned asylum somewhere more distant from the Soviet zone.

The recourse to violence in the case of the *Kazachi Stan* and Caucasian Division alone did not arise from any unanticipated exigency. While the 'shoot to kill' policy decided upon at the Corps Commander's conference on 22 May was issued to all divisions, in the event its gratuitous use was directed uniquely against Cossacks in the Drau Valley (the *Kazachi Stan*).[17] It was 78th Infantry Division alone which was informed the next day that

> As security will be broken at first mention of disarmament it is proposed at that time to notify destination in clear and our intention to complete the move in an operational manner.

This explanation is deceptive, in that the Cossacks predictably co-operated with their disarmament some days before the operation. No one involved on the ground believed – or had reason to believe – that they would object to disarmament. Clearly, it is the fate of all prisoners of war to be disarmed at some stage. Nor is there any record of a Cossack's objecting to the procedure, although some evaded compliance.

Thus the anticipated resort to extreme violence must have arisen from a distinct consideration.

Within the 78th Infantry Division preparations were undertaken for what was envisaged from the outset would prove a ferociously violent operation. On 25 May, the 2nd Inniskilling Fusiliers war diary recorded:

> The Bn was to move as for battle with first line ammunition. The reason for this move was approx 30,000 Cossacks who had been fighting with the German army, and who were now our POW,[*] and did not want to leave their camp in the Drau valley, and return to Soviet Russia, which had been ordered, and a certain amount of trouble was anticipated.

On 28 May the battalion commander learned what was the prime purpose of the operation in the Drau valley:

> **The removal of the Cossack officers was carried out. As we had been warned that this was the crucial point in the whole operation**, everybody was more than usually vigilant.[18]

On the eve of the Cossack officers' handover, the 36th Infantry Brigade issued this letter:

> The following message from Brig. G.R.D. Musson, D.S.O., Commander 36 Inf Bde Gp, will form the basis of a talk to be given under unit arrangements to All Ranks of the Brigade Group on morning 27 May.
>
> 1. It has been decided by Higher Authority that all surrendered t[roo]ps in the B[riga]de area will be disarmed today. After 1400 hrs any surrendered tps found in possession of arms or ammunition will be arrested immediately and will be liable to the death penalty.
>
> 2. In order to ensure that this order is carried out peacefully, additional tps have been brought into the B[riga]de area. I hope that the order will be complied with and that there will be no outbreak of trouble.
>
> 3. It is our responsibility to maintain law and order amongst surrendered personnel and keep them in their areas.
>
> 4. It is our responsibility to ensure that their camps are secure from attack [by whom?].
>
> 5. I realise that **we are dealing with people of many nationalities**[†] whose languages we cannot talk and that **there are many women and children amongst them**.
>
> 6. You are faced with a problem that will demand great patience and tact and I am sure that you will overcome the many difficulties with which

---

[*] As such, the Cossacks were unequivocally protected by the terms of the 1929 Geneva Convention on Prisoners of War. Cf. Appendix A.

[†] That is to say, a substantial number were overtly acknowledged not to be Soviet citizens.

you may be faced. Be firm. Remember that quick and determined action taken immediately may save many incidents and lives in the future.

7. If it is necessary to open fire you will do so and you must regard this duty as an operation of war.

8. In order to give you some idea as to the action you should take in case of emergency, I will give you three examples.

(a) If a person or body of people attempts to escape you will order them to halt by shouting at them. If they deliberately disregard your order and run away you will open fire, aiming at the legs if you consider this will be sufficient to stop the attempted escape; if not, **shoot to kill**.

(b) If you are approached by an uncontrollable crowd you must **shoot to kill** the apparent leader. You must not fire overhead or in the air. If you do this the bullet will kill or wound some innocent person a long way away [strolling in the surrounding mountains, presumably].

(c) If you see any member of the surrendered persons attempt to use a weapon or attack you or any British officer or man, you will open fire immediately.

9. I have published the following orders for all ranks of the Brigade G[rou]p:

(a) Personal arms will be carried by all ranks at all times,

(b) Officers will have an escort,

(c) No one will go about alone.[19]

Next day Musson reiterated the dangers facing troops engaged in an operation, whose implementation was envisaged as hazardous in the extreme:

Above all else try to avoid casualties to yourselves, your officers and your comrades. This will be achieved if you are always on your guard.[20]

In the event the Cossacks' resistance unexpectedly reflected the spirit of Tolstoy or Gandhi, although this was scarcely the reaction to be anticipated from men of their legendary martial qualities. When the disarmament of the Cossacks took place, it was an operation of necessity rough-and-ready, and largely reliant on Cossack co-operation. A thorough search was in the circumstances impossible, and it was Cossack good faith rather than British efficiency which ensured the general absence of firearms in possession of the Cossacks.[21] As a 5th Corps report noted afterwards:

Disarmament was completed without incident on 27 May. Subsequent searchings of camps showed that the majority of weapons were handed in; isolated instances occurred later of Cossacks and Caucasians who had escaped from their camps still being in possession of firearms when they were encountered by our patrols. There is little doubt that the officers of both forces did all they could to ensure compliance with the disarmament orders issued to them by the British battalions concerned.

But before the handover operations occurred it was impossible to know what arms still lay concealed among the tens of thousands of formidable warriors encamped at the foot of mountains affording ideal cover for the guerrilla warfare at which they excelled. Their predicament being desperate, fighting could have lasted for days, causing severe casualties among British troops. This was the risk Keightley went out of his way to encounter, when by obeying his orders emanating from AFHQ he could instead have seen the Cossacks peacefully entrained for Radstadt or Bruck under SHAEF control, making their disarmament an American responsibility.

It is needless to labour the point further, save to emphasize the added singularity that the shoot to kill policy was uniquely planned to be deliberately employed against that body of Cossacks which included a very high proportion of non-combatant civilians. **It seems that force was anticipated as essential to repatriate the *Kazachi Stan* and neighbouring Caucasians, because deception in their case alone was considered incompatible with a decisive consideration undeclared in 5th Corps orders**.

The 5th Corps policy required an announcement to be made *en clair* before what was plausibly anticipated would become 'an uncontrollable crowd', against whom (as has been seen) it would then in all probability be necessary to

> open fire, aiming at the legs if you consider this will be sufficient to stop the attempted escape; if not, shoot to kill.

At the Nuremberg Tribunal, prosecuting counsel emphasized that

> It is clear ... that the Geneva Prisoners of War Convention imposes upon its signatories the strictest obligations to protect its prisoners of war from violence.

The context related to the shooting of prisoners of war who resist obeying orders issued by their guards.[22]

At the same time, Keightley was concerned not to alert AFHQ to the fact that extensive violence was anticipated to a degree that shocked General McCreery and Field Marshal Alexander (to say nothing of the Red Cross), when they were belatedly alerted to what had occurred. Brigadier Musson's letter to his Brigade reveals the extent to which British lives as well as Cossack were anticipated as being at serious risk. What overriding consideration induced Corps Headquarters to undertake this exceptional course, unique in its danger, inhumanity, flagrant violation of international law, and expressed AFHQ policy; while at the same time so curiously contrasted to the 'humane' practical stratagem of 'deception' (lying) successfully employed elsewhere throughout the Corps area?

What that consideration was seems clear beyond contention. **Deception could not be employed in the case of the mass of the *Kazachi Stan*, because it was intended to employ it in the first instance to extract those Cossack and Caucasian officers on whom it has been seen the Soviets were primarily concerned to lay hands.**[23] As 5th Corps 405/G letter of 24 May explained,

> It is of the utmost importance that all the offrs and **particularly senior comds** are rounded up and that none are allowed to escape. The Soviet forces regard the safe delivery of the offrs as a test of British good faith.[24]

Once the leading Cossack generals and officers failed to return from 'the conference that never was', it was correctly anticipated that their families and followers must inevitably become aware of the betrayal, and consequently the terrible fate that awaited them in their turn.

Thus, the requirement to rely on force in the Drau Valley alone to repatriate soldiers and civilians arose as an inevitable consequence of the decision to segregate and dispatch their officers in advance of the major handover. It can now be seen that 5th Corps' perceived need for violence was contingent on the predominating aim: **the safe extraction and delivery to the Soviets of the Cossack and Caucasian officers held at Lienz, Dellach and Oberdrauburg. Behind that necessity lay the overriding concern to fulfil the Soviet demand of 11 May for the return of the Cossack officers in general, and the tsarist generals Krasnov, Shkuro and Kelich-Ghirei in particular. Yet it was they above all whose non-Soviet citizenship should have ensured their retention.**[25]

General Musson told me that 36th Infantry Brigade lacked resources for implementing screening of non-Soviet nationals on an individual basis. This, even if true, is scarcely relevant. Had he received an order reflecting that consideration, he would have been entitled to question it on those grounds. In fact, he never received such an order.[26]

Brigadier Low was at pains to raise with 8th Army the question of use of force. But why did he not raise the other equally material consideration of screening? After all, AFHQ message FX 79904 of 22 May, of which 5th Corps received a copy, stipulated that only those Cossacks 'who are

Soviet citizens' according to the 'definition ... given in AFHQ letter CR/3491/G1-British of 6 May [*recte* March]' 'should [be] returned direct [to the Soviets] by Eighth Army'. Why did Low and his successor Major-General de Fonblanque not explain to higher command the purported practical difficulty of putting the order into effect?

The 5th Corps' plea to 8th Army of 23 May included these justifications for use of indiscriminate force to hand over Cossacks.

> **Cossacks will view any move with suspicion as to destination. Consider therefore may be necessary use force to move Cossacks at all from present area. Longer they remain present area more likely force have to be used. Request you confirm our freedom of action in this.**

The first sentence further betrays the extent of Keightley's and Low's duplicity. In the first place, they encountered no serious problem in implementing carefully-planned deception, with regard to both Cossacks and Yugoslavs, whenever it was (in all cases but one) considered appropriate. In any event, no one in 5th Corps could seriously have imagined that the Cossacks would regard evacuation *northwards or westwards in American trucks* with suspicion.

A few days later Keightley himself arranged the elaborate deception, whereby the Cossack officers were persuaded to travel *eastwards* in the direction of the Soviet zone, under the pretext that they were to attend a conference with Field Marshal Alexander.[*] Thus, the 5th Corps commander was confident that *a lie* ('on the word of a British officer') would suffice to dupe the 2,000 *disarmed* Cossack officers into travelling *eastwards*, in the direction of their remorseless enemies. Was the truth likely to be less effective in inducing *armed* Cossacks (it will be recalled that the plan was to disarm them at their destination within the American zone) to travel to obvious safety in the direction of SHAEF-controlled territory *in the west or north*?

The purpose of Keightley's glib falsehood can only have been to ensure that the Cossacks should *not* be rescued by the Americans. Ensuing events confirm this conclusion. At this very time, parallel Corps policy towards their Yugoslav prisoners presents a revealing anomaly. The 5th Corps headquarters was as determined to hand over Yugoslav citizens as it was Cossacks, yet no comparable request was issued for freedom to use force to effect the former. Why was permission requested in one case and

---

[*] Similar 'deception' tactics were employed by the Turks when perpetrating genocide against the Armenians in 1919 (Peter Balakian, *The Burning Tigris: A History of the Armenian Genocide* (London, 2003), p. 338).

not the other? Given the obvious risk of refusal the reason must have been a weighty one, and it is clear from the evidence what it was.

A week earlier Brigadier Low anticipated that Yugoslav nationals whom he was anxious to hand over to Tito would view any move with deep suspicion. A simple solution was at once devised: on 17 May the Corps order requiring their handover to Tito included the instruction that 'these forces will not be told their destination'. This euphemism concealed the reality. Plainly, the Yugoslav prisoners had every reason 'to view any move with suspicion as to destination', and Low's bland written instruction masked his oral instruction that they should be deceived into believing they were being transported to safety in Italy.* At the same time, Keightley made no request to be permitted to use force to repatriate Chetniks and other Yugoslav prisoners. Why the distinction?

By 23 May four days had passed since 5th Corps began repatriating tens of thousands of Croats. All had been successfully duped into returning without incident as a result of successful deception in fulfilment of Low's duplicitous order. If this policy were considered feasible in the case of the Yugoslavs, why was 5th Corps not content to employ it in the case of the Cossacks? Yet again, why the anticipated need for extreme force uniquely in the case of the *Kazachi Stan*?

In the event, the Cossack officers were successfully returned by means of dishonorable 'deception'. On 25 May divisional staffs were informed of the planned operation. As Anthony Crosland, on the staff of 6th Armoured Division, recorded that day in his diary:

> We have now received orders that all Cossacks, White Russians, Ukrainians, etc. must be handed over to the Russians. There must in all be well over 100,000 of them. So once again we start the sordid business we had with the Croats. This time we are building several huge stockades, surrounded by wire: into this the victims will be shepherded, disarmed, but not given an inkling of their future: then on a given date they will be marched into the Russian area under heavy guard. The Russians say they want the rank-and-file for forced labour, but the officers they propose to treat as traitors.

In this manner thousands of Cossacks held by 46th Infantry Division and 7th Armoured Brigade were taken in trucks to be handed over to the Soviets at Judenburg. With a few individual exceptions, they were induced to do so under the belief that they were being moved to other camps. The Cossack officers at Lienz were deceived into travelling to a wired camp at

---

* Telephone communication between 5th Corps and 8th Army was still inoperative at this time (WO.170/4184).

Spittal where they were assured of being received by Field Marshal Alexander, while in reality they were dispatched onwards under heavily armed guard to the Soviet-occupied zone of Austria.

Once again, it is important to recall that the only substantial group of Cossacks against whom use of savage force was anticipated from the outset was the mass of other ranks and civilian refugees encamped in the Drau Valley around Lienz and Spittal. Although this anomaly has never before been remarked, let alone subjected to examination, its explanation becomes evident from consideration of the records.

Following the Corps decision of 21 May effectively to define all Cossacks as Soviet nationals liable for return, the senior staff officer (GSO1) to the BGS at 5th Corps, Lieutenant-Colonel Ralph Turton, conferred with his counterpart at 78th Infantry Division Headquarters, Lieutenant-Colonel Henry Nicholl. After discussing logistical arrangements for the transport of Cossacks and Caucasians, the report of their discussion concluded:

> Time and date for complete disarmament is requested from HQ 5 Corps. It is requested that this date be nominated 24 hrs in adv[ance] and 48 hrs before time of departure of first train.
>
> As security will be broken at first mention of disarmament it is proposed at that time to notify destination in clear and **our intention to complete the move in an operational manner.**[27]

A copy of this instruction was sent on 23 May to 36th Infantry Brigade, responsible for Cossacks (the *Kazachi Stan*) and Caucasians held by 78th Infantry Division in the Drau Valley, commanded by Major-General Robert Arbuthnott. It is significant that no equivalent order was issued by 5th Corps to the three other formations responsible for handing over Cossacks. That they had already been disarmed without demur confirms that 5th Corps had no reason to fear violent resistance on the part of Cossacks held in the vicinity of Lienz.

The 6th Armoured Division remained obstinately opposed to use of force or deception. Its commander, General Murray, informed me in 1975 that he never received orders to use force or deception, and would not have obeyed them if he had:

> But funnily enough I never got orders [to use force] - if I got orders like that I wouldn't have obeyed them. And I'm *astonished* that Arbuthnott sat down under them ... and then to have the conference which never was going to take place is something I thought *absolutely unbelievable* ... Keightley ... was rather apt to take short cuts. He didn't get any change out of my outfit in the sense that he got it out of Arbuthnott, because

Arbuthnott stooped to such a level, which I wouldn't have thought any British officer would ever do.* And I must say (I can't help it) I attribute it all to Charles Keightley ... he knew that I was unlikely to be a very helpful subordinate in this way ... I mean, to go and intervene in the way that Arbuthnott did, and carry out operations such as he did: we couldn't have done it, I'm absolutely certain. And we certainly didn't in the event.[28]

As has already been described, Keightley, who throughout recognized himself as obliged to tread very carefully in the matter, adroitly arranged for the majority of Cossacks held by Murray to be transferred that day (22 May) to the less scrupulous Major-General Weir's command at 46th Infantry Division. The majority of the 15th Cossack Cavalry Corps was accordingly handed over by Weir's Division, this being effected as elsewhere by effective use of deception:[†]

It is certain that, if they had known of this plan, there would have been wholesale attempts at desertion and suicide.[29]

It is gratifying to record, however, that most soldiers in the Division were as disgusted by the operation as their comrades in 78th Infantry Division and 6th Armoured Division. Lieutenant-Colonel C.E. Bond, then serving in 46th Infantry Division, informed me that

When it was learned that the Cossacks, including the German officers, were to be handed over, we made our protest in the strongest possible terms available to serving officers, first to General McCreery at Eighth Army, and, through him, to Field Marshal Alexander. Our protest was fully supported and we heard that it had been referred to the Prime Minister itself.[30]

Needless to say, Keightley did not permit the protest to reach McCreery, let alone Alexander or Churchill. This falsehood can only have originated with 5th Corps command. British officers were lied to in much the same way as were the Cossacks.

---

* This was inadvertently unfair to Arbuthnott, who (unknown to General Murray) had protested vigorously, until given a flat order to obey by Keightley himself.

† Article 26 of the 1929 Geneva Convention stipulates that prisoners-of-war must be informed of their destination when being transferred from one location to another (Gustav Rasmussen (ed.), *Code des prisonniers de guerre: Commentaire de la convention du 27 juillet 1929 relative au traitement des prisonniers de guerre* (Copenhagen, 1931), p. 116). I doubt the signatories envisaged providing a false destination in order to lure prisoners-of-war into death or slavery as a legitimate interpretation of this provision.

Colonel Bond's revulsion was widely shared within units of 46th Infantry Division. Lieutenant David Nockels, serving in the Royal Horse Artillery, recounted his grim experience.

> My troop sergeant went with the first convoy, and on his return he related to me what had happened. He was white with anger & wept when he told me of some of the prisoners leaping off the bridge to try & escape the Russian guards. Some of them mere boys of not more than 13 or 14 years, through the age range to quite elderly men.
>
> The attitude of the other ranks was one of disdain toward the officers. It was apparent that in their eyes we had let them down – we had cheated the Cossacks. We officers of course knew no more than any of the men, but at that time some of the men were as near to mutiny as any I had ever seen. The position was extremely distasteful and unstable.[31]

So far as can be assessed, such distaste was almost universal at the time. Thus Major Lawrence Stringer, of the Durham Light Infantry, recalled the operation to have been 'the unhappiest episode in the whole of my military career ... my view represents the view of all our chaps'.[32]

Captain Michael Frewer (also of the Durham Light Infantry), at the time Intelligence Officer with the Royal Artillery at 46th Infantry Divisional Headquarters, described to me the stratagem devised by his command.

> The plan, as I remember it, was this. It was known that the Cossacks (the White Russians) would *not* want to be returned to the Red Russians. In fact it was known that they had deliberately surrendered to the British Army rather than either to the French or the Americans - obviously not the Red Russians - because they hoped to get a fairer deal. And so the plan roughly was this: that the men, the officers and men of these Cossack brigades or Cossack divisions were told that they were going to be moved to a new camp in Italy, *i.e.* south of their position. A vast fleet of three-ton trucks was assembled on various days (I think four or five days in succession); and the Cossacks were loaded into these trucks, all of which, besides having their driver and co-driver in the front of the truck, had two British soldiers in the back of the truck with loaded rifles (I remember clearly the instructions).
>
> The route that these trucks was to take was very carefully chosen. For the first ten miles or so it pointed south, so that the deception plan could appear to have some realism, but then there was to be a quick change of direction so that the convoy of trucks started to move north towards the Russian line. And at that point onwards at very frequent intervals of ten to twenty-five yards along the road on each side there were to be British soldiers, again with loaded rifles, to prevent anyone leaping out of the

trucks and getting away.

All this clearly was connected with the feeling that these White Russians would do anything they could to not be handed over to the Soviets. As soon as the trucks turned north towards the Russian lines, the instructions to the drivers were to put their foot down on the accelerator and drive as fast as they could (which was probably then forty or fifty miles an hour) up this main road artery, which was to be cleared of all other transport and civilians, so that the trucks would get straight through at high speed, and the chances of anyone getting out of the trucks surviving were practically nil.[33]

Sergeant George Rhodes, who was seconded to this escort duty *en route*, remembered how effectively the plan worked in the field.

I think a different lot of troops were used each day. It was an unpleasant but peaceful business when our turn came, probably because the Cossacks had been told they were going to an American camp.[34]

One of the German officers dispatched with the Cossacks, Karl-Gottfried Vierkorn, was among those who could never forget the moment when their column arrived in Judenburg: it was not until then that it belatedly dawned on him that they had been betrayed.[35]

Precisely the same ruse was employed within 7th Armoured Brigade, independently attached to 5th Corps. General K. C. (Ted) Cooper, then commanding the Brigade, told me how

we drove them during the night as far south as we could so as to confuse them... [The Cossacks were told they were going to a] new camp. We moved them south, and then during the dawn we brought them up to Judenburg. I had one or two posts out in case there was any trouble once they realized I had them on *this* road more, because there it was getting dawn and they might have then appreciated what was happening to them. Which indeed they did. About dawn they began to realize that they weren't going south: they were going north. They were no fools. And they spotted it. And they simply came up to Judenburg, and then they got out of the lorries, and they had to march over the bridge. And I suppose the most frightful sight that I saw was the - the General went first, and he said: 'well, this is it, chaps!' Over he went. The others, as they went over, they took off every single thing they'd got: wristwatches, rings - as they got on to the bridge and said, 'well, here you are chaps - Tommies!' - and they threw them back...

And it was a very nasty one put over on the soldiers. They didn't like it at all - my soldiers. They felt *very* badly about it. Very, very badly.[36]

This successful deception, like those perpetrated with other divisions, was devized at Corps Headquarters, as General Cooper again clearly recalled:

> ... it was all planned. We all had conferences and that sort of thing: we gave our ideas - at Corps. And worked it out, yes.

> ... We all discussed it: how were we going to do it, and we all put up our suggestions, and that sort of thing ... I remember some of those meetings where we thrashed it out.* It was very detailed in the end, it had to be, so as the timing was correct.

> Because it was a lot of people to move - a lot of people to move.

Further east, 5th Corps's extensive resort to perfidy had proved equally effective with regard to Croats handed over to Tito's executioners, who slaughtered the great majority in their thousands. Corps Headquarters planned to employ the same method in effecting the repatriation of Cossacks, and expected it to prove similarly efficacious. In the event, thousands of Cossacks *were* successfully repatriated by means of deception. Few could be brought to believe that British officers would willingly lie to them. The question must then be reiterated: with the policy of 'deception' proven generally successful, why did 5th Corps Chief of Staff find it necessary to appeal to 8th Army to be permitted to use force against the Cossacks? After all, one prime advantage of deception was that it could be claimed that its victims returned freely.

Of course, no one could be certain that deception would prove wholly effective on any occasion, and unforeseen contingencies might occur. But the parallel case of the Yugoslavs, together with Cossacks held in other divisional areas, illustrates just how anomalous appears the intention to employ indiscriminate violence uniquely in the case of the Cossack other ranks, civilians, women (a number of them pregnant), children, and babies at Peggetz. It will also be recollected that the explicit AFHQ prohibition on use of force when repatriating Soviet citizens issued to 5th Corps on 13 March remained effective throughout this time – as was emphasized by General McCreery himself in his order to 5th Corps of 13 June.

On or about 18 May, 5th Corps received from 8th Army a copy of AFHQ order FX 77268 requiring 'Chetniks and dissident Yugoslavs' held in Southern Austria to be evacuated to safety in North Italy. 5th Corps responded with an urgent plea to 8th Army to be permitted to fulfil their

---

* General Cooper's allusion is doubtless to the key conferences held on the mornings of 21st and 22nd May. Since minutes of the meetings have not survived, his memory of what occurred at them is valuable.

plan to hand the Chetniks* over to Tito. The 8th Army forwarded the request to AFHQ, which responded on 23 May with order FX 80836:

> Agree that all Jugoslav Nationals in Eighth Army area should be returned by you to Jugoslavs **unless this involves use of force** in which case they should be dealt with in accordance with AFHQ 77268 of 17 May.

AFHQ policy in the case of the Yugoslavs thus replicated that issued the previous evening with regard to the Cossacks:

> You have authority to pass Cossacks direct to Russians **provided force has not repeat not to be used**.

The predictable effect of Keightley's secret decision to flout McCreery's orders by authorizing indiscriminate force to be used against the Cossacks at Lienz and neighbouring Caucasians will be described in Chapter Thirteen. Meanwhile the next chapter will consider the murky part played by the Minister Resident for the Mediterranean, the Right Honourable Harold Macmillan.

---

[1] General Sir William Jackson and Group Captain T.P. Gleave, *The Mediterranean and Middle East* (London, 1988), vi (part iii), p. 362. Nigel Nicolson (Alexander's biographer) also proposed this consideration to me. Alexander's alleged slackness in this respect may in part have arisen from his being a fighting general, who liked to be up with the men at the front line as much as possible (John North (ed.), *The Alexander Memoirs 1940-1945* (London, 1962), p. 14).

[2] FO.1020/42,92.

[3] FO.1020/42.

[4] FO.916/126558.

[5] Derry and May were presumably despatched to 5th Corps in response to McCreery's AC/189 enquiry sent to 15th Army Group and AFHQ early the previous morning (14 May).

[6] Trial Transcript, Day 12.

[7] 'Comd 5 Corps late but we eventually arrived there and had a tremendous party. 2015 hrs Arrived back at HQ. (The worse for wear)' (Norrie diary).

[8] FO.916/1020.

[9] In his journal, compiled some years later, Major-General de Fonblanque recalled of the period 21-23 May that 'The Cossack problem was on us and in connection therewith I had at least two conferences with Russians at Wolfsberg'.

[10] *The Trial of German Major War Criminals: Proceedings of the International Military Tribunal Sitting at Nuremberg Germany* (London, 1946-51), ix, p. 329.

---

* Yugoslav royalists who had fought for the Allies, whom Macmillan and Keightley felt should be killed too.

---

[11] WO.170/4473. 27 May '3 W[elsh.G[uards]. L.O. <u>Exercise Cossack</u> ... (N.B. Shoot to kill if it becomes necessary)' (Nicolson Log Book, p. 113): in the event it did not. In 1944 German authorities in Croatia received disturbing reports of outrages allegedly perpetrated by soldiers of the 15th Cossack Cavalry Corps (Peter Broucek (ed.), *Ein General im Zwielicht: Die Erinnerungen Edmund Glaises von Horstenau* (Vienna, 1980-88), iii, pp. 292, 371, 392). The reports were challenged by an officer representing the Corps (*ibid.*, p. 372; Erwein Karl Graf zu Eltz, *Mit den Kosaken: Kriegestagebuch 1943-1945* (Donaueschingen, 1970), pp. 89-90). No charge against the alleged perpetrators appears to have been raised by the Yugoslav Government. Finally, and most significantly in the present context, *no* reports of such crimes were lodged with British 5th Corps in Austria. There is some evidence of licentious – on occasion, violent - behaviour by Cossacks following their initial plunge into the chaotic civil war in Croatia, but effective measures were swiftly implemented by their German officers to impose discipline. Philipp von Schoeller, who served as *Rittmeister* in the Cossack Corps, emphasized to me the stern punishment accorded all ranks found guilty of war crimes. 'We would have immediately been court-martialled and heavily punished for breach of law of war as for instance was the case with Lieutenant-Colonel Paul Baron von Wolff who had given the order to shoot five hostages after a transport of wounded Cossacks had been raided and butchered... Wolff was degraded, sent to a punishment battalion as a private ...' (letter of 7th March 1989). Cf. also my *Victims of Yalta* (London, 1977), p. 226; Samuel J. Newland, *Cossacks in the German Army 1941-1945* (London, 1991), pp. 152-53).

[12] Attempts have been made to palliate the forced repatriation in Austria by representing the Cossacks as universally guilty of unspeakable war crimes. A characteristic example is that of Sir Peter Wilkinson, who served with an SOE unit in wartime Slovenia. In his memoirs, he asserts that 'in Slovenia and particularly in Croatia, we had suffered greatly at the hands of the Cossacks who were the cruellest of the cruel and apparently licensed by their German officers to rape and loot at will' (*Foreign Fields: The Story of an SOE Operative* (London, 1997), p. 241). In reality, Sir Peter knew full well that the Cossacks were never stationed in Slovenia. Moreover, the claim that 'we had suffered greatly at the hands of the Cossacks' appears on closer examination to be untrue. Challenged by me, Sir Peter in a letter dated 19th January 1998 sought to defend his charge, explaining 'that my reference to the Cossacks to which you refer is a fair description of the reputation they enjoyed among the peasants who were the victims of their foraging parties ...' So it transpires that his accusation rested, *not* on heroic first-hand personal experience ('we had suffered greatly'), but on hearsay accounts originating with local inhabitants who possessed no practical means of distinguishing between Cossacks (who were not there anyway!) and notoriously

undisciplined 'Caucasian' units who *were* operating in Slovenia. Nor was this the sole obstacle to his extracting accurate information in the Slovenian countryside. In a letter of 10 November 1989 to Messrs Rubinstein Callingham he described Slovene as 'a language I neither speak nor understand'. In fact *at the time* it was 'Mongols' (Kalmucks, or possibly Caucasian levies) whom Wilkinson (27 April 1944) accused of being responsible for appalling acts of violence and rapine, in a lengthy and detailed report containing no mention of Cossacks (Thomas M. Barker, *Social Revolutionaries and Secret Agents: The Carinthian Slovene Partisans and Britain's Special Operations Executive* (Boulder, 1990), p. 107). Wilkinson was in close contact with Low (Aldington) following his arrival in Austria in May 1945 (cf. his *Foreign Fields*, pp. 233-37, 239). It may well be that Wilkinson was the principal or sole source of allegations of Cossack war crimes propagated from 5th Corps Headquarters by his friend Toby Low.

[13] 6th Armoured Division intelligence at the time (5 May sitrep) knew nothing of the 'war crimes' charge, recording on the contrary that the Cossacks [*i.e. Kazachi Stan*] were 'reported willing to surrender to British but NOT to YUGOSLAVS or Communist partisans [and] complain that their families are being slaughtered by GARIBALDI partisans' (WO.170/4337). As Anthony Crosland noted in his diary on the eve of their arrival in Austria, 'Another fantastic complication here is the presence in the mountains of no fewer than 35,000 Cossacks! These unfortunate men were anti-Soviet Russians from the Don & Kuban, who (complete with wives & families) evacuated c. the Germans in 1943, & were settled by them in a hilly area here in N. Italy. Many Italians were turned out to make room for them, & the local pop. merely wants to be rid of them. They themselves have not formed an active fighting unit on the German side: their only military activity has been local defence of a Home Guard nature v the patriots. Another pretty little refugee problem for us'. Following the Division's arrival in Austria Crosland came to believe that the Cossacks had after all been guilty of war crimes. However, since he possessed no means at that time of acquiring reliable information on the topic, it seems likely that his comment originated in Corps Headquarters disinformation.

[14] D. P. Vertepov (ed.), *Русский Корпус на Балканах во Время II Великой Войны 1941-1945 г.г.* (New York, 1963), p. 104.

[15] Trial Transcript, Day 26.

[16] Letter of 6 April 1988. Zoe Polanska, whose horrific experiences during the bloody operation at Peggetz are recounted in Chapter 13, was among refugees who made their way from Vienna to join the Cossacks at Lienz (Trial Transcript, Day 27).

[17] Francis Carr was serving in 1945 as a platoon commander in 1st Battalion of the 60th Rifles. He informed me that 'The only operation we had to perform was lining the route the Cossacks took to Judenburg in Styria ... We were not

told to shoot them if they broke away. As far as I can remember, such a possibility was never mentioned' (letter of 13th January 1989). This was in 6th Armoured Division, commanded by the humane General Murray.

[18] WO.170/5018.

[19] WO.170/4396.

[20] WO.170/4461; WO.170/4396.

[21] A young Cossack in the *Kazachi Stan* recalled that, while heavy and automatic weapons were handed over to the British during the official disarmament on 25 May, many Cossacks secretly retained small-arms such as carbines and pistols (Nikolai Vasiliev, 'Записки юного казака', in N. S. Timofeev and S. D. Bodrov (ed.), *Война и судьбы* (Nevinnomyssk, 2002-5), i, p. 17).

[22] *The Trial of German Major War Criminals*, iii, pp. 40-41, 42.

[23] The British Government's explanation for prior removal of the Cossack officers at Lienz is that it 'was to prevent the officers from leading their followers in opposition to the repatriations' (Brigadier Anthony Cowgill, Lord Brimelow, and Christopher Booker Esq, *The Repatriations from Austria in 1945: The Report of an Inquiry* (London, 1990), p. 108; cf. p. 118). Although this motive is advanced as though it were established fact, in reality it represents mere conjecture, being found nowhere among the voluminous contemporary sources. Besides, had such a pragmatic consideration really existed, why should General Musson and Colonels Malcolm and Odling-Smee have withheld it from me throughout our lengthy discussions? In fact it is normal military practice when transferring large bodies of prisoners of war to retain their officers, in order to preserve order with greater facility. Thus, on 20 May the U.S. 20th Corps war diary noted of the situation in Austria that 'To the southeast, two entire German cavalry divisions, 75,000 armed Cossacks, and numerous scattered fragments of other enemy units were supposed to have surrendered to the meager British forces in that area. German officers had been permitted to retain their weapons and remain in control of their units' (*The XX Corps: Its History and Service in World War II* (Osaka, 1984), p. 404; cf. FO.1020/42,136, 137). Brigadier Clive Usher, who was responsible for all Germans and Cossacks in 6th Armoured Division custody, informed me that 'The senior officers of the Cossack Corps were German and after a time I allowed them to be given their revolvers to maintain discipline and check the indiscriminate slaughter of Austrian cattle' (letter of 4 June 1974). Since the practice is customary in most armies when dealing with surrendered formations, it does not require further substantiation here.

[24] WO.170/4241.

[25] As Brigadier Tryon-Wilson explained to me, 'It was entirely on the basis, which was perfectly straightforward, that how the devil could one carry out the instruction of dividing individuals into sectors in such an integrated operation such as the Cossacks were, without a certain amount of force being necessary? Because apart from there being women and children apart from

there being men, there were troops as well ... you could not separate them without a possible degree of force ...' The explanation could hardly be clearer: resort to otherwise unjustifiable force arose from the necessity of 'dividing' the Cossacks quartered around Lienz. The only 'division' planned or practised was that of the officers from their men.

[26] 'We have again had it confirmed in [unspecified!] verbal evidence that, in the operational situation in which 5 Corps found itself, to conduct detailed screening would have been out of the question' (Brigadier Anthony Cowgill, Christopher Booker Esq, Lord Brimelow, and Brigadier Teddy Tryon-Wilson, *Interim Report on an Enquiry into the Repatriation of Surrendered Enemy Personnel to the Soviet Union and Yugoslavia from Austria in 1945 and the Alleged 'Klagenfurt Conspiracy'* (London, 1988), p. 404).

[27] WO.170/4388,128.

[28] Interview with the author on 12 February 1975.

[29] WO.204/7211. Suicides were awkward – better the Soviets should conduct the killing.

[30] Letter to *The Observer*, 5 March 1978.

[31] Letter to the author of 23 June 1985.

[32] Imperial War Museum Sound Recordings, reel 12: http://www.iwm.org.uk/collections/item/object/80017280. I am indebted to Michael Frewer's son Christopher for drawing my attention to this vividly recounted source.

[33] Information from M. A. C. Frewer.

[34] *Western Morning News*, 7 June 1990.

[35] Information from Karl-Gottfried Vierkorn. Cf. *idem, Gefangen in Sibirien: Achteinhalb Jahre hinter Stacheldraht* (Oberaudorf, 1994), pp. 20-21.

[36] Interview with General Cooper.

CHAPTER XI
HAROLD MACMILLAN

Ay, now the plot thickens very much upon us.
George Villiers, Duke of Buckingham, *The Rehearsal* (1671)

Although Harold Macmillan later sought to transfer responsibility for the Cossack handovers wholly onto his 'friend' Alexander's shoulders,[1] it is abundantly clear that the Field Marshal was duped throughout these events by Macmillan, Minister Resident (*i.e.* political adviser) at AFHQ. Alexander's friend Field Marshal Alan Brooke, Chief of the Imperial General Staff, noted in his diary for 8th July 1944, 'I am afraid Macmillan has him [Alexander] entirely fooled, he likes his company as he believes that he receives from him an insight into political affairs'.[2] On 13 May 1945, the Minister made his unexpected dash to Klagenfurt, on receipt of Keightley's unexpected request for advice on how to respond to the Soviet demand for the leading émigré Russian generals. He went well beyond his authority in giving Keightley 'advice' to comply with this blatant violation of Allied policy on screening: 'advice' that was conveyed in such authoritative terms as to lead Keightley to report that '**We** have decided to hand them over ...' When ten days later this decision came under challenge, Keightley declared that it had been authorized, not by higher military command (which it had not), but by a 'verbal directive from Macmillan to Corps Comd at recent meeting' – where 'directive' unmistakably amounted to an order. Keightley, as he explained, accepted it as such, in consequence of which he had entered into what he clearly considered would otherwise constitute an unauthorized commitment:

> we [again] have undertaken to return all Soviet nationals in Corps area to Soviet forces.

Here the specific 'Soviet nationals' was deliberately designed to deceive his superiors at 8th Army and above. Under pressure from Macmillan, Keightley had already secretly committed himself to including the White Russians among those to be handed over.

It is clear from what ensued that Macmillan on his return to Naples withheld from Field Marshal Alexander all mention of his 'advice' to

Keightley. Instead, on the next day he obtained an order for handover of the Cossacks from the compliant General Robertson, Chief Administrative Officer at AFHQ. The true bone of contention between 5th Corps and the Red Army had been obscured by concealing the presence of the distinguished White Russian officers and other old émigrés, through use of the tendentious phraseology 'all **Russians** should be handed over to Soviet forces at agreed point of contact' – the correct terminology (in the context of repatriation, almost invariably employed elsewhere) being 'all **Soviet nationals**'.

The day after Brigadier Tryon's visit to Voitsberg on 11 May 1945, Field Marshal Alexander, exercised by Tito's truculent threat to incorporate Venezia Giulia and Southern Carinthia into a Communist Greater Yugoslavia, suggested to Macmillan that he pay 'a short visit to 8th Army Headquarters and 13th Corps tomorrow in order to put Generals McCreery and Harding fully in the picture'.[3] Accordingly, Macmillan on 12 May flew to 8th Army commander General McCreery's headquarters at Treviso in North Italy, whither he returned the same evening after paying a flying visit to General Harding, commanding 13th Corps facing the Italo-Yugoslav frontier.

It was shortly after his arrival that morning that General Keightley at 5th Corps, alerted to Macmillan's arrival at Treviso, telegraphed the Minister[*] with a request for guidance on the Soviet demand for the senior White Russian commanding officers among the Cossacks.[†] As Brigadier Tryon-Wilson explained to Dr. Lyn Smith of the Imperial War Museum,

> ... he'd told him what the problem was [*i.e.* of the Cossacks], and he had mentioned - or perhaps he'd mentioned that we had some White Russians.

Macmillan's memory was plainly accurate in recalling that his additional journey to Austria arose from an unexpected request from Keightley, since neither he nor Alexander had anticipated any need for the Minister to include 5th Corps command in his brief tour, nor had any unexpected exigency affecting 5th Corps arisen during the previous twenty-four hours with regard to the threat posed by Tito.[4] But what precisely was the issue faced by General Keightley that unexpectedly required Macmillan's counsel, rather than that of his (Keightley's) superior, General McCreery?

---

[*] At this time telephone communications between 5th Corps and 8th Army had temporarily broken down (WO.170/4059).

[†] 'Macmillan's own recollection years later was that he had responded to an urgent *ad hoc* request for a visit from General Keightley' (Horne, *Macmillan: 1894-1956*, p. 258).

That Soviet citizens were to be handed over to the Soviets was at this time established policy. On the morning of 11 May, the day before Macmillan's arrival at McCreery's Headquarters, 8th Army issued this instruction to 5th Corps:

> Understand 1789 Russians in WOLFSBERG? Camp.
>
> Request you make every endeavour ensure they are handed over to Russian forces for repatriation at earliest opportunity. This has been agreed on governmental basis between Britain, US and USSR.[5]

Since these Russians were almost certainly Soviet citizens, whether liberated prisoners of war or refugees, whose return was as noted stipulated by the Yalta Agreement (with whose terms Keightley was fully acquainted), there was no call for Macmillan to advise Keightley on the issue.

What overridingly urgent reason was there then for Keightley to consult Macmillan on the subject? As the government-sponsored Cowgill Inquiry[*] has repeatedly stressed, the Minister possessed no authority to issue instructions to soldiers. Still more remarkable, why did Macmillan suddenly decide that it was necessary to fly north to Austria to confer with Keightley in person, rather than respond to the latter's enquiry by return of telegram?[†] Unfortunately, the motive for Harold Macmillan's unaccountable intervention remains broadly mysterious and controversial, although that his intervention was decisive remains incontrovertible.[‡]

Macmillan's own account is to be found in his diary for 13 May.

> Left the camp at 8.30 for the airfield. Went by Dakota (Broad, Brigadier Floyd, Con Benson, and one or two other Eighth Army officers and I) to Klagenfurt... We landed safely at Klagenfurt airfield about 10 a.m. The field is a grass one, small and rather bumpy, but the DC3 machines land well in such circumstances. We were met by General Charles Keightley (Fifth Corps) and some of his staff. This officer, whom I have met from time to time, is an admirable soldier and a very level-headed and sensible

---

[*] The British Government's covert role in suppressing important public documents and perverting the course of justice is so extensive as to require a further book to set out the evidence *in extenso*.

[†] Telephone communication between 5th Corps and 8th Army was still inoperative at this time (WO.170/4184).

[‡] From time to time friends have suggested I should address the question of Macmillan's motive for his actions, lest hostile critics arraign my failure to do so. On the other hand, as any hypothesis in the present state of knowledge would be confessedly tentative and speculative, I prefer to leave readers to draw their own conclusions on the basis of the evidence here presented.

[amenable?] man. He is well suited for his difficult and embarrassing task ... among the surrendered Germans are about 40,000 Cossacks and 'White' Russians, with their wives and children. To hand them over to the Russians is condemning them to slavery, torture and probably death.[*] To refuse, is deeply to offend the Russians, and incidentally break the Yalta agreement. We have decided to hand them over ...[6]

Here it is important to recall the fact that Keightley possessed his own 'political adviser', in the person of his chief of staff Brigadier Toby Low. Tryon-Wilson recollected that Low was not present at his meeting with Keightley on his return to Corps headquarters, but the General must certainly have mentioned the Soviet request to his Chief of Staff that day. Low's background was very different from that of the brusque and unimaginative Keightley. A lawyer by profession, he nurtured strong political ambitions. He had managed to ingratiate himself with no less a figure than the Foreign Secretary Anthony Eden, with whom he conducted regular correspondence throughout his wartime military service. He was certainly in a position to appreciate the politically sensitive issue of White Russians among the Cossacks.

The authors of the Cowgill Inquiry ingeniously claimed that Macmillan's reference to 'White Russians', whose handover to the Soviets he concerted with Keightley on 13 May, represents an allusion to the White Russian *Russkii Korpus*, a military body of some 4,000 largely emigrant Russians from Yugoslavia, who had surrendered to 1st Guards Brigade on the previous day. Were no other evidence available, the conjecture might almost appear plausible. It would be yet more so had Macmillan himself, or anyone else involved at the time, ever advanced it. Unfortunately for his apologists, he never did so on successive occasions that he discussed the subject both in public and private. On the contrary, when obliged to address the topic he invariably accepted that the White Russians whose handover he urged were distinctive individuals embedded in the Cossack formations. Again, within twenty-four hours of his conference with Keightley, he wrote of both 'Cossacks and 'White Russians'' that 'We have decided to hand them over'. Significantly, there exists no record at any stage of an intention to hand over members of the

---

[*] Although Macmillan's chilling dismissal of the Cossacks' certain fate was exceptional among figures involved at the time, it enjoyed an unfortunate precedent. In 1854, on the eve of the Crimean War, Lord 'Palmerston first suggested dealing with an anticipated 30,000 Russian prisoners in Sevastopol by setting them free to go to Odessa on foot, anticipating that many would starve, die of exposure, or be killed by peasants en route' (Paul W. Schroeder, *Austria, Great Britain, and the Crimean War: The Destruction of the European Concert* (Ithaca, NY, 1972), p. 204).

Russkii Korpus, whom Brigadier Toby Low himself ruled as early as 21 May 'not [to] be treated as Soviet Nationals until further orders'. No such orders were ever issued: the reason for which is uncertain, but presumably reflected the well-established fact that they had travelled direct from their homes in Yugoslavia, while few of its complement had ever been near the Soviet Union.[7] The Robertson order of 14 May was issued in response to Macmillan's advice to Keightley to hand over 'Cossacks and 'White Russians''. Although it required 'all Russians' in 5th Corps area to be handed over to the Soviets, at no time did 5th Corps command interpret this as applicable to the *Russkii Korpus*.

In 1985, when invited to speak at Winchester College on the forced repatriation of Russians at the war's end, I mentioned Toby Low's participation as chief of staff. Lord Aldington (as he had become) was at the time of my talk Warden of the College, and greatly perturbed arranged to speak to the boys in response to my charges (on condition I be not present!). The session occurred on 1 March, when in the course of his address he mentioned that

> the [Cossack] divisions also included Russians who had not either served in the Russian Army or been in Russia for the last 15 years. Amongst them were officers who belonged to what has become known as the White Russian community, many of them living in France and other parts of Western Europe. Some of these were distinguished people who were wanted by the Soviet Russians.

Here in Aldington's original version, before making his telling deletion, we have both *explicit* allusion to the leading émigré Cossack generals, whose names featured in capital letters in the list handed Brigadier Tryon-Wilson at Voitsberg, together with *implicit* recognition that their inclusion among Cossacks he arranged to have handed over was better withheld from his audience. Aldington subsequently gave a copy of this first draft of his Winchester address to the Government agent Brigadier Cowgill, who among other blundering initial moves to gain my confidence passed it to me. At the 1989 libel trial Aldington acknowledged this draft text as his own, but was unable to provide a satisfactory explanation for his original inclusion and subsequent deletion of the revealing description 'distinguished'.[8]

From this it is evident that Keightley's Chief of Staff, whose own 'Definition' of 21 May explicitly excluded the *Russkii Korpus* from handover, acknowledged that the White Russians in question were individual officers – some of 'distinction' – who had lived 'in France and other parts of Western Europe' – *i.e. not* Yugoslavia, whence the *Russkii Korpus* originated.

When Keightley wired Macmillan in Italy on 12 May regarding the Soviet demand for the leading White Russians in 5th Corps custody, the effect was electric. The Minister immediately abandoned his planned return to Naples the next morning, and flew instead to Klagenfurt aerodrome. Following his arrival, he conferred for two hours with Keightley. Brigadier Tryon-Wilson emphasized to me that Low *must* as Chief of Staff have participated in so important a meeting, although Low himself cautiously denied it.[9] That night Keightley reported to 8th Army troublesome activities of Yugoslav troops in the region occupied by his Corps, together with his need to dispose of extensive 'straggling formations and refugees of all nationalities'.[10] However, by Macmillan's own account nothing had transpired of such significance as to require a fresh unplanned flight.

'He [Keightley] gave us his story, and we gave him ours'.

On the other hand, what *did* require a decision was a response to the insistent Soviet request for the handover of leading émigré Cossacks. Accession to the Soviet demand for White Russian officers, whose handover to the Soviets was expressly prohibited by Allied policy directives represented the *sole* issue requiring a decision not covered by existing orders. Yet Macmillan's wording betrays the fact that he played a protagonist role ('**we** have decided') in that decision. Above all, his diary entry gives the game away, where he includes 'White Russians' as a distinct and prominent category among Cossacks whose return the Soviets demanded.

The fate of the majority who were undoubted Soviet citizens did not require any additional journey by Macmillan to Klagenfurt. On the morning of the previous day Keightley encountered Brigadier Pat Scott, commanding 38th Irish Infantry Brigade, near Lavamund. Scott's force had just accepted the surrender of thousands of Cossacks crossing the Yugoslav frontier. As he reported afterwards:

He [Keightley] told me that by our agreement with the Russians, the Cossacks should have been handed over to them, and that my action might produce some international incident'.[11]

This further confirms that Keightley required no instruction with regard to treatment of Soviet citizens, beyond that which he had earlier received from 8th Army. So far as this factor was concerned, all Macmillan needed to do was confirm what Keightley already knew, *viz.* that Allied policy provided that 'All persons of undoubted Soviet citizenship must be repatriated irrespective of their own wishes...'[12]

There is an intrinsic oddity in Macmillan's sudden decision to extend his journey to Austria. Brigadier Tryon-Wilson was emphatic that it was the fate of the Cossack generals that Keightley wished to discuss. Why should Macmillan have found the Soviet demand for a score of émigré Cossack generals of such overriding importance as to require a face-to-face meeting with General Keightley, when a simple telegraphed response would have sufficed? After all, no one was more familiar than he with the authoritative Foreign Office ruling of 19 February that year (a week after the signing of the Yalta Agreement), which informed him *in response to his own enquiry* that

> The line which we have taken and you should follow is that all persons who are Soviet citizens under British law must be repatriated and that any person who is not (repeat not) a Soviet citizen under British law must not (repeat not) be sent back to the Soviet Union unless he expressly desires to be so...[13]

That he suddenly flew north in order to persuade Keightley to flout it confirms that Macmillan already possessed some overriding reason for acquiescing in the Soviet demand. It has been seen that, so long ago as the previous October, he had received a full report on the Cossack presence in North Italy, and it is probable that he was kept abreast of their activities thereafter. Furthermore, SOE reports and other sources of information are likely to have mentioned the well-known prominence of tsarist generals like Krasnov among their command. Soviet concern with recovering their inveterate foes was made plain at the time of the surrender of German forces in Italy.

On 29 April 1945, a delegation acting on behalf of General Heinrich von Vietinghoff, German Commander-in-Chief Southwest, arrived at AFHQ headquarters in the palace of Caserta outside Naples, where it formally accepted the instrument of surrender of all forces under his command.[14] Macmillan was absent from headquarters at the time, but returned next day. He claimed that he felt it 'important that the Russians should not suspect us of anything *political*, and I thought it discreet to be absent from Caserta'.[15] However that may be, he must surely have been consulted by Alexander during the days following his return, when the Soviet representative at AFHQ raised a particularly contentious issue.

Major-General Alexei Pavlovich Kislenko was a serving officer in Soviet Military Intelligence (GRU), attached to the Allied command.[16] On 3 May and thereafter he sought to persuade AFHQ to include specific reference to 'Vlasovskie [members of the so-called Vlasov army recruited by the Germans] **and others** [bold inserted]' in the surrender terms. The reference was plainly to the Cossacks around Tolmezzo. AFHQ joint planning staff objected that 'We consider that these forces are already covered by the wording of paragraph 1 of Appendix 'A' to the Instrument of Surrender', adding subsequently that

> The two remaining points raised in your letter, namely the disposal of Soviet citizens ... are under further examination. In the meantime the disposal of Soviet citizens will continue to be regulated in accordance with the present agreements between the United States, British and Soviet Governments.[17]

Kislenko can scarcely have been satisfied with what he probably took for prevarication. He would also have been aware that handover of non-Soviet citizens was frustratingly not permitted under 'the present agreements between the United States, British and Soviet Governments'.

SMERSH (which undoubtedly maintained a presence within the Soviet mission at AFHQ) had also long been well-informed of the presence of notable White Russian émigrés among the Cossacks in North Italy,[18] and it is improbable to suppose that Kislenko and his colleagues had not long previously raised with Macmillan the delicate question of their eventual handover.

What remains unknown is what consideration persuaded the Minister Resident to espouse Soviet policy in this respect with the secrecy and vigor subsequent events indicate.

It is now time to consider the startling extent to which Keightley, following Macmillan's 'advice' delivered in person during his visit on 13 May, began a studied course of deception of his superiors – deception broadly dictated by the potent figure of the Minister Resident. The night following his visit, Keightley telegraphed Major-General Brian Robertson, Chief Administrative Officer at AFHQ. Headed 'Please inform MACMILLAN', it reads as follows:

> Approximately 300,000 PW surrendered personnel and refugees in Corps Area. further 600,000 reported moving North to AUSTRIA from JUGOSLAVIA. I am taking all possible steps to prevent their movement along roads, but this will NOT completely prevent them as they are short of food and are being harassed. Should this number materialize, food and guard situation will become critical. I, therefore suggest that all possible steps are taken to dispose soonest of all surrendered personnel in this area whether German, Austrian or Russian by moving them to Northern Italy or their homes, whichever may be the policy. Certain SS troops already causing trouble, but this being dealt with. On advice

MACMILLAN, have today suggested to Soviet General on TOLBUKHIN's HQ that Cossacks should be returned to Soviets at once. Explained that I had NO power to do this without your authority, but would be glad to know TOLBUKHIN's views and that if they coincided with mine, I would ask you officially. Cannot see any point in keeping this large number Soviet Nationals, who are clearly great source contention between Soviets and ourselves. This area now becoming clearing house for all stragglers, straggling formations and refugees of all nationalities, who require food and shelter...[19]

Copies of relevant sections of Keightley's signal were also forwarded to 8th Army and 15th Army Group. The deceptive reference to 'this large number Soviet Nationals' presumably originated with Macmillan. However, return of 'Soviet Nationals' covered by the Yalta Agreement was emphatically not a 'great source contention between Soviets and ourselves'. As has been seen, both within 5th Corps and elsewhere the provisions of the Yalta Agreement were accepted and implemented without hindrance. At this time, the sole source of contention was the proposed inclusion of Macmillan's 'White Russians' among Cossacks whose return was demanded by SMERSH – a crucial factor suppressed in Keightley's message.

It is telling that Macmillan henceforth became acutely concerned to make it appear that his unplanned flight to Klagenfurt comprised an integral part of the original mission to North Italy suggested by Alexander. In 1980 Macmillan informed the Cabinet Secretary Sir Robert Armstrong:

> On 13 May I went to Klagenfurt at Field Marshal Alexander's request to report on the dangerous situation arising from the Yugoslav invasion of Italian territory.[20]

Interviewed by Ludovic Kennedy on BBC1 in 1984, he yet again stressed that he had been sent to Klagenfurt at Alexander's behest. Macmillan's diary also suppresses the fact that his diversionary flight occurred in response to an unanticipated request from Keightley.

It is incontrovertible that Macmillan did *not*, as he was at such repeated pains to assert, fly 'to Klagenfurt at Field Marshal Alexander's request'. On 11 May he informed the Foreign Office:

> At Field Marshal Alexander's suggestion I am making a short visit to 8th Army Headquarters and 13th Corps tomorrow in order to put Generals McCreery and Harding fully in the picture.[21]

Thus, on the eve of his departure, it was not anticipated that his journey would include a visit to General Keightley at 5th Corps.

To acknowledge that he extended his impromptu journey at Keightley's request might have raised questions as to what was the unexpected issue that so urgently required his presence in Austria, being evidently too delicate to be openly resolved by telegram from 8th Army headquarters.

Further suggestive is the fact that Macmillan's first report, dispatched from Naples to the Foreign Office at mid-day on 14 May, on his mission of the past two days omitted mention of his unanticipated flight to Austria:

> I visited while I was away General McCreery (Commander of the 8th Army) and General Harding who is in charge of the 13th Corps at Monfalcone.

It was not until the late afternoon of the following day (15 May) that Macmillan dispatched a second message, in which he added that

> I made a brief flying visit to General Keightley at Headquarters 5th Corps at Klagenfurt in Carinthia... In North Carinthia there is a pocket of some 30 Cossacks* including women and children...

> Of course I have got to know these three generals pretty well during the campaign. The chief object of visiting them was because Field Marshal Alexander thought it would do good to put them in the political picture. This I did and I think it was useful.[22]

Why did Macmillan omit reference to his unanticipated additional flight in his first telegram? And why did he mislead the Foreign Office in the second into believing that it was arranged in advance by Alexander? In my book *The Minister and the Massacres* I suggested that his initial intention had been to withhold mention of his unanticipated visit to Keightley.[23] Christopher Booker, a member of the Cowgill Inquiry, claimed in response that the signals

> ... were transmitted to London separately, as is standard Foreign Office procedure, which is to start a new telegram when the subject-matter of a report changes; and it was only because the second message arrived the following day that Tolstoy read them as different messages.[24]

I suspect the reader will at once have noted that 'the subject-matter' had in this instance *not* changed. Secondly, while it is true that signals (normally of some length) were occasionally transmitted in separate sections, it is pretty clear that this was not what occurred on this occasion.

---

* '30,000' in Macmillan's Birch Grove Archives (Cowgill, Brimelow, and Booker Esq, *The Repatriations from Austria in 1945: The Documentary Evidence*, 116; Booker, *A Looking-Glass Tragedy*, p. 119). However, 'pocket' seems a curious term for 30,000 people.

The first message was dispatched to the Foreign Office at 12.30 pm on 14 May, while the second was sent well over a day later, at 5.20 pm on 15 May. There was nothing to prevent so cursory a report's being composed as a whole. According to his own account, Macmillan was certainly not busy during this time. As he noted in his diary, on 14 May 'I stayed in bed or lounged in the garden all the day', while the next day he 'Took the morning off, motoring up for luncheon at Caserta in the old villa (which the Russells still have)'.

Again, Macmillan begins the first message by explaining that 'I visited while I was away General McCreery ... and General Harding ...' Why was Keightley's name omitted at this prefatory juncture? It is only in his second telegram that Macmillan mentions his visit to Keightley, falsely asserting that it was at Alexander's behest that he visited all three generals. An air of deception hangs over these two brief telegrams, separated as they are by over a day, during which Macmillan declared himself to have enjoyed all the spare time in the world. And why was he so concerned to emphasize that he made no more than 'a brief flying visit to General Keightley', when all his visits during those rushed two days were brief and flying? Why did he not mention the subject-matter of their discussion, which after all represented a direct concern of the Foreign Office? Of course, such considerations would be of secondary significance, were there not much weightier evidence of Macmillan's consummate duplicity.

The natural interpretation of the two signals is that Macmillan initially intended to withhold reference to his unanticipated visit to Keightley from the Foreign Office, and that some unexpected exigency arising during the ensuing twenty-four hours led to his feeling compelled to add it to the account of his journey. The suppression in the second message of his 'advice' to Keightley to hand over the Cossacks – let alone the delicate matter of compliance with the Soviet demand for the old émigré generals – unmistakably intimates what it was he wished to hide.

The likeliest explanation of Macmillan's belated decision to inform the Foreign Office of his flight to Austria is that it arose from his American counterpart Alexander Kirk's unexpected forthright objection to Robertson's callous authorization of the handovers of Cossacks and Yugoslavs, dispatched to the State Department late on the evening of Macmillan's return on 14 May. The relevant sections of the 'Robertson order' read as follows:

ref Eighth Army AC/189 of 14 May.

1. all Russians should be handed over to Soviet forces at agreed point of contact est by you under local arrangements with Marshall

TOLBUKHIN's HQ. steps should be taken to ensure that Allied PW held in Russian area are transferred to us in exchange at same time...

3. all surrendered personnel of established Yugoslav nationality who were serving in German forces should be disarmed and handed over to Yugoslav forces.

Originator: CAO Auth: B.H. ROBERTSON, LT GEN Information: SACS ... RESMIN

Concurred: BR RESMIN [*i.e.* Macmillan].[25]

Robertson would undoubtedly have informed Macmillan of Kirk's forthright objection (cited below) to this order, together with the latter's intention of referring the matter to the US Government. It must further have appeared probable that the State Department would take up the disputed issue with the Foreign Office - in which case Macmillan's unplanned visit to Keightley could no longer be concealed. Hence arose the necessity for Macmillan's incongruously-worded second message.

Yet more suspicious is Macmillan's suppression in his diary of his 'advice' to Keightley to arrange the Cossacks' handover, and his collaboration with General Robertson in providing formal authorization for the operation. As though this were not enough, he concealed his support for the proposed surrender to Tito of thousands of Yugoslav fugitives, for whom in his diary entry he hypocritically expressed sentimental concern, at the very time he was colluding with Robertson to authorize their surrender to their vindictive foe Tito – who in the event obligingly slaughtered his compatriots almost to the last man. As Kirk indignantly pointed out, the latter order violated concerted British and American policy.

These points established, we may return to the crucial question why Macmillan felt that Keightley's query about the Cossacks required him to fly in person to advise the General. So far as the great majority of Cossacks was concerned, he had only to refer the 5th Corps commander to the Yalta Agreement of 11 February (with which Aldington declared himself to have been then familiar) on the one hand, and the ensuing 6th March AFHQ message copied to 8th Army that 'All persons of undoubted Soviet Citizenship will be repatriated irrespective of their own wishes'[26] on the other.

As we know, the *sole* issue requiring resolution when Keightley approached Macmillan was the vexed question of disposal of senior White Russian officers recently demanded by SMERSH at Voitsberg. Who was better placed to resolve so sensitive and essentially political an issue than the Minister Resident?

Thus, so far as Keightley was concerned, the only issue not explicitly covered by extant orders was that which he raised when he contacted Macmillan to request his advice: *viz.* how should he respond to the Soviet demand for the White Russian officers singled out on the list handed to Brigadier Tryon two days earlier? This issue alone represented what the latter subsequently described as 'the hot potato'.

All this explains (as nothing else does) Keightley's abrupt and otherwise inexplicable shift from his initial disgusted rejection of the Soviet demand for the White Russian officers, to insistence on delivering them up to the Soviets. On the afternoon of 11 May he had reacted with revulsion to the Soviet demand for their handover, but two days later he became immersed in increasingly delicate and duplicitous machinations for surrendering them to their enemies.

On the night of Macmillan's visit on 13 May Keightley dispatched a signal to General McCreery at 8th Army, in which he informed him:

> on advice Macmillan have today suggested to Soviet General on Tolbukhins HQ that Cossacks should be returned to Soviets at once. explained that I had no power to do this without your authority but would be glad to know Tolbukhins views and that if they coincided with mine I would ask you officially. cannot see any point in keeping this large number Soviet nationals who are clearly great source contention between Soviets and ourselves.[27]

McCreery, who possessed no means of knowing that any of the Cossacks were old emigrants, passed on this request for a ruling to 15th Army Group and Alexander's Chief of Staff (General Morgan) at AFHQ.[28] As events were to show, the latter appears at a time of maximum crisis to have overlooked the implications of this message, which was in any case not directed to him for action.

It is at this juncture that 5th Corps deception of higher command begins. In the first place, McCreery's headquarters had two months earlier issued its order to 5th Corps that 'All persons of undoubted Soviet Citizenship will be repatriated irrespective of their own wishes'. Why should Keightley require a repetition of the order, if he wished to hand over only 'Soviet nationals'? The answer is provided by the last sentence of his signal:

> cannot see any point in keeping this large number Soviet nationals who are clearly great source contention between Soviets and ourselves.

Keightley knew, as McCreery did not, that 5th Corps' sole difficulty with the Soviets arose, *not* from repatriation of Soviet citizens (whose return had besides yet to be formally requested by the Soviets), but with the contentious demand for the leading non-Soviet Cossack officers. His deceptive description of the Cossacks as 'this large number Soviet nationals' can only have been intended to mislead McCreery into believing that *all* Cossacks in 5th Corps custody were Soviet nationals. What Keightley now sought, on Macmillan's 'advice', was an order specifying that *all* Cossacks should be handed over, without any inconvenient rider to the effect that 'In cases where nationality is in doubt, personnel concerned will be sent to 373 PW Camp for adjudication', nor any troublesome emphasis on 'undoubted Soviet Citizenship'.

The net was beginning to close around Generals Krasnov, Shkuro, and their senior colleagues singled out on the SMERSH list handed to Brigadier Tryon on 11 May.

The continuing influence of Macmillan on policy from this time on is further confirmed by Keightley's dispatch that night to Allied Force Headquarters at Naples of a copy of the relevant section of his signal to McCreery. Headed 'Please inform MACMILLAN', it was addressed 'ACTION: CAO'.[29] As has been seen, CAO was the Chief Administrative Officer, Major-General Sir Brian Robertson. At the same time, when Macmillan dined with Alexander on his return to AFHQ on the evening of 13 May, it appears from his diary and immediately ensuing events that he withheld any mention of the intended fate of the Cossacks, despite the fact that it, and the proposed handover of Yugoslav fugitives, were the sole contentious issues to have arisen during his two-day visit to North Italy and Carinthia.

All Alexander's subsequent actions and reactions confirm that he was being kept wholly in the dark by Macmillan and Keightley on these key issues.

From the outset of his arrival at AFHQ, Macmillan had established a close rapport with Robertson. In January 1944, he 'Called to see Major-General Brian Robertson (son of the old Field Marshal) - a very intelligent and efficient officer. He does not suffer fools gladly ...' A year later he noted that 'I like doing business with General Robertson, for he is a very clever man'. They were together frequently: two days after Keightley's message reached Robertson, Macmillan recorded that 'As part of regular routine, I had a conference with General Robertson on various Italian questions'.[30]

That Robertson was a diligent and able administrator is well-attested, but that there was another, harsher aspect to his character appears from what ensued.

Meanwhile, as mentioned earlier, late on the evening of Macmillan's return to Naples (14 May), his American counterpart at AFHQ, Alexander Kirk, sent this report to the Secretary of State in Washington.

Situation of surrendered enemy personnel in British Fifth Corps area has been reported by CG Eighth Army as follows:

Unmanageable numbers of refugees and prisoners of war are materially deteriorating from operational capacity of the corps. It is suggested negotiations be opened with Marshal Tolbukhin for return of 28,000 Cossacks to Russian lines.

This afternoon General Robertson, Chief Administrative Officer AFHQ requested us to concur in a draft telegram to CG British Eighth Army authorizing him to turn over 28,000 Cossacks (see our 797 of October 16, 1944, Midnight), including women and children to Marshal Tolbukhin, and further instructing him to turn over to Yugoslav Partisans a large number of dissident Yugoslav troops with exception of Chetniks.*

General Robertson stated that Macmillan, who talked with CO Eighth Army yesterday, had recommended this course of action.† We asked whether the Russians had requested that these Cossacks be turned over to them, and Robertson replied in the negative and added "but they probably will soon". We also asked General Robertson what definition he proposed to give to "Chetniks" and he was very vague on this point. We then stated we could not concur without referring the matter to our Government. CAO expressed disappointment that we did not seem to agree with him on this point but added that he was faced with a grave administrative problem with hundreds of thousands of German POWS on his hands and could not bother at this time about who might or might not be turned over to the Russians and Partisans to be shot. He would have to send his telegram in spite of our non-concurrence.

Department's views would be appreciated urgently.[31]

This was the signal which evidently necessitated Macmillan's hasty post-scriptum to the Foreign Office, in which he belatedly added that he had visited Keightley, in addition to McCreery and Harding. It seems that Macmillan contacted Robertson directly (in person, or by telephone) on his return to Naples. Robertson's order concludes 'Concurred: BR[itish] RES[ident]MIN[ister]', which confirms that Macmillan spoke directly to him on his return, and that he urged, or concurred with, the 'draft telegram' also shown to Kirk, which included the deceptive allusion to the Cossacks as 'all Russians'. For how could Macmillan be held to have 'concurred' with the text of an order unless he had seen and discussed it?[32] Kirk's

---

* Yugoslav royalists fighting for the Allies.
† It is important to note that Macmillan urged the handover, not only of Cossacks, but also Yugoslavs. In his diary entry he was careful to withhold inclusion of the latter category among groups he urged to be handed over. Instead, he unctuously expresses sympathy with their plight.

refusal to concur with the proposed intruction made Macmillan's
agreement essential to legitimation of Robertson's deceptive ('all
Russians') order.

Later that year, on 14 August, long after the handovers were
completed, Kirk returned to the charge, protesting to Field Marshal
Alexander that

> It was stated that SAC [Supreme Allied Commander: *i.e.* Alexander]
> took note of our non-concurrence [with the Robertson order] and pointed
> out that Brit Resmin [Macmillan] had concurred in proposed action [*i.e.*
> authorizing the handover of Yugoslavs]... In conversation with
> Alexander this morning, he stated to us that he was obliged to receive
> surrender of almost one million Germans in mid-May and could not deal
> with anti-Tito Yugos as he would have liked. We stated we had nothing
> to add to our memorandum under reference except to point out to him
> again that Resmin acted contrary to policy agreed upon after consultation
> by [State] Dept and For[eig]noff[ice].[33]

This significant message is reproduced in the Cowgill Inquiry's 'Key
Papers'. At the same time it is omitted in their 'Report of an Inquiry', and
mentioned in passing without citation or discussion in Booker's sequel.
This is unsurprising. After all, the message 'Brit Resmin [Macmillan] had
concurred in proposed action' confirms that Macmillan and Robertson
discussed the issue in person, just as Kirk's parallel 'non-concurrence'
occurred at a discussion between the two men.[34] The 'proposed action'
cannot be other than promulgation of the Robertson order.

It is also significant that Alexander Kirk, who in all probability knew
much more than he committed to these two signals, assigned responsibility
for the handover to Macmillan alone. He clearly understood who bore
prime responsibility for authorizing blatant violations of concerted Allied
political policy.[*]

Macmillan's authority as Minister with direct access to Churchill and
the Foreign Office presumably sufficed to persuade the ambitious
Keightley to overcome his initial instinctive concern for humanitarian
legalities, and implement what was transmuted a few days later into a
'verbal directive' from the Minister. Any reservations Keightley might
have retained are likely to have been stilled by his aide and adviser,
Brigadier Toby Low. Low nurtured strong political ambitions. Despite

---

[*] Kirk confined his August protest to the return of Yugoslavs. His failure to include
mention of Cossacks doubtless reflects the fact that he was denied means of knowing
that Alexander's prohibition on use of violence and insistence on screening had in
their case been violated by Keightley.

their marked differences in age, status, and social standing, he was close to the Foreign Secretary Anthony Eden. On 23 May, Low left 5th Corps for England,[35] where he successfully stood for Parliament in the July General Election which saw Churchill's departure from office.

With Macmillan's concurrence, Robertson promptly issued order FX 75383 of 14 May to 8th Army for transmission to 5th Corps, of which the relevant passage reads:

> all Russians should be handed over to Soviet forces at agreed point of contact est by you under local arrangements with Marshall TOLBUKHIN's HQ.[36]

Although the order was issued formally in Field Marshal Alexander's name, it was in fact issued by Robertson as Chief Administrative Officer. It is clear from everything that follows that Alexander was kept in ignorance of the order until it was belatedly drawn to his attention a week later on 22 May.

It is unlikely that substitution of the catch-all expression 'all Russians' for the normal unambiguous usage 'Soviet citizens' reflected carelessness on the part of so meticulously efficient an officer as General Robertson. The probability is that this unmilitary lack of precision reflected the Minister's suggestion. In his diary account of his discussion with Keightley the day before, Macmillan had employed comparably ambiguous terminology, when he urged 'scrupulous adherence to the agreement in handing back **Russian subjects** ...' Krasnov, Shkuro, and many of their fellow-officers had been Russian subjects, but never Soviet citizens. The loose blanket term can only have been intended to mask a deliberate decision to hand over every Russian, regardless of his or her wishes or nationality.

Macmillan's deception of London on this delicate issue continued throughout his tenure of the post of Minister Resident at AFHQ. On 18th May he described the situation in the British zone of Austria to Sir James Grigg, Secretary of State for War, as follows:

> ... The utter confusion in these areas is really astonishing ... In Austria one British corps seemed to be charged with ...

> Dealing with the White Russians and Cossacks, together with their wives and families, serving in these German forces ...

That 'White Russians' refers here to individual old émigrés from Western Europe, and not the *Russkii Korpus*, is borne out by a letter from Jack Nicholls, Foreign Office representative at 5th Corps, who three days later explained similarly that

I am being confronted with similar problems; if captured Cossacks fighting with the Germans are to be handed over to the Russians, what should be done with White Russians with French nationality?[37]

Grigg, as Macmillan was doubtless aware, was a statesman strongly sympathetic to the plight of helpless Russians threatened with betrayal to their Soviet persecutors.[38] Consequently the Minister did not alert him to the fact that 'Dealing with the White Russians and Cossacks' in Carinthia no longer represented 'confusion', so far as policy directives were concerned. Four days earlier he had given his fatal 'advice' to Keightley to hand over 'White Russians' in 5th Corps hands, and next day 'concurred' with General Robertson in ordering delivery of *all* Cossacks to the Soviets. Macmillan's duplicity is here so evident as to lead the authors of the Cowgill Inquiry to adopt an unusual precaution, in order to occlude their paragon's regular resort to lies and deceit. After Macmillan's words 'Dealing with the White Russians and Cossacks, together with their wives and families, serving in these German forces', the Inquiry *added to the quotation* the words 'We have decided to hand them over ...'[39] In this way they made it appear that Macmillan had *not* suppressed his decisive intervention! Yet again, such it seems is the new official historiography.

As for the Cossacks, the *sole* reason given for their return was that Macmillan had forcefully urged it ten days earlier. Keightley's wording makes it clear that it was this, rather than General Robertson's order the next day, which bound him. It was on 13 May that Keightley 'on advice Macmillan ... today suggested to Soviet General on Tolbukhins HQ that Cossacks should be returned to Soviets at once', and it was two days later that Robertson's order approved by Macmillan arrived at 5th Corps Headquarters.[40] In short, the only motives advanced for the repatriation were political, and the only authority for proceeding with it was that provided by Harold Macmillan's 'advice', shortly afterwards to be defined expressly as an authoritative 'verbal directive'.

It seems too that Macmillan adroitly withheld reference to the Cossacks during his brief visit to England at this time to report to Churchill on the troubled situation in Venezia Giulia, and the measures required to check Tito's aggression in the region.[41] The day he arrived, Saturday 19 May, Macmillan was driven straight to the Prime Minister's official residence at Chequers. Churchill's private secretary, Jock Colville, recorded his impression in his diary:

Harold Macmillan, summoned from Italy because of the Venezia Giulia crisis, arrived at tea-time ... I don't like the ingratiating way in which Macmillan bares his teeth.[42]

There he remained closeted with the Prime Minister with only two other guests until the early hours of the morning. Churchill was in expansive mood, and eager to learn all the Minister Resident's news. In Macmillan's own words: 'After dinner, a short film, and then a lot of talk (till about 2 a.m.) about Tito. I did my best to explain to P.M. the whole position, as we saw it at A.F.H.Q., and **all** [bold inserted] the various problems which we had to face locally'. Macmillan stayed the night, and did not leave for home until the following afternoon.

Among 'all the various problems which we had to face locally', Macmillan plainly went out of his way to omit mention of the Cossack problem. He might well have thought it one that would exert a dangerous appeal to Churchill's marked love of the picturesque and romantic, particularly in view of his ardent championing of the Cossack cause during the Russian Civil War. His speeches urging support for the Whites in 1919, declared Lord Robert Cecil in the House of Commons, gave him a mental picture of Churchill 'riding at the head of Cossacks making a triumphant entry into Moscow'.[43] Still more pertinently, on 29 April 1921 he sent his advisers this firm instruction: 'No loyal [*i.e.* anti-Bolshevik] Russian can be sent back to Russia against his will'.[44]

In view of all the great issues that were discussed at Chequers that night it might be suggested that Macmillan's reticence arose from no more than remarkable oversight – but for the fact that it was during his visit that Churchill evinced concern for those very Cossacks whose fate now hung in the balance. Two days before Macmillan's arrival at Chequers, Churchill received a copy of the message from Eisenhower informing him of Alexander's request that SHAEF should *inter alia* assume responsibility for the Cossacks held by 8th Army, and explaining that he (Eisenhower) had agreed to do so. During the night before Macmillan's arrival, Churchill urged Eisenhower to comply:

> You have no doubt read NAF/974 from Alexander. I shall be most grateful if you will do what you can to help him.[45]

What memories mention of the Cossacks conjured up we do not know, but there can be no doubt that the Prime Minister was concerned. It would be absurd to suppose that he failed to discuss the issue at all with the Minister, whom he had summoned specifically to discuss critical issues arising from Operation Coldstream, as the strategic move was named by Eisenhower on the following day.[46] Yet it was on the following day that Churchill interrupted talk with Macmillan to send an enquiry to General Ismay, his Chief of Staff:

> Could I have a further report on the 45,000 Cossacks of whom General

Eisenhower speaks in his SCAF.399. How did they come in their present
plight? Did they fight against us?[47]

The concluding queries suggest a sympathetic attitude, and we know that
the Prime Minister shared Alexander's chivalrous outlook. In the
following month he addressed the Field Marshal on this question,
expressing 'great apprehension as to future of all those peoples who
refused to return to their native countries because of opposition to political
regimes', and going on to urge Alexander 'to be particularly careful to see
to it that no force was used to persuade anyone to return to his native
country'.[48] Alexander responded within a month by prohibiting forcible
repatriation altogether, an action that aroused considerable indignation at
the Foreign Office, where it was held with some justification that he had
exceeded his powers.[49] It is further significant that Alexander encountered
no adverse reaction from the Soviets in consequence of his firm refusal to
meet their principal demands.

    Whether Churchill held or expressed such views in May concerning
the Cossacks is conjectural. What is pertinent to the present enquiry is that
he found it necessary to direct the question to Ismay at all. For there, seated
opposite him, was Alexander's closest colleague: a man more likely than
any to know the answer. Not only were the Cossacks held within a region
covered by Macmillan's ministerial responsibility, but he had himself
flown into Austria a week before to assess the situation: a fact he cannot
have avoided mentioning during the prolonged discussion of Tito's
designs in the region. Did Churchill not think to ask Macmillan the
question whose answer it took Ismay a fortnight to unearth? It seems
implausible to suppose so. It was not just a question of sentiment or
honour, but 5th Corps' relief of responsibility for thousands of prisoners
of war was an essential factor in the success of Operation Coldstream.
Churchill was anxiously pursuing a satisfactory outcome of the Yugoslav
crisis throughout these critical days, and followed events with closest
attention.[50] It seems Macmillan withheld from him any mention of his
'advice' to Generals Keightley and Robertson to deliver the Cossacks to
the Soviets, as well as Robertson's order of 14 May that this should be put
into effect. As has been seen, it appears equally certain that Macmillan
failed to inform Alexander of this 'advice' when they dined together on
the evening of his return to Naples.

    In describing these convoluted intrigues, it will I trust be noted that I
have adopted at every stage the natural interpretation of each source cited.
It is surely telling that, in almost every case, Government-inspired
conclusions require doing precisely the opposite.

HAROLD MACMILLAN INTERVIEWED BY LUDOVIC KENNEDY ON BBC TELEVISION IN 1978
(BBC transcript)

'MACMILLAN AT WAR

'M. The Field Marshall asked me to go up to Klagenfurt to see what was happening. So I flew up and I found one brigade [*sic*] we'd got there, just before the/Tito's people who were also claiming that -ER-ER-Carinthia and there were about, I should think, 80 to 100,000 of them. We got there just -CHUCKLE- in time to put up notices on the/on the Town Hall to say 'we are the Military Government of Carinthia' and it was a very difficult situation, we only had one brigade and there were thousands of them.

'K. Were we near war at all with them?

'M. Well, it w-was extremely awkward; the British Army wasn't in a very/much of a mood to fight another war, particularly against Tito's partisans who we'd been told had been a splendid support to us against the Germans for years. It wouldn't have been very easy to fight a war. I mean, morally, they'd, I suppose, done their duty, but it wouldn't have been a popular war with the Army. It was just owing to Alex's skill that he made this agreement with Tito. But at Carinthia was more difficult. However, the poor General Keightley, who had the Army, he had only one brigade. In addition to the partisans, there were a mass of people called, I think they called them Moustachi [Ustashi] who were Croats and Serbs, anti-part/thing [Partizan], and they'd arrived in considerable numbers, either as refugees or to fight/settle in Carinthia, we didn't quite know. In addition, there was a Russian Army approaching of about 2 or 4/300,000 troops which we certainly didn't either wish to quarrel with or in a position with one brigade to quarrel with. Then there were about 30,000 Cossacks, who had been recruited by the Germans when they had gone right into Ge/into Russia early in the war and, of course, were rebels against Russia, been fighting for Germany. Then there were a lot of so-called White Russians who w-were with the Germans, for what re/in order to support Germany against Russia, I suppose.[*] I suppose, they –stumbling- and what were we to do with all these people? Well, actually, we hadn't the physical power to do very much, but General Keightley was extremely good –ER-sensible, wise man and he made quite good terms with the Russian General, who was of course, was in an overwhelming position actually.

---

[*] Macmillan clearly recalled the distinct status of the White Russians.

And we thought the only thing to do was to carry out what had been agreed at the Yalta Treaty.

'K. What was that?

'M. It was agreed that when the armies met, all/everybody should good/give back each other's nationals, so to say. For instance, the Russians found among the Germans 3 or/2 or 3000 of our soldiers who were prisoners, you see, and a fair number of wounded and various other English people. Well, they were/we wanted them very much back. Then we were to give back to the Russians the Cossacks and other Russian people, Russian subjects who'd been fighting or supporting Germany and the only thing to do was to carry out. It was harsh in some ways, because no doubt some of these White Russians were people who'd been –PAUSE- well, were against the Communist regime for years. Still, they were on Germans' side and working with the Germans and we hadn't a great – PAUSE- you must remember the conditions at the time, Russia was, after all, our great ally and we'd made the agreement and so we carried it out.

K. You say in your diaries: 'To hand them over to the Russians' – that's this Cossacks and White Russians –ER- 'is condemning them to slavery, torture and probably death'.

M. Yes, probably.

K. So, whatever had been decided at Yalta –ER-ER- surely that shouldn't have been done?

M. It had to be done. We had no power to stop it. And not to do it would have meant they would have not sent back our British prisoners.

K. D'you know who gave the orders for this?

M. Well – I, no, not re/well, we –STUMBLING-ER- I suppose the combined Chiefs of Staff. We had our instructions from them.

K. -ER- the information that I have is that they – they were not in favour of it and nor was the Foreign Office.

M. Well, those were our instructions; they sent us round instructions before we went there.

K. So-so did the executive order come from General Keightley or –

M. Oh no, from the Field Marshall.

K. From the Field Marshall.

M. And to him from the Combined Chiefs.

K. From Alexander?

M. But before-before the crisis, I mean some weeks before, we had our orders what we were to do under the Yalta Agreement.

K. So it/this was Alexander's carrying out?

M. Well, I mean, but not at the moment of crisis, at –PAUSE- I mean they'd come back/they'd gone round about a month before.

K. Yes, I mean, all I was trying to find out, if you can remember, is who –

M. I can't remember exactly; all I do remember is reporting to Alexander.

K. Reporting what?

M. Well, that Keightley and I both thought that we had better carry out the agreement. There was nothing else we could do.[*]

K. In view of what has happened, of what we know happened to them all, did you have any –PAUSE- thoughts about this afterwards? Any regrets?

M. Well, of course, but then you know, –PAUSE- we know much more than we did.

K. Of course.

M. –PAUSE- I often think –PAUSE- it's so easy to criticise the English government before the war; Neville Chamberlain, Halifax were called – because they wanted to have peace with Germany – were called defeatists and guilty men. I opposed them strongly, but I think they couldn't believe that a man could be so evil as Hitler –PAUSE- I couldn't believe really that he'd really killed 1 million Jews, and certainly in the war when the Russians were allies, I didn't know that Stalin had killed 6 million people –PAUSE- enemies of the regime. I mean it/when he went mad, killed 6 million people –PAUSE- just/I don't think we thought these things would happen. I felt that they might treat them very badly. Of course, the Cossacks they would, but they were practically savages, they were –PAUSE-

K. But the White Russians, some of them had never been in Russia. They were children of people who'd come out of Russia in the Revolution.

M. Well, why were they up there?

K. Well, they were fighting with the Germans, weren't they?

M. Yes, they were fighting with the/I mean, they weren't/we'd been fighting the Germans for 6 years; they're not friends of ours –UNCLEAR-

K. Russia wasn't their/they were White Russians; Russia wasn't their Motherland any more, was it?

M. Well, that was laid down according/it was a very strict rule according to the date of their birth, or-or leaving of Russia. If they'd left between certain dates, they weren't handed over.

K. Now I wasn't asking this by way of a –

M. No. No, but I –

---

[*] At no time is Macmillan recorded to have reported the problem to Alexander.

K. –ER- criticism, but simply that-that, because of what did happen, whether afterwards, you thought: 'well – '

M. Well, of course.

K. I wonder, if I did the right thing?

M. It was terrible. Well, I'd really nothing much to do with it except carry out our instructions, but –ER- I think, it was right probably, because I don't think we'd have got our British soldiers back and we naturally thought a lot about them. I didn't realise they would be quite so bad, because – I put that in – but that's it! But they did terrible things, of course, because people did do terrible things.[51]

The Times, 30 October 1990

Sir, Writing of the forced repatriation of captured Cossack and White Russian troops in 1945, Mr Daniel Johnson says:

> interviewing an unprepared Macmillan in 1984, Ludovic Kennedy relied entirely on Count Tolstoy's tendentious interpretation. Closely quizzed, Macmillan was made to appear evasive...

If Mr Johnson had had the courtesy to telephone me before he published this, I would have told him that far from being unprepared, Mr Macmillan said that he would be happy to be questioned on any matter arising from his book *War Diaries* which was the subject of the interview.

I did not rely entirely, or indeed at all, on something that Count Tolstoy had written, for at that time I had not read anything he had written (*The Minister and the Massacres* was not published until 1986). If Macmillan was evasive in his replies, he had every reason to be, for he had written in his War Diaries that the repatriations of the Russian troops was "condemning them to slavery, torture and probably death".

Yours etc.,

LUDOVIC KENNEDY,

Ashdown,

Avebury, Wiltshire'.[52]

---

[1] In his televised interview with Ludovic Kennedy aired on BBC1 (21 December 1984), Macmillan asserted that 'The Field Marshall [Alexander] asked me to go up to Klagenfurt to see what was happening'. This was manifestly false. Macmillan further asserted that large numbers of liberated British POW were delivered by the Red Army in exchange for the Cossacks. This was also untrue. On 16 May 'Exchange of liberated P.W. between Eight Army and Russians agreed' (FO.916/1207). This was a week before 5th Corps agreed to hand over the Cossacks and White Russians, and it was made clear

throughout that the exchange of prisoners of war and Cossack handovers fell into entirely distinct categories.

2 Alex Danchev and Daniel Todman (ed.), *Field Marshal Lord Alanbrooke: War Diaries* (London, 2001), p. 568. On 31 January 1945, Brooke wrote again: 'I had a long and useful interview with Alex... Finally told him that some of us had doubts as to whether Macmillan or Alexander was Supreme Allied Commander of Mediterranean!' (p. 652). Cf. also pp. 645, 646, 661, 657, 672. Alexander, not unreasonably, accepted the division of labour more or less to the letter: 'The role of Minister Resident was a political appointment – he was the Prime Minister's personal representative within a defined theatre of operations. As such he acted as adviser to the commander-in-chief on all political issues, thereby leaving him free to devote his main energies to the problems of the battlefield' (John North (ed.), *The Alexander Memoirs 1940-1945* (London, 1962), pp. 109-10).

3 FO.371/48814.

4 The successive Cowgill Inquiries, following a suggestion by Lord Brimelow, assert as though it were fact that Macmillan's unanticipated visit arose in response to Keightley's query (10 May) to General McCreery at 8th Army whether he could open fire on Yugoslavs who disobeyed orders from British commanders (FO.1020/42,67). According to this speculative reconstruction, McCreery informed Macmillan of Keightley's query, which caused the Minister to extend his journey to Austria (Brigadier Anthony Cowgill, Lord Brimelow, and Christopher Booker Esq, *The Repatriations from Austria in 1945: The Report of an Inquiry* (London, 1990), pp. 16-17; Booker, *A Looking-Glass Tragedy*, pp. 171-73). In response, it may be questioned why Macmillan failed to mention this factor, both in his diary at the time and later: in particular, when closely questioned on the topic by Ludovic Kennedy. Moreover, ensuing signals establish that the 'shooting' issue had been promptly passed upwards by Alexander, who informed McCreery that 'Macmillan will explain it to you when he arrives' (FO.1020/42,73). No suggestion had arisen at AFHQ of Macmillan's extending his itinerary to repeat his explanation to Keightley in person, and by the time of Macmillan's arrival at 8th Army Headquarters on 12th May the situation in Austria had in any case become temporarily defused (*ibid.*, 76, 79, 80). Thus there was no call for the Minister to act as messenger boy in the manner suggested. Yet again, in his report to the Foreign Office despatched following his return to Naples, Macmillan asserted that it was Alexander who arranged his visit to Klagenfurt, *not* McCreery. Brigadier Tryon-Wilson, who was throughout this time present at 5th Corps Headquarters, recalled that it was the vexed question of the Cossack officers alone that caused Keightley to request advice from Macmillan, who at no time then or thereafter intervened on the basis of the specious Cowgill conjecture. Unsurprisingly, the Cowgill Inquiries were as ever unable to cite any evidence in support of their imaginative

reconstruction of events.

[5] WO.204/10126. Enforced repatriation of Cossacks in Austria does not appear to been considered an issue during the first few days of British occupation in Austria. The Russians at Wolfsberg were not Cossacks.

[6] Harold Macmillan, *War Diaries: Politics and War in the Mediterranean January 1943-May 1945* (London, 1984), p. 757.

[7] Aldington himself recalled that 'The reason for that was that to our knowledge the majority of it [*Russkii Korpus*] were people who had not been in Russia, who had lived outside Russia for many years and who included also Rumanians. We thought that was clearly a non-Soviet national formation' (Trial Transcript, Day 4).

[8] *Ibid.*, Day 8.

[9] In detailed notes recounting her interviews with Aldington, Alistair Horne's research assistant Serena Booker recorded in December 1980 that 'Aldington claims to know nothing about H[arold]M[acmillan]'s visit (despite being BGS!!)'. In the following month, she pressed him further, saying '"I have been told that you were at the meeting with HM" – "Who by?" – Tryon, Musson and in HM's diary he talks of a "Brigadier, and meeting Keightley's senior officers" – "Does he mention me by name?" – "No". "No, I can't remember being there..." After successive lengthy interviews with Aldington, Serena concluded in a letter to me of 15 January 1982: '.. my thanks again for your help over Aldington – it would be so nice to nail him down, but he is like a box of eels as regards wriggliness, so I doubt one will be successful!' It seems Horne accepted her estimate, as he advanced potent (if understandably cautiously worded) reasons for believing that Low did in fact attend Keightley's conference with Macmillan on 13 May (*Macmillan: 1894-1956* (London, 1988), pp. 478-79). In June 1974 (my first contact with him), Aldington assured me: 'I do not remember being involved in any matters concerning the Cossack Divisions'. In February 1983 he similarly explained: 'Thank you for letting me know you are preparing a piece on the handover of Yugoslav citizens to Tito in May/June 1945. I do not remember that problem arising in my time in Austria'. Yet, under examination in court fifteen years later, all of a sudden his memory extended to details of meetings he attended, reports he despatched, etc, etc!

[10] FO.1020/42,86.

[11] Jerome Jareb and Ivo Omrčanin, 'The End of the Croatian Army at Bleiburg, Austria in May 1945 according to English Military Documents', *The Journal of Croatian Studies* (New York, 1977-78), xviii-xix, p. 160.

[12] WO.32/11119,230A. The Cowgill Inquiry sought to discount the possibility of any conspiratorial discussion between Macmillan and Keightley at Klagenfurt, on grounds that 'the two men ... [were] sitting in a room in an airfield building with at least half a dozen others' (Christopher Booker, *A Looking-Glass Tragedy: The Controversy over the repatriations from Austria in 1945* (London, 1997), p. 175; cf. Cowgill, Brimelow, and Booker Esq, *The*

Repatriations from Austria in 1945: The Report of an Inquiry, p. 17). Once again, this is speculation dressed up as fact: nothing is recorded of the circumstances of the meeting. Even that it occurred at the aerodrome remains unknown. On 23rd May 1985 Brigadier Tryon-Wilson, who was in a better position to know than anyone then alive, told me he was certain the conference took place in Keightley's sophisticated headquarters caravan by the Wörthersee. This issue is, however, unimportant. The 'others' (apart from his aide Philip Broad) accompanying Macmillan were Brigadier Floyd, Chief of Staff to 8th Army, his AMG colleague Con Benson, and some of Floyd's subordinate officers. Their reason for joining the flight had nothing to do with Macmillan, being 'to discuss moves of remainder 46 Div, 4 MED, 26 MED & 61 HY regts' into Austria (WO.170/4183). It is accordingly most unlikely that they were invited to attend Macmillan's *tête-à-tête* with Keightley. Low's signal O539 of 23 May to Floyd explains that 'As a result of verbal directive from Macmillan to Corps Comd at recent meeting we have undertaken to return all Soviet nationals in Corps area to Soviet forces'. This suggests Floyd had hitherto been unaware of Macmillan's directive. Macmillan's deputy Broad was incidentally an uncritical admirer of Communism in Yugoslavia, even to the extent of withholding communications from the royalist resistance leader Mihailovich to the Yugoslav Government-in-Exile (Michael Lees, *The Rape of Serbia: The British Role in Tito's Grab for Power 1943-1944* (San Diego, Tex., 1990), pp. 129-30).

[13] WO.32/11119,230A.

[14] General Sir William Jackson and Group Captain T.P. Gleave, *The Mediterranean and Middle East* (London, 1988), vi (part iii), pp. 328-33, 417-18.

[15] Macmillan, *War Diaries*, p. 746.

[16] Allen Dulles, *The Secret Surrender* (London, 1967), p. 204. The principal function of GRU officers seconded to embassies abroad was to conduct espionage in the host country (Frank Gibney (ed), *The Penkovskiy Papers: by Oleg Penkovskiy* (New York, 1965), pp. 65-93).

[17] WO.204/1593, WO.204/1596.

[18] 'I found out these details later from our NKGB agents, who had been with Krasnov for a long time. They had played the parts of Cossack officers who had gone over to the Germans and were handed over to us along with the others' ('A.I. Romanov' [Captain Boris Bakhlanov], *Nights are Longest There: Smersh from the Inside* (London, 1972), p. 154).

[19] WO.1020/42,82.

[20] Cowgill, Brimelow, and Booker Esq, *The Repatriations from Austria in 1945: The Report of an Inquiry*, p. 212. Macmillan's statement here further refutes the Cowgill Inquiry's speculative assertion that he flew to his meeting with Keightley to discuss lawless Yugoslav behaviour *in Austria* (*ibid.*, p. 17).

[21] FO.371/48814,98.

[22] FO.371/48816; WO.106/4059.

[23] Tolstoy, *The Minister and the Massacres*, p. 121.

[24] *A Looking-Glass Tragedy*, pp. 118-19.

[25] WO.170/4184,569; FO.1020/42.

[26] NA. 383.7-14. Keightley's message to Macmillan was almost certainly sent on the morning of the latter's arrival at 8th Army on 12th May.

[27] WO.170/4241.

[28] FO.1020/42,86.

[29] WO.1020/42,82.

[30] Macmillan, *War Diaries*, pp. 367, 640, 641, 726, 760.

[31] NA 740.00119 Control(Italy)/5-1445.

[32] Booker claimed that there was no consultation between Macmillan and Robertson on the 14th (*A Looking-Glass Tragedy*, pp. 117-18). He was enabled to do this only by ignoring all pertinent evidence.

[33] Rogers P. Churchill, William Slany, John G. Reid, N. O. Sappington, and Douglas W. Houston (ed.), *Foreign Relations of the United States: Diplomatic Papers, 1945, Europe*, (Washington, Volume V (Washington, 1969), p. 1250. Macmillan could scarcely have been described as having 'acted contrary to policy', had his intervention really been confined to proffering a suggestion to McCreery.

[34] As a former senior Foreign Office official, Thomas Brimelow was familiar with the terminology employed. In a letter to Lord Aldington of 30 July 1985, he took it for granted that Macmillan 'mentioned it [the Cossack problem] to Robertson on that date': *i.e.* on his return to Caserta.

[35] WO.218/248; WO.170/7491.

[36] WO.170/4184,569; FO.1020/42.

[37] FO.371/46609.

[38] Nikolai Tolstoy, *Victims of Yalta* (London, 1977), pp. 63, 64, 92.

[39] Cowgill, Brimelow, and Booker Esq, *The Repatriations from Austria in 1945: The Report of an Inquiry*, p. 63.

[40] FO.1020/42,92.

[41] FO.371/48816.

[42] John Colville, *The Fringes of Power: Downing Street Diaries 1939-1955* (London, 1985), p. 600. On 29 June 1984, Sir John Colville wrote to me: 'I agree with you in thinking it improbable that Alex. approved the hand-over. It would have been wholly untrue to his form. Whether Harold Macmillan was responsible I doubt if we shall ever know, for I expect the orders were not committed to paper and it seems clear that the C.O.S., the F.O. and No 10. were not informed. But I doubt if General Keightley would have taken such a step without higher authority'.

[43] John Silverlight, *The Victors' Dilemma: Allied Intervention in the Russian Civil War* (London, 1970), p. 286.

[44] PRO Colonial Office papers 730/13. I am grateful to the late Sir Martin Gilbert for providing me with this reference.

[45] FO.1020/42,108; WO.219/290.

[46] WO.219/290.

[47] Winston S. Churchill, *Triumph and Tragedy* (London, 1954), p. 647.

[48] PREM.3 364/17, 748-50. For Macmillan's visit to England, see Macmillan, *War Diaries*, pp. 761-63.

[49] NA.800.4016 DP/8-145; FO.371/4910,77.

[50] Churchill, *Triumph and Tragedy*, pp. 483-87.

[51] BBC transcript (including sections not screened) kindly provided me by Sir Ludovic Kennedy.

[52] The Cowgill Report likewise claimed that 'Kennedy sprung on an unprepared Macmillan a series of apparently probing questions about the hand-overs ..' (Cowgill, Brimelow, and Booker Esq, *The Repatriations from Austria in 1945: The Report of an Inquiry*, p. 214), Like Daniel Johnson, the authors of the Report were careful not to check the veracity of their accusation with Kennedy.

CHAPTER XII
ENTER SMERSH

Tolstoy's narrative was by now studded with sinister references to SMERSH – 'the secret pact made between 5 Corps and SMERSH at Voitsberg', a 'SMERSH-inspired announcement read to the Cossacks on 29 May', 'the White Russians were handed over to SMERSH'.

Christopher Booker, *A Looking-Glass Tragedy*, p. 45

Received from the English command, through the representatives of RKKA,[*] Vlasovite-Generals Shkuro and Domanov with their adjutants: hand over to the representatives of OKR[†] "SMERSH".

Records of the Central State Archive of the Soviet Army

Following their demand on 11 May for the surrender of the senior White Cossack commanders, the Soviets proved surprisingly dilatory in pursuing the issue. Ten very busy days passed by, when on the afternoon of 21 May Keightley's Corps Commander Royal Artillery (CCRA), Major-General de Fonblanque, travelled to Wolfsberg, where he conferred with the Soviets.[1] As the Phantom signals unit at 5th Corps Headquarters reported next day,

Representatives of 5 Corps & Russian Force met yesterday at WOLFSBERG Y6305. **NO final decision was made** [bold added] but both agreed 1) that Russians accept COSSACKS & CAUCASIAN surrendered personnel in Corps area with their German Cadre 2) that they be moved by train to JUDENBERG B 2565 & evacuation completed by 11 June 3) that Russians and PW be returned on 22-24 May & Russian civilians 26 May.

Russian representative returns tomorrow after speaking with Russian higher commander.[2]

Thus, no formal commitment had yet been entered into for the handover of the Cossacks. Nor did the Soviets appear in any pressing hurry over the matter. The 5th Corps war diary noted that 'Conference with

---

[*] Red Army.
[†] 'Counter-Intelligence Branch'.

Russians at Wolfsberg today may be repeated 23 May'.[3] The next meeting accordingly took place on the afternoon of the 23rd, when de Fonblanque paid his second visit to the Soviet zone.[4]

At 7.15 that evening the 5th Corps BGS sent this revealing signal to 8th Army (cited in Chapter Eight).

> O539. Secret. Personal BGS for C of S.[*]

> Ref AFHQ sig F80197 dated 22 personal for Gen McCreery and copy to 5 Corps. As a result of verbal directive from Macmillan to Corps Comd at recent meeting we have undertaken to return all Soviet Nationals in Corps area to Soviet forces. Macmillan mentioned no proviso about use of force and we have issued instructions that force may be used if absolutely necessary. Consider quite impossible to guarantee to return Cossacks and so honour our verbal agreement with Soviet forces unless we are allowed free hand in this matter. Cossacks will view any move with suspicion as to destination. Consider therefore may be necessary use force to move Cossacks at all from present area. Longer they remain present area more likely force have to be used. Request you confirm our freedom of action in this.[5]

As has just been seen, 'NO final decision was made' at the previous conference on 21 May, and it was not until the 24th that the commitment was finally undertaken. Early that morning a fresh Soviet delegation arrived unannounced, demanding immediate further talks. The significance of this belated urgency on their part will be made clear shortly. The 5th Corps headquarters was taken by surprise, but managed to arrange a conference that afternoon at Wolfsberg. As 5th Corps war diary records on 24 May,

> At conference with reps 57 Russian Army at Wolfsberg. Russians agreed to accept Cossacks from 6 Brit Armd Div and 78 Div areas by train at Judenburg and those from 46 Div by march route at Voitsberg.

On this occasion Keightley decided that the British delegate should be Lieutenant-Colonel Ralph Turton, senior staff officer to Major-General de Fonblanque, who had succeeded Toby Low as Brigadier General Staff on the latter's departure the previous day. I have been unable to learn much of Colonel Turton, but events suggest that he had been wholly in Low's pocket. Indeed, he would hardly have been selected for the post were he not. It is surely telling that Keightley decided to retain de Fonblanque at Corps Headquarters on the occasion of this, 5th Corps's most important

---

[*] The style and content of this signal suggest that it was composed by Toby Low before his departure for England that day.

transaction with the Soviets. Indications are strong that the latter was not party to the conspiracy to hand over the White generals.

Although yet again no minutes of the meeting have been preserved, what passed is briefly summarized in the text of a subsequent Corps order:

> This letter sets out the provisional plan for the move of Cossacks from the British to the Soviet area as agreed by Chief of Staff 57 Soviet Army and GSO.1 5 Corps [Turton] on 24 May.
>
> 1. Definition
>
> Throughout this order the term "Soviet nationals" is taken to mean those tps of Soviet nationality incl their Camp followers who have fought with or co-operated with the enemy. For definition of Soviet nationals see this HQ letter 405/G dated 21 May.
>
> 2. Disarming and Segregation
>
> On 28 May
>
> (a) all Cossacks t[roo]ps will be completely disarmed ...
>
> (c) the off[ice]rs will be segregated from the other ranks and placed in confinement. German offrs will be separated from Cossack offrs. All will be disarmed.
>
> 3. Move of offrs ...
>
> (c) **It is of the utmost importance that all the offrs and particularly senior comds are rounded up and that none are allowed to escape. The Soviet forces regard the safe delivery of the offrs as a test of British good faith** [bold inserted].[6]

Omitted here are detailed outlines of routes, dates of delivery and other logistical matters. The introductory reference to 'the provisional plan for the move of Cossacks' suggests that all de Fonblanque had managed to establish at the previous conference three days earlier was broad concurrence that repatriation would be agreed and shortly take place.

What Colonel Turton had now concerted with his amiable Soviet colleague may be succinctly summarized:

> (i) *Every* Cossack was to be disarmed and handed over.
>
> (ii) *All* are to be treated as Soviet nationals: a classification explicitly reflecting Brigadier Low's Machiavellian 'definition of Soviet nationals ... this HQ letter 405/G dated 21 May'.
>
> (iii) German officers and NCOs are to be treated as Soviet nationals (on what conceivable grounds?), and handed over separately.

(iv) Stringent precautions are to be adopted to ensure the safe delivery of *all* Cossack officers, *above all the senior commanders.*

It will be seen shortly how closely these stipulations tally with a uniquely revealing Soviet account of this negotiation.

It goes without saying, that the transfer of German prisoners-of-war (which under international law incidentally included Russians in German uniform) to a third power – a power which had notoriously declined to become a signatory to the Geneva Convention on Prisoners of War in 1929, and was certain to treat them with extreme barbarity - represented deliberate violation of the Hague and Geneva Conventions on a shocking scale.[7] It is a matter of grave concern that none of the apologists for forced repatriation has ever expressed the slightest concern for this factor. On the contrary, blatant violations of international law have been openly defended by spokesmen for the British Government (Cowgill *et al.*), on grounds that they were justified by considerations of *Realpolitik.* Yet at the Nuremberg tribunal it was of primary concern in the prosecution of Nazi war criminals 'that the Geneva Prisoners of War Convention imposes upon its signatories the strictest obligations to protect its prisoners of war from violence'.[8]

It seems that for some even today there exists one law for Germans, and another for British.

Provision (iv) above points unmistakably to the celebrated tsarist generals, whose names were singled out on the list handed to Brigadier Tryon on 11 May, which he in turn passed to General Keightley. Specifically wanted was General Shkuro, who alone is identified by name as liable to handover in the Corps 'Definition' of 21 May. Despite characteristic evasiveness, Lord Aldington felt he had no choice in court but to acknowledge that he was aware of Shkuro's identity and status, when he singled him out by name for delivery to his enemies.[9] As will be seen in Chapter Fourteen, within three days 5th Corps was to detach Shkuro from his fellow-generals at Lienz, secretly abduct him by night from his quarters, and hold him in solitary custody apart from all other Cossacks prior to delivering him up to the Soviets on 29 May.

The 5th Corps command's actions appear so atrocious, insubordinate and deceptive, that some otherwise fair-minded people have felt chary of accepting the indictment. Appearances look bad, it is true, but may what transpired not be ascribed either to muddle or pragmatic decisions adopted in haste, without due consideration of their implications or consequences? Are conclusions to be drawn from British military records really such, that extensive conspiracy and treacherous intent provide the sole logical explanation consistent with available evidence?

Such a reaction is understandable. A conspiracy of the extent indicated represents something so alien to any normal person's experience, that there exists strong inducement to assume that there must be some explanation more in accord with everyday experience. In addition, I fear that the timid reluctance of some academic historians with relevant expertise to address themselves seriously to what has become a political issue dangerous to anyone espousing a viewpoint unacceptable to the British establishment, has done little to assist the general public in arriving at an informed conclusion. Nor have Government censorship and disinformation assisted in establishing what the evidence plainly indicates.

My overall conclusion, although now greatly substantiated by documents previously undiscovered or inaccessible, remains in essence that which I first advanced in Chapter Eleven of my book *Victims of Yalta* (published in 1978), and last set out in detail in 1985 in *The Minister and the Massacres*. It is one which was reliant primarily on analysis of British military records, combined with extensive first-hand accounts by participants in the operations. Nevertheless, as I emphasized then, 'one half of the source material needed for the story unfolded in this book is inaccessible to scholars', since 'research in Soviet and Yugoslav archives is not permitted ...'[10]

Since then, however, an astonishingly revealing source unexpectedly appeared in the form of an interview published in the Soviet newspaper *Golos Rodinii*, No. 34. The extent to which it illuminates the tragic events in Austria from an entirely fresh perspective is so remarkable that a full translation is here provided. Headed 'OPERATION "END OF ATAMAN SHKURO"', it reads as follows:

'May 1945 had arrived. Hitler had already done away with himself, the Reich was eking out its last days, but traitors to the Motherland, inveterate adventurers, counter-revolutionary ringleaders, still dreamed of bloody operations

'"I will knock half this world into the next, before they catch me!" cried Ataman Shkuro furiously. "My "wild divisions" and "wolf squadrons" will drive through death and pave the way for us".

'Not two months had passed before Shkuro and Krasnov and their comrades in arms fell into the power of Soviet Chekists.* Ever since

---

* The term 'Chekist' is taken from *Cheka*, adopted by the Soviets from the original 'ChK' (Extraordinary Commission) as a generic term for its successor political police organizations OGPU, NKVD and SMERSH.

various fanciful accounts of their capture have been provided. Today we recount how this operation was conducted in reality ...

'The Army in which the Chekist Captain Soloviev was serving finished the War in the Austrian town of Graz. Victory, spring, inclined everyone to long-anticipated relaxation, peaceful occupations. But Mikhail Soloviev was preparing operations for capture of the ringleaders of the White Guardist[*] gang, who had been serving fascism: General Krasnov, Ataman Shkuro, the commander of the Wild Division Prince Sultan-Ghirei Klich, SS General von Pannwitz ...

'General Krasnov, on the second day after the October [1917] victory,[†] had advanced his army on Petrograd, against the Revolutionaries. But his units were defeated, while Krasnov himself became a prisoner. Crossing himself, he gave his word of honour that he would cease his struggle against Soviet power. But he broke his word and fled to the Don, where he gathered counter-revolutionary forces and became famous for punitive operations. Later he offered his services to the fascists.

'Shkuro: an adventurer, a robber, who with exceptional cruelty made short work of the peaceful population. The bloody track of the torturer and bestial Shkuro remained as a yoke upon the entire country. Not for nothing was he known to the people as Ataman Shkuro.

'Not far from Graz lay a camp for repatriated people with deportation stations.[11] They were buzzing like bees. Here were gathered hundreds of thousands of displaced persons, prisoners-of-war, the remains of Cossack squadrons. In the mornings among the multitude there often passed a short, thickset man in a brown field shirt. This was Soloviev. He struck up conversations with former concentration camp prisoners, Cossacks.

'"And where are you from?" enquired in friendly tones a former Kuban Cossack, domiciled abroad.

'"I'm looking for my adopted brother".

'"Then you may even find him. Yesterday they said that Krasnov has appeared, and today already it is said that Shkuro has been seen a hundred versts from here. He's scared of the Cheka, who are digging about everywhere".

'Each evening the Chekists gathered, delivering reports, summarizing facts; while each morning the Captain reported everything to the head of the Smersh unit attached to the Army, Colonel Feodor Ivanovich Okorochkov.

---

[*] 'White Guardist' was employed by the Soviets as a derogatory term for Russians hostile to the Soviet regime.
[†] *i.e.* the Bolshevik *coup d'état* in Moscow and Petrograd.

'Soviet representatives urgently raised the question of armed military units. "Oh, it's dangerous", objected the English; "they are drunk and shooting". At the time of the negotiations there was talk about General Krasnov, Ataman Shkuro and other war criminals. All our attempts to ascertain their whereabouts produced no results. The English representative declared: "If we find them, then certainly we will hand them over to the Soviet authorities, as has been agreed".

'At the next meeting near our mission there appeared a new English interpreter. We spoke together. He turned out to be an inhabitant of Poltava, [named] Antonenko. But here he was called Galushka. Through him the Soviet representatives tried to get something across:

'"Your bosses are arranging these talks, but in fact they are hiding entire formations. You are hiding the White Generals Krasnov and Shkuro, but you declare that you want to be our allies and friends. Something is not quite as it should be".

'"Well, a day or two ago they were in a camp at Glaisdorf".

'But at that point he cut himself short, feeling he had said too much.

'On this occasion Soloviev went to the end of the columns, thinking he would get to the camp which Antonenko had inadvertently mentioned. The journey was extremely dangerous: everywhere there were armed Cossacks. This is what passed. The Captain looked at his driver, Sergeant Deyev. The other threw him a glance:

'"Time to go? The motor needs repairing!"

'He stopped and began tinkering with the engine. Suddenly the car was surrounded by police in armoured cars and motorcycles: "What's going on?"

'Soloviev, not getting out of the car, said calmly:

'"A minor breakdown. We're moving on".

'So the English departed, the Chekists remaining alone. Soon they came to a large village. A woman and a soldier were standing by a well. Soloviev descended in order to drink some water, glanced across, and glimpsed a sailor's striped shirt beneath his English jacket. The lad ran up to the car:

'"What, have you lost your way?"

'"No, we're travelling on a mission".

'"But brothers, they'll shoot you in the twinkling of an eye".

'"And who are you?"

'"I was a prisoner, and I want to get back to my own people".

'The Captain grasped the sailor's hand:

'"Do me a favour: tell me where are Krasnov, Shkuro?"

'"It's said they've gone".

'"Where? Who knows?"

'"Lena, Shkuro's mistress. She's in a camp. If you like, she'll be with you in your car; but, mind you, you must let me come along too".

'The sailor set off on his way, and Soloviev sat alongside his colleague as if on hot coals. They knew: one false step - and all would be lost. They checked their pistols and placed grenades in their pockets. As before they did not take their eyes from the square. What if suddenly bandits [Cossacks] were to spring out with submachine guns?

'Finally the sailor reappeared with a girl. Chattering cheerfully, they approached the car. Seeing strangers, the girl stopped apprehensively. The youth opened the car door and hustled her into the car. Soloviev turned to her with his pistol in his hand. She said coolly: "That doesn't scare me. One yell from me and you'll be gunned down from all sides".

'"If you want to live you'd better shut up!" warned Soloviev.

'And the car abruptly shot forward.

'Mikhail Soloviev recounts:

'On that day Lena and the sailor told us a great deal. It was well known that Krasnov, Shkuro and other ringleaders had raised anti-Soviet military formations, and sent a message to the Allied armies in Italy, in which they petitioned 'to be taken under their protection' and proffered their services for the 'struggle against Communism'.[*]

'The facts obtained allowed the member of our mission in a final meeting to advance much more keenly the question of the handover to the Soviet Army of the remainder of the enemy force, together with the White Guard generals.

'During one of the intervals in the conference, Soloviev went out into the garden. The deputy head of the English mission joined him there.

'"They are wanted without delay in the Motherland", said Soloviev; "but

---

[*] The reference is unmistakably to General Krasnov's letter to Field Marshal Alexander, which he composed on 8 May. It probably fell into British hands by the next day, although how it became known to SMERSH at the early stage implicit from Soloviev's account is hard to say. Was it brought by Keightley and Low to their first meeting with the Soviets at Voitsberg on 10 May? If so it would account for the latter's being so well-informed about the émigré Cossack officers when Brigadier Tryon arrived for the second meeting on the following day.

here are your colleagues holding back".

"'It's odd to me too", agreed the Lieutenant-Colonel. Then, after remaining silent for a moment, he suddenly murmured: "And are the Atamans worth much?"

"'I should think so! They've been plundering all their lives", responded Soloviev, noting that his account secretly interested the Lieutenant-Colonel. "My view is as follows: among the people being repatriated, give us these Atamans. Who wants them now? Send them off to us, and the treasure can stay behind with you!"

"'But how can we deliver the Generals to you?" And then there came an idea to the man with whom Soloviev spoke, with which the Captain [Soloviev] concurred. "These Generals have appealed to Alexander's staff concerning their final destination.[12] Well, certainly, we'll grant them the opportunity of going for a drive in our covered trucks to the Commander's staff".

'On receipt of Soloviev's report the Chekists worked out a plan for the final stage of the operation. Every other day occurred mass repatriations. The handover location chosen was Judenburg. They surrounded it with units of frontier guards.

'The English sought out the Generals by the Italian frontier and invited them to come to the conference with Alexander's staff in connexion with their message. The first truck appeared in the evening, covered with black tarpaulin. They stopped on the bridge. The flaps were opened, and with the help of English soldiers General Krasnov appeared from the vehicle, and from the second: Ataman Shkuro. Immediately after came other trucks. All the bandits were swiftly disarmed and lodged in the building of a disused factory. Afterwards under strong guard they were sent to the east.[13]

'Ataman Shkuro always sought an opportunity to commit suicide. He even tried to throw himself on a bayonet. But the troops were on the alert.

'Shkuro asked Soloviev:

"'What will happen to me?"

"'The People's Court will decide that".

'In January 1947 the Military College of the Supreme Court of the USSR sentenced the accused Krasnov P.N., Shkuro A.G., Sultan-Ghirei Klich, Krasnov S.N., Domanov T.I. and von Pannwitz to be punished by death by hanging.[14] The just sentence was fulfilled'.

The author of the article, Mikhail Osipovich Stepichev, a special correspondent of *Pravda*, also introduced a Soviet television interview with Soloviev shown on 18 December 1988. Questioned in what appeared to be his sitting-room while leafing through his photograph album of the period, Soloviev provided with minor variations and one or two interesting additions a résumé of the account provided in the newspaper. Still photographs included glimpses of the British handover of Cossacks at Judenburg, while another showed Shkuro and Domanov seated in the back seat of an open-top car driving along a city street (presumably Graz). Shkuro is in Cossack uniform, and both are seen to be smiling cheerfully. Stepichev conceded their extraordinary courage. Quoting the photographer, he explained:

> They noticed the camera ... and [Shkuro] put on this jolly expression ... after his arrest, after they had been brought to Moscow. Putting a good face on a bad situation.[15]

Broadly speaking Soloviev's account speaks for itself, and its significance is immediately apparent. If his version of events be authentic, then any claim that the handover of Shkuro resulted from administrative oversight on the part of 5th Corps, rather than deliberate policy, must be abandoned at once. Nor can there any longer be question that retrieval of Krasnov, Shkuro and the other White Generals was the particular responsibility of SMERSH. A document held in the Central State Archive of the Soviet Army reports:

> Received from the English command, through the representatives of RKKA [the Red Army command], Vlasovite-Generals* Shkuro and Domanov with their adjutants: hand over to the representatives of OKR "SMERSH".[16]

'Captain SOLOVIEV' is listed in Red Army archives as a member of the Commission headed by a Colonel Shorokhov for 'the Reception of Soviet citizens and prisoner-of-war former soldiers and commanders of the Red Army'.[17] Analysis of Soloviev's story not only confirms its remarkable accuracy, but confirms that it adds so much to our understanding of events as to complement at almost every stage that provided by British sources. It should be remembered, too, that much of the account deriving from British documents is here published for the first time, and is

---

* General Vlasov was a captured Red Army general, whom the Germans placed in charge of an anti-Communist 'army' of several hundred thousand captured and exiled Russians. 'Vlasovite' became a Soviet term of abuse effectively corresponding to 'quisling'. His reputation is now widely rehabilitated in contemporary Russia and elsewhere, Vlasov being with some justice regarded as a Russian de Gaulle. Cf. Catherine Andreyev, *Vlasov and the Russian Liberation Movement: Soviet reality and émigré theories* (Cambridge, 1987); K.M. Alexandrov, *Офицерский Корпус Армии Генерал-Лейтенанта А.А. Власова 1944-1945* (Moscow, 2009), pp. 9-48.

consequently unlikely to have been accessible even to Soloviev's resourceful superiors.

Besides, it does not appear that Soloviev's concern was with disinformation. No attempt to denigrate the British, nor even the Cossacks to any exorbitant degree, is to be detected, and his words and complacent outlook suggest no interested motive beyond that of lauding the resource and courage of Captain Soloviev – and by extension, that of the all-powerful organization which he served. In fact, the interview was one of a series authorized by the KGB to promote its record as prime defender of the Motherland.

It will assist to take the narrative step by step, reminding ourselves first of what is established in British sources. Four (or possibly five, if the issue were discussed with General Keightley during his visit to Voitsberg on 10 May) relevant meetings are known to have taken place between British and Soviet representatives before full agreement on the Cossack handovers was reached.

> 11 May. Brigadier Tryon's visit to Voitsberg, at which he was handed the list of 'wanted' Cossack officers, the names of Krasnov and other leading émigré Generals being emphasized by capital letters.

> 21 May. Major-General de Fonblanque's conference at Wolfsberg, at which 'NO final decision was made but both agreed 1) that Russians accept COSSACKS & CAUCASIAN surrendered personnel in Corps area with their German Cadre.[18]

> 23 May. De Fonblanque's second conference at Wolfsberg, which appears to have been inconclusive save for broad agreement that the Cossack handovers should take place.

> 24 May. Colonel Turton concludes arrangements for the handovers at Voitsberg in the Soviet zone – above all with regard to inclusion of the leading (principally White) Cossack officers.[19]

Although one might not expect factual precision in a retrospective description such as Soloviev's, his account dovetails strikingly with British contemporary records. His account of the negotiations begins:

> **At the time of the negotiations there was talk about General Krasnov, Ataman Shkuro and other war criminals.**

The first 'talk about General Krasnov, Ataman Shkuro and other war criminals' occurred during the visit of Brigadier Tryon to Voitsberg in the Soviet zone on 11 May. That it amounted merely to 'talk' reflects the fact that Tryon was empowered to do no more than bear the list of names back to 5th Corps Headquarters.

> **All our attempts to ascertain their whereabouts produced no results. The English representative declared: "If we find them, then certainly we will hand them over to the Soviet authorities, as has been agreed".**

Initially, as will again be seen shortly from previously inaccessible Soviet evidence, 5th Corps command remained for a week or more ignorant of General Krasnov's whereabouts within the Corps area. Finally, on 17 May a search was initiated in accordance with the Soviet demand, which (since he was not in hiding) must have achieved success within twenty-four hours.

> **At the next meeting near our mission there appeared a new English interpreter. We spoke together... Through him the Soviet representatives tried to get something across:**
>
> **"'Your bosses are arranging these talks, but in fact they are hiding entire formations. You are hiding the White Generals Krasnov and Shkuro, but you declare that you want to be our allies and friends. Something is not quite as it should be".**
>
> **"Well, the other day they were in a camp at Gleisdorf".[*]**
>
> **But at that point he cut himself short, feeling he had said too much.**

The account of this episode bears more authority than do Soloviev's oblique allusions to the earlier approaches, given that this time he was present at the meeting. Although much may be conceded to mutual misunderstanding, it seems that the continuingly evasive reaction ascribed de Fonblanque by the suspicious Soloviev meant no more than that he (de Fonblanque) was at this prefatory stage ignorant of Keightley's privy decision to accede to the SMERSH demand for Krasnov and Shkuro.

Broadly speaking, there is no means of establishing precisely who on the staff at 5th Corps was or was not complicit in the secret decision to comply with the Soviet demand for the old émigré generals. That it was a secret scarcely requires reiterating, nor that those responsible sought to restrict to a minimum the number of people aware of the true nature of what was being planned. The decision to ignore screening was withheld from 8th Army, and obscured from divisional commanders, who knew

---

[*] The reference to Gleisdorf is mysterious. At the time of Soloviev's cloak-and-dagger operation, the town lay well within the Soviet zone in Styria.

nothing more of official screening provisions than what was contained in Low's deceptive 21 May 'Definition' of Soviet citizenship.

In a letter sent to Toby Low on 13 June, not long after his return to England, General Keightley expressed a low estimate of de Fonblanque's talents:

> Dolly [de Fonblanque] is functioning [as BGS] at the moment and it is a sorry business compared to our recent days.

Keightley might well have thought it undesirable, as well as unnecessary, to inform his new and evidently unsatisfactory BGS of a policy which was undoubtedly being kept secret from other senior officers in 5th Corps.

On 12 August 1978, General de Fonblanque responded to an enquiry from Lord Aldington as follows:

> Now back some 34 years – I fear I can offer nothing about discrimination [*i.e.* screening] among those Caucasians [and Cossacks] we sent back to the Russians. My feeling is that we sent them all. What I can say, however, is that increasingly Charles Keightley resisted sending anyone until finally overridden by the F.O. You are perfectly right that we wanted to get shot of the clutch of P.O.W. but as the fate awaiting the [Cossacks and] Caucasians became more clear so the resistance to their despatch increased.

De Fonblanque went on to recount circumstances relating to the handover of Shkuro, which suggest he was unaware that it involved any violation of Allied policy. Particularly significant is de Fonblanque's firm understanding that the handover was forced on a reluctant 5th Corps command under Foreign Office pressure. This was the deceptive line consistently peddled by Keightley and Low, both at the time and after.

Given the privacy and tone of their correspondence, it is reasonable to assume that de Fonblanque was confiding a genuine recollection to his former colleague Aldington. It seems he was in that case unaware of the secret decision to disobey 8th Army rulings on screening, while his concluding sentence suggests that he could have been among those officers on 5th Corps Staff whose 'resistance to their despatch increased'.

There is a further intimation that de Fonblanque was not privy to secret machinations at 5th Corps Headquarters, after he succeeded Low as BGS on 23 May. Although the return of Shkuro must have been decided no later than 21 May, when Brigadier Low included him in his 'Definition' of that date, SMERSH officer Soloviev's account shows that Soviet demands for their return were received with frustrating lack of receptiveness at successive conferences, until at the final session 'the deputy head of the

English mission', an unidentified lieutenant-colonel, agreed to delivery of Shkuro and his fellow Atamans. This English officer can only have been Lieutenant-Colonel Turton, who acted as deputy successively to Brigadier Low and Major-General de Fonblanque during the negotiations, and presided over the decisive meeting on 24 May. It was only when Keightley deputed Turton to head the negotiations that the fatal concession was formally agreed. It seems that he was privy to a covert arrangement from which de Fonblanque was excluded.

To return to Soloviev's story. Following his allusion to what was apparently the conference of 23 May at Wolfsberg, he continues:

> **On this occasion Soloviev went to the end of the columns, thinking he would get to the camp which Antonenko had inadvertently mentioned. The journey was extremely dangerous: everywhere there were armed Cossacks.** *

There follows the melodramatic account of the abduction of Shkuro's mistress, which some readers may have found a little *ben trovato*.

In reality it provides as remarkable evidence as any of Soloviev's reliability as a witness. Stripped of its anecdotal refinements, the adventure is simply summarized. Immediately following the conference Soloviev sets off on an unauthorized expedition to hunt down Shkuro. Although checked and implicitly ordered to leave the British zone by British military police, he manages to abduct the unfortunate Lena *en route* and returns to Soviet lines.

In his television interview, Soloviev added a further detail of his return:

> **We came to the barrier boom at the demarcation line, it was a temporary boom. I said to the driver: "ram it!" We got past the boom. British soldiers carrying submachine guns ran out of a tent. We could see our own soldiers sitting on a tank not far away. But the boom was open. They didn't take any action at all.**

The essential veracity of Soloviev's account of his brush with British troops is suggested by the fact that what must surely be the same trifling incident is recounted in British records. Some time between 3.30 and 7.30pm on 23 May, 128th Infantry Brigade notified 46th Infantry Division:

> Party of 3 Russian offrs arrived at St Andra stating that they had come to find out strength of the traitors i.e. Cossacks in our area. matter referred to Corps. 128 Bde told to tell them that we cannot have them

---

* It was not until 27 May that the Cossacks around Lienz were disarmed.

swanning in our area without authority of their Corps HQ and our Corps HQ. the whole matter of [Cossack] traitors is being discussed this afternoon between Marshal Tolbukin's reps and our reps in Wolfsberg.[20]

A trifling discrepant detail lies in the reference to *three* Russian officers, since Soloviev's account suggests he was accompanied by his driver alone.

Underlying assumptions of this account are worth noting. Allusions to the Cossacks being armed, likewise the identity of date, locality, and declared purpose of the Soviet party, it is hard to suppose that the description does not in each source refer to the same trifling incident. So far as the number of officers is concerned, the British contemporary record is presumably to be preferred. It is not unlikely, therefore, that British soldiers peering into Soloviev's staff car mistook his driver and the sailor for fellow-officers. That they were accompanied by an attractive young woman may in the circumstances of the time not have been thought worth mentioning.

St. Andra lies in the British zone a few miles south of Wolfsberg. It seems that Soloviev, despairing of obtaining a collaborative reply from de Fonblanque on the vexed question of the elusive Atamans, decided to slip away with his SMERSH colleagues during or immediately after the conference, in order to pursue their inquiries in the cloak-and-dagger manner congenial to their sinister organization.

What follows in Soloviev's story contributes further to confirm this reconstruction:

> On that day Lena and the sailor told us a great deal. It was well known that Krasnov, Shkuro and other ringleaders had raised anti-Soviet military formations, and sent a message to the Allied armies in Italy, in which they petitioned 'to be taken under their protection' and proffered their services for the 'struggle against Communism'.

Once again Soloviev is well-informed. Krasnov had indeed written such a letter early in the second week of May,[21] which was intercepted by the British within a day or so of its dispatch. That they in turn accommodatingly passed such incriminating messages to SMERSH was attested by no less an authority than the villainous NKGB chief Vsevolod Nikolaevich Merkulov. As he gloated in his Lubianka lair to General Krasnov's nephew Nikolai:

> Did you get anything out of your petition which your uncle, the Ataman, drew up in French and sent from Spittal? What, do you think we didn't know about that?

The British were indeed dancing to SMERSH's tune, as he exultantly boasted.[22]

The SMERSH interrogation of Lena and the sailor took place 'that day', which was probably the evening of 23 May. According to Soloviev's account, he (and by implication his superior, Colonel Okorochkov) believed that the British were concealing Shkuro's whereabouts in order to evade handing him over. General de Fonblanque, who had succeded Low as BGS that day, may well have been ill-informed concerning Shkuro. (In the Soviet mentality, such a protestation was almost invariably taken to signify deceptive cunning rather than simple ignorance). Whether Lena was in a position to know that Shkuro was at Lienz also seems doubtful. St. Andra is far from the Drautal, and as an inveterate womanizer Shkuro may well have kept more than one mistress. Soloviev's words suggest no more than that he possessed sufficient information to be aware that the Ataman was held by the British somewhere in Austria.

Now that he was at last in possession of this information, Soloviev makes it clear he wasted no time in renewing his demand, and once again we find his moves reflected in the British records. At 7.30 on the morning of 24 May a message was passed up to 5th Corps from a British unit facing Soviet lines, to say that the Soviets had informed them that a representative of Marshal Tolbukhin would be arriving to consult with a 5th Corps representative at nine o'clock.

The 5th Corps Headquarters replied testily:

> Impossible for us to send rep at one hrs notice. We would like 12 hrs notice and fuller details of the meeting. If the matter is urgent would the rep like to go to Corps.

Shortly afterwards they sent a further message:

> Re Marshal Tolbukhin's rep. If going to Corps get details of visit and pass to Corps BEFORE rep leaves for Corps.

At 10.50, 138th Infantry Brigade (which controlled the area contiguous to the Soviet zone) passed on further information concerning the unexpected visitors:

> Russians awaiting to go to 5 Corps are at present at their Div HQ opposite Köflach. They wish to talk about repatriation of Cossacks. Ranks not known. Escort standing by. 5 Corps G1 informed - will ring and notify shortly.

The 5th Corps G1 was, as has been noted, Lieutenant-Colonel Ralph Turton, senior staff officer to the BGS throughout this time. In view of the urgency, 5th Corps notified 46th Infantry Division:

G1 5 Corps wishes one Russian officer of G1 Corps level to be at Y[orks] & L[ancs] HQ Köflach 1530 hrs today. (138 [Bde] infm).[23]

As 5th Corps records show, the request was complied with, and the principal Soviet negotiator proved to be the Chief of Staff of 57th Soviet Army. It was he who agreed with Turton the details of routes and timing set out above.

Accompanying this high-ranking Red Army officer was Captain Soloviev of SMERSH, who as it proved was empowered to discuss a particularly sensitive matter. Reverting to the memoir published in *Golos Rodinii*, we find precious details both of the manner and content of his discussion with Colonel Turton.

> **The facts obtained allowed the member of our mission in a final meeting to advance much more keenly the question of the handover to the Soviet Army of the remainder of the enemy force, together with the White Guard generals.**
>
> **During one of the intervals in the conference, Soloviev went out into the garden. The deputy head of the English mission joined him there.**
>
> **"They are wanted without delay in the Motherland", said Soloviev; "but here are your colleagues holding back".**
>
> **"It's inexplicable to me too", agreed the Lieutenant-Colonel. Then, after remaining silent for a moment, he suddenly murmured: "So the Atamans [Krasnov and Shkuro] are of great value?"**
>
> **"I should think so! They've been plundering all their lives", responded Soloviev, noting that his account secretly interested the Lieutenant-Colonel. "My view is as follows: among the people being repatriated, give us these Atamans. Who wants them now? Send them off to us, and the treasure [*dragotsennosti*] can stay behind with you!"**
>
> **"But how can we deliver the Generals to you?" And then there came an idea to the man with whom Soloviev spoke, with which the Captain [Soloviev] concurred. "These Generals have appealed to Alexander's staff concerning their final destination. Well, certainly, we'll grant them the opportunity of going for a drive in our covered trucks to the Commander's staff.**

More than any other section of Soloviev's narrative, this passage confirms to a remarkable degree the accuracy of his memory. He recalls correctly that the British representative was a 'Lieutenant-Colonel', whom he also rightly identified as 'the deputy head of the English mission'. His rank and role are specified as accurately as might be wished. By the morning of the 24th he was Major-General de Fonblanque's deputy, since the latter had succeeded Brigadier Low as BGS to 5th Corps on the previous day.

Soloviev's reference to the émigré generals' approach to AFHQ is likewise accurate. Krasnov addressed a second appeal for asylum to Alexander in the third week of May, while British war diaries mention with regard to Shkuro 'two letters written by him to Commander 36 Inf Bde [Brigadier Musson] and forwarded to 78 Div [General Arbuthnott] under 36 Inf Bde letters 129/G dated 23 and 24 May'. In the event 5th Corps withheld the letters from Alexander, passing them instead secretly to SMERSH. Consequently, they are not to be found among the voluminous British records.

Here may be noted a significant consideration consequent on Soloviev's reproach that the 5th Corps delegation was 'holding back' on surrendering the White generals. Despite this obstruction, Soloviev provides no trace of a suggestion that the Soviets might retain liberated Allied prisoners-of-war were their demand not to be fulfilled. Yet Macmillan and his advocates have claimed this as the prime threat that obliged the British to surrender the Cossacks! Not only is there no evidence that such a threat ever occurred, but here we have direct testimony that it was not one the Soviets cared to deploy.[*]

We possess here a precious glimpse of the extent of covert co-operation between 5th Corps command and SMERSH. Brigadier Tryon-Wilson confirmed to me that General Krasnov's petitions were received at 5th Corps headquarters. He assumed they were destroyed there, but as Soloviev's and Merkulov's accounts show, they were in fact covertly passed to the Soviets.

In January 1993, at the personal invitation of President Yeltsin, my authorized inspection of the Soviet archives relating to the forced repatriation included a visit to the Lubianka. There I was received by KGB Major-General Alexei Kondaurov. After discussing the material I was researching, I asked him whether I might visit the room where the Krasnovs were interrogated by his predecessor Merkulov. The General proved obliging, and I was much moved to find myself in the large hall where the brave Krasnov family's ordeal began. I showed Kondaurov a copy of young Nikolai Krasnov's account of his reception by Merkulov, which the General confirmed rang true. His only criticism was that it

---

[*] One possibility is that Stalin, being deeply concerned to secure the return of the White Russian officers in British hands, did not wish that delicate operation to be imperilled by a lesser side-issue. But since there exists no evidence that the hypothetical 'exchange' was ever considered, it is needless to pursue the issue.

represented Merkulov as a brutal thug, whereas he was in fact a cultured man. Such indeed was his reputation among his Soviet confrères,[24] although it did not prevent his being at the same time a sadistic bully.

Merkulov's sneering reference to the 'petition which your uncle, the Ataman, drew up in French and sent from Spittal' came in the context of mocking allusions to the abject compliance of the British with Soviet demands. The 5th Corps' secret transmission of the petitions not only appears bizarrely sinister, but particularly despicable, in that it must have been apparent that Soviet acquisition of the petitions would compromize the elderly General even more than was already the case.

As was seen, during one of the intervals in the conference Soloviev slipped out into the garden. There he was joined by the acting head of the English mission: *i.e.* Colonel Turton. Was it chance that brought about this private exchange: a brief sortie by both men to enjoy a quiet cigarette, perhaps, followed by an encounter under the shade of a tree? It seems unlikely. In the first place, it is surely implausible to suppose that the senior officer in the British delegation would have wandered off alone in the midst of so important a conference. He had much to discuss with his Red Army opposite number, one might suppose. More significantly, is it conceivable that under normal circumstances so significant an agreement would have been settled by Turton at a chance encounter with a subordinate officer of undefined standing from his opposite number's entourage?

The likeliest explanation is that the exchange was deliberately conducted out of earshot of the other officers, British and Soviet. The Chief of Staff of the 57th Red Army could arrange details of reception points and train timetables, but the secret handover of Shkuro and the other White officers in deliberate contravention of Field Marshal Alexander's orders was a delicate business to be handled in secret. Turton's concern to hold a private discussion with Soloviev in the garden is understandable in light of indications that other officers on 5th Corps staff were not privy to Keightley's agreement to include the White generals in the handover. As will be seen, Soviet records never before revealed show that the reception of the Cossacks at Judenburg was handled almost from the outset entirely by SMERSH.

Immediately on his return to 5th Corps headquarters, Turton drew up a 'provisional plan for the move of Cossacks from the British to the Soviet area', which included the clause reflecting his secret pact with Soloviev:

> It is of the utmost importance that all the offrs and particularly senior comds are rounded up and that none are allowed to escape. The Soviet

forces regard the safe delivery of the offrs as a test of British good faith.[25]

Or, as Soloviev put it,

They are wanted without delay in the Motherland ... but here are your colleagues holding back.

A curious detail may be of significance. Soloviev mentions that he suggested an exchange with Turton:

My view is as follows: among the people being repatriated, give us these Atamans. Who wants them now? Send them off to us, and you can keep the treasure (*Отправим их к нам, а драгоценности можете оставить себе*)!

The authors of *The Mitrokhin Archive* were struck by the sensational 'claim in a KGB file that a British army officer (and perhaps two of his colleagues) had been bribed into handing over the White generals'.[26]

In his Soviet TV-1 broadcast on 18 December 1988, Soloviev provided a more explicit account of his exchange with the British officer, whom we know to have been Turton.

In a conversation with a British lieutenant-colonel, deputy head of the mission, the following deal was proposed: We take the generals, and the gold and other valuables of these generals [Krasnov and Shkuro] can remain with you. He made one condition: Our deal must be kept a total secret. And as if jokingly, he asked for my word as a gentleman. I gave him my word as an officer, and I have kept my word right up to now.[27]

The Russian word for 'treasure' in the *Golos Rodinii* article is *драгоценности*, which is translated in *The Mitrokhin Archive*, from what appears to be a variant account of Soloviev's mission, as 'gold'. However, the reader may have noted a curious incongruity. If the British were *already* in possession of the 'treasure', what additional benefit could they derive from Soloviev's concession? And what might this 'treasure' have been? The British had taken a valuable bejewelled sabre from General Shkuro, which thereafter vanishes from the records. One can only suppose that it ended up as plunder in the hands of 5th Corps – possibly the unprincipled General Keightley himself. But this appears insufficient inducement in the context of the proposed momentous exchange.

Soloviev's proposal and Turton's cautious proviso suggest the presence of something of substantial value *in 5th Corps hands*, which, if revealed, was likely at the least to prove embarrassing to the Corps command.[28] In fact there did exist such a 'treasure', which 5th Corps was indeed at great pains to conceal. On 26 May 1945, in the Cossack camp at Peggetz,

Without any prior notice a truckload of British soldiers arrived at the Cossack Bank and, using the name of a senior officer as their authority, demanded the keys to the safe. They checked its contents with the Bank's director looking on, and then, despite his protest that the safe contained only the money belonging to individuals who had deposited their life savings with him and that it did not represent any money belonging to the paymaster of the Cossack Land, they locked the safe and loaded it on to the truck and drove away.

The news of this traveled fast from camp to camp, and the depositors rushed to town to see if they could recover a little of their loss. There was not a penny left. Six million marks* and an equivalent amount in Italian lira had all gone.[29]

No reference to this confiscation is to be found in British military records, and the fate of the Cossack Bank remains a mystery to this day. As the account indicates, many Cossacks had deposited their savings in the bank,[30] and it would not have been difficult for SMERSH to have learned of this expropriation by the British military authorities. While it cannot be certain that this was what Soloviev and Turton had in mind, at present no preferable alternative presents itself.[31] No reference to the expropriation is to be found in 5th Corps records, although that it occurred is certain.

The Soviet proposal, then, did not constitute an absurd offer to 'give' 5th Corps command a 'treasure' (whatever it constituted) which was already in their possession, but to preserve as a close secret its expropriation by the British in partial exchange for the White generals. At the same time, this cannot have been the true governing motive for 5th Corps command's secret agreement to hand over non-Soviet citizens generally, and the senior non-Soviet officers in particular, since as has been seen this intrigue originated with Harold Macmillan, who can have had no concern with the Cossack bank.

That SMERSH chose to conduct its affairs in its own way, frequently without the knowledge of the Red Army, is in keeping with all that is known of the organization's *modus operandi*. Indeed, one of its prime duties was to maintain vigilant watch on the Red Army itself.[32] Although SMERSH operatives frequently used Red Army ranks and uniforms for discretionary

---

* About $2,400,000 at the time. The estimate is not excessive if it be recalled that there could have been 20,000 or more deposits confided for safety to the well-guarded bank during the Cossacks' hazardous stay in North Italy. On the other hand, the value of the 'treasure' would have become dramatically reduced at a time when the Reich had collapsed in ruins.

purposes, its chain of command was wholly distinct, being answerable directly to the Main Administration of Counter-Intelligence (GUKR), whose headquarters was at 2, Dzerzhinsky Square in Moscow.[33] The recovery of the Cossack Generals was regarded as a task of such delicacy that negotiations for its implementation were entrusted entirely to SMERSH, while Marshal Tolbukhin's staff officer, who arrived at Wolfsberg on 17 May expressly to discuss repatriation of Soviet citizens from Austria, was not empowered even to address the issue of the Cossacks on a general basis.

Soloviev's reasons for conducting negotiations separate from those of his military colleagues are sufficiently apparent. But what of Colonel Turton? In his television interview Soloviev implicitly suggests that the Englishman wished to raise matters too sensitive for his companions' ears. From whom did Turton wish their deal kept secret? Not from Soloviev's superiors, who must inevitably be informed of details of any agreement. The implication can only be that Turton did not wish this aspect of the agreement brought to the attention of those of his colleagues who were not in the know. This would explain the private discussion in the garden, out of earshot of other participants at the conference.

At the same time this begs a further question. The pressing requirement for secrecy on Colonel Turton's part would make it incredible that he should have sought out at random a junior officer apparently on the Soviet colonel's staff, in order to conduct what he expressly regarded as a discussion of exceptional sensitivity. It seems Turton had reason to know that Soloviev possessed authority beyond his modest rank.

The conclusion that it was from his own colleagues Turton was anxious to withhold the substance of their discussion is borne out by Soloviev's opening words: Shkuro, Krasnov and the other Generals 'are wanted without delay in the Motherland ... *but here are your colleagues holding back*'. What can this mean, other than that an official demand for Krasnov and Shkuro advanced at the conference ('here') had recently been rejected – or, at best, treated evasively - by Turton's superior Major-General de Fonblanque? Turton himself adopts a different approach, however. He seizes opportunity to confer privately with Soloviev in the garden, where the deception plan for luring the Atamans into Soviet hands is agreed.

Details of Soloviev's résumé of the discussion are consistent with other sources:

> My view is as follows: among the people being repatriated, give us these Atamans. Who wants them now?

Repatriation of the Cossacks generally had been agreed by the British (they are 'being repatriated'), but the Atamans for some reason are being treated as a special case and withheld. To Soloviev this is puzzling: from a Soviet viewpoint distinctions of citizenship and the provisions of the Yalta Agreement are of no account. The Cossack generals were inveterate foes of Soviet power, who should be returned without differentiation.

Although it is clear that Turton was personally only too anxious to comply with the demand from SMERSH, he is inhibited by a practical consideration:

But how can we deliver the Generals to you?

The difficulty clearly cannot have derived from the Soviet side, and consequently must have arisen within 5th Corps command. Turton goes on to suggest the ingenious ruse which was put into effect four days later. The episode bears only one possible explanation. Although Corps Headquarters has agreed to 'the [Cossack] people being repatriated', it lacked authority openly to enforce inclusion of the Atamans. Deception was the only viable alternative: deception required to evade 8th Army orders restricting repatriation to Soviet citizens, in order to dupe the Cossack generals.

Soloviev suggests that Turton spontaneously improvised both the general agreement to return the Atamans and the specific nature of the deception. That this was what really occurred is of course implausible. Turton could not have undertaken such a commitment without prior instruction from General Keightley. This need not affect the credibility of Soloviev's tale, however. The nuances inevitably reflect his subjective understanding. Besides, even if we accept the wording of the dialogue more literally than it might deserve, there is no means of knowing to what extent Turton chose to keep his cards close to his chest.

In summary, then, the version of 5th Corps policy implicit in Soloviev's reminiscence is as follows:

1. The Soviets had demanded the return of Shkuro, Krasnov and the other Atamans the moment their surrender to the British became known.
2. The ensuing conference at Wolfsberg on 21 May was presided over by General de Fonblanque, who was not party to the planned betrayal, and was kept in ignorance of the undercover compact to hand over the White Generals.
3. Lieutenant-Colonel Turton, although aware that 8th Army orders denied 5th Corps authority to deliver the non-Soviet Atamans, arranged with the SMERSH representative evasion of the prohibition by means of the deception tactic he (Turton) proffered.

Soloviev's narrative matches that implicit in the British records so consistently and in such detail as to carry conviction.

Here we may pause briefly to consider a fundamental difficulty I
encountered in conducting an investigation that has preoccupied me off
and on over the past 40 years. The official British 'Inquiry'* headed by the
former MI6 officer Brigadier Cowgill concluded that

> In the light of all the evidence now available, it is impossible to sustain
> the charge that there was any kind of 'conspiracy' involved in the
> repatriations. This charge could only have been made on the basis of
> conjecture, drawing on fragmentary evidence.[34]

So far as the Cossacks are concerned, the principal allegation of
conspiracy rested on my conclusion that 5th Corps deliberately entered
into a secret agreement with the Soviets to add the White émigrés to the
Soviet nationals among the Cossacks handed over. The Cowgill Inquiry
prefaces its collection of facsimile documents with the curious claim that
'**The Documentary Evidence** [bold in original] includes the full texts of
all the Key Papers''.[35] This literally bold assertion must puzzle
professional historians, since it is rare indeed that it can be justifiably
assumed that *all* evidence on a particular topic is known at a given time.
However, I was informed by Brigadier Cowgill that the authors of his
Inquiry, being apparently unable to recruit a professional historian
amenable to their purpose, employed Christopher Booker, a journalist
much given to conspiracy theories on climate change and the like, to
'polish' their text.[36]

By a freakish chance of history, public attempts (such as Horne's
commissioned biography of Macmillan, the repetitive publication of
successive editions of the Cowgill Inquiry's official report, the 1989
Aldington trial, etc) to close the debate on the 1945 forced repatriations
coincided closely with major international political upheavals. At the
beginning of 1990 the Communist regime in Yugoslavia was overthrown,
and the country began dramatically fracturing into its component nations.
About the same time the totalitarian order in Soviet Russia collapsed with
contrasted lack of violence. The dramatic effect of the Yugoslav
Communist debacle on my prior published account remains a story yet to

---

* Cowgill claimed his 'Inquiry' was independent of outside authority. Originally, I had
intended to set out the evidence for its covert establishment by the British government
in an appendix to this book. However, the documentation has become so voluminous
and intriguing (in both senses), that it would require a further book to establish, not
merely the fact, but the extraordinarily devious and wide-reaching nature of British
government scheming in relation to this story. Cf. Appendix C for well-informed press
coverage of this issue.

be told, but the fall of Soviet Communism was to prove revelatory in the present context to an astonishing degree.

My work had long enjoyed warm support from Alexander Solzhenitsyn while he lived in exile, and it was he who arranged publication of a Russian-language edition of my earlier book *Victims of Yalta*, by the well-known émigré firm YMCA in Paris. Once he was free to return to his homeland, the great writer took every opportunity to endorse my work on Russian television and elsewhere. In particular, he denounced in ringing terms the blatant judicial corruption and government interference surrounding the 1989 Aldington trial.[*]

Many books on the subject were being published in Russia, Russian investigative television documentaries pursued the topic, *Victims of Yalta* became required reading at the Russian Military Academy, and surviving victims added their numerous voices to the outcry. The talented director Alexei Denisov produced a penetrating and widely viewed television documentary on the subject. The bitter resentment with which I was regarded by the British Establishment was now counterbalanced by vigorous support from the Russian Government, media, and people. At a military parade the Ataman of the Don Cossacks presented me with a ceremonial saber, I was elected an *essaul* of the Terek Cossack Host at a ceremony in the Caucasus, and President Yeltsin personally granted me Russian citizenship.

Above all, in January 1993 a presidential decree granted me privileged access to inspect the relevant state archives. Before being taken in an official car to the various ministries in Moscow, I was received by General Dmitri Volkogonov, who was responsible for historical archives in the capital. As author of acclaimed biographies of Lenin, Trotsky, and Stalin, Volkogonov was familiar with the background of my work, as well as with official efforts in Britain to suppress or distort the story. After explaining the range of archives I was about to visit, he glanced at me with a quizzical smile, and enquired:

> How is it that the British do not accept what everyone in Russia knows is true?

To this he added benignly,

> At any rate, you will find that your name still carries weight in this country!

---

[*] Cf. Appendix 'B': 'Solzhenitsyn's Declaration'.

Excited as I was at the prospect of viewing sources to which I had little dreamed of gaining access, I was at the same time seized by a certain apprehension. During my lengthy researches on this subject, I frequently had occasion to reflect on the precarious nature of the grounds on which historians form their judgments on topics as controversial as that to which I have devoted so many years of research. For long, major sources of information had been denied me. Not only was it frustrating in the absence of direct evidence to be obliged to resort on occasion to reasoned speculation, but there remained the inescapable danger that information of which I was currently ignorant might one day come to prove some of my most fundamental conclusions unequivocally wrong, and my enraged critics right! Most significant of potential sources to which I had naturally possessed no access before the early 1990s were the archives of the Soviet Union. They, if anything, must surely possess potential power to prove me broadly right – or direly wrong – on almost all essential issues.

To return to one significant example, how reliable was the first-hand account of Captain Soloviev's secret negotiations with the representative of British 5th Corps at Wolfsberg on 24 May 1945? Although Soloviev's description can be shown to correspond in telling detail with entries in British records, it must be acknowledged that it is written in somewhat melodramatic style. The broadcast television series, of which his description is a slightly abbreviated résumé, was intended to glorify the deeds of the Soviet security services in protecting the Motherland from Western intrigues. This called for a lively treatment. But what if Soloviev went further, editing or even falsifying details of the event?

British defenders of forced repatriation are united in asserting that the White émigrés were handed over to the Soviets in consequence of oversight, inability to conduct screening, inadvertent misinterpretation of orders – anything, indeed, other than that they were deliberately betrayed in consequence of a secret agreement with the Soviets, concealed from Keightley's superiors at 8th Army, 15th Army Group, and AFHQ, as well as from Churchill and Eisenhower. However, thanks to General Volkogonov, and unfortunately for the true conspiracy theorists, there lies before me a copy of the War Diary of the 57th Red Army for May 1945, with whom the negotiations at Wolfsberg were conducted. On or about 24 May it records,

> On the basis of arrangements with the allied military command the latter finally agreed to hand over in their entirety the 15 Cossack Corps / Vlasovites/ the whole collection of Russian traitors to the Motherland **and the White emigrants**. Point of handover – JUDENBURG.[37]

The wording confirms that allusion is to the agreement, which as has been seen was concluded on the 24th, and not retrospectively to the handover operation itself. 'The allied military command' can only mean 5th Corps, while 'Vlasovites' is a loose pejorative classification of Soviet nationals notionally under the command of General Vlasov. Thus 'the White emigrants' unequivocally constitute a distinct category. Futhermore, the wording of the Red Army war diary entry echoes Harold Macmillan's categorization of the victims to be handed over as 'Cossacks and 'White' Russians' too closely to be coincidence.

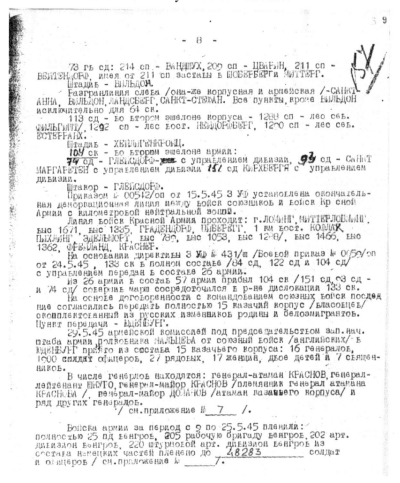

Extract from 57th Red Army War Diary

Here we have definitive proof, whether reliance be placed upon British or Soviet records, or both, that by the afternoon of 24 May a secret agreement was concerted between 5th Corps and Red Army representatives for the return of White Russian emigrants among the Cossacks, by force where necessary. At the same time Colonel Turton entered into a conspiratorial arrangement with the SMERSH envoy, whereby Krasnov, Shkuro and the other generals should be duped into accompanying the Cossacks, in this way denying them opportunity to raise dangerous protest with their British escorts.

The 5th Corps command's agreements violated the authoritative 8th Army order of 13 March, together with successive official reminders that screening must be undertaken in order to ensure that Soviet citizens alone were repatriated. In addition, there were the *two* AFHQ orders of 22 May prohibiting use of force to repatriate *any* Cossack, whether White émigré or Soviet citizen.

The ruse revealed by Colonel Turton to Captain Soloviev ensured that evasion of screening provisions would pass undetected by 8th Army. Neither before nor after the operations did 5th Corps headquarters reveal to 8th Army that prominent Tsarist generals, together with a substantial number of other non-Soviet foreign nationals and holders of League of Nations passports, were dispatched to the Soviet zone by means of elaborate subterfuge.

Since no one in 5th Corps besides General Keightley and one or two of his senior colleagues at Corps Headquarters was in a position to know of any order regulating categories of Russians liable for return beyond 5th Corps' own 'Definition' - which with legalistic duplicity implicitly classified *all* Cossacks indiscriminately as Soviet nationals - no serious obstacle to the treacherous chicanery appeared likely to be encountered. With the old generals eliminated in Soviet gaols, and White emigrants dying by their thousands in GULAG camps, there should have been a convenient end to any possibility of public exposure.

I confess that this consideration has played a large part in sustaining my determination never to let the sufferings of the victims be forgotten – still less condoned. It is as well, too, to expose the nefarious activities of various branches of the British Establishment and its more subservient supporters employed to bury the story as effectively as were the thousands of murdered Cossacks, Caucasians, Serbs, Slovenes, and Croats during that grim summer of 1945. Ironically, it was pressures applied to silence me that compelled me repeatedly to return to the subject - when official acknowledgment of guilt, and atonement honestly accepted, would have left me free to pursue other topics of close interest to me.

When 8th Army commander General McCreery came to enquire into the matter immediately after the unhappy event, he was assured by

Keightley that 'cases of hardship or irregular repatriation were chiefly due to the impossibility of accurately classifying the inmates of the camps before repatriation commenced'.[38] Ironically, as we now know, it was specifically the White Russian officers who *had* been 'accurately classified'!

Looking back over these conspiratorial events, it is not difficult to envisage the plausible Macmillan, Minister Resident with wide-ranging authority at the highest levels, impressing the overridingly ambitious Keightley with claims of high reasons of state for an exceptional necessity of ignoring orders received from AFHQ. Brigadier Tryon and General de Fonblanque were certainly duped into believing that the policy was instituted by the Foreign Office. And, given Keightley's deep involvement in all this chicanery, it is more likely than not that he likewise was deceived by Macmillan. It is easy to picture the latter's presenting an impressively plausible account of the Foreign Office's concern to avoid antagonizing the powerful Red Army facing the Corps boundary to the east. While 5th Corps in reality enjoyed cordial relations throughout with Marshal Tolbukhin's forces, Macmillan must naturally have appeared best placed to assess the larger picture. In any case, all that is known of Keightley's character suggests that he would instinctively have been inclined to oblige the influential politician.

The day after the Minister's visit, Keightley signalled 8th Army:

on advice Macmillan have today suggested to Soviet General on Tolbukhins HQ that Cossacks should be returned to Soviets at once. cannot see any point in keeping this large number Soviet nationals who are clearly great source contention between Soviets and ourselves.[39]

Thus, it was exclusively 'on advice Macmillan' that Keightley was persuaded 'this large number Soviet nationals ... are clearly great source contention between Soviets and ourselves'. He himself had encountered no such problem, as he emphasized the day after Macmillan's visit.

Met Lt Gen on Tolbukhins staff today and after very cordial meeting all arrangements with Soviets and Bulgars confirmed. all relations with Soviets most friendly with much interchange whisky and vodka.

It must, then, have been Macmillan who persuaded Keightley that the Cossacks were a 'great source contention between Soviets and ourselves'. It was in reality the White émigrés whose fate was in dispute. Whence did Macmillan obtain this knowledge? Was it from the Soviet Mission at AFHQ, which had on an earlier occasion raised with him the issue of repatriation of captured Soviet citizens?[40]

The emphatic assertion that the Cossacks in question were all 'Soviet nationals' can only have been deliberately deceptive. The fact that hundreds, possibly thousands, among them were old émigrés, exempt under undeviating Allied policy from surrender to the Soviets, was known to 5th Corps Headquarters from at least 8th May, when General Arbuthnott and Brigadier Musson interviewed the Cossack delegation headed by the tsarist General Vasiliev at Tolmezzo, all of whom were old emigrants. On 10th May, 56th Recce Regiment reported the 'surrender of an old Cossack Gen. Schkuro, who had fought under [the White commander, General] Denikin'. The fact that Shkuro bore the Order of the Bath bestowed by King George V attracted from the outset much interest and admiration among British officers.

That the unimaginative and ambitious Keightley accepted without question Macmillan's seemingly authoritative 'advice' at their meeting on 13 May is understandable. What is harder to explain, however, is why Keightley continued to adhere to his commitment to what he subsequently described as Macmillan's 'verbal directive' to hand over all the Cossacks (the presence of the considerable body of 'White Russians' still being consistently concealed) *after* his receipt of fresh orders from AFHQ requiring the Cossacks to be removed to safety under Eisenhower's control. The Corps Commander was regarded by many who knew him as narrow-minded and unpleasantly arrogant, but nothing suggests that he himself professed any political understanding or competence. Above all, it is inconceivable that so ruthlessly ambitious a commander would have committed himself to deliberate disobedience and recurring deception of his superiors, without some overriding undeclared motive.

Here we may turn to consider the man who stood at his side throughout most of this critical period, whose duty it was to provide advice at every turn. This was his Chief of Staff, Brigadier Toby Low. Thirty-one years old, he had enjoyed a good military career, and was much valued by Keightley as an efficient and reliable staff officer, upon whose judgment he could rely. However, unlike other senior 5th Corps officers, Low was not a regular soldier. He had qualified as a barrister in 1939, and nurtured strong political ambitions. He maintained a correspondence throughout the War with Anthony Eden, the Foreign Secretary, with whom despite their considerable difference in age and social status he had managed to curry favour.

On 23 May 1945 Low left Austria for England to stand as a candidate in the General Election. Immediately on his return he visited Eden and conferred with Harold Macmillan.[41] He was shortly afterwards elected MP for the safe Conservative seat of Blackpool North. When Harold

Macmillan became Prime Minister in 1957, Low was first knighted and then raised to the peerage. He also pursued a career in business, whose results were not always happy. As chairman of the Port of London and afterwards Chairman of Westland Helicopters, he presided over the virtual collapse of both. At the same time, it was noted that

> Aldington's view, understandably in view of his post-war career, was that there were few problems which could not be solved by nudging the right elbow.[42]

The reputation for lack of scruple and deviousness which pursued him throughout his years in business was borne out during and after his involvement in the notorious libel trial of 1989. He was subsequently shown to have repeatedly perjured himself, above all constantly lying in order to establish an alibi absenting him from the decision on 22 May to employ extreme brutality against Cossacks, whether men, women, or children, whose delivery to the Soviets he arranged. He brought forward his date of departure from those to which he had adhered prior to the trial, to dawn on the 22nd, in order to absolve himself from responsibility for decisions made at the conference where the fatal 'shoot to kill' decision was settled. Overwhelming evidence that he in fact left after that date was dismissed by the judge at the 1989 trial,[*] only to be decisively confirmed within a few months of his verdict by discovery of the official signal from Corps headquarters giving his true date of departure.[†]

Aldington subsequently continued to perjure himself repeatedly, in particular asserting in affidavits framed by his pliable solicitors Allen and Overy that his half-million pound costs of the trial had been borne by him personally, which he was at great pains to recover from me. Eventually, following repeated denials at the company's annual general meetings, it was reluctantly conceded by the Chairman of the Sun Alliance Insurance Company, of which Aldington had fomerly been Chairman, that his costs had in reality been secretly borne throughout by the Company. It is a measure of the manner in which the British Establishment conducts its

---

[*] The trial Judge Michael Davies was discovered shortly after the trial to be a member of the same small private Rye Golf Club as Lord Aldington, while their homes lay within eight miles of each other in the countryside. When Davies selected himself as trial judge, he withheld mention of this surely pertinent consideration. That a succession of appeal court judges implicitly found the arrangement perfectly acceptable provides an interesting insight into the close-knit workings of the English judiciary.

[†] Phantom Operational Log (1920 hrs on 24th May): 'BGS left 5 Corps for England on FLIAP on 23rd May' (WO.218/248).

affairs when faced by what it regards as a critical emergency, that Aldington, his solicitors Allen and Overy, and the Sun Alliance were happy to collude in seeking to swindle me out of half a million pounds.

While all this confirms the man's character as manipulative, devious, deceptive, greedy, and coldly inhuman, it does not of course establish that it was specifically he who exercised major influence over 5th Corps' deception of higher command with regard to arranging and brutally implementing the handover of the Cossacks. We have his acknowledgment that 'I do remember being involved in the drafting of the signal to General McCreery': *i.e.* the signal O.410 of 14 May, citing Macmillan's 'advice' that *all* Cossacks (implicitly including 'White Russians') should be dispatched to their Soviet foes.[43] And we know too, from the testimony of Brigadier Tryon-Wilson, that direct communication was maintained between 5th Corps and Macmillan throughout much of this time.

If the evidence indicates Macmillan's continuing influence on 5th Corps policy after his return to Naples, there is likewise reason to suspect that he exerted it primarily through his future political protégé, the energetic, compliant, and notoriously none too scrupulous Toby Low.

In 1995 my wife and I were invited by our friend and neighbour, Brigadier Ian Weston-Smith, to dine together with an old friend of his, Major Anthony Gell, who had expressed concern to meet me. After dinner, the three of us left the ladies and withdrew to the study, where Major Gell told his story. With his permission I tape-recorded it, while accepting his request that I should not make his name public during his lifetime. Major Gell died in 1998, leaving me now at liberty to tell his story.

The gist of his tale is as follows. In 1945 he was serving with British Military Intelligence in Germany, working alongside his American counterparts at Frankfurt. The head of US Military Intelligence there was Colonel Anthony J. Drexel Biddle Jr., pre-war and wartime US ambassador to Poland.[44] In January 1944 Biddle resigned from the State Department and joined the US Army, with the rank of lieutenant-colonel, to serve on General Eisenhower's staff. His contacts with underground movements and resistance units in occupied Europe provided intelligence for planning the Allied invasion of Normandy.

By 1945 Biddle was Chief of the Allied Contact Section of SHAEF, with offices in a building belonging to the German chemicals firm I. G. Farben in Frankfurt. Biddle's chief staff officer was a Major Bob Neiman,[*] while Major Gell as his British counterpart maintained close personal

---

[*] I am not entirely sure about the spelling of this name.

contact with Biddle. As Major Gell informed me, in May 1945 Biddle learned through his intelligence networks that Brigadier Toby Low was planning to hand over the Cossacks and Royalist Yugoslavs in Austria to certain death at the hands of the Communists.[45] When I pressed to know why it was Low's name, rather than Keightley's, that featured in this connexion, Major Gell explained that his sources emphasized that 'Low was running rings around Keightley in this affair'.[*] Both Biddle and Gell were horrified by the news, which they reported back to their respective government departments with urgent recommendations that the operations be halted. Major Gell believed that his own protest went to the British Foreign Secretary, Anthony Eden, who was unfortunately a close friend of Low! Certainly nothing more was heard of it. Gell did not know where Biddle's protest went, nor what became of it, but presumed that it was directed to an equally high US authority.

NOTE
TOBY LOW AND THE COMMISSAR

My previous book on this topic, *The Minister and the Massacres*, was concerned as much with the parallel tragedy of tens of thousands of fugitives from Tito's tyrannical regime in Communist Yugoslavia as with the fate of the Cossacks. The victims were duped into returning across the frontier to be massacred by assurances that they were being transported to join a large body of their compatriots held in North Italy. The ruse was suggested by Brigadier Low, when conferring with Tito's representative Colonel France Hočevar. Although Low (Aldington) denied this when challenged in court, when I subsequently interviewed Dr Hočevar in a recorded interview conducted at his home in Slovenia on 16 January 1990, he volunteered without any prompting from me:

> I think that one or two days after the 15th when Toby Low said: 'we shall tell them that they were going to Italy'...

> It is sure, without doubt, that he said to me that he would tell them that they would be sent to Italy...

> I [Hočevar] didn't expect that we would get them back so easily, in such a regular way: that we would get them *all* back...

> Just without any bargaining! I expected that I would have to convince

---

[*] When on 4th March 1975 I interviewed Edward Renton, 2 i/c of 6th Special Force commanded by Low's close friend Major Charles Villiers, he (Renton) emphasized that 'The really operative person at that time was the BGS, who was Toby Low'.

them, try to convince them, that nothing would happen to these people before they would release them.

Low's eagerness to oblige the Communist regime (acting of course as General Keightley's right-hand man) in perpetrating mass murder is patent, and requires no comment. The telling deletion in his 1985 speech at Winchester College betrays his concern to shift responsibility from himself to subordinate command for ordering lying to the defenseless victims – in flagrant violation both of orders from higher command and Article 26 of the Geneva Convention on Prisoners of War. As he wrote in his preparatory draft,

> Prisoners 'will NOT be told of their destination': 'Normally such an order would have been issued following a conference between the Corps Commander, General Keightley, and the Divisional Commanders. The purpose of it, I guess, was to reduce to the minimum the need for our British soldiers to use force with the Yugoslavs. ~~Subterfuge~~ Silence was thought to be better than violence. The order was translated lower down the line into a statement to the Yugoslavs that they were going to Italy.[*]

Aldington's despicable role is clear and uncontroversial. What remains intriguing is a further incident in the following year, in which he was the protagonist.

Here follows an account by Captain Laurence G. Tanner of the Intelligence Corps.

> In the latter part of 1946 I was posted as GSO 3 (Intelligence) to 13th Corps HQ at Duino, Trieste. There I was one of four Intelligence Staff Officers and my responsibility was to record Yugoslav infringements of the Morgan Line and anti-Allied activities in Trieste, Montfalcone and other areas. As a date which I cannot now remember, I was instructed to lunch with General, later Field Marshal, Harding (GOC 13th Corps) and Harding introduced me to Brigadier Toby Low who was a civilian by then, having been demobbed from HM Forces on becoming a Member of Parliament.

> I was told that the reason for Low's visit to Trieste was that he wished to acquaint himself with the current situation there prior to speaking in a debate on the Yugoslav problem in the House of Commons. General Harding told me to entertain Low next day and drive him along the Morgan Line so that he might appreciate the nature of the terrain, but,

---

[*] In reality officers required to implement the 'subterfuge' were outraged by the betrayal. As Colonel Robin Rose Price recorded in 3rd Welsh Guards war diary: 'Order of most sinister duplicity received i.e. to send Croats to their foes i.e. Tits to Yugoslavia under the impression they were to go to Italy' (WO.170/4982).

'on no account get yourselves picked up by the Jugs'. The day after, I was ordered to drive Low into Yugoslavia to a village in the hills which I think was called Apaciacella (phonetic spelling). When we got there it appeared to be something of a ghost village. There were no inhabitants or shops but a few Yugoslav soldiers were lounging around. I drove to the only important looking building which seem to be a minor town hall. Leaving the jeep in the square, Low and I went up the steps and entered a large chamber which was unfurnished except at the far end, about 75 feet away, there was a long trestle table and seated on the far side was a Yugoslav general flanked on either side by an aide. In the corner, sitting with legs crossed and picking his teeth with a toothpick, was a rather sinister figure whom Low later told me was a Political Commissar. In my recollection the meeting lasted about an hour. I did not know what subjects were discussed or what was said, since presumably the conversation was in Serbo-Croat, with which I was unfamiliar. It was, however, a rather ill-tempered meeting with the General glancing frequently towards the Political Commissar, of whom he seemed to stand in some awe. At no stage where we offered refreshments or even a cigarette. When the meeting was over, Low and I walked to the door, but just as we came to the entrance steps the Yugoslav General forced his way between us from behind, embraced us both in his out-stretched arms, and at that stage a man came forward with a camera and took a photograph. Immediately thereafter the General thrust us aside and strode off. I was told later in Duino that the photograph was published by a newspaper in Dubrovnik to demonstrate the cordial relations of Tito's forces with their Anglo-American allies.[46]

Today I regret not having taken up a pertinent point with Captain Tanner. Low's discussion with the Yugoslav general cannot have been conducted in Serbo-Croatian, which he would not have understood. It is to be suspected that Tanner, as would in any case have been proper, was seated too far away to overhear the discussion, which can only have been conducted through an interpreter.

Low's consultation with the communist envoys poses the question: what was its true purpose? His visit is unlikely to have been concerned with 'a debate on the Yugoslav problem in the House of Commons'. Not only is Low not recorded to have participated in any such debate during parliamentary proceedings recorded in Hansard for that year – but in fact no such debate occurred. It will be recalled that Tito had every reason for being grateful to Low for playing a key role in handing over for mass slaughter thousands of anti-Communist Serbs and Slovenes. Nor can he have been ignorant of the fact that 5th Corps co-operation with his regime was conducted secretly, subverting consistent Allied policy of preserving anti-Communist Serbs and Slovenes from being handed over against their will.

Again, if the purpose of Low's meeting with the 'General' was 'to demonstrate the cordial relations of Tito's forces with their Anglo-American allies', why was it arranged in such strangely secretive circumstances?

As with so much in Low's career, there exist rather more questions than answers.

---

[1] 5th Corps Commander's conference: 'CCRA [de Fonblanque] reported on his discussions of 21 May: they will be confirmed or otherwise by Russians at Wolfsburg p.m. 23 May' (WO.170/4241).

[2] WO.218/7491.

[3] WO.170/4352,291.

[4] On 23 May, 5th Corps's war diary recorded: 'Negotiations for handover of Cossack tps to Russians opened' (WO.170/4241). Some years later General de Fonblanque recalled that 'The Cossack problem was on us and in connection therewith I had at least two conferences with Russians at Wolfsberg'. His first visit was on the 21st, and the second must have been on the 23rd, since final negotiations on the 24th were handled by Colonel Turton.

[5] FO.1020/42,141.

[6] WO.170/4241.

[7] Cossacks in German uniform were entitled to prisoner-of-war status under international law. Cf. my paper 'The Application of International Law to Forced Repatriation from Austria in 1945', in Stefan Karner, Erich Reiter, and Gerald Schöpfer (ed.), *Kalter Krieg: Beiträge zur Ost-West-Konfrontation 1945 bis 1990* (Graz, 2002), pp. 131-53. In 1952 the legal position of prisoners of war threatened with handover to a third party was confirmed by United Nations General Assembly resolution 610 (VII), which ruled that 'force shall not be used against prisoners of war to prevent or effect their return to their homelands' (Allan Rosas, *The Legal Status of Prisoners of War: A Study in International Humanitarian Law Applicable in Armed Conflicts* (Helsinki, 1976), p. 479). Cf. William C. Bradbury, Samuel M. Meyers, and Albert D. Biderman (ed.), *Mass Behavior in Battle and Captivity: The Communist Soldier in the Korean War* (Chicago, 1968), pp. 334-35. Precedents for British denial of POW status to Cossack soldiers in the German Army had been set by Nazi Germany in its maltreatment of Polish, Yugoslav, and Italian prisoners of war (Richard D. Wiggers, 'The United States and the Denial of Prisoner of War (POW) Status at the End of the Second World War', *Militär-geschichtliche Mitteilungen* (Oldenbourg, 1993), lii, p. 93).

[8] *The Trial of German Major War Criminals: Proceedings of the International Military Tribunal Sitting at Nuremberg Germany* (London, 1946-51), iii, pp.

40-41.

[9] Trial Transcript, Day 8.

[10] Nikolai Tolstoy, *Victims of Yalta* (London, 1977), p. 498; *idem, The Minister and the Massacres* (London, 1986), p. 361.

[11] For the huge Soviet transit camp at Graz, cf. Pavel E. Nazarenko, *В Гостях у Сталина: 14 Лет в Советских Концлагерях* (Melbourne, 1969), pp. 9-11; Nikolai Tolstoy, *Victims of Yalta* (Corgi, 1979), p. 21; *idem, The Minister and the Massacres*, pp. 273-74.

[12] Long before the publication of Soloviev's memoir I conjectured that the deception tactic arose out of collaboration between Keightley's Headquarters and the Soviet security forces: 'The ruse whereby the Cossack officers were deceived into going peacefully to their deaths appears also to have been adopted at 5 Corps HQ from a suggestion obligingly provided by Smersh' (*Stalin's Secret War* (London, 1981), p. 313). Clearly I had underestimated the resourcefulness of 5th Corps senior staff officers.

[13] All these details are accurate: cf. *Victims of Yalta*, pp. 220-35.

[14] Among these officers only Domanov was a Soviet citizen.

[15] I am obliged to the late Dr Ludmilla Foster, from whom I obtained the copy of Soloviev's account.

[16] I am grateful to the Director of the Central State Archive of the Soviet Army for copies of this and other relevant documents. Cf. also 'A.I. Romanov' [Captain Boris Bakhlanov], *Nights are Longest There: Smersh from the Inside* (London, 1972), pp. 153-54.

[17] Central State Archive of the Soviet Army.

[18] WO.218/7491. 'May 20. CK & I attended 'Conference' with Russians beyond Judenberg 2.30 pm – 12.30 am' (de Fonblanque journal). The journal was compiled some years after the event, and as no conference occurred on 20 May, the allusion must be to that which took place on the 21st.

[19] 'At conference with reps 57 Russian Army at Wolfsberg Y.60. Russians agreed to accept Cossacks from 6 Brit Armd Div and 78 Div areas by train at Judenburg and those from 46 Div by march route at Voitsberg B.6255' (WO.170/4241).

[20] WO.170/4352.

[21] General V. Naumenko (ed.), *Великое Предательство: Выдача Казаков в Лиенце и Других Местах (1945-1947); Сборник материалов и документов* (New York, 1962-70), i, p. 140; Peter J. Huxley-Blythe, *The East Came West* (Caldwell, Idaho, 1964), p. 121.

[22] N.N. Krasnov, *Незабываемое 1945-1956* (San Francisco, 1957), p. 80.

[23] WO.170/4352.

[24] Strobe Talbott (ed.), *Khrushchev Remembers* (Boston, 1970), pp. 339-40.

[25] WO.170/4241.

[26] Christopher Andrew and Vasili Mitrokhin, *The Sword and the Shield: The Mitrokhin Archive and the Secret History of the KGB* (New York, 1999), p. 135.

[27] I am grateful to Alyona Kojemikova of Keston College for a transcript of the broadcast.

[28] As General Shkuro's confiscated sword is mentioned openly in 36th Infantry Brigade War Diary, it was evidently not regarded as a secret at the time.

[29] Huxley-Blythe, *The East Came West*, pp. 125-26. Huxley-Blythe's book being intended for a general readership, no reference is given. However, there can be no doubt that the account is authentic. As the list of his informants on p. 7 attests, the author had acquired numerous first-hand accounts from witnesses in a position to know the facts. Detailed confirmation of the expropriation is in any case to be found in Vasily Frank's 7 April 1954 report from Lienz to the Tolstoy Foundation.

[30] The Cossack *Feldbank* had accompanied the *Kazachi Stan* under cavalry escort throughout the Cossacks' time in Italy. Among local Italians a tradition was preserved of a Cossack treasure buried mysteriously somewhere in the Carnian Alps near the Italo-Austrian frontier. It was said that in subsequent years small parties of Cossacks returned to the region in search of the treasure (Pier Arrigo Carnier, *L'armata cosacca in Italia (1944-1945)* (Milan, 1965), p. 241; Claudio Magris, *Enquête sur un sabre* (Paris, 1987), pp. 55-59). Among the scattered and impoverished survivors of the butchery at Lienz, such rumours might readily have circulated. Few if any survivors of the slaughter at Peggetz are likely to have had direct knowledge of the bank's fate.

[31] On 12 December 2000, Mr. K. G. Spayer informed me of a business visit he paid to the investment manager of the Dresdner Bank in the British zone of Germany during the 1950s. *En passant*, the manager recommended investment in gold. Many clients, he explained, 'were investing in gold at that moment 'and, not only locals, but foreigners as well, including a British general who has 1 cwt of gold deposited in our vaults!' Although there is no suggestion that this represents the Lienz 'treasure', it illustrates the extent to which not every British general's hands were clean at that time.

[32] 'Romanov', *Nights are Longest There*, pp. 69-70.

[33] Vadim J. Birstein, *SMERSH: Stalin's Secret Weapon* (London, 2011), p. 183.

[34] Brigadier Anthony Cowgill, Lord Brimelow, and Christopher Booker Esq, *The Repatriations from Austria in 1945: The Report of an Inquiry* (London, 1990), p. 227.

[35] *Ibid.*, p. x.

[36] The journalist Christopher Booker ('Esq.') seems to have nurtured a loftily dismissive attitude towards academics generally. Thus, of a seminar held at the London School of Economics, he described its organizer David Regan, Francis Hill Professor of Local Government at Nottingham University, in comically snobbish terms as 'a Professor D.E. Regan, of 1 Florence Boot Close, Nottingham'. Regan's introductory exposition on the nature and composition of committees of enquiry was dismissed with heavy sarcasm as

a 'dazzling parade of logic and erudition' (*A Looking-Glass Tragedy: The Controversy over the repatriations from Austria in 1945* (London, 1997), p. 130). Booker's obituary in *The Guardian* (4 July 2019) noted that 'In his weekly columns he regularly annoyed and frustrated scientists, climatologists and doctors with his assertions that asbestos was not dangerous, speed cameras caused accidents, fossil fuels were necessary, global warming was a hoax and Darwinian evolution was not proved'.

[37] 57th Soviet Army Журнал, p. 157.

[38] FO.1020/2838,31A.

[39] WO.170/4241.

[40] Harold Macmillan, *War Diaries: Politics and War in the Mediterranean January 1943-May 1945* (London, 1984), p. 75.

[41] Trial Transcript, Day 3.

[42] Magnus Linklater and David Leigh, *Not with Honour: the Inside Story of the Westland Scandal* (London, 1986), p. 29.

[43] Letter of 11 February 1981 to Serena Booker (copy in my possession).

[44] He was 'a most devoted friend of the Polish Nation and much beloved by it' (Edward J. Rozek, *Allied Wartime Diplomacy: A Pattern in Poland* (New York, 1958), p. 165).

[45] For Biddle's antipathy to Soviet maltreatment of PW, and his extensive contacts with underground agents in Austria and elsewhere in Eastern Europe, cf. John M.G. Brown, *Moscow Bound: Policy, Politics and the POW Dilemma* (Eureka, CA, 1993), pp. 318, 339, 395.

[46] Letter of 11 October 1989. Mr. Archie Vack recalled that 'When I was on John Harding's staff in Trieste in 1946, my wife and I had to give a formal drink party for an officer visitor – Toby Low' (letter of 24 April 1989).

CHAPTER XIII
BLOOD IN THE SQUARE

Article 23 of the Hague Conventions of 1899 and 1907:

... it is particularly forbidden ...

to kill or wound an enemy who, having laid down his arms or having no means of defending himself, has surrendered on discretion.[1]

It was, and will remain, one of the blackest deeds in British history. The memorial to the victims of Yalta should have the same inscription as Dachau and Auschwitz (both of which I have seen): THIS MUST NEVER HAPPEN AGAIN.

(Lord Boothby to Sir Bernard Braine MP, 16 April 1981).

Thank you for your letter of 28 January about the Yalta Victims' Memorial. I was horrified to hear of the vandalism against the Memorial. Such desecration is the act of barbarians and we must hope the police will be able to catch them. I hope the second Memorial will escape the fate of the first.

(Prime Minister Margaret Thatcher to Lord Bethell, 1 February 1983).

Entrapment and betrayal of the old émigré generals and officers represented the prime concern of General Keightley and the few members of 5th Corps command privy to the secret agreement with SMERSH. It has also been seen that it was this conspiratorial aspect of the ensuing operations that uniquely required covert separation of the officers of the *Kazachi Stan*, held by units of 78th Infantry Division in the neighbourhood of Lienz, from the greater body of other ranks and thousands of civilian camp followers.

Apart from the Cossacks held within the 78th Infantry Division's area, further substantial bodies were held by 6th Armoured Division, 46th Infantry Division, and 7th Armoured Brigade. In each of the latter cases, Cossack officers (including Germans) were sent to their fateful destination at the same time of others of their rank. Furthermore, officers and other ranks of the 15th Cossack Cavalry Corps held by 6th Armoured Brigade were confined together on the eve of their handover within wired camps,[2] whereas the *Kazachi Stan* Cossack camp at Peggetz was unwired.

Deception was widely employed to ensure that the operations were conducted efficiently, avoiding any danger to British troops involved. From a pragmatic point of view, this policy proved eminently successful, with few casualties (suicides) among the Cossacks, and no British casualties. At the same time tens of thousands of Yugoslav fugitives from Tito's murderous regime were similarly duped into being entrained for return from British camps, on the pretext that they were (as AFHQ policy in fact required)[3] travelling to safety in the designated reception area in District One in North Italy. Once again, officers and men were not obviously separated during the handovers.

The 78th Infantry Division's implementation of the handovers in late May and early June was conducted on a radically distinct principle. On 28 May the Cossack officers were informed that they were being transported to a meeting with Field Marshal Alexander himself, who would explain arrangements for their future. No name could have exerted a more potent effect on the Cossack officers. His reputation as a paragon of chivalry and honor was legendary. Furthermore, the pretended meeting was cunningly designed to appear as a response to General Krasnov's appeal to his former comrade-in-arms. As we know, Keightley and Low had in reality intercepted the General's letters, passing them surreptitiously into the hands of SMERSH, while keeping their existence secret from 8th Army and the Supreme Allied Commander.

Dangers inherent in handing over the *Kazachi Stan* as a single cohesive body to the Soviets presented a grave problem, on the following grounds:

1. Since it was the Cossack officers, the overwhelming majority of whom were old émigrés, whose surrender SMERSH particularly desired, it was essential that they be handed over in a controllable body. The camp at Peggetz was not wired, while many officers (especially the senior ones identified in the SMERSH list presented to Brigadier Tryon on 11 May) were housed in Lienz or other suitable venues in the vicinity. Thus, 'wanted' officers might easily have escaped in the predictable event of confusion at the time of their transportation. It will be seen in the next chapter that exceptional measures were adopted to ensure the safe delivery of the daredevil General Shkuro to his executioners.

2. Among officers of 78th Infantry Division, vigorous objection

was raised to handover of the Cossacks generally, and above all the White officers, who should have been retained in accordance with successive orders received from higher command. Major-General Arbuthnott, the divisional commander, had himself raised repeated indignant protest against Keightley's order.

3. On 15 March, Keightley's Headquarters received a copy of the 8th Army directive containing the uncompromising stipulation that 'All persons of undoubted Soviet Citizenship will be repatriated irrespective of their own wishes. In cases where nationality is in doubt, personnel concerned will be sent to 373 PW Camp [in North Italy] for adjudication'. Before Macmillan's intervention on 13 May, Keightley was declaredly averse to betrayal of people who had never been citizens of the USSR.

4. Among Arbuthnott's subordinate officers, many manifested rooted objections to the planned betrayal, above all to the patent injustice of including non-Soviet citizens. Colonel Odling-Smee, who was responsible for 4,000 Caucasian troops, developed a warm rapport with General Kelich-Ghirei, a White émigré whose name had been among those picked out in capitals in the SMERSH list. He was horrified by receipt of the order to hand him over. Lower down the ranks, Major 'Rusty' Davies bore responsibility for the huge camp at Peggetz. Ignorant of considerations influencing his superiors, he became so disturbed by the protests of non-Soviet nationals, that he took it upon himself to establish a small screening post within the camp. One or two other officers acted similarly.[4]

5. Amid the confusion of rounding up tens of thousands of scattered Cossacks, escape into neighbouring forests and mountains was clearly likely, and in fact occurred on a considerable scale. Such fugitives included White emigrants, whose escape was facilitated by the fact that most spoke fluent German, French, or even English.

That safe delivery of the White officers to the Soviets represented the prime consideration in the operation is illustrated by a further consideration. Deception of the Cossack officers, who could not credit that British officers would repeatedly lie in order to send prisoners-of-war to certain death, was cynically anticipated to prove effective. As General

Krasnov's nephew Nikolai, a dashing young Cossack subaltern from Yugoslavia, reflected,

> My God! Being prisoners of the Anglo-Saxons cannot be bad, they assured themselves. The English are gentlemen! We are not dealing with some ephemeral Hitler, but with officers of His Majesty the King. An English officer does not give his word on his own behalf, even if he is a Field Marshal! He speaks in the name of the highest, supreme power. In the name of the Crown![5]

But what of the mass of Cossack other ranks who remained behind after the officers' departure? The British command appreciated that their true predicament would become immediately apparent with the officers' failure to return from the 'conference', and that their turn must follow. As it was, a couple of Cossack officers succeeded in escaping *en route*, changed into civilian clothes provided by a sympathetic Austrian farmer, and returned to Peggetz with the sinister news.[6]

On 19 May, Eisenhower was informed that among the prisoners it was proposed to transfer to SHAEF command '45,000 [who] are Cossacks still fully armed'. Although disarmament took place in the camps on 25 and 27 May, many Cossacks retained their side arms, which in the circumstances were not difficult to conceal. Had they decided to resist British orders, there can be no question but that they would have represented a formidable force to overcome. In the mountains around Lienz, thousands of young and active soldiers, trained and experienced in guerrilla warfare, and driven to desperation by the proposed betrayal, would have presented dangerous adversaries. Of course, the British could bring overwhelming force to bear on them – but at what cost to British lives?

At Keightley's corps commander's conference held on the morning of 22 May, operational orders included the grim instruction: 'Divs will be prepared to shoot at Cossacks to enforce the evacuation plan'. Since Toby Low did not depart until the following day, it will have been he who was responsible for issuing the directive. That evening 5th Corps received a copy of a signal from Field Marshal Alexander that 'You have authority to pass Cossacks direct to Russians provided force has not repeat not to be used'.[7] This unambiguous instruction was blithely ignored by 5th Corps command, who continued with preparations for deploying whatever degree of force they adjudged necessary for rounding up and entraining the Cossacks.

Ignorant of these machinations, in his operational instruction of 26 May, Brigadier Musson commanding 36th Infantry Brigade included these chilling words:

... there are many women and children amongst them. You are faced with a problem that will demand great patience and tact and I am sure that you will overcome the many difficulties with which you may be faced. Be firm. Remember that quick and determined action taken immediately may save many incidents and lives in the future. If it is necessary to open fire you will do so and you must regard this duty as an operation of war...

If a person or body of people attempts to escape you will order them to halt by shouting at them. If they deliberately disregard your order and run away you will open fire, aiming at the legs if you consider this will be sufficient to stop the attempted escape; if not, shoot to kill.[8]

Many similar orders were issued by Waffen SS commanders,[9] and it is grim indeed to find British officers prepared to implement so brutal a measure – with the striking distinction, moreover, that their operation occurred in peacetime. Furthermore, Keightley and Low were fully prepared to risk the possibility of losing substantial numbers of British lives in order to ensure the safe delivery of the émigré officers.

It is now time to turn to events on the ground, in order to appreciate the terrible consequences of 5th Corps's illicit policy.

'Have our supper ready: we'll be back this evening!' some of the Cossack officers had shouted cheerfully as they were deluded into boarding trucks for the 28 May 'conference' at Spittal, where they were promised the meeting with Field Marshal Alexander.[10] But the evening drew on, and no officers reappeared. In her hotel room Lydia Krasnov watched the hours passing – six o'clock, seven, eight – it was now past the latest time her 76-year old husband General Peter Krasnov had named for his return. Feeling increasingly agitated, she went below, where she found Major Davies and the Battalion chaplain, the Rev. Kenneth Tyson.

'Are the officers not coming back?' she asked anxiously.

'Well, not here, at any rate', Davies admitted.

'But shall we see our husbands again soon? Where are we to meet them?'[11]

Davies replied awkwardly that he did not know. Lydia turned pleadingly to Kenneth Tyson and implored his assistance. But the Argylls' chaplain could only utter calming platitudes: he himself did not yet know what was the fate in store for the Cossacks. Lydia Krasnov suffered a sinister premonition that she would not see her husband again.

In the camp at Peggetz, the English-speaking emigrant Olga Rotova, from Yugoslavia, also fearfully awaited news. At eight o'clock she was told that her services were again required as interpreter. She was taken to

two British officers, whom she recognized as having accompanied the
convoy bearing off the Cossack officers that afternoon. By them stood one
of the trucks, ominously empty. Olga turned pale.

'Where are our officers?' she asked.
'They're not coming back here'.
'But where are they?'
'I don't know'.
'But you told me four times that they were returning', she protested;
'then you were deceiving me?'

Unable to meet her gaze, the British officer replied in embarrassed
tones: 'We are only British soldiers and are obeying the orders of our
superiors'.[12]

Shortly afterwards it was announced that Major Davies wished to see
all senior non-commissioned officers at his office in the camp at Peggetz.
The meeting was to be held that evening at nine o'clock, when they were
to bring with them lists of the various regiments and *stanitsas,* with names
and ranks written in English. This was done, and the men assembled at the
designated time. But hours passed, until by midnight they assumed that
Davies would not appear. Even so commonplace a mischance seemed to
strike a chill among the men assembled there in the gloom. They
concluded that the meeting must have been deferred until the following
morning, and that all should return to their quarters. Before doing so,
however, in the sinister absence of their officers they decided to elect one
of their number as representative and leader, in place of the absent Ataman
Domanov. Their choice fell upon Kuzma Polunin, a senior sergeant much
respected by the men.

Olga herself stayed on, when the electric light suddenly failed. Settling
down in the darkness, she tried to doze a little. But she stayed awake, like
most people in the camp that night. At 2.30am, a torch flashed around, and
Olga sat up to find Major Davies before her. He wanted the list of camp
inmates, and when she told him that all had dispersed for the night, he told
her the meeting would now take place at 8.30 am.

When the time arrived, all were assembled outside Davies's office.
Davies did not appear, and the suspense grew. Then, at nine o'clock, a
British lieutenant arrived. Accompanying him was an interpreter, but it
was to Olga Rotova that he turned. 'Read this out!' he ordered abruptly,
handing her a sheet of paper. The document contained an order worded in
Russian, and the assembled Cossacks listened in silence as Olga recited its
contents:

1. Cossacks! Your officers have betrayed you and led you on a false path.

They have been arrested and will not return. You can now, no longer fearing or guided by their influence or pressure, discuss their lies and speak out about your wishes and beliefs.

2. It has been decided that all Cossacks must return to their homeland.

The text, with its formulaic Marxist emphasis on class conflict and liberation of the oppressed underdog, smacks of those sinister Soviet 'interpreters' and 'liaison officers' from SMERSH, who, authorized by 5th Corps command, played a shadowy role throughout the operations.[13] Certainly, it is hard to imagine a British officer's penning such a text. There followed general instructions to the Cossacks to continue to preserve their internal organization, and obey the commands of the British military authorities.

Major J. W. French, then second-in-command of the Argylls, later informed me:

... two Red Army officers were sent to Lienz to supervise the deportation of the Cossacks and see that the Yalta provisions were complied with ...[14]

It was in fact SMERSH officers in Red Army uniforms who were assigned authority to ensure 'deportation of the Cossacks'. It is significant that 5th Corps military records suppress any mention of the significant role played by these covert emissaries of Soviet power.

Olga's clear voice died away, to be followed by a deathly silence. By now there must have been few in Peggetz who did not fear the worst, but to hear this order read out, so calmly consigning them to death, torture, or some icy hell north of the seventieth parallel. At last a loud voice rang out in protest, declaring that the words slandering their officers were lies, that all Cossacks loved and respected their officers, and that if only they would be returned to them they would follow them anywhere in the world.

The British lieutenant listened in silence to this speech, tersely informed the Cossacks that he was now handing them over to Major Davies, and departed.[15]

Davies himself was still in Lienz. He had been allocated what was perhaps the most appalling role a British officer has ever been compelled to undertake. His job was to break the news to the officers' wives, now gathered in the Goldener Fisch Hotel, which had hitherto been Domanov's Headquarters. Davies was obliged the night before to mislead Lydia Krasnov, but now the truth had to come out. Not only had all their husbands been dispatched to an horrific fate, but the hundreds of women there assembled were now to follow them.

Davies made his announcement in as sympathetic a fashion as he could, assuring his audience that there was no reason to suppose that the worst had happened to their husbands, and that arrangements were in any case being made for the wives to join them. Before the torrent of protest and agony that his words unleashed, Davies could only reply that, as a soldier, he had no choice but to obey his orders. But what orders! Extricating himself from the crowd of despairing women, he drove in his jeep to the camp at Peggetz. When the possibility of handing the Cossacks over to the Soviets was first bruited, he mentally dismissed their fears 'because he could not believe they would be sent to the Soviet Union'. He considered Stalin a crueller tyrant even than Hitler: 'From his knowledge of Stalin and what people had told him, he knew their fate would be death'. At one point he was confronted by an old lady who held out her hands before him. This is what they did to me', she explained. Her fingernails had all been torn out by the roots.

From an early stage of their captivity, Davies was made aware that many of the Cossacks and their families were not Soviet citizens. As he later recalled,

> People showed him their passports or other documents (eg certificates) to show as he understood it, they were not Soviet citizens. Cannot say what proportion were not Soviet citizens but there were quite a number. Learnt this from the first week onwards.

He vainly urged Colonel Malcolm, commanding 8th Argyll and Sutherland Highlanders, to institute a screening procedure, asking 'Can we not screen out the obvious ones?' Unsympathetic to the Cossacks, and acting as he was under orders, Malcolm brushed off all such protests. Davies became increasingly distressed, particularly as he believed screening to be perfectly practicable. As he continued,

> [They] could have paraded everyone and asked them to bring out documents [and be] therefore segregated. People could have been given a chit or a stamp. As for those without documents, they could have been interrogated.

> There was the capability to carry this out. Although he only had 120 men in his company, there were more than enough intelligent soldiers in the battalion. There was also the education corps and the intelligence corps. From his knowledge screening could have been carried out.[16]

In the camp the news had been broken an hour before, but Davies still had the daunting task of facing those with whom he had become on terms of close friendship, to tell them that he had lied repeatedly in assuring the officers of the reality of the 'conference', and that now all must return willy-nilly to the Soviet Union. Speaking through Olga Rotova, he explained that 31 May, two days hence, was fixed for the date of their repatriation. The regiments would be entrained in the order Don, Kuban, Terek, with the charitable intention of keeping families together. Everything would be done to enable them to keep their possessions with them, to preserve the *stanitsa* (Cossack settlement) groups, and in general to make the journey as comfortable as possible. Special arrangements would be made for those incapacitated by age or infirmities from travelling in the general crowd. So he had been told, but when the time came

> He realised that the Cossacks were being treated as something inhuman, as little better than animals. He was horrified.[17]

Davies was doing his best, but those present could see he was deeply disturbed. Questioned by the Cossack schoolmistress Evgenia Polskaya, he reassured her that Stalin would settle all those repatriated on 'farms'. Evgenia, who was fully aware of the nature of 'farms' in the gulag system, found this apparent naivety hard to swallow.[18] Shouts arose that the Cossacks would never go willingly; many of the women were weeping, while a large number stood stunned. Major Davies's anguished reassurances about the conditions of the journey (even they proved false) appeared a cruel mockery. Were the British vicious as well as treacherous, or so gullible as to surpass belief?

Davies departed, declaring before he left that he would be back again in the afternoon. Soon afterwards two trucks arrived, in which it was announced that the luggage of the officers should be placed for transmission to its owners. (They had been told to bring nothing to the 'conference', in order to convince them they would be back the same evening). The weeping wives took the opportunity of sending off numbers of letters and parcels, but what happened to them is not recorded. By now the officers were in the hands of SMERSH in Judenburg. This cruel hoax led many wives to believe that they might yet see their husbands, and conceivably deterred some who might otherwise have escaped.

After this the Cossacks of Peggetz gathered together with improvised black flags and placards. The latter bore pleas scrawled in faulty English: 'Better death here than our sending into the SSSR!!'[19]

When trucks arrived with their midday meal, the Cossacks declared they would refuse to eat. The soldiers shrugged their shoulders, dumped the food in piles, and drove off. At four o'clock Davies reappeared. He seemed momentarily unnerved by the black flags, placards, and milling crowd crying out reproaches and pleas. He explained that he had received orders, decided upon at the highest level, that all Russians must go back to the Soviet Union. He had no choice but to obey. When this had been interpreted to the crowd a number pushed their way forward, thrusting before him passports and Nansen certificates. 'We are not Soviet citizens', they explained forcefully. In law they were, as their documents proved, French, Italians, Yugoslavs, or bearers of League of Nations passports. 'How can you do this?' cried one. 'In 1920 the British sent warships to the Dardanelles to rescue us from the Bolsheviks, and now you are handing us back again!'

Davies was aghast and for the first time realized that something was seriously wrong. But the orders passed down to him and Colonel Malcolm were unmistakable: *all* Cossacks in the Drau Valley must be handed over. That people who were not Soviet citizens should be delivered by force to a regime under which they had never lived, and to which they plainly could not legally belong, seemed inconceivable, and Olga Rotova, dropping her role of interpreter and speaking in her own person, asked: 'Will the Vlasov troops have to go?' 'Yes', Davies replied. 'And the old emigrants?' 'The old emigrants as well'. 'Then I must go too?' For Olga had lived for the past quarter-century in Yugoslavia, where she learned her fluent English working for the Standard Oil Company.

'Yes, you too. All Russians without exception'.

'But look, Major: the men are weeping'.[20]

Once again few slept that night. The improvised churches were filled with congregations confessing and receiving communion. The next morning was 30 May, and it was at dawn on the following day that the Cossacks were to be delivered into the hands of their enemies. Under the leadership of Kuzma Polunin, meetings were held to decide what to do should the British resort to use of force. A few still refused to believe that they were capable of fulfilling such brutal threats; others thought that it was all a terrible misunderstanding. A petition was drawn up and handed to Colonel Malcolm. It declared that:

> WE PREFER DEATH than to be returned to the Soviet Russia, where we are condemned to a long and systematic annihilation. We, husbands, mothers, brothers, sisters, and children PRAY FOR OUR SALVATION!!![21]

Other petitions, to King George VI, the Archbishop of Canterbury, and Winston Churchill were handed to Major Davies.[22] It was afterwards alleged that he threw them into the wastepaper basket;[23] but, as he told me, this was untrue. The petition from which an extract is quoted in the previous paragraph certainly reached brigade headquarters, but the ultimate fate of the remainder of these documents is unknown – though not hard to guess.

Throughout 30 May, the valley of the Drau presented a grim spectacle. On the barrack huts and tents, and even along the main Lienz-Oberdrauburg road, black flags were hung out. A hunger strike was declared, and food brought into the camp by the British authorities was left piled up and untouched. Into each heap was thrust a pole supporting a black flag. Continuous services were conducted by the priests, and agitated groups of Cossacks gathered under the leadership of Polunin and his aides to consider what desperate action they might take. Weeping mothers clutched their children, well aware that by the following evening they would very likely be separated from them for ever.[24] Bitter words were spoken against the sanctimonious advocates of the Four Freedoms and democracy.[25]

As the day drew on, there came a temporary reprieve. Major Davies reappeared in the camp to announce that the operation had had to be postponed for twenty-four hours, as the following day was the Catholic Feast of Corpus Christi. The Cossacks began to feel a glimmer of hope, and wondered whether some last-minute intervention might not yet save them.[26] The real reason for the delay was, however, less consoling. The Soviet authorities had declared they could receive only 2,000 prisoners on the first day, and so two trains had been cancelled.[27]

Only one trainload could leave on 31 May, and it was decided that the first batch should come from the Caucasians encamped east of Oberdrauburg. It has been necessary to ignore them temporarily while relating the plight of the Cossacks. It will be recalled that several thousand of the mountain 'tribes' were also held under guard by 36th Infantry Brigade.[28] Like the Cossacks, they had been deprived of their officers. The first the men and their families knew of their fate was when a British officer and 'interpreter' entered the camp to announce that their officers had been delivered to the Soviets, and that their turn must now follow. In this way, the brutal violence that ensued was predictable. This was at five o'clock on 28 May, and the officer in charge was Colonel Odling-Smee, commander of 5th Buffs. Although prepared for a hostile reaction, he was visibly taken aback by the outbursts of weeping, shrieks and protest that greeted his announcement.

Colonel Odling-Smee placed strong guards on the camp that night and ordered constant Bren gun carrier patrols. Despite this, some two hundred Caucasians succeeded in escaping to the forests. Of these, half left in a single body, led by a determined Karachaev tribesman. It is not unlikely that Odling-Smee, a true gentleman who loathed the whole treacherous operation, was happy to turn a blind eye to this disappearance of at least some of the intended victims.

Some old men and children got away with them. Among them was an Ossetian under-officer, Tuaev, who set off with a close friend. He heard the English shooting at the unarmed fugitives, but with his companion succeeded in crossing the mountains to Italy.[29]

The next day a petition was presented to Odling-Smee. Setting out the history of their sufferings, it begged the British to provide them with a refuge from persecution.[30] The British CO replied enigmatically 'that the USSR was our ally and promised that when they returned they would be sent to depopulated areas of the USSR'. The second part of the statement was true enough, but appeared to offer the mountaineers small comfort. It should, however, again be emphasized that Colonel Odling-Smee, was like most other soldiers in 78th Infantry Division, profoundly opposed to the treacherous policy of forced repatriation. In later years he explained to his son how distressed he had been, both at the time and since, at having to send helpless people to their deaths. He also reflected on the Nuremberg Tribunal, finding it hard to distinguish between the orders he was required to obey, and those implemented by Nazis tried for comparable actions. As he explained to his son,

> The only reason he finally gave in, and accepted the order, was that he was eventually persuaded by [Brigadier] Musson that the Soviets would not return the Allied P.O.W.s they were holding, unless all the Cossacks were first handed over to them. In effect there was a stark choice between saving our own people or saving the Cossacks.[31]

This was in fact yet another lie put out by 5th Corps command. At no time did the Soviets threaten any such action, and in reality the procedure for returning British ex-POW in Austria was throughout treated by both the British and Soviets as an entirely separate issue.

On the afternoon of 30 May, the first men of the Kabardinar tribe were detailed for entrainment at Dellach station. D Company of 5th Buffs arrived at 2pm, to find that the prisoners had made little arrangement for their departure while others were preparing a stubborn passive resistance. Major McGrath, commanding the Company, reported on his difficulties afterwards:

> Next to the track leading to the road a party of men, women and children approximately 200 strong, had formed themselves into a circle. It appeared that they had no intention of moving, for they had put up a black flag, and were chanting hymns and wailing.
>
> I ordered four 3-tonners to back up to them and with about 20 men tried

to get them into the vehicles. The wailing increased and a number indicated that they wished to be shot by us rather than [be] sent to the USSR. With great difficulty a few were forcibly put on one of the trucks, but it was impossible to prevent them from jumping off, which they all did. It appeared that certain men were the ringleaders of this sit-down strike and as an example I ordered four men to forcibly put one of these ringleaders on a vehicle. However he created such a disturbance that I was compelled to hit him on the head with an entrenching tool handle (a number of my men were armed with these) and blood was drawn. This appeared to have a sobering effect on the crowd, for from then onwards they dispersed to their carts and belongings. About half an hour later they had all dispersed and were eventually directed onto the road with the rest of the tribe as my men rounded them up.

These prisoners were held in a guarded pen at the railway station all night; they were then entrained with a further batch of prisoners without difficulty. With the Kabardinars were also dispatched 169 presumably homesick Caucasians who had actually petitioned to return to their homeland.[32] It is important to note that for whatever reason there were among both Caucasians and Cossacks a minority who genuinely volunteered to return 'home'. It was in part this factor that assisted Keightley and his henchmen to assure higher command that virtually all handed over were authentic volunteers.

In fact, the Kabardinar families had good reason for their reluctance to return to Russia. They had fled after the Germans had occupied their homeland in 1942, leaving behind them a scene of horror. In the tiny Kabardino-Balkar Soviet 'autonomous republic' in the Caucasus, near the city of Nalchik, a molybdenum *combinat* of the NKVD operated with convict forced labour. When the Red Army retreated from the region, several hundred slaves, for technical transport reasons, could not be evacuated in time. The director of the *combinat,* by order of the Commissar of the Kabardino-Balkar NKVD, Comrade Anokhov, machine-gunned the unfortunates to the last man and woman. After the area was in due course 'liberated' from the Germans, Anokhov received his reward, becoming President of its Council of People's Commissars, the highest office in the autonomous region.[33]

If any Kabardinar were fortunate enough to be sent home rather than to the coalmines of Kemerovo oblast, he could be sure of a welcome from Commissar Anokhov.

Altogether, on the two days 31 May and 1 June, 3,161 Caucasian men, women and children were sent off in three trainloads to Judenburg. The men were bolted in, thirty-six to a wagon, while the women and children were loaded on afterwards with the baggage.[34] So they pass out of our story.

Meanwhile, the Cossack families had just another twenty-four hours in which to make their farewells to each other – a necessary ritual since it was an invariable rule with the Soviet authorities to break up family groups when dispatching them to the labour camps.[35]

Many a son gazed with sadness at aged grandparents who had travelled on their wagon the hundreds of *versts* leading from the Kuban to Poland, and from Poland to Italy and Austria. How long would they survive in Karaganda or Pechora? A month? A fortnight? And the wives, the children ... everybody knew what was the fate of a woman in the gulag, especially if she were young and pretty.[36] A number of the women were pregnant, but even that did not prevent their enforced return to a regime where beatings and gang rapes by camp criminals were the norm.

Another separation was, to many, almost as agonizing. During that Thursday, Cossacks everywhere could be seen talking fondly to their horses, stroking their manes and muzzles, and spoiling them with lumps of sugar. Weeping openly, they comforted their intelligent beasts, companions of their travels and hardships. Sometimes a Cossack, shamefaced and heart-broken, led his friend under the trees, where a revolver-shot put an end to any possibility of neglect after his master's departure. Professor Verbitsky witnessed a scene where an ill favored old Cossack was offering his equally plain but much loved grey cow to an Austrian family. The family was as delighted with the gift as the old man was with the thought that at least his cow had found a good home.[37]

The night of 31 May 1945 was one that no survivor of the camp at Peggetz would ever forget. Those who had not been present at Major Davies's announcement were swiftly made aware of their impending fate, as the news spread from one barrack hut to another.

> "I went to Number 6 barrack",* recalled one woman: "Everyone was talking about it. The women were in a state of deepest distress, but all their discussion was pointless. For me that evening recalls a feeling of utter despondency. The situation was worse than the games cats play with mice. One sat at the table for a while, as though playing some part in a play, while all around a universal state of agitation reigned. My heart was paralyzed: everything was terrible, wretched, and in fact hopeless".

Wild rumours abounded, and schemes for evading their fate were abandoned as swiftly as they were raised. The camp was effectively

---

* No 6 barrack was occupied by Major Davies as his administrative office in the camp.

unguarded, and a trickle of terrified people made their way singly or in family groups through the darkness into the surrounding forest. However, few seized this opportunity to flee, and the overwhelming majority stayed put within the barracks complex. Converging motives served to bring about this seemingly fatalistic response.[38]

A large proportion of the inmates of Peggetz Camp were women, children, and old people, and the relatively few able-bodied men were in no position to provide protection for their helpless families. Moreover, while the camp was enclosed only by a wooden fence, the valley of the Drau was overshadowed on either side by precipitous snow-covered crags, which for the most part only an experienced mountaineer might hope to surmount.

The British guardhouse in No. 6 barrack provided no more than a token presence of the occupying forces. However the route to the south was effectively blocked by the swollen torrent of the river Drau, whose wooden footbridge was guarded night and day by British sentries. Beyond the railway line skirting the northern perimeter of the camp lay the main road from Lienz to Spittal, along which armored cars drove ceaselessly checking that no refugees were attempting to seek refuge in the forest. Foot patrols were constantly on the move in surrounding fields and lanes, and in the confusion of darkness any attempt at mass break-outs afforded the risk of incalculable casualties. Despite this, not a few Cossacks managed to slip away.

Unable to contemplate the abyss upon which they found themselves poised, desperate people sought to allay their terror with agonized discussions continuing throughout the night. To most it was clear that the worst had happened, and that there was no avoiding the most terrible fate anyone could contemplate. The extensive lying 'on the word of a British officer', which had enabled their captors without risk to themselves to place the Cossack officers at the disposal of their remorseless foes, did not permit even the most sanguine to repose any confidence in British honor and humanity. Unaware of the extent to which British soldiers had themselves been duped by their superiors, the genuine sympathy evinced by Major Davies and many of his 'tommies' appeared as little more than a characteristic example of that hypocrisy which continental nations traditionally ascribed to *Albion perfide*.

Then there was the cowardly (as the Cossacks saw it) circumstance of their recent disarmament: a ruse which enabled heavily-armed British troops to attack defenseless men, women, and children at almost no risk to themselves. British officers had repeatedly assured the Cossacks that their purpose was to replace the heterogenous collection of arms supplied them by the Germans with up-to-date British weaponry. A widespread and seemingly plausible belief had arisen that they were to be replaced when the Cossacks came to be employed as a foreign legion in British service, probably in the Pacific against the Japanese.

The Cossacks could scarcely expect British troops voluntarily to concede them means of inflicting casualties on their assailants. But their formal act of surrender at Kötschach on 8 May, regardless of its lack of specific conditions, entitled them to the full protection of international law, enshrined in the Hague and Geneva Conventions on treatment of prisoners-of-war. Their voluntary surrender of arms provided superfluous but nevertheless seemingly valid confirmation of the fact.

Prior removal of the officers was designed to ensure that none of the old émigrés, whose abduction represented Stalin's prime priority, escaped or raised potentially embarrassing protests with British officers. A dangerous consequence of this move was that the mass of Cossack other ranks and civilians was unexpectedly deprived of their leadership. As has been seen, high command at 5th Corps headquarters, as well as at Divisional and Brigade level, anticipated that extensive bloodshed was likely to prove necessary to entrain a leaderless and panic-stricken crowd.

At six o'clock on the previous evening they had been told to prepare themselves with their luggage for the journey, and Rusty Davies told the young interpreter Olga Rotova to meet him at the main gate at 7am.[39] As soon as this was known, the Don Cossack priest Father Vasily Grigoriev told his fellow clergy to assemble all the Cossacks in their *stanitsas* for a service in the camp square. This was to take place an hour before the arrival of Major Davies.[40] It was only to God they could now look for aid. A Cossack told the Austrian family with whom he was staying: 'No bread this morning, my sister. This morning we are to die'.[41]

But one thing the Cossacks were resolved to show the world. Major Davies had begged them to co-operate in the arrangements made for the morrow. They knew that if they did so, it could afterwards be said that they had voluntarily returned to Russia. The British would have to compel them to go. Never should the British escape the moral consequences of their actions.

In fact, where repatriated Russians did *not* resist, as in the camps where they were interned in Britain, officials did indeed claim, suppressing the evidence, that they had gone willingly. The Cossacks knew nothing of this, but their instinct was right. Although their 40,000 people were a comparative drop in the ocean of wretched victims delivered up to Stalin by the Western Allies at this time, it was the terrible events of

1 June at Peggetz that most vividly illuminated the massive tragedy of the betrayed Russian prisoners.

The night of 31 May to 1 June was cloudy, with the moon barely visible. A Cossack waiting sleepless with his wife and two small children recalled eight years later the first sinister manifestation of the coming day's work. Before daybreak, for the first time since the end of the war, a rattling of wagon wheels could be heard stealthily approaching along the railway line from the direction of Lienz. Brakes squealed furtively as it ground to a dead halt at the little station of Dölsach, just north of the Cossack camp.[42]

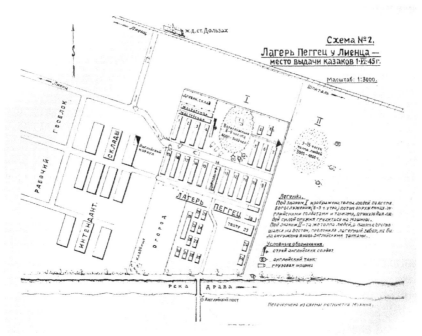

The camp at Peggetz

1. At the top is the station at Dölsach, and the railway line where cattle-trucks awaited transportation of the Cossacks to Judenburg on 1 June.

2. On the right is the field into which the terrified crowd spilled in the afternoon.

3. At the bottom is the river Drau, with its narrow wooden bridge, where many suicides occurred. (Today's bridge lies a hundred yards or so distant, and did not exist at the time).

Sleepless thousands emerged from their barrack buildings to congregate around an improvised altar erected in the camp square. The

Cossack priests, dressed in full vestments and carrying icons, mounted the rostrum and began to intone the liturgy. The vast congregation took up the familiar chant. It was their holy Orthodox faith that had enabled their ancestors to emerge intact from the dark time of the Mongol conquest; and who knew whether, whatever the outcome of this day's events, God might not yet intend the salvation of His faithful children?

Olga Rotova was in the congregation, supporting the sick wife of a colonel who had attended the Spittal 'conference'. Joining in the comforting responses, she could not help listening for another sound that must come soon. Then suddenly she heard the hum of a vehicle entering the gates, and saw Major Davies being driven into the camp in a jeep. Beside him was the under-officer Kuzma Polunin, whom Davies vainly hoped might assist him in enforcing compliance with his orders.

It was 7.15 a.m. Rusty Davies estimated that there were about four thousand people assembled in the barrack square, and it was abundantly clear that they had no intention of co-operating in any way.

Having formed up his Company, who had jumped out of their trucks behind him, he waited some minutes to see if the service was ending. Then he ordered his interpreter, a young officer sent from divisional headquarters, to give an order through a loudspeaker that he was giving them ten minutes in which to finish the service. The ten minutes passed, after which he gave them a final five minutes. Numerous pale faces were turned in his direction, but the singing and praying continued.

Meanwhile, Colonel Malcolm, commanding 8th Argylls, appeared, and instructed Davies to move in and start loading the Cossacks onto the waiting trucks. A platoon was ordered forward, but immediately the Cossacks reacted in a clearly concerted fashion. As the vast crowd shifted and surged away from the advancing soldiers, it could be seen that there was an outer ring of the younger and fitter men, whilst behind them was gathered the mass of women, children, sick, and aged. As the British troops approached, the mass of Cossacks nearest them knelt or crouched on the ground, interlocking their arms and making it hard to extract individuals. Faced with this passive resistance, the troops returned to Davies.

Davies realized that moves against the main mass of people were likely to be fruitless, or, if pressed to the limit, cause bloodshed. His prime responsibility was to his own men, but he was also deeply concerned to complete the task without injuring the Cossacks. He and the other men of the Argylls had never liked the task assigned them, but now that they were face to face with an unarmed crowd, which included innumerable women and children, the toughest amongst them became distressed. As the

Battalion Chaplain, the Rev. Kenneth Tyson, emphasized to me: 'They could not believe that this was what they had been fighting the war for. They were repelled by the whole business'.

Rusty Davies had a job to do, and although he would make every effort to accomplish it with a minimum of violence, he was determined to fulfil his orders. Following regular procedure for crowd control, he now sent forward a platoon to move in and cut off one of the corners of the crowd. Armed with rifles and pickaxe-helves, the platoon was formed into a wedge and successfully forced their way through a section at the edge. About two hundred Cossacks were thus forcibly detached, though still huddled together in a small body. As the gap opened between them and the remainder, Davies ordered in his two remaining platoons to ensure that the two parties continue separate.

Now the first platoon advanced upon the sundered group in order to start loading them on to the waiting trucks. What followed was described by Davies in his report made shortly after:

> As soon as the platoon approached to commence loading, the people formed themselves into a solid mass, kneeling and crouching with their arms locked around each others' bodies. As individuals on the outskirts of the group were pulled away, the remainder compressed themselves into a still tighter body, and as panic gripped them started clambering over each other in frantic efforts to get away from the soldiers. The result was a pyramid of hysterical, screaming human beings, under which a number of people were trapped. The soldiers made frantic efforts to split this mass in order to try to save the lives of these persons pinned underneath, and pick helves and rifle butts were used on arms and legs to force individuals to loosen their hold. When we eventually cleared this group, we discovered that one man and one woman [had] suffocated. Every person of this group had to be forcibly carried onto the trucks.[43]

As each truck received its complement of prisoners, it tore out of the camp gates and drew up a few hundred yards to the north where the train was waiting. This consisted of fifty cattle-trucks, their windows strongly barred. In the middle was an open freight-car, on which sat a couple of shirt-sleeved soldiers of the Lancashire Fusiliers with a machine gun. As each wagon received its complement of thirty-six Cossacks, it was strongly bolted down; all that could be seen was an occasional hand thrust through the grille, waving an imploring handkerchief to powerless friends.[44]

In Peggetz camp, Major Davies now sought to hive off a second group. After a vain appeal to Father Grigoriev to end the resistance, he ordered his men in once again. With weapons advanced menacingly, the soldiers made towards the huddled mass of Cossacks, seeking further to break their way through and split off another section. But the crowd had watched with increasing horror the brutal treatment meted out to those already taken. They now realized what they hitherto could not quite bring themselves to believe, that British soldiers acting under orders would employ any methods, however brutal, to shift them.

As the first soldiers began smashing their way through the densely-packed throng, a wild fear gripped the people. A young mother later recalled:

> There was a great crush; I found myself standing on someone's body, and could only struggle not to tread on his face. The soldiers grabbed people one by one and hurried them to the trucks, which now set off half-full.

> From all sides in the crowd could be heard cries: 'Avaunt thee, Satan! Christ is risen! Lord have mercy upon us!'

> Those that they caught struggled desperately and were battered. I saw how an English soldier snatched a child from its mother and wanted to throw him into a truck. The mother caught hold of the child's leg, and they each pulled in opposite directions. Afterwards I saw that the mother was no longer holding the child and that the child had been dashed against the side of a truck. What happened then I don't know. The altar was knocked over, the vestments of the clergy were torn ... we were so crushed in the crowd that mother (who wore on her chest an ikon of Our Lady of Kazan) began to look livid and gasped for breath.

> 'Oh Lord', I prayed, 'why did I have a child in such a time? Lord! What shall I do? St. Theodosius of Chernigov, save my daughter! If I can only preserve her just through this terrible Friday, I promise to fast rigidly every Friday so as never to forget this one!'

> And so it was that a miracle took place: that very crowd which had just been on the point of crushing us now began gradually pushing us out, releasing us. And how they shoved ... not towards the chain of soldiers, but in the opposite direction in such a way that now there opened before us a way leading to the bridge, across the river and into the forest.[45]

As panic swept across the crowd, the whole mass began to move. While elements broke from the main body and made for the narrow wooden bridge across the Drau, the rest huddled together and began to move in a blind struggling mass away from the British, who were engaged in slicing off another group for loading. Above the infernal noise, Cossack leaders could be heard shouting to all to keep together. This was in accordance with the agreed plan that only by doing so could they hope to avoid being picked up in detached groups by the soldiers. Now borne along by its own momentum, the crowd of terrified and shrieking Cossack men, women, and children was pressed against a strong fence of planks that bounded the camp to the east. The pressure built up unbearably until it seemed that hundreds would there be crushed to death, when suddenly a portion of the stockade collapsed and the people gushed out into a field beyond. Eventually the majority of the crowd of thousands had moved into this open field. While Cossacks moved around shouting for friends and relatives, the priests resumed their interrupted service. Gasping from heat and exhaustion, the people began to recover a little. Huddled together in a forlorn and frightened group, those nearest the gap in the fence glanced fearfully back, expecting to see British soldiers springing through. A cordon of troops was hastily thrown round the field, and at first they were allowed to remain where they were. [46] Before long, however, a force of ten armored cars arrived from the direction of Dölsach. Under the merciless threat of their machine guns, the crowd helplessly stumbled back into the camp. [47]

There were in fact enough stragglers left in the camp for Davies's needs at that moment, and as he noted in his report:

> Quite a number left the crowd voluntarily now in order to search for, or join lost relatives and children. This gradual trickle of "volunteers" provided sufficient numbers to complete our first train load.

In fact there were not enough, but Colonel Malcolm feared the situation was getting out of hand and decided for the present to call it a day. As his report stated, he ordered Major Davies

> to stop collecting people forcibly and to start clearing the huts of those who had by then returned to them. By this means 1,252 persons were loaded on to the train by 1130 hrs. The full complement should have been 1,750, but I decided not to continue the forcible methods in view of the inevitable injuries inflicted. [48]

Among the panic-stricken crowd was Zoe Polanska, together with her friend Tonia. As sixteen-year-old schoolgirls, they had been abducted by the Nazis from their home near Odessa, and before long were condemned to the horrors of Auschwitz. There the girls were subjected to protracted ghastly medical experiments under supervision of the infamous doctors Capesius and Mengele, which left Zoe permanently unable to bear a child. Eventually, the two girls were 'fortunate' enough to be transferred to Dachau. [49] At the end of 1944 they managed to escape, when an Allied bombing raid fortuitously destroyed part of the wired perimeter. They made their way to Vienna, where they were tended by a kindly nun. As the

war drew on, Allied air-raids intensified over the city, while Gestapo
activities were on the increase, and the nun advised them to seek refuge in
Italy. It was in this way that they came to join the Cossacks withdrawing
across the mountains to Austria.

Now they were to suffer brutalities which appeared as dreadful as
those they had suffered at the hands of the Nazis.[50] As Zoe recalled,

> During the Lord's Prayer, I watched the soldiers' bayonets glisten in the
> sun as they advanced on the mass. At the first tug by the soldiers the
> earth shook violently underneath us, like a volcano: our bodies were
> crushed together so closely that a needle could not have passed in
> between them. Another tug ... and the Lord's Prayer was drowned in
> screams as the soldiers pitched forward insanely, moblike and barbaric,
> with an enthusiasm well beyond the bounds of control. The mass of
> humans huddled together, delirious with despair, like animals hypnotised
> by the sight and smell of blood. We were crouching with our arms
> interlocked.

> There was a pause for a moment, then the soldiers answered in the same
> way they would have gone into battle. At first they attacked us with their
> rifle butts and big sticks while trying to pull away a group of people from
> the outermost perimeter of the circle. At that point, a fight broke out as
> women from inside the circle tried to help their men to resist the soldiers.
> The soldiers then fired shots. The song of bullets and shells snarled directly
> over the crowd: some on the outside fell in grotesque agonies from their
> injuries, others were stunned by sheer fright.

> I was in the center of the circle and only just managed to hear Tonia, who
> by then was some distance behind me: she was screaming and waving her
> hand. 'Come on!' she roared, 'We'll all be killed if we stay here'.

> I lost sight of her hand when I was suddenly hoisted up above the crowd
> like a football. I could feel the humid flesh and the heads underneath my
> feet, but could do nothing except watch the hysterical battle in full view
> below me. There were many howls and decisive blows as the soldiers
> dragged away first the men, then the women, children and tiny babies,
> loading them into the waiting army trucks.

> The bayonets were now in full use; the rifle butts were swinging amongst
> the helpless crowd. In their swift and deadly rushes to attack the men the
> British soldiers yelled like lunatics. Just two yards away from the circle
> one soldier was bending over a man who was lying flat on the ground with
> blood spurting from his head. The blood soiled the soldier's face, but
> another soldier came quickly to help him and together they lifted the
> unconscious man and threw him into the truck.

> On the south side of the square a group of Cossacks wrestled with the

soldiers, leaping like hounds. Underneath their feet lay a woman in the last month of pregnancy. She lay on her back in a most uninhibited fashion, her hands flung above her head and her legs parted – unable to protect the small life inside her. Today, the baby boy crushed in his mother's abdomen is a living reminder of that evil event. He was born spastic and totally unable to comprehend the injustice he was subjected to in the warmth of his mother's womb. In 1975, when I made my first pilgrimage to Lienz, that very child had grown into a tall young man: he was living in the suburbs of Lienz – only a short distance from that scene of death.

The sun shed its light over the fighting men, but light alone does not convey the wisdom of understanding this form of persecution. I really thought by now that the soldiers' minds must have blacked out. Why had they been so kind in the first instance only to behave so badly and turn against us so cruelly? Indeed, I realised even then that they must have been compelled by political powers beyond their control to act as they did, astonishing as it was. They were infused with such madness that it was almost unnatural. To me, it was even more unnatural to see the soldiers crying even as they proceeded with their actions.

No amount of crying or begging from the kneeling mother could stop the soldier pulling her little girl from her arms and flinging her into the truck. Another freckle-faced, red-headed soldier slowly lifted his rifle and grabbed the priest by his dark robes. Tears were streaming from his undefinably coloured eyes as he pursued his 'enemy', but the priest pushed him away with a large wooden cross. The priest then deposited himself firmly on the platform before yet another attack plunged deeper into the circle and the altar collapsed with its icons and decorations showering the crowd. In the resulting chaos a pyramid of screaming humans clambered over each other, frantically trying to free themselves and get away from the soldiers' hands. More blood and destruction.[51]

At the time of writing these words, *no* British official source has ever expressed a shadow of regret for these and innumerable other deliberate violations of Article 3 of the 1929 Geneva Convention.

Prisoners of war have a right to respect for their personality and their honour. Women shall be treated with all the consideration due to their sex.[52]

Worse was to follow for Zoe. Frantic with fear in face of the brutality of the British troops, the crowd began to stampede. Many of all ages were crushed to death in the press. Zoe's experiences that day speak for many others, save for its eventual outcome.

At that moment I was lifted once more by the mob and thrown like an eggshell against the window of a hut. Through the split glass, the upper part of me fell through inside the hut: but my legs were trapped on the other side and my knees impaled on the jagged glass. I was pinned tightly on both sides. At first the pain was severe, but then I could no longer feel anything from the waist down. People were swarming over me. It seemed hours until Tonia, too, was pushed to the hut; she managed somehow to throw my legs inside.[53]

There was a little bridge across the Drau, which bounded the south side of the camp. In early summer the river flows with incredible swiftness from melting mountain snows, and as the hard-pressed flood of fugitives poured over the bridge, the girl whose account was cited earlier[*] saw another mother clasp her child and deliberately hurl herself into the fiercely rushing waters. The writer and her family got away safely into the mountains after several more hazardous encounters; she kept her vow and from that day onwards confined her diet on Fridays to bread and water.[54]

Meanwhile Zoe and Tonia made their way likewise across the bridge, witnessing similar scenes of horror: suicides in the river and neighbouring woodland, children trampled to death. After a brief respite, they were recaptured and dragged back to the camp. There they felt momentary pity for Major Davies, whom they saw weeping.[55] Mothers were desperately searching for their children, while lost children wandered tearfully in their hunt for parents they would never see again.

Zoe and Tonia, together with a ten-year old girl were flung into a truck which was already filled with battered victims. When the vehicle was replete with captives, it was driven swiftly to the railway line, where the victims were dragged out and hurled into a cattle-truck. Screams echoed from other wagons, whose inmates were already bolted into the darkness. Zoe and her companions were flung into a wagon, where they became momentarily separated by the crush of bleeding victims. Gazing round, she saw an old man mopping blood from his bleeding head, a bucket in the corner in which prisoners regardless of age or sex were expected to relieve themselves.

She could stand no more. As the truck which brought them pulled away, Zoe struggled to the door of the wagon, and managed to extend her wounded legs over the edge of the doorway. Just outside, the 8th Argylls Medical Officer, Dr. John Pinching, was tending a battered victim on the ground. Glancing up, he saw the bruised and bleeding girl dangling above

---

[*] Not a few of the survivors remained so fearful that the British might yet betray them to the Soviets, that they continued to retain their anonymity years after the event.

him. Without hesitation, he pulled her out, and took her aside to bandage the bleeding gashes in her legs.[56]

Such were the chances of life and death on that hideous day. Its only difference, so far as Zoe was concerned, from her earlier abduction by Waffen SS troops from the Ukrainian town of Pervomaisk in 1942, was that it was vastly more brutal. While Zoe miraculously escaped and lived to tell the tale, her friend Tonia was taken away in the train to Judenburg, and thence to the slave-labour camps of Kemerovo oblast, thousands of miles to the east. She was never heard of again, and the fate of a pretty teenage girl at the hands of camp criminals in the remotest reaches of the gulag is neither pleasant nor difficult to imagine.

In later years few, if any, of the numerous Cossack survivors whom I knew bore resentment against British troops involved in these bloody events. After reading my book *Victims of Yalta* they had come to recognize that the great majority of officers and men of the Argylls and other regiments involved were themselves victims of a policy of which they were profoundly ashamed. However, they were less charitably inclined towards the principal authors of the policy. Nor did it increase their respect for Britain's honor, when one of the leading figures responsible was in 1989 granted a legal judgment of £2,000,000.[*] Lord Aldington publicly bewailed the fact that in the event he only obtained a modicum of the reward to which he felt entitled. No record exists of his expressing even momentary regret for those who suffered so terribly in consequence of his actions in 1945.

To the Cossacks the men of the Argylls seemed to have gone berserk. Lashing out with their heavy weapons, they inflicted fearful blows which rained down indiscriminately on male and female, young and old alike. The priests and their assistants were dashed to the ground and dragged away, their vestments and icons trampled in the dust. A middle-aged Kuban Cossack, who was bearing an icon of the Virgin during the service, had been so badly beaten that blood was splashed over his neck, face, hands, shirt - and even on the icon itself.

Eight years later another Kuban Cossack wrote:

> On my memory is impressed the following scene. [A British] soldier was escorting with his gun a young Cossack wife with a year-old baby in her arms. The hand of the baby was slightly wounded or scratched. The soldier, stopping ten metres from the edge of the crowd, bound a field bandage round the baby's hand, gave him water to drink from his flask;

---

[*] As Lord Aldington's costs were secretly paid by the Sun Alliance insurance company of which he had been Chairman, they effectively amounted to additional damages.

and then, in spite of the mother's pleas, took him off to the truck.[57]

Here may be noted a further provision of the Geneva Convention (Article 25):

> Insofar as the continuance of military operations does not prevent it, sick and wounded prisoners of war shall not be transferred so long as their recovery may be hindered by the journey.[58]

It was about this time that Dr. Pinching, Zoe Polanska's saviour, arrived on the scene. Summoned the moment it became apparent that people were becoming seriously hurt, he remembered treating a dozen or so middle-aged casualties, mostly for head-wounds. In some he inserted stitches on the spot; two or three semi-concussed victims had to be sent to hospital in Lienz. It was while he was tending these people on a nearby grassy bank that Olga Rotova came upon him.

> The doctor expressed to me his indignation over the use of arms against our people. 'It's inhuman', he said, weeping openly.[59]

Despite the savagery inflicted on them, Cossack eyewitnesses repeatedly attest to the acute distress manifested by Dr. Pinching, Major Davies, and others among British troops acting under orders they dared not disobey. However, historical veracity requires that other, less palatable attitudes be recorded. One such example, likewise recorded by Olga Rotova, occurred at this moment.

> A Scottish officer came up to him [Dr. Pinching]. He had a swollen hand. Evidently, in the attack on the unhappy people, he had bruised it. I personally saw this officer mercilessly beating the protestors with a stick. Unfortunately, I forgot his name.

In fact he was almost certainly the officer whose photograph appears in plate XXIX of General Naumenko's great compendium devoted to the tragedy, whose caption declares that he 'displayed especial cruelty' on that black 1 June 1945. When I showed it to Major Davies, he identified him as a battalion intelligence officer named Smellie. It was possibly another who mercilessly beat a cowering woman with a rubber truncheon, swearing savagely as he did so. The Cossack Likhomirov having been killed in the square, his widow and three children were hurled into a cattle-truck, and like the remainder dispatched to the gulag. Professor Verbitsky never forgot the sight of a bearded old man fleeing from the line of trucks waiting to deliver the Cossacks to their persecutors. A British soldier clubbed him on the head, and left him stumbling away with blood coursing down his face.[60]

Some British soldiers did not scruple to profit from the slaughter. In her position as official interpreter, Olga Rotova had regular occasion immediately afterwards to visit the headquarters building of the Argylls in Lienz.

> When I was taken in the large jeep to the hotel, I saw there heaps of articles, silver and gold objects, boots, shoes, etc.

The deserted barracks buildings at Peggetz had been exhaustively plundered by British troops.[61]

A priest, Father Timofey Soin, described how his wife was separated from him in the press and knocked to the ground. Fortunately, just as she felt she was about to go under, she was helped to her feet. As the crowd was swept this way and that, she saw on the ground a mother and child – crushed to death. Everywhere children were screaming for their parents, and parents, immovable in the throng, were gazing around for their offspring. Where possible the men of the Argylls grabbed children first and thrust them into the trucks. This was not to save them from danger, but because it frequently happened that the agonized parents then rushed forward and could be seized likewise. Despite this, both the despairing, instinctive efforts of parents and the more detached desire of Rusty Davies to keep families united were generally of little avail.[62]

'Three unknown Russians and one Cossack child' (military cemetery at Lienz).

The casualty list was indeed heavy. Apart from the large number who had been wounded by the soldiers or crushed in the press, many deaths arose directly or indirectly from the morning's work. Colonel Malcolm stated that, when the Cossacks clung to each other,

> it was necessary to hit the men hard to make them let go, and then many had to be dragged by three or four soldiers to the trucks. Many minor struggles and scuffles developed in the course of which a number of Cossack men got hurt and cut. My troops were using axe helves and the butts of their rifles, but bayonets had been fixed and some wounds were caused accidentally, none deliberately, by them ... four people apparently got knocked down in the crowd and were killed: or it is possible that they had previously been suffocated under the heaps of people who had thrown themselves down in many cases several deep.

Rusty Davies wrote that, during the second assault,

> one of the crowd clutched at one of the soldiers' rifles and deliberately pulled the trigger in an effort to shoot himself. The bullet killed a youth standing alongside. During this stampede a man was trampled to death.

In the Argylls' War Diary the total enemy casualty list after the unequal battle was given as '5 Killed; 3 Evacuated with gunshot wounds; 7 head injuries; collapsed 2; Women and children 2'.[63]

Not only do these figures fall far short of what is known from numerous eyewitness accounts and existing graves, but it seems that the reference is in any case to deaths in the camp area alone. There were many more in the countryside around. Even before the handovers began, two Cossack officers who held a cynical view of the value of British assurances had shot themselves in the woods. During the operation itself soldiers were firing constantly at the continuing trickle of escapers, particularly those who succeeded in crowding across the footbridge over the Drau.[64] A surviving Kuban Cossack, Daniel Kolomeic, recalls how he escaped into the mountains, but his companion was gunned down as they fled.[65] A Cossack woman hiding in the undergrowth was given away by the barking of her dog and killed in a burst of automatic fire.

Many escapers, perhaps twenty or thirty, were drowned in the waters of the Drau. A woman doctor, Praskovia Voskoboinikova, deliberately hurled herself in, accompanied by her whole family: children, mother and sister.[66] Numerous similar cases were witnessed, many likewise involving the sacrifice of children whom mothers sought in their despair to save from the unending torments of a slave labor camp upbringing.[67] An eyewitness saw a Cossack strap himself to his saddle and spring with his horse into the whirling current of the Drau.[68] In a hospital in Lienz, a sick

Cossack threw himself from a window to his death when the troops came for him.[69]

Many other British soldiers were horrified by these instances of total despair. Kenneth Tyson recalled seeing a corpse suspended from a branch in the trees near Dölsach station, and Rusty Davies remembered seeing 'several' such during the day. The worst case of all was perhaps that which the latter came across whilst walking about the site after the morning's proceedings. In a woodland glade lay five bodies. Four were those of a mother and her three children, the youngest of whom was a baby girl just one year old. They had each been shot once in the back. Some way off sprawled a man's corpse; beside him lay a revolver, with which he had shot himself through the head. It was this scene which brought home to Davies more than anything else the fear which gripped the Cossacks at the thought of returning to the Soviet Union. For there could be only one interpretation of the tragedy: the father, in what frame of mind we can only surmise, had killed all his family one by one. He had then walked a little way off and put an end to his own sufferings.[70]

That evening the scene in the camp at Peggetz and its environs resembled the aftermath of a battle. Bloodied figures wandered about, seeking for lost relatives. Masterless horses cantered here and there, their plaintive whinnying accompanied at times by the harsh cries of the Cossacks' camels. Small groups of people made off furtively for the mountains, whilst others returned in despair from skulking in the woods to take up quarters once again in the quietened camp.[71] Everywhere the wounded and the dead lay around.

How many people died on that day, either by their own hands or killed by British troops? British sources suggest only about a dozen, but this is undoubtedly far too low. The normally accurate Olga Rotova estimates around 700 victims, including people crushed to death, shot, drowned in the river and self-immolated. Of these she knew of well over a hundred who were killed.[72] In the forests around there were undoubtedly casualties of which the British knew nothing and cared little.

A reliable statistic is that provided nine years after the event by Vasily Frank, representative of the international charitable Tolstoy Foundation. After visiting the spot and interrogating survivors, Frank reported to the Foundation on 7 April 1954 that

> A number was killed during the operation or committed suicide and are buried at the grave-yard at the actual place of operation – now the site of a memorial monument consecrated by Archbishop Anastasius – holds the bodies of 126 persons. Many more are buried in the fields and forests nearby. Others were drowned whilst attempting to escape and are buried

further downstream.

A list of graves in the vicinity of Peggetz and Lienz compiled by a Cossack visitor to the spot in 1963 includes no less than eighteen mass graves.[73]

An Austrian living at nearby Nikolsdorf, Bartholomäus Plautz, suffered from nightmares as he recalled the scenes around his home on 1 June 1945. With a friend, he set off with a horse-drawn wagon to collect and bury the dead Cossacks. He remembered all too vividly finding women clutching their dead babies, lying in the fields with their throats cut. Few could be identified

By the site of the camp at Peggetz is the little cemetery mentioned by Vasily Frank, where some of the victims lie buried. The 28 gravestones are purely symbolic, and do not reflect the number of bodies buried there. An Austrian lady, Erika Patzold, who as a young girl was present at the time of the atrocities, explained that

> underneath the 28 neatly arranged tombstones and the tall memorial head tombstone lie over 700 people – one of the larger mass graves dug by British army bulldozers during the massacre. "Those who chose to die rather than be sent forcibly to the Soviet Union were just thrown into these big holes".[74]

> Every year on the anniversary Russians come from all over the world to hold commemorative services and pray for the souls of the departed. Latterly, a fine traditional wooden chapel has been erected beside the cemetery. There is also in Lienz a charming little Orthodox church, constructed at the expense of a Russian benefactor. When I first visited the town, the cemetery was zealously supervised by a small, one-eyed old Cossack named Ivan Gordienko.[*] He was himself a survivor of the events described above, and conducted me over the scenes of thirty years earlier

> It was not only in the camp at Peggetz that scenes of violence and tragedy occurred that day. Further to the east, at Oberdrauburg, men of 6th Royal West Kents and 56th Recce Regiment were faced with a similar task in rounding up and dispatching to Judenburg nearly two thousand more

---

[*] Today the church, cemetery, and little museum are sustained by the selfless labours of my friend Father Georg Kobro. Given the honourable extent of German atonement and recompense for Nazi crimes, it is distressing to note that *no* contribution to maintenance of the cemetery and chapel at Lienz, nor any other memorial, has ever been considered by the British Government. On the contrary, the British official view apparently remains unaltered that the beatings, killings, suicides, and transport to Macmillan's 'slavery, torture, and probably death' were justified in view of 'grave operational necessity'.

members of the *Kazachi Stan.*[75] As at Peggetz, on the two previous days black flags were hung out, and petitions against return submitted. Some Cossacks expressed a desire to return to the USSR and were placed for their own protection in a detention barracks east of Lienz.[76]

On 1 June arrangements were made for entraining similar to those at Peggetz. Once again, the Cossacks made a concerted and desperate effort to resist. Lieutenant E.B. Hetherington, of 6th Royal West Kents, remembered the opening of the operation.

> On entering the camp it was very evident that the vast majority of Cossacks had no intention of being evacuated. This was borne out by the fact that they bunched together at the end of the camp, the outer ring linking arms to prevent any infiltration by our troops. I ordered the men of 11 Pl[atoon] to fix bayonets in an attempt to rouse the Cossacks into surrender, but it was without success. They replied by taking off their shirts and asking the British soldiers to stab them. The interpreter was then called for and he spoke to them telling them it was foolish to act the way they were acting and that if they did not come quietly now they would be taken by force. Loud cheers greeted this statement.

The leader of the Cossacks had already been seized and placed in the waiting train, and it was decided to employ as forceful methods as were necessary to accomplish the task laid down. So determined was the passive resistance of the prisoners, however, that the West Kents were obliged to call for assistance. They were joined by 45 men of the Lancashire Fusiliers, who had been detailed for escort duties on the train. After prolonged beating and use of firearms, 1,749 Cossacks (including 102 women and 4 children) were loaded into the cattle cars. Lieutenant R. Shields of the Royal Inniskilling Fusiliers, watching the operation, wrote:

> I was witness to many amazing incidents of fanatical fear and dread of the future they thought was in store for them. Men outstretched on the ground baring their chests to be shot where they lay. There were many women in a state of frenzy amongst the Cossacks also.

Eight hundred of the Cossacks on this train came from another camp a little further up the line. Lieutenant Shields now travelled on to this camp, where a company of his regiment had arrived to supervise the entraining.

> By this time [runs Shields's eye-witness account] Capt Campbell had arrived with the main body of A Coy. Then the trouble started again. The minute we moved to remove them to the train they immediately sat down where they were with arms inter-laced, refused to move, and demanded that we 'shot them where they lay'. Capt Campbell decided that this was no time to be gentle and try and coax them to move – it was a case of

move them by force. The troops fixed their bayonets, and started breaking the body into small groups. This proved no easy job. After 10 mins of beating with sticks, rifles, and even to the extent of bayonets points being used, and not too gently either.

The men were by this time very much aroused, and it was then that someone opened up with an automatic. This gave the troops the thing they had waited for. Weapons were fired above the heads of the Cossacks, and into the ground in front of them. Scenes were pretty wild by this time, and the big worry was that we might shoot up our own people, fortunately that did not happen. By this time quite a number had moved to the trucks to embus for the train, but the main body still would not move an inch despite the really rough handling they had received. One man in particular, I thought he must have been the ringleader because he seemed to have all the control over them. He by the time he had been dragged to the trucks was bleeding from the blows he had received and the leather coat (which was a very good one too before the fight started) was in shreds, likewise the jacket and shirt underneath.

With his removal plus the additional firing which was becoming more erratic as the men's tempers became aroused, they started moving towards the trucks with the exception of about 200 who tried to make their escape through the woods.

They of course were met by the Bren fire, out to stop any such attempt. This stopped most of them but not before there were casualties.[77] The few that did manage to escape were eventually rounded up by the RWKs in the adjoining camp.

From then on the job was easy. We cleared the camp, collected the wounded and killed which amounted to 3 killed and 4 wounded, two of them serious who were sent to hospital.

All told it took the Coy 2 hrs to clear one camp which totalled some 800 Cossacks.

All this ruthless bloodshed was employed to drive eight hundred people at bayonet point onto trucks, a good number of whom were women and children. Yet at the same time, a few miles to the west, Major Davies with exactly the same number of men managed to deal with a crowd of about four thousand with less deliberate brutality. It is relevant to note that while the men of the Argylls had been living for three weeks in close association with the Cossacks, the Inniskillings had newly arrived from Villach to assist in the operation. Curiously, however, not a single Cossack memoir appears even to mention the Inniskillings, while the Argylls are held up to near universal execration. After their prolonged dealings with them at Lienz, the names of Major Davies and the Argyll and Sutherland

Highlanders have passed into Cossack history. Many Cossack writers were apparently unaware that other units were called in to assist in the entraining; indeed, they are scarcely likely to have retained the names of formations they encountered so briefly. It may be, therefore, that events at Oberdrauburg became conflated in some Cossacks' memory with those at Peggetz. Equally, it is possible that the harsh action of Lieutenant Shields and his men ensured that no survivors remained to tell the tale.

It would be wrong, however, to assume that Irish soldiers were any happier than their Scottish counterparts in participating in so much gratuitous brutality. Mr. L. Birch, then serving with the Inniskillings, described to me his harrowing experience in dealing with the fugitives:

> During the day we came across small groups carrying pitiful bundles – men – women and the odd child. It was my bitter experience to have a woman stand before me, pull her dress open at her breast saying "Bitte schossen" ['please shoot me'] – she was one of a party of half-a-dozen - I told her to go and pointed to the mountains and safety. I have often wondered if any of those ever made it to the freedom they sought. Most of the lads taking part in this operation felt certain revulsion as to what was taking place.

The concern of 5th Corps command that these supposedly creditable operations should be perpetrated under conditions of absolute secrecy is illustrated by the experience of an official Army film crew dispatched on a roving mission to record operations in Southern Austria at this time. Based near 5th Corps Headquarters on the Wörthersee, they had been issued a free hand by Allied Force Headquarters to film where they chose. What happened is recorded in an interview with cameraman Alan Wilson.

> I remember that we filmed a lot of Cossacks coming in... And they [Wilson's crew] were filming and photographing the camp where the British troops – and I recall that they were the Royal West Kents, this particular incident – they were told to move the Russians out of the camp and get them loaded on to lorries which were taking them to the railways station... And apparently the Russians suspected that something nasty was going to happen to them. And they refused to leave the camp... And I gather that in the end the West Kents were told to fix bayonets and go in and sort of winkle them off the ground, use the point of the bayonet to encourage them. And the whole thing was very distasteful...
>
> And an officer came up to them and took the film off them and confiscated it.
>
> The camera team registered vociferous protest at this high-handed action.

They protested because this sort of thing should not have happened because we had a pass which permitted us to film anything[,] signed by Allied Military Headquarters, and said that all the material shot or photographed by us was liable to censorship [at AFHQ], and we should not be obstructed in our work.

John Cotter, the officer in charge of the film unit, was furious.

And he went straight away down to I think it was corps headquarters or he may have gone down to division. I don't know. But I know he had a session with General Arbuthnot. But I think Gerald [General] Keightley who was corps commander. I don't know who it was he actually saw ... Well, I think it must have been Arbuthnot told him that ... Told him, you know, that he'd best keep quiet about this. You know, he upheld the destruction of the film basically.

Asked whether orders were given that all filming was to cease forthwith, Wilson responded that it had been planned to film on the train taking the Cossacks to their destination.

And we were going to put our camera on one of the trucks. And nothing more was heard of that. So I would believe that instructions must have been given that the whole thing was out as far as coverage was concerned ...

And I think the reason that this sticks rather vividly in my memory is the troops involved ... were the Royal West Kents. And that was my regiment. So this thing really, you know, hit me, that my own regiment had been involved in this, you know, rather disgusting sort of conduct.[78]

It seems that AFHQ was not informed of this censorship, and was clearly not intended to be made aware of its imposition.

The first and most terrible day of the repatriation operation was over.[79] For thousands of people it had been one of horror or remorse. Obviously, the Cossacks now in the hands of SMERSH in Judenburg were the real sufferers. But there were others on whom the day's events would leave a lasting and agonizing impression. The ordinary soldiers of 'Y' Company of the 8th Argylls were seen by many to be weeping as they conducted their incomprehensibly detestable task.

The Reverend Kenneth Tyson, battalion chaplain, described to me how many came to him afterwards, asking in bewilderment and obvious distress what they should do. He could only answer that they must continue to obey their orders; but he himself did not feel satisfied. His duties had not permitted him in the preceding weeks to see as much of the Cossacks as others, but the whole grim business seemed to him quite contrary to everything that Christ's teachings enjoin. He had arrived halfway through the morning's proceedings, when the main crowd of Cossacks had broken through the camp fence and reassembled in the neighbouring field. He witnessed no violence, only troops inexorably pushing unresisting Cossacks towards the trucks. But the sight preyed on his mind, and on 3 June, a Sunday, he preached on the text:

> And Jesus, when he came out, saw much people, and was moved with compassion toward them, because they were as sheep not having a shepherd: and he began to teach them many things (Mark 6, 34).

The soldiers assembled in the Lienz cinema, which was used as an improvised chapel, heard Tyson preach movingly and with obvious feeling on the necessity for compassion in war.

> 'I didn't criticise the commanding officer at all', he recalled to me, 'and I wouldn't dream of doing so, as I had no responsibilities. But I left no doubts in anyone's mind what *my* thoughts about the whole thing were: that it was wrong, that it was completely contrary to our Christian tradition and what we'd fought for'.

He remembers that his congregation was still profoundly agitated by what they had experienced: 'They were perplexed, stunned, at what they had been asked to do'.

The two men who bore immediate responsibility, Colonel Malcolm and Major Davies, also disliked what they had been obliged to undertake, although in differing degree. Colonel Malcolm, whom I found a somewhat chilling personality, thought then and afterwards that the Cossacks were traitors to their country and deserved to be sent back to whatever punishment lay in store for them. Many of his regiment had been captured before Dunkirk, and, as he subsequently asked me, 'what fate would they have deserved had they volunteered to fight for the Germans?' But whatever one may think of this argument, based on utterly different considerations and circumstances, it does not cover the substantial number of unfortunates who were women and children, or those who had never been Soviet citizens. British soldiers in 1940 were not fighting for a barbaric regime which oppressed its own citizens like a savage foreign oppressor, but were citizens of a decent law-abiding state. Nor would even British traitors on their return home have been condemned to slavery, torture, or most likely both. Finally, the Cossacks had never fought against Britain, and immediately after their willing surrender to British forces they proffered their services to work – and, if required, fight – for British interests. *

---

* Colin Mitchell, at the time a lieutenant in the Argylls, was it is to be hoped rare in

However, it is not impossible that this callous and, I fear, shameful justification originated retrospectively in Malcolm's mind.

Colonel Malcolm also felt that the force employed in loading the Cossacks was no more than was necessary. And of course it is true that if his orders were to be fulfilled, then some degree of force or violence was unavoidable in view of the Cossack refusal to co-operate. He was repelled by the bloodshed and panic his orders were causing and, as has been seen, ordered the loading to cease prematurely despite the fact that the train should have included a further five hundred. It is impossible to determine now how far this reflected compassion for the victims, or how far the shameful effect of the brutal operation was affecting the morale of his men.

Shortly after giving this order, Colonel Malcolm walked from the camp to the railway line where he found Brigadier Musson, who had driven over from Oberdrauburg. Malcolm told Musson that he would not be prepared to employ the same degree of force in continuing the operation the next day, to which Musson replied only with a grunt. That evening, Malcolm spoke again to Musson on the telephone on the subject, stating further that he would no longer issue the troops with live ammunition.

For his part, Rusty Davies was unhesitating in expressing sympathy and affection for his unfortunate charges, and condemned outright the policy he was obliged to implement. Moreover, he considered his superiors' assertion, that any screening of non-Soviet citizens was impractical, to be unjustified. After all, he had himself conducted improvised screening, albeit on a small scale. He was disgusted by the dishonourable role foisted upon him of having to lie to people who looked upon him as their friend. Finally, he felt that the violence required for the entraining on 1 June should in itself have been enough to have the measure cancelled forthwith.

In some Cossack records, the name of Major Davies is one mentioned with contempt and opprobrium. All they knew was that he had lied to them and deceived them, and that he had supervised the brutal events of 1 June. But what could he have done? Two alternatives to obeying his orders existed: to disobey them, or resign his commission. Neither of these courses was to be contemplated by any soldier at that time without the

---

espousing a repellently racist view. 'On the whole my sympathies were not over-extended. These people had a tough record as L of C anti-Partisan troops. But because they were so primitive, accompanied by their household goods and families, it was difficult to equate them with the Germans we had been fighting some weeks earlier' (cited approvingly by Sir Carol Mather, *Aftermath of War: Everyone Must Go Home* (London, 1992), p. 170).

greatest misgiving. Corporate loyalty had been built up in the battalion over the past years of hard fighting in North Africa and Italy. Davies had the highest respect for his CO's judgment, was not a regular soldier, and was moreover a youthful 26 years old. Even if he had refused to obey the order, he would have been punished and replaced by another officer.

A moving testimony to the anguish of Major Davies is supplied by Olga Rotova, a witness little likely to mitigate British actions or individuals. That evening she described in her diary standing in the crowd watching the first onslaughts by the Argylls. Suddenly she was summoned out of the crowd to appear before Major Davies.

'At last I've found you! Why didn't you meet me at the entrance?' he cried.

'My place is with my own Russian people', she replied.

Davies passed on to explain hurriedly that he was anxious to find Domanov's wife, so that she might be properly treated, away from the milling crowd.

'I'm not sure that I believe you, Major', replied Olga dubiously.

After a vain search for the general's wife, Davies, 'pale and upset', made a new request.

'Tell them not to resist', he said, indicating the frenzied crowd.

'Major! Produce a great stove with a fire in it and give orders to jump in. Would you jump?'

'I don't know'.

'You know very well, Major, that you would not. To return to the Soviets is worse than the fire of a stove!'

'But I, a British officer, cannot watch longer the beating of unarmed people ... women, children. I can't authorise any more violence, I can't any more, I can't!'

He was weeping copiously.

'I can't go on, I can't!'[80]

Once again, it should be recalled that Olga's account was drawn not from memory years later but from her diary written that evening. Moreover, as a fluent English-speaker, she was in a privileged position to understand what she witnessed.

Davies in addition went to some lengths to retain a few of the more obvious old emigrants, such as General Krasnov's wife Lydia. These were placed in an improvised guard hut during the confusion, and thus evaded the repatriation intended for them by 5th Corps command. In subsequent years, Davies received Christmas cards from several of these people, who lived in the West. The Rev. Kenneth Tyson, who sought to console Lydia Krasnova at the time, bequeathed to me a copy of one of General Krasnov's novels that she had given him, in which Tyson wrote: 'She awaited her husband's return or news of him in vain'.

Lydia died five years later, according to those who knew her unwilling to the last to accept that her husband was really dead.

Grave of Lydia Krasnov

Another remarkable case was that of Domanov's intelligence officer. He had formerly been an officer of the British Crown, serving in the Hong Kong Police and decorated with the MC by King George V. To hand such a man over to the Soviets for execution was more than the Argylls could stand. He was provided with civilian clothes and allowed to escape.[81] Those Cossack accounts which lay major blame on Major Davies or Colonel Malcolm are inadvertently committing a real injustice. We must search higher up the chain of command for the true culprits, and above all in the political hierarchy. It was after all Harold Macmillan who wrote in his diary a fortnight earlier:

> To hand them over to the Russians is condemning them to slavery, torture and probably death. To refuse, is deeply to offend the Russians, and incidentally break the Yalta agreement. We [he and General Keightley] have decided to hand them over ...

So appalling were even muted reports of the events of 1 June and in the days thereafter that the Red Cross threatened to withdraw its personnel from the area. Any leakage of this embarrassing move would of course have been acutely embarrassing to 5th Corps command. In the following month General Keightley called on Lady Limerick, head of the Red Cross Relief Department, when on leave in London to reassure her that, during the operation,

> there was evidently some protest, as he said they only had to "shoot twice" and in neither case hit anybody. They [the Cossacks] were then interviewed and agreed to return to Soviet territory together with their wives and children. The men went back without any more pressure; the women protested at first under the instigation of their priest, but subsequently followed him into the train, and they all went back together.[82]

I imagine most readers would conclude from this that Keightley was not only a hardened bully but also a shameless liar. To Christopher Booker, however, spokesman for the official Cowgill 'Inquiry', his lies represented no more than a perfectly legitimate 'exercise in damage limitation', while he assured his readers that Keightley had in any case no more than 'glossed over the details'.[83] We may imagine how a comparably emollient plea employed by defense counsel on behalf of a major German war criminal would have been received at the Nuremberg Tribunal. And was not the Cowgill Inquiry itself one extended 'exercise in damage limitation', undertaken on behalf of the British government?

Some Cossack survivors of the atrocity, however, sensed where real responsibility lay. In 1989 Lord Aldington, who as Brigadier Low had issued the orders that resulted in all this bloodshed and terror, successfully persuaded a court of law to rule that he was entirely innocent of war crimes he played a major part in implementing in 1945. Among witnesses called for the defense was Major Davies. He afterwards confessed to having been apprehensive lest he be attacked by Cossack witnesses also testifying. When he arrived, two survivors of the carnage at Lienz, Maria Platonova and Anna Bratjakina, were waiting in the corridor outside the courtroom to take their turn as witnesses. Before Davies could realize what was happening, the ladies rushed up and embraced him, crying out 'we know it wasn't your fault!' He was profoundly moved, as were they.

By the end of a fortnight a total of 22,502 Cossacks and Caucasians was dispatched by 36th Infantry Brigade from the Drau Valley to the Soviet-occupied zone of Austria. Colonel Malcolm's threat to refuse further use of extreme violence was never put to the test, as subsequent entrainments passed much less violently. Nevertheless, there were further individual tragedies,[84] and on 2 June the Royal West Kents once again resorted to beatings when loading a party of 1,750 Cossacks of the 2nd Don Regiment at the Nikolsdorf Station.[85] But in general, the prisoners seemed to have been cowed into resigned submission by the terrible events at Peggetz and Oberdrauburg on 1 June.

A macabre epilogue to the handovers in Austria occurred not long afterwards. The abducted Cossacks left behind them thousands of their beloved horses. The 5th Corps appears to have made no attempt to find a home for these sturdy beasts, many of which could surely have found welcome homes with Austrian farmers. Horrified Cossacks who had escaped the handovers witnessed a grim scene. Kuzma Kostrominov, of 1st Don Cossack Regiment, saw how,

> using bulldozers the British dug trenches into which they forced horses and camels, where they shot them with machine guns mounted on armoured cars.

Officer cadet Yushkin Kapitonovich shared the love of horses common to all his race, and also watched the operation with utter horror:

> During all of World War II I did not witness anything more terrible. Camels were crying, horses were trembling, awaiting their fate.

During this holocaust, an estimated eight thousand horses were slaughtered in the colossal pit, together with fifteen mature camels and three of their calves.[86]

A very few were saved, a number of the finest mounts being appropriated by senior 5th Corps officers. One in particular, a beautiful mare named Katinka, proved the focus of admiration at point-to-points held by officers that summer across British-occupied Carinthia. In addition, 60 Cossack grooms were withheld from repatriation to tend the commandeered steeds.[87] It seems 5th Corps command could exercise mercy when circumstances were deemed appropriate.

With large numbers of Cossacks and Caucasians living in unwired camps, it will come as no surprise to learn that many managed to escape, both before and after the tragic events described. British sources estimated that 'those that had managed to escape evacuation amounted to well over a thousand, probably considerably more',[88] and General Naumenko's edited collection of Cossack letters and memoirs contains numerous references to successful escapes by groups and individuals. One outstanding case was that of Kuzma Polunin, the young NCO whom the Cossacks had chosen as their leader after their officers had been lured to Judenburg on 29 May. He had entered Peggetz camp on the fatal morning of 1 June in Major Davies's jeep. How he escaped is not known, but Olga Rotova met him in the camp (to which he had returned) two months later.[89]

On 26 May, 36th Infantry Brigade HQ issued elaborate instructions to all units concerned, detailing various posts and passes to be guarded and patrolled.[90] But despite this, and the formidable natural obstacles facing anyone wishing to leave the Drau Valley, large numbers made their way into the forested foothills and attempted the dangerous journey across the snow-covered heights beyond.[91] Determined efforts were made to comb the mountains and recover the scattered groups. A report made by 56th Recce Regiment noted that:

> In the early days parties of Cossacks and Caucasians were large and reluctant to expend energy in evading patrols. As time went on they were seldom found in parties of more than 12 and sat high up on the snow line during the day with sentries out who gave the alarm by shouting. By night they often occupied summer farms or bivvied in the woods on the lower slopes. The regular Cossacks and Caucasians requested to be shot rather than handed over, but having been taken they made no determined efforts to escape and readily obeyed British orders.[92]

Kenneth Tyson described to me such a search party which he accompanied on 3 or 4 June, and remembers also the Cossacks' resigned acceptance of their fate. The patrol he was with ascended a pass leading below the Spitzkofel Mountain south of Lienz. After ascending two or three thousand feet they came upon a group of 50 or 60 men, women and children. Without resistance, these turned round and were escorted back to the camp. On other occasions, however, patrols fired on and even killed would-be escapers. On occasion 5th Corps Headquarters authorized Soviet officers (undoubtedly from SMERSH) to participate in such murders.[93]

From 7 to 30 June, 1,356 Cossacks and Caucasians were recaptured in the mountains. On 15 June, 934 of these were taken in trucks to Judenburg; the Soviet authorities requested that they be taken on to Graz, where they arrived the following morning. British troops guarding this convoy learned that many of the prisoners delivered were massacred by the Soviets shortly after their arrival.[94]

A British soldier who accompanied a subsequent convoy bearing Cossacks to the NKVD reception camp at Graz glimpsed what awaited their victims. He was Troop-Sergeant Donald Lawrence, of 56th Recce Regiment, which provided the escort. As they crossed the viaduct over the river Mur, he was horrified to see a woman throw first her baby, and then herself into the waters below. The remainder of the prisoners, male and female, were herded on arrival into a huge wired concentration camp. There Lawrence saw drunken Soviet guards firing bursts of machine-gun fire into the helpless throng. He himself managed to smuggle one of the women back to Lienz in his armored car, and never forgot his nightmare journey.[95]

During the first week of June, thousands of Russians travelled on the one-way journey from the Drau Valley to Judenburg. For nine hours, they were packed together in sealed cattle wagons. In June 1998, I visited Evgenia Polskaya, one of the survivors of the tragedy, at her home in the Caucasus. She still recalled with horror the terrified scream which arose from the helpless prisoners when the train in which she travelled was suddenly plunged into total darkness on entering a tunnel.[96] They included hundreds of children, and all knew that they were beginning their long journey to Harold Macmillan's complacent vision of 'slavery, torture, and probably death'. She compared their treatment in the sealed train with that recently accorded Jews in Europe. Was she wrong?

Immediately after the operations had taken place, Captain Thomson, a liaison officer from AFHQ dispatched by Field Marshal Alexander to Keightley's Headquarters to investigate the atrocities, was informed that

> ... the handover of the Cossacks ... was much less difficult than had been anticipated.[97]

So it had blithely been expected to be *worse*!

Although it does not fall within the remit of this book to describe the ghastly fate of the Cossacks and Caucasians following their handover to SMERSH in the detail it deserves, ample evidence attests to the fact that the holocaust of prisoners was as bad as may be imagined. Professor Stefan Karner's researches among the archives of GULAG provide a partial statistical breakdown of the mortality rate. Victims delivered up in consequence of Keightley's acquiescence in Macmillan's 'verbal directive' were mainly dispatched to GUPVI camp 525 in Kemerovo near Tomsk in Siberia. Of 17,330 slaves in Camp 525, 3,540 are specifically identified as 'Vlasovites and White emigrants', as identified both by Harold Macmillan and in the 5th Corps secret agreement with SMERSH. By 1 January 1946, 284 were already dead, almost certainly (in the case of adults) as a consequence of their barbaric treatment as slaves working in the Kuzbas coalmines.

We now also know something of the fate of a specimen body of Cossack women and children held in Camp 525. Of the 808 recorded Cossacks, more than half were under the age of 21, one in about every seven was not yet five years old, and around five per cent were babies born in 1945. Of the 269 women between fifteen and 35 years of age, a total of 26 were pregnant in Kemerovo at the end of October 1945, some still breastfeeding their babies. One baby succumbed to the strain and died practically during the recording of the lists ... The death rate at the entire complex was alarmingly high and amounted for the duration of the camp administration, until 1949, to approximately ten per cent! The NKVD mentions in its camp report in this connection bad living conditions for the first contingents brought into the camp, to which the Cossack wives and children had been assigned: crowded barracks, housing in mud huts, two- to three-tiered bunk beds, extremely low temperatures in the living quarters, no sick bays, no sanitary facilities, no recuperation facilities in the entire area of the camp administration. Also, little food, the same diet day in, day out, lack of warm clothing, insufficient bed sheets and, on account of the difficulty of transportation, no opportunity of procuring the requisite equipment.

Finally, and perhaps most horrifically, the NKVD report complacently mentions infiltration of the camp staff by 'criminal elements'. The effect of this factor on the helpless Cossack women in particular is too horrible to contemplate.[98]

At the other end of the 130-mile journey, a young British soldier watched the daily procession of trains arriving at Judenburg. Towards the end of May 1945, 25-year old Sapper Reg Gray of the 192nd Railway Operating Company, Royal Engineers, found himself near Judenburg, where he was detailed to act as driver to an engineering officer, Lieutenant Sykes. One night he drove the lieutenant to an officers' mess outside the town. As Reg Gray sat in his jeep waiting in the road, he could hear from some distance off the sound of great crowds of men singing. Occasionally this was punctuated by bursts of rifle fire, and a red glow burned in the darkness from where the sounds emanated. At that moment another jeep drew up alongside, and Gray asked the driver what was going on. The other explained that 40,000 Russians were gathered there to be sent back to Russia.

Just then, Lieutenant Sykes reappeared and gave Gray instructions to pick him up next morning at four o'clock. 'It was perishing cold' when they set off, he recalled. However, there was little time for reflection, as

Sykes now told him they were to drive north to Judenburg. As they sped up the valley, the officer explained that he had been detailed to act as liaison officer at the handover point where the returning Russians were to pass under Soviet control.

As they approached their destination they were waved to a halt. A column of trucks was coming down the highway and made for the bridge over the Mur. In them were seated Cossack officers in German uniforms. As the convoy streamed slowly over the bridge there was a brief halt, and in a flurry of excitement word was passed back to those waiting that a Cossack had hurled himself over the parapet to his death. Eventually the road was cleared, and Reg Gray's jeep drove over the high-arched bridge to the Soviet-occupied side of the town. The first thing that struck him was an extraordinary change in the atmosphere. On the British side all was cheerful noise and bustle. On the other, the very houses seemed drab, and the people around looked terrified. An eerie feeling of fear permeated the atmosphere.

At the railway station, half-a-dozen Red Army soldiers sat playing cards on the deserted platform. After some time, there was a trembling of the lines, and a train came slowly steaming in. As it drew up, Gray could see that the windows of the trucks were sealed with barbed wire. Between the strands of wire fluttered hands dangling watches and other valuables. There were no guards in sight, only engine personnel. At once two Soviet soldiers jumped into the seats of a nearby 37mm light anti-aircraft gun and swung the barrel round menacingly to cover the train. A Soviet officer began walking the length of the wagons, banging each one in turn with a length of twisted steel cable. After a while the doors were unlocked and the prisoners descended, blinking in the sunlight.

They were lined up in a great queue, men, women, and children intermingled. They were not allowed to bring a single article of luggage with them and all portable personal possessions were left piled in the trucks. A Jew acting as interpreter to the British officer was standing nearby, and Reg Gray asked him if he knew what was going to happen to the Cossacks. The interpreter went off, to return with the reply that all the officers would be shot and the rest sent to Siberia. To Gray, young and apolitical, this meant little at the time, and he admitted subsequently that his first thought was for the pickings to be had from the empty train.

Inside he found pathetic little bundles of cherished possessions – battered suitcases, clothes, blankets, watches. Everywhere were festooned pieces of German insignia torn from uniforms, and welcoming heaps of Italian *lire* and Austrian *schillings*. There was a Singer sewing-machine, which an old woman was pleading in vain to be allowed to take with her.

In another was a pair of abandoned gold wedding-rings which Reg Gray retained. With disgust he discovered that each wagon-load of forty people had been supplied for the needs of nature with half a forty-gallon oil drum. The squalor could be imagined. At least one of the returning victims had decided he would escape the fate for which he had been destined. In the corridor of a Pullman car lay the blanket-covered body of a Cossack suicide. Moving hastily past this macabre sight, Gray completed his search of the train. His pockets were bulging with Austrian and Italian notes, which were of course useless to the Russians. Perhaps the oddest item he encountered was a box of fifty tins of Players cigarettes in the guard's van of this and every subsequent train. They had evidently been placed there for the use of the prisoners, but remained at the same time completely inaccessible! The humane provision of a last smoke, however, may have looked good in some report.

For the first fortnight of June, Gray drove Lieutenant Sykes every day from their billets on the British side of the river to meet the trains shuffling into Judenburg station. Each arrival was the same: the train drew up, hissing. There were no guards on board, only the personnel to drive the engine – and they were never permitted to descend. Soviet soldiers unlocked the wagons and led away the prisoners. What happened to them Reg Gray never saw; he had only the report of the interpreter to go by.

What he did witness was the fate of the prisoners' belongings. As each train was unloaded, every Cossack was stripped of all his possessions. These were dumped nearby in an ever-growing heap, which by the end of the fortnight had assumed massive proportions; it was 'as big as a gasometer'. And when the last train had left, Soviet guards poured kerosene on to the base of the pile and watched it go up in a column of black smoke.

His duty over, Reg Gray returned to his unit. In the other direction endless columns of bowed figures set off on the long journey eastwards. Their ordeal had begun.

POST SCRIPT

THE BRITISH GOVERNMENT'S
OFFICIAL VERSION OF EVENTS

'You ... raise allegations of crimes committed by British soldiers in Austria against Russian soldiers and civilians. We are not aware of any evidence to support such allegations' (Letter of 13 July 1999 to the author from Mrs. Catherine Mackenzie, of the Human Rights Policy Department of the Foreign Office)

'Our reply to Count Tolstoy did say, quite properly, that we were not aware of any evidence to support his allegations that British soldiers in Austria at the time had committed "savage crimes"' (Letter of 20 September 1999 to Zoe Polanska from Mr J. L. Howgate, of the Eastern Department of the Foreign Office)

It is revealing to note the contrasted attitude where comparable maltreatment of *British* troops was concerned. On 25 February 1944, the Foreign Office requested that the Swiss Government (the Protecting Power) make 'a strong complaint to the German Government regarding the conditions in which British prisoners-of-war were transferred from Italy to Germany'.

> Reliable information has been received by the War Office of disgraceful conditions during the transfer of 1,500 British prisoners of war from Stalag III D to Stalag IV G. and other Stalags in the area of Wehrkreis IV during during November, 1943. These conditions give grounds for serious complaint.

> It appears that during the journeys referred to above prisoners of war were crowded into cattle trucks at the rate of 45 men to each truck and were also compelled to march at a pace which forced them to jettison food and personal effects which were irretrievably lost.

> Further it appears that during these journeys prisoners of war were struck so severely with bayonets and and rifle butts that several had to receive medical attention.

> Such treatment indicates a total disregard of the obligations imposed by the Prisoner of War Convention.[99]

The British official history of the events recounted in this chapter acknowledges assistance rendered by some three-score individuals, some of whom were participants in the events of 1945. Not one, however, was drawn from among victims of the operations extolled in the report. On the other hand, an entire tearful concluding chapter is devoted to 'THE ORDEAL OF HAROLD MACMILLAN'.[100]

---

[1] James Brown Scott (ed.), *Les conventions et déclarations de La Haye de 1899 et 1907* (New York, 1918), p. 116.

[2] 'Here it was Cossacks, vaguely reputed to have been fighting for the Germans, who had first of all to be escorted from the concentration area in the hills to some hurriedly but very efficiently built cages put up by German pw, before being entrained for Russia in accordance with an agreement made with Marshal Stalin at Yalta. The encaging went well and at the end of the day

about 3,600 horses, 1,225 grooms, 3,872 ORs, 105 Cossack Officers, 6 Priests, 8 women, 2 Vets and a 2 M.Os had been netted' (WO.170/4982).

[3] AFHQ – 8 Army (17 May 1945): 'Chetniks and dissident Jugoslavs infiltrating into areas occupied by Allied troops should be treated as disarmed enemy troops and evacuated to British concentration area in Distone. Total numbers including eleven thousand already in Distone believed about thirty five thousand' (FO.1020/42,116).

[4] General V. Naumenko (ed.), *Великое Предательство: Выдача Казаков в Лиенце и Других Местах (1945-1947); Сборник материалов и документов* (New York, 1962-70), i, pp. 231, 262; Zoe Polanska-Palmer, *Yalta Victim* (Edinburgh, 1986), p. 137; Gordon and William Dritschilo, *Survivors of Lienz: A Dritschilo Family Memoir* (Bethesda, Md., 2006), pp. 102, 104, 105.

[5] N.N. Krasnov, *Незабываемое 1945-1956* (San Francisco, 1957), p. 20.

[6] 'Воспоминания Галины Захарьевны Блашинской', in Elena Shupilina (ed.), *Станичный Вестник* (Montreal, 2005), xxxix, p. 39.

[7] FO.1020/42,135.

[8] WO.170/4396.

[9] Cf. Omer Bartov, *The Eastern Front, 1941-45, German Troops and the Barbarisation of Warfare* (Basingstoke, 1985), pp. 106-19.

[10] Naumenko (ed.), *Великое Предательство,* i, p. 156.

[11] *Ibid.,* i, pp. 158-59.

[12] For another testimony to this regrettable justification, with its echoes of the defense plea at Nuremberg, cf. Viktor Karpov, 'Долгая дорога в Лиенц', in N.S. Timofeev and S.D. Bodrov (ed.), *Война и судьбы* (Nevinnomyssk, 2002-5), ii, p. 67.

[13] Cf. Ariadna Delianich, *Вольфсберг - 373* (San Francisco, 1950), p. 60; Father Michael Protopopov, *"Живых Проглотим их...": Пут от Георгиевского Креста к Голгофе* (Melbourne, 2000), p. 255; Dritschilo, *Survivors of Lienz,* pp. 103, 104-5.

[14] Letter of 2nd December 1975.

[15] Dritschilo, *Survivors of Lienz,* pp. 181-83.

[16] Davies sworn witness statement, 1989.

[17] Nicholas Bethell, *The Last Secret: Forcible Repatriation to Russia 1944-7* (London, 1974), p. 148.

[18] Evgenia Polskaya, *Это мы, Господи пред Тобою...* (Nevinnomyssk, 1998), p. 29.

[19] Naumenko (ed.), *Великое Предательство,* i, plate XXVIII.

[20] *Ibid.,* pp. 183-6. Where possible, I checked Olga Rotova's invaluable diary account with Major Davies, who confirmed its accuracy. For his denial on the morning of 29 May that he knew the officers would not return, cf. the account by another English-speaking Cossack woman (*ibid.,* p. 123).

[21] WO.170/4461.

[22] Naumenko (ed.), *Великое Предательство*, i, pp. 124, 147, 199; ii, p. 60.

[23] *Ibid.*, i, p. 124; Józef Mackiewicz, *Kontra* (Paris, 1957), p. 188.

[24] In the gulag it was widespread policy to separate children from their mothers, the former being regarded as state property (B.K. Ganusovsky, *10 Лет за Железным Занавесом 1945-1955: Записки Жертвы Ялты. Выдача XV Казачего Корпуса* (San Francisco, 1983), pp. 97-100).

[25] Naumenko (ed.), *Великое Предательство*, i, pp. 124-25.

[26] *Ibid.*, p. 186; Mackiewicz, *Kontra*, p. 189.

[27] WO.170/4461.

[28] 'The alleged ration strength of the Caucasians totalled 4,800 men, women and children... it was not possible to hold a physical check of numbers; there is little doubt that the figure was exaggerated' (WO.170/4461).

[29] Naumenko (ed.), *Великое Предательство*, i, pp. 106-7; ii, pp. 171-73.

[30] WO.170/4461.

[31] I am grateful to the late Colonel Odling-Smee and his son John for this and much other relevant information.

[32] *Ibid.*; WO.170/4993.

[33] Victor Kravchenko, *I Chose Freedom: The Personal and Political Life of a Soviet Official* (London, 1947), p. 405. Kravchenko learned of this incident when working for the *Sovnarkom* in Moscow, the authority which controlled such plants.

[34] WO. 170/4993; WO.170/4461.

[35] Cf. David J. Dallin and Boris I. Nicolaevsky, *Forced Labor in Soviet Russia* (London, 1948), pp. 270-73; Robert Conquest, *The Great Terror: Stalin's Purge of the Thirties* (London, 1968), pp. 339-40.

[36] Instances from voluminous literature recounting the degrading and horrific maltreatment of women in the gulag are to be found in Elinor Lipper, *Eleven Years in Soviet Prison Camps* (London, 1951), pp. 7-8, 15-17, 27-29, 120, 124-41, 214, 294-5; Dimitri Panin, *The Notebooks of Sologdin* (London, 1976), pp. 178-81; Robert Conquest, *Kolyma: The Arctic Death Camps* (London, 1978), pp. 28, 30-34, 176-99; Ganusovsky, *10 Лет за Железным Занавесом 1945-1955*, pp. 97-102.

[37] Naumenko (ed.), *Великое Предательство*, ii, pp. 74-5. Cf. the touching account of an Astrakhan Cossack's farewell to his camel, in Peter J. Huxley-Blythe, *The East Came West* (Caldwell, Idaho, 1964), pp. 71-72.

[38] Elena Yakovlevna Shupilina (ed.), *Лиенц – Казачья Голгофа* (Ottawa, 2005), p. 14.

[39] Naumenko (ed.), *Великое Предательство*, i, p. 190.

[40] *Ibid.*, p. 259.

[41] 'Die Kosakische Tragödie', *National Zeitung* (30/5/75), p. 6.

[42] Naumenko (ed.), *Великое Предательство*, i, p. 224. The 36th Infantry Brigade Order 17 of 29th May stipulated that 'it is hoped that all trains will arrive at loading points by 0500 hrs on the day of departure' (WO.170/4396).

[43] WO.170/4461; Naumenko (ed.), *Великое Предательство*, i, pp. 225-26.

[44] WO.170/4461; Naumenko (ed.), *Великое Предательство*, i, p. 229.

[45] *Ibid.*, pp. 199-203. Boris Borisov, a White émigré from Bulgaria bearing a Nansen Certificate, was present when the service was brutally interrupted. 'The trucks were backed up and the soldiers began throwing people into the trucks. They tried to grab children so the mothers would follow them into the trucks. They used rifle butts, clubs and bayonets (weren't the king's soldiers brave against innocent women, children and the elderly)' (Trial testimony of 8 August 1989).

[46] Naumenko (ed.), *Великое Предательство*, i, pp. 205-6, 228-29; ii, p. 54.

[47] *Ibid.*, pp. 228-30, 260-61; Huxley-Blythe, *The East Came West*, p. 156. It is not always clear whether the vehicles (*танкетки*) mentioned in Cossack eyewitness accounts were armoured cars or Bren-gun carriers. A contemporary photograph shows one of the former in the square at Peggetz on 1st June (Naumenko (ed.), *Великое Предательство*, i,, plate XXIX). Some Cossacks believe that tanks were employed to cow the defenceless victims, but Professor Verbitsky, an intelligent eyewitness, emphasizes that they were not tracked vehicles but armored cars with rubber tyres (G.G. Verbitsky, *Остарбайтеры: История Россиян Насильственно Вывезенных на Работы в Германию (Вторая Мировая Война)* (Vestal, NY, 2001), p. 260). Colonel Malcolm also emphasized to me that no tanks were present.

[48] WO.170/4461.

[49] Polanska-Palmer, *Yalta Victim*, pp. 51-82.

[50] Evgenia Polskaya found the day bloodier than anything she had experienced throughout four harrowing years of war (*Это мы, Господи пред Тобою*, p. 40).

[51] Polanska-Palmer, *Yalta Victim*, pp. 128-29.

[52] Gustav Rasmussen (ed.), *Code des prisonniers de guerre: Commentaire de la convention du 27 juillet 1929 relative au traitement des prisonniers de guerre* (Copenhagen, 1931), p. 109.

[53] Polanska-Palmer, *Yalta Victim*, p. 130.

[54] Naumenko (ed.), *Великое Предательство*, i, pp. 200-3.

[55] Alexei Somoff, who was present as a small boy, recalls seeing 'an English officer or an N.C.O. He looked at us and covered his face with his hands. He appeared to be sobbing or was in a state of shock (shame)'.

[56] Polanska-Palmer, *Yalta Victim*, pp. 129-37; personal communications from Dr Pinching and my late dear friend Zoe.

[57] Naumenko (ed.), *Великое Предательство*, i, pp. 227-30.

[58] Rasmussen (ed.), *Code des prisonniers de guerre*, p. 115.

[59] *Ibid.*, p. 209. Dr. Pinching told me he did not recall this brief exchange, but believed it consistent with his state of mind at the time. He himself saw the battalion's tough 2 i/c, Major Leask, also weeping.

[60] Polskaya, *Это мы, Господи пред Тобою*, pp. 23, 49, 76; Verbitsky, *Остарбайтеры*, p. 260.

[61] Naumenko (ed.), *Великое Предательство*, i, pp. 209, 210.

[62] Cf. Polskaya, *Это мы, Господи пред Тобою*, pp. 39-44.

[63] WO.170/4988.

[64] Polskaya, *Это мы, Господи пред Тобою*, pp. 40-41. One of Christopher Booker's two trumpeted discoveries during a 'research' visit to Peggetz was that 'the solid wooden bridge across the Drau is still there' (Christopher Booker, *A Looking-Glass Tragedy: The Controversy over the Repatriations from Austria in 1945* (London, 1997) , p. 407). In fact, what he saw was a subsequent bridge of different construction at another location. By his own account, the nearest he ever came to meeting an eyewitness of the event was an encounter with a local Austrian youth, who recalled his grandmother's mentioning dimly-remembered Cossacks (*A Looking-Glass Tragedy*, p. 407). Although these two incidents (the wrong bridge and the dead grandmother) constituted the sum total of Booker's discoveries during his expedition, his researches at Lienz are grandly described in the index to his *magnum opus* as 'how [Cossacks are] remembered in Austria today' (*ibid.*, p. 463). It is characteristic of Gregor Dallas's deeply muddled account of these events that he thinks there were *two* bridges in 1945. He also believes that General Krasnov commanded the Cossack Corps in Croatia, and that Christopher Booker 'spent several decades researching and disputing Tolstoy's account' (*Poisoned Peace: 1945 – The War that Never Ended* (London, 2005), pp. 389, 521-24). In fact Booker conducted no research, and spent the first years of his effusions in the press vigorously *endorsing* my conclusions.

[65] *National Zeitung*, 6/6/75.

[66] Naumenko (ed.), *Великое Предательство*, ii, pp. 110-12. For the incident with the dog, see also *ibid.*, i, p. 233.

[67] *Ibid.*, i, pp. 134, 201, 233; ii, p. 54; *National Zeitung*, 30th May 1975; Polanska-Palmer, *Yalta Victim*, p. 131.

[68] Naumenko (ed.), *Великое Предательство*, i, p. 210.

[69] *Ibid.*, p. 233. Dr. Pinching recalled a 'four- or five-storey hospital' in Lienz, but could not confirm or refute the authenticity of this account. On 29 June 'a Medical Officer at NUISDORF Hospital informed the Coy Commander there, that most of the people intended to commit suicide' (WO.170/5018).

[70] Cossack sources, which give the names of the family, list only two children (Naumenko (ed.), *Великое Предательство*, i, p. 233; ii, p. 111).

[71] *Ibid.*, i, p. 234.

[72] *Ibid.*, p. 210.

[73] A. Petrovsky, *Unvergessener Verrat!: Roosevelt - Stalin - Churchill 1945* (Munich, 1965), p. 27.

[74] Vera Lafferty (née Bratjakina), 'Lienz revisited, sixty years later', in Elena Shupilina (ed.), *Станичный Вестник* (Montreal, 2005), l, p. 38. The figure

of 700 interred beneath the cemetery at Peggetz may reflect the estimated total of casualties around Lienz, since Mrs Patzold is presumably unlikely to have counted them. Nevertheless, there is no reason to doubt her account of the mass grave. Eyewitness descriptions of the comparable British use of bulldozers to inter thousands of Cossack horses are recounted below. Another local witness, Bartholomäus Plautz, recalled the 'common grave' (*Massengrab*) in the cemetery at Peggetz (Wenzel, *So gingen die Kosaken durch die Hölle*, p. 39).

[75] WO.170/5022; WO.170/5018.

[76] WO. 170/4396.

[77] 'At OBER DRAUBURG are the corpses of eight COSSACKS shot whilst trying to escape' (WO.170/4389).

[78] Imperial War Museum Department of Sound Records, Accession No 003896/07.

[79] This account of operations near Oberdrauburg is taken from the War Diaries: WO.170/5022; WO.170/5018; WO.170/4461.

[80] Naumenko (ed.), *Великое Предательство*, i, pp. 206-8.

[81] Information from Major J. W. French.

[82] FO.371/51227.

[83] Booker, *A Looking-Glass Tragedy*, pp. 294-95, 434.

[84] Cf. Naumenko (ed.), *Великое Предательство*, ii, pp. 55-56.

[85] 'When the Company of 6 RWK responsible for the loading arrived at the first camp they found about 1000 Cossacks kneeling, praying and singing hymns. A few moved voluntarily to the transport provided. The remainder, after a few had been hit with pick helves and rifle butts, followed shortly afterwards' (WO.170/4461, Appx B).

[86] Verbitsky, *Остарбайтеры*, p. 262.

[87] For the history of these horses and Katinka in particular, cf. Lt.-Col. A.D. Malcolm, *History of the Argyll and Sutherland 8th Battalion 1939-47* (London, 1949), pp. 252-8; Lt.-Col. G.I. Malcolm of Poltalloch, *Argyllshire Highlanders 1860-1960* (Glasgow, 1960), pp. 116-17). Retention of the sixty Cossack grooms is described in Naumenko (ed.), *Великое Предательство*, ii, pp. 81-85.

[88] WO.170/4461. Elsewhere in the same file the much higher estimate of 'some 4,100' is given.

[89] Naumenko (ed.), *Великое Предательство*, i, p. 191.

[90] WO.170/4396; WO.170/4461.

[91] For a vivid account of the hazards of one such successful crossing, *vide* Naumenko (ed.), *Великое Предательство*, i, pp. 201-3. Nikolai Krasnov's wife Lily stayed hidden in the mountains, returning to Peggetz when she learned of the amnesty belatedly extended to old émigrés. Her husband learned of this from a Cossack in the Kamyshlag forced labour camp complex near Omsk (N.N. Krasnov, *Незабываемое 1945-1956* (San Francisco,

1957), p. 227). Mrs. Tatiana Danilievich described to me how she lay concealed in a Lienz cellar throughout the time of terror.

[92] WO.170/4396.

[93] WO.170/4461. Cf. Naumenko (ed.), *Великое Предательство*, ii, pp. 35-6; Bethell, *The Last Secret*, pp. 151-56; Verbitsky, *Остарбайтеры*, p. 261; Protopopov, *"Живых Проглотим их..."*, p. 255; Dritschilo, *Survivors of Lienz*, pp. 103, 104-5.

[94] WO.170/4461; information from Duncan Macmillan, o/c the convoy.

[95] Nikolai Tolstoy, *Victims of Yalta* (Corgi Books, 1979), p. 21. For an eyewitness description of the NKVD reception camp at Graz, cf. Petrovsky, *Unvergessener Verrat!*, pp. 249-51.

[96] Cf. *Это мы, Господи пред Тобою*, pp. 49-50.

[97] FO.1020/39.

[98] Stefan Karner, *Im Archipel GUPVI: Kriegsgefangenschaft und Internierung in der Sowjetunion 1941-1956* (Vienna and Munich, 1995), pp. 20-24. Cf *idem*, 'Zur zwangsweisen Übergabe der Kosaken an die Sowjets 1945 in Judenburg', in Harald Stadler, Rolf Steininger, and Karl C. Berger (ed.), *Die Kosaken im Ersten und Zweiten Weltkrieg* (Innsbruck, 2008), pp. 145-46; V.N. Zemskov, *Возращение советских перемещенных лиц в СССР. 1944-1952 гг.* (Moscow, 2016), pp. 340-48.

[99] FO.916/888.

[100] Brigadier Anthony Cowgill, Lord Brimelow, and Christopher Booker Esq, *The Repatriations from Austria in 1945: The Report of an Inquiry* (London, 1990), pp. xi, 211-17.

CHAPTER XIV
THE SECRET BETRAYAL
OF THE WHITE GENERALS

When Germany collapsed, it was found that very large numbers of Soviet Russians – mostly, no doubt, from non-political motives – had changed sides and were fighting for the Germans. Also, a small but not negligible proportion of the Russian prisoners and Displaced Persons refused to go back to the U.S.S.R., and some of them, at least, were repatriated against their will. These facts, known to many journalists on the spot, went almost unmentioned in the British Press, while at the same time Russophile publicists in England continued to justify the purges and deportations of 1936-8 by claiming that the U.S.S.R. 'had no quislings'.

George Orwell, 'The Prevention of Literature' (1946)

The resolutions of the Yalta and Potsdam conferences were the subject of daily discussion and criticism [in Butyrki NKVD gaol]. No one could grasp how America and England could make concessions which they could never retrieve. How could Roosevelt and Churchill agree to hand over their own prisoners to the Bolsheviks? Had the western world learnt nothing at all of Soviet policy during the years since the Revolution, when it could allow the Red power to spread over one country after the other, right to the heart of Europe?

Unto Parvilahti, *Beria's Gardens: Ten Years' Captivity in Russia and Siberia* (London, 1959), p. 60.

The chronology of events has been diverted somewhat by the tragic events recounted in the last chapter. This is because it is essential to show what were the deadly consequences of the 5th Corps's decision to detach the officers of the *Kazachi Stan* from the great mass of Cossacks with their womenfolk and children, in order to fulfill to the letter the secret Soviet demand for Generals Krasnov, Shkuro, and other Cossack officers.

As we have seen, the extensive bloodshed and cruelty described in the previous chapter occurred only in the case of Cossacks and Caucasians held by 36th Infantry Brigade in the vicinity of the towns of Lienz and Oberdrauburg. Everywhere else, substantial bodies of Cossacks were handed over to the Soviets with little or no violence. Instead, large-scale deception was widely employed, the victims being duped into believing they were being diverted to other camps. Britain's widespread reputation for honor and decency accounts for the relative ease with which this uncharacteristic resort to mendacity was effected.

The disparity of treatment in the case of the Cossacks and Caucasians around Lienz can only be accounted for by 5 Corps's overriding requirement to ensure safe delivery of the Cossack officers, the majority of whom were not Soviet citizens and hence not liable to repatriation under the terms of the Yalta Agreement. As 5th Corps's order of 24 May 1945 emphasized,

> It is of the utmost importance that all the off[ice]rs and particularly senior com[man]d[er]s are rounded up and that none are allowed to escape.

When, on 11 May, Brigadier Tryon delivered the Soviet demand for the leading White Russian generals to General Keightley, the latter initially expressed strong distaste at the idea of complying ('over my dead body'). Nevertheless, appreciating that it represented a request going well beyond the relevant remit (*i.e.* the 8th Army screening order of 13 March), he seized opportunity to request advice from Harold Macmillan, Resident Minister in the Mediterranean, who was at that moment fortuitously visiting the neighbouring 13th Corps.

As we know, Macmillan issued Keightley with 'advice', subsequently confirmed as an unequivocal 'verbal directive', to deliver up all the Cossacks, among whom he expressly included 'White Russians'. The politically ignorant but coldly ambitious Keightley was sufficiently overawed by – or concerned to ingratiate himself with – the influential politician to implement this instruction. Particular satisfaction was expressed by the Soviets for inclusion of the leading White Russian generals Krasnov and Shkuro. As an immediately ensuing Soviet report puts it:

> The generals included: general-ataman KRASNOV, lieutenant-general SHKURO, major-general KRASNOV /nephew of general ataman KRASNOV /, major-general DOMANOV / ataman of the cavalry corps/ and a number of other generals.

Of these named commanders, only Domanov was a Soviet citizen.

This sinister factor in the agreement was throughout withheld by Keightley from higher command.

In his television interview with Ludovic Kennedy broadcast on 21 December 1984, Macmillan declared:

> Then there were about 30,000 Cossacks, who had been recruited by the

Germans... Then there were a lot of so-called White Russians who were with the Germans, in order to support Germany against Russia, I suppose... It was harsh in some ways, because no doubt some of these White Russians were people who'd been against the Communist regime for years. Still they were on the Germans' side and working with the Germans, and we hadn't a great – you must remember the conditions at the time. Russia was, after all, our great ally, and we'd made the agreement and so we carried it out'...

Kennedy: 'But the White Russians, some of them had never been in Russia. They were children of people who'd come out of Russia in the Revolution'.

Macmillan: 'Well, why were they up there?'

Kennedy: 'Well, they were fighting with the Germans, weren't they?'

Macmillan: 'Yes, they were fighting with the/I mean, they weren't/we'd been fighting the Germans for six years – they're not friends of ours –

Kennedy: 'Russia wasn't their/ they were White Russians; Russia wasn't their motherland any more, was it?'

Macmillan: 'Well, that was laid down accordingly. It was a very strict rule according to the date of their birth, or of leaving Russia. If they'd left between certain dates, they weren't handed over'.

Macmillan's evasiveness in this exchange is patent, and struck Kennedy (as he informed me) at the time. The last sentence Macmillan knew to be wholly false. By his own admission, recorded immediately following his meeting with Keightley on 13 May 1945, it was he who uniquely directed the handover of White Russians as a designated entity. Another of his obfuscating exculpations is telling:

> ... there may have been some unfortunate people who managed to get to Paris or something, picked up by the Germans, got somehow into a camp and were claimed as Russian citizens. These would be ... like our friends Prince Obolensky and all the people we knew. There may have been some, but I wouldn't have thought very many, but there may have been. [1]

Macmillan's citing of Prince Obolensky as the type of White Russian he had in mind is suggestive. A glamorous older contemporary of his at Oxford was Prince Serge Obolensky, who might well have struck him as a typical distinguished White Russian. He was a striking figure, who during the Second World War became a Colonel in OSS, the American counterpart of British SOE and forerunner of the CIA, and perhaps yet more glamorously danced with Marilyn Monroe. In late 1943, he and General Theodore Roosevelt (son of President Theodore Roosevelt) called on Macmillan in Algiers. The purpose of their visit was to urge the Minister's support for General Draža Mihailović's royalist resistance movement in Yugoslavia. He and Obolensky offered to fly to Mihailović's headquarters to establish a liaison with the Allies. Macmillan was dismayed by the proposal, explaining firmly that it was current British policy to support the communist Tito over the royalist Mihailović. Roosevelt and Obolensky were horrified by what they regarded as a betrayal of the patriotic resistance in Yugoslavia, and vigorously urged a change of policy. Macmillan, however, remained adamant in supporting the communists, as a predictable consequence of which,

> Tito delivered into the hands of the Reds some two million Yugoslavians – good, stable, religious, conservative people, who could have formed a solid support for a pro-Allied government in Yugoslavia.[2]

Although Macmillan significantly omitted mention of this dramatic contretemps from his published war diaries, it was surely this Prince Obolensky that he had in mind, rather than some less distinguished relative. Moreover, the issue under dispute with Serge Obolensky – the betrayal of anti-communist Yugoslavs – might well have triggered a disturbing memory, given that forcible handover of thousands of anti-communist royalist Serbs by 5th Corps to Tito's butchery occurred in 1945 alongside the similarly savage policy adopted towards the Cossacks. This inhuman and unauthorized action was urged by Macmillan on General Robertson, Chief Administrative Officer at Allied Force Headquarters.

Macmillan was well aware both of the protected status of Russians who had never been Soviet citizens, and the presence of the distinctive and substantial number of White Russians held by 5th Corps, who included notable figures on whom Stalin was particularly concerned to wreak vengeance. Macmillan himself said so; the SMERSH officer Soloviev, who conducted the secret agreement with 5th Corps, explained that it was *primarily* the White generals whom the Soviets sought. The 57th Red Army war diary records their specific inclusion as the salient factor in the handover agreement. Macmillan responded to Keightley's request for a ruling on the fate of the White émigrés with 'advice' that they be expressly included in the handover – 'advice' which, when his favored policy became threatened by Field Marshal Alexander's humane intervention, was strengthened into an emphatic 'verbal directive' which Keightley explained he regarded as operative.

In view of this overwhelming body of evidence, a candid reader might wonder how the British Government's subsequent version of events, which asseverated that Macmillan bore no responsibility whatever for inclusion of the old émigrés, might conceivably be sustained? The answer is neither credibly nor creditably. Brigadier Cowgill and his collaborators, working under instructions from the British government of the day, undertook successive desperate attempts to exculpate Macmillan by drawing attention to a few instances – in almost every case unconnected with the Cossacks held by 5th Corps – where the term 'White Russians' was used loosely or ignorantly with reference to anti-communist Russians generally, and contended that it was to these that Macmillan alluded in his diary. In reality, such slipshod usage cannot have been applicable to the Cossacks whose handover Macmillan urged on 13 May, when he drew the identical distinction among the Cossacks, with his reference to '40,000 Cossacks **and White Russians**', as did the 57th Red Army war diary's description at the same time of the agreement to hand over 'the whole collection of Russian traitors to the Motherland [*i.e.* those Cossacks who were Soviet citizens] **and the White emigrants**'.

Realizing the weakness of their 'argument', the apologists slyly shifted their ground to espouse an entirely distinct consideration, drawing attention to an authentic White Russian formation in 5th Corps hands, which they sought to identify as the 'White Russians' to whom Macmillan referred.[3] This was the 4,500-strong *Russkii Korpus*, recruited from émigré remnants of Baron Wrangel's army following its evacuation from the Crimea in 1920, who had been granted refuge by King Alexander of Yugoslavia, and eventually succeeded in effecting a fighting retreat into Austria in May 1945. The trouble with this ingenious defense is that handover of the *Russkii Korpus* is not recorded at any time even to have been considered, whether by the British or (perhaps surprisingly) the Soviets.[4] Their presence in Austria is wholly irrelevant to the issue. It is in addition telling that neither of these specious prevarications was advanced by Macmillan himself, who acknowledged to his authorized biographer Alistair Horne that he 'was prepared to 'take the blame' for sending back the White Russians 'by mistake''. That Macmillan 'was prepared to 'take the blame'' can only mean that it was he who authorized the handover, and that he was wrong in having done so – now that the issue had unexpectedly become public. His cautious acceptance of blame also contradicts the claim advanced on his behalf that 'In military matters, Macmillan could only advise. He could not direct'.[5]

Faced with this awkward admission, Horne proffered yet another casuistic defense

> Had he been involved in some underhand conspiracy, he would hardly have allowed the entry about the 'White Russians' ... to stand in his diary

entry for 13 May, or then to publish it after the Tolstoy attack had been made.[6]

Macmillan's *War Diaries* were published in 1984, some time after my earliest suspicion of his responsibility for the Cossack betrayal appeared in print. However, in his eagerness to exculpate his employer, Horne ignored or suppressed the fact that Macmillan had *already* made public reference to his part in the decision to hand over 'about 40,000 Cossacks and White Russians, with their wives and children' – in his memoirs, which were published a decade before I came to write anything on the topic.[7] Indeed, it was this allusion that first aroused my suspicions about his involvement in the tragedy.[8] Obviously, Macmillan could not have withheld the reference from his *War Diaries* without arousing the likelihood of questions being asked concerning the prior reference in his memoirs.

Again, it is telling that Macmillan himself never adopted any of the spurious defenses of his conduct advanced by the Cowgill Inquiry, Alistair Horne, John Keegan, Christopher Booker, Hugh Trevor-Roper, and the like. He doubtless recognized their vulnerably fallacious nature, and was too wary to risk exposure by endorsing them.

Macmillan's own words to Ludovic Kennedy ('some unfortunate people who managed to get to Paris or something') confirm that he had in mind old émigrés scattered about Western Europe since the Russian Revolution.

More might be adduced to confirm Macmillan's active role, both in the Cossack handover generally and the illicit inclusion of the White Russians in particular. However, I suspect any open-minded reader will already have accepted the overwhelming evidence for his culpability, and return now to events on the ground in Austria. These further confirm the impossibility of ascribing the inclusion of the White Russians generally, and of Generals Krasnov and Shkuro in particular, to mere blunder or misunderstanding. That there was indeed a 'Klagenfurt conspiracy' is I believe now established beyond contention.

Evidence never before published confirms that the illicit handover of Generals Krasnov, Shkuro, and Kelich-Ghirei represented, not an unfortunate ancillary outcome, but *the primary concern* of General Keightley and his Chief of Staff, Brigadier Low. The conspiratorial nature of their betrayal will now be made yet more manifest, while 5th Corps's withholding of any reference to their handover from Keightley's superiors at 8th Army, 15th Army Group, and AFHQ is established beyond dispute.

We may now resume the personal history of Generals Krasnov, Shkuro, and Kelich-Ghirei, following their surrender to the British in May 1945. As was seen at the conclusion of Chapter 7, following their few months' turbulent sojourn in Northern Italy, the Cossacks had withdrawn before the final triumphant advance of the Allied armies in Northern Italy into Austria.

General Keightley and his chief of staff, Brigadier Low, now found themselves in an awkward quandary. On 13 May they had received 'advice' from Harold Macmillan to deliver *all* Cossacks in their hands to the Soviets. This 'advice', confirmed ten days later in more explicit terminology as a 'verbal directive', specifically included 'White Russians' among categories to be surrendered to the Red Army. However anxious Keightley proved himself to be to oblige the influential Minister, the fact remained that Macmillan possessed no formal authority to issue orders to the military, who continued bound by the 8th Army directive of 13 March, which stipulated in unambiguous terms that

> All persons of undoubted Soviet Citizenship will be repatriated irrespective of their own wishes. In cases where nationality is in doubt, personnel concerned will be sent to 373 PW Camp for adjudication.

The fundamental issues are as follows.

1. Why did Keightley on 13 May seek a ruling from Macmillan regarding the response he should give to the Soviet demand handed to Brigadier Tryon? After all, he was *already* in possession of the order from 8th Army to return all Cossacks (*i.e.* the great majority) who were 'of undoubted Soviet Citizenship', while 'in cases where [Soviet] nationality is in doubt' individuals were required to be dispatched to Italy for screening. Nothing could be more explicit, or easy of fulfilment, with regard to either category.

2. The 8th Army order of 13 March reflected Foreign Office instructions to Macmillan, sent on 19 and 20 February 1945, the crux of which was that 'All persons of undoubted Soviet citizenship must be repatriated irrespective of their own wishes', while any individual of Russian origin who was not a Soviet citizen 'must not (repeat not) be sent back to the Soviet Union unless he expressly desires to be so'. Why then did Macmillan find Keightley's request so unusually sensitive that he suddenly extended the itinerary agreed with Field Marshal Alexander in order to fly to advise the General in Austria? Could he not simply have reminded Keightley of

settled British policy regarding both Soviet citizens and White emigrants?[9] Macmillan, after all, was as much bound by the ruling as was Keightley.

Since Keightley was already in possession of an order requiring return to the Soviets of all Soviet nationals, Cossack or otherwise, the sole bone of contention lay in the request handed to Brigadier Tryon for the inclusion of some twenty prominent officers, all save one of whom were patently not Soviet citizens. Their handover was expressly prohibited under Allied policy directives, and constituted the sole matter of controversy contained in the Soviet demand. How is it possible to avoid the conclusion that Macmillan considered the issue raised by Keightley so delicate as to require a private face-to-face discussion? Both Macmillan and Keightley withheld from 8th Army all mention of the Soviet demand for the old émigrés, and colluded to obtain General Robertson's directive deceptively calling for 'all Russians' (as opposed to the precise 'Soviet citizens') to be handed over. We do not need to look further for an explanation of Macmillan's concern to engage in an immediate covert discussion in person with Keightley.

No one was better placed than Brigadier Tryon-Wilson to address this issue, and he was explicit when I spoke with him in a conversation recorded on 17 December 1985. To my enquiry 'I wonder what was the reason you went up there [Voitsberg on 11 May]: the main reason?', he responded:

> I think to find out from General Keightley's point of view as to what exactly it was that they were expecting in the context of handing over those who were not affected by the Yalta Agreement.

This indicates that his Red Army hosts had already approached Keightley on the topic during his visit on 10 May – possibly at a general level, not identifying individual Cossack leaders. As Tryon-Wilson further attested, the demand for General Shkuro, who had been appointed a Knight Commander of the Bath by King George V, was regarded as particularly shocking, and Keightley's reaction on being shown the list on the afternoon of 11 May was 'over my dead body!'

First-hand evidence thus confirms that the great bone of contention lay, not in the handover of Cossacks generally (an issue which had in any case yet to be formally raised by the Soviets), but in the proposed inclusion of émigré White Russian officers, whose 'return' was prohibited by the Foreign Office's instructions to Macmillan of 19 and 20 February 1945, and the relevant 8th Army order to 5th Corps of 13 March. At his 1989 libel trial, Aldington claimed that this order provided

> a very loose definition, and I do remember it being ambiguous, that's
> why in fact questions were asked ... why we had to try and answer some
> questions –

presumably those posed by the divisional commanders concerned. Revealingly, Aldington here let slip that he was *at the time* familiar with the text of the 13 March order. At the same time, he was well aware that its provisions were in no way 'ambiguous'. The text states succinctly and unequivocally that no Russian is to be handed over who is not 'of undoubted Soviet Citizenship', which actually goes beyond retention of those who could *prove* their non-Soviet status on the evidence of a Nansen Certificate, foreign passport, or other documentation (which in fact almost everyone affected possessed). Under the Foreign Office ruling, lack of positive proof of Soviet citizenship sufficed to protect suspects from handover.

Where doubt existed 'personnel concerned will be sent to 373 PW Camp for 'adjudication'. Here 'adjudication' is plainly synonymous with screening, which is what in fact occurred in the case of captured Russians dispatched there. At the 1989 trial Aldington sought to dismiss this provision, on grounds that

> it has some extraordinary statements about sending them all to some 373
> PW Camp, which is not relevant to the time about which we are talking.[10]

In reality, 373 PW Camp was throughout the time the Cossacks' fate was being decided conveniently situated across the Italian frontier, near Mestre inland from Venice.[11] That is to say, it was situated at much the same distance from Lienz as Judenburg, where Cossacks required to be screened were instead handed over to SMERSH. Nor is Aldington's claim acceptable that 373 PW Camp lacked adequate facilities for screening large numbers of prisoners. On 10 June, for example, 8th Army reported to AFHQ that '2500 of 3000 Russians held at Mestre NOT Soviet citizens'.[12]

About this time, too, a body of several thousand Ukrainian troops in German service was transferred from Austria to Northern Italy. Although some delay was necessarily incurred, no insuperable problem was envisaged in subjecting them to individual screening. Nor was any other ill effect anticipated or incurred, such as a Soviet refusal to return liberated British prisoners of war, etc.

As a report of 18 June to AFHQ explained after their arrival,

> Approx 11000 Ukrainians in sep concentration area. Of these, some 70
> per cent believed to come from pre-1939 Russia but nearly all disclaim
> Soviet citizenship. Will therefore have to be interrogated in detail by

Russian speaking Officer now being despatched by you. This process
will take time and will therefore be unable to have Soviet citizens among
them sorted in time to despatch at end of present programme.[13]

Besides, had some insuperable difficulty in screening the Cossacks
really existed, why did 5th Corps not raise the problem with 8th Army?
Setting aside emergency conditions on the battlefield, it is unheard of in
regular military practice for an order deemed impractical of fulfilment to
be simply ignored, without raising the problem with higher command.

In addition, subordinate units within 5th Corps were kept in ignorance
by Corps Headquarters of the requirement to screen Russians potentially
liable for repatriation. The afternoon following the betrayal of the White
officers a report from 8th Argylls at Lienz raised this pertinent query.

> Germagen Rodionoff was evacuated yesterday with the Cossack officers.
> He is not a Russian subject and has been living in Paris for 15 years.
> Apparently, he is a teacher. His family is in France, and it would appear
> that he has been put in the Cossack camp by mistake. May we have your
> advice. It seems highly probable that there are a large number of persons
> at present in the Cossack camp who are not of Russian origin. What is
> the position regarding these people.[14]

No response from 5th Corps headquarters is to be found in the records.
Why not?

Nor in fact was there any pressing necessity to conduct the screening
on the southern side of the Carnian Alps. Captain A. P. Judge was at the
time attached to Brigadier Musson's staff at 36th Infantry Brigade. As he
explained to me,

> ... I am surprised that the handover of the Cossacks should have been
> done with no attempt at screening. For the officers this would have
> presented no great problem in the Spittal P.W. camp. It might initially
> have been rough and ready but ... many genuine cases could have been
> easily established and the proportion would certainly have given food for
> thought.

Shortly afterwards he was engaged in checking DPs in the Brigade area.

> With a Slav interpreter but speaking mostly French and German, I spent
> a whole day going through their documents and their backgrounds. There
> were 120 persons all told, men, women and children and they split down
> into 19 different nationalities, including a Czech national of Turkish
> extraction! The largest single group were White Russians from France
> and Belgium, carrying the appropriate carte d'identite and permis de
> sejour, etc. etc. One I remember well had worked in Rumania for the Red
> Cross and still carried a letter of commendation from a Capt. Mackenzie

for services rendered to Russian refugees in 1919-20. I reported back to
Brig. Musson that none were Soviet citizens and all had documentation
to show it. My information seemed to be greeted with some relief.

(This was after Field Marshal Alexander's personal intervention during his
visit to 5th Corps on 4-5 June). However, despite Captain Judge's evidence
of the relative ease with which screening might have been conducted, as
General Musson emphasized to me, 'it came from the top that everybody
[among the Cossacks] had to go'.

Yet further confirmation that screening would have been well within
the capacity of 5th Corps to implement came from General Sir Horatius
Murray, then commanding 6th Armoured Division with responsibility for
19,000 troops of the 15th Cossack Cavalry Corps. As he explained to me,

> I was surprised that ... so little was done to "Filter" these prisoners, and
> the scenes further North of us must have been terrible to witness. That
> no attempt was made by Vth Corps Headquarters to provide the
> necessary machinery is, to me, incredible. It would be interesting to
> know why nothing was done in this field as Corps either had the
> machinery or could easily have provided it. [15]

That this was no *ex post facto* speculation on Murray's part is shown
by the fact that an impressive instance of improvised screening was
effected within his divisional area, despite its prohibition by the 5th Corps
oral order that *all* Cossack officers should be handed over. As 6th
Armoured Division war diary recorded on 31 May,

> 60 offrs with Cossacks but not deemed Soviet citizens sent to White
> Russian camp Klein St Veit. [16]

Furthermore, there existed no pressing emergency which prevented
the Cossack handovers from being deferred for weeks or even months if
required. The Soviets could scarcely have raised formal objection to an
effective screening process – indeed, they do not appear ever to have done
so. The 5th Corps's retention of the 4,500-strong *Schutzkorps* (*Russkii
Korpus*) on implicit grounds that many of its complement were White
Russian émigrés aroused not the mildest protest from the Soviets.

Long before any question of a libel action had arisen, Aldington
privately acknowledged that, far from being 'ambiguous', 'There was a
sensible definition of who was a Russian Cossack and who was not and ...
this definition had been established much earlier in the year, I think
March'! [17] That being the case, why he did not implement the 'sensible
definition'?

What in fact transpired was that a uniquely novel approach was laid
down at the 5th Corps conference on the morning of 21 May, when

Brigadier Low issued his treacherous 'Definition' discussed earlier, in which *all* members of Cossack and Caucasian units were designated Soviet citizens. All mention of the 'sensible definition of who was a Russian Cossack and who was not' was suppressed in Low's document.

During his cross-examination at trial in 1989, a clearly flustered Low provided this overall explanation of his 'Definition':

> We were an operational Corps Headquarters. We were at the time deployed operational. We had at the back in reserve a plan for operational action. We were not a Military Government or a District. We were a fighting Corps and organised as such. If we had to move people, therefore, we expected to move not individuals but formations. It's not unusual, in my experience, to deal with formations and to describe things in that way.[18]

It is a great deal more unusual to employ so obviously specious a pretext for wilful disobedience to orders. Were the difficulty real, why were the Cossacks not retained until they could be transferred to 373 PW Camp in nearby Italy? If Keightley and Low found their orders in any way difficult of fulfilment, why did they not explain as much to 8th Army? Anticipating this objection, during his final address to the libel action jury, Aldington's counsel Charles Gray QC (afterwards a judge), declared that

> there was **on the evidence** [bold added], at least one officer from 8th Army present at this discussion which took place on 21st May in the morning [which provided the basis for the 'Definition' circulated to divisions that afternoon].[19]

In fact, no such 'evidence' was submitted at trial, nor does it exist.[20] However, since Judge Davies failed to correct this falsehood in his summing-up, it was presumably accepted by the jury. On the other hand, a copy of the resultant 'Definition' was sent to 8th Army, its equivocal wording being designed to pull the wool over General McCreery's eyes, as well as those of divisional commanders within 5th Corps. Not being an operational order, it in any case did not call for immediate consideration on the army commander's part.[21]

That the deception was successful is shown by McCreery's response when he was belatedly informed by Red Cross officials of the reality of 5th Corps's treatment of the Cossacks:

> The General was shocked by the evidence and forthwith issued instructions that <u>no</u> sick people were to be moved and <u>no</u> D.P.s were to be repatriated against their will. Further, **he rescinded an outrageous instruction that in cases of doubt refugees were to be classified as Soviet Nationals**.[22]

More might be written on this topic, but here I am concerned with 5th Corps' overriding concern to deliver the émigré generals to the Soviets. It was seen earlier that in 1985 Aldington privately acknowledged the significant status of the émigré generals.

> Amongst them [the Cossacks] were officers who had belonged to what has become known as the White Russian community, who had not served in the Russian Army or been in Russia in the last 15 years. Some of them were distinguished people who were wanted by the Soviet Russians.

Despite this, Christopher Booker brazenly asserted on Aldington's behalf that 'No one at 5th Corps was aware that each of the four formations included a small minority of émigrés, who were not Soviet citizens (this was only to come to light later)'.[23] This claim had already been authoritatively refuted by Brigadier Tryon-Wilson, Senior Administrative Officer at 5th Corps, who told Macmillan's biographer Alistair Horne that 'verbal instructions to divisional and brigade commanders were in accordance with the decision not to screen formations to be sent back'.[24] Besides, were Booker's unsubstantiated claim true, what need was there for Low's detailed 'Definition' in the first place?

The fact is that Aldington's claim that military emergency meant that 'we expected to move not individuals but formations' was flatly contradicted by himself, in a letter he wrote to Serena Booker on 11 February 1981, in which he declared:

> All I can say now is what I remember distinctly; and what is confirmed by the records; namely, that right up to the time when I left the policy of H.Q. 5th Corps was to follow Yalta strictly and to separate those you call "White Russians" from the Cossacks and to follow very closely the definition in 8th Army Order of March 1945.

This affirmation confirms in addition that by 21 May he (Low) was fully apprised of the fact that 5th Corps held a sufficient number of White Russians to require their separation from Cossacks who were Soviet nationals.

Perhaps the most sinister aspect of Low's 21 May Definition is the implicit falsehood that some form of screening had already occurred, which in particular resulted in the exclusion from handover of the 4,500-strong Russian *Russkii Korpus*.

Still more remarkable in the Definition is the absence of any reference to the 30,000-strong *Kazachi Stan*, which contained not only by far the largest number of readily-identifiable White Russians, but above all those very émigré generals on whom the Soviets were expressing pressing concern to lay hands! This striking omission can only have been deliberate, and it is hard to envisage its purpose as being other than to avoid drawing 8th Army attention to the presence of the *Kazachi Stan*'s émigré officers in the catalogue of sacrificial victims. Given the principled hostility of Major-General Arbuthnott, commander of 78th Infantry Division, to the brutal policy of forced repatriation, the omission of any reference to the Cossacks in his charge can only reflect yet another aspect of the Machiavellian policy pursued by his superiors at 5th Corps headquarters.

A recurring theme among advocates of the handovers in Austria is that little or nothing was known at 5th Corps headquarters of the extensive number of non-Soviet citizens among the Cossacks and Caucasians in their hands, and still less of the presence of what Aldington himself recalled as 'distinguished' White generals. The Cowgill Inquiry's claim was emphatic:

> it is clear that '*the presence and status of the non-Soviet Cossacks*' was not considered by anyone at 5 Corps until detailed consideration was given to the hand-over operations at the time when the 21 May Definition order was drawn up... Even at the time of the drafting of the 21 May Definition order, the evidence suggests that attention was only very hazily focused on the possibility that there might be some emigres among the main bodies of Cossacks ... in general '*the presence and status of the non-Soviet Cossacks*' is something which only gradually came to assume its present significance in retrospect and after the repatriations had taken place.[25]

In the third edition of the Inquiry's Report, Booker emphatically assured his readers that on 21 May,

> No one at 5 Corps was aware that each of the four formations included a small minority of émigrés, who were not Soviet citizens (this was only to come to light later).[26]

This is hard to believe, given that General Krasnov was most prominent among the '~~distinguished~~ people' Aldington had recalled four years earlier as being held by 5th Corps. This also reads strangely in light of Brigadier Tryon-Wilson's repeated descriptions (recorded in writing and on tape) of Keightley's receipt of the list of émigré Russian officers whose delivery was requested by the Soviets during his visit to Voitsberg on 11 May 1945. Thus Tryon-Wilson reminded Lord Aldington on 20 August 1987:

> Further to your letter of the 30th July and my acknowledgment dated the 14th of August, I am now ready to roll!
>
> The "bit of paper" that you mention was handed to me by one of the

Russian Officers as I was getting ready to leave the conference and through an interpreter I was informed that it was a list of individuals believed to be held in our area and who they, the Russians, would be particularly interested in having returned to them, or words to that effect.

The list contained some 20 to 25 names and although obviously I read it through[*] - names at that particular time meant nothing to me - and I am sure that we had no knowledge at Corps H.Q. of a roll-call of officers of Cossacks and Germans held in our area. What I do remember clearly about the list is that it contained some 5 names which were in block capitals as against the remainder in normal type. I can only conjecture that the names in block capitals referred to the White Russian Generals or Emigrés and I certainly don't remember details as regards nationalities etc.

I handed the list to General Charles [Keightley] that evening before the usual evening conference and we were on our own. General Charles read the list through and made some initial comment which I don't remember but concluded with "Over my dead body," - clearly this was a humanitarian observation as I had explained to him when handing over the paper that they were officers or individuals which they, (the Russians,) particularly required. General Charles could quite easily have recognized some of the names of the old Emigrés and it would be a natural expression of a caring officer.

Since Keightley was at the time fully prepared to repatriate Soviet citizens in accordance with the Yalta Agreement, his objection 'over my dead body!' can *only* mean that he recognized the names on the list as those of individuals who were *not* Soviet citizens.

Today it might be supposed that British officers at the time would have known and cared little about leaders of the White Army during the Russian Civil War. However, Tryon-Wilson's understanding that Keightley recognized some of the names is in this case credible. A year after the events in Austria, Krasnov testified at his secret trial in Moscow that he

> ... wrote a letter to the Supreme Commander of Allied Forces in Italy Marshal Alexander, in which he wrote at great length that he represented the Kazachi Stan and its military units and expressed readiness to act fully in accord with the instructions of the British command. Of himself personally Krasnov wrote that he did not wish to continue as head of the "main administration of the Cossack Army", but was ready to be an advizer to the British on all questions.

---

[*] Presumably the names were typed in English.

During further interrogation, Krasnov explained that the letter was twenty pages long, that it was compiled immediately on his arrival in Austria (i.e. on 8 May), and that he gave it to a German officer who offered to convey it to Field Marshal Alexander. General Shkuro had joined him at Kötschach two days earlier, a fact Krasnov might well have mentioned in his letter, given the fact that Shkuro had been appointed a Companion of the Bath by King George V. Since this occurred on the day of Germany's formal surrender, it cannot have been more than a day or so before the unnamed German officer fell into British hands. Its contents were plainly of considerable interest to the British command in Austria, and must have been passed with a minimum of delay to 5th Corps headquarters. All this (and very likely more, of which no record is preserved) readily accounts for Keightley's immediate recognition on 11 May of the names of Krasnov and 'the old boy with the CB'.

Not only this, but 5th Corps headquarters's failure to forward Krasnov's letter to 8th Army for upward transmission to Alexander confirms that *rigorous measures were being undertaken from 13 May onwards to prevent the Field Marshal from learning that a significant body of White Russian émigrés was held by the British in Austria.*

I now turn to one of the more remarkable archival discoveries in this grim historical event, imbued as it is throughout with secrecy, suppression of significant documents, and vengeful actions of the British legal and political establishment directed against any attempt to arrive at the truth of this murky history. I little dreamed, throughout long years of investigating the story, that the day would come when the Russian government would assist me in uncovering relevant evidence from their hitherto secret archives. Thanks to the active personal support of President Yeltsin, that day finally arrived. Would this unexpected trove establish that my conclusions were right or wrong? Here was the unexpected test.

Beria reported to Stalin on 26 May 1945 that the tens of thousands of Cossack men, women, and children delivered by British military authorities in Austria to Stalin were to be dispatched by SMERSH to the Kemerovo Gulag camp complex in Western Siberia.[27] As may be imagined, conditions there were horrific almost beyond belief. Husbands were separated from their wives and both from their children.[28] All were treated as slaves, clad in rags in which they slept in unheated rooms on bare boards, and allotted starvation rations. Beatings and torture were inflicted unceasingly, the casualty rate being estimated at fifteen to twenty a day. The brutal local commandant, MVD General A.V. Shamarin, issued this ruling in response to prisoners' requests to be paid for their work in construction and flooded coalmines:

I shall pay you nothing, you will deliver up to us, as traitors to the Motherland, as self-seekers, the profit of your labors.[29]

As Macmillan had foreseen, it was indeed 'slavery' of the cruellest character to which his 'verbal directive' consigned them.[30] Indeed, the old emigrants, whose status entitled them to protection under international law, were often treated worse than ordinary slaves within the Gulag administration. On 23 January 1950, MVD Minister Sergei Kruglov reported to Stalin that especially harsh camps were being built for enemies of the people, including 'White émigrés'.[31]

Among punitive measures designed to make life unbearable for the slaves were mindlessly repetitive nocturnal interrogations conducted by the NKVD at their headquarters in the local town of Prokopevsk.[32] A striking example of this practice is contained among documents provided me from the Russian archives.

EXTRACT FROM THE MINUTES OF THE EXAMINATION of the accused OVSIANNIKOV Arkadii Aleksandrovich

on 14 March 1946.

town of Prokopevsk.

Question: In the examination of 27 November 1945 you gave evidence that in May 1945 together with general DOMANOV you participated in discussions with the English command. Describe that in more detail?

Answer: Regarding my participation in the discussions with the English command in the month of May 1945 together with general Domanov, I give the following evidence: after the retreat from Italy, in Austria 14-15 May 1945 I was appointed to the staff of general DOMANOV and was provided with the duty of an officer with a special commission - interpreter in the English language. Since I had mastered the English language well, it fell to me to enter into talks with representatives of the English command at the time when already the Cossacks had been disarmed and made prisoner by the English.

On 17 May 1945 in general DOMANOV's room in the town of Lienz (Austria) appeared general MUSSON, representative of the English command, who was concerned with two questions, where and how the Krasnovs were living[;] and was authority given by DOMANOV to hold discussions through the German colonel, whose surname I do not know[,] with Field Marshal ALEXANDER on the question of deciding the fate of the Cossacks.

DOMANOV gave the reply to general MUSSON through me, as interpreter, that he did not know where the Krasnovs were living, and also that he did not provide the authority for the German colonel to enter into discussions with Field Marshal ALEXANDER on the question of the fate of the Cossacks.

I have been unable to discover more concerning the unfortunate officer Ovsiannikov, save that his mastery of English suggests he was one of the many old émigré officers handed over at Judenburg. Momentarily withdrawn from the frozen hell to which he had been consigned, his testimony unexpectedly sheds unique light on some of the most controversial aspects of this murky history. Presumably he was returned the night following his interrogation to join his comrades, the majority of whom perished in the death-camps.

The first point to note is Musson's concern with discovering any channel through which General Krasnov might attempt to contact Field Marshal Alexander.

The second is the oddity of the brigade commander's personal intervention on the spot, which if merely routine could have been transmitted by telephone or wireless communication from Musson's headquarters at Oberdrauburg to the Argylls' battalion headquarters in Lienz. Long before I gained access to the Soviet record, Musson assured me that 'I certainly did not visit Domanov's Headquarters'.[33] That was clearly incorrect.

That Musson was initially ignorant of General Krasnov's whereabouts is explicable. As has been seen, the latter's wish to remain in the Hotel Van Gogh at Kötschach-Mauthen was declined, and on 9 May he and his wife Lydia were taken away in a British staff car.[34] They were reinstalled in the elegant Amlacher Hof at Amlach village in the countryside outside Lienz.[35] That their whereabouts had become temporarily overlooked at 36th Infantry Brigade headquarters a week later is natural enough, given that Krasnov held no official position in the *Kazachi Stan*, and consequently maintained no direct contact with the British command.[36] Furthermore, as the Argylls' chaplain the Rev. Kenneth Tyson informed me, the General could speak almost no English (hence his writing to Field Marshal Alexander in French).

Striking conclusions may be drawn from Ovsiannikov's account of Brigadier Musson's discussion with General Domanov in the latter's room in the Goldener Fisch hotel in Lienz. It represented the obvious initial port of call for discovering General Krasnov's whereabouts. Since neither Musson nor his superior General Arbuthnott could have possessed any personal interest in identifying the domicile of an elderly general playing no part in the Cossack command structure, it must surely be that the former was fulfilling an enquiry emanating from 5th Corps headquarters. As nothing is reported to have ensued on Musson's enquiry, it further appears that it was confined to establishing where Krasnov was to be found when required. In addition, there would have been little point in identifying his whereabouts were surveillance of the Amlacher Hof not maintained from then onward.

It appears that General Krasnov had initially been forgotten by 36th Infantry Brigade for the space of a week or more. Now, however, despite Musson's drawing a blank at Domanov's headquarters, he would have encountered no difficulty in speedily discovering his whereabouts from Colonel Malcolm, commanding 8th Argylls. All this suggests that Musson's concern to locate Krasnov arose from some recent unexpected consideration. What that was is evident. On the previous day (16 May), Field Marshal Alexander's chief of staff, General William Morgan, had flown to 5th Corps headquarters. There he conferred with Keightley and his staff, apprizing himself of the situation on the ground, and informing the Corps Commander of developments affecting his command. At midday he sent the following message to Alexander:

> Personal for Field Marshal Alexander from Gen Morgan.
>
> 5 Corps situation difficult owing to very widespread commitments and guards required for prisoners and surrendered personnel.
>
> Prisoners and surrendered personnel total about 220000 of whom 109000 Germans 15000 Hungarians 46000 Cossacks 25000 Croats 25000 Slovenes. Consider that SHAEF should be asked to take over 5 Corps front ...[37]

This confirmed Alexander's plan to 'clear the decks' in Austria, among other moves by transferring responsibility for all Cossack and German prisoners in 5th Corps hands to the U.S. 12th Army Group. This move would have superseded Macmillan's and Keightley's planned handover of the Cossacks to the Soviets. Above all, it threatened to abort the planned delivery of the White Russian generals and other old émigrés, whom the Americans would undoubtedly have retained as non-Soviet citizens. It is further clear that Keightley took care not to inform General Morgan of the Robertson order received on the previous day, requiring 5th Corps to deliver all 96,000 Cossacks, Croats, and Slovenes to Stalin and Tito, which was now to be superseded by Alexander's solution, as practical as it was humane.

The British government's apologia for 5th Corps' illicit actions requires it to be believed that the handover of Krasnov and his fellow émigrés was conducted in consequence of ignorance and haste on the part of Keightley and Low, rather than conspiracy. In the third version of the

Cowgill Inquiry, Christopher Booker went further, assuring his readers that 5th Corps only appreciated the presence of old émigrés after it was too late to retain them. (As will shortly be seen, Booker felt impelled to doctor evidence lying before him when advancing this assertion). Aldington himself claimed at the 1989 libel trial that 'I don't remember knowing about Krasnov'.[38]

However, Ovsiannikov's testimony to his NKVD interrogator less than a year after the event establishes incontrovertibly that, no later than 17 May (four days after Macmillan's fateful visit), Keightley and Low at 5th Corps headquarters were not only fully aware of 'the presence and status of the non-Soviet Cossacks', but were already taking steps to ensure the handover of General Krasnov in particular. It is poignant to reflect that the wretched Ovsiannikov, who was returned the same night to months or years of bitter suffering in the adjacent slave-labour camp at Tygransky Slope, has now from the grave provided testimony decisively confirming the criminal guilt and treachery of his British betrayers.

His response incidentally confirms the falsity of the canard espoused by some surviving Lienz Cossacks that they had in some way been betrayed by the former Soviet officer Domanov.[39] In fact the latter had remained in close communication with Krasnov throughout May, and presumably denied knowledge of his whereabouts in order to protect him.

Listening again to my successive recorded interviews with General Musson (as he had become) in 1974, given his key role in the handovers I find him unusually reticent – not to say, cagey – concerning the deliberate inclusion of White Russians for handover, in comparison with almost everyone else involved whom I interviewed (Aldington being the obvious exception).[*] It is true that Musson repeatedly emphasized that his orders were that all Cossacks should be returned, *without screening, and above all including the officers* (which is of course true). However, he made no mention of his visit to General Domanov, nor of elaborate measures with which he was closely involved to ensure the return of the 'listed' Cossack officers. He also implied that the leading Cossack generals were identified in the 21 May 'Definition' as liable to return. As he ventured to me:

---

[*] It it remarkable that Musson declined to testify at the Aldington trial in 1989, where his evidence would have been of the first importance. A charitable view (which I am cautiously inclined to espouse) would be that he was deeply troubled in his conscience, while unprepared to perjure himself at the trial (as one or two others of Aldington's scanty array of witnesses were happy to do). Captain A. P. Judge, who was on his staff at the time, informed me that 'I formed a strong personal attachment to the Brigadier. He was quite one of the kindliest regular officers I met all through the war'.

But look, I don't know whether you've got this: there also appears at the head of the [21st May] list the name 'Ataman Group'. Is this as I imagine a reference to Ataman Peter Krasnov and his personal entourage?

In fact, as will be revealed in the next chapter, the Ataman Group was a wholly distinct body. I suspect that Musson likewise recollected its existence, for reasons which will appear when the Ataman Group comes under consideration. It may be significant, too, that he casually employed Krasnov's Christian name, which I had not mentioned during our lengthy interview.

Secondly, and of equal significance, is the importance Musson ascribed in his questioning of Domanov to obtention of further information concerning Krasnov's attempt to establish contact with Field Marshal Alexander. Given that his letter was retained at 5th Corps Headquarters and withheld from higher command, it is clear that General Keightley was concerned to block any further attempt on Krasnov's part to establish contact with the Supreme Allied Commander.

Thus, irrefutable evidence confirms that the handover of the White emigrant Cossack commanders arose from no last-minute oversight, but was arranged with meticulous care in consequence of Macmillan's 'verbal directive'. Were confirmation of this required, it becomes yet further manifest in the circumstances of the handovers of the two most prominent figures in the list.

Early on the morning of 26 May, Ariadna Delianich, an old émigré from Yugoslavia acting as emissary from the *Russkii Korpus* to General Domanov at Lienz, set off on her mission. In her memoir, written in Russian, she describes how,

> Picking up my rucksack, I went out onto the highroad to catch a lift from cars travelling to Lienz. After several fruitless attempts I risked stopping a small tank (*небольшой танк*) [presumably an armored car] bearing British markings.* Heads popped up out of the tank. I held out my pass.
>
> "Where to?" curtly enquired a curly-haired head in a black beret.
>
> "Lienz!"
>
> "Okay! Jump in!" [in English]
>
> They opened the lid on the turret, and for the first time in my life I was being driven in a tank. There were only two men in the tank. Both were captains, in black berets with tank insignia.† They indicated a place for

---

* That morning 56th Reconnaissance Regiment received orders to 'maintain regular armed C patrols along rd Dellach – Lienz' (WO.170/4396).
† Personnel of the 56th Recce Regiment wore black berets.

me in the rear part of the machine. The tank moved on.

It was dark. The lids of the vision slits were closed. The road was not visible to me, only past their heads through the front window could I see shadowy shapes. I listened to the officers' conversation. I was surprized that they were speaking in French. The rumbling of the vehicle muffled sounds, so that I could only catch snatches of their words. Suddenly I pricked up my ears. I heard names: Shkuro, Krasnov, Domanov... Disarming... Peggetz. Further on they spoke of certain special units, which had been especially transferred from Italy.[40] Again they spoke of Shkuro and the prison at Spittal.

There was something dangerous and alarming in their words. A horrifying conjecture did not give me tranquility. I wanted to learn more, but they broke off the discussion... It was the 26th May 1945.[41]

While this ominous incident was occurring, a great stir brought the Cossacks swarming from their barracks onto the square at Peggetz. Driven slowly through in a small car was *batka* Shkuro in his Kuban Cossack uniform, a legendary hero to every Cossack man, woman, and child. All struggled to shake his hand, pressing on him cigarettes, tobacco, or cakes, and at his departure the joyful crowd followed him some way beyond the gate as he was driven back to Lienz.[42]

That evening Shkuro dined in the Goldener Fisch with General Solamakhin, chief of staff to Field Ataman Domanov. Next day Solamakhin told Olga Rotova what transpired afterwards.

At 3 o'clock in the morning of 27 May Shkuro burst into his room, sat on his bed and burst into tears.

"That ... Domanov has betrayed me," he exclaimed. "He invited me round, gave me drink, and betrayed me. Now the English are coming to arrest me and hand me over to the Soviets. They are giving me, Shkuro, over to the Soviets... They are handing me, Shkuro, to the Soviets..."

He struck himself on the chest, and tears rolled from his eyes. At 6 o'clock in the morning he was taken away by two English officers.[43]

Meanwhile, under circumstances so secret that they feature nowhere in 36th Infantry Brigade or 8th Argylls war diaries, it was on the same day that General Krasnov was placed under house arrest in his quarters at Amlach. During his lengthy interrogation in the Lubianka prison a year later, the General mentioned that on

27 May I was imprisoned by the English and after two days I was placed at the disposal of the Soviet military command.

Yet the authors of the government 'inquiries' consistently maintained that Krasnov and Shkuro were included in the handovers purely in consequence of administrative oversight!

Thomas Dennis was at the time a young artillery officer attached to 78th Infantry Division. On arrival at Spittal, in the Drau Valley, he and some of his fellow subalterns were instructed to conduct enquiries among the vast multitude of refugees crowding the fertile narrow plain beneath the mountains. Encouraged to act on his own initiative, he established an improvised interrogation point at the barracks gate. Although he spoke French, and was joined by a German-speaking major, he soon discovered that the fugitives spoke a multiplicity of further languages, ranging from Italian to Hungarian, Czech, Serbian, Croatian and Russian. However, by retaining the assistance of bilinguals among them, he was swiftly able to utilize them in three-way conversations. His experience convinced him that it would have been perfectly possible to screen Cossacks and others, had a settled attempt to do so been implemented at divisional headquarters. Many of their officers in particular had been living in France, and spoke to him in French. The Cossacks were only too anxious to co-operate with the British, and expressed a constant fear lest they fall into the hands of the Soviets. Dennis himself was well aware that a grisly fate awaited any Cossack to whom this might occur.

Later, Dennis recalled the arrival of Shkuro at Spittal:

I think probably in the fourth week of May I discovered that a gentleman called Schkuro had also just been given quarters. I cannot remember who told me but I think it was probably Major Smith. I understood from whoever did tell me that Shkuro was a senior Cossack officer. I immediately went to see him and discovered that he and his Headquarters staff of about 15 or 16 people had been given quarters on the first floor patrolled by British Troops. I did not know where Shkuro had come from or who had arranged for him to be quartered there. I assumed that, for him to receive such preferential treatment, it must have been arranged by the higher British command.

I went into Shkuro's room, and immediately noticed from his insignia and dress that he was a General and indeed he told me this. Our conversation was conducted through his Aide de Camp who spoke perfect French. My purpose in seeing Shkuro was to discuss the Cossacks in the context of my responsibilities as a liaison officer. He then told me that he had enormous faith in the British people and that he had been decorated by King George V with the 'Commander of the Order of the Bath' for his service to Britain in World War I... General Shkuro was extremely pleasant and friendly although he certainly commanded respect. I used to see him every day and we built up a very good relationship...

Two days later Shkuro was joined by the other Cossack officers from Lienz, who had been repeatedly assured 'on the word of a British officer' that they were being taken to a consultation with Field Marshal Alexander, who would decide upon their ultimate asylum. When Dennis was informed of this treacherous action,

> I was utterly shocked, dazed and numbed by all this. I could not believe that the British Army would be so callous as to treat these people in this way. Indeed, I was so upset that when I attended the briefing meeting, I asked to be relieved of my command saying that I wished to have no part in the handover as I felt I and the Cossacks had been grossly deceived by what I said was trickery of the worst kind. I was told that, as a British officer, it was my duty to obey my orders and that we mere junior officers were not aware of the complexities of the situation. I was also told that any refusal would be dealt with as 'a refusal to obey an order in the field' and, in that event, our orders would be carried out by other troops who would not be so sensitive as I was. I realised that I had no option but to obey my orders and I steeled myself for what was to come...

> After the meeting, I went to the main barracks and up to the first floor to meet General Shkuro. Through his Aide de Camp I understood that he knew of the impending handover. However, it appeared he realised my shame and embarrassment and he very quickly told me that he bore me no malice and again thanked me for the kindness which I had shown to the Cossack community at all times. He then produced a most beautiful ceremonial sword which was decorated with many jewels and which he said had been presented to him when he received the decoration from King George V. He said he wished to present the sword to me as a personal gift. I explained that, as a British Officer, I could not accept the gift on a personal basis, but could do so on behalf of the British Army. He seemed to understand this and asked me to include his wishes in my report. He then gave me the sword, which together with my daily situation report I handed in to my Headquarters. I never saw either the sword or General Shkuro or any of his staff again.

> I then called my Troop together and explained the position to them and the orders which I had received. I made no attempt to gloss over any of the facts. I remember I felt my men had to be told only the truth which I did not disguise from them. My men made it abundantly clear to me that they found the whole business thoroughly distasteful and did not wish to carry out the orders. I felt I was teetering on the edge of a mutiny. Eventually they accepted that there was no option but to go through with everything as it was appreciated that there was no possible alternative.[44]

The magnificent sword has vanished from the record.[45] In 1985 Brigadier Tryon-Wilson told me that it was brought to Corps HQ, and he saw Major-General de Fonblanque with it. The suspicion rests that it was either he or General Keightley who expropriated it as plunder of war.

Two days later (29 May) General Shkuro was driven, together with his fellow-officers, to Judenburg, where they were delivered into the incredulous but gleeful hands of the Red Army. Ariadna Delianich was among those who witnessed his departure from Spittal.

> Several brief orders were issued. The soldiers drove the curious spectators further back. From the house emerged some English [soldiers] and General Andrei Shkuro, in full [Cossack] uniform, with accompanying [Cossack] officers. I immediately recognized Peter Babushkin, [Prince] Chegodaev and another of our Belgrade émigrés…

> I pushed further forward. The voice of Andrei Shkuro was borne across to me. He was protesting loudly, explaining that he was a Knight of the English Order of the Bath. "Give me a revolver! I don't fear death, but I don't want to fall into the hands of the Red scum alive!"

> Shkuro sat down in the truck. With him came the remaining Russian officers. With shrieking sirens motorcyclists roared forward. The tragic procession moved on. The Knight of the English Order of the Bath, the fighting General, was being delivered by our former allies to the Communists.[46]

Her description is borne out by the War Diary of 36th Infantry Brigade:

> The last party to be loaded was General Shkuro and his staff of 25. General Shkuro had been in the camp [Spittal] for some 36 hours. When informed by O.C. 1 Kensingtons, on the evening of the 28th May, that he was to be returned to Russia, he requested to be shot. When ordered to mount on the lorry the following morning, he and his staff complied without difficulty.[47]

Shkuro's initial cordial reception by Red Army officers at Judenburg, his fearless bearing and contemptuous comparison of their open Soviet enemies with the treacherous British have been described by eyewitnesses.[48] It is important to note the extent to which British troops were similarly deceived by their superiors. Shkuro's prior abduction was thus explained by 36th Infantry Brigade:

> General Shkuro (of the Cossack Reserve Regiment) had been sent to Spittal two days earlier, as the move of his Regiment was then complete.[49]

This was a lie: his regiment's move and his consequent separation from it had occurred at least a week earlier. As 36th Infantry Brigade war diary itself recorded: 'During the period 16 to 20 May they [Domanov's force] were joined by some 1,400 persons of the Cossack reserve regiment under the command of General Shkuro'.[50] All this chicanery indicates that Shkuro's betrayal was meticulously planned from an early stage. Implementation of this elaborate conspiracy was no doubt regarded as particularly requisite in his case, given that he had received so high a British honour for his services alongside British troops in 1919. This provoked much sympathetic comment and corresponding indignation among British soldiers dismayed by the prospect of his betrayal.

General Peter Krasnov was likewise marked down by the Soviets as a 'wanted' figure. Once Brigadier Musson had discovered his residence at Amlach on or immediately after 17 May his days were numbered. On 24 May, concerned at having received no reply to his appeal to Field Marshal Alexander transmitted over a fortnight earlier, Krasnov penned a further letter to the Allied commander.[51] As Brigadier Tryon-Wilson recalled, this suffered the fate of its predecessor, being retained at 5th Corps Headquarters. Both appeals were withheld from higher command (8th Army), while at the same time being surreptitiously passed to SMERSH.

On 27 May, the Cossack officers were informed that they had been invited to discuss their predicament with Alexander himself at Spittal. Krasnov regarded this as a response to his appeal (as he was doubtless intended to do), while 5th Corps correspondingly found in it a potent means of duping the elderly General. However, the British command was taking no risks. That evening Domanov's English-speaking ADC Captain Butlerov was visited in the Goldener Fisch hotel by Major Davies from the camp at Peggetz. The latter laid particular emphasis on the necessity of General Krasnov's joining the Cossack officers on the morrow:

> And ... please, don't forget to notify general Krasnov. The army commander [*i.e.* Alexander] is very concerned to meet him.[52]

Next morning (28 May), Butlerov arrived to request the General's attendance at the 'conference'. Krasnov prepared himself, confident that all would be well. Lydia, however, with a wife's instinct, feared something terrible. Before long a car arrived, dispatched by Ataman Domanov. Peter Krasnov embraced his wife, crossed himself, kissed her on the cheek, and said: 'no need for sadness!' She smiled, embraced him, crossed herself, and accompanied him to the car. As her husband set off, he called out: 'I'll be back between 6 to 8 o'clock this evening!' However, as she recalled two years later, he did not come back: 'In 45 years it was the first time he did not fulfil what he promised. I understood that misfortune had inopportunely come upon me ...'[53]

About this time, 'there appeared at General Domanov's hotel a tall English general who repeated the order given by Major Davies, adding: 'Please don't forget to pass my request to old Krasnov. I request this of you most earnestly'.[54] This could only have been one of the two generals commanding in the district. Of these, Major-General Arbuthnott was short, while Brigadier Musson was tall.

Still incredulous that the British had betrayed him, Krasnov headed the column in a car. Behind him a large bus carried the principal Cossack officers, while the remainder were packed into forty or fifty trucks. Together they travelled under heavy armed escort eastward to Spittal. After a while British tanks, armored cars, and motorcyclists emerged from the surrounding forest to escort the convoy. Alarmed by this display of lethal force, the officers in the bus began questioning their British driver. Smiling, he explained that their escort was designed to protect them from armed SS units still at large in the region. This implausible claim increased some Cossack officers' mounting fear and suspicion.

After a drive of more than two hours, they arrived on the outskirts of the town of Spittal, where they were taken to a nearby wired former German refugee camp surrounded by British sentries.[55] From a window of the upper story of a stone building near the entrance the imprisoned General Shkuro welcomed his comrades with a defiant wave.[56] His British captors were taking no chances with the fearless and resourceful Kuban Cossack.

Descending from the bus, young Nikolai Krasnov was delighted to find his great-uncle, father, and Uncle Semeon, whose car had become detached from the convoy. The old General appeared convinced still that the British would treat them correctly. 'Well, all will be clarified today at the conference and sorted out. Isn't that true, Nikolai?' But other members of the family remained dubious.

Late that evening any lingering hope of honorable treatment was abruptly dispelled, when a distraught General Domanov burst into the Krasnovs' room. 'Tomorrow morning we are all to be sent to Judenburg, where every one of us is to be handed over to the Soviets!' he exclaimed frantically. Rising from his bed and supported by his cane, the old General declared that he must be mistaken in accusing the British of such flagrant treachery. In his despair Domanov blurted out that there could be no mistake, since just now at supper they had repeated their intention to him. The word 'repeated' struck an indignant chord. So Domanov already knew of the forthcoming betrayal, and had failed to warn them! Was he not a traitor? Amid the universal alarm, Domanov apparently found no opportunity of explaining that he had been cursorily informed of their destination by Brigadier Musson during a brief stop of the convoy en route to Spittal, when it was too late for any escape.[57]

General Krasnov intervened to urge calm upon all present, pointing out that panic and dispute were of no use now. It was necessary to draw up a petition to King George VI, and another to the International Red Cross in Geneva. This was swiftly done, and the text (written in French, and signed by Krasnov and other officers) was given to an English major, who expressed doubt of its efficacy, given that all Cossack and Caucasian officers were due to be delivered up to the Soviets the next day. In fact its existence was withheld from 8th Army command, and it was instead delivered by 5th Corps directly to the Soviet authorities. As noted earlier, it was a strange situation, wherein 5th Corps headquarters kept SMERSH informed of matters withheld from their own superiors at 8th Army.

Could it be that Keightley and Low were not averse to providing their Soviet colleagues with incriminating evidence that might assist in ensuring the permanent silencing of awkward witnesses to British perfidy and duplicity towards their Cossack charges and their own superiors alike?

Few if any of the condemned officers slept that night. Two or three committed suicide by hanging themselves on lavatory chains, while another was cut down and resuscitated by British soldiers.[58] At dawn on 29 May, the officers emerged from their huts into the camp square. From the precinct watchtowers their guards watched curiously. The Cossacks knelt on the dusty ground to pray *en masse* under direction of three priests. As the British commander acknowledged, 'The service they held was a most impressive affair and the singing was magnificent'. When General Domanov declined Colonel Bryar's request that he require his officers to board the trucks, the latter gave orders for force to be employed. A moment later, and a platoon of the Kensingtons advanced through the gateway of the barbed-wire precinct, armed with rifles and pickaxe helves. As they were dragging the hapless prisoners towards the transport, one Cossack officer bit the hand of one of his captors. The guards promptly set upon the prisoners, striking right and left at them, until they were driven into the waiting vehicles.

Lastly, as Colonel Bryar further reported:

> The final party to leave was General SHKURO and his staff amounting to about 25. This General had been housed in a Barrack Block as opposed to the prison camp for 36 hrs. On the night of the 28th he was informed by OC 1 KENSINGTONS that he was to return to RUSSIA and immediately replied by asking if he could be shot. This was refused and

on the morning of 29th he and his staff obeyed orders and created no trouble whatever.[59]

Even at this stage 5th Corps was not prepared to risk escape of 'the old boy who had the CB'. The SMERSH list presented to Brigadier Tryon earlier in the month must be fulfilled at all costs.[60] Although nothing would have been easier at this stage than to conduct screening and retention of non-Soviet citizens, under 5th Corps's secret policy no provision was allowed for such procedure. Lieutenant Petrie, a subaltern responsible for embussing the Cossack officers, reported afterwards:

> A number of last-minute pleas of associations with the Allies, e.g. "Worked 25 yrs in France".

> Such protests were ignored, since the order was to dispatch *all* Cossack and Caucasian officers.

> The column departed at speed, escorted as before by armored cars and motorcyclists. Skirting the town of Villach, the convoy hurtled on its way, until a sign was glimpsed proclaiming that they had arrived at Judenburg. There they drew up at the entrance to a narrow stone bridge. Far below in its deep ravine coursed the turbulent waters of the boulder-strewn river Mur. At the far end stood a Red Army soldier. After a brief pause, the trucks trundled across, their slow passage permitting two officers to fling themselves over the parapet, to be shattered on jagged rocks far beneath.

As the officer commanding the armored car escort reported (it may be suspected with suppressed indignation) in the regimental war diary:

> On arrival at Judenburg one officer leapt over a hundred foot precipice, but was recovered and handed over mangled and dying to the Soviet forces. As the officers were being debussed, and just after the Soviet guard had taken them over, one officer cut his throat with a razor blade and slumped dying across my feet... All the prisoners requested frequently to be shot whilst in our custody, rather than be handed over to the Soviets.[61]

At the far end a barrier was raised, and the convoy deployed onto Soviet-occupied territory. Nearby, a Red Army soldier with a harmonica played a popular tune 'Wait for me'. Like Harold Macmillan when he directed General Keightley to deliver up the Cossacks, all knew that they were entering the gates of Hell, beyond which lay 'slavery, torture, and probably death'.[62] In all, 1,736 Cossack officers, the greater part of whom had never been Soviet citizens, were handed over.[63]

[1] Christopher Booker, *A Looking-Glass Tragedy: The Controversy over the repatriations from Austria in 1945* (London, 1997), p. 42).

[2] Serge Obolensky, *One Man in his Time* (New York, 1958), p. 253.

[3] Brigadier Anthony Cowgill, Lord Brimelow, and Christopher Booker Esq, *The Repatriations from Austria in 1945: The Report of an Inquiry* (London, 1990), pp. 63-64; Booker, *A Looking-Glass Tragedy*, p. 174. It is amusing to note again the pompous emphasis on rank and title among the authors, possibly designed to stress the semi-official status of the 'Inquiry'.

[4] In 1946 a Soviet report mentions without comment the presence of Colonel Rogozhin's *Russkii Korpus* in western Austria ('Отчет о выполнении решений Правительства Союза ССР по проведению репатриации граждан СССР и граждан иносранных государств периода Великой Отечественной Войны (1941 – 1945 г.г.)', p. 93). I am indebted to Professor Stephan Karner for a copy of this document. It appears to have been tacitly conceded by Stalin that no request would be made for the unit's handover.

[5] Brigadier Anthony Cowgill, Christopher Booker Esq, Lord Brimelow, and Brigadier Teddy Tryon-Wilson, *Interim Report on an Enquiry into the Repatriation of Surrendered Enemy Personnel to the Soviet Union and Yugoslavia from Austria in 1945 and the Alleged 'Klagenfurt Conspiracy'* (London, 1988), p. 44.

[6] Alistair Horne, *Macmillan: 1894-1956* (London, 1988), p. 276. The same point is advanced by Ludovic Kennedy, *On my Way to the Club* (London, 1989), p. 378.

[7] Harold Macmillan, *The Blast of War: 1939-1945* (London, 1967), p. 609.

[8] Nikolai Tolstoy, *Victims of Yalta* (London, 1977), p. 277.

[9] Christopher Booker asserted that 'this definition ... was drawn up solely to exclude people from the annexed territories, the Balts and Poles ...' (Booker, *A Looking-Glass Tragedy*, p. 219). Once again, he deliberately distorts the content of a document. Macmillan had no concern with 'Balts and Poles', but sought a ruling on treatment of 'Soviet ex-prisoners-of-war' held within the Mediterranean command (WO.32/1119,230A, 281A).

[10] Trial Transcript, Day 8.

[11] WO.170/7250.

[12] NA. 383.7-14. Mr F. G. Bradley, then serving with the RASC, provided me with a detailed account of the repatriation in the latter part of June 1945 of the 500 prisoners at Mestre deemed to be Soviet citizens (letter of 2 September 1985). On 12 June General Golikov, head of the Soviet Repatriation Commission, complained to Molotov that the British in North Italy were withholding Soviet citizens, of whom 2,500 were still held in Camp 373 at Mestre. No recorded repercussion resulted from the British refusal to enforce their handover.

[13] NA. 383.7-14.

[14] WO.170/4988.

[15] Letter of 29th December 1974.

[16] WO.170/4337. For a detailed account of this striking event, cf. my *Victims of Yalta*, pp. 241-47. It is evident that General Keightley did not issue the recalcitrant General Murray with the oral order he transmitted to 78th Infantry Division. Instead, he hastily transferred the majority of Cossacks held by 6th Armoured Division to the care of 46th Infantry Division.

[17] Letter of 23 January 1981 to Brigadier Tryon-Wilson. Despite this first-hand evidence of receipt of the 13 May screening order at 5th Corps headquarters, Christopher Booker insisted that 'In fact, even AFHQ's three instructions of 6, 7 and 15 March were only passed down as far as Eighth Army' (*A Looking-Glass War*, p. 219). This provides a characteristic specimen of Booker's shameless casuistry. In fact the signal of 15th March *was* transmitted to 5th Corps, while the key signal is in any case that of **13th** March, which was likewise received at 5th Corps headquarters. He was enabled to make this deceptive assertion in consequence of the Cowgill Inquiry's omission in its so-called 'Key Papers' of 5th Corps signal A/3013 dated 15 March, which records that a copy of the crucial 13 March screening order was forwarded *inter alia* to 78th Infantry Division. Booker will have seen the relevant signal, since he regularly attended the 1989 libel trial as an assistant to Lord Aldington and his lawyers. A copy was included among court documents in Bundle A 39. All reference to it is likewise omitted from the Cowgill Inquiry report, whose authors assured its readers contained every relevant paper.

[18] Trial Transcript, Day 8.

[19] Trial Transcript, Day 36.

[20] Aldington himself declared: 'I would guess that there was somebody from 8th Army present... I really cannot remember. I do not remember anything about the conference at all other than what is in the document' (Trial Transcript, Day 4); 'I would have thought there would have been somebody present from 8th Army, but I cannot remember and it is very unfortunate that there is no list available'; '8th Army, as I say, were present - were either present at the meeting - I can't prove that' (Day 8). It is not difficult to see why the presiding Judge Michael Davies adopted the unusual precaution of withholding the trial transcript from the jurors when considering their verdict (Trial Transcript, Day 38).

[21] The British Government's 'Inquiry' asserted that receipt of Low's Definition instigated 8th Army's 21 May A 4073 request to AFHQ for a ruling on the fate of the Cossacks (Cowgill, Brimelow, and Booker Esq., *The Repatriations from Austria in 1945: The Report of an Inquiry*, p. 101). This is untrue: A 4073 begins 'Reference your FX-75383 dated 14 ...'.

[22] Rose-Gibson Report of 10 July 1945.

[23] *A Looking-Glass War*, p. 222; cf. p. 224.

[24] *Macmillan: 1894-1956* (London, 1988), p. 265; note: 'Statement by Brigadier C.E. Tryon-Wilson to 'Cowgill Group'' (p. 480).

[25] Cowgill, Brimelow, and Booker Esq, *The Repatriations from Austria in 1945: The Report of an Inquiry*, pp. 199-200.

[26] Booker, *A Looking-Glass War*, p. 222; cf. p. 224.

[27] V.A. Kozlov and S. V. Mironenko (ed.), *Архив новейшей истории России Том I: «Особая папка» И.В. Сталина; Из материалов Секретариата НКВД-МВД СССР 1944-1953 гг. Каталог документов* (Moscow, 1994), p. 113; V.N. Zemskov, *Возращение советских перемещенных лиц в СССР. 1944-1952 гг.* (Moscow, 2016), pp. 51-52.

[28] General V. Naumenko (ed.), *Великое Предательство: Выдача Казаков в Лиенце и Других Местах (1945-1947); Сборник материалов и документов* (New York, 1962-70), ii, p. 53.

[29] Zemskov, *Возращение советских перемещенных лиц в СССР*, p. 261. For Shamarin's role in the GULAG administration, cf. A.I. Kokurin and Yu.N. Morukov (ed.), *Сталинские Стройки ГУЛАГА 1930-1953* (Moscow, 2005), pp. 107, 109, 111.

[30] For first-hand accounts of conditions in Kemerovo Oblast, cf. Victor Kravchenko, *I Chose Freedom: The Personal and Political Life of a Soviet Official* (London, 1947); pp. 316-41; *Le procès Kravchenko contre Les Lettres françaises: Compte Rendu des Audiences d'après la Sténographie suivi d'un index des noms cités* (Paris, 1949), pp. 342-400, 436-37, 446-50; Naumenko (ed.), *Великое Предательство*, ii, pp. 266, 304-6; A. Petrowsky, *Unvergessener Verrat!: Roosevelt - Stalin - Churchill 1945* (Munich, 1965), pp. 329-31, 336; Karl-Gottfried Vierkorn, *Gefangen in Sibirien: Achteinhalb Jahre hinter Stacheldraht* (Oberaudorf, 1994), pp. 51-55; E.B. Polskaya, *Это мы, Господи пред Тобою...* (Nevinnomyssk, 1995), pp. 89-283; Viktor Karpov, 'Долгая дорога в Лиенц', in N.S. Timofeev and S.D. Bodrov (ed.), *Война и судьбы* (Nevinnomyssk, 2002-5), ii, pp. 69-74.

[31] Dmitri Volkogonov, *Сталин: Политический Портрет* (Moscow, 1994), i, pp. 516-17. This incidentally attests to the large number of émigrés handed over by the British, whose detention required construction of entire camps.

[32] Naumenko (ed.), *Великое Предательство*, ii, pp. 308-9. 'One of the most frequent forms of interrogation was the "conveyor" method, where several investigators took turns in the non-stop interrogation of a prisoner for several days without sleep, forcing the prisoner to stand or sit in uncomfortable positions. Often such conveyor interrogations involved beatings and other forms of torture' (Oleg V. Khlevniuk, *The History of the Gulag: From Collectivization to the Great Terror* (Yale, 2004), p. 151). For individual experiences of this practice, cf. W.G. Krivitsky, *I was Stalin's Agent* (London, 1939), pp. 213-25; Elinor Lipper, *Eleven Years in Soviet Prison Camps* (London, 1951), pp. 40-42.

[33] Letter to the author of 16th April 1979.

[34] Naumenko (ed.), *Великое Предательство*, i, p. 117.

[35] The Cossack cadet school, commanded by a Colonel Medynsky, was also

established at Amlach (*ibid.*, i, pp. 152-54, 241-43; WO.170/4988). As a notable White émigré, care was taken to include Medynsky among Cossack officers handed over to SMERSH on 29 May.

[36] Naumenko (ed.), *Великое Предательство*, ii, pp. 139-40. Krasnov had formally transferred his authority to Domanov on 18 February 1945 (*ibid.*, p. 107).

[37] WO.170/4184,674.

[38] Cowgill, Brimelow, and Booker Esq, *The Repatriations from Austria in 1945: The Report of an Inquiry*, pp. 199-200; Booker, *A Looking-Glass Tragedy*, p. 309; Trial Transcript, Day 8.

[39] Cf. Nicholas Bethell, *The Last Secret: Forcible Repatriation to Russia 1944-7* (London, 1974), pp. 104, 113.

[40] On the day of Ariadna's journey (26 May) 36th Infantry Brigade recorded that 'additional tps have been brought into the Bde area' (WO.170/4396). The accuracy of such details, established by documentary evidence of which she could have possessed no knowledge, attests to the credibility of her account of the journey.

[41] Ariadna Delianich, *Вольфсберг - 373* (San Francisco, 1950), pp. 58-59. Booker sought to discredit the embarrassing authority of Ariadna's testimony by rejecting a horrifying description elsewhere in her book of the final delivery of Slovene soldiers despatched by 5th Corps to Tito. Declaring that her account represents 'one of the most shocking passages in *The Minister and the Massacres*', he pronounced it incredible on grounds that 'There is not a shred of evidence to corroborate this account ... It is now clear that Delianich's account is imaginary' (Booker, *A Looking-Glass Tragedy*, p. 254). The *non sequitur* is too obvious to require notice. Why should there necessarily have been corroboration? It does not appear that any victim escaped that day's operation, and British sources might well have been chary of recording the appalling action. The brutality, although undeniably horrible, involved a single death, and pales into insignificance when compared with atrocities perpetrated at Peggetz, Oberdrauburg, and elsewhere. In fact, wherever Delianich's memoir can be checked, it is demonstrably accurate. Furthermore, her description of the atrocious killing of a fugitive by machine-gun fire can by no means be dismissed as lurid fantasy. On the previous day at Spittal a burst of machine-gun fire was employed to deter an escaping Cossack officer (WO.170/4396, Appx 'A'). Had he continued to run, he would doubtless have suffered a similar fate: 'Any attempt whatsoever at resistance will be dealt with firmly by shooting to kill' (WO.170/5025).

[42] Naumenko (ed.), *Великое Предательство*, i, pp. 191-92; Zoe Polanska-Palmer, *Yalta Victim* (Edinburgh, 1986), pp. 121-22.

[43] Naumenko, *Великое Предательство*, i, p. 192.

[44] Trial Transcript, Day 30. Dennis's lengthy first-hand testimony is discreetly ignored in Booker's *magnum opus*, although he devotes three laborious

chapters to the Aldington libel trial at which it was submitted.

[45] GSO1 5 Corps (Turton) - 78 Inf Div: 'Ref Gen Shkuro's sword. This not to be handed over to Russians yet. 78 Div will hold and ask for further instrs from 5 Corps. Other offrs swords to be handed over as previously arranged' (WO.170/4389).

[46] Delianich, *Вольфсберг - 373*, pp. 83-84. An old emigrant from Serbia, Ara was employed by the British as an interpreter (does this account for the oddity that the British soldiers who gave her a lift in their armoured car adopted the precaution of speaking in French?). On the previous day she had been acting as interpreter at Weitensfeld (Naumenko (ed.), *Великое Предательство*, ii, pp. 156-57).

[47] WO.170/4461.

[48] Naumenko, *Великое Предательство*, ii, p, 301; N.N. Krasnov, *Незабываемое 1945-1956* (San Francisco, 1957), pp. 41, 44-47; B.K. Ganusovsky, *10 Лет за Железным Занавесом 1945-1955: Записки Жертвы Ялты. Выдача XV Казачего Корпуса* (San Francisco, 1983), pp. 38-39; Polskaya, *Это мы, Господи пред Тобою*, p. 55.

[49] WO.170/4461.

[50] *Ibid.*

[51] Naumenko (ed.), *Великое Предательство*, i, p. 140; Peter J. Huxley-Blythe, *The East Came West* (Caldwell, Idaho, 1964), pp. 124-25.

[52] This is another significant piece of evidence to emerge from the death-camps of GULAG. It was in the notorious gold-mining complex of slave labour camps at Karaganda that Krasnov's nephew Nikolai obtained this information from his fellow-prisoner Captain Butlerov (Krasnov, *Незабываемое*, pp. 25-27).

[53] Naumenko, *Великое Предательство*, i, pp. 158-59. Cf. Krasnov, *Незабываемое*, p. 27. Lydia Feodorovna received much comfort at this fraught time from the Rev. Kenneth Tyson, Chaplain to the Argylls.

[54] Naumenko (ed.), *Великое Предательство*, i, p. 141.

[55] Cf. Gabriela Stieber, *Nachkriegsflüchtlinge in Kärnten und der Steiermark* (Graz, 1997), pp. 238-40, plates 5-8.

[56] Naumenko (ed.), *Великое Предательство*, ii, plate between 96-97: cf. p. 300.

[57] Information provided me by Captain A.P. Judge, who was present at the occasion.

[58] Cf. Naumenko (ed.), *Великое Предательство*, i, p. 145.

[59] WO.170/4461.

[60] Christopher Booker claimed that the release at Spittal of Colonel Kuchuk Ulagai, on grounds of his Albanian citizenship, proves that regular screening of prisoners at Spittal was put into effect: 'It was agreed, under the terms of the 21st May definition order, that he should not be included in the party for repatriation the following day' (*A Looking-Glass Tragedy*, p. 249). As ever, Booker's claim is false. In none of the sources is it suggested that Ulagai was

reprieved in consequence of Low's 'Definition' (*e.g.* WO.170/5025; WO.170/4461; Krasnov, *Незабываемое*, p. 34). What happened is this. Suspicious of Ulagai's failure to return, his wife showed his Albanian passport to Colonel Odling-Smee of 5th Buffs. The latter promptly telephoned Spittal, gaining thereby what he understood to be a reprieve (information to the author from Colonel Odling-Smee). To his family, Ulagai explained subsequently that he was released through the intervention of King Zog of Albania, who was then living in Cairo as the guest of King Faroukh (information from Colonel Ulagai's nephew Murat Natriboff). In reality it would have been impossible for Ulagai to have made such a contact at that time. A possible explanation is that he mentioned his connexion with King Zog to Colonel Bryar at Spittal, and pursued it subsequent to his release.

[61] WO.170/4396.

[62] The foregoing narrative is based primarily on the detailed eyewitness account by General Krasnov's great-nephew Nikolai (*Незабываемое*, pp. 28-40). For further details, cf. WO.170/4461, Appendix 'C'; Naumenko (ed.), *Великое Предательство*, ii, pp. 144-301; Pavel E. Nazarenko, *В Гостях у Сталина: 14 Лет в Советских Концлагерях* (Melbourne, 1969), pp. 5-9; G.G. Verbitsky, *Остарбайтеры: История Россиян Насильственно Вывезенных на Работы в Германию (Вторая Мировая Война)* (Vestal, NY, 2001), pp. 255-57.

[63] WO.170/4461.

CHAPTER XV
STALIN'S VENGEANCE

Biding his time, this man [Stalin] has taken revenge sooner or later upon everyone who ever criticized him vitally.

W. G. Krivitsky, *I was Stalin's Agent* (London, 1939), p. 243.

Those who dispatched the Cossacks and Yugoslavs to their enemies nurtured no illusions as to their likely fate. General Robertson, on issuing the order intended to implement the violent handovers, confessed that he 'could not bother at this time about who might or might not be turned over to the Russians and Partisans to be shot'. When Harold Macmillan authorized the handover of the Cossacks and White Russians, he noted without apparent regret that, 'To hand them over to the Russians is condemning them to slavery, torture and probably death'.

Within 5th Corps, virtually everyone shared this grim premonition. Captain Anthony Crosland, a young intelligence officer with 1st Guards Brigade of pronounced left-wing views, recorded impressions in his diary on 29 May:

> I witnessed today one of the less agreable aspects of peace, or rather retribution: the handing over to the Soviet Army of large numbers of Russian nationals who had been fighting in the ranks of the Wehrmacht. There are thousands & thousands of these men all told, mainly Cossacks, Ukrainians & White Russians. What prompted them to join the Germans I do not in any detail know: mainly, probably, the prospect of food & release from German prison camps. When we first came into Austria, they all made strenuous & ultimately successful efforts to surrender to us rather than to the Russians or Tito. But now the Russians have demanded them back, & this was apparently agreed at Yalta: they say they will shoot the officers as traitors, & use the remainder as forced labour. So, rather cold-bloodedly, we hand them over disarmed to the Russians.
>
> There have been difficulties already. The secret of their fate somehow leaked out a few days ago; some have already committed suicide, others tried to escape and were shot. This morning a deputation arrived, asking if they could be shot on the spot instead of being handed over. Eventually, however, the gt. majority are got away somehow or other.

The scene of this particular hand-over was the bridge at Judenburg which is the frontier between our zone & the Russians. The road down to the bridge was lined for half a mile with armed British soldiers, & armoured cars sat at vantage points in the town, to guard against any last-minute break-away. Across the bridge was the Russian committee of welcome, composed mostly of a smart-looking Guards unit with green-topped caps, partly of a scruffy Mongol-looking tank unit; they nearly all had medals on their chest, & were generally a well turned-out and pleasant-looking crowd.

At length the convoy rolled up under heavy guard. They were mainly Cossacks: rough, brutish-looking peasant types in fur hats, most of them men of middle age, but with some boys. One knew that these Cossacks had committed some of the worst atrocities of the war:[*] one knew they thoroughly deserved a traitor's fate: yet as they craned their heads out of the trucks to try & see what lay in front of them, one forgot all that, & felt nothing but pity. All one saw was a lot of simple uncomprehending men being shepherded off under guard to a black & hopeless future: in the case of the officers, going off to certain death; and for a few moments, as I looked at the youngsters particularly, I could hardly stand the whole scene, & nearly broke down.[1]

The barbaric treatment inflicted by the Soviet regime on more than two million of its citizens returned under the terms of the Yalta Agreement is today sufficiently well known. Here the focus is specifically on the fate of General Krasnov and other old émigrés among the Cossacks: those whom no interpretation of the Agreement could envisage as liable for enforced 'return' to a Soviet Union in which they had never lived.[†]

After being rushed from the cage at Spittal to the Soviet lines at Judenburg, the Cossack officers were placed in custody under guard by troops of Marshal Tolbukhin's army. Just across the bridge over the river Mur (where some Cossacks had seized opportunity of hurling themselves to their deaths) was a huge concrete steel mill. Its machinery had already been dismantled and removed by the Soviets, and a large chamber within

---

[*] It has been seen that this groundless charge was circulated by 5th Corps headquarters in order to induce British troops to approve the Cossacks' betrayal (cf. Chapter Ten, notes 11 and 12).

[†] Morally, it goes without saying, the return of the mass of Cossacks by force against Alexander's explicit orders was just as bad. My focus on the White émigrés arises in major part from their acting as 'the canary in the cage': their betrayal was so flagrantly treacherous and contrary to orders as to highlight the conspiratorial nature of the Cossack handovers overall. The accompanying dispatch of tens of thousands of fugitives from Tito's regime to certain death in Yugoslavia is described in my book *The Minister and the Massacres*, censored in Britain since 1990.

the empty structure, 250 metres by 50, was now employed as a temporary prison for the Cossack officers. Red Army officers, agog with curiosity, came to visit them. For the wretched Domanov and other former Soviet citizens, they displayed nothing but contempt; they were traitors to their Motherland

But for the White officers, veterans of the Civil War who had neither acknowledged Soviet power nor ever lived in the USSR, they displayed marked politeness and respect. They were especially delighted at encountering in person the legendary Shkuro, whose racy reminiscences of their old battles in 1919, interlarded with an inimitable range of obscene language, brought him a circle of admiring listeners. What the Soviet officers could not understand, however, was how the British had come to include their old allies among those returned. Their commanding officer, General Dolmatov, expressed astonishment at finding tsarist officers among the prisoners.[2]

Shortly afterwards arrived a body of interrogators from SMERSH, who were rather less gentlemanly in their attitude. However, they, too, appeared surprised that the British had made so uncalled-for a concession.

'Surname, Christian name, patronymic, date and place of birth? Where were you living before 1939?' asked a Chekist, stopping before one of the old émigrés, who was one of the few to survive to recount his experiences.

'I named a town in the Balkans. He stopped writing and glanced up at me:

'Then you're an emigrant? You're not liable for repatriation. Comrade Stalin did not claim the old emigrants. Why are you here?' 'They handed me over by means of a trick. I was never a Soviet citizen. I am a Bulgarian citizen'.

The Cossack felt a brief moment of rising hope, to be dashed by his interrogator's next words:

'You're not liable for repatriation, but once you end up here you don't get out again. I myself worked in Germany, but now I have returned against my wishes'.

A few days later, when the Cossacks had been moved to a fresh transit point, the same old emigrant encountered identical incredulity from a SMERSH investigator:

'Émigré? You're not liable for repatriation, but once in our hands you don't get out of here!'[3]

That the lower echelons of the SMERSH team were apparently ignorant of the secret agreement including old émigrés in the handover may suggest that up to the last minute their superiors were by no means confident that the British really would make so abject a concession - one for which the Soviets were offering no known *quid pro quo*.

SMERSH officers who came to watch the departure of the Tsarist generals on the next stage of their journey were at once contemptuous of British duplicity and bewildered by their motivation. One of the group later mused over a puzzling aspect of the deal.

> One evening when I was looking through the list of Cossack officers, before they were dispatched to Moscow (we received these lists from our investigation branch), I went over the whole affair in my own mind. How could the British have done this? Perhaps it was the work of their socialists, who, after all, were also in the government. But Churchill, the Prime Minister! You could hardly call him a socialist! Yes indeed, there was a lot I couldn't understand.[4]

Many Cossacks travelled no further than the Judenburg steel-mill. Within it, British troops across the river heard repeated bursts of small-arms fire during the next few days. They were able to guess what a Russian man and wife living in the town confirmed, both from their own observation and that of other local informants.

> Under the roar of the factory engines shootings continued day and night. On the right of the highroad, opposite the factory, was a workmen's settlement. Some of them (former Communists) managed to gain entry to the factory where they saw and heard much. One day the inhabitants of this settlement, as well as those in the town, were astonished: the factory had begun to operate! Smoke was rising from the factory chimneys, but all the workers remained unsummoned at home. Every gaze was turned towards what was happening in the factory. Scouts were sent out. Their report was regarded as absurd and incredible, and nobody believed it: the Soviets were cremating the Cossacks ... However, they swiftly came to accept it as soon as work began again for the settlement, and after the whole town was oppressed by the stench of burning human flesh. The factory was 'working' for five and a half days. After this came the last detachments of Cossacks (it was 15 July 1945),[5] and Russian girls formerly working in the district were summoned to the factory. Their task was to 'scour the factory of Cossack parasites'. This was the expression used by one of the Soviet officers.[6]

Not all victims were murdered in the factory. Sergeant George Rhodes of the Royal Artillery travelled with a truckload of Cossacks to Judenburg. In his case the convoy was directed to cross over into the Soviet zone.

On both sides of the bridge stood the Russian soldiers armed with tommy guns. They wore green coloured anoraks, and looked a really vicious lot. We crossed the bridge, turned right and a bit further on down the road we turned left into a kind of quarry, then we stopped. The Russians dropped the tailboards, and with quick crisp commands had the Cossacks jumping out of the trucks like fire crackers. They gave us short shrift and told us to clear off, which we did. On going back up the hill we heard the sound of machine gun fire.[7]

Major Claud Hanbury-Tracy-Domvile, who served with Military Government in Judenburg following its absorption into the British zone of Austria, remembered 'finding roadside graves of desperate attempts to escape. The whole operation shocked the local Austrians'.[8]

For the most distinguished of the old émigrés, those tsarist generals whom 5th Corps had taken such particular precautions to inveigle into their trap, a special fate was reserved. First an English officer presented the Soviet colonel with a carefully compiled list of prisoners being handed over. Then, even as the leading Cossack generals were descending from their vehicle after crossing the bridge at Judenburg, a senior Red Army officer approached, calling out, 'Who in this group is General Peter Krasnov?'

The old Ataman identifying himself, he and his companions were at once separated from the other Cossack officers. With General Krasnov were his nephews General Semeon Nikolaevich and Colonel Nikolai Nikolaevich Krasnov, and the latter's young son, also Nikolai Nikolaevich. It was young Nikolai who miraculously survived ten nightmare years of slave labour to reemerge in the West, where he wrote the memoir from which this account is principally drawn. Accompanying the four Krasnovs were Generals Shkuro, Vasiliev, Solamakhin, Domanov, and Sultan-Ghirei, together with old General Krasnov's aide-de-camp, Colonel Morgunov. Of these only Domanov was a Soviet citizen. Treated for the most part with respectful politeness by their Red Army guards, they were confined in the former factory office. There they were joined by General Helmuth von Pannwitz, German commander of the 15th Cossack Cavalry Corps.

Shortly thereafter, a Red Army captain entered to request that Generals Krasnov and Shkuro visit the Soviet general commanding in the Judenburg district. As they were leaving the room, Shkuro cynically contrasted the polite attitude of their declared enemy with that of those treacherous 'friends' who had presented him with one of their highest decorations, and with equal equanimity now arranged his coming murder:

Very likely it will be pleasanter talking with 'our people' than with 'those others'.

General Dolmatov proved to be the best type of Red Army officer. In his mess was assembled a group of his colonels, who greeted the White commanders with studied courtesy. It turned out that they had been fighting in 1918 and 1919 on opposite sides of the same front. At once reminiscences were exchanged in lively manner, all reflections of a political nature being studiously avoided. As the conversation drew to a close, Dolmatov declared with evident sincerity:

> I would like to think that you both are not distressed at the prospect of returning to the Motherland. Believe me, the war has changed many things. Soviet power is no longer something to fear. You, as I am told, are travelling to Moscow. They won't hold you long there. They'll talk to you, find out what they need, and send you away. You'll meet many old friends, recall old times and live out your own lives in the Motherland. Good luck!

Throughout their brief period in the hands of the Red Army, the White officers received the same courteous treatment. Dolmatov's feelings reflected a sentiment widely held in the Red Army at this time. After the unparalleled victory over Hitler's hordes, a feeling of euphoria affected much of the population of the Soviet Union. All their unparalleled sacrifices and dauntless heroism could not have been for nothing, and the new world promised in official propaganda must now surely have arrived![9] Stalin sensed this mood and dreaded it: now that the external enemy was miraculously defeated, he would have to turn once again on the yet more feared internal foe – the Russian people.

From time to time the prisoners received callers of a different stamp from the gentlemanly officers and friendly men of the Judenburg garrison. Young Nikolai Krasnov (the source of the account which follows) recalled:

> We were called upon by silent visitors – officer agents of Soviet counter-intelligence: SMERSH and the military branch of the NKVD. They entered the room, took us in with a glance, as if counting heads, and went away, shutting the door firmly behind them.

These in turn were replaced by another distinguished, highly decorated army general whose name they did not learn. He talked much with General Krasnov, appearing intensely interested in all the old Don Ataman had to say on the situation in their country. Repeating Dolmatov's assurances of honorable treatment and a new future for the postwar Soviet Union, he went on to ask how Krasnov envisaged developments. Deeply impressed by what he had just seen of the Red Army, Krasnov thought for a few moments, then declared:

> The future of Russia is a great one! Of that I have no doubt. The Russian people are immovable as a fortress. They are forged in steel. They have endured not just a single tragedy, nor just a single yoke. The future lies with the people, and not with the government. Regimes come and go, and Soviet power will pass. Neros are born and vanish. Not the USSR, but Russia will deservedly regain her honorable place in the world.

The Soviet general was visibly struck by these words, on which he stood reflecting, untroubled by the presence of a number of other Red Army officers. Then, as he turned to leave, he asked suddenly whether among the 'gentlemen' present there were any Soviet people. Domanov and another ex-Red Army man reluctantly acknowledged themselves. The General gazed sternly at them, then said:

> Look, these people, whom we call "Whites", in 1918 and thereabouts fought against us with arms and propaganda. Openly. They held to their ludicrous reactionary ideology. They are our enemies, but to some extent I can understand them. The Soviet Union nurtured you,[10] made you what you are, gave you a position, and how did you repay her? Well, as it happens they'll be talking about all that with you in Moscow. You haven't got long to wait!

With which he departed abruptly.*

Not long afterwards the whole party was driven in trucks to Graz, where their guards were replaced by SMERSH officers. After a night in prison, they travelled to a SMERSH operational base at Baden-bei-Wien, where they were photographed and subjected to that repetitive questioning to which the Soviet security services were so addicted. Old General Krasnov was questioned at length about his career as a novelist; young Nikolai was surprised by the interrogators' familiarity with the general's works. It seemed that his literary prowess was regarded as a greater threat to the Soviet Union than his military activities in 1917 and 1918.

On 4 June the party was flown to Moscow. At the aerodrome they were transferred to prison vans – marked 'Bread' on the outside to mislead Western journalists – that drove them at speed through the streets to another large prison. Guided along endless corridors past rows and rows of cells, Nikolai Krasnov was eventually thrust into a recess smaller than a telephone kiosk, in which he could neither sit nor stand. It was a strange homecoming to the country he had left within a few months of his birth,

---

* Could this unidentified general have been Marshal Tolbukhin?

of which he naturally possessed no memory. He was in the Lubianka, headquarters of the NKVD.

> I winced at a terrible shriek which – it seemed to me – rang out almost from within my own cell. It was a woman's scream;
>
> 'Kill me, you devils, but let me breathe! Aaaah!'
>
> I felt as if my hair stood on end. My heart froze. In the years that followed I often seemed to hear that woman's scream. For then I knew nothing of the fate of my wife and mother, nor of any of the wives and mothers of our officers.

Everything in the building was calculated, whether deliberately or not, to induce in its involuntary inmates a surreal state of alienation. The innumerable identical passages, the deadly silence, the bizarre regulations and purposeless rituals – all these were enough in themselves to affect a prisoner's mental equilibrium.

> We passed through corridors. Not once was there a turning. Doors. Doors. More corridors. It seemed to me that they were conducting me through a labyrinth in order to destroy my sense of direction. It is possible that we traversed the same route more than once, but everything was so monotonous and featureless that I had no means of knowing.

Finally, Nikolai was shown into a room where he was stripped and searched with extraordinary minuteness from head to foot. Dissatisfied even with this, a supervising colonel of the MVD (Ministry of Internal Affairs) drove his finger unexpectedly up the young man's rectum, elegantly wiping it afterwards on his own handkerchief. Satisfied at last, the colonel ordered the guards to dress Krasnov in his uniform, 'and take him at once to "him"'. Once again, they passed through the succession of passages and ascended an unknown number of floors in a silent lift, until Krasnov found himself unexpectedly taken down a richly carpeted passage and ushered into a large, luxuriously-furnished chamber. With a pang of anguish and delight, he found himself standing before his father. But before they could exchange more than a few words, they were taken on through a high doorway into an even larger hall, carpeted in deep piled Bokhara, whose walls were decorated with a three yard-high portrait of Stalin, and another of his security chief, Lavrenty Beria. In the far depths of the room, the Krasnovs saw before them, seated at a magnificent writing-table, a general in the uniform of the MVD. 'Merkulov!' came a whisper from behind their backs. So this was the mysterious 'him' whom Nikolai was to see! Every Russian, Red or White, knew the name of the dreaded Minister of State Security, second only to Beria in the Soviet hierarchy of terror.

Vsevolod Nikolaevich Merkulov had risen to power in December 1938, after Beria replaced the criminal dwarf Yezhov as head of the NKVD. At the time of the Revolution, he had been a student in Baku with Beria, who continued to entrust him with commissions of great importance. In 1940, he travelled to Berlin as colleague-cum-watchdog with Molotov during the latter's discussions with Stalin's ally Hitler. That same year he and Beria implemented Stalin's decision to massacre the Polish officers at Katyn,[11] and in 1941 he organized the mass deportation of citizens from the occupied Baltic States.[12] After the shift in alliances, when Hitler's invasion threw Stalin into the arms of Britain, Merkulov was responsible for arranging for British engineers to destroy the Baku oil wells in the event of a victorious German Army's conquering the Caucasus. Now, as his ensuing words were clearly to imply, he had been assigned control of delicate negotiations with the British resulting in the secret surrender of the tsarist veterans.[13]

Merkulov plainly attached great symbolic importance to the capture of the famous Civil War generals, and though normally far from loquacious he could not resist the temptation to unburden himself before two victims who were unlikely to live to repeat the tale. His words are of great significance and merit repeating from Nikolai Krasnov's detailed memoir. As we will see, there are strong reasons for accepting the accuracy of his account.

> The General remained silent. We – did not stir. Then he slowly raised his great head and examined us boldly and openly, just as people examine the exhibits at a waxworks exhibition. The officer, like a statue, stood behind our backs.

'Have some tea and a bite to eat, "gentlemen" Krasnov!' Merkulov suddenly said in a sharp voice. 'And provide them with cigarettes'. An obliging hand set out an open packet of Kazbek cigarettes on our little table. The officer went out.

Once again there was silence. A long drawn-out silence. Merkulov was clearly waiting for us to take our tea. A tray appeared with the steaming drink, deliciously bitter to smell. An attractive service. On the plates – 'all sorts of "honors"', as my father liked to say. 'Go ahead!' ordered the general. There were just the three of us. 'Don't be shy, "gentlemen"! Eat up and drink your tea,' continued Merkulov, rising to his feet. 'It is not often we have tea parties in the Lubianka. Only for special guests!' A peculiar smile appeared on his face, quite masking his intentions.

'When you've finished eating, I shall tell you something. They have probably already told you who I am. I am – Merkulov, one of your future – well, let's say it – bosses!'

A pause. The General walked backwards and forwards by his desk, softly swaying at the hips and turning lithely on his heel.[*]

'How was your journey? You weren't airsick?' (What was that, a hint at Shkuro?) Has anything upset you? Is there anything you need?' And not waiting for a reply swiftly, as if it were no concern to him, Merkulov addressed himself directly to Father:

'Why don't you smoke, Krasnov, and why not drink your tea? It seems to me that you're not very chatty or friendly! I've a feeling that by this silence you are trying to conceal your agitation, your fear; but there's no need for concern. At least, not in this room. Look, when they summon you before the interrogator, I advise you to speak only the truth and find an answer to every question otherwise ... we shall have to string you up'. Merkulov laughed softly.

'Do you know how they hang people here? First of all slowly, by easy stages ... even not too painfully ... but afterwards ... Haven't you read the detailed accounts of such interrogations in Ataman Krasnov's books?

My fingers grew cold. In my temples a pulse beat out a furious "tom-tom". My heart beat so loudly, that the noise might have been heard by Merkulov, standing at his desk a bare ten metres away. My father was silent. His face was pale but perfectly composed. I envied him.

'Don't hope for freedom', continued the General; 'you're not children! However, should you not be obstinate, all formalities will be concluded easily, you will sign something-or-other, you will serve a couple of years in ITL[†] and there you will become accustomed to our way of life – you'll find it a delightful part of the world. Then, perhaps we'll let you go. You'll live'.

Again a pause.

'There it is, Colonel Krasnov, choose between telling the truth and staying alive, or refusal and death. Don't think I'm scaring you. On the contrary! Why, Peter Nikolaevich, Semeon Nikolaevich and you – are

---

[*] 'Beside Beria had been standing a man with an athletic figure and a splendid head of thick dark hair flecked with grey ... This was Merkulov, my future boss, first People's Commissar and then Minister' ('Romanov', *Nights are Longest There*, p. 55).

[†] *ispravitelno-trudovoi lager*: 'corrective labour camp'.

our old acquaintances!

'In 1920 you managed to slip like quicksilver out of our hands, but now it is we who hold all the cards. You're not getting away...'

He took several steps back and forth. His hands were clasped behind his back, and he twiddled his crossed fingers. I could not help noticing that a ring gleamed on one of them.

'So, Colonel, shall we have a little talk?'

'I have nothing to talk to you about!' my father replied sharply. 'What do you mean by "nothing"?' laughed the Chekist quietly. 'Agreement is worth more than money, Krasnov. Your past doesn't interest us. We know all about that. But there are certain small details about your recent activities which it would do no harm to hear from your lips'.

'I've nothing to tell you! I don't understand what all this procrastination is about. Finish the whole business now. A bullet in the back of the neck and ...'

'Oh, no, "Mister" Krasnov'. Merkulov smiled crookedly as he lowered himself into an armchair. 'Things are not as simple as that. Just think. A bullet in the back of the neck, and that's all? Nonsense, Your Excellency. You'll have to work. There's plenty of time before you get in your coffin. Time enough before you fertilize the ground. But first you will work for the good of the Motherland! A spot of timber-felling, a spell in the mines with water up to your belt. You will spend time, my dear, up by the 70th parallel. That'll be interesting. 'You'll see life', as we say. You don't know "our" language. You don't know the camp slang which has sprung up in the polar region. You'll be hearing .... You'll walk with macaroni legs', the general roared with laughter. 'But you'll work. Hunger will keep you at it'.

We sat in silence. My head buzzed. The palms of my hands were sweating from impotent rage. 'We've got to build, Colonel Krasnov! And where shall we find the hands? There's no great profit from the gallows and the "blindfold". Times have changed. We shoot people only rarely. We need hands that work, that don't need paying. We've waited twenty-five years for this joyful meeting with you. You émigrés have had quite long enough deluding your young people abroad'.

Merkulov was a little out of breath after his monologue. A thick vein stood out on his forehead. His eyes became sharp with spite and hatred. 'You're scared? What of? Scared of work? But what is the point of all this? You don't believe a word I say, and I don't believe any of yours. To me you are a White bandit, and to you I am Red scum. However, we Reds are on top now. So it was in 1920, and so it is now. Power is with us. We don't flatter ourselves with the hope that we'll manage to reeducate Krasnov and convert him into an obedient Soviet sheep; you'll never be smitten with love for us. But we'll make you work for communism, build it up, and that will provide the greater moral satisfaction'.

Merkulov fell silent, fixing his eyes expectantly on Father. 'Why all this long introduction?' replied Father in a tired voice. 'I understand everything perfectly without explanations, general. I am quite aware how hopeless is our position. My son and I are soldiers. We have both fought. We have both looked death in the face. It makes no difference to us on which parallel, the seventieth or the hundredth, he sweeps his scythe. I only kick myself for one thing: why did we trust the English? However, my head will be off.

'Ah! If it were only death!' sneered Merkulov. 'You can drop those resounding words about "a soldier's death". That's – outdated rubbish. Death came past you, without even noticing you. But, that you trusted the English – that was true stupidity. They are – a nation of shopkeepers! They will sell their best friends without blinking an eyelid. Their policy is – prostitution. Their Foreign Office – is a brothel, in which sits a *premier* – a great diplomatic "madam". They trade in other people's lives and their own conscience.

'We? We don't trust them, Colonel. That's why we took the reins into our own hands. They don't know, that we have them checkmated and now we have made them dance to our tune, like the last pawn. Sooner or later there will come the battle between the communist bear and the Western bulldog. There will be no mercy for our sugared, honeyed, grovelling, fawning allies – there will be none! They'll fly away to the devil's mother with all their kings, with all their traditions, lords, castles, heralds, Orders of the Bath and Garters, and white wigs.

There'll remain under the lash of the bear's paw nothing of all those, who nurture the hope that their gold will rule the world. Our healthy, socially strong, young idea – the idea of Lenin – of Stalin – will conquer! That's how it'll be, Colonel!'

Merkulov stood up and, concluding these last words, crashed the side of his hand sharply on to the table.

After a similar tirade directed at Nikolai Krasnov, Merkulov dismissed the prisoners. Nikolai saw his father once again, in October of that year, and then no more. The colonel, like his son, was sent to one of the northern labor camps where the harsh conditions killed him even more swiftly than Merkulov had anticipated. This verbatim account of the interview with Merkulov is, like all reported conversations, a reconstruction from memory. However, despite its melodramatic content, there are compelling reasons for accepting it as accurate in essential details. When Nikolai Krasnov came to write the memoir from which these excerpts are drawn, he noted:

> Despite the fact that eleven years have elapsed, this meeting with Merkulov and everything he said made such an indelible impression on my memory that I believe I have reproduced it exactly as it happened. I may have omitted some things, but I have added nothing.

Long years later I was deeply moved to stand in the room that provided the stage for this grim drama. It was on 14 January 1993 that I was received in the Lubianka by Major-General Alexei Kondaurov of the FSB, as the KGB had by then become. He read a copy I had brought of Nikolai Krasnov's account of his reception, after which I asked if I might be permitted to visit the scene of the Krasnovs' grim encounter. He recognized the large room from Nikolai's description and escorted me there. In early years I had once or twice dreamed of being confined in the dreaded Lubianka, but never conceived of the remarkable circumstances in which the visit eventually occurred.[*]

Nikolai Krasnov's total recall was not due solely to the exceptional nature of what had passed, nor to the years of solitary suffering which burned all he had undergone into his consciousness. Immediately after this unnerving interview, Nikolai was parted from his father and taken down to the Lubianka bathhouse, where to his delight he found his great-uncle, Ataman Peter Krasnov. The General was resigned to his coming end, but avowed his confidence that his nephew, young and fit, would somehow win through and return to 'our own people' in the West. He then went on to impose a sacred duty on the young man:

> If you do survive, fulfil this testament of mine. Describe everything you experience, what you see or hear, whom you meet. Describe it as it was. Don't exaggerate the bad. Don't paint in false colors. Do not depreciate what is good. Do not lie. Write only the truth. Keep your eyes wide open. Here, under these circumstances, you will have no chance to write, not even brief notes, so use your mind as a notebook, as a camera. This is important, gravely important. From Lienz to the end of your journey of sufferings, remember it all. The world must learn the truth about what has happened and what is happening, from the betrayal and treachery to

---

[*] During a visit to Moscow in the following year, General Kondaurov invited me to lunch at the Hotel Metropole, formerly headquarters of the Comintern. The reader may be amused to learn that the purpose of our meeting turned out to be a polite invitation to head operations of the Menatep Bank abroad. Since I encounter great difficulty in compiling even a tax return, I felt obliged to decline.

– the end.[14]

Nikolai solemnly vowed and, by what can only appear as a miracle, fulfilled his vow as his 'grandfather' had foretold. After more than ten years in forced labor camps, where he underwent experiences more harrowing even than Merkulov's gloating account could have led him to believe, he was among the tiny number of surviving old émigrés amnestied by Khrushchev and permitted to return to the West. Just after Christmas 1955, he was set free in Berlin, and made his way at once to a cousin in Sweden. There he sat down and did not cease writing until he had completed his story, exactly as required by the old novelist and general.

> Today [he concluded] is January 28, 1956. It is a month today since I came to freedom, to the free world, in Stockholm. In that month I wrote this memoir. I wrote frantically every night. It seemed to me that every extra day distancing me from that boundary landmark, painted red and white and crowned with the five-pointed star, might wipe from memory or introduce new impressions into the mental notebook I had compiled in the USSR. Today I completed my book. I do not know when or under what circumstances it will appear, nor who will publish it; but I have kept my promise given to grandfather in the basement bathroom of the Lubianka Prison.[15]

A year later the book was published in Russian by an émigré publishing house in San Francisco. Although it was widely read by Russians in emigration, and appeared in a slightly inaccurate English translation in New York in 1960,[*] it aroused scant interest in the world at large. Not long after completing his task, the author, his health undermined by years of appalling suffering, died suddenly in Argentina. At least he was able to spend a few precious years with his beloved wife Lily, who had so narrowly escaped suffering the same fate at the hands of the British in Lienz.

It might have seemed to Krasnov and those around him that all had been to little avail, but the old general was surely right. The book has survived, preserving an indestructible testimony. Above all, it has preserved the extraordinary colloquy with Minister of State Security Vsevolod Nikolaevich Merkulov.

Merkulov's rantings, as reported by Krasnov, epitomize much that was endemic in Soviet thinking. There was the bullying tone, the undisguised relish in cruelty, and the obligatory grandiloquent boasts of the invincibility of Soviet power, which can be paralleled almost word for

---

[*] In the translation Major Davies becomes 'Major Stone', a change I can only suppose reflecting the publisher's fear of libel proceedings.

word in comparable declamations of the period. We can also detect the criminal's love of deception for its own sake: the gratification deriving from hoodwinking clever or sanctimonious persons in authority. Then again, a tacit admission of inferiority runs through the whole harangue in face of the superior culture of old Russia and Western Europe; compensated by vindictive sarcasm and a genuinely chiliastic sense of destructive rejuvenation.[16]

In the same month that the Krasnovs were interviewed by Merkulov, the Polish resistance leader Zbygniew Stypułkowski was interrogated by one of his underlings, a Major Tikhonov, in another part of the building. The tone and content of Tikhonov's threats were remarkably similar to those of his superior. 'When we came to discuss my probable sentence', wrote Stypułkowski, 'Tikhonov said it was easy enough to part with one's life, but not so easy to face life-long internment in the Siberian *lagry* (camps)'. His interrogator went on to remark contemptuously:

> What are you waiting for? For an armed conflict of Russia with Great Britain and the U.S.A.? That is only an illusion. Before we reach that stage, you will be watching events from the other world. Besides, there never will be a war with Great Britain – we'll finish her in another way. Once our foot is on India's threshold she won't budge. What can Great Britain do in such circumstances? She is a colossus which we can help to die naturally.[17]

A recurrent theme in Merkulov's train of thought is the treachery and duplicity of the Soviet Union's British ally. Gratification, bemusement, and contempt are intermingled in his assessment. If Merkulov's reactions reflect those of the rest of the Soviet leadership it is clear that, whatever the motive for the British handover of the Cossack generals, their betrayal aroused neither gratitude nor incentive for reciprocity, but merely contempt and mistrust. Nothing in his words intimates that the British received any compensatory concession in return for their remarkable compliance.

Despite the victory of the Bolsheviks, the harassed existence of many Whites in emigration, and the fact that the Krasnovs now lay entirely at his mercy, Merkulov was still possessed by virulent resentment of what he perceived as their pretensions to superior culture and civility. This was perhaps one of the motives which made the Soviet leadership so extraordinarily determined to destroy what to outsiders must have appeared an utterly negligible threat.

Possibly the most tantalizing point in Merkulov's monologue is that in which he alluded to the British public figure who had betrayed the

Whites into his power. His words unmistakably intimate that he had a particular highly-placed official figure in mind. He does not speak of 'the British government'. What makes the glancing reference so suggestive is the strong likelihood that Merkulov knew the identity of his mysterious opposite number on the British side. On 4 June, the date of the interview in the Lubianka, the covert arrangement to include old émigrés in the handover of Soviet citizens was just three weeks old. That it was NKGB general Merkulov who summoned the Krasnovs to crow over their discomfort suggests that it was he who, on the Soviet side, was ultimately in control of exceptionally delicate and important negotiations conducted behind the backs of the British and American governments, and the Allied military command in the Mediterranean. As few people as possible would have been let into the secret, and he was at gloating pains to make it plain that he was *au courant* with all that had passed – even to the petition drawn up in French by General Krasnov in the Kensingtons' cage at Spittal. The Soviet security apparatus was clearly exceedingly well informed of everything on the British side pertaining to the surrender of the Cossacks. As a former SMERSH officer explained, 'our NKVD agents had been with Krasnov for a long time. They had played the parts of anti-Soviet Cossack officers who had gone over to the Germans and were handed over to us along with the others'.[18]

Soviet intelligence officers were included among the personnel of the Soviet military mission attached to Allied Force Headquarters in the palace of Caserta, one of whose prime objectives was the recovery of Soviet nationals in British custody. As this was a political issue, they must naturally have looked to the Minister Resident, Harold Macmillan, for co-operation.[19]

That Merkulov's phraseology was accurately recalled by young Krasnov seems likely. The latter had no reason to associate the British Foreign Office with his betrayal, since the Cossacks knew nothing of the provisions of the Yalta Agreement, and insofar as they considered the matter at all presumed the order for their repatriation had been decided by Churchill and transmitted by Alexander through the normal military channels.[20]

Equally, there is no likelihood that Merkulov was indulging in a general tirade against the Foreign Office for its connection with the Yalta Agreement, into which he subsumed the issue of the unauthorized return of White émigrés. The official British standpoint on the necessity for screening repatriated Russians was undeviating outside Austria, as Soviet representatives at all levels were continually reminded when attempting to overreach their legitimate demands under the terms of the Yalta

Agreement. Equally, if the deliberate inclusion of White émigrés among the Cossacks handed over in Austria resulted from an *ad hoc* military arrangement by 5th Corps or 8th Army, there would be no reason for Merkulov to bring the Foreign Office 'madam' into the picture at all. To Merkulov the distinction between the two operations, the one authorized and the other prohibited by the British Government, was unmistakable. His reference to the buying and selling of 'their own friends' could have no application to the return of Soviet citizens under the Yalta Agreement. In no context could Merkulov have conceived of Britain's sustaining any sense of obligation towards liberated Soviet prisoners, many of whom had served in the German armed forces. Nor would he have envisaged their handover as a betrayal, since from his perspective they were being returned to the State to which their loyalty was due.

Merkulov's words indicate that it was to the old émigrés that he alluded as having been 'sold' by an influential figure whom he associated with the Foreign Office. His reference to this unnamed personality is curious. 'Their Foreign Office [the term is in English in the text] is a brothel, in which sits [or presides] a [or 'the'] "premier", a great diplomatic "madam"'. At first glance this could be taken as an allusion to the Foreign Secretary, Anthony Eden. There are, however, good reasons for rejecting such a conclusion. First, it is hard to envisage any circumstances in which Eden could have played a part in the secret unauthorized arrangement to include White Russians in the surrender. Not only did he possess no means of communicating directly with British generals in the field, but for most of the critical period was not even in England. On 13 April he flew to the United States to attend President Roosevelt's funeral and participate in discussions at the San Francisco Conference. He did not return to England until 17 May, four days after the conspiracy had been put into effect at Klagenfurt.[21] Indeed, far from being in cahoots with Macmillan, it was at this time that Eden expressed annoyance with him for exceeding his powers by 'interfering with Italian and Balkan affairs', claiming, too, that Macmillan 'usurped functions' properly exercised by the Foreign Office.[22]

Although Macmillan's motive for giving Keightley the remit to hand over 'White Russians' along with the Cossacks remains unclear, that he did so is incontrovertible. Could it be that Merkulov or his informants in the Soviet security services mistakenly assumed that Macmillan was a 'Foreign Office' 'premier'? His role as Minister Resident was essentially diplomatic, and his principal aides (Roger Makins, Harold Caccia, Philip Broad, et al.) received their postings from the Foreign Office. The precise nature of his newly-minted function remained ambivalent even to his American counterpart, Robert Murphy.[23]

There is no article in Russian, so 'premier' may signify either 'a' or 'the' premier. The Russian word 'premier' has two distinct meanings, both corresponding to foreign usages. It means, first, 'premier', 'prime minister'; and, second, a leading or 'star' actor. Merkulov's contemptuous allusion, in view of the conventional inappropriateness of the term, suggests that he was indulging in a slighting sneer at the expense of a leading political functionary, whose character he regarded in a showy but contemptible light.

In the overall context of Merkulov's tirade it seems that he considered the anonymous organizer of the White officers' betrayal as something of an effete poseur, 'a leading actor'. By 1945 Macmillan had long adopted what he took for the languid drawl and other attributes of a world weary aristocrat, which were certainly not those of his upbringing. The Duke of Devonshire's family, into which he had married, regarded him (and to some extent treated him, to his mortification) as a clever *arriviste*.[24]

In selling the Whites down the river, Merkulov's shadowy 'premier' and his collaborators had gone further than simply collaborating with legitimate Soviet interests or fulfilling diplomatic obligations; they had 'traded away their own consciences'. Again, the passage employing metaphors drawn from chess may indicate that Merkulov considered his coup to have resulted less from an unexpectedly favorable response to a forceful demand, than from a series of adroit moves, resulting in a concession by no means to Britain's advantage.

However suggestive such considerations might appear, Macmillan's motive will, I fear, always remain obscure. The historian is placed in an awkward situation when considering so tantalizing an issue. Should he ignore it altogether, hostile critics will seize opportunity to assert that this weakens his case (of course it doesn't, but that is another matter). Yet, should he be bold enough to raise the issue, the attempt will as vociferously be condemned as groundless speculation. All that the available evidence is capable of establishing with any degree of certitude is *what* Macmillan did – not *why*.

Further to these considerations may be noted the Soviet concern to suppress public mention of the decisive British role in the betrayal of General Peter Krasnov and his family. This was evident from the start. Transferred from the Lubianka to Lefortovo Prison, on 4 June 1945 young Nikolai Krasnov was shown a document, which to his indignation contained the following concealment of the decisive British role in his abduction:

Citizen Krasnov Nikolai Nikolaevich, born in 1918, a Yugoslav citizen, temporarily detained by organs of SMERSH on former Austrian territory in the zone of occupation of our armed forces, to be taken into custody, and investigations started by organs of the NKGB of the city of Moscow under Article 58 (4 and 1) of the legal code of the RSFSR.[25]

The official Soviet encyclopedia of the Russian Civil War likewise asserts that General Peter Krasnov was 'captured by Soviet forces' (захвачен сов. войсками) in 1945.[26]

The Soviet intelligence chief Pavel Sudoplatov, who was at the time Beria's Director of the Administration for Special Tasks, claimed that the British exchanged General Krasnov for Admiral Raeder, whom they wished to put on trial for alleged crimes perpetrated during the U-boat campaign.[27] This is impossible, as Sudoplatov must have been aware. Raeder remained at large three weeks *after* the Krasnovs' handover by the British, until his capture by Soviet troops on 23 June! Again, it was not until the end of August that the Soviets began to initiate the process for Raeder's delivery to the court at Nuremberg.[28] In reality the British were reluctant to try any German admiral, and in the event Raeder was brought directly from Moscow to face the Nuremberg tribunal.[29]

It seems that Soviet security chiefs were concerned so far as possible to withhold or occlude mention of British participation in the betrayal.

Finally, it may be asked why the show trial of the Cossack generals was conducted in secret. The establishment of a such a court, where the verdict was decided in advance, indicates its essentially ideological and propaganda purpose. Its proceedings, first made available during my 1993 visit to Moscow, convey outward appearance of being fairly conducted, being almost exclusively concerned with the defendants' testimony concerning their activities. No 'confessions' were extracted. One can only infer that Soviet secrecy with regard to British complicity in the fate of the Cossack generals arose from a need to conceal their collaboration in the illicit handovers generally, and specifically to cloak the identity of Merkulov's effete and treacherous 'premier'.

Young Nikolai Krasnov survived his ordeal, thanks to his youth and hardiness. Released with a handful of other White émigrés under Khrushchev's amnesty in 1955, he was reunited with his beloved wife Lydia (Lily) in Argentina, only to die four years later in consequence of heart failure: a belated consequence of the maltreatment he suffered in consequence of British perfidy and Soviet cruelty throughout his ten years of suffering as a slave in the gulag. None of the others of the elite group flown to Moscow was so fortunate. His father (also Nikolai) died in one of the northern camps a few months after his delivery into the hands of SMERSH.[30]

Nikolai and Lydia (Lily) Krasnov in 1959[*]

Stalin's vengeance against General Krasnov and other White Russian leaders, with whom he had waged open and covert war for more than a quarter of a century, was now complete. I conclude this history with intriguing formerly classified Soviet evidence indicating why, even in the aftermath of the defeat of Nazi Germany in 1945, the despot believed he had reason to fear, as well as loathe, General Krasnov's White Army in exile.

---

[*] This touching photograph was sent by Nikolai Krasnov from Argentina in 1959 to my late friend Peter Huxley-Blythe, who in turn bequeathed it to me.

Within a few days of the surrender of Domanov's Cossacks to the British in Austria, the war diary of 8th Argyll and Sutherland Highlanders recorded:

Russian Kantemir Gp. (cf sitrep 15 May)

A group consisting of 4 Offrs, 56 men, 5 women and 2 children from the Cossacks, led by Capt Kantemir who was a leader of a group of agents in the Cossack Div some two years ago. They were recently all trained by the Germans in the N. of Italy in organisation of Partisans, sabotage, and espionage, behind the Soviet lines. Capt Kantemir offered his services in this respect on the 13th, and it was not considered wise to leave the group on its own with the Cossacks. They were therefore despatched to Div today.[31]

The next day 78th Infantry Division cheerfully reported:

BM 36 Bde Require instrs for disposal of 77 ex-PW Russian Saboteurs (willing to go and sabotage Russia). FSS [field security] say they are too dangerous to keep. If no instrs by 0900 hrs 15 May they will be sent to sabotage Div HQ![32]

A grimmer note was struck by their being singled out in Brigadier Low's duplicitous 'Definition' of Russians to be handed over to the Soviets:

405/G 5 Corps - Divs:

Following will be treated as Soviet nationals:- Ataman Group.[33]

It has been widely assumed that 'Ataman Group' was a reference to the leading Cossack generals Krasnov, Shkuro, Domanov, and von Pannwitz, all of whom bore (or had borne) the Cossack honorific rank of Ataman. It can now be seen that this was not the case.

On an unspecified date in June, not long after the British handover of the Cossacks at Judenburg, Lieutenant–Colonel Sokolov of NKVD command at the rear of 3rd Ukrainian Front issued instructions to Colonel Pavlov, commanding the NKVD unit in the town, to adopt rigorous measures ensuring retention in prison of Cossack intelligence officers, and emphasizing the need for prevention of suicides or escapes.

Sokolov particularly stressed the importance of discovering the whereabouts of a group of officers commanded by *essaul* (Cossack captain) Kantimir, son of a White officer, who had assembled an elite parachute unit trained to undertake sabotage operations behind Red Army lines. Trained at a German sabotage school in Kråkow, Kantimir had been seconded to Shkuro, who was then living in Berlin, in the autumn of 1944. The latter knew his father, with whom he had served during the Civil War, suggesting that Kantimir was a White émigré Cossack. Although the British, in fulfilment of Brigadier Low's directive of 21 May, had included Kantimir's force among the thousands of Cossacks handed over at Judenburg, it appears that he and his followers had succeeded in concealing their identity among the thousands repatriated during the early days of June.[*]

Sokolov's instruction concluded:

> Take immediate action to find KANTEMIR. If successful, radio the result. Entrust the examination of KANTEMIR to Major Comrade ROSTILOV.

It is to be suspected that Major Rostilov was a specialist in the NKVD's well-known methods of extracting information from recalcitrant prisoners. However, it seems that the resourceful Captain Kantimir and his men continued in their successful evasion.

Further investigation by SMERSH extracted information that in February and March 1945, following the Cossacks' arrival in Italy, General Shkuro had proposed to the German command that Cossacks be recruited to operate as units conducting sabotage behind Red Army lines. On 4 October 1945 General Domanov, lately commanding the *Kazachi Stan* and now a prisoner in the Lubianka, was interrogated concerning this specialized unit with which SMERSH appeared deeply concerned.

> QUESTION:- In the examination of 29 July you provided evidence for the existence in the "Kazachi Stan" of a spy-sabotage school. Give details of the circumstances, in which this school was created?
>
> REPLY:- Roughly in December 1944 or January 1945 (I don't remember precisely) to me in the "Kazachi Stan", stationed at that time in the town of Tolmezzo, there appeared before me an unknown *essaul* [Cossack captain] who presented himself by the name of Kantimir (whether it was really his name, I don't know). After introducing himself to me, Kantimir declared that he was commander of the spy-sabotage school called "Ataman" and that he had with with him 10 Cossacks from Berlin, trained in the school "Ataman", among whom was a *sotnik* [Cossack lieutenant], who declared himself his aide. (The names of those who accompanied Kantimir were not identified).
>
> QUESTION:- Did Kantimir tell you, who were the complement of the

---

[*] Something of the daredevil nature of the Ataman Group is conveyed by the nickname borne by one of their number. Sympathetic British soldiers at Spittal 'freed a Cossack juvenile, agent of the special parachutist group 'Ataman', nicknamed "Ginger" and "Tracer Bullet"' (Naumenko (ed.), *Великое Предательство*, i, p. 145).

spy-sabotage school "Ataman" and who was nominated their chief?

REPLY: - Kantimir informed me that he personally directed the spy-sabotage school "Ataman", and that it was created with the permission of the head of the Cossack "Reserve" of the White General Shkuro, at a time when Kantimir and his people found themselves with the "Cossack Reserve" in Berlin.

As confirmation of his words Kantimir showed me a letter of recommendation from General Shkuro, in which the latter asked me, as Field Ataman of the "Kazachi Stan" to render assistance to Kantimir and his people with regard to living quarters and rations. He produced General Shkuro's letter.

Generally speaking, Domanov's account was unsatisfactory. He explained that

KANTIMIR told me that those who graduated from the spy-sabotage school were to be sent to the rear of the Red Army with the task of conducting espionage activities. To carry out sabotage on defense facilities, to carry out anti-Soviet agitation among the local population.

The Captain was also authorized to recruit further members of the Ataman Group as required from among the Cossacks. Domanov described him as being about 35 years old, of medium height, with blond hair and grey eyes.

He was unable to specify whether the Ataman Group had actually undertaken any missions, nor could he throw any light on their current whereabouts. The extent of the Soviet leadership's concern with Captain Kantimir and his little group of saboteurs is evidenced by the fact that the existing four-page SMERSH report is in fact a summary of an interrogation that lasted from 11.30 in the morning to 4 o'clock that afternoon.[*]

Not only this, but the obsessive search continued well into the following year. Towards the close of a lengthy interrogation in the Lubianka on 19 September 1946, General Peter Krasnov was questioned concerning

... the Cossack unit of 35 men, called "Ataman".

Question: For what purpose was the "Ataman" unit formed?

Answer: The "Ataman" unit was formed from elite Cossacks for gathering espionage intelligence, and also to conduct anti-Soviet

---

[*] Shkuro's interrogation confirmed evidence already provided by Domanov with regard to Kantimir's activities.

propaganda in the rear of the Soviet Army.

This unit was for a long time trained in parachuting and in methods of conducting subversive operations. Of the final fate of this unit I know nothing.

Krasnov's concluding response suggests that Kantimir and his men continued to evade capture. It is to be feared that even so they would have been swallowed up among their tens of thousands of Cossack comrades dispatched to slavery in Siberia. On the other hand, given their ingenuity, courage, and specialized military skills, it would be gratifying to think that they somehow managed to escape the Soviet maw. More pertinently, readers may be puzzled by the Soviet leadership's obsessive concern with the threat posed by a body comprising a few score hostile troops operating behind Red Army lines. After all, Marshal Tolbukhin's 3rd Ukrainian Front comprised at this time five armies numbering 407,000 officers and men, almost 7,000 guns and mortars, and 407 tanks and specialist guns. In addition, the associated 17th Air Force disposed of 965 warplanes.[34] Furthermore, its rear area was covered by well-equipped NKVD units, whose primary functions were to prevent Red Army desertions and mop up resistance within the occupied zone.

Is it credible that this fearsome war machine felt threatened by a handful of Cossack paratroopers, however courageous and well-armed? Might it not be that they had another target – one consistently identified by General Krasnov's Brotherhood of Russian Truth, and implicitly anticipated in his novel *The White Coat*? Was Stalin personally disturbed by the fact that this highly trained sabotage squad had succeeded in evading the best efforts of SMERSH to track it down, leaving it at large to pursue its goal within the Soviet Union? Where was it now? Could it be that Captain Kantimir was intended to become the Russian Stauffenberg?

Despite its triumphant destruction of the once invincible *Wehrmacht*, Soviet control of the interior in the immediate postwar period was far from monolithic. In one particularly alarming incident in February 1944, Ukrainian resistance fighters succeeded in ambushing a Red Army armored column, when they killed General Nikolai Vatutin and narrowly missed shooting his companion Nikita Khrushchev, First Member of the Military Council.[35] The resistance was far from being extinguished with the defeat of Germany, and in June 1945 and thereafter Stalin received alarming reports of continued armed resistance by 'bandits and armed anti-Soviet formations' in the trackless forests of Ukraine and Belorussia, where pitched battles occurred between NKVD military units and rebels of various anti-Soviet persuasions.[36]

Throughout his accession to power in the Soviet Union, Stalin lived in dire fear of assassination.[37] He himself was a fervent believer in the effectiveness of murder as a political weapon, and employed a department (the Administration for Special Tasks) of the NKVD, which specialized in assassination and abduction abroad. Leading political figures were favored targets, their most celebrated victim being Trotsky in 1940, while before that abortive attempts were made on such prominent figures as King Boris of Bulgaria, General Franco in Spain, and *Reichsmarschall* Goering.[38] The extent of Stalin's personal cowardice is hard to assess, and is in any case largely irrelevant in the present context. The number of his victims ran into millions, and for every victim there existed survivors with every reason to avenge their loss. Concern here is however not with the broader picture, but with the exceptionally potent threat posed by White emigrants – whether in reality or in Stalin's fevered estimation.

As Christopher Andrew observes in his penetrating study of the KGB and its predecessors,

> Remarkably, many otherwise admirable studies of the Stalin era fail to mention the relentless secret pursuit of "enemies of the people" in western Europe. The result, all too frequently, is a sanitized, curiously bloodless interpretation of Soviet foreign policy on the eve of the Second World War which fails to recognize the priority given to assassination.[39]

What remains unique in the case of the abduction and murder of General Peter Krasnov is the extent to which Stalin succeeded in manipulating a well-placed British figure (or figures) into collaboration with the crime.

Reverting to Stalin's obsessive personal fear of the White émigrés, in 1933 an alleged monarchist plot to assassinate him resulted in 26 arrests of former gentry figures, several of whom were women.[40] In 1939 the Japanese sent a party of ten White Russians across the Manchurian frontier, who were assigned the mission of assassinating Stalin – a project which continued attractive to the Japanese Government.[41] In practical terms, such a task could realistically *only* prove successful if undertaken by Russians, who alone were capable of merging undetected into the population at large. When considering the implications of the extraordinary disappearance of Captain Kantimir and his squad of trained parachutist saboteurs, Stalin's security chiefs will have recalled reports such as that received by Beria in 1943 of a special Messerschmidt Arado-332 being prepared by the German command to drop a trained group of saboteurs from Vlasov's Liberation Army well behind Red Army lines.[42]

Still more apt to Stalin's personal fear is the story of a Red Army soldier named Peter Ivanovich Tavrin (real name Shilo). In the course of a lengthy report, People's Commissar for State Security Vsevolod Merkulov reported that in May 1942 Tavrin had defected to the Germans.

From September 1943 till August 1944, [Tavrin] was personally trained as a terrorist for committing terrorist acts against the USSR leaders... The goal of sending [him] is to organize and conduct a terrorist act against C.[omrade] Stalin, as well as, if possible, acts against the other members of the government: Beria, Kaganovich and Molotov.

In September 1944 Tavrin was flown in a four-engined *Luftwaffe* bomber across Red Army lines, when he was however eventually arrested near Smolensk. In consequence of a lively fear that related operations might continue in being, Tavrin was incarcerated and constantly interrogated by SMERSH (afterwards MGB), and it was not until on 28 March 1952 that he was executed.[43]

The extremity of Stalin's fear of assassination by White agents at this time is illustrated by the extraordinary case of Pavel Kutepov, son of the White leader General Alexander Kutepov, who was murdered by OGPU terrorists in Paris in 1930. At the end of the war, Pavel was captured by the Red Army outside Belgrade and shortly afterwards brought to Moscow. Although he had in reality worked for the pro-Soviet underground in Yugoslavia, and at the time of his arrest was acting as a translator for the Red Army, he was put on trial for having allegedly planned to infiltrate the Soviet Union for the purpose of assassinating Stalin. The evidence proving shaky in the extreme even for a Soviet trial, Pavel Kutepov was sentenced to a mere twenty years' imprisonment. When professing his innocence, he enquired why he had been singled out. 'You are your father's son', was the terse reply.[44]

When Stalin withdrew to his *dacha* at Sochi towards the end of the war, extensive measures were implemented by his security for liquidating the threat of 'terrorists' feared to be lurking in the vicinity.[45] However, nothing more is recorded of the elusive Captain Kantimir and his group.

Finally, on 17 January 1947 *Pravda* announced that a military court had tried and sentenced the following

agents of German Intelligence, leaders of armed White Guard units during the period of the Civil War, Ataman P. N. Krasnov, Lieutenant-General of the White Army A. G. Shkuro, the commander of the "Wild Division" - Major-General of the White Army Prince Klich Sultan-Ghirei, Major-General of the White Army S. N. Krasnov, and Major-General of the White Army T. I. Domanov, and also the German Army General of the SS Helmuth von Pannwitz.[46]

General Peter Nikolaevich Krasnov was 76 years old at the time of his death. His NKGB medical examination in the Butyrka Prison found him to be suffering from advanced sclerosis, emphysemia, cardiac breakdown, and senile decrepitude, amounting to a progressively chronic condition of ever-increasing debility. He and his companions were executed by hanging in the courtyard of the Lefortovo Prison in Moscow, possibly by the drawn-out process described so exultantly by Merkulov.

Stalin's vengeance was now complete. As a leading NKVD officer recalled after his defection to the West,

> ... the critics referred to the so-called Stalin's "theory of sweet revenge" which he expressed one evening, in the summer of 1923, in a friendly conversation with Kamenev and Dzerzhinsky. "To choose one's enemy", said Stalin, "to prepare every detail of the blow, to slake an implacable vengeance, and then go to bed.... There is nothing sweeter in the world!"[47]

AFTERMATH

The sole claim to novelty in Christopher Booker's strange book *A Looking-Glass Tragedy* lay in a single sensational assertion. Publicizing the work under the banner headline CONSPIRACY OF LIES in the *Daily Mail* on 22 November 1997, the author announced that

> the fate of the Cossacks and Yugoslavs who were handed over, although tragic, turned out to have been seriously exaggerated ... Despite the general impression that almost all the 45,000 Cossacks returned to the Soviet Union were either shot or died in Stalin's labour camps, it [has] emerged that the majority were actually released from the camps a year later.

Writers like Solzhenitsyn and Nikolai Tolstoy, declared Booker, anxious 'to build up maximum sympathy for them as innocent victims', now stood exposed as having been speciously engaged in 'blurring over much of what really happened to the Cossacks when they returned to Russia'.

While *A Looking-Glass Tragedy* reposes securely on the shelves of libraries throughout Britain, my *The Minister and the Massacres* has been largely removed by obedient librarians. British reviewers lavished praise on what Alistair Horne, official biographer to Harold Macmillan, termed 'Booker's work of remarkable, painstaking diligence'. John Keegan, a military historian, believed the subject 'deserves the fullest historical investigation. Christopher Booker is in a position to undertake the task'.[*]

---

[*] These encomia are the more odd, in that Booker never actually conducted any

Norman Stone, formerly Professor of Modern History at Oxford, likewise declared himself convinced by the work, affirming that 'Booker does a wonderful job in explaining the context'. His praise, however, has a history. When the Cowgill Inquiry published its 'Report' in 1990, the author Robert Harris boldly published an excoriating review of the work in the *Sunday Times*, whose title makes its content clear enough:

HERE'S A WAY OUT FOR EVERY WAR CRIMINAL.[48]

Unlike Cowgill and Booker, Harris had spoken at length with victims of Macmillan's policy: in particular, Major Rusty Davies, who wept as he described the appalling scenes he witnessed in Peggetz camp on 29 May 1945. Greatly alarmed, lawyers were employed (by whom does not appear, as Cowgill's publication was privately subsidized),[49] who threatened to sue for libel on his behalf. Unusually, the newspaper capitulated at once without consulting Harris,[*] and paid the apparently indigent Brigadier an undisclosed £30,000. In addition, Norman Stone was commissioned to write a fresh 'balancing' review, which duly found that 'the three authors have produced a reconstruction of very high quality ... Macmillan can be completely exonerated'.[50]

Booker's 'discovery' that, contrary to popular belief, few Cossacks had died in Soviet captivity was vigorously endorsed by commentators. 'Of the Cossacks repatriated to Russia, few were actually killed; horrendous as their privations were, the vast majority survived the Gulag', declared Horne. Robert Knight of the University of Loughborough likewise swallowed Booker's assertion that 'many of the lower ranks seem to have been released from the Gulag surprisingly soon'.

Booker's dramatic revelation derived from a single source: a brief memoir included in the collection of Cossack memoirs painstakingly assembled by the veteran General Vyacheslav Naumenko, whose two volumes were published in New York in 1962 and 1970. Booker explained that

> *Velikoye Predatelstvo (The Great Betrayal)* was significant because it remains to this day the most comprehensive account of what happened to the Cossacks and Germans during the years after they had been handed

---

research worth the name. As Nigel Nicolson reminded the Cowgill 'Inquiry', well over 90% of the evidence they cited was taken unacknowledged from my two books on the subject and archival material I discovered subsequently, while Booker obtained a smattering of unimportant additional material provided by Cowgill and Brimelow (cf. *A Looking-Glass Tragedy: The Controversy over the repatriations from Austria in 1945* (London, 1997), pp. 10-11).
[*] Information kindly supplied by Robert Harris.

over - and in this respect, it again provides a rather different picture from that given later by Tolstoy.

Moving on,

> The fullest and most detailed account of this story contained in Naumenko's book was that provided in three letters sent to him in 1954 by Gerhard Petri, a senior lieutenant [*Oberleutnant*] on von Pannwitz's staff ...

This assertion of the unique authority of Petri's account appears not a little arbitrary, comprising as it does fewer than six pages of a 719-page collection, and it is hard to see why a solitary German account should be accorded canonical preference over the predominating wealth of Cossack memoirs contained in Naumenko's collection.

However that may be, what Petri's account proved, according to Booker, is that relatively few of the Cossacks repatriated from Austria in 1945 stayed for long in the camps, let alone died there. As he explained,

> The 'Cossack rank and file', on the other hand, Petri wrote, were 'as early as 1946 released from their prisoner status ... even among the officers and Germans, probably the majority survived their sufferings, to be released between eight and twelve years after the war. The vast majority of the [Cossack] rank-and-file, possibly amounting to well over 30,000, were released from the camps into 'internal exile' after a year and freed three years later.[51]

In fact Booker never read (as he implies he did) Naumenko's great collection, since he knew not a word of Russian – no more than did his admirers Horne and Knight. The passage upon which he relied for his astonishing claim that more than 30,000 Cossack rank and file soldiers were freed in 1949 comprises two sentences from Petri's account, a translation of which he borrowed from Cowgill's acclaimed *Report of an Inquiry*:

> At the end of 1949 the Reds condemned all the Germans and all the officers of the Cossack Corps to 25 years collectively. **The rank and file were sent home** [emphasis inserted].[52]

The first sentence is correctly translated. The second, however, reads in the original Russian:

> Рядовых **немцев** посылали домой.[53]

Russian readers will at once observe that a word has been omitted from the Cowgill version: rather a significant one, as it happens. For what the sentence actually states is:

The **German** rank and file were sent home.

Anyone with a cursory knowledge of post-war history will at once recognize the allusion. During the last quarter of 1949 the Soviet Union authorized the repatriation of German and Austrian prisoners of war, in consequence of which 158,195 returned to their homes. The Soviet motive was to sweeten relations with the newly-elected Chancellor of West Germany, Konrad Adenauer.[54]

Thus Petri was referring to the small number of German other ranks serving in the Cossack Corps (in which he served), and *not* the great mass of Cossack rank and file, as Booker and his co-authors wished their readers to believe.[55] That suppression of the key term 'German' was deliberate is unmistakable. On the other hand, since Booker could not read Russian, it presumably was not he who originated the falsified record. Fortunately, it is not difficult to establish who did.

It has been seen that Booker copied his assertion from the Cowgill report, of which he was in some way co-author (although not researcher). The only member of the Cowgill Inquiry who could read Russian was the late Thomas (in due course Lord) Brimelow, who at the time of the forced repatriations had been Second Secretary at the Northern Department of the Foreign Office. His earlier posting at the Moscow Embassy from 1942-45 evidently left him with a particularly soft spot for Stalin's Russia. A confirmed socialist, he was one of the most callous proponents of Britain's forced repatriation policy, strongly backing the Foreign Office's covert violations of English law required to return unwilling Russians held in Britain, and raising vigorous objection when in 1946 General McCreery halted forced repatriation in British-occupied Austria. In June 1945 he welcomed the brutal Soviet occupation of Eastern Europe as introducing a more equitable distribution of property.[*]

Emphasizing Lord Brimelow's meticulous attention to matters of detail, Booker acknowledged that

We [the Cowgill Inquiry] also benefited greatly from his ability to read documents, books and diaries in both German and Russian.[56]

It must have been Brimelow who mistranslated the passage upon which Booker relied for his 'no Holocaust' claim, and his omission of the crucial word 'German' can only have been deliberate. Not only was

---

[*] This confident assertion was at least applicable to the Red Army's attitude towards women. For just one victim's nightmare experience of Soviet occupation in 1945, I commend my late friend Gunild Walsh's moving memoir *The Silent Crime: As Lived Through by my Twelve Year Old Self* (blurb.com, 2011).

Brimelow both a stickler for accuracy and fluent Russian-reader, but he had especial reason to recall the repatriation of German prisoners of war in 1949, which came directly within his field of responsibility at the Northern Department of the Foreign Office.

It may well be that the gullible Booker was himself deceived by Brimelow's shameless distortion of the historical record. On the other hand, ample evidence exists of the extent to which he did not scruple to doctor the most explicit of evidence when it conflicted with the propaganda function of the Cowgill Inquiry. The biggest hurdle the Inquiry had to overcome in order to establish that everything happening in Austria in 1945 was entirely admirable and above board, was the unauthorized inclusion of White emigrants among Cossacks handed over to the Soviets.

It was to buttress his central claim that no one in the British command was aware of the White émigré presence in Austria until it was too late, that Booker wrote of a group of fourteen surviving White officers handed over on 29 May 1945:

> They admitted it was only **after they had been handed over** that they learned from the Russians that their repatriation had been under an agreement with the allies which applied only to Soviet citizens (**in other words, they had not protested to the British at the time**) [bold added in each case].[57]

Thus he made it appear that the inclusion of non-Soviet citizens arose, not from deliberate policy, but in consequence of tragic oversight.

Booker's cited source for his account was Peter Huxley-Blythe's book *The East Came West*. In it, Booker read the following passage, contained in a sworn statement by the White Russian officers concerned.

> On May 28, 1945, at 6:00 P.M. we learnt that we were to be handed over to the Soviets. **We lodged a formal protest and produced our documents to prove to Lieut. Colonel Malcolm that we were old émigrés** [bold added]. He told us that we could show our documents to Joseph Stalin.[58]

Booker's distortion of this evidence can only have been deliberate.

As a consequence of Khrushchev's 'thaw' following the death of Stalin, a 'Decree of Amnesty' was promulgated in Moscow on 17 September 1955, which provided for the release from captivity of categories of prisoners condemned under the notorious Article 58.[59] By the following year a pitifully small group of surviving 'foreigners' (White émigrés bearing non-Soviet citizenship, together with German officers of the 15th Cossack Cavalry Corps) was finally permitted to leave the Soviet Union.

The handful of old emigrant Cossack officers just mentioned, who had been released after the extermination of their comrades in the gulag camps, found themselves free in Austria and West Germany - but utterly destitute. Following the protracted harsh treatment they had suffered, they were now 'old, ill, and therefore unable to work for our living'. In May 1958 they compiled an appeal to the British government for modest financial support, in compensation for their unlawful handover by British forces to a regime of which they had never been citizens. They also established contact with Peter Huxley-Blythe, pioneering historian of the Great Betrayal.

Huxley-Blythe assembled the petition and related evidence, which on 4 September 1958 he forwarded to the Prime Minister, the Rt. Hon. Harold Macmillan. It would be fascinating to know what memories this might have stirred concerning events in which Macmillan had played so significant a role thirteen years earlier. However, it may be that he never saw Huxley-Blythe's letter and enclosures, which were passed to the Foreign Office.

A fortnight later Huxley-Blythe received the official response, which explained that

> The case submitted by these officers was carefully considered in connexion with their petition to Her Majesty the Queen in December 1957. A thorough examination of the facts led to the conclusion that no action could be taken to assist the persons named in your letter.

In his published account of these exchanges, Huxley-Blythe tactfully concluded the cited Foreign Office response:

> 'I am,
> Sir,
> Your obedient Servant,
> (signature)'.[60]

However, in a letter of 10 June 1998 to Christopher Booker, in which he protested against the latter's doctoring of evidence in *A Looking-Glass War*, Huxley-Blythe revealed the identity of the Foreign Office functionary who penned this chilling response.

> You wrote in respect of the Petition that I submitted, "On 17 October a reply was sent to Huxley-Blythe that a 'thorough investigation of the facts led to the conclusion that no action could be taken to assist the persons named'". What you failed to mention was that the person who signed this letter was none other than Thomas Brimelow whose role in this entire affair gives rise to much disquiet.

[1] Crosland Diary.

[2] A. Petrowsky, *Unvergessener Verrat!: Roosevelt - Stalin - Churchill 1945* (Munich, 1965), p. 104.

[3] General V. Naumenko (ed.), *Великое Предательство: Выдача Казаков в Лиенце и Других Местах (1945-1947); Сборник материалов и документов* (New York, 1962-70), ii, pp. 242, 246.

[4] 'A.I. Romanov' [Captain Boris Bakhlanov], *Nights are Longest There: Smersh from the Inside* (London, 1972), pp. 153-55.

[5] On 10 July 1945 Alexander ordered 8th Army to 'hand over to Russians those Cossacks who can be returned without use of force...' (NA.740.00119 Control (Italy)/7-1045).

[6] Naumenko (ed.), *Великое Предательство*, i, pp. 173-75. The witness identified himself by the intials 'A.V.F'. Doubtless he and his wife nurtured a fear that they too might be delivered up by the British (the Red Army withdrew from Judenburg and the rest of Styria on 21 July 1945). The author explained that they continued living in Judenburg for a considerable time after the handovers. As Russian refugees, they may have been inhabitants of the Judenburg DP camp (for which cf. Siegfried Beer, *Judenburg 1945 - im Spiegel britischer Besatzungsakten* (Judenburg, 1990), pp. 45-48; Gabriela Stieber, *Nachkriegsflüchtlinge in Kärnten und der Steiermark* (Graz, 1997), pp. 258-62). An eyewitness account of an individual Soviet murder at Judenburg during the handover is to be found in N.N. Krasnov, *Незабываемое 1945-1956* (San Francisco, 1957), p. 51. Christopher Booker assured his readers that 'Apart from this solitary instance, there is no direct evidence that any of those handed over by the British were killed in Judenburg' (*A Looking-Glass Tragedy: The Controversy over the repatriations from Austria in 1945* (London, 1997), pp. 250-51). Evidently his inability to consult Russian sources denied him access to the detailed first-hand testimony contained in General Naumenko's collection. Mass killings in large buildings, with noisy machinery employed to override the cacophony of shooting and screaming, represented standard NKVD and SMERSH practice (Nikolai Tolstoy, *Victims of Yalta* (London, 1977), pp. 129-30).

[7] Letter to the author of 2 November 1998.

[8] Letter to the author, 13 November 1974.

[9] Gregory Klimov, *The Terror Machine: The Inside Story of the Soviet Administration in Germany* (London, 1953), pp. 74-75.

[10] The beneficence of this 'nurture' is illustrated by the fact that throughout much of his career Domanov had suffered repeated terms of imprisonment at the hands of the NKVD, while in the autumn of 1937 his brother was condemned to ten years' slave labour (K.M. Alexandrov, *Офицерский Корпус Армии Генерал-Лейтенанта А.А. Власова 1944-1945* (Moscow, 2009), pp. 381-82).

[11] Cf. R. G. Pikhoya and A. Geishtor (ed.), *Катынь: Пленники необъявленной*

войны (Moscow, 1997), pp. 350 *et seq.*

[12] N.L. Pobol and P.M. Polyan (ed.), *Сталинские Депортации 1928-1953* (Moscow, 2005), pp. 215-17, 222-24.

[13] For a summary account of Merkulov's career cf. V.N. Khaustov, V.P. Naumov, and N.S. Plotnikova (ed.), *Лубянка: Сталин и НКВД-НКГБ-ГУКР «Смерш» 1939 – март 1946* (Moscow, 2006), p. 584.

[14] Krasnov, *Незабываемое*, pp. 41-84.

[15] *Ibid.*, pp. 325-26.

[16] It is striking that similar characteristics represent salient facets of the mind of the common criminal (Alfred Adler, *The Neurotic Constitution: Outlines of a Comparative Individualistic Psychology and Psychotherapy* (London, 1921), p. 157; *idem, Problems of Neurosis: A Book of Case-Histories* (London, 1929), pp. 129-30).

[17] Z. Stypułkowski, *Invitation to Moscow* (London, 1951), pp. 266, 294. Comparison may also be made with a speech delivered by Merkulov's colleague Abakumov to an audience of SMERSH officers at almost exactly the same time ('Romanov', *Nights are Longest There*, pp. 237-39.

[18] *Ibid.*, p. 154.

[19] 29th April 1943: '5 p.m. Two Russians, who have come to look after Russian internees in the internment camps and to arrange their transport to Russia *via* England. Simple in principle, difficult in practice' (Harold Macmillan, *War Diaries: Politics and War in the Mediterranean January 1943-May 1945* (London, 1984), p. 75). Nothing more is recorded in Macmillan's diary of this Soviet mission, although the importance of its remit can only have increased enormously over the ensuing two years. The oddity of Macmillan's silence on its significant activity at AFHQ was drawn to my attention by the late Professor Norman Stone. The function assigned the Soviet officers indicates them to have been representatives of SMERSH ('Romanov', *Nights are Longest There*, pp. 170-71).

[20] Naumenko (ed.), *Великое Предательство*, ii, pp. 36-38.

[21] The Earl of Avon, *The Eden Memoirs: The Reckoning* (London, 1965), pp. 528-37.

[22] Kenneth Young (ed.), *The Diaries of Sir Robert Bruce Lockhart* (London, 1980), pp. 328, 519-20.

[23] Robert Murphy, *Diplomat among Warriors* (London, 1964), p. 206. Cf. Winston S. Churchill, *Closing the Ring* (London, 1952), p. 375.

[24] A perceptive analysis of Macmillan's 'False Self, the protective mask that eventually became one of the most distinctive personalities of the century' is provided by Richard Davenport-Hines, *The Macmillans* (London, 1992), pp. 161-78.

[25] Krasnov, *Незабываемое*, p. 106; cf. p. 58.

[26] S.S. Khromov (ed.), *Гражданская Война и Военная Интервенция в СССР: Энциклопедия* (Moscow, 1983), p. 300. A Soviet account of Shkuro's

wartime activities baldly concludes: 'Together with von Pannwitz Shkuro found himself in the hands of Soviet justice' (M. K. Kasvinov, *Двадцать Три Ступени Вниз* (Moscow, 1979), p. 70).

[27] Pavel Sudoplatov, *Спецоперации: Лубянка и Кремль 1930-1950 годы* (Moscow, 1997), pp. 265-66.

[28] Vadim J. Birstein, *SMERSH: Stalin's Secret Weapon* (London, 2011), pp. 378-79, 382-83, 387.

[29] Ann Tusa and John Tusa, *The Nuremberg Trial* (London, 1983), pp. 93, 125. In reality little enthusiasm was evinced by the British for prosecution of German naval commanders (*The Trial of German Major War Criminals: Proceedings of the International Military Tribunal Sitting at Nuremberg Germany* (London, 1946-51), xiv, pp. 64-319).

[30] Krasnov, *Незабываемое*, p. 180; Zoltan Toth, *Prisoner of the Soviet Union* (Old Woking, 1978), p. 180.

[31] WO.170/4988.

[32] WO.170/4388.

[33] WO.170/4241.

[34] John Erickson, *The Road to Berlin* (London, 1983), p. 512.

[35] 'Romanov', *Nights are Longest There*, pp. 101-3.

[36] V. A. Kozlov and S. V. Mironenko (ed.), *Архив новейшей истории России Том I: «Особая папка» И.В. Сталина; Из материалов Секретариата НКВД-МВД СССР 1944-1953 гг. Каталог документов* (Moscow, 1994), p. 120. Cf. pp. 81, 126-27, 131. The struggle to repress armed resistance in Ukraine and Belorussia continued into 1946 and beyond (pp. 145, 151, 155, 161, 166, etc.). Cf. also Dmitri Volkogonov, *Сталин: Политический Портрет* (Moscow, 1994), ii, pp. 425-26.

[37] The astonishing extent of precautions to protect Stalin within the walls of the Kremlin are described by a former officer of the guard (Peter Deriabin and Frank Gibney, *The Secret World* (London, 1960), pp. 111-22). Cf. W.G. Krivitsky, *I was Stalin's Agent* (London, 1939), p. 177.

[38] Boris Bajanov, *Bajanov révèle Staline; Souvenirs d'un ancien secrétaire de Staline* (Paris, 1979), p. 259; Christopher Andrew and Vasili Mitrokhin, *The Sword and the Shield: The Mitrokhin Archive and the Secret History of the KGB* (New York, 1999), pp. 67-70.

[39] *Ibid.*, pp. 74-75.

[40] Stephen Kotkin, *Stalin: Vol. II: Waiting for Hitler, 1928-1941* (London, 2017), p. 145.

[41] *Ibid.*, p. 640; *The Trial of Major German War Criminals*, i, p.73.

[42] Volkogonov, *Сталин*, ii, pp. 374-75. The Arado-332 was a highly sophisticated transport aeroplane, capable of flying 332 kilometres.

[43] Birstein, *SMERSH*, pp. 226-29.

[44] *Ibid.*, pp 276-77, 470; Unto Parvilahti, *Beria's Gardens: Ten Years' Captivity in Russia and Siberia* (London, 1959), p. 45.

[45] Volkogonov, *Сталин*, ii,, p. 428.

[46] Quoted in Naumenko (ed.), *Великое Предательство*, ii, pp. 296-97.

[47] Alexander Orlov, *The Secret History of Stalin's Crimes* (London, 1954), p. 39.
     Cf. Stephen Kotkin, *Stalin: Volume I: Paradoxes of Power, 1878-1928* (New
     York, 2014), pp. 715-16.

[48] *Sunday Times*, 21 October 1990.

[49] The 'Inquiry' mysteriously appeared under the imprint of Christopher Sinclair-
     Stevenson, although it emerged later that an unidentified source had met the
     printer's expenses (*Boardroom Magazine*, February 1991).

[50] Norman Stone, 'Judgment best left to history', *Sunday Times*, 30 December
     1990. My old friend Norman's conduct on this occasion was uncharacteristic,
     and those who knew him may wonder whether he was altogether sober when
     persuaded to write his eulogy.

[51] Christopher Booker, *A Looking-Glass Tragedy: The controversy over the
     repatriations from Austria in 1945* (London, 1997), pp. 314-17.

[52] Brigadier Anthony Cowgill, Lord Brimelow, and Christopher Booker Esq., *The
     Repatriations from Austria in 1945: The Report of an Inquiry* (London,
     1990), p. 180.

[53] Naumenko (ed.), *Великое Предательство*, ii, p. 322.

[54] Stefan Karner, *Im Archipel GUPVI: Kriegsgefangenschaft und Internierung in
     der Sowjetunion 1941-1956* (Vienna and Munich, 1995), pp. 201-203, 217;
     idem, 'Das sowjetische Kriegsgefangenenwesen 1941-1956', in *Niemiecki i
     Radziecki System Jeniecki w Latach II Wojny Swiatowej. Podobienstwa i
     roznice*' (Opole, 1997), p. 60; Erwin Peter and Alexander E. Epifanow,
     *Stalins Kriegs-Gefangene: Ihr Schicksal in Erinnerungen und nach
     russischen Archiven* (Graz, 1997), p. 286. A commission from Moscow
     arrived at GULAG camps in October 1949 to select German prisoners for
     repatriation (Naumenko (ed.), *Великое Предательство*, ii, p. 326).

[55] Karl-Gottfried Vierkorn lists 82 of his German and Austrian fellow officers in
     the 15 KKK, who perished in gulag camps between 1945 and 1949 (*Gefangen
     in Sibirien: Achteinhalb Jahre hinter Stacheldraht* (Oberaudorf, 1994), pp.
     261-63).

[56] Booker, *A Looking-Glass Tragedy*, p. 138. A lengthier and still more fawning
     encomium to Brimelow's impartiality and analytical skills appears on p. 421.

[57] *Ibid.*, p. 313.

[58] Peter J. Huxley-Blythe, *The East Came West* (Caldwell, Idaho, 1964), p. 206.

[59] Naumenko (ed.), *Великое Предательство*, ii, pp. 318-19. Cf. Pavel Polyan,
     *Жертвы Двух Диктатур: Остарбайтеры и Военнопленные в Третьем
     Рейхе и их Репатриация* (Moscow, 1996), pp. 328-32.

[60] Huxley-Blythe, *The East Came West*, pp. 202-10.

APPENDIX A
FORCED REPATRIATION FROM AUSTRIA AND THE GENEVA CONVENTION

On the basis of asserting the universality of standards which had not been quite universally accepted, were the Nuremberg and Tokyo tribunals justified in finding the great majority of their defendants guilty? It is easy – and it was well done by the defense lawyers at the trials – to point out that there had been terrible deeds on both sides in the war, and that in some areas, such as submarine warfare and city bombing, the Allies, as much as the Axis powers, had ignored existing treaties and legal principles. However, there was one major category of crime in respect of which there was little comparison between the Allies and the Axis powers, and it was this category which, in the end, formed the basis for the conviction of most of the major war criminals. It concerned not combat, but treatment of those more or less *hors de combat*. The Axis atrocities against many of those who were directly under their control – whether Jews, prisoners of war, or inhabitants of occupied territories – formed the one really strong ground for conviction. It cannot have been wrong to punish these clear violations of the most elementary principles of decency, which in most cases were also contrary to the Geneva prisoners of war convention and the Hague land war convention. Thus, the convictions in the Nuremberg and Tokyo trials were in the end not so much about the initiation or conduct of military hostilities as about the treatment of largely defenseless people in the hands of the adversary.[*]

At the 1989 libel action, undertaken by Lord Aldington over accusations contained in a leaflet I wrote entitled 'War Crimes and the Wardenship of Winchester College', one of my principal accusations (as the title indicated) was:

> Were all that Lord Aldington claims to be true he would still stand arraigned in gross violation of the laws of war and humanity. The

---

[*] Adam Roberts, 'Land Warfare: From Hague to Nuremberg', in Michael Howard, George J. Andreopoulos, and Mark R. Shulman (ed.), *The Laws of War: Constraints on Warfare in the Western World* (New Haven and London, 1994), p. 135.

deliberate inclusion of German and Austrian officers of the 15 Cossack Cavalry Corps for example was authorised by Lord Aldington in flagrant contravention of the Geneva Convention on prisoners-of-war.

The issue was discussed in detail at a closed hearing on Day 32 of the trial, to which press and public were denied access. The relevant passages of the transcript are here published for the first time, as being of considerable interest to historians and lawyers, and relevance to the murky history of the forced repatriation.

Charles Gray QC, acting for Lord Aldington, claimed that the provisions of the 1929 Geneva Convention did not apply at the time of the handovers. The grounds for his assertion were twofold. First, Germany having surrendered and the war being over three weeks before the grim events occurring in Austria at the end of May and beginning of June, the Convention was no longer applicable. With the cessation of hostilities, the Cossacks were not prisoners of war, but fell under a newly-introduced category of Surrendered Enemy Personnel. This alteration of status, Gray asserted, deprived them of any rights to which they might have been entitled under the terms of the Convention.[1] As he put it:

> ... the fundamental problem ... is that the Geneva Convention does not actually apply to surrendered personnel.

Gray further assured Judge Michael Davies,

> Your Lordship will be familiar from the documents in this case, the distinction was always drawn of [by?] 8th Army above and below between Surrendered Enemy Personnel and prisoners of war, the distinction being the obvious one, that the prisoner of war is a person who has been taken captive during hostilities, whereas the surrendered person is somebody who has surrendered either during or (as in this case) after the cessation of hostilities. One thing that is abundantly plain from the Geneva Convention is that it applies only to prisoners of war.

It is untrue, as Gray insinuated, that this 'obvious' distinction reflected customary practice 'always drawn' under international law. In reality, it was adopted as an embarrassing innovation, never employed before or since.[2] The distinction between POW and SEP was tied on a pragmatic extra-legal basis to the date of the capitulation of *Germany* (the emphasis is explained below), and the dire problems that arose therefrom. It arose from particular circumstances of the close of hostilities, and was not a legally inexorable outcome of that contingency.

As a leading Red Cross lawyer pointed out afterwards,

> The spirit of the 1929 Convention, and even any reasonable interpretation of it, were certainly against any such subterfuge. But the

letter of the Convention was not sufficiently clear on the point.[3]

Differential treatment between the categories of Prisoners of War and Surrendered Enemy Personnel reflected in pragmatic terms modification of Clause 11 of the 1929 Geneva Convention, which required POW to receive the same rations as their captors.[4] With millions of German soldiers falling into Allied hands following the German surrender at Rheims on 8 May 1945, it was impossible to fulfil this obligation. Accordingly, the novel category of Surrendered Enemy Personnel* was introduced, whereby the Allies treated their prisoners as best they could, without being liable to meet a condition far beyond their resources in the ruinous conditions of Central Europe prevailing at the war's end.

This improvised abrogation of the Geneva Convention aroused widespread embarrassment on the part of the British and American governments – in the latter case, leading to formal restoration of POW status in March 1946.[5] At the same time, the introduction of SEP status was never intended as an instrument to deprive prisoners of their basic human rights under international law.[6]

As Sir Patrick Dean, legal adviser to the Foreign Office, explained on 7 July 1945:

> To obviate the necessity of treating vast numbers of surrendered Germans as prisoners of war and giving to them standards of treatment which it is in fact impossible to fulfil, a great number of the German armed forces are being treated as "disarmed German persons" and not prisoners of war... The distinction between treatment of German prisoners in the strict sense [of the Geneva Convention] and German disarmed persons is therefore in this respect artificial.[7]

It was urged by jurists not long after that it would have been preferable for the Allied governments not to have reneged from the Convention, instead conceding that the practical difficulty of fulfilling Article 11 made it for the present inoperable.[8] Here, however, the concern is with the specific issue of the Cossacks' status as prisoners of the British. Since they had surrendered on or immediately after VE Day (8 May 1945), Charles Gray contended that, as SEP, they could no longer claim the protection of the Geneva Convention.

It was on this assumption that Gray maintained at the 1989 trial that my central accusation concerning Lord Aldington's responsibility for war crimes (in the strict legal sense) could not stand up. In response, the defense called a leading expert on international law to expound the legal

---

* The American equivalent status was that of Disarmed Enemy Forces (DEF).

background. Christopher Greenwood (subsequently Sir Christopher, a judge at the International Court of Justice and professor at the London School of Economics) was at the time of the Aldington trial a barrister specialising in international law. He was invited by the defense to make submissions on the crucial question of the applicability of the 1929 Geneva Convention on Prisoners of War to the Cossacks at the time of their delivery to the Soviets.

Greenwood's exposition is of major significance, not only with regard to the particular case of the Cossacks, but to the legal status of prisoners of war generally. Indeed, acceptance of Gray's misrepresentations could affect the welfare of British prisoners of war in current or future conflicts. Here follows the relevant extract from the trial transcript (Day 32), omitting only the Judge's more irrelevant interruptions.

***

MR. GREENWOOD: ... My submissions relate purely to the question of war crimes within the technical meaning of international law, and it is for that reason that I wanted to begin by referring your Lordship to the case of 'Tremtex v the Central Bank of Nigeria', reported in 1977 1, King's Bench Reports, page 529. The point in that case has nothing to do with war crimes as such. The point in that case, as the headnote makes clear, concerned the rules of international law relating to sovereign immunity which could be applied by the English courts. The decision of the Court of Appeal was that they could, and the reason for that is given most clearly by Lord Denning on page 554 at points G and H on that page, where he says that:

> 'Seeing that the rules of international law have changed and do change, and that the courts have given effect to the changes without any Act of Parliament, it follows to my mind inexorably that the rules of international law as existing from time to time do form part of our English law'.

It is on that basis my Lord that we submit that the rules of international law relating to war crimes liability are something of which the court may take judicial notice...

However complicated the rules of international law might be regarding war crimes, the submission that we wish to make is really very simple. It turns on three propositions. First of all, that there was a duty on the part of the United Kingdom to treat members of the German armed forces humanely, whenever the members of those armed forces came into the power of the United Kingdom.

Secondly, my Lord, that that duty of humane treatment includes a duty to protect captives from inhumane treatment by anybody else, and that a duty to protect from inhumane treatment would be violated if members of enemy armed forces were handed over to another state in circumstances where it was known or suspected that they would be massacred or in any other way ill-treated.

Our third proposition, my Lord, is that if it is found that the plaintiff was in some way responsible for a breach of that kind, then as a matter of international law he would be guilty of a war crime.

My Lord, before turning directly to those three propositions, I would like to make one or two brief submissions about some preliminary matters. The first concerns the definition of a war crime in international law, and it is for that purpose that I have asked your Lordship to look at the first of the papers in the bundle that was handed up to you, the Manual of Military Law 1929, and turn to the second sheet, paragraph 441, about half way down on the left hand side of the page.

"The term 'war crime' is the technical expression for such an act of enemy soldiers and enemy civilians as may be visited by punishment or capture of the offenders. It is usual to employ this term, but it must be emphasised that it is used in the technical military and legal sense only and not in the moral sense".

My Lord, a rather more exhaustive definition of war crime is provided by the second paper in the bundle, the extract from International Law by L. Oppenheim. Again my Lord, on the second sheet of that document, paragraph 251:

"In contradistinction to hostile acts of soldiers by which the latter do not lose their privilege of being treated as lawful members of armed forces, war crimes are such hostile or other acts of soldiers or other individuals as may be punished by the enemy on capture of the offenders. They include acts contrary to International Law perpetrated in violation of the law of the criminal's own state, such as killing or plunder for satisfying private lust and gain, as well as criminal acts contrary to the laws of war committed by order and on behalf of the enemy state. To that extent, the notion of war crimes is based on the view that states and their organs are subject to criminal responsibility under International Law".

The third document I want to refer your Lordship on this point is the third paper handed up to you, the Charter of the International Military Tribunal of Nuremberg. This Tribunal my Lord, as Article 1 of the Charter shows, was set up in pursuance of an agreement concluded between the principal Allied powers for the trial and punishment of the major war criminals...

The International Military Tribunal at Nuremberg was set up as the first attempt by states to apply the international law principles of war crimes liability. We would submit that the Charter which defines its jurisdiction to try war crimes should be regarded as an authoritative interpretation of what that concept entails. If we turn to the second page of the Charter my Lord, Article 6B lists what are to be regarded as war crimes for the purposes of the Tribunal's jurisdiction:

> "Violations of the laws or customs of war. Such violations shall include, but not be limited to, murder, ill treatment or deportation to slave labour, or for any other purpose, of civilian population of or in occupied territory; murder or ill treatment of prisoners of war or persons on the seas".

The rest of the definition, my Lord, does not come within the scope of this argument.

My Lord, the sources of international law on which war crimes liability are based, we would submit, consist of treaties such as the Geneva Convention on Prisoners of War of 1929, and the Hague Convention of 1907, and the Rules of General Customary International Law, on which many of the provisions of those treaties were based. These provisions my Lord, would continue to apply, we submit, even after the German surrender of 8th May 1945. Here my Lord, if I might refer you to the case of *ex parte* Kochenmeister, 1947, 1 King's Bench, page 41. This case concerned an application for *habeas corpus* by an applicant who was in terms an alien enemy. The application was brought in 1946 more than a year after the German unconditional surrender.[9] The second paragraph of the head note makes clear:

> "By English law the King alone can make peace with the State with which this country has been at war, and thereby bring the state of war to an end, and a certificate of His Majesty's Secretary of State for Foreign Affairs to the effect that His Majesty is still at war with a state is conclusive evidence that the state of war is not at an end".

My Lord, that was given over a year after the German unconditional surrender and the Court, in that case, accepted a state of war between the United Kingdom and Germany remained in effect at that date.

Nevertheless, my Lord, the United Kingdom and the other Allied governments did make the distinction between those members of the German armed forces who surrendered before 8th May, 1945 and those who surrendered after 8th May, the latter category being described as Surrendered Enemy Personnel.

Our principal submission is that whether or not the Geneva Convention and Prisoners of War Convention of 1929 was formally applicable to Surrendered Enemy Personnel, the duty to afford humane treatment contained in article 2 of that convention and in Article 4 of the Hague Regulations of Land Warfare of 1907, was applicable to all those members of the German armed forces who surrendered to the United Kingdom ...

In effect, our submission is that the principle laid down in Article 2 is applicable in any event and is applicable to all the Surrendered Enemy Personnel who fell into the power of the United Kingdom. We base that submission on the fact that the International Military Tribunal at Nuremberg and the other war crimes tribunals held consistently that Article 2 of the Geneva Convention was declaratory of the existing customary international law and, therefore, could be applied by those tribunals, irrespective of whether the Convention was formally applicable or not.

My Lord, if we turn to the Nuremberg judgment, the fourth document in the bundle, this was an important point in the Nuremberg judgment because the USSR was not a party to the 1929 Geneva Prisoners of War Convention. If we turn to page 48, final sheet of the extract, the column on the left-hand side, the part I would like to direct your Lordship's attention to is -

MR. JUSTICE MICHAEL DAVIES: Is this part of the judgment?

MR. GREENWOOD: It is, my Lord. The Defence had submitted in the Nuremberg trial, my Lord, that the ill-treatment of Soviet prisoners of war by German troops was not a war crime because the 1929 Prisoners of War Convention was not binding between Germany and the Soviet Union, the Soviet Union never having been a party. The Tribunal rejected that argument and it based its rejection on the fact that the principal humane treatment of prisoners of war reflected the general principles of international law applicable to captives in wartime and the Tribunal quotes the Memorandum written by Admiral Canaris, Head of Naval Intelligence, relating to the treatment of Soviet prisoners. He then stated:

"The Geneva Convention for the treatment" -

MR. JUSTICE MICHAEL DAVIES: You had better start: "The argument".

MR. GREENWOOD: My Lord, yes:

"The argument in the defence of the charge with regard to the murder and ill-treatment of Soviet prisoners of war, that the USSR was not a party to the Geneva Convention, is quite without foundation. On the 15th

September, 1941 Admiral Canaris protested against the regulations for the treatment of Soviet prisoners of war, signed by General Reinecke on the 8th September, 1941. He then stated: 'The Geneva Convention for the treatment of prisoners of war is not binding in the relationship between Germany and the USSR. Therefore only the principles of general international law on the treatment of prisoners of war apply. Since the 18th century these have gradually been established along the lines that war captivity is neither revenge nor punishment, but solely protective custody, the only purpose of which is to prevent the prisoners of war from further participation in the war. This principle was developed in accordance with the view held by all armies that it is contrary to military tradition to kill or injure helpless people. The decrees for the treatment of Soviet prisoners of war enclosed are based on a fundamentally different view-point".

The Tribunal concluded:

"This protest which correctly stated the legal position, was ignored".

My Lord, we would submit that the matter was even more clearly picked up by the United States Military Tribunal in the 6th document, Trial of Wilhelm Von Leeb, sometimes described as the German Wehrmacht trial. If I might make one supplementary submission in this respect, the United States Military Tribunal that tried this case was set up by the four Allied powers under the Control Council Law, number 10, the 5th document in the bundle and, therefore, its jurisdiction to try the members of the German High Command stems not simply from an act by the United States Government, but an act to which the United Kingdom Government was a party.

MR. JUSTICE MICHAEL DAVIES: Where do we find that?

MR. GREENWOOD: Control Council Law number 10, the preamble on the first page, my Lord.

"In order to give effect to the terms of the Moscow Declaration of 30 October 1943 and the London Agreement of 8 August 1945, and the Charter issued pursuant thereto ..."

That is a reference to the Charter of the International Military Tribunal.

"... and in order to establish a uniform legal basis in Germany for the prosecution of war criminals and other similar offenders, other than those dealt with by the International Military Tribunal, the Control Council enacts as follows".

So, my Lord, this was not a purely United States decision, it was a decision of the Tribunal created by the four major Allied powers at the end of the Second World War.

My Lord, the same argument about the inapplicability of the 1929 Prisoners of War Convention was raised for the Defence in the Von Leeb trial, at the bottom of page 89 of the extract, then on page 93 we find the Tribunal's response to that. Paper 6, the penultimate paragraph:

> "Most of the prohibitions of both the Hague and Geneva Conventions, considered in substance, are clearly an expression of the accepted views of civilized nations and binding upon Germany and the defendants on trial before us in the conduct of the war against Russia".

The Tribunal goes on in the final paragraph:

> "We cite in this category the following rules from the Hague Rules of Land Warfare".

Over the page on page 90 there is a long list then from the Hague and Geneva Conventions but, my Lord, I expressly direct your attention to Article 4 of the Hague Regulations:

> "Prisoners of war are in the power of hostile Government, but not of the individuals or corps who capture them. They must be humanely treated".

Then, a little further down the page:

> "From the Geneva Convention: 'They must at all times be humanely treated and protected, particularly against acts of violence, insults, and public curiosity'".

So, my Lord, we submit, therefore, that the Tribunals which, with the authority of the British Government - the express authority of the British Government - applies the rules of international law on war crimes to the German defendants at the end of the Second World War, started on the assumption that the principle in Article 2 of the Geneva Prisoners of War Convention applied whether the Convention was formally applicable or not. It thus applied to all members of enemy forces who became prisoners, who came into the power of the detained state.

So, I would submit, my Lord, we are not seeking to open up any kind of new area here. We are tying the submission to Article 2 of the Prisoners of War Convention in this way.

The second proposition that I say I wish to try and establish was that once it is accepted that there is a duty to treat surrendered enemy personnel in a humane fashion, that duty would necessarily include a duty to protect them from inhumane acts by others. We would submit, my Lord, that is implicit in article 2 of the Geneva Prisoners of War Convention and in the customary international law, that if it is forbidden to massacre prisoners themselves, it must also be forbidden to hand them over to someone else, knowing they are going to be massacred by the people to whom they are handed over.

Again, in this context, my Lord, I refer you to the 6th document, the decision in the Von Leeb case, this time at page 92. One of the charges raised in the High Command trial concerned a German order for the execution of Allied Commandos who were captured in combat. Commandos are members of special forces captured behind enemy lines, handed over to the SD.[*] At page 92 the Tribunal dealt with the responsibility of officers of the Wehrmacht for handing over prisoners of war to the SD. The first full paragraph on page 92, my Lord:

"Also it is the opinion of this Tribunal that orders which provided for the turning over of prisoners of war to the SD, a civilian organisation, wherein all accountability for them is shown by the evidence to have been lost, constituted a criminal act, particularly when from the surrounding circumstances and published orders, it must have been suspected or known that the ultimate fate of such prisoners of war was elimination by this murderous organisation".

My Lord, our submission is that that passage is indicative of a general principle relating to the duty of humane treatment; that that duty is violated if someone is handed over to another authority in circumstances where it is foreseen that they will be ill-treated, murdered, tortured and so forth.

Our third proposition, my Lord, is that although, as Mr. Gray has pointed out, the obligations under international law are binding upon states, the war crimes trials held at the end of the Second World War clearly indicate that there is individual criminal responsibility on the part of those members of armed forces or civilians who, knowingly, played a part in the commission of violation of the laws of war.

My Lord, we would submit that that is clear in the Nuremberg judgment, it is clear from the Charter of the International Military Tribunal.

If one turns to the final page of the Charter of the International Military Tribunal, my Lord, the last paragraph of Article 6:

"Leaders, organisers, instigators and accomplices participating in the formulation or execution of a common plan or conspiracy to commit any of the foregoing crimes are responsible for all acts performed by any persons in execution of such plan"...

My Lord, our submission is that if it is established that someone participates in an act which is a violation of the international law of war in

---

[*] *Sicherheitsdienst*, the intelligence agency of the SS and Nazi Party in Nazi Germany.

such circumstances that he is responsible in whole or in part for that violation, then he is a war criminal within the sense of international law. My Lord, in relation to staff officers -

MR. JUSTICE MICHAEL DAVIES: You would add to that, would you, whether he is doing it in obedience to an order from a superior officer or not?

MR. GREENWOOD: Indeed so, my Lord. The Defence of superior orders was not accepted. If one looks at Article 8 of the International Military Charter, document 3:

"The fact that the Defendant acted pursuant to order of his Government or of a superior shall not free him from responsibility, but may be considered in mitigation of punishment if the Tribunal determines that justice so requires".

My Lord, one finds the same principle accepted in the judgment of the International Military Tribunal in the judgment in the Von Leeb case. Would your Lordship like me to refer you to the passage?

MR. JUSTICE MICHAEL DAVIES: Not at the moment, Mr. Greenwood. If Mr. Gray argues contrary to Article 8, then you shall have an opportunity to refer to it.

MR. GREENWOOD: Thank you, my Lord. Our submission is that if somebody participates with a sufficient degree of responsibility in the violation of the laws of war, they are guilty of a war crime. If one looks at the von Leeb case, my Lord, document 6, at page 80, the Tribunal there begins to deal with the special position of the responsibility of staff officers, on the facts of this case, the members of the German ...

Under the heading: "The Responsibility of Staff Officers" I read the following paragraph:

"There has also been much evidence and discussion in this case concerning the duties and responsibilities of staff officers in Connection with the preparation and transmittal of illegal orders. In regard to the responsibility of the Chief-of-Staff of a field command, the finding of Tribunal V in Case No. 7"

- that is a reference to the case of Von Leeb to which I would like to turn in a moment, with your permission:

"as to certain defendants has been brought to the attention of the Tribunal. It is pointed out that the decision as to Chiefs of Staff in that case was a factual determination and constitutes a legal determination only insofar as it pertains to the particular facts therein involved. We adopt as sound law the finding therein made, but we do not give that finding the scope that is urged by defence counsel in this case to the effect that all criminal acts within a command are the sole responsibility of the commanding general, and that his Chief-of-Staff is absolved from all criminal responsibility merely by reason of the fact that his commanding general may be charged with responsibility therefore".

My Lord, if one then turns to page 81, the third paragraph on that page, the Military Tribunal there states:

"In the absence of participation in criminal orders or their execution within a command, a chief of staff does not become criminally responsible for criminal acts occurring therein".

I submit the natural inference to be drawn from that passage is that he can become criminally responsible, and if one goes over to page 82, the first paragraph there:

"As stated heretofore, the responsibility allowed a chief of staff to issue orders and directives in the name of his commander varied widely and his independent powers for exercising initiative therefore also varied widely in practice. The field for personal initiative as to other staff officers also varied widely. That such a field did exist, however, is apparent from the testimony of the various defendants who held staff positions and in their testimony have pointed out various cases in which they modified the specific desires of their superiors in the interests of legality and humanity. If they were able to do this, the same power could be exercised for other ends and purposes and they were not mere transcribers of orders".

My Lord, if I may make a very brief reference to the other two cases in the bundle of documents, number 7, the trial of Wilhelm List and Others. My Lord, this was also a trial conducted under the terms of Control Council Law number 10 by United States Military Tribunal acting on behalf of the four principal Allies. The two Defendants to which I particular draw your Lordship's attention are Generals Foertsch and von Geitner, both of whom were chiefs of staff. Page 42. In relation to General Foertsch, the Tribunal said:

"The Chief of Staff was in charge of the various departments of the staff and was the first advisor of the Commander-in-Chief. It was his duty to provide all basic information for decisions by the Commander-in-Chief and was responsible for the channelling of all reports and orders. He had no troop command authority".

Then, a little later down, my Lord, half-way through the paragraph beginning: "It was the testimony of Foertsch":

"For all practical purposes, the accused had the same information as the Defendants List and Kuntze during their tenures as Wehrmacht

Commanders Southeast. He knew of all the incidents described earlier in the outline of evidence dealing with the defendants List and Kuntze. The defendant Foertsch did not, however, participate in any of them. He gave no orders and had no power to do so had he so desired".

My Lord, it is our submission that von Leeb and List decisions set out the nature of responsibility of staff officers for the violation of the laws of war. That they make clear that a staff officer's status as such did not preclude his liability as a war criminal provided he had been - the phrase used in von Leeb – "more than a mere transcriber of orders".

If I might briefly refer your Lordship to the 8th and final document, the trial of Lieutenant General Harukei Isayama. This was a trial, my Lord conducted by United States Forces in the Far Eastern theatre. We submit it is relevant as a purely persuasive authority in relation to the interpretation of war crimes liability. On page 63, the fourth paragraph on that page begins:

"Isayama, a Lieutenant-General, as Chief of Staff of the 110th Area Army, was in a position to advise Ando, the commander on all matters. His connection with the trials of the American airmen"

- the alleged trial and execution of some American airmen -

"lay in his discussions with the commander and with Furukawa, Chief of the Judicial Department, at the time when the original request for instructions was sent to Tokyo on 14th April, 1945; in his consideration of the charges against the defendants on or about 16th May, 1945; in his discussion with the chief judge and members of the judicial department at the close of the trial on 21st May, 1945; in the preparation of a request to Tokyo for final instructions on 22nd May, 1945; in his receipt and passing on of the instructions received from Tokyo; in his receiving and passing on to the commander the protocol of judgment and order for execution; in his instruction to Furukawa that the records of trial be filed; and in his instructions to all involved in the trial to state to the Americans as the purported records of trial show".

I submit there must be a misprint in that final line, but I cannot identify what it is.

We submit this decision, he was convicted and sentenced to life imprisonment by the United States Court, the case illustrates the way in which that notion, the distinction between a mere transcriber of orders and someone who took a consenting part in the commission of violation of laws of war, was applied in practice.

Finally, my Lord, we would submit that where somebody with that degree of responsibility participated in the violation of the laws of war, the fact they did so respond to superior orders was not accepted as a defence at Nuremberg or any of the other trials, nor is it sustained by any of the authorities.

My Lord, that concludes the submissions I was instructed to make.

***

Thus, Dr. Greenwood showed conclusively that reclassification of prisoners of war as Surrendered Enemy Personnel could not lawfully deprive captured soldiers in British hands of the protection of the 1929 Geneva Convention, whose provisions were enshrined in British law as securely as they were under international treaty.

This said, General Keightley and Brigadier Low could not be expected to be aware of these legal considerations, had they (as Charles Gray QC asserted) received orders to treat their prisoners as Surrendered Enemy Personnel, depriving the Cossacks of the protection of the Geneva Convention. It was not for them to question decisions of higher command over issues beyond their competence.

Nevertheless, the fact remains that the issue is entirely irrelevant. For the evidence incontrovertibly shows that the Cossacks were *never* relegated to the status of SEP. On the contrary, as prisoners of war throughout their time in Austria they unequivocally retained all protective rights enshrined in the 1929 Geneva Convention. In his Court submission, Gray omitted to mention the fact that the novel category of SEP became applicable throughout Eisenhower's SHAEF command in Germany, *but not in Alexander's CMF command in Italy and Austria.*

The German Army South-West, commanded by General von Vietinghoff, covering enemy forces in Italy and southern Austria, entered into terms of surrender with Field Marshal Alexander at the palace of Caserta on 2nd May 1945. The terms of the capitulation include the following provisions.

> 8. All personnel of the German Armed Forces shall be subject to such conditions and directions as may be prescribed by the Supreme Allied Commander. **At the Supreme Allied Commander's discretion, some or all of such personnel may be declared to be prisoners of war...**

Further clauses establish that Alexander never exercized his discretion in order to adopt the SEP policy ruling obtaining at the time under SHAEF command in Germany. On the contrary, he formally endorsed maintenance of the legal rights of prisoners of war as defined by the Geneva Convention.

> 12. The German Authority will release in accordance with the

instructions of the Supreme Allied Commander all [Allied] prisoners of war (naval, military or air) at present in their power and will furnish forthwith complete lists of these persons with the places of their detention. **Pending release of such prisoners of war, the German Authority will continue to protect them in their persons and property, and accord them such treatment and facilities as are prescribed under the Geneva Convention.**

Thus the Convention remained effective throughout Alexander's command under the terms of the surrender agreement. As the Field Marshal himself wrote:

After the surrender I visited prisoners of war to satisfy myself that their treatment was in accordance with those rules of conduct which we as a nation consider right and proper.[10]

The surrender terms continue:

13. The provisions of paragraph 12 preceding will be applied by the German Authority equally to all other persons who are confined, interned or otherwise under restraint for political reasons or as the result of any action, law or regulation originating from discrimination on grounds of nationality, race, colour, creed or political belief.[11] **Such persons as are not entitled to treatment in accordance with the Geneva Convention will be afforded comparable rights and amenities in accordance with their rank or official position.**

Once again, we find the Geneva Convention explicitly accepted as continuing effective throughout regions administered by AFHQ following the German capitulation on 2 May. Although not every unit surrendering to Allied forces was classified as POW, the distinction was made clear in each instance. The radical distinction between treatment of prisoners of war under SHAEF administration and those held by CMF was that Eisenhower formally reclassified *all* enemy troops surrendering after 8 May 1945 as SEP, whereas Alexander disallowed POW status solely in the case of surrendered Yugoslavs (Chetniks) whose status was ambivalent.

The next day (3 May), 8th Army implemented the terms of surrender with Operation Instruction No. 1465, whose relevant clauses read as follows.

1. The object of this instruction is to consolidate present rules for dealing with PW and Surrendered Personnel...

'Distinction between PW and SURRENDERED PERSONNEL.

5. Chetnicks, troops of Mihailovitch and other dissident Yugoslavs ...

will be regarded as surrendered personnel and will be treated accordingly. The ultimate disposal of these personnel will be decided on Government levels.

Evacuation of PW and treatment of SURRENDERED PERSONNEL.

6. PW will be evacuated in the normal way.

7. 5 Corps will be responsible for evacuating PW from CONEGLIANO-BELLUNO area prior to taking over this area from 13 CORPS.[*]

With the exception of the above CORPS will be responsible for PW evacuation within their own areas.[12]

Captured Germans are, as the Instruction repeatedly emphasizes, to be treated as Prisoners of War (PW). 'Surrendered personnel' applies *only* to 'Chetnicks, troops of Mihailovitch and other dissident Yugoslavs'. The heading 'Distinction between PW and Surrendered Personnel' plainly implies that all formations surrendering to Allied forces within CMF (Central Mediterranean Force) fall into one or the other category.[13] Germans and Cossacks in German service are implicitly included among prisoners to be treated as PW. Classification of Chetniks as 'surrendered personnel' was never employed to authorize cuts in their rations and other comparable deprivations applied to SEP in Germany. Still less was it envisaged that they might be delivered up to another state certain to treat them with gross inhumanity. On the contrary, Alexander resolutely refused to surrender any Chetniks to Tito against their will.[14] It is clear from this that the expression 'surrendered personnel' as applied in Instruction No 1465 represents little more than common military parlance ('personnel who have surrendered'), and can bear no comparison to the prescriptive legal classification of German prisoners interned under SHAEF administration as Surrendered Enemy Personnel.[15]

Nowhere in Central Mediterranean Force records, from the signing of the capitulation terms onwards, do the terms 'surrendered personnel' or 'surrendered enemy personnel' correspond to those of SEP or DEF, as obtaining under Eisenhower's command in Germany.[16] When on 19 May Eisenhower informed Alexander that he was prepared to accept Cossacks and other prisoners under SHAEF control, he explained that they would be accepted under 'the status of "disarmed enemy forces" [DEF]'.[17] This confirms (what the evidence in any case attests) that this category did not exist in territory administered by Alexander's CMF.

---

[*] On 1-2 May 3rd Welsh Guards captured 5,000 Germans at Conegliano, whom they evacuated to Belluno (WO.170/4982).

The 8th Army's Instruction 1465 is marked for 'Distribution 5 Corps', and implicitly designates Germans and Cossacks in German service as POW. Any doubts as to this conclusion are dissipated by the consistent usage within 5th Corps.

Major Geoffrey Shakerly of the King's Royal Rifle Corps described to me how he accepted the surrender of a body of Cossacks:

> ... through the interpreter I asked the Adjutant to tell his CO that I had come to demand his surrender to the British Army under the terms of the Geneva Convention... I clearly remember the German Adjutant stressing the point that it was the British Army they were surrendering to & under the terms of the Geneva Convention.[18]

On 26 May the 12th Honourable Artillery Company war diary recorded:

> Move of Cossack Div into Regtl area [Weitensfeld]. This Div had fought against Russia and were therefore now treated as PW.[19]

Next day, 1st Guards Brigade war diary recorded that it was 'Of great political importance that PW [Cossacks] should be delivered to Russians complete'.[20]

On 18 July General Keightley himself informed Lady Limerick of the British Red Cross that

> several thousand Cossacks were taken prisoner, but had been for the last 3 1/2 years fighting in the German ranks; **they were dressed in German uniform and were taken prisoners of war.**[21]

Yet again, on 28 July a Foreign Office minute noted that 'the Cossacks in Austria ... are prisoners of war'.[22]

Thus, delivery of the Cossacks to 'slavery, torture, and probably death' in the Soviet Union, which to compound the issue was not a signatory of the 1929 Convention on Prisoners of War, undoubtedly constituted a major war crime.

---

[1] Gray further made a further attempt to justify forced repatriation by citing Article 75 of the 1929 Geneva Convention, which provides for speedy mutual repatriation of prisoners of war after the close of hostilities. What he failed to remind the court was that the Soviet Union was not a signatory of the Convention, being in this instance as in others generally regarded at the time of its ratification as a despotic regime, which *inter alia* maintained a system of slavery unparalleled since the days of the Roman Empire. The unique position of the USSR in this respect is reflected by the fact that

The international practice after World War I shows that no prisoners of war were forcibly extradited to their countries of origin. At that time, the problem only arose between certain powers and Soviet Russia.

From 1918 to 1921, the Soviets signed twenty-seven international treaties and agreements concerning the repatriation of prisoners of war and civilians. All were based on the principle of voluntary repatriation only and contained almost identical clauses explicitly precluding any forced repatriation (Julius Epstein, *Operation Keelhaul: The Story of Forced Repatriation from 1944 to the Present* (Old Greenwich, Conn., 1973), p. 14; cf. pp. 14-16).

[2] René-Jean Wilhelm, *Can the Status of Prisoners of War be Altered?* (Geneva, 1953), pp. 5-8.

[3] *Ibid.*, p. 11.

[4] Article 11 of the 1929 Geneva Convention requires prisoners of war to receive the same rations as those alloted their captors (Gustav Rasmussen (ed.), *Code des prisonniers de guerre: Commentaire de la convention du 27 juillet 1929 relative au traitement des prisonniers de guerre* (Copenhagen, 1931), p. 112).

[5] Richard D. Wiggers, 'The United States and the Denial of Prisoner of War (POW) Status at the End of the Second World War', *Militär-geschichtliche Mitteilungen*, (Oldenbourg, 1993), lii, p. 102.

[6] Ironically, it was in the same year that Charles Gray contended that introduction of SEP status deprived POW held in British occupation zones of any protection under international law, that the Canadian author James Bacque similarly argued (although from a very different perspective) that introduction of the parallel DEF status in US occupied zones was deliberately intended to permit inhumane treatment of prisoners of war (James Bacque, *Other Losses: An Investigation into the Mass Deaths of German Prisoners at the Hands of the French and Americans After World War II* (Toronto, 1989), pp. 161-62). However, historians are generally united in dismissing Bacque's accusation, which now appears almost as much a conspiracy theory as Gray's claim (cf. *Militär-geschichtliche Mitteilungen*, lii, p. 92). The major difference is that Bacque argued his case publicly on the basis of an extensive range of evidence, whereas Gray asserted his in conditions of secrecy on the basis of no evidence – or rather distortions of evidence.

[7] FO.371/46773. Cf. *Militär-geschichtliche Mitteilungen*, lii, pp. pp. 91-104.

[8] Wilhelm, *Can the Status of Prisoners of War be Altered?*, pp. 7-8. Eventually Article 6 of the 1949 Geneva Convention formalized the obvious intent of the 1929 Convention: 'No special agreement shall adversely affect the situation of prisoners of war, as defined by the present Convention, nor restrict the rights which it confers upon them' (Adam Roberts and Richard Guelff (ed.), *Documents on the Laws of War* (Oxford, 1989), p. 219). Cf. Christiane Shields Delessert, *Release and Repatriation of Prisoners of War at the End of Active Hostilities: A Study of Article 118, Paragraph 1 of the Third Geneva Convention Relative to the Treatment of Prisoners of War* (Zürich, 1977), p. 62.

⁹ The United States was similarly slow to sign peace treaties with Germany, Japan and other defeated enemy states following their defeat in 1945 (Delessert, *Release and Repatriation of Prisoners of War at the End of Active Hostilities*, p. 64).

¹⁰ John North (ed.), *The Alexander Memoirs 1940-1945* (London, 1962), p. 150.

¹¹ The reference is to concentration camp inmates held hostage by SS troops in South Tyrol (Allen Dulles, *The Secret Surrender* (London, 1967), pp. 243-44).

¹² WO.170/4182.

¹³ Thus on 14 May Alexander's Chief of Staff General Morgan informed Eisenhower: 'Refugee and PW situation in 5 Corps area becoming unmanageable and prejudicing operational efficiency of Corps' (WO.170/4185,451). Such references could be multiplied.

¹⁴ This reflects the policy urged by Churchill on 29 April to Sir Orme Sargent at the Foreign Office. 'There is no doubt that ... they [Chetniks and other anti-Tito Yugoslavs] should be disarmed and placed in refugee camps, [it] is the only possible solution' (FO.371/48812).

¹⁵ The terms 'surrendered personnel' and 'surrendered enemy personnel' are regularly employed interchangably without capital letters. Field Marshal Alexander's order of 4th June confirms just how imprecise and informal such definitions were: 'Yugoslavs who bore arms against Tito will be treated as surrendered personnel ... All this personnel will be regarded as displaced personnel ...' (FO.371/48825).

¹⁶ On 15 May Brigadier Low described Croats and Slovenes held by 5th Corps as 'surrendered ex-enemy personnel' (WO.170/4243). Two days later his senior staff officer referred in similarly loose terms to 'personnel surrendered to date' (WO.170/4184,712).

¹⁷ WO.219/290.

¹⁸ Letter to the author of 18 September 1975.

¹⁹ WO.170/4832. 'During the previous week [before the transfer of Cossacks to 46th Infantry Division] we had been fortunate to have been called upon to act solely in accordance with the Geneva Convention and not to take part in the forced repatriation that followed' (Lt-Col. Brian Clark of the Royal Irish Fusiliers, 1988, Witness Statement).

²⁰ WO.170/4404.

²¹ FO.371/51227. Note Keightley's specific acceptance, implicit in the Geneva Convention, that uniform determines a prisoner's status.

²² FO.371/47903,16.

APPENDIX B
SOLZHENITSYN'S DECLARATION

THE SUNDAY TIMES · 12 MAY 1996

Nobel support

I AM ready to sign a collective letter in defence of Count Nikolai Tolstoy's rights to his research archives, which are in danger of being taken away from him as reported in News Review (April 7).

The story of the shameful betrayal by the British authorities of Russian people to destruction at the hands of Stalin — a saga that has dragged on for 50 years, and one in every manner hushed up by the United Kingdom — calls out for far more severe judgment of the rule of law in Britain.

Alexander Solzhenitsyn
Moscow, Russia

Solzhenitsyn: 'I'll sign'

RUSSIAN TELEVISION INTERVIEW WITH A.I. SOLZHENITSYN

Broadcast on 30 September 1994 and published in *RUSSKAYA MYSL* on 12 October 1994

Interviewer:
You are speaking about those people whom Stalin hated and liquidated. But in reality the Americans and British helped him to do it? They perpetrated a dreadful betrayal ...

Solzhenitsyn:
Yes. And now we're coming to this in the next book. Because with this book I want to concern myself only with the prisoners.

I have to say that I feel very strongly about this subject. I was arrested at the front in 1945. I had a completely clear conscience: I was arrested because I criticized Stalin. And I was not in the least resentful: I sat and sat, I was trapped. But I saw those children with whom I sat in gaol - they waged war against them! They were sentenced by the Motherland! And yet again they were sentenced by the Motherland: there, in prison, they were abandoned; and again, a third time, they were sentenced, when they took them away and arrested them once more. What for?

I took their fate deeply to heart. And I consider this matter one of the greatest importance, one that must be fully understood. Yes, it was in the West - why in the West is there such general silence about this matter? The West stays quiet about their fate - not only were they handed over, but I'm talking about the governments. Why do they remain silent? Three American presidents were in some degree indirectly guilty of their handover and that of other fugitives in the West: Roosevelt, Truman, and Eisenhower. And the British Government was utterly tarnished. And a few lovers of justice and truth among Western and our own émigré scholars unearthed it with difficulty, barely penetrating the full truth. And now for the next book, that by Nikolai Tolstoy.

Nikolai Tolstoy - he is the great-nephew. Broadly speaking, it's like this: Nikolai Tolstoy's great-grandfather was the first cousin of Lev Nikolaevich - a close relative of Lev Nikolaevich. Earlier in "The Gulag Archipelago", not suspecting the implication, I wrote: "What Tolstoy will some day write about this? About the prisoners-of-war?" And a Tolstoy appeared, and he wrote.

He wrote a superb book: "Victims of Yalta". *Victims of Yalta*. Here it is [Solzhenitsyn shows the photograph on the back cover], who today is fighting heroically for truth - *today*! This is what I have to say about it.

He wrote the history of the Yalta Agreement, how Roosevelt and Churchill agreed that *they would deliver up by force* all those Soviet citizens who found themselves in the West (whether they were prisoners, or abducted to the West by the Germans to work, or refugees - all of them were to be handed over by force). And then something terrible began: that dreadful period of 1945 -1946, when our Allies - the British and the Americans - by force, with bludgeons, delivered hundreds of thousands of our Soviet citizens into the hands of the Soviet counter-espionage organization SMERSH.

I spoke about this. Much is now - *now*! - generally known about this. But the British Government customarily retains its secrets for thirty years, while much documentation is withheld for fifty years. Already fifty years have passed - they remain inaccessible.

When I was in England, I immediately addressed the English people on the radio, and said that it is a disgrace, this British betrayal: it is burned into our memory, and it must somehow be atoned. They handed over not only those who fought in the second World War. They handed over General Krasnov, who was an ally of the British in the first World War, who scarcely participated in the second. They gave him up to be hanged by the Bolsheviks, together with other Cossacks: old and young, with their Cossack wagons ...

Interviewer:
With children and women ...

Solzhenitsyn:
With children and women. People committed suicide on the spot. The "democratic" British drove them at bayonet point, or by deception, to the handover point - as happened at Judenburg, where they were told they were going to a conference. All the officers believed in the "conference" concerning the fate of their army - and were promptly handed over to SMERSH.

And now there is a further extraordinary story. Tolstoy wrote this work. And he showed that the British Government and Macmillan in particular were guilty of all this, and he identified individual senior officers. Moreover, he drew attention to one of the commanders, whom he mentioned, and a leaflet was published (*not by him!*): "look, here's a war criminal!" A war criminal – Warden of such-and-such a College, an honourable lord, so it appears – well, a highly honourable peer. This occasioned a trial of the pamphlet's author. But Tolstoy nobly said: since the evidence comes from my book, I will place myself in the dock.

And so the trial began. I have to say that justice in present-day Britain ... many of us in Russia have the impression that British democracy has created a judicial system incredible in its fairness and its democratic procedure. Don't believe it!

British justice, the evils of which were exposed by Dickens, has become more rotten after a century – after a century and a half. I have had experience of it – I've experienced it twice over. Once I was involved in an action lasting eight years: an action over half a line, half a phrase, in my book "The Oak and the Calf". A rascal brought an action against me, claiming I had libelled him in that book. And thus a work of literature is brought to court to be evaluated by a jury.

Our people fancy that a jury means something open and fair ... selected by lot, these were people who sleep at night under London's bridges: dock labourers, and prostitutes, who haven't any idea what literature is. And they sat in literary judgment! They sat for seven days, but afterwards the proceedings dragged on for eight years, and I was found guilty of defamation. And this very rascal published a book about me, filled with lies and calumnies occurring in just about every sentence.

I never went to court over that. But a noble émigré involved himself in court proceedings lasting ten years. Justice was done! They proved him to be a scoundrel, who swinishly wrote this book; proved him to be a common criminal - in every sentence. Never mind - never mind! He refused to pay: "I am bankrupt, I possess nothing, I am not guilty".

And the English court excused everything. Do you appreciate that? And then this English court ordered Nikolai Tolstoy to pay his fine for telling the truth: one and a half million pounds sterling ...

Interviewer:

Three million dollars, almost.

Solzhenitsyn:

Two and a half million dollars to pay. And still the judicial proceedings go on. Now he is completely bankrupt, and may be put in prison: "How can we fleece him further? He has children ..." Everything is lost. He is still researching the matter, he has discovered new facts, he is unearthing the whole business. But for *them* it is distasteful and boring.

I was unable to contain myself, and several years ago I wrote a letter to the British Queen. I wrote: "Your Majesty, I appreciate that you do not control British justice. I understand that British justice is completely independent of you. But the blot of this betrayal will lie on the whole of Britain: this unbearable betrayal of your allies, this betrayal of defenceless people. Take a moral step: it is within Your Majesty's power to distance yourself morally from what British justice is doing".

I received a reply from some official: "Her Majesty read your letter with interest". That was it.

Interviewer:

And you received no further reply?

Solzhenitsyn:

There was no further response, and there won't be - and I don't expect it.

APPENDIX C

RICHARD NORTON-TAYLOR, 'MYSTERY OF A MISLAID FILE'

The Guardian, 28 May 1992
Documents relating to one of the most controversial episodes in recent British history – the forced handover of tens of thousands of Cossacks and Yugoslavs at the end of the Second World War – were removed from the Public Record Office five years ago to help a Tory peer prepare for a trial to which he was awarded record £1.5 million libel damages.

They were removed in 1987 shortly after Aldington sued over an intemperate pamphlet written by the historian, Nikolai Tolstoy, and distributed by Nigel Watts, a property developer with a personal grievance against the peer.

The subsequent trial focused on Aldington's role as Chief of Staff in Austria in 1945 when British troops were ordered to participate in what the FO was later to describe as "a ghastly mistake".

The FO has admitted it removed the files from the PRO for Aldington. It also made them available to members of the committee involved in what the FO called a "private investigation" into the controversy. The committee was chaired by Brigadier Anthony Cowgill, and included among its members Lord Brimelow, a wartime FO official criticised in Victims of Yalta, published in 1978 – Tolstoy's first (and well-received) foray into the controversial issue which he will not let go.

One file the FO made available to Aldington and Cowgill – and which was in practice unavailable to anyone else – deals with a central issue raised during the two-month trial: the argument that the British Army, threatened by Tito's forces, was under pressure to "clear the decks" and was simply carrying out orders to repatriate the Cossacks and Yugoslavs under its control.

References to the FO file appeared in the court bundles prepared by Aldington's lawyers. When Tolstoy's lawyers first appreciated the significance of the file two weeks into the trial in October 1989, the FO came up with photocopied documents. These represented less than 20% of the complete file, FO 1020/42, which, we now know, was taken from the foreign office in 1987, mysteriously lost, suddenly found in an FO cupboard, and finally returned to the PRO at the end of last year.

The loss of the file was acknowledged by the FO for the first time on August 21, 1991. In response to a letter from Sir Bernard Braine, then Father of the Commons, Lady Chalker, FO minister of state, said the file was "recalled from the PRO for use by them (the Cowgill team)" and was held in the FO for more than a year. Officials were "on the point of confirming to the Public Record Office that the file went missing whilst on requisition to department". The loss was "deeply regretted".

Three months later Foreign Secretary Douglas Hurd told Sir Bernard the loss of the file "came to light in mid-1989". The PRO, he said, had confirmed that it was "marked out" to the FO in 1987 and had not been available to researchers at the PRO since then.

In December 1991, Hurd informed Sir Bernard that the document had been "misfiled" but was now "available to researchers". Sir Bernard, who by now was becoming deeply suspicious about what the FO had been up to, responded by sending Hurd a 15-page letter.

Hurd responded in February: "Our records of files requisitioned from Lord Aldington in 1987 are incomplete but it would seem he made two visits, the wrong reference having been supplied by him before the first visit". He said that although officials did not know when the file was lost, "from papers found with it in November last year [1991] it appears that it was incorrectly put away with other papers in early 1988 . . . The file was later found by the records staff when routinely clearing out a cupboard of unconnected material". The PRO was not told of the loss until October 1991.

The file refers to a plan, drawn up between May 20-23, to despatch a column of 800 US trucks to evacuate all Cossacks in the British 5 Corps area to safety in the American zone of Germany. A War Office document (which has also been unavailable at the PRO) confirmed the offer of US help in a plan code-named Operation Coldstream. Far from being in a desperate state, 5 Corps reported on May 22 that all was well. A War office record states: "Confirmed conversation, Chief of Staff, BGS, to Main 8th Army from Main 5 Corps, situation report, 22 May. 'Situation in Lienz (where the Cossack men, women and children were being held) well in hand and can be organised by one unit'".

Records from American archives found by Tolstoy record that US Army headquarters reported on May 22, 1945: "Apparently the British had the situation under control and did not need our assistance". They also suggest that, whatever the British were saying about the threat posed by

Tito, the US took a different view. "If Tito wants a fight", General Patton, commander of the Third U.S. Army told his men, "do a good job".

Another question which arose during the trial was the date when Aldington, then Brigadier Toby Low, left for home. His recollection was that he had left Austria on May 22, 1945. The date is important; on that day, allied headquarters issued orders forbidding the British Army 5 Corps to use force against the Cossacks, and referring it to an earlier instruction to screen all Russians to see whether they were Soviet nationals. It was the time when plans for the Americans to take the Cossacks west to Germany were coming to a head. And on that morning a decision was made at a 5 Corps conference to order British soldiers to shoot Cossacks who resisted being handed over.

A separate War office document, discovered at the PRO after the trial, is a record of 2 GHQ Liaison Regiment, one of the British Army's "Phantom" signals units. Dated May 24, 1945, it states: "BGS (Brigadier General Staff, the position held by Aldington) left 5 Corps for England on FLIAP (overdue leave) on 23 May." The document was not available at the trial.

It is not clear whether a consistent record is taken of the dates Whitehall departments take files away from the PRO. Last month, Miss G.L. Beech, head of the PRO's reader services department, told a researcher: "we are not ... able to provide details or dates at which individual documents have been requisitioned by government departments," she said. However, the Guardian has since been told that this does not reflect official PRO policy.

Tolstoy followed up Victims of Yalta with another book, The Minister and the Massacres. The title is a reference to the role played by Harold Macmillan, the minister responsible for executing British policy in Italy and Austria at the time. The book, which was published in 1986 and sold 10,000 copies in hardback, also refers in passing to the role played by Aldington.

After the jury gave its verdict on the libel trial, a statement was read in open court disclosing that in 1988, Century Hutchinson, Tolstoy's publishers, made a private settlement with Aldington, paying him £30,000 and undertaking not to issue any further copies of the book.

In 1990 – four years after the book was published – Aldington's lawyers, Allen & Overy, wrote to local authority librarians throughout the country telling them that by "continuing to loan the book out the libraries under your control and republishing the libels contained in the book and are themselves libelling our client. We should be grateful if you would confirm that you will arrange for all copies of the book within your libraries' possession to be withdrawn from circulation".

Attached to the letter was a document referring, not to the agreement between Aldington and Century Hutchinson, but to the libel trial which concerned a quite different publication – the pamphlet written by Tolstoy and distributed by his co-defendant, Nigel Watts. In a letter to Ian Mitchell, editor of Topical Books, who has taken up Tolstoy's case, Allen & Overy put this apparent confusion down to a "a clerical error".

How did libraries react to a letter which had no legal force? They succumbed. For example David Vaisey, the librarian of the Bodleian at Oxford University, has instructed the book to be withdrawn from circulation. "I believe that in all the circumstances", he wrote to Peter Gwyn, a historian, in December 1990, "I have acted in the best interests of the library and its readers by not laying the Bodleian open to an action for libel".

Richard Wise, director of Arts and Libraries in Kent, said that were he to permit copies of The Minister and the Massacres to remain in circulation, he would be acting "recklessly". This was after he was told by Dallas Manderson, Century Hutchinson's group sales director, that the book was "was deemed libellous". The fact is that no court of law has so deemed it.

Last year Tolstoy's book, which includes additional material, was published in Croatia. In Britain, Cowgill's report The Repatriations From Austria in 1945, published by Sinclair-Stevenson in 1990, says there was no question that many British soldiers involved in the episode felt that they were asked to carry out actions which they found deeply distasteful. But it absolves Macmillan and senior army officers on the spot from criticism and blame, and dismisses Tolstoy as a conspiracy theorist.

The origins of the libel trial lay in a dispute over an insurance claim between Nigel Watts and Sun Alliance, of which Lord Aldington was then chairman. The judge said that dispute was irrelevant to the trial. Later Sun Alliance acknowledged that it had advanced £500,000 to help Aldington pay for his legal costs.

After the trial, Aldington obtained an injunction freezing Tolstoy's Forced Repatriation Fund, but did not sequestrate its assets to help pay for the libel award. In 1990, the Court of Appeal blocked Tolstoy's attempt to contest the verdict and the damages on the grounds that he could not put up sufficient security for costs.

The European Commission of Human Rights recently decided the Government has a case to answer over the way Tolstoy was treated in the English courts. The controversy is far from over. But the story of the missing documents raises a broader issue, namely the absolute discretion the Public Records Act gives to Whitehall departments to withhold, or take away, documents from the nation's archives. The Act allows departments to keep, or requisition, documents for what it calls "administrative purposes", or for "any other special reason".

APPENDIX D

TIM RAYMENT, 'THE MASSACRE AND THE MINISTERS'

The Sunday Times, 7th April 1996

Bankrupts don't live badly these days. Count Nikolai Tolstoy, the biggest libel loser in British history, enjoys a 17th-century farmhouse in Oxfordshire, his son at Eton and a Volvo estate in the drive.

True, the house is cold because the heating is low, and he doesn't know where the money will come from to keep Xenia, his 15-year-old daughter, at her £12,420-a-year private school. But it is as if his £2m debt never happened.

It is more than six years since the writer and historian turned pale in the High Court, his wife fighting tears beside him, as he was ordered to pay £1.5m damages to Lord Aldington, a former deputy chairman of the Conservative party. He had accused the peer of complicity in war crimes committed just after the defeat of Germany in 1945.

To friends of Aldington, a former brigadier and barrister on first-name terms with ministers in every Tory government since the war, a crank had got his comeuppance. Yet if you visit Tolstoy in his study, a converted wagon shed heated by one panel of a portable gas fire, he will tell you a compelling story.

It is an account he wants to make public in the courts, but cannot: of how the machinery of government seemed to tilt the scales of justice, and the state supposedly interfered in a private court case.

A few years ago, before the Scott report and the furore over three businessmen who faced prison because the government would not come clean on its arms-to-Iraq policy, nobody would have believed such a tale. Now perhaps they might.

Today, 2,320 days after his defeat, Tolstoy has not paid a penny of the £1.5m damages and more than £500,000 costs he owes his elderly foe. Instead, he has been busy with legal challenges.

At the European Court of Human Rights he won a ruling that the size of the award violated his freedom of expression. In Britain, in actions that have sometimes been heard in secret, he has fared less well.

He was not allowed to appeal against the libel verdict because he could not lodge £124,900 to pay Aldington's likely costs if the case failed. Later he issued a writ for fraud, claiming that new evidence showed the baron obtained his award through perjury. This action, deemed "frivolous" and "vexatious", was struck out by a judge.

At first Tolstoy's legal activities look like delaying tactics, to keep a lovely house a little longer. However, his supporters include some surprising names.

Writers such as Chapman Pincher and Alexander Solzhenitsyn, academics such as Roger Scruton and Gavin Stamp, and politicians of the calibre of Viscount Cranborne, the Conservative cabinet minister and leader of the House of Lords, are patrons of the fund that maintains the Tolstoys and their four children.

Taki, the socialite and Sunday Times columnist, paid for the Volvo. Xenia's school fees for this year are underwritten by a Conservative peer whom Tolstoy wants to remain anonymous. Eminent lawyers such as Richard Rampton QC, Lord Lester QC and Alun Jones QC have acted for Tolstoy free.

Why do these people believe in him? Could he be the victim of rough justice?

"There were babies, there were pregnant women. It's really quite indescribable. These were British soldiers with bayonets ... I had a lot of pain and punishment in Auschwitz, but at least I didn't have bayonets at my back. To see people being shot at and bayoneted, it was just sheer bestiality".

Zoe Polanska-Palmer, a retired businesswoman who lives near Dundee, witnessed one of the incidents at the heart of this affair. In 1945 she was 14. She had been one of Dr Mengele's victims in Auschwitz, but it is British behaviour that haunts her. Polanska-Palmer is from Ukraine. Taken by the Germans for child labour, she eventually escaped to the Austrian mountains, joining 70,000 Cossacks, emigré Russians and Yugoslavs who had surrendered to the British.

They were not a very military slice of humanity: men exercised their horses, wives hung washing and children played in the grass. Some were Soviet citizens who hated communism and had fought on the German side. Some had fled Russia before the Soviet Union existed. A number had been part of a savage struggle against Tito's partisans in Yugoslavia. Others, like Polanska-Palmer, had fought nobody.

Many had families with them; according to a telegram from Field Marshal Alexander, who was in charge of operations in Austria, 11,000 of the Cossacks were women, children and old men. "To return them to their country of origin immediately might be fatal to their health", he said.

Yet all were handed back — to the Soviet Union or Tito's partisans.

It was official allied policy to hand over Soviet nationals, under the Yalta agreement of February 1945, to ensure the return of British prisoners of war "liberated" by the Red Army. Witnesses insist, however, that the British command in Austria made almost no attempt to distinguish Soviet from non-Soviet citizens, and even handed over emigré Russians waving French passports and one wearing a British medal awarded for his conduct in the first world war.

Soldiers, some in tears, used deception and force to get their hysterical charges into the trucks and cattle trucks. "Many of them kept coming to me to ask me to shoot them, and to fetch their wives and children and shoot them as well", said a lieutenant in the Royal Artillery, years later.

Some women cut their babies' throats. Polanksa-Palmer watched others save themselves from Stalin's camps by jumping from a bridge to their deaths.

Across the line, Cossack officers were murdered as soon as they were received by the Russians. They tried to die with dignity, singing as they were shot. "That night and the following day, we started to count the small-arms fire coming from the Russian sector, to the accompaniment of the finest male voice choir I have ever heard", said Edward Stewart, of the Royal Corps of Signals. "The voices echoed round and round the countryside. Then the gunfire would be followed by a huge cheer".

The anti-communist Yugoslavs handed over to the communist partisans suffered a similar end. Thousands were slaughtered.

Tolstoy, a distant relative of Leo Tolstoy, the giant of Russian literature, has investigated the handovers since the first war papers were released to the Public Record Office in 1973. Two of his nine books are on this subject: Victims of Yalta, published in 1977 to general praise, and The Minister and the Massacres, released in 1986.

He believes the emigré Russians were forcibly repatriated because Harold Macmillan, "minister resident" in the Mediterranean and later prime minister, wanted to please Stalin. The Minister and the Massacres claims Macmillan persuaded a British general to ignore a Foreign Office telegram ordering that "any person who is not (repeat not) a Soviet citizen under British law must not (repeat not) be sent back to the Soviet Union unless he expressly desires".

Aldington - then a politically well-connected, 30-year-old brigadier called Toby Low - was chief of staff to the general commanding British forces in the area. On May 21, 1945, he issued the orders as to how to define Soviet citizenship. "Individual cases will NOT be considered unless particularly pressed ... In all cases of doubt, the individual will be treated as a SOVIET NATIONAL". In Tolstoy's view, the fate of the emigré Russians was sealed.

Within weeks of the war's end, Aldington returned to England to secure a seat as a Tory MP. After a ministerial career, he was ennobled by Macmillan and became chairman of the Sun Alliance insurance company. Bizarrely, it was this role that led to his conflict with Tolstoy.

A property developer called Nigel Watts, who had read The Minister and the Massacres and was fighting Sun Alliance over a disputed life insurance claim, drew up a leaflet about Aldington's role in Austria and sent it to Tolstoy. It was wrong in places, so Tolstoy rewrote it and Watts circulated 10,000 copies to politicians, the press and Aldington's acquaintances. Unlike the book, the language of the leaflet was wildly uncompromising and Aldington sued.

At first he acted against Watts alone, and did not want Tolstoy involved. He issued a second writ only after lawyers drew up an affidavit in which Tolstoy, who was confident of his claims, demanded to be sued.

Who did what in Austria was now for a jury to decide. In Whitehall, however, others were also getting involved.

After The Minister and the Massacres was published, a private "committee of inquiry" had been set up under Anthony Cowgill, a retired brigadier in regular contact with Bernard Ingham, spokesman for No 10. Cowgill was to investigate the charges against Macmillan, and he enlisted Aldington's help.

In a letter to the Ministry of Defence, seen by The Sunday Times, Cowgill describes a study "in conjunction with . . . Lord Aldington ... This study is being done in the national interest".

Two of Cowgill's three co-authors had an interest in the outcome. Brigadier Teddy Tryon-Wilson had played a part in the repatriations, and Lord Brimelow, a Soviet specialist and Labour peer, had been a junior official at the Foreign Office. Tolstoy had accused Brimelow of the "remarkable falsehood" of claiming that the repatriations had been without violence. The final inquiry member was Christopher Booker, a journalist.

In spring 1986, Cowgill introduced himself to Tolstoy, who took him for an independent investigator. Cowgill said he ran a business organisation and was forming a committee to look into events in Austria in 1945. He explained that he was planning a business conference in Cambridge, which Aldington was to chair, and wondered, in the light of Tolstoy's book, if the peer were a fit person to do so. Tolstoy invited him round and they went for a pub lunch.

It was the first of more than half a dozen visits in which Cowgill would settle himself in the worn armchair in Tolstoy's study, pat the children's heads and go through the evidence against Macmillan and Aldington. Tolstoy handed it all over, including records he had obtained from America under the Freedom of Information Act.

His wife, Georgina, grew concerned. When Tolstoy gave away copies of his microfilms she was furious. "I remember saying to him, 'What are you doing?'" she said. "I suppose he was pleased that somebody was trying to follow it up".

While Tolstoy was out of the country, Cowgill held a press conference to announce the results of his investigation. "An independent inquiry", The Times reported, "has found Mr Harold Macmillan (later Lord Stockton) innocent of 'the gravest charges ever levelled at anyone who has become a British prime minister' ... An interim report to be published next week rebuts the allegations made by Count Nikolai Tolstoy in his books The Victims of Yalta and The Minister and The Massacres". Tolstoy "was not available for comment", making it seem he was hiding. Only *The Sunday Times* took the trouble to find him.

There was to be another twist. "The inquiry which last week cleared Harold Macmillan of wrongdoing in the Balkans in 1945 has produced evidence that will be used in a libel case which the defence has branded as Britain's first war crimes trial", The Sunday Telegraph reported.

Who commissioned the inquiry, and who paid for it? Cowgill - who would later deny links with British intelligence – says it was a private venture, funded by the team members. He started work after Ingham told him there would be no public inquiry into events in Austria in 1945.

"I said, 'Look, there must be an Establishment picture on this', and he came back in a couple of days and said, 'No there isn't, we just don't know. If by any chance you are doing any work obviously we would like to know'", Cowgill said last week. He reported his findings in an hour-long meeting with Robert Armstrong, the Cabinet secretary.

Soon Tolstoy had another surprise. Officials at the Foreign Office and the Ministry of Defence removed from the Public Record Office several files of war papers that he needed for his defence in the libel case. When his researcher asked for these documents, including reports and signals relating to Aldington, she was told they were not available.

Only after the nine-week trial had started in October 1989 was Tolstoy given a photocopy of the most important of the files. Four-fifths of the contents were missing.

Aldington, however, was not finding access to war records a problem. "Dear George", he wrote to George Younger, the then defence secretary, on March 8, 1987. "... you are a friend who will understand my distress ... if the files can be brought to the Westminster area in a series of bundles, that would be very helpful".

"If I had received a letter of that sort from Tolstoy, 1 would have done the same for him", Younger said this weekend.

It was 1991, 19 months after the trial had ended in disaster for Tolstoy, before he began to make new inquiries about the missing papers. The question was taken up by Sir Bernard Braine, the Conservative MP who was then father of the House of Commons (he is now Lord Braine of Wheatley).

"I have had a complaint that your department has not so far returned a file to the Public Record Office concerning certain events in Austria in the spring and summer of 1945", Braine wrote to Douglas Hurd, then foreign secretary, in August 1991. "The file no is FO1020/42. I hope you can assure me that the file will be returned to the Public Record Office and made available to researchers. If there is some special reason for retaining it, then perhaps I could be told. As a privy counsellor, I myself would like to see the file".

Lynda Chalker, a minister of state, replied. The file was "one of many" that had been recalled for use in the Cowgill investigation, and the papers had been held at the Foreign Office for more than a year for the team to research. Now, after four years, the Foreign Office was "on the point of confirming to the Public Record Office that the file went missing ... The loss of this or any file, apparently while in the custody of the FCO, is deeply regretted".

Braine, "astonished at ... the sheer carelessness", wrote again. Why, he asked, had the Foreign Office lent Cowgill "exceptional assistance" for a campaign of attacks on Tolstoy's honesty and integrity? "I think any reasonable person would agree ... this massive and prolonged propaganda campaign could have influenced the jury".

This time Hurd replied. "The help given to the private Cowgill inquiry", he said, "amounted to no more than making available some Foreign Office papers already in the public domain for consultation in the FCO". The loss of the file was "very regrettable".

Five days later, Hurd had an announcement. "The missing file has been found", he wrote to Braine. "It had been misfiled. It has been returned to the Public Record Office, where it is again available to researchers".

Braine, however, thought Hurd was being evasive. He wrote the foreign secretary a personal letter in the strongest terms, which has never [before] been published. "This disgraceful activity ... was designed to pervert the course of justice in a case concerned with one of the most shameful episodes in British history", the father of the House declared. "I have been in parliament for 42 years, and have held office under two prime ministers. I cannot recollect a previous instance of officials conniving at the suppression of records in order to prevent justice being done in the courts".

After further correspondence with Hurd, Braine wrote to Tolstoy, again in terms that have not been revealed before. "Douglas Hurd's last letter to me (March 5) saddens me", said the MP, who had held Hurd in high regard. "He is now engaged in a cover-up. If he did not think his officials had behaved improperly, all he had to do was to provide an answer to my questions".

Hurd was unavailable for comment yesterday. Lord Howe, who was foreign secretary when the papers were removed - and who, incidentally, had been appointed by Aldington to the board of Sun Alliance in 1974 - was also unavailable, on holiday.

Nor have Aldington's dealings with the Ministry of Defence been fully explained. On January 11, 1988, he wrote to Lord Trefgarne, the minister of defence procurement. "Dear David", he began. "You have kindly offered to help me with the documents relating to the Cossack/Yugoslav repatriations in Austria in May 1945 ..." Aldington reported that he had been through "all the files I wanted", but there was "one small matter in which you may be able to help in corroboration". What was the date of his departure from Austria, which "may prove to be vital in a simple rebuttal of most of the outrageous charges made against me"?

Trefgarne, despite "a thorough search", was unable to find the required corroboration. Aldington asked Trefgarne to look in his wartime personal file.

It is Ministry of Defence policy not to allow direct access to personal files, but Trefgarne complied. "As the two papers in question are, in themselves, fairly innocuous, 1 am happy to provide the attached copies", he wrote. "I must ask that they be treated in strict confidence, for use by yourself and your counsel only and that the source of the documents (ie, your personal file) should not be revealed". The papers showed that Aldington had arrived in Britain on May 24; but his day of departure from Austria was still a puzzle.

The date mattered. If Aldington could show that he had left after breakfast on May 22, as he told the libel trial, it would prove he was absent from a conference that day at which it was decided to shoot at Cossacks resisting forced repatriation.

When Tolstoy finally gained access to the key Foreign Office and defence ministry files, he found apparent discrepancies with Aldington's statements in court. One discovery was that the American forces in Austria had sent 800 vehicles, apparently to take the Cossacks to safety in Germany on the orders of General Dwight Eisenhower, the allied supreme commander. When the vehicles arrived at the border of Aldington's territory, however, the British said they were not required. This rebuff came in a signal from the Brigadier General Staff (BGS) for 5 Corps, Aldington's title. But he says he was no longer Brigadier General Staff at 5.14 pm on May 22, when the signal was sent, having handed over to a successor that morning.

On May 23, the BGS of 5 Corps - Aldington again denies being the BGS concerned - sent another signal. "As a result of verbal directive from Macmillan to corps commander at recent meeting", it said, "we have undertaken to return all Soviet nationals in corps area to Soviet forces". Despite earlier instructions from Field Marshal Alexander that there was to be no force, the signal sought permission to use it, explaining that otherwise the Cossacks could not be returned.

Aldington told the libel trial that he had left Austria on May 22 for Naples, where he spent two days before returning to Britain. He was unable to produce witnesses to confirm his time in Italy, and the curious thing is that he used to say he had left on May 25 or 26, or even May 29. In 1981, for example, Aldington wrote to Serena Booker, a researcher helping Alistair Horne with the authorised biography of Macmillan: "You really must believe me when I tell you again that I did not know that 'White Russians' (that is, as I understand it, Russians resident in Paris or elsewhere in western Europe during the 20s and 30s) were returned". He insisted: "I left on May 25".

Further confusion arose when an historian studying Eden's papers in the library of Birmingham University came across a handwritten letter from Aldington. It was dated May 21 and postmarked in Austria on May 22. "My dear Anthony", it began. "I hope to fly home on May 24 - at last after so long - a fortnight in England".

This does not conflict with Aldington's account, but when Tolstoy's lawyers drew attention to the letter it was withdrawn from access. The library told him: "The trustees [of the Eden papers] have ... informed us that they do not wish you to have access to the archive".

In parallel to the research, Tolstoy continued his legal battle, after declining an offer from Aldington to settle for £300,000 and losing his application to appeal. To his frustration, most of the legal infighting has been heard in secret. The details are revealed here for the first time.

His writ alleging fraud, claiming that Aldington had obtained his £1.5m libel award through perjury, was struck out in chambers by Mr Justice Collins in October, 1994.

Alun Jones, Tolstoy's QC, was so outraged by the running of the closed three-day hearing, in court 23 of the High Court, that he contemplated walking out. He continued after being assured that a tape recording of the proceedings was being made. When the case was over he was told that no recording would be available.

According to Tolstoy's handwritten notes, Collins dismissed new evidence - a signal apparently recording that Aldington left Austria on May 23 – "because it disagrees with Lord Aldington's testimony". The judge also refused an application to bring to court under subpoena a tape-recorded interview given by Aldington to the Imperial War Museum.

"Ah, you are going to listen to it and analyse it". Collins said. He brushed aside a letter from Aldington to the museum, dated August 26, 1993, and seen by The Sunday Times, in which the peer says: "I do not want to complicate affairs by having on record for the public any statements different from those I made on oath in the courts".

Collins then ordered Tolstoy's lawyers to pay 60% of Aldington's costs, reasoning that as they had acted for nothing, they had made themselves a party to the case. In effect, this was a new legal principle with wide implications, putting at risk any lawyer who decided to act for a client *pro bono* (for the public good). Last December, the Court of Appeal ruled that although Collins's reasoning was wrong, the decision itself was right.

"No barrister or solicitor will be allowed to represent him because of the extraordinary financial penalty", one QC said last week. "The whole thing has just been silenced".

Tolstoy's legal friends feel it is fair to point out that, before becoming a judge, Collins had been prosecuting counsel for the Customs & Excise in the 1992 Ordtech case, and incorrectly assured the court that the crown possessed no evidence helpful to the defence. He was reproached over this in the Scott report.

Tolstoy is now preparing for a final court case to defend himself from ruin. He is acting for himself, as no lawyer will risk being seen to help. In February, he delivered bundles of evidence for an appeal against Collins's judgment, and now awaits a date for the hearing.

After exchanges with the official overseeing his bankruptcy, he fears for the books in his chilly study, running to 4,000 volumes collected since the age of 12. If they are taken away to be sold, it will stop him writing further about the events of 1945.

His wife says the strain of the past six years has marked all her family. Xenia, the youngest, was glad to go to boarding school and escape the atmosphere at home. Alexandra, the eldest, had to resit her A-levels. Tolstoy himself has changed.

"His confidence in his writing has been very knocked", she said. "He feels, 'Who's going to be interested? Who's going to believe in what I write?' The feeling that his books are going to be taken away is a living nightmare to him. He sleeps very badly. He listens to Classic FM all through the night".

"I've had regrets but no serious ones", says Tolstoy of his £2m debt. "It was a terrible event by any standards. It just offends one's whole sense of justice that this could happen and the official view, enshrined in the Cowgill report, is that nobody is responsible for it. The only person who is a criminal in British eyes is me".

His supporters are standing by him. "You are talking about one of my heroes", said Braine. "I have admired him all the years I have known him. He is a seeker of truth".

That is not how he is seen by the Establishment figures in this affair. "All this story about new evidence is nonsense", Aldington said. "They have always been trying to reverse the verdict. The fact is that 1 have now had something like 15 or 16 judges deciding for me, which is quite a lot".

"It's complete nonsense", agreed Collins. "It has been known for litigants to get somewhat obsessed with the cases they are involved in, and not to be able to know what is truth and what is fantasy".

Cowgill concurred. "We certainly went in heavily impressed by Tolstoy's very vivid writing", he said. "But the more we went into it, the more we found what had been written was almost 180 degrees different from reality. It was quite astonishing".

As for the ministers, the Foreign Office said Hurd would stand by his replies to Braine's letters.

"I can't truly remember what happened at all", said Trefgarne, who is no longer at the Ministry of Defence. "I am quite certain that I would not have been allowed by officials to do anything that was not perfectly proper. Any allegation of impropriety by Count Tolstoy is, of course, without foundation".

BIBLIOGRAPHY

n.b. I have long adopted the practice of rendering titles of books published in Russian in the Cyrillic alphabet. An English phonetic alphabet is all but meaningless for Russian readers and monoglot English readers alike. On the other hand, I feel that providing authors' names and places of publication in the English alphabet makes titles at least recognizable. For some this may appear incongruous, but in my view represents the least awkward compromise.

Jonathan R. Adelman, 'Soviet Secret Police', in *idem* (ed.), *Terror and Communist Politics: The Role of the Secret Police in Communist States* (Boulder, 1984).

Alfred Adler, *The Neurotic Constitution: Outlines of a Comparative Individualistic Psychology and Psychotherapy* (London, 1921).

Alfred Adler, *Problems of Neurosis: A Book of Case-Histories* (London, 1929).

K.M. Alexandrov, *Офицерский Корпус Армии Генерал-Лейтенанта А.А. Власова 1944-1945* (Moscow, 2009).

Svetlana Alliluyeva, *Only One Year* (London, 1969).

Christopher Andrew and Vasili Mitrokhin, *The Sword and the Shield: The Mitrokhin Archive and the Secret History of the KGB* (New York, 1999).

Catherine Andreyev, *Vlasov and the Russian Liberation Movement: Soviet reality and émigré theories* (Cambridge, 1987).

Alexei Arseniev, 'Русская диаспора в Югославии', in A. Arseniev, O. Kirillova, and M. Sibinovich (ed.), *Русская змиграция в Югославии* (Moscow, 1996).

The Earl of Avon, *The Eden Memoirs: The Reckoning* (London, 1965).

Paul Avrich, *Kronstadt 1921* (Princeton, 1970).

James Bacque, *Other Losses: An Investigation into the Mass Deaths of German Prisoners at the Hands of the French and Americans After World War II* (Toronto, 1989).

'Geoffrey Bailey', *The Conspirators* (London, 1961).

Boris Bajanov, *Bajanov révèle Staline; Souvenirs d'un ancien secrétaire de Staline* (Paris, 1979).

Peter Balakian, *The Burning Tigris: A History of the Armenian Genocide* (London, 2003).

Thomas M. Barker, *Social Revolutionaries and Secret Agents: The Carinthian Slovene Partisans and Britain's Special Operations Executive* (Boulder, 1990).

Omer Bartov, *The Eastern Front, 1941-45, German Troops and the Barbarisation of Warfare* (Basingstoke, 1985).

I.I. Basik, S.N. Ivanov, S.O. Panin and V.S. Khristopherov (ed.), *Русская Военная Змиграция 20-40-х годов XX века: Документы и Материалы* (Moscow, 1998-).

P.N. Bazanov, *Братство Русской Правды – самая загадочная организация Русского Зарубежья* (Moscow, 2013).

Nicholas Bethell, *The Last Secret: Forcible Repatriation to Russia 1944-7* (London, 1974).

Vadim J. Birstein, *SMERSH: Stalin's Secret Weapon* (London, 2011).

Alexander Bobrinskoy, *Дворянскіе Роды внесенные въ Общій Гербовникъ Всероссійской Имперіи* (St. Petersburg, 1890).

Christopher Booker, *A Looking-Glass Tragedy: The Controversy over the repatriations from Austria in 1945* (London, 1997).

Viktor Bortnevsky, *Белое Дело: (Люди и события)* (St. Petersburg, 1993).

Alexander von Bosse, *The Cossack Corps* (Headquarters US Army European Command, 1950).

William C. Bradbury, Samuel M. Meyers, and Albert D. Biderman (ed.), *Mass Behavior in Battle and Captivity: The Communist Soldier in the Korean War* (Chicago, 1968).

Gordon Brook-Shepherd, *Iron Maze: The Western Secret Services and the Bolsheviks* (London, 1998).

Peter Broucek (ed.), *Ein General im Zwielicht: Die Erinnerungen Edmund Glaises von Horstenau* (Vienna, 1980-88).

Robert Paul Browder, 'Kerenskij Revisited', in Hugh Maclean, Martin E. Malia, and George Fischer (ed.), *Russian Thought and Politics* (*Harvard Slavic Studies*, iv) (Cambridge, Mass., 1957), pp. 421-34.

John M.G. Brown, *Moscow Bound: Policy, Politics and the POW Dilemma* (Eureka, CA, 1993).

Ortwin Buchbender, *Das tönende Erz: Deutsche Propaganda gegen die Rote Armee im Zweiten Weltkrieg* (Stuttgart, 1978).

Pier Arrigo Carnier, *L'armata cosacca in Italia (1944-1945)* (Milan, 1965).

Pier Arrigo Carnier, *Lo Sterminio Mancato: La dominazione nazista nel Veneto orientale 1943-1945* (Milan, 1982).

E. Malcolm Carroll, *Soviet Communism and Western Opinion 1919-1921* (Chapel Hill, 1965).

Alfred D. Chandler and Louis Galambos (ed.), *The Papers of Dwight David Eisenhower* (Baltimore and London, 1970-2001).

Konstantin Cherkassov, *Генерал Кононов: (Ответ перед Историей за Одну Попытку)* (Melbourne, 1963-65),

V.Y. Chernaev, 'Писатель генерал Краснов', in V.G. Bortnevsky (ed.), *Русское Прошлое: Историко-Документальный Альманах* (St. Petersburg, 1993), iv, pp. 352-59.

Rogers P. Churchill, William Slany, John G. Reid, N. O. Sappington, and Douglas W. Houston (ed.), *Foreign Relations of the United States: Diplomatic Papers, 1945, Europe,* (Washington, Volume V (Washington, 1969).

Winston S. Churchill, *Closing the Ring* (London, 1952).

Winston S. Churchill, *Triumph and Tragedy* (London, 1954).

John Colville, *The Fringes of Power: Downing Street Diaries 1939-1955* (London, 1985).

Robert Conquest, *The Great Terror: Stalin's Purge of the Thirties* (London, 1968).

Robert Conquest, *Kolyma: The Arctic Death Camps* (London, 1978).

Robert Conquest, *Stalin and the Kirov Murder* (London, 1989).

E.H. Cookridge, *Gehlen: Spy of the Century* (London, 1971).

Georges Coudry, *Les camps soviétiques en France: Les «Russes» livrés à Staline en 1945* (Paris, 1997).

Brigadier Anthony Cowgill, Christopher Booker Esq, Lord Brimelow, and Brigadier Teddy Tryon-Wilson, *Interim Report on an Enquiry into the Repatriation of Surrendered Enemy Personnel to the Soviet Union and Yugoslavia from Austria in 1945 and the Alleged 'Klagenfurt Conspiracy'* (London, 1988).

Brigadier Anthony Cowgill, Lord Brimelow, and Christopher Booker Esq, *The Repatriations from Austria in 1945: The Report of an Inquiry* (London, 1990).

The Repatriations from Austria in 1945: The Documentary Evidence Reproduced in Full: Cowgill Inquiry (London, 1990).

Geoffrey Cox, *The Race for Trieste* (Letchworth, 1977).

Gregor Dallas, *Poisoned Peace: 1945 – The War that Never Ended* (London, 2005).

David J. Dallin and Boris I. Nicolaevsky, *Forced Labor in Soviet Russia* (London, 1948).

Alex Danchev and Daniel Todman (ed.), *Field Marshal Lord Alanbrooke: War Diaries* (London, 2001).

V. Danilov, T. Shanin, L. Dvoinykh, V. Vinogradov, and O. Naumov (ed.), *Филипп Миронов: Тихий Дон в 1917-1921 гг.* (Moscow, 1997).

R.W. Davies, 'Soviet Defence Industries during the First Five-Year Plan', in Linda Edmondson and Peter Waldron (ed.), *Economy and Society in Russia and the Soviet Union, 1860-1930: Essays for Olga Crisp* (Basingstoke, 1992), pp. 244-74.

Christiane Shields Delessert, *Release and Repatriation of Prisoners of War at the End of Active Hostilities: A Study of Article 118, Paragraph 1 of the Third Geneva Convention Relative to the Treatment of Prisoners of War* (Zürich, 1977).

Ariadna Delianich, *Вольфсберг - 373* (San Francisco, 1950).

Peter Deriabin and Frank Gibney, *The Secret World* (London, 1960).

Isaac Deutscher, *Stalin: A Political Biography* (Oxford, 1949).

Milovan Djilas, *Conversations with Stalin* (London, 1962).

John Donovan (ed.), *'A Very Fine Commander': The memoirs of General Sir Horatius Murray* (Barnsley, 2010).

Gordon and William Dritschilo, *Survivors of Lienz: A Dritschilo Family Memoir* (Bethesda, Md., 2006).

Allen Dulles, *The Secret Surrender* (London, 1967).

S.V. Dumin (ed.), *Дворянские Роды Российской Империи* (St. Petersburg, 1993-98).

Dwight D. Eisenhower, *Crusade in Europe* (New York, 1948).

Mark R. Elliott, *Pawns of Yalta: Soviet Refugees and America's Role in Their Repatriation* (Urbana, 1982).

Erwein Karl Graf zu Eltz, *Mit den Kosaken: Kriegestagebuch 1943-1945* (Donaueschingen, 1970).

Laura Engelstein, *Russia in Flames: War, Revolution, Civil War 1914-1921* (New York, 2018).

Julius Epstein, *Operation Keelhaul: The Story of Forced Repatriation from 1944 to the Present* (Old Greenwich, Conn., 1973).

John Erickson, *The Road to Berlin* (London, 1983).

Orlando Figes, *A People's Tragedy: The Russian Revolution 1891-1924* (London, 1996).

Orlando Figes and Boris Kolonitskii, *Interpreting the Russian Revolution: The Language and Symbols of 1917* (New Haven and London, 1999).

George Fischer, *Soviet Opposition to Stalin: a case study in world war II* (Cambridge, Mass., 1952).

William C. Fuller, Jr., *The Foe Within: Fantasies of Treason and the End of Imperial Russia* (New York, 2006).

Michael Futrell, 'Alexander Keskuela', in David Footman (ed.), *St Antony's Papers · Number 12: Soviet Affairs Number Three* (London, 1962), pp. 23-52.

B.K. Ganusovsky, *10 Лет за Железным Занавесом 1945-1955: Записки Жертвы Ялты. Выдача XV Казачего Корпуса* (San Francisco, 1983).

Lennard D. Gerson, *The Secret Police in Lenin's Russia* (Philadelphia, 1976).

Frank Gibney (ed), *The Penkovskiy Papers: by Oleg Penkovskiy* (New York, 1965).

Elliot R. Goodman, *The Soviet Design for a World State* (New York, 1960).

Gabriel Gorodetsky, *The Precarious Truce: Anglo-Soviet Relations 1924-27* (Cambridge, 1977).

Gabriel Gorodetsky (ed.), *The Maisky Diaries: Red Ambassador to the Court of St James's 1932-1943* (New Haven and London, 2015).

Frank Grelka, „Zwischen Kollaborationismus, Kriminalisierung und Kanonenfutter", in Harald Stadler, Rolf Steininger, and Karl C. Berger (ed.), *Die Kosaken im Ersten und Zweiten Weltkrieg* (Innsbruck, 2008), pp. 93-112.

Colin J. Gunner, *Front of the Line: Adventures with the Irish Brigade* (Belfast, 1991).

C.R.S. Harris, *Allied Military Administration of Italy 1943-1945* (London, 1957).

John Harris (ed.), *Farewell to the Don: The Journal of Brigadier H.N.H. Williamson* (London, 1970).

Tsuyoshi Hasegawa, *Crime and Punishment in the Russian Revolution* (Cambridge, Mass., 2017).

Norman Hillson, *Alexander of Tunis: A Biographical Portrait* (London, 1952).

Joachim Hoffmann, *Die Geschichte der Wlassow-Armee* (Freiburg, 1984).

Alistair Horne, *Macmillan: 1894-1956* (London, 1988).

Matthias Hoy (Ph.D. thesis), *Der Weg in den Tod: Das Schicksal der Kosaken und des deutschen Rahmpersonals in zweiten Weltkrieg* (Vienna, 1991).

Sir David Hunt, 'H.R.L.G. Alexander', in E.T. Williams and C.S. Nicholls (ed.), *The Dictionary of National Biography: 1961-1970* (Oxford, 1981), pp. 18-23.

Peter J. Huxley-Blythe, *The East Came West* (Caldwell, Idaho, 1964).

Miroslav Iovanovich, 'Россия в изгнании: Границы, масштабы и основые проблемы исследования', in A. Arseniev, O. Kirillova, and M. Sibinovich (ed.), *Русская эмиграция в Югославии* (Moscow, 1996).

The Memoirs of General the Lord Ismay (London, 1960).

I.B. Ivanov, *Русский Обще-Воинский Союз* (St. Petersburg, 1994).

General Sir William Jackson and Group Captain T.P. Gleave, *The Mediterranean and Middle East* (London, 1988), vi (part iii).

Jerome Jareb and Ivo Omrčanin, 'The End of the Croatian Army at Bleiburg, Austria in May 1945 according to English Military Documents', *The Journal of Croatian Studies* (New York, 1977-78), xviii-xix, pp. 115-82.

Robert H. Johnston, *"New Mecca, New Babylon": Paris and the Russian Exiles, 1920-1945* (Kingston and Montreal, 1988).

Sharman Kadish, *Bolsheviks and British Jews: The Anglo-Jewish Community, Britain and the Russian Revolution* (London, 1992).

Heinrich-Detloff v. Kalben and Constantin Wagner, *Die Geschichte des XV. Kosaken-Kavallerie-Korps* (Münster, 1988).

B.K. Ganusovsky, *10 Лет за Железным Занавесом 1945-1955: Записки Жертвы Ялты. Выдача XV Казачего Корпуса* (San Francisco, 1983).

Stefan Karner, *Im Archipel GUPVI: Kriegsgefangenschaft und Internierung in der Sowjetunion 1941-1956* (Vienna and Munich, 1995).

Stefan Karner, 'Das sowjetische Kriegsgefangenenwesen 1941-1956', in *Niemiecki i Radziecki System Jeniecki w Latach II Wojny Swiatowej. Podobienstwa i roznice* (Opole, 1997), pp. 43-67.

Stefan Karner, 'Zur zwangsweisen Übergabe der Kosaken an die Sowjets 1945 in Judenburg', in Harald Stadler, Rolf Steininger, and Karl C. Berger (ed.), *Die Kosaken im Ersten und Zweiten Weltkrieg* (Innsbruck, 2008), pp. 141-49.

Viktor Karpov, 'Долгая дорога в Лиенц', in N.S. Timofeev and S.D. Bodrov (ed.), *Война и судьбы* (Nevinnomyssk, 2002-5), ii, pp. 52-169.

M.K. Kasvinov, *Двадцать Три Ступени Вниз* (Moscow, 1979).

George Katkov, 'German Foreign Office Documents on Financial Support to the Bolsheviks in 1917', *International Affairs* (London, 1956), xxxii, pp. 181-89.

George Katkov, 'The Kronstadt Rising', in David Footman (ed.), *St Antony's Papers · Number 6: Soviet Affairs Number Two* (London, 1959), pp. 9-74.

George Katkov, *Russia 1917: The February Revolution* (London, 1967).

George Katkov, *The Kornilov Affair: Kerensky and the break-up of the Russian army* (London, 1980).

Robin Kemball (ed.), *Marina Tsvetaeva: The Demesne of the Swans; Лебединый Станъ* (Ann Arbor, 1980).

John Keane, *Tom Paine: A Political Life* (Boston, MA, 1995).

Peter Kenez, *Civil War in South Russia, 1918* (Berkeley, 1971).

George Kennan, *Memoirs 1925-1950* (Boston, 1967).

Ludovic Kennedy, *On my Way to the Club* (London, 1989).

Erich Kern, *General von Pannwitz und seine Kosaken* (Göttingen, 1964).

Michael Kettle, *The Road to Intervention: March-November 1918* (London, 1988).

Michael Kettle, *Churchill and the Archangel Fiasco: November 1918-July 1919* (London, 1992).

V.N. Khaustov, V.P. Naumov, and N.S. Plotnikova (ed.), *Лубянка: Сталин и НКВД-НКГБ-ГУКР «Смерш» 1939 – март 1946* (Moscow, 2006).

Oleg V. Khlevniuk, *The History of the Gulag: From Collectivization to the Great Terror* (Yale, 2004).

S.S. Khromov (ed.), *Гражданская Война и Военная Интервенция в СССР: Энциклопедия* (Moscow, 1983).

Gregory Klimov, *The Terror Machine: The inside story of the Soviet Administration in Germany* (London, 1953).

Amy Knight, *Beria: Stalin's First Lieutenant* (Princeton, 1993).

G.A. Knyazev, 'Из записной книжки русского интеллигента за время войны и революции 1915-1922 г.', in V.G. Bortnevsky (ed.), *Русское Прошлое: Историко-Документальный Альманах* (St. Petersburg, 1991), ii, pp. 97-199.

A.I. Kokurin and Yu.N. Morukov (ed.), *Сталинские Стройки ГУЛАГА 1930-1953* (Moscow, 2005).

Mikhail Koriakov, *I'll Never Go Back* (London, 1948).

Andrei Korliakov, *Русская Эмиграция в Фотографиях Франция 1917-1947* (Paris, 2001).

Wolodomyr Kosyk, *La Politique de la France à l'égard de l'Ukraine: Mars 1917 - Février 1918* (Paris, 1981).

Stephen Kotkin, *Stalin: Volume I: Paradoxes of Power, 1878-1928* (New York, 2014).

Stephen Kotkin, *Stalin: Vol. II: Waiting for Hitler, 1928-1941* (London, 2017).

V.A. Kozlov and S. V. Mironenko (ed.), *Архив новейшей истории России Том I: «Особая папка» И.В. Сталина; Из материалов Секретариата НКВД-МВД СССР 1944-1953 гг. Каталог документов* (Moscow, 1994).

N.N. Krasnov, *Незабываемое 1945-1956* (San Francisco, 1957).

P.N. Krasnov, 'На внутреннемъ фронтѣ', in I.V. Gessen (ed.), *Архивъ Русской Революцiи* (Berlin, 1921), i, pp. 97-190.

P.N. Krasnov, 'Всевеликое Войско Донское', in I.V. Gessen (ed.), *Архивъ Русской Революцiи* (Berlin, 1922), v, pp. 191-321.

P.N. Krasnov, *Бѣлая Свитка* (Berlin, 1928).

Werner H. Krause, *Kosaken und Wehrmacht: Der Freiheitskampf eines Volkes* (Graz, 2003).

Victor Kravchenko, *I Chose Freedom: The Personal and Political Life of a Soviet Official* (London, 1947).

Petr N. Krikunov, 'Collaborationism: Some Issues in Participation of Cossacks in the Second World War', in Harald Stadler, Rolf Steininger, and Karl C. Berger (ed.), *Die Kosaken im Ersten und Zweiten Weltkrieg* (Innsbruck, 2008), pp. 119-29.

W.G. Krivitsky, *I was Stalin's Agent* (London, 1939).

T. Kubansky, *A Memento for the Free World* (Paterson, N.J., 1960).

P.I. Kuleshov, *Хождение по этапам* (Sydney, 1987).

Aino Kuusinen, *Before and After Stalin: A Personal Account of Soviet Russia from the 1920s to the 1960s* (London, 1974).

François de Lannoy, *Les Cosaques de Pannwitz 1942-1945* (Paris, 2000).

Michael Lees, *The Rape of Serbia: The British Role in Tito's Grab for Power 1943-1944* (San Diego, Tex., 1990).

George Leggett, *The Cheka: Lenin's Political Police* (Oxford, 1981), pp. 171-203).

Duke G. Leuchtenberg, 'Какъ началась «Южная Армія»' in I.V. Gessen (ed.), *Архивъ Русской Револющи* (Berlin, 1923), viii, pp. 166-82.

Lars T. Lih, Oleg V. Naumov, and Oleg V. Khlevniuk (ed.), *Stalin's Letters to Molotov 1925-1936* (Yale, 1995).

Magnus Linklater and David Leigh, *Not with Honour: the Inside Story of the Westland Scandal* (London, 1986).

Elinor Lipper, *Eleven Years in Soviet Prison Camps* (London, 1951).

Nikita D. Lobanov-Rostovsky, *Эпоха. Судьба. Коллекция* (Moscow, 2010).

Emil Ludwig, *Leaders of Europe* (London, 1934).

Józef Mackiewicz, *Kontra* (Paris, 1957).

Claudio Magris, *Enquête sur un sabre* (Paris, 1987).

Harold Macmillan, *The Blast of War: 1939-1945* (London, 1967).

Harold Macmillan, *War Diaries: Politics and War in the Mediterranean January 1943-May 1945* (London, 1984).

V.G. Makarov and V.S. Khristoforov (ed.), *Высылка вместо Расстрела: Депортация Интеллигенции в Документов ВЧК-ГПУ 1921-1923* (Moscow, 2005).

Lt.-Col. A.D. Malcolm, *History of the Argyll and Sutherland 8th Battalion 1939-47* (London, 1949).

Col. G.I. Malcolm of Poltalloch, *Argyllshire Highlanders 1860-1960* (Glasgow, 1960).

Andrei Malyunas and Sergei Mironenko (ed.), *A Lifelong Passion: Nicholas and Alexandra; Their Own Story* (London, 1996).

Vasily Matasov, *Белое Движение на Юге России 1917-1920 годы* (Montreal, 1990).

Carol Mather, *Aftermath of War: Everyone Must Go Home* (London, 1992).

Evan Mawdsley, *The Russian Revolution and the Baltic Fleet: War and Politics, February 1917-April 1918* (London, 1978).

Sean McMeekin, *The Russian Revolution: A New History* (London, 2017).

Roy A. Medvedev, *Let History Judge: The Origins and Consequences of Stalinism* (London, 1971).

S.P. Melgounov, *La "Terreur Rouge" en Russie (1918-1924)* (Paris, 1927).

Michael A. Meyer and Hilaire McCoubrey (ed.), *Reflections on Law and Armed Conflicts: The Selected Works on the Laws of War by the late Professor Colonel G.I.A.D. Draper, OBE* (The Hague, 1998).

Lord Moran, *Winston Churchill: The struggle for survival* 1940-1965 (London, 1966).

Robert Murphy, *Diplomat among Warriors* (London, 1964).

V. Nabokov, 'Временное Правитьелство', in I.V. Gessen (ed.), *Архивъ Русской Револющи* (Berlin, 1921), i, pp. 9-96.

General V. Naumenko (ed.), *Великое Предательство: Выдача Казаков в Лиенце и Других Местах (1945-1947); Сборник материалов и документов* (New York, 1962-70).

Pavel E. Nazarenko, *В Гостях у Сталина: 14 Лет в Советских Концлагерях* (Melbourne, 1969).

Hans Werner Neulen, *An deutscher Seite: Internationale Freiwillige von Wehrmacht und Waffen-SS* (Munich, 1985).

Samuel J. Newland, *Cossacks in the German Army 1941-1945* (London, 1991).

John North (ed.), *The Alexander Memoirs 1940-1945* (London, 1962).

Bogdan C. Novak, *Trieste, 1941-1954: The Ethnic, Political, and Ideological Struggle* (Chicago, 1970).

Serge Obolensky, *One Man in his Time* (New York, 1958).

A.V. Okorokov, *Русская Змиграция: Политические, военно-политические и воинские организации 1920-1990 гг.* (Moscow, 2003).

Alexander Orlov, *The Secret History of Stalin's Crimes* (London, 1954).

George Orwell, *Down and out in London and Paris* (London, 1933).

Dimitri Panin, *The Notebooks of Sologdin* (London, 1976).

Unto Parvilahti, *Beria's Gardens: Ten Years' Captivity in Russia and Siberia* (London, 1959).

Erwin Peter and Alexander E. Epifanow, *Stalins Kriegs-Gefangene: Ihr Schicksal in Erinnerungen und nach russischen Archiven* (Graz, 1997).

Vladimir and Evdokia Petrov, *Empire of Fear* (London, 1956).

A. Petrowsky, *Unvergessener Verrat!: Roosevelt - Stalin - Churchill 1945* (Munich, 1965).

R.G. Pikhoya and A. Geishtor (ed.), *Катынь: Пленники необъявленной войны* (Moscow, 1997).

Richard Pipes, *Struve: Liberal on the Right, 1905-1944* (Cambridge, Mass., 1980).

Richard Pipes, *Russia under the Bolshevik Regime 1919-1924* (London, 1994).

Richard Pipes (ed.), *The Unknown Lenin: From the Secret Archive* (New Haven, 1996).

Richard Pipes, 'The Kornilov affair: A tragedy of errors', in Tony Brenton (ed.), *Historically Inevitable?: Turning Points of the Russian Revolution* (London, 2016), pp. 109-22.

Harvey Pitcher, *Witnesses of the Russian Revolution* (London, 1994).

N.L. Pobol and P.M. Polyan (ed.), *Сталинские Депортации 1928-1953*

(Moscow, 2005).

Zoe Polanska-Palmer, *Yalta Victim* (Edinburgh, 1986).

Evgenia Polskaya, *Это мы, Господи пред Тобою...* (Nevinnomyssk, 1998).

Pavel Polyan, *Жертвы Двух Диктатур: Остарбайтеры и Военнопленные в Третьем Рейхе и их Репатриация* (Moscow, 1996).

Elisabeth K. Poretsky, *Our Own People: A Memoir of 'Ignace Reiss' and His Friends* (Oxford, 1969).

Dimitry V. Pospielovsky, *A History of Soviet Atheism in Theory and Practice, and the Believer* (Basingstoke, 1987-88).

Dimitry V. Pospielovsky, 'The Survival of the Russian Orthodox Church in her Millennial Century: Faith as *Martyria* in an Atheistic State', in Geoffrey A. Hosking (ed.), *Church, Nation and State in Russia and Ukraine* (London, 1991).

B. Prianishnikoff, *Новопоколенцы* (Silver Springs, Md., 1986).

Le procès Kravchenko contre Les Lettres françaises: Compte Rendu des Audiences d'après la Sténographie suivi d'un index des noms cités (Paris, 1949).

Father Michael Protopopov, *"Живых Проглотим их...": Пут от Георгиевского Креста к Голгофе* (Melbourne, 2000).

Ingomar Pust, *Titostern über Kärnten 1942-1945* (Klagenfurt, 1984).

Oliver H. Radkey, *The Unknown War in Soviet Russia: A Study of the Green Movement in the Tambov Region 1920-1921* (Stanford, 1976).

Marc Raeff, *Russia Abroad: A Cultural History of the Russian Emigration, 1919-1939* (New York, 1990).

Helen Rappaport, *The Race to Save the Romanovs* (New York, 2018).

Gustav Rasmussen (ed.), *Code des prisonniers de guerre: Commentaire de la convention du 27 juillet 1929 relative au traitement des prisonniers de guerre* (Copenhagen, 1931).

Peter Reddaway, 'Literature, the Arts and the Personality of Lenin', in Leonard Schapiro and Peter Reddaway (ed.), *Lenin: The Man, the Theorist, the Leader; A Reappraisal* (New York, 1967), pp. 37-70.

Thomas Riha, *A Russian European: Paul Miliukov in Russian Politics* (Notre Dame, Ind., 1969).

Gerhard Ritter, *The Sword and the Sceptre: The Problem of Militarism in Germany* (London, 1972-73).

Gábor Tamás Rittersporn, 'The omnipresent conspiracy: On Soviet imagery of politics and social relations in the 1930s', in J. Arch Getty and Roberta T. Manning (ed.), *Stalinist Terror: New Perspectives* (Cambridge 1993).

Adam Roberts and Richard Guelff (ed.), *Documents on the Laws of War* (Oxford, 1989).

Adam Roberts, 'Land Warfare: From Hague to Nuremberg', in Michael Howard, George J. Andreopoulos, and Mark R. Shulman (ed.), *The Laws of War: Constraints on Warfare in the Western World* (New Haven and London, 1994), pp. 116-39.

Paul Robinson, *The White Russian Army in Exile 1920-1941* (Oxford, 2002).

'A.I. Romanov' [Captain Boris Bakhlanov], *Nights are Longest There: Smersh from the Inside* (London, 1972).

Allan Rosas, *The Legal Status of Prisoners of War: A Study in International Humanitarian Law Applicable in Armed Conflicts* (Helsinki, 1976).

Nikolai Ross, *Врангель в Крыму* (Frankfurt, 1982).

Edward J. Rozek, *Allied Wartime Diplomacy: A Pattern in Poland* (New York, 1958).

Marquis of Ruvigny, *The Titled Nobility of Europe* (London, 1914).

Leonard Schapiro, *Russian Studies* (London, 1986).

Felix Schneider, '„Freeborn" und „Coldstream" – Vorboten des Kalten Krieges in Österreich und Venezia Giulia 1945', in Karner, Reiter, and Schöpfer (ed.), *Kalter Krieg*, pp. 115-29.

Paul W. Schroeder, *Austria, Great Britain, and the Crimean War: The Destruction of the European Concert* (Ithaca, NY, 1972).

James Brown Scott (ed.), *Les conventions et déclarations de La Haye de 1899 et 1907* (New York, 1918).

Lt. Gen. Pavlo Shandruk, *Arms of Valor* (New York, 1959).

K.F. Shatsillo (ed.), *Дневники Императора Николая II* (Moscow, 1991).

General S.M. Shtemenko, *Генеральный Штаб в Годы Войны* (Moscow, 1973).

Elena Yakovlevna Shupilina (ed.), *Лиенц – Казачья Голгофа* (Ottawa, 2005).

John Silverlight, *The Victors' Dilemma: Allied Intervention in the Russian Civil War* (London, 1970).

Greta N. Slobin, *Russians Abroad: Literary and Cultural Politics of Diaspora (1919-1939)* (Boston, 2013).

A.V. Smolin, 'Кронштадт в 1921 году: новые документы', in V.G. Bortnevsky (ed.), *Русское Прошлое: Историко-Документальный Альманах* (St. Petersburg, 1991), ii, pp. 348-60.

Douglas Smith, *Former People: The Last Days of the Russian Aristocracy* (London, 2012).

Walter Bedell Smith, *Moscow Mission 1946-1949* (London, 1950).

Boris Sokoloff, *The White Nights: Pages from a Russian Doctor's Notebook* (New York, 1956).

A. Solzhenitsyn, *Архипелаг ГУЛаг: Опыт Художественного Исследования 1918-1956* (Paris, 1973-75).

Raymond James Sontag and James Stuart Beddie (ed.), *Nazi-Soviet Relations 1931-1941: Documents from the Archives of The German Foreign Office* (Washington, 1948).

Mark D. Steinberg and Vladimir M. Khrustalëv, *The Fall of the Romanovs: Political Dreams and Personal Struggles in a Time of Revolution* (Yale, 1995).

Vladimir Stepanov, *Свидетельство Обвинения: Церковь и государство в Советском Союзе* (Moscow, 1980).

Gabriela Stieber, *Nachkriegsflüchtlinge in Kärnten und der Steiermark* (Graz, 1997).

Lieutenant-General John Strawson, 'McCreery, Sir Richard Loudon', in E.T.

Williams and C.S. Nicholls (ed.), *The Dictionary of National Biography: 1961-1970* (Oxford, 1981), p. 690-91.

Wilfried Strik-Strikfeldt, *Against Stalin and Hitler: Memoir of the Russian Liberation Movement 1941-5* (London, 1970).

Z. Stypulkowski, *Invitation to Moscow* (London, 1951).

Pavel Sudoplatov, *Спецоперации: Лубянка и Кремль 1930-1950 годы* (Moscow, 1997).

Strobe Talbott (ed.), *Khrushchev Remembers* (Boston, 1970).

John W. Thompson, *Russia, Bolshevism, and the Versailles Peace* (Princeton, 1966).

D.R. Thorpe, *Supermac: The Life of Harold Macmillan* (London, 2010).

Zoltan Toth, *Prisoner of the Soviet Union* (Old Woking, 1978).

Jürgen Thorwald, *The Illusion: Soviet Soldiers in Hitler's Armies* (New York, 1975).

L.N. Tolstoy, *Не Могу Молчать (О смертныхъ казняхъ)* (Berlin, 1908).

Nikolai Tolstoy, *Victims of Yalta* (London, 1977).

Nikolai Tolstoy, 'The Klagenfurt Conspiracy', *Encounter* (London, 1983), lx, pp. 24-37.

Nikolai Tolstoy, *The Tolstoys: Twenty-Four Generations of Russian History 1353-1983* (London, 1983).

Nikolai Tolstoy, *The Minister and the Massacres* (London, 1986).

Nikolai Tolstoy, 'The Application of International Law to Forced Repatriation from Austria in 1945', in Stefan Karner, Erich Reiter, and Gerald Schöpfer (ed.), *Kalter Krieg: Beiträge zur Ost-West-Konfrontation 1945 bis 1990* (Graz, 2002), pp. 131-53.

Nikolai Tolstoy, 'The Mysterious Fate of the Cossack Atamans', in Harald Stadler, Rolf Steininger, and Karl C. Berger (ed.), *Die Kosaken im Ersten und Zweiten Weltkrieg* (Innsbruck, 2008), pp. 151-67.

V. Tretyakova (ed.), *Тайны Истории в романах повестях и документах* (Moscow, 1996).

The Trial of German Major War Criminals: Proceedings of the International Military Tribunal Sitting at Nuremberg Germany (London, 1946-51).

The XX Corps: Its History and Service in World War II (Osaka, 1984).

Robert C. Tucker, *Stalin as Revolutionary 1879-1929* (London, 1974).

Ann Tusa and John Tusa, *The Nuremberg Trial* (London, 1983).

Adam B. Ulam, *Stalin: The Man and his Era* (New York, 1973).

Richard H. Ullman, *Britain and the Russian Civil War: November 1918-February 1920* (Princeton, NJ, 1968).

George Urban, 'A Conversation with Milovan Djilas', *Encounter* (December, 1979), pp. 10-42.

Nikolai Vasiliev, 'Записки юного казака', in N.S. Timofeev and S.D. Bodrov (ed.), *Война и судьбы* (Nevinnomyssk, 2002-5), i, pp. 4-63.

G.G. Verbitsky, *Остарбайтеры: История Россиян Насильственно Вывезенных на Работы в Германию (Вторая Мировая Война)* (Vestal, NY, 2001).

D.P. Vertepov (ed.), *Русский Корпус на Балканах во Время II Великой Войны 1941-1945 г.г.* (New York, 1963).

Karl-Gottfried Vierkorn, *Gefangen in Sibirien: Achteinhalb Jahre hinter Stacheldraht* (Oberaudorf, 1994).

Dmitri Volkogonov, *Троцкий: Политический Портрет* (Moscow, 1992).

Dmitri Volkogonov, *Ленин: Политический Портрет* (Moscow, 1994)

Dmitri Volkogonov, *Сталин: Политический Портрет* (Moscow, 1994).

Solomon Volkov, *Testimony: The Memoirs of Dmitri Shostakovich* (London, 1979).

Gunild Walsh, *The Silent Crime: As Lived Through by my Twelve Year Old Self* (blurb.com, 2011).

August Walzl, *Kärnten 1945: Vom NS-Regime zur Besatzungsherrschaft im Alpen-Adria-Raum* (Klagenfurt, 1985).

Piotr S. Wandycz, *Soviet-Polish Relations, 1917-1921* (Cambridge, Mass., 1969).

Alexander Watson, *Ring of Steel: Germany and Austria-Hungary at War, 1914-1918* (London, 2014).

Edgar M. Wenzel, *So gingen die Kosaken durch die Hölle* (Vienna, 1976).

John H. Wheeler-Bennett, *Brest-Litovsk: The Forgotten Peace March 1918* (London, 1939).

Elizabeth White, 'The Legal Status of Russian Refugees, 1921-1936', *Zeitschrift für Globalgeschichte und Vergleichende Gesellshaftsforschung* (Leipzig, 2017), xxvii, pp. 18-38.

Richard D. Wiggers, 'The United States and the Denial of Prisoner of War (POW) Status at the End of the Second World War', *Militär-geschichtliche Mitteilungen* (Oldenbourg, 1993), lii, pp. pp. 91-104.

Allan K. Wildman, *The End of the Russian Army: The Old Army and the Soldiers' Revolt (March-April 1917)* (Princeton, 1980).

René-Jean Wilhelm, *Can the Status of Prisoners of War be Altered?* (Geneva, 1953).

Sir Peter Wilkinson, *Foreign Fields: The Story of an SOE Operative* (London, 1997).

Andrew Wilson, *The Ukrainians: Unexpected Nation* (New Haven and London, 2000).

Lieutenant-General Sir James Wilson ('The Repatriations from Austria in 1945: The Cowgill Inquiry – Report and Documentary Evidence', *Army Defence Quarterly Journal* (London, 1991), cxxi, pp. 61-63.

Bertram D. Wolfe, *Khrushchev and Stalin's Ghost* (New York, 1957).

E.L. Woodward and Rohan Butler (ed.), *Documents on British Foreign Policy 1919-1939: First Series* (London, 1949), iii.

Alexis Wrangel, *General Wrangel: Russia's White Crusader* (New York, 1987).

Kenneth Young (ed.), *The Diaries of Sir Robert Bruce Lockhart* (London, 1980).

V.N. Zemskov, *Возращение советских перемещенных лиц в СССР. 1944-1952 гг.* (Moscow, 2016).

Libushe Zorin, *Soviet Prisons and Concentration Camps: An Annotated Bibliography 1917-1980* (Newtonville, Mass., 1980).

INDEX

CPSIA information can be obtained
at www.ICGtesting.com
Printed in the USA
BVHW090815140122
626145BV00004B/59/J